DOING BUSINESS RESEARCH

DOING BUSINESS RESEARCH

A GUIDE TO THEORY AND PRACTICE

NICK LEE
WITH IAN LINGS

Los Angeles | London | New Delhi
Singapore | Washington DC

First Published 2008
Reprinted 2011

SAGE Publications Ltd
1 Oliver's Yard
55 City Road
London EC1Y 1SP

SAGE Publications Inc.
2455 Teller Road
Thousand Oaks, California 91320

SAGE Publications India Pvt Ltd
B 1/I 1 Mohan Cooperative Industrial Area
Mathura Road
New Delhi 110 044

SAGE Publications Asia-Pacific Pte Ltd
33 Pekin Street #02-01
Far East Square
Singapore 048763

Library of Congress Control Number: 2007935303

British Library Cataloguing in Publication data

A catalogue record for this book is available from the British Library

ISBN 978-1-4129-2878-6
ISBN 978-1-4129-2879-3 (pbk)

Typeset by CEPHA Imaging Pvt. Ltd., Bangalore, India
Printed in Great Britain by the MPG Books Group
Printed on paper from sustainable resources

This work is dedicated to John Cadogan, who inspired me to follow this path in the first place, and to all the research students I have interacted with, who inspire me to continue to follow it.

Nick Lee

Contents

Foreword

Research is a process. Often, it is represented as a mechanical process in which one just has to follow the rules, and everything should be OK. The trouble is, what the rules are seems to differ pretty much with who's laying down the law. Positivists, realists, phenomenologists, ethnomethodologists, critical realists, feminists and many more, all have quite definite and different views of what research is and how it should be done. And within each camp, there will be rival factions.

For students beginning their research career, the plethora of different accounts can often be confusing. This is hardly surprising: in my experience, most of their instructors are just as confused and seek to cover their confusion by affirmation of one or other of the rival camps and denouncement of the others. While this makes for good sectarian politics, it is not always a lot of help to the introductory student. It leaves them with little option other than finding out which camp they should belong to if they are to maintain peace with their supervisors.

There is a better way, dear reader, and I believe that this book introduces it. The great value of the book is that it is systematic in its accounting and coverage of the research process; hence, you don't just get one side of the fence being presented, but receive a clear and comprehensible outline of the various positions that can be found in the research literature. Moreover, the book demonstrates very clearly that, even in practically oriented disciplines such as marketing and management, we ignore the foundational and fundamental philosophy of science and measurement issues at our peril.

If you have had the typical undergraduate business student's education, you will probably be a good technician, ready to go and gain work, eager to apply the techniques that you have learnt in business school. However, if you are the less typical student who wants to contribute to the research knowledge of the communities of practice to which you aspire to belong, the things that you learnt as an undergraduate will only take you so far. It will be unusual if you have read much philosophy, or methodology, or 'how-to-do-research' books.

There are many books in the market-place addressed to matters of research, philosophy of science, methodology and writing, but there are few books that enable you to bring it all back home in one volume. I believe that this book does that – and it does so in a way that is lively, informative, substantively useful and comprehensive in its topics. Of course, it is not an in-depth account of the topics that it addresses – that is not the point – but it is a great orienting device, a compass that will help you steer your way through that very personal journey that is called research. Every research student will need many guides for their journey, and this is a very good one with which to get started.

Professor Stewart Clegg
Aston Business School 2007

Acknowledgements

For some reason, I love writing acknowledgements. In fact, not many people know that I actually began the first draft of the acknowledgements page for my Ph.D. dissertation at least 18 months before even writing a word on the first draft of the actual thesis! This time around, I forced myself to wait till the end before writing them. But I have still been looking forward to it for the last two years. Now that the time has come to write them, however, I fear that I cannot adequately express my gratitude to the many people who deserve it so richly, so please excuse my somewhat ham-fisted efforts. Of course, any mistakes or omissions in the book are entirely their responsibility – oh, hang on, I mean mine!

First, and in all probability foremost, this book would never have happened without a number of people. Without Delia Alfonso (nee Martinez) at Sage's constant prodding (some might say 'whining', but not I, of course) to write a book, I most definitely would not have ever considered the possibility seriously. Whether or not this is a good thing remains to be seen! But I will be honest and say that at no point did I regret my decision (the limoncello is on me – again!). Secondly, without the long and fruitful planning discussions with Ian Lings, I probably wouldn't have ever gotten off my backside and done the book. Ian, it's a shame that things didn't go to plan and you went off to Sydney and had far too much fun to write 50 per cent of this, but rest assured that without you it wouldn't have happened. Although I *am* taking all the money.[1] Perhaps the most important people in this context, however, are Professor Geoff Durden and Professor John Cadogan. Geoff was my postgraduate dissertation supervisor, and if he hadn't taken a risky decision (his words) on a long-haired slacker (also his words) then I would probably be stacking supermarket shelves somewhere. Through Geoff I met John, who eventually became my Ph.D. supervisor and great friend. It is not going overboard to say that everything I know I owe to John in some way. Apart from the haircut. Through John I met Dr Anne Souchon, who has also been unstinting in her support and friendship over the years, and both John and Anne have proved inspirational friends and colleagues.

At the time of writing this book, a vast number of people helped me out in various ways. In particular, while doing her own Ph.D., Laura Chamberlain took time out to read and

[1] Just kidding!

comment on every single chapter of the manuscript. This was amazingly helpful, and she came up with a number of great ideas which have made this book immeasurably better, including the 'why is it important to know this stuff' feature. Most importantly, she always had the courage to tell me if I was writing incomprehensible rubbish, or to prick my ego when it (often) expanded beyond its usual size. As well as this, I was humbled by the enthusiasm and generosity of all 31 individuals who contributed to the viewpoints at the beginning of each chapter. Without fail, every single one of you made a contribution to this book which would have been impossible in any other way, and I feel incredibly lucky to have been able to collect together the thoughts of so many outstanding thinkers in one place. Speaking of which, many thanks to Anouche Newman, who thought up the 'view from the trenches' idea, Jennifer Walker for her kind permission to use a figure from her M.Sc. dissertation and Mirella Kleijnen and Martin Wetzels for letting me use the figure in Chapter 10. Thanks also to SPSS (www.spss.com) and QSR International (www.qsrinternational.com) for kind permission to reproduce various images of their software in the analysis chapters. Also, after Delia took maternity leave, Anne Summers came on board this project at Sage, and has been nothing but supportive and entertaining along the whole process. I wish you the best of luck in your adventures in India, but Delia can drink more than you any day (sorry!). After Anne left for her Indian adventure, Clare Wells took over for the final push, and deserves thanks for keeping me going at the end. A number of research students and academics offered specific comments on various pieces of this work, and all deserve great thanks. In alphabetical order: Evert Gummeson, Bill Rozeboom, Anna Sandfield and Seraphim Voliotis. Finally, thanks to Gareth Williams (Development Editor at Sage) and a number of anonymous Sage reviewers for their helpful comments on chapter drafts. If I have forgotten anyone, I truly apologise, and please let me know (but please read to the end before going off on a rant at me!).

From 1999 I have worked at Aston University, and the colleagues I met there have undoubtedly had a major impact on this book. I am deeply appreciative of the support and opportunity to indulge myself I have been given at Aston, and the diversity of theory and method I have been exposed to, not just in the Business School, but across the university. Although there are too many people to mention individually, I believe the 2000–2007 Marketing professoriate do deserve some specific acknowledgement for giving me the time and space to develop my thinking, and having the courage to support me (or at least to try to ignore my activities), even when I may have sometimes seemed to go wilfully against their own thoughts on what 'a good career move' might be. So, Gordon Greenley, Graham Hooley, John Saunders and Veronica Wong, thanks.

In a more general sense, my ideas about research that together form this work were shaped by conversations and (sometimes) arguments with my many colleagues, friends and not-so-friends in this weird and wonderful business. It is completely impractical to list all of these people, but I would like to acknowledge the generosity of spirit shown to me by so many exalted scholars over the years, who engaged with me in my sometimes random and ill-informed rantings at conferences and other occasions. Many of you are probably unaware of the influence you had on my thinking, even with so little a gesture as a smile and a nod of the head, but thank you. I am also indebted to many of you for the generous support you have shown me over the years in various ways. Among the many, I feel I must specifically acknowledge Adamantios Diamantopoulos, Rod Brodie, Rob Morgan, David Jobber, Greg Marshall, Costas Katsikeas, Nigel Piercy, Felix Brodbeck, Marnik Dekimpe and Stewart Clegg for their inspiration, support and material contribution to my thinking on these issues over the years. Your examples have shown me the true meaning of the word 'professor'.

In my career as a marketing academic, I have also been blessed with some wonderful colleagues over the years, who have provided support, inspiration, companionship and, most importantly, friendship. Each one of you has inspired this work in some way, directly or indirectly. There are an uncountable number of people in this category (many of whom have already been mentioned), but my particular appreciation is extended to those who have been subjected to my long and boring rants about methods and things like that: Amanda Beatson, John Rudd, Andrew Farrell, Paul Hughes, Maria Saaksjarvi, Alex Nicholls, Teck-Yong Eng, Walter Hertzog, Jan Weiseke, David Gilliland and Andrew Smith. Furthermore, the research students within Aston Business School and the Marketing Group have proved an endless source of inspiration, as well as the students in the Aston M.Sc. in Marketing Management and 2001–2006 final year B.Sc. in Marketing. Of special note are Joanne Brown, Stephanie Feiereisen, Xia Wu, Aarti Sood, Yannis Angelis, Yves Guilliaume and Catherine Demangeot. Your constant encouragement and complimentary words about this work in a general sense kept me going during the times that I lost confidence[2] in my ability to do this, or wondered whether in the end anybody would get anything out of the book.

Of course, without my non-marketing researcher friends and family, I would have gone totally mad in the last couple of years while writing this book. It's been impossibly valuable to get away from the hothouse and just have some fun, and also to be reminded that – however important and world-changing I think my work is – in the grand scheme of things, there are many other important things in life.[3] You all also helped remind me that, to most people, writing a book (any book) is far more impressive than writing a paper in some obscure academic journal which no one outside the field will ever see. In the 'publish (as long as they are journal articles) or perish' world that most academics like me live in, this was invaluable motivation. There are many in this category, but my particular appreciation goes out to Caroline Burrow, JooBee Yeow, Scott Beatson, Mark and Monique Goodson, James and Jen Tohill, Geert and Susan Van de Vorstenbosh, Carl Senior, Mike Butler, Mark and Jo Talbot and Didier Souchon. Super thanks also to Longdon Cricket Club and my Thursday and Friday Afternoon Football Massives for giving me outlets for my pent-up energy (sorry for all the swearing, guys). As I always listen to music while writing, I was going to acknowledge the many excellent artists I listened to over the last few years, but then

[2] It *did* happen on occasion!

[3] I can't yet bring myself to admit that they are *more* important!

I realised Andy Field already did that in his book, and it would look kind of lame if I copied. You can find me on www.last.fm as nj_lee. And of course, last but not least, many thanks to my Mum, Meg and Jess my sisters, and my new nephew Brylie (thank God, another male in the family!).

Nick Lee is not sponsored or endorsed by any brand of computer, electronics, software, stimulant, relaxant, sporting goods or musical equipment. However, as many were used in the creation of this book, sponsorship managers should feel free to send him as many gratuitous things as possible.

Nick Lee, 2007

How to use this book

This is a book about doing scholarly research. As such, it is a book designed to be read by scholarly researchers, or those who intend to become them. What does this mean? Well, broadly speaking, it means anybody who is involved in doing some kind of academic research project, and there will be some discussion of what 'academic' or 'scholarly' research actually means in Chapter 1. In practical terms, it means that this book is definitely intended for those who conduct research aimed at advancing theory and knowledge. Of course, I think most commercial, governmental and other forms of research would benefit greatly by absorbing the material in this book; but let's stay in the realms of reality here. Who should read it? Well, if you are doing any kind of postgraduate research in the social sciences, I think this book is going to be very useful to you. I also think this book is well-suited to final year undergraduate dissertations as well. Nonetheless, I didn't write this book just for students, I also wrote it for academic researchers. I wrote it for any academic researcher who feels a little lacking in confidence in his or her knowledge of the underlying fundamentals of research, who is looking for a central source of information from which to start. I also wrote this book for supervisors of research students, who may be looking for something to help them structure their programme of education for their students – or even just something to ask them to read right at the start of the process. In fact, that was the original vision for what this book could be. Certainly, I am well aware that it is the minority of academics in the social and applied fields who are actually interested in research methods, so I feel a coherent and comprehensive account of the conceptual, philosophical and technical underpinnings of scholarly research will be very valuable. For, indeed, that is what this book is.

Just as important is what this book isn't. It is not designed to show you all the technical details; it is designed to help you understand the *thought processes* involved in doing good scholarly research, and *how to make decisions* about what to do. There are plenty of books out there that cover the technical stuff for each of the different concepts I will discuss. However, there are very few (I actually suspect there are none) which give a holistic view of scholarly research, focusing on philosophy, methodology and dissemination all together. So, you should use this book as a central source, or a springboard for further learning. In this spirit, I have provided plenty of further reading for you to get your teeth into. It's not 'everything you need to know', but it will show you how you – in my opinion – need to *think* to conduct scholarly research in the social sciences and applied disciplines successfully. Importantly, I do not aim to make some kind of original contribution to the philosophy of science or methodology. While I do think there are some nice ideas in here which are in some small way 'original-ish', my aim is to provide information on existing theories and methods of research, and allow you to move from there. There are no 'new' methods in here, because it is my view that in order to create, you need to understand what is already out there in depth first.

In terms of background knowledge, I do not really assume anything specific about the readers of this book. I personally think this material can be understood by almost any reader of some intelligence. Of course, most of the readers of this book will have an undergraduate degree, or at least one or two years of undergraduate-level education, and I think that you could usefully consider this to be a good basic assumption about the type of background you will need to get the most out of this book. But, that said, if you do not fall into this category, please don't be put off. Probably the most important qualification you need to read this book is an interest in research.

So, how should you go about using this book? You'll find plenty of information about the specific features of the book in Chapter 1, but in essence, open the front cover (you've already done that, good start), read, keep going until you reach the end! I know that sounds flippant, but I really do think that a good researcher needs to grasp all of the information in this book in order to make informed decisions about how to conduct their work. Too many researchers only understand or want to understand a small part of the vast cornucopia and history of scholarship, and I would love to play even a tiny role in opening up more researchers to the vista of alternatives available to them – even if they never use them. So, in my dreams I see everybody (vast armies of researchers) who buy this book sitting down in a comfy chair and reading the book cover-to-cover. In reality, however, I realise this is unlikely, and you will probably dip in and dip out of the book using the chapter headings to direct you. That's why at many points you will see cross-references to other parts of the book which I think are relevant. When you come across these, I think you should follow them up, go to the relevant chapter and read on! You'll also see a number of boxouts. I'll explain these in more depth in Chapter 1, but suffice it to say that these are not necessarily to be ignored! Sometimes they are kind of 'asides', but more often they actually provide important additional information. At the end of each chapter, you'll also see plenty of exercises to do. Please do these, but don't expect to turn to the back to find answers. The exercises are more about conceptual thinking than technical details.

Finally, this book has been a constant part of my life for the last 25 months, and I consider it to be a work in progress. I am always learning, and I hope this to be the case for my entire career. In the process of writing this, I have learnt things I wish I had known many years ago, and I hope that this book saves you from the many mistakes I have so far made in my career. Doubtless, I will make more mistakes, and learn more things, which I hope to use to update this book (if anyone buys it). This book has most definitely been a labour of love, but even so I want this book to do the best job it can for you, the reader. Therefore, I genuinely welcome feedback from you.

Best wishes for your research, and good luck!

Nick
Email: thinkingresearch@you-think-too-much.co.uk
Web: www.you-think-too-much.co.uk

HOW TO USE THIS BOOK

Chapter 1
What is research, and why would anyone want to do it?

Nick Lee and Ian Lings

SUPERVISOR'S VIEW: PROFESSOR KWAKU ATUAHENE-GIMA

Research, contributions, knowledge and who knows what! As you embark on an academic career, the two potholes that will make or break that journey are in the form of two words: 'contribution' and 'new'. When I was in graduate school, my professors always told me to endeavour to 'make a contribution' – not only that, but also that the conrtibution must be 'new'. When I began my academic career, the emphasis on these two words became deafening at research conferences, seminars and workshops. When pressed for better explanations of what is a 'new contribution', many presenters would respond with something like: 'say something interesting', 'create new knowledge', 'develop new theory', etc. Hardly ever would anyone explain what 'interesting' and 'new' meant. More important, how one judges the 'interestingness' and 'newness' of a research contribution is a question that is often left unanswered.

Coupling my industry and research experiences, I have come to realise that research is about *conversations*, and that I am on a personal journey of learning and discovery – learning from what others have done and are doing to discover how and why I can contribute to their conversations. I believe that I do not create knowledge with my research and publications – rather, I participate in a conversation about issues of interest to academicians and practitioners. To the extent that my participation leads the audience to judge that I have enhanced the conversation with insights and understandings that are *new to them*, I have contributed new and interesting knowledge. Yet, I have not created new knowledge – rather the audience has created new knowledge that helps in their continuing the conversation along new and different avenues of understandings. As you read onwards, think about this and how you will offer opportunities for your academic and practitioner audiences to create their own new and interesting knowledge. This, in my view, is the beauty of research and is what makes the research journey interesting and worthwhile in spite of the deep potholes.

VIEW FROM THE TRENCHES: ANOUCHE NEWMAN

When I try to explain to my friends and family what I do, nobody really understands me, or their eyes glaze over and I change the subject. A friend recently asked me what I would do when I finished my Ph.D.: 'Are you going to get a real job afterwards?' Well, this *is* my real job. Why do I do research? I don't know why I am doing what I am doing. I just fell into it and here I am. Some days I wake up and think it is the worst thing in the world. Research is not easy and it can be incredibly frustrating. On other days the very reason I hate being a researcher is why I love my job, because I like to be faced with research problems that are exciting and challenging at the same time.

When I first started 'doing' research, I had no idea what 'research' really meant. I just thought it was cool that I was getting paid to carry on studying. To be honest, I am still getting to grips with what doing research involves, and my views and opinions regarding what research actually means are evolving as I gain more experience. Research can mean different things to different people. And what constitutes 'good' research can also mean different things to different people. It is important that you form your own opinions. That's one of the things that makes your research unique – along with the fact that you are supposed to be doing something that no one else has ever done before. Some people might disagree with what you believe; that's what research is all about. You have to show those people *why* your opinion is valid. Of course, there is no right or wrong answer to any one research problem and, on occasion, your best ideas are from people who see the world in a different way to you. Be open to the different views and opinions that exist around you.

I cannot offer you a definition of research that will help you understand what it is or how to do it. You have to live it to know it and you will always be learning something new about what you think research is supposed to be.

So, you stand here at the beginning, or somewhere along the way, of a journey, that of **discovery**. You've already heard from some people who have successfully negotiated many of the hazards of that journey (Professors Clegg and Atuahene-Gima), and from Anouche – soon to be Dr Newman – who is only just beginning to lose sight of the early shores (we like to call this 'leaving the beach'). If you are reading this book, we can only assume that you are interested in research in some way (well, you could be one of our Mums we guess, hello Mum – you appear later so keep reading!) You might be a research student who is only just starting out, you might be a more experienced researcher who is looking for some ideas, or like us, you might just be interested in reading and writing about research itself. Whoever you are, as long as you are interested in thinking about research, we are writing this book for you.

This chapter is about setting out very clearly a perspective on research, and also about explaining exactly what this book is trying to do, and maybe more importantly what it is *not* trying to do. Furthermore, we are hoping desperately that you will enjoy it enough to keep reading the rest! After all, it's taken us two years to get this far so we'd really like you to read it.[1] This chapter is being written about 30,000 feet above the Atlantic Ocean on a flight to Reykjavik in Iceland. While we are there we will present the results of various research projects, some conducted with our students. Two weeks ago Nick was invited to Helsinki to speak on a panel about research, and in a month or so he will be doing the same in Disneyworld, Orlando, in the US. Research has provided each of us with what many would see as an amazing life so far. We've been to places we'd only ever heard about as kids growing up in small towns in New Zealand (Nick) and England (Ian). We've done things we'd never have dreamed of, and met some of the most amazing people in the world, many of whom have done us the honour of working with us (in fact, lots of them will appear throughout this book), and it never ceases to amaze both of us that even one person is interested in what we have to say. It's fair to say that this thing called 'research' is responsible for all of this. Well, it certainly can't be our respective good looks!

But what *is* research? This chapter is aimed at explaining that question in some way. However, as you will see as you read on through this book, there are many, *many*, different perspectives and answers to that question. We have our own perspective for sure, but we really want to give you enough information so that you can make your own mind up. Nevertheless, one really important thing to keep in mind is that to be a great researcher, you can never stop learning. We spoke above about the idea of this being a journey, and it is exactly that. However, the *journey of discovery never ends*. Every day we learn something new, and the day we stop being excited by that is the day we will think about finding a new job.

Moving on, at the end of this chapter we really hope you have come to terms with these key ideas:

- What is the purpose and added value of *this* book over other books on the same general subject?
- What is academic research, and what is knowledge?
- How can you 'contribute' to knowledge?

---

[1] In case you are wondering, this chapter was written last, it hasn't taken us two years to write ten lines! Actually, maybe it did take *Ian* two years to write ten lines....

- There are many ways of doing research, and no one single right way.
- What the four 'ologies' are, and how they link together.
- How research can link the theoretical world, to the real world, and how this then relates to knowledge creation.

Why is it Important to Know This Stuff?

This chapter is a very important one for a number of reasons. First of all, it 'sets the scene' for all of the information to come. This is necessary because there is a heck of a lot of information, theories, ideas and questions all about to hit you. You are going to need some kind of structure in place to help you try to absorb all of that information, or else you will get overwhelmed. In fact, the information in this book is the culmination of probably a decade of doing, thinking and writing about this kind of thing, so mainlining it straight into your brain is probably going to be a bit of an overdose!

We are hoping that this chapter will give you an idea of what the book is about, and also about our own personal perspective on research. From here, you're going to be in a good position to learn more, or even decide whether you want to learn more, before you commit to the whole thing (you have bought this already haven't you? If not, go and buy it, then come back and continue reading).

In this chapter, we are going to try to set out a few key things we wished we'd known before starting out, which would have helped us a lot. We are also going to try to give you some indications of the unique features of this book, and why we spent two years writing it, rather than just recommending some other book to people who ask. With this knowledge in hand, you should be able to get the most benefit out of the book, which is very important to us.

However, maybe the most important idea we are trying to get across is that **research is fun**. Well, perhaps it's more accurate to say research *can be* fun, when you are confident in yourself and what you are trying to do. The task we set ourselves at the start of this project was to give you that confidence. Research is also a *human process*; it's done by people like you and us, not computers or robots. Researchers are real people, who have alternative opinions; they disagree, argue, make mistakes and are subject to all of the other natural social interactions like any other group. We want to get this feeling across here, and in the rest of the book. Ignoring these processes paints a very inaccurate picture of how most academic research gets done. So, read on, learn and laugh (or at least pretend to laugh when it looks like we are making a joke – that's just common courtesy).

Why (yet) another research book?

Trust us, you don't have to ask that question! Over the last couple of years we have asked ourselves that question so many times we've lost count. Actually, there are two questions: (a) why did we start writing the book; and (b) why did we continue writing it when things got tough? The answers to both are linked, but also quite separate. And both those answers illuminate the purpose of this book nicely.

The idea behind this book came from a conversation between us, Dr Nick Lee and Dr Ian Lings, in a bar called 'The Sacks of Potatoes'. If you want to find it, it's pretty well located on the campus of Aston University in Birmingham (that's in the UK, not Alabama). They do a lovely pint of bitter. Both of us had had our Ph.D.s for a couple of years, and we had each been teaching at Aston for maybe five years . We had just been given the opportunity to create a course in 'Marketing Science', which was designed to give students the academic research skills to do a good research dissertation, and maybe inspire some of them to go on to do a Ph.D. We took this as a chance to teach students 'our way' of doing research. In other words, the way we had been taught by our own supervisors and senior colleagues. However, when it came to finding a textbook for this course, we were shocked to discover that there was no single book which set everything out in one place. In fact, we had to take chapters from maybe 10 or 15 books and put them together in a readings pack. At the same time Nick was trying to teach research methods to our Doctoral students, and again finding it very hard to locate appropriate material all in one place.

What we were looking for was not a book which went through the fine details of statistical formulae or sampling, or the 'technical' side of research. That kind of thing is pretty easy to find (and you know what, it's not really the hard part). No, what we wanted was a book which taught you how to **think** about doing research. We wanted an easy-to-follow resource which showed how philosophical issues linked with practical and technical issues, and then how students should think and write about those things. In other words, *how do you make decisions about* ***what to do*** *when you are doing research*, and then *what are the implications of those decisions for your research*? Bits and pieces of this were available in many different books and articles, but we couldn't locate an integrated source. As well as this, we were beginning to find that we were continually answering the same questions asked of us by research students. We began to think 'wouldn't it be great if we could somehow clone ourselves in miniature, and sit on people's bookshelves ready to answer those fundamental questions'. This would save a lot of time. However, we were informed that such technology was not available right now (and to be fair it might be a bit weird). So, we decided that the next best thing would be to try to pack all of the experiences and things we had discovered about research (mainly through making mistakes) into a book. Then, we could just force – I mean suggest – that people buy that book.

This is the book you now hold in your hands. To us, it's the cumulative result of a lot of mistakes, a lot of questions, not as many definitive answers and a heck of a lot of fun over the last ten years since we both started researching. We both hope you enjoy it, and, most importantly, that you learn from it.

So, what *is* research?

If you open up any research methods text, you'll get a definition about what research is. However, most texts, even those which are supposed to be aimed at doctoral and postdoctoral-level researchers, will give you a definition which is implicitly (or explicitly) based on the viewpoint of the author. You may, or (more likely) may not yet, understand that there are many different definitions of research, based on many different philosophies and opinions about the world. As you move through the book, you'll discover the characteristics of these opinions and views, and you will begin to clarify your own personal view of the world and research.

Chapters 2 and 3 will spend a lot of time and ink on outlining two very different approaches to research, and Chapter 15 will look at how they are incontrovertibly opposed and undeniably similar at the same time. But right here we don't want to get into that. What we do want to do is define research in such a way that it does not overly bias one position over another, and taps into the real commonality of what research is all about. So, um, here goes: ***Research is about generating knowledge about what you believe the world is***.

Pretty simple huh? Well, actually, it's deceptively so. As you will come to see, there are very different definitions about what knowledge is, what the 'real world' is and also about what 'type' of knowledge we can generate – and even about what the knowledge generation process should be. In other words, within this definition can live an almost unlimited number of different flavours and styles – most of which are founded on reasonably solid principles. So don't get too complacent! The rest of this section will deal with a few key principles of research, which will be of varying relevance to each of you, depending on how you got here in the first place.

Induction and deduction

The two concepts of induction and deduction are vitally important for any consideration of research, and they will appear repeatedly throughout the book. They are both concepts from elementary logic,[2] and can help you link together the 'thinking' parts of research with the 'getting out there and doing' parts. **Deduction** is basically the process of drawing conclusions from rational and logical principles. In the terms of logic a valid argument is one in which there is no situation where the principles (which are called premises) are true and the conclusion is not true, and this is a good place to start talking about research. Let's look

---

[2]Learning the basics of logic is quite handy actually; if you are interested we will suggest a book to start off with in the 'further reading' section.

at an example. The classic principles of deduction (and induction) were laid down by the Ancient Greeks – who you will hear about later – and concern the idea of moving from a general law to a conclusion about a specific instance. For example, the premises that 'writing a book always makes the author(s) rich' and 'Nick and Ian are writing a book' together lead to the conclusion that 'Nick and Ian will become rich'. That is only valid, however, if the premises are true. If only it were so! You can consider the premises to be examples of 'theory', which you will learn about later. In most scientific situations, and especially social science, we are not sure about whether our theories are true. In this case we need to go and somehow test our theories, usually by designing some kind of *research*, most often collecting some real-world data.

Induction is essentially the opposite of deduction. It is the process of moving from specific observations to a more general theory. So using the example above, we might observe Nick and Ian finishing the book, and then accruing vast quantities of wealth, and perhaps other authors doing the same, and therefore come to the inductive conclusion that 'writing a book makes the author rich'. So in this case you are moving from observations of the world to general theories about it. However, it's not quite as simple as it seems. In most real-world research contexts, induction and deduction tend to be linked together, almost sequentially in some cases. Figure 1.1 shows this in graphical terms.

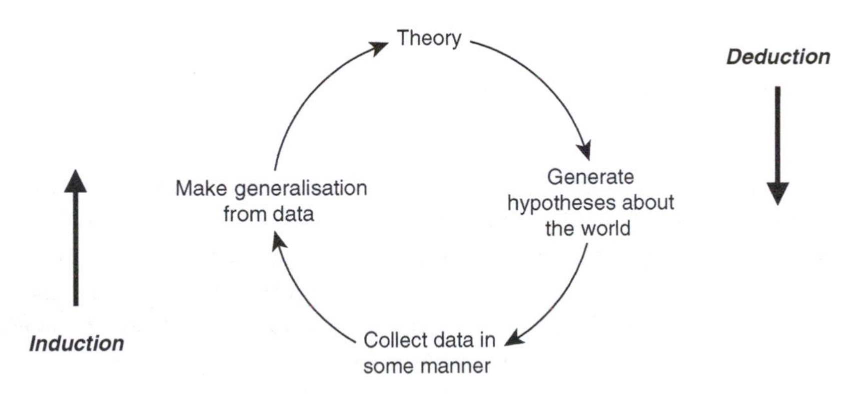

Figure 1.1 Induction and deduction in social science theory

Different research traditions and philosophies tend to emphasise either induction or deduction. But in the real world these distinctions are rarely as clear as advocates of each position would have you believe. Figure 1.1 implies that in the real world we often alternate between deduction and induction. Figure 1.2 shows the process as more of a 'spiral' which is similar to how you could interpret Nick's own Ph.D. project. This begins from his supervisor's (Professor John Cadogan's) incidental observations during the course of his own M.Phil. research in 1993–4, to an inductive idea generation phase, until Nick came on board in 1998 and took the project on in a deductive fashion to begin with, followed by an

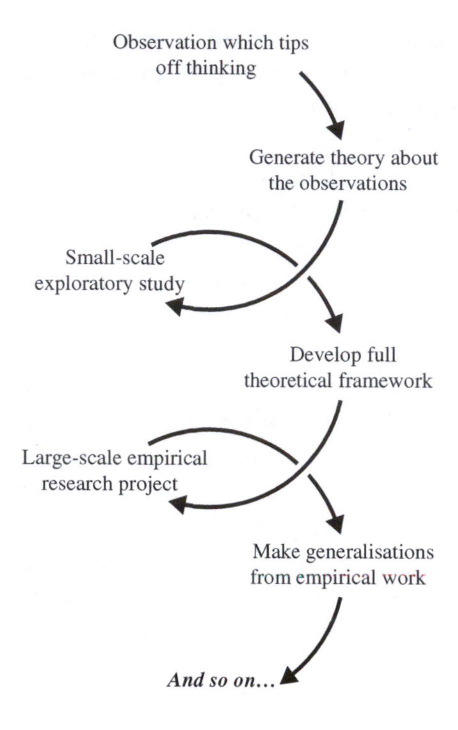

Figure 1.2 Induction and deduction in practice

inductive stage, and so on. In fact, the project as a whole is still continuing in this spiral, and you may be able to follow the trail of research studies which come out of it over the coming years (hopefully!). In this figure is the first use of an important word for the rest of this book; **empirical**. The word empirical refers to something which is observable by the senses. In other words, to most intents and purposes, it means observable data from the world around us. Unfortunately, there is sometimes confusion over the use of this word. We have both been made aware of situations where 'empirical' has been used to refer to 'quantitative' or experimental observations. The use in this book, however, will be the more general one, where empirical refers to *all* observable data, both quantitative and qualitative. That said, don't get 'empirical' confused with **empiricism**, which is a distinct philosophy that will be discussed in the next chapter.

It's likely you will feel more or less comfortable with either the inductive or deductive approach, and this opinion will begin to form more firmly after you have read the first three chapters. However, it is important to realise that (a) there are valid arguments for both positions, and (b) in the real world we tend to incorporate more of a spiral process over the course of an entire research project, particularly in the social sciences where theories are much less fully formed than in the natural sciences such as physics.

Commercial versus academic research

Or, the 'real world' versus the 'ivory tower' as some have put it. You might see some of the ideas in this short section discussed using the names 'pure' and 'applied' research in other books; however, there are some important differences which need discussion. First things first, this is not a book about how to do 'commercial research' – although in our opinion a lot of commercial (e.g. consultancy) research projects would be far better if they used the principles discussed here. Many of you reading this book will have come from commercial backgrounds, where you will have had experience of either doing, commissioning, or interpreting the results of market and commercial research. While this will give you a decent start, you should be aware that the academic research environment is *very* different from the commercial environment. In the commercial research world, a client comes up with a brief for research, aimed at tackling a specific problem for their organisation. What is important is *solving the problem*. For example, if the brief is 'find out why sales of my Fizzy Sugar Water drink are falling', the company only wishes for an answer to that question. Furthermore, that answer is likely to be guarded jealously by the company as a competitive advantage. Without an understanding of much of the rest of this book, it is hard to show how this is different from an academic study, but we can give you some brief ideas. For example, there is very seldom any 'theory' underlying the commercial research project, instead the researcher simply goes out into the world and looks for answers. This approach ignores vast swathes of prior work that has been done, which may be applicable to the situation. Furthermore, commercial researchers tend to be led by the data they collect (we call it being 'data driven') rather than interpreting data in the light of prior theory. This can lead to answers which are applicable to the single situation – which is of course the objective of commercial work – but have little value to other contexts. However, as you will see later on, academic research takes a far broader approach.

Academic research is usually concerned with generating new knowledge about something. This knowledge can be general or applied to a specific situation. However, the important distinction from commercial research is that it *rests on a theory of what knowledge is and what it is not*. What we mean is that for commercial research the 'knowledge' is not important for its own sake, just for solving a problem, whereas in academic research it *is* important. Our knowledge of the world increases in incremental fashion as more and more researchers discover new things, which add on to other things which we already 'knew'. In order for this process to be coherent, we must understand exactly what knowledge is, and how we can generate it. In doing so we can develop some level of appreciation as to how that piece of knowledge fits with the rest of cumulative human knowledge. In a commercial context, this is not important in the slightest. You tend to find that academic research projects are concerned with general theories rather than specific problems. For example, you might find a study on 'factors which influence the sales of fast moving consumer goods', rather than one aimed at a specific brand of fizzy sugar water. Such a study would often have to spend considerable time on understanding previous theories before ever going out into the field to collect data. The aim of such a project would not necessarily be to solve a management problem, but to further develop theory. This type of research is often called **pure research**. It is research done for the sake of improving knowledge. It is part of the duty of academic researchers to disseminate the findings of their work in an open fashion, such as through books, research articles in journals, and things like that. Such work can be aimed at discovering new things, or extending existing knowledge and theories into new contexts. The key, however, is that every academic/pure research study should make a *contribution to existing knowledge*. In other words, it must (a) **tell us something we didn't know before**, and (b) **be conducted in a rigorous way**. The rest of this book will be about how you can do that.

This is not to say that the findings from academic research are of no use to anyone except other researchers. Indeed, in the social sciences (and especially the business research fields) it is often part of the remit of the academic researcher to produce findings which are of some use to the relevant practitioner. That's why in many management and business research journals you will find a section marked 'managerial implications', where the researchers try to show how managers can take this new knowledge and improve their performance in some way. The term **applied research** is often used to refer to research that is aimed at solving a particular problem. However, it is our opinion that it should not be confused with the commercial research above. Applied research, to us, should be considered as a form of academic research which is aimed at providing answers to a specific problem, *as well as contributing to theory*. Often, we can take existing theory and apply it into a specific business context. But this work must still be based on theory and knowledge, rather than just starting from scratch every time. Sometimes, applied research is funded by private organisations, who wish to use the findings to improve their processes or performance. In this case it is vital that you (and they) understand the rights you have to publish that work in academic journals, or more importantly your final thesis (if you are doing one). If possible, get a signed agreement before you put in any of your own efforts and resources.

What is knowledge?

In the previous section, we repeatedly used the term 'knowledge' as an important distinction between different types of research. What then is knowledge? Actually, it's a really hard question. Many people never really think about what characteristics a belief or piece of information must have in order for it to be classed as 'knowledge', but Chapters 2 and 3 deal with knowledge in much more detail, and will show you that there are in fact a lot of smart people who have thought about it. Perhaps you remember as a child being told about something which was called 'common sense'? We never quite uncovered what this common sense was, but it seemed to be something which was quite obvious to anyone, and you didn't have to be really intelligent to understand that it was right.[3] But what makes this 'common sense' worth believing? There never seems to be any evidence attached to common sense, it is just there, blindingly obvious. Nick once got a review back from a very well-regarded academic journal, saying that he had merely provided some evidence to support 'common sense that all sales managers would surely know already'. And herein lies to our mind the difference between 'common sense' and 'knowledge'.

In order for something to be knowledge, *it must rest upon some kind of reliable evidence* at least. Now there are different ideas as to what makes evidence reliable, which will be discussed in the followings chapters. However, you must somehow be able to justify a piece of information in order for it to be knowledge. Common sense by itself is not knowledge, unless it rests on a body of evidence (induction) or a reliable theory (deduction). The need to switch off the power before changing an electrical socket is both common sense and knowledge. It is deductive knowledge for most of us because it rests on a reliable theory of electricity; it is inductive knowledge as well for Nick as he once electrocuted himself trying to fix something. Common sense which is not also knowledge is questionable, so make sure you do question it when someone next says to you 'but it's just common sense'.

But how are you supposed to contribute to this thing called 'knowledge', if you don't even know what it is? Well, as you move through the book, you will begin to understand the different ideas about what knowledge can be and how you can generate it. Before then, you need to have some tools in your armoury. These are what we call the 'ologies'. They are four key terms for different concepts of the knowledge generation process, which can differ according to how you perceive the world and what we can know about it:

- **Ontology:** Ontology is the study of the nature of reality. For our purposes, you can think of an ontology as being a set of beliefs about *what* the world we are studying actually is. For example, is reality objective and independent of our perception of it, or is it constructed by those who experience it? Does it exist apart from our experience of it?
- **Epistemology:** An epistemology should follow from an ontology. Epistemology is the study of what we can know about reality, and is dependent in many ways on what you believe reality to be. For example, can we generate unbiased, generalisable knowledge about the world, or is this knowledge specific to a particular time and place?
- **Axiology:** Axiology is in essence about the 'aims' of your research, and receives a little less attention than the other three in this list. In a basic sense, what are you trying to do? It follows again from ontology. For example, do you try to explain and predict the world, or are you only seeking to understand it? Can you even do one without the other?

---

[3]In fact, one of Nick's (many) sayings is that 'common sense is what dumb people use to make smart people feel stupid'.

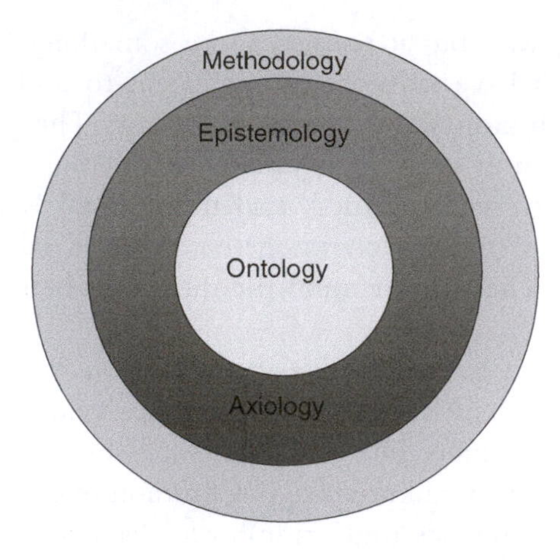

Figure 1.3 Linking the 'ologies' together

- **Methodology:** Finally, methodology is the least important, but most discussed, of these concepts for most researchers. Methodology is basically *how* you are going to go about your research. It is fundamentally dependent on the first three, as you will discover in the rest of this book. For example, are you going to use qualitative or quantitative methods?

Figure 1.3 shows one way of looking at the link between these four concepts. In fact, one way of looking at the rest of the book is as a long discussion on each of these concepts, and how they link together.

Theory, knowledge, research

So, we've discussed quite a few different bits and pieces so far, but let's have a go at linking them all together in some way. First, consider the idea of **theory**. Theory is a strange kind of concept, and Ian will deal with it in some depth in Chapters 4 and 5. There are many complex ways of defining theory, but we won't belabour the point at this stage. In simple terms, you can think of a theory as being a set of interrelated ideas, which is an attempt at explaining some aspect of the real world. Many people think of theory as being represented by words and statements; however, theories can be represented in different ways, and they sometimes get given different names when this is done. For example, a **model** is a representation of a theory, usually in some graphical or mathematical form. While we might wish our theories to include all things relevant to the aspect of the real world we are studying, this is generally impossible. Instead, theories are *simplifications* of the real world. Part of the researcher's job is to work out just how much simplification can be done beyond which nothing of interest can be found. One interesting distinction for our purposes is between **normative** and **positive** theory (Nick will discuss this in some more depth in the next chapter). Positive theory is what most of this book is implicitly concerned with, it is that type of theory which is concerned with what is actually happening, not what ought to happen. In fact, Babbie (2006) says that this is all that social science theory is concerned with. **Normative** theory, on the other hand, is about the 'right' way to do things. This can be concerned with ethical right and wrong, or a more rational type of right and wrong, such as how to make the 'right' decision in a business context. Indeed, it is the case that a reasonable amount of managerial and organisational research could be considered to have normative overtones at least. Interestingly, it is only in the relatively recent past that the great minds have focused solely on positive theory. If you begin to study philosophy in any depth at all, you'll no doubt find that philosophers in history tended to mix considerations of what *was* happening, with what *should* be happening. But that is by-the-by.

We've discussed knowledge in some more depth already, so let's talk about research now. In simplistic terms, and drawing from all of the previous discussion so far, research can be thought of as the process of generating some kind of evidence with which to support (or refute) your theory. Well, that would be a deductive way of looking at it, anyway. An inductive way of considering research would be as the process of generating information with which to form some kind of theory. In fact, we like to think of the research process as one of *linking together the theoretical world and the 'real' world*. This is exemplified in Figure 1.4, which will form an overarching structure for this book. Each chapter is designed in some way to illuminate this link in a different way.

The *theoretical world* is the world in which our ideas, theories, and concepts exist. Part of the research process exists solely in this world. That part concerns linking together different

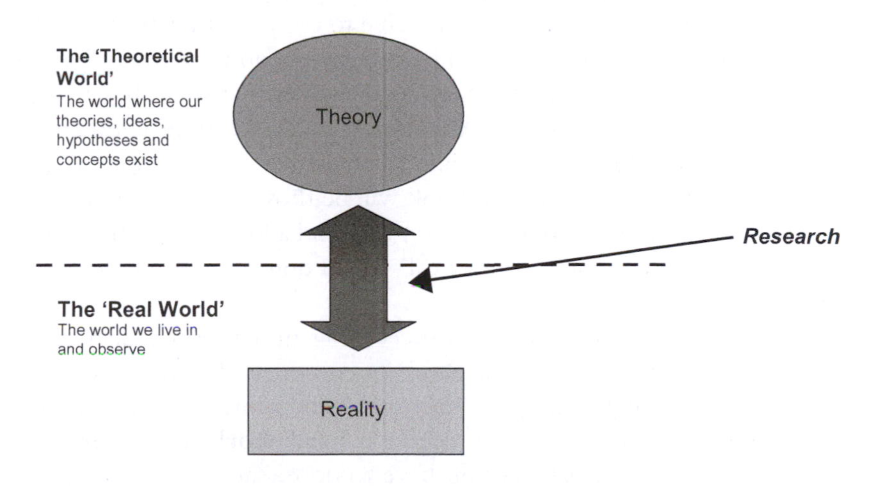

Figure 1.4 Theory, reality, research

ideas, theories, concepts, laws, generalisations, and the like. If this process results in something which makes enough of a contribution to our knowledge in itself, it can be the subject of an entire research project or dissertation. However, this book is more about the type of research which tries to link theory with 'reality' – whatever your beliefs about the nature of reality. The conception of knowledge we've outlined earlier is the *result of research*. Whichever way that research is conducted, if it is done so in a justifiable way, then it should either (a) create new knowledge, or (b) add evidence to our existing knowledge. Both of these are contributions to knowledge, and are appropriate to different situations. As you move through the rest of this book, you will begin to learn about the different ways you can justifiably conduct research and create knowledge, and how proponents of one view may differ from, and disagree with, proponents of another.

Some practical tips and advice

So, after the information about what this book is about, it would be useful to tell you what it is *not* about. Although before you read on, perhaps you should go to the counter and purchase this? Go on, you know you want to!

Now you've paid for the book, here's the bad news. This book is *not* a handbook on how to do your research degree from choosing a topic to writing your dissertation. There are a number of very good books on that topic (some of which we refer to at the end of this chapter). This book is – as we have already mentioned – for somebody who wants to learn how to *think* in the way that is required to become a good researcher. It's not a 'cookbook', or a step-by-step guide. It's designed to show you the different ingredients, explain how they link together, and then allow you to design your *own* recipes. Then, each time you have to do research, you won't have to find a recipe to copy, you'll have the skills to design your own. So you won't be finding sections on how to choose a topic, how to manage your supervisor and your time, and all of that. You can get that stuff elsewhere. It's useful, but it won't make you a good researcher. Although you may become a good mimic of one! Which is fine until you hit something you didn't prepare for ... However, we do recognise that a large amount of the audience of this book will be those who *are* candidates for higher research degrees. So even though we don't want to spend a lot of time on it, we would like to dispense some helpful advice on the 'practical' side of doing a research degree. Which we shall do so here.

First of all, we believe the key factor in succeeding in a research degree of whatever form is not intelligence, is not having a good supervisor, and is not choosing the right topic. These things are useful for sure, and they make you more likely to succeed (usually). However, the key to success in a research degree is **hard work**. If you are willing to put in the required effort, and do whatever you have to do to succeed, then you *will* succeed almost every time (barring unforeseen catastrophes and the like). This is true whatever your research goal is,[4] whether it be to publish in the top journal in your field, or achieve a big research grant; anything is possible if you are *genuine* in your willingness to do whatever it takes to get there. So ask yourself before you start, are you willing to make sacrifices to get through? If not, think very carefully about starting a research degree, and a research career, because it is *not* an easy ride. The other question you need to ask yourself is **why are you doing this**? It is very important that you have a goal in mind which completing a research degree will help you achieve. Both of us did Ph.D. degrees because we wanted to be academics, and this goal helped us when times get tough. If you are just doing it because you don't have anything else to do, then you are setting yourself up for disaster.

Secondly, while learning the conceptual, technical, and methodological tools outlined in this book should give you a huge head-start on becoming a great researcher, you also need to realise that researchers like us, you, and your supervisors and colleagues are **human**. These collections of humans in academic departments are just the same as all other social systems. They are subject to (sometimes huge) egos, politics, emotional entanglements, romantic intrigues, friendships, nemeses, and all of the rest. And when you start going to academic conferences things will get even more interesting! With this in mind, as a research student you should make yourself aware of the political situation in your department, and your academic field. Who is powerful? What viewpoints on the subject are dominant? Things like that are very important to your success. Not that you have to follow the crowd at all. Please be different and original. However, if you are going to be controversial you need to pay attention to who is likely to be with you, and who is likely to be against you. Don't go barging in like you are the greatest thing ever seen (even if you think that you are[5]). Remember, even though *you* think your work is the most important thing in the world, academics have many other demands on their time and mental resources. So do try to balance your demands with the other demands on your supervisor and colleagues. Our advice is to try to integrate yourself with your academic department socially, but don't feel you have to become 'best friends' with anyone in particular. Of course rules are made to be broken, but do remember that close personal relationships can make your life more difficult. If you are happy with that, then go for it. Conversely, being likeable and respectful, and participating in social activities, can help you immensely. So what we are saying is try to understand the social situation of being a researcher, and balance these things out.

Finally, let's talk briefly about topic choice. Simply put, there are no real rules here. It's important not to do something you hate or fundamentally disagree with, but then again this could lead to some very interesting angles on a topic. Most books advise you to do something you are 'interested in', but sometimes this advice is not very helpful. In fact, if

---

[4]Incidentally, it's true of pretty much everything in life!

[5]For those of you who knew Nick as a Ph.D. student, yes he is aware of the irony of these statements, thank you.

you get too involved in your topic, you will have major problems writing it up – since most of the time this involves some ruthless cutting of prized work (we'll talk about this in Chapter 16). We've both seen Ph.D. students have real problems finishing off as they just didn't know when to stop, and didn't want to take advice on changing things to give them the best chance of passing the examination. Their topic was so special to them that they couldn't look at it rationally. What *is* very important is that your *supervisor is interested in the topic*. Remember, they have many demands on their time, so if they love your work they are much more likely to engage with it. Topic choice should really be in conjunction with your supervisor in our opinion, but some good tips on choosing a topic are:

- Do try to be interested in some way in the topic, it does help.
- Make sure your supervisor is interested in it, and is competent to supervise the topic.
- It also helps if your supervisor has an idea of the methods you will use and can assist you in learning about them.
- Make sure you are not doing something too outrageous. It is attractive to do something 'radical', but it often leads to major difficulties later on.
- That said, make sure you are doing a topic which has scope for development and flexibility. You need to make sure you can make enough of a contribution to knowledge to justify your degree.

Final points, and how to use this book

We hope that this chapter has given you a flavour of what this book is about and how it can help you. As you have probably worked out already, we think research is a wonderful business to be in, even though it can sometimes be incredibly frustrating! Our idea is that you will be able to use this book as a central source for your development as a researcher. When you need something more specific, you can begin by referring to the sources which are presented at the end of each chapter. Most definitely we don't think this book is everything you need to know to be a great researcher. But we do think it is the best *starting point* available to someone who wants to become an academic researcher in a social or organisational research field.

One of the reasons we believe this is that it contains an integrated and in-depth view of things which you don't often find in a single source. For example, it is rare to find such attention given to philosophy of science in a foundational book (see Chapters 2, 3, and 15), as well as information on measurement (Chapters 6 and 7), literature and theory development (Chapters 4 and 5), and both qualitative and quantitative research methods. However, we think that a key strength of the book is its integration. At many points we have tried to link together philosophical issues with practical and technical ones, to show how they are inseparable.

With this in mind, a key goal was to write the book in such a way that a reader would feel comfortable reading it from cover-to-cover (as well as being able to dip in and out).

We don't feel that one can truly appreciate the research process in a piecemeal fashion. As we have hopefully hammered you over the head with in this chapter, research is a set of inextricably interlinked parts – like a puzzle with an almost infinite variety of answers. We do appreciate (more accurately, our Ph.D. students have forced us to accept) that many of you will dip in and out of this book as you hit on certain problems. However, we have tried very hard to cross-reference throughout, so maybe you will be inspired to read other parts of the book as well.

Before we finish, we'd like to draw your attention to some of the more unique features of the book – to help you get the most out of it. You'll no doubt be aware that the first section of this chapter contained three interesting things you might not have seen before in a research book, and these are repeated at the start of each chapter. First, we have a viewpoint from a leading scholar who is an acknowledged expert in their field, with special knowledge or skills in the topic of the chapter. These academics have been specifically selected as having interesting and important information about the topic, and maybe even viewpoints that differ from ours! As we keep saying, research is about different perspectives, and we hope to give you as many as possible in this book, while still being somewhat coherent. Secondly, we have a corresponding viewpoint from a researcher who is closer to the beginning of their careers, perhaps a research student, or someone who has recently finished a research degree. We call this the 'View from the trenches' as it is a view from the front lines of actually doing research. These contributors were selected specifically as they dealt with the topic of the chapter in some depth when they were 'learning the ropes'. We hope they will let you in on a few secrets that your supervisors and more experienced colleagues might not tell you about, and show you how to avoid common pitfalls. Finally, there is a section entitled 'Why is it important to know this stuff?' We developed this section because we were told that – to our shock – students tend not to read things just for the sake of it. This section will tell you *why* the topic of the chapter is vital to your development as a researcher, whatever research path you travel down.[6]

Within each chapter you will also find two different types of box. **Alternative views** show that there are indeed different ways of looking at a particular topic, and give you pointers about how you can find out more, or extend your own knowledge. On the other hand, **Illustrations, Definitions and Examples (IDEs)** extend the body text a little more, sometimes giving examples of how you can apply concepts practically, sometimes giving extended definitions of concepts which don't 'fit' in the main body. At the end of each chapter you will find a list of our favourite books and articles on the topic of that chapter, with some brief details about why we think they are so great. The full reference for each of these is provided in the Bibliography section at the end of the book. Finally, you'll find

[6]At this point Anouche Newman and Laura Chamberlain deserve significant thanks for coming up with the ideas of the 'View from the trenches' and 'Why is it important to know this stuff?' sections respectively.

some exercises which you can go through to help you cement the content of this chapter in your mind. The exercises are designed to be (at least a little) fun, and also to help you realise that – even though it may sometimes feel like it – your research career is not the only thing of importance in life!

Finally, we'd just like to make a short note on who we are, and our own research standpoints and backgrounds. As you already know if you were paying attention earlier, this book was jointly conceptualised by both of us, while we were colleagues at Aston Business School. However, Ian subsequently moved to the University of Technology in Sydney, and thus the lion's share of the writing was done by Nick, with Ian's contributions explicitly noted at the beginning of the relevant chapters. Both of us did our Ph.D. degrees at Aston Business School in the UK, and we share a similar view on research. This view on research would most clearly be expressed by the content of the next chapter – so we won't go into it here in any depth. While this may seem self-explanatory to many, we both believe that there is an external world out there to be observed, explained, and ultimately predicted, and that the knowledge we generate in one situation can (within limits) be generalised to other contexts. However, we are aware that this is not the view held by all researchers, and we have tried very hard to provide enough information about alternative views to allow you to make your own minds up on what you believe about reality, knowledge, and research (see especially Chapter 3). Nevertheless, methodologically speaking we are both eclectic, having published work using qualitative and quantitative methods, as well as work which has been purely theoretical.

So, onwards into the great wide open! We hope you have taken the following points from this chapter:

- Being a researcher can be a rewarding choice of career; but it is a process of constant learning as well.
- This book is about learning how to *think* about doing research, much more than it is about technical processes such as formulae and numbers.
- Research has many different definitions, but one overall common characteristic is that it concerns the generation of knowledge about the world.
- There are some differences between inductive and deductive processes of research, but in practical terms we often incorporate both in any given project, especially in the social sciences.
- Academic research must make a contribution to knowledge, or in other words, tell us something we didn't know before. That said, there are many ways of conceptualising just what a contribution to knowledge actually is.
- Knowledge is information which has some degree of justification, but that justification can differ according to one's epistemology and ontology.
- Ontology, epistemology, axiology, and methodology are key concepts, and are all linked together.
- On one level, research is the process of linking theory to reality, whatever your beliefs about these things, and it results in the creation of knowledge.
- This book is about knowledge creation through research, and we hope it adds something to the already vast literature on the subject.

Further reading

There are many, many outstanding books on research and research methods out there in the world. In some ways, we would like this book to act as a central point, from which you can go out and learn more as required. With this in mind, and as we already mentioned, at the end of each chapter we will provide a list of our favourite books and articles on the topic, for your reading delight. We refer to many books which have relevance to the content of this chapter later on, in other chapters, but some which do not appear later are:

- *The Practice of Social Research* by Earl Babbie. This book is popular in the US, but not so much in Europe. This is a shame, as we think it offers an excellent insight into the theory of research, as well as the social practice of it.
- *How to Get a Ph.D.* by Estelle M. Phillips and D. S. Pugh. This book is as much about the process of the Ph.D. as it is about research itself. It is a useful resource on lots of things we don't cover here – like managing your supervisor, time management, and all of that stuff.
- *Logic* by Wilfred Hodges. Logic is a useful tool for aspiring researchers in many ways, and this book is a nice introduction to it.

There are what seem like hundreds of other books on the market which are called things like 'Doing a Dissertation', 'Research Methods for …' and the like. We wouldn't want to recommend any specific ones from this group. After all, if they did what we wanted, we wouldn't have written our own! Nevertheless, each of them offers some unique insight, and they can all contribute to your development.

EXERCISES

Unlike the rest of this book, we have only one exercise for you this time. However, we think it might be the most important of the lot!

1. Write down in less than 300 words an answer to the question: *Why are you doing research?* In it, consider the following points:

   a. What are the aims of your project?
   b. What do you hope to get out of it?
   c. How committed are you to this goal?
   d. What are the implications of the first three issues on the effort you are willing to put in to the project?

It's important to note that there are no right or wrong answers here, but clarifying your feelings at the start will help you immensely to direct and channel your efforts, as well as set your expectations as to the likely outcomes. Remember, you can be as successful as you want, as long as you are willing to put the effort in. It's up to you!

Chapter 2
The scientific approach to research

SUPERVISOR'S VIEW: EMERITUS PROFESSOR WILLIAM W. ROZEBOOM

The Enigma of Hypothesis Testing: Although it is generically a sound principle of hypothesis appraisal that verifying some previously uncertain consequence *c* inferred from a hypothesis *h* increases *h*'s credibility, the hypothetico-deductive (HD) model of scientific inference standardly proclaimed in introductory science texts (you'll see it later in this very chapter) is operationally helpful to roughly the same degree as would-be driver training that never mentions traffic signals. The HD training slogan's counterpart neglect is failure to recognise, much less suppress, two potential confirmation corruptions, *hypothesis inflation* and *consequence dilution*: if hypothesis *h* entails consequence *c* (abbreviate this as $h \rightarrow c$) while *a* and *d* are additional propositions such that *a*&*h* is not logically false nor *c-or-d* logically true (that is, ignoring trivialising extremes), then also $a\&h \rightarrow c$ [h-inflation] and $h \rightarrow$ *c-or-d* [c-dilution]. These seem to allow HD confirmation to make dubious conjectures plausible by appending them to some theory generating a strong track record of successful predictions, and to diminish prediction failures of theories we love by disjunctive cushioning of their more dubious implications. And though common sense surely shields us from inferences so egregiously perverse, we still want some metatheory clarifying how such arguments go wrong and some concern for whether subtle versions of these may not sometimes degrade our real-life reasoning.

Hypothesis inflation is as common as food mold and often not merely benign but operationally unavoidable. Almost always in scientific research, and scarcely less frequently in everyday life, our hypothesis-based deductive predictions take the form 'If *h*, then *c* always occurs in circumstances *a*', or more briefly, 'If *h*, then *c*-wherever-*a*'. (Inference this ideally determinate is in practice usually softened to probabilistic import. But problems of strict-entailment rationality don't vanish from probabilistic inference; they just get murkier there.)

When empirical research on prospect *h* finds or experimentally contrives an instantiation *i* of observable condition *a*, whether *i* also manifests *c* is a test of inflated hypothesis *a(i)&h* which, however, focuses its confirmational impact just on *h* since *a*(*i*) retains its truth presumption. But an *h* with non-trivial real-life implications can almost always be analysed as a conjunction of constituent propositions; and *h*'s confirmation as a whole by HD consequence verification seldom if ever confirms all conjunctive constituents of *h* equally. Indeed, it may even disconfirm some.

An important admonition for science praxis follows immediately from this: **Never interpret results of a hypothesis test holistically**. For your research to advance our understanding of the topic addressed by hypothesis *h*, it is nearly worthless for us to learn simply that your test of *h* has confirmed/disconfirmed this by verifying/refuting *h*'s data implication *d*. Unless *h* is trivially simple, it is logically a conjunction of many propositions, not all of which are needed for *h* to entail your declared prediction. Those which are not inflate a more austere portion *h** of *h* sufficient to imply *d*, and have no manifest claim to any of the belief change warranted by our learning whether *d*. So far as you are able you should try to identify components of *h* that can be expunged from *h* without impairing the deflated *h**'s import for your study's results. It does not, however, follow that whenever *h* is logically equivalent to *g&h** with *h** alone sufficient to predict your experiment's *d*-outcome, our *g*-credence should be indifferent to that result. If *g* has explanatory import for *h**, confirmation of *h** by your *d*-finding should also pass some confirmation back to *g*. And if we suspect that *d* may be overdetermined, i.e. has multiple sources perhaps including *g* that can bring about *d* even absent *h**, our current belief repertoire may approve an adjustment of our *g*-credence in light of your *d*-finding independent of how that affects our *h**-belief. It is impractical for a research report to attempt updating the credibilities of all propositions to which its results are relevant, but it's important to appreciate that its *h* is generally a conflation of many ideas and needs separate appraisals of its most salient parts.

Consequence dilution, on the other hand, seems to be more a metatheoretic curiosity than an operational threat insomuch as commonsense should scorn reasoning this manifestly perverse even though disjunctive predictions such as parameter intervals aren't always objectionable. But we still want some understanding of how diluting a HD test's prediction corrupts that, and the provisional account I would proffer were more space available here challenges us to clarify our notions of 'because'. You would appreciate that explication more, however, were you to develop it on your own. Although it's far too early in your career for you to fly solo on that, you might give it a try to test your potential at concept analysis – not expecting to reach an articulate conclusion but to see if philosophy-of-science puzzles turn you on.

VIEW FROM THE TRENCHES: DR JAN WIESEKE

When I started my Ph.D. I was struggling with the practical and scientific requirements of my work. I felt that my thesis had to make both a scientific as well as a practical impact. At that point of time I found this tightrope walk to be a key challenge for me. Now, looking back after completing the thesis, I still think that this point is of crucial importance. My feeling is that talking to practitioners and their main problems significantly helps to develop exciting research. The quest for a researcher is then to abstract from the concrete problem to a generalisable phenomenon. But it is difficult early on to fully understand even what the ideal of generalisability means.

If there is one other thing that I found to be helpful in this challenge I would say multidisciplinarity. If you are stuck entirely within a single discipline you can sometimes miss out on key aspects of scientific methods and philosophies, depending on the development of your discipline. In my case I had a detailed background in psychology, doing my Masters in this area. During my Ph.D. in the business/marketing field this background was of immense help. With the knowledge about psychological methods, philosophies, theories and current research topics, it was much easier to develop research questions and to find research gaps in the marketing area. Moreover, due to my earlier studies I also had a broader equipment of methodological approaches in my mind, compared to other Ph.D. students with no interdisciplinary background. Crucially, it also helped me to more clearly understand key scientific concepts, which weren't as clearly explicated in the marketing literature I was reading for my Ph.D. That said, it is important to realise the extra-effort that is necessary to delve into two disciplines. Nevertheless, from my experience this effort has had a large and long-term pay off. Therefore the best suggestion that I can give is to gain interdisciplinary insights as early as possible within the Ph.D.-time.

The word 'science' means many different things to different people. To some it conjures up images of white-coated people in high-tech laboratories performing experiments with Bunsen burners or particle accelerators. To others the image of a wizened, white-bearded man (often suspiciously like Albert Einstein) writing formulae on a blackboard dominates. I'll be discussing some of these stereotypes later in this chapter. However, even though the 'sociology' of science will prove important throughout this book, in the main I want here to talk about science in terms of the *philosophy and methods* of science, not the type of people who *conduct* science. Again though, stereotypes dominate many people's thinking on this issue. To a large part of the population, real science is solely concerned with what could be called the *natural* world – rocks, atoms, chemicals, forces, flora and fauna, and the like. Others, often those who, like me, work in the area, consider the *social* world to be part of the concern of science. But even among social researchers there is contradiction over what science is. Some see 'science' as an honorific term for a discipline to work towards, others as an irrelevant label held over from the past – a 'cringe' towards the so-called real sciences which betrays a lack of confidence. I will also talk about some of these issues in the coming chapters.

I prefer to think of science in a rather less judgemental way. The term 'science' certainly implies some rather important things about the characteristics of a field, which will be considered in the following sections. However, to call one discipline a 'science' does not mean it is *better* than another. Science in one sense is simply a label which one can put on a field or discipline to distinguish it from another type – such as an art, or practice. Of course, it's important to label disciplines, as it implies certain characteristics about what one can and can't do, the type of knowledge one can gain from the discipline, and how it should be used. Even so, this does not imply that one type of knowledge is always better than another – although in certain circumstances this may be the case. Nevertheless, just as 'red' is not inherently better than 'blue', science is not inherently better than art, for example. However, science is also a term which can be applied to a specific *method* for generating knowledge, which has developed from the work of many eminent philosophers – some of whom will be introduced in this chapter. The aims of the following chapter are thus twofold. Firstly, I want to give you the knowledge of what science *means* and what the scientific method *is*. This involves in part a brief but fascinating journey through the lives and work of some very interesting people over the past 2,500 years. Secondly, at the end of this chapter I would like you to be able to think of science in a non-judgemental way, and begin to be able to determine *for yourself* whether you want to be a 'social scientist' or not.

But in order to answer this question, you need to have come to terms with the following key concepts that are covered here:

- How notions of science developed throughout the history of philosophy.
- Different ideas about what science and scientific knowledge are.
- The scientific method as a way of conducting research.
- The implications of such a viewpoint for *social* scientists.

Why is it Important to Know This Stuff?

Firstly, you should also understand that the concepts I am about to mention in this little box apply equally to the next chapter, but let's not complicate things right now – I'll do a very good job of that later on. Anyway, if you recall Figure 1.4 in the previous chapter, you know, the link between theory and reality, you can see where philosophy of science fits in. It's concerned with exactly how we can link theoretical ideas to the reality of our world, but also about the nature of that reality, and how much we can ever know about it. Figure 2.1 expresses the position of philosophy in this little model of research. Philosophy is often thought of as dry, boring, and irrelevant – rather like research methods themselves, or music theory in fact (you know, notes, scales, time signatures, keys, melodies, all that stuff). 'Why is this relevant?' I hear you ask. Well, most of us listen to music – and I listen to, write, and play *a lot* of music. So when I'm not thinking about research, I'm thinking about music (well, almost always anyway). Now it's perfectly possible to write a great song without *knowing* the first thing about music theory, and which melody fits with which key and all that – I can name hundreds of them (unfortunately none written by me). But those songs are great by *luck*, or instinct if you would rather call it that. That doesn't make the song less great, but it does make it rather more difficult to consistently keep writing great songs – since you don't know *why* they worked. Just that it 'felt' right at the time.

Philosophy of science is like the music theory of research – it tells you what knowledge itself should be, which questions you can ask about the world, which methods are appropriate to collect data to answer those questions, and even what answers you can logically give to your questions. You can do great research without knowing a jot of philosophy, but again it will be by luck, instinct, or by simply slavishly following a model laid down earlier – say, by your supervisor. The former means you are not likely to do consistently good research, and the latter means you are doomed to simply repeat that which has gone before and never create anything original (I can name a few musicians who take the same approach!)

So it's important to have a grasp of the philosophy of science in general. It's also important, however, to have a good grounding in the 'scientific' approach to research – which with most of this chapter is specifically concerned. This approach was the backbone to many of the great discoveries of natural science, and also underpins the social scientific methodology. The approach discussed in this chapter forms the bedrock of social science, so it's a really important starting point for you. While (as Chapter 3 will explore) criticisms have appeared, one needs a grounding in the traditional scientific approach in order to criticise it – if that's what you want to do. Without this grounding, any criticisms are uninformed, or just copies of those made by others. So whoever you are, and whatever you want to do, the content of this chapter is vital to your research education.

Furthermore, the story of the philosophy of science is full of weird characters with strange ideas – it's the great soap opera of Western history (and I am just going to present the 'clean' version)! Finally, my stated goal of this book is for you to leave it being able to think for yourself, and if you want to think for yourself, you should concern yourself with the thoughts of great thinkers in the past. You might just find it interesting.

Oh yeah, I make some pretty good jokes in here too, if I do say so myself!

To begin, we will together travel back over two thousand years to Ancient Greece (if it helps, you can imagine swirling colours and whooshing sounds to enhance the illusion)!

Philosophy and the roots of science

Although the specific details of this are subject to some debate, it is generally accepted that the first true philosophers were the Milesians, who lived in Miletus, a city on the coast of what is now Turkey in the 6th century BC, which sounds nice. Unlike many other humans at that point it would seem that they had quite a lot of spare time, since they began to ask the question 'what is reality made of?' If you go back to the first chapter, it is easy to see that this is a fundamental question concerning the philosophy of science! In fact, it is often surprising for non-philosophers to discover that questions of the philosophy of science seem to be those which have exercised the minds of many of what we consider the 'great' philosophers. Moving back to the Milesians, the reason which we consider them to be the first true

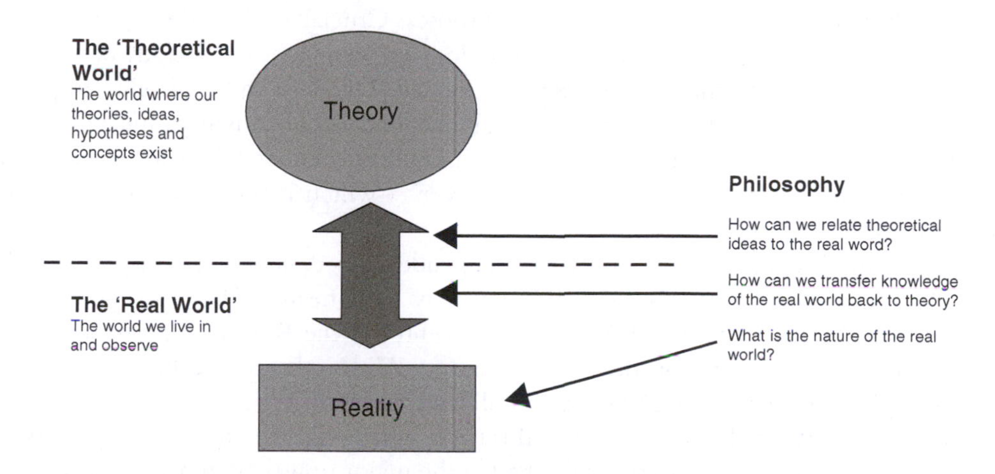

Figure 2.1 Philosophy's place in the research model

philosophers is that they were unwilling to rely on supernatural (e.g. religious) explanations for phenomena. In other words, they did not want to 'explain away' anything they didn't understand by appealing to an all-powerful God or Gods. Pythagoras (571–496 BC), who lived in Greece, was also concerned with the nature of reality. You may remember him from your geometry and mathematics classes. He had some strange beliefs (such as eating beans was sinful), but he also believed that truth should not be accepted but instead *proved*. Of course, considering as he did that the only truth is mathematics, makes this doctrine somewhat easier. Fortunately for today's students, most supervisors have given up on his rather harsh method of dealing with student debate – he once drowned one of his students for revealing the existence of irrational numbers (such as Pi) to the world. Heraclitus (*circa* 500 BC) believed that one can never trust the knowledge from our senses. Instead, true knowledge comes from reason, not observation. These and many other 'pre-Socratic' philosophers contributed much to early philosophy of science, even though most of the specifics of their ideas have since been disproved. This is an important illustration of *scientific progress*. New ideas inevitably build on those prior to them, either extending or debunking them with additional knowledge. We are all but one small link in the vast and constantly growing chain of knowledge.

Socrates (470–399 BC) is generally considered to be the 'father' of Western philosophy. One of his primary contributions was to move philosophy away from questions of reality, and towards questions of *morality*, which do not really concern us here. However, his fundamental doctrine is a compelling one to all good researchers: **question everything**. He is credited with inventing Socratic Dialogue, which essentially involves a constant questioning of ideas, which he believed should ultimately lead to the truth. He must have been a rather exasperating dinner party guest, and perhaps this was why he was eventually condemned to death by his erstwhile allies. Many of those who followed Socrates, such as Plato (427–347 BC), have much importance to philosophy in general, but Aristotle (384–322 BC) is particularly relevant to our purposes. Crucially, Aristotle appears to have first articulated the concepts of deduction and induction, which you've already come across in Chapter 1. This led to the idea of *generalisation* (see IDE 2.1), and the ability to predict events from theory. Aristotle also thought long and hard about causality, and why things behave as they do. Ultimately though, he talked himself into something of a corner, tracing all events back to one single cause or 'prime mover' – which is uncomfortably close to a supernatural explanation.

It is at around this point that history begins to intrude on our tale. In fact, one of Aristotle's pupils, Alexander the Great (356–323 BC, you may have heard of him) swept all before him across the Mediterranean and Asia Minor. Eventually the Roman Empire supplanted Alexander to become the major force across Europe. Within this period little concerns us, and philosophy was mainly concerned with politics and morals.

Another major event also occurs around this time, which you may have already guessed – Christianity. Once the Church was established as the major power within Europe, it held a monopoly on all types of thought. Philosophy became concerned with religious questions,

IDE 2.1: Generalisation

Generalisation is a key concept in research, and you'll be spending much more time learning about it in later chapters. Generalisation is in essence the idea that we can apply our specific results to a wider context than just the one that we studied. Aristotle's thinking about induction paved the way for generalisation in a number of ways. Induction, as you should remember, is the idea that we can theorise from the observations we make. So if Aristotle observed a number of fish swimming in the river, he is able to make an educated assumption from this data that all fish can swim. This concept gives science the ability to predict rather than simply report what is happening. But as we shall see in Chapter 3, not all social researchers think that this is a good thing

i.e. *Theology*. Questions of science were subservient to questions regarding the nature of God, Evil, or suchlike. Explanations of phenomena also required consideration of the role of God. One can imagine that the Milesians would not have been best pleased.

Renaissance, enlightenment and empiricism

The period of Church domination of Western thought is often termed 'The Dark Ages', and not without reason. In fact, it is not until the 14th century that European philosophers began to ask questions about the nature of science again. In fact, the great philosophical works and ideas we've already discussed were only kept alive in the Islamic world, by the Abbasid Caliphs (rulers of what is now approximately Iran, Iraq, Saudi Arabia, Egypt, and surrounding countries). The Abbasids played a major role in transmitting the thoughts of the classical philosophers to the Christian West, and as such contributed significantly to the eventual Enlightenment.

According to some schools of thought, it was the rediscovery and translation into Latin of the Islamic collections of the work of the classical philosophers which kick-started the Renaissance in Catholic Italy, and particularly 13th century Florence. The Renaissance was an explosion of artistic and scientific endeavour, while in Protestant countries the Reformation was also associated with an increase in scientific thinking. Great scientists such as Galileo (1564–1642) employed experimentation, induction and observation to make fundamental discoveries (although this did not impress the Catholic Church overly). At the same time Francis Bacon (1561–1626) began to elucidate the idea of physical causes, and laws of nature which can be discovered by scientific methods. But the man commonly accepted as the originator of modern philosophy is René Descartes (1596–1650). Descartes was profoundly sceptical of the evidence provided by his senses, and looked to determine a method to discover accurate scientific knowledge. Ultimately, it is arguable whether he ever did, but he did come up with a rather nice catchphrase; 'cogito, ergo sum', *I think, therefore I am*. Descartes' belief that observed data were inferior and untrustworthy compared with pure reason (termed **rationalism**) kick-started one of the key debates of modern philosophy of science, which I will come to next.

At the same time, the Enlightenment was raging throughout Europe, bringing in a new era of belief in the primacy of science and reason over superstition and dogma. One of the major contributions to philosophy of science made at this time was that of John Locke (1632–1704), one of the founders of **empiricism**. Empiricism holds that the only knowledge we have can come from our observations, and that humans have no innate ideas which are not from experience (see IDE 2.2). One can see that this is almost diametrically opposed to Descartes' position, and the debate between rationalism and empiricism as the foundation of knowledge has continued in various forms ever since.

IDE 2.2: Rationalism and Empiricism

The debate between rationalism and empiricism is possibly the key one in modern philosophy of science, and it can be argued that it has still not been satisfactorily resolved. Descartes considered reason to be more trustworthy than observation, because he was of the opinion that our senses could be easily fooled. In fact, the only things he considered to definitely exist were thoughts – because even doubting them was a kind of thought. This is where the famous 'cogito' comes from. The only thing Descartes was sure of was that he was thinking. This idea naturally leads to the contention that our reasoning must be of a greater value than mere empirical observation – since we know that our senses can be fooled.

In contrast, Locke's empiricism considered that rationalism was subservient to empirical observation. He argued that at birth the human mind was a blank slate (or as he put it a *tabula rasa*), and that therefore in order to reason about the world we first had to observe it. From this idea, it is easy to get to the stage where one can consider empirical data to be of primary importance over mental reasoning. More specifically, the 'blank slate' idea implies that all your reasoning must in some way depend on empirical observations, since you had no capacity to reason before observation. Combining the two positions of empiricism and rationalism has since occupied the minds of many eminent philosophers.

David Hume (1711–1776) was an empiricist, but he also discredited the contention that inductive reasoning can be a source of true knowledge, and this assertion is a key component of the modern scientific method. Specifically, Hume argued that scientific findings based on observation are not 'proved', but are merely conjecture. No matter how many times you observe something, it only takes a single contradictory observation to disprove your idea. Hume also believed that causality was only human belief based on prior experiences. It would pay to remember these ideas, since I shall return to both in some more detail later in this chapter – so don't worry if you haven't quite got a handle on them yet.

Immanuel Kant (1724–1804) was heavily influenced by Hume, and he will also appear (somewhat controversially) in the next chapter. Kant can be thought of as something of a mid-point between rationalism and empiricism. He considered that observations must be constituted by the mind to create knowledge, and that the mind does contain some inherent knowledge with which to categorise our observations.

Georg Hegel (1770–1831) is also important to the philosophy of science. Hegel proposed that ideas evolve towards a better representation of reality through a *dialectic* process. An idea is a *thesis*, which automatically creates an *antithesis* (its opposite). A struggle between these ideas naturally occurs until a *synthesis,* or more truthful idea, is achieved. This process is fundamental to conceptualisations of science. Hegel believed that eventually through the dialectic process we could achieve true knowledge.

Betrand Russell (1872–1970) also operated within the empiricist framework, at least in his early years. He considered that in order to understand anything, we must break it down into its component parts (philosophers term this **analysis**). He also argued that direct experience was the only route to certainty, and anything else must be created through logical construction from its component parts (i.e. **synthesis**). However, it was at around this time that *scientists* rather than philosophers began to make their presence felt in debates regarding the philosophy of science.

The Vienna Circle, logical positivism, logical empiricism and the scientific method

The Vienna Circle were not philosophers of science, but instead were practising scientists. In fact, they generally considered all philosophy to be rubbish and concerned with irrelevant, unsolvable 'pseudo-debates' (you may think the same about now). The primary members of the Vienna Circle were Moritz Schlick (1882–1936), Otto Neurath (1882–1945) and Rudolf Carnap (1891–1970), although others were involved as well. They believed that the only true knowledge was through science, with philosophy relegated to an activity which clarifies concepts and clears up confusions. They are generally associated with a philosophy of science termed **logical positivism**. In many ways, logical positivism can be seen as an evolution of empiricism. To the logical positivists, ideas were only meaningful if they were *verifiable*, or could be empirically tested. Further, knowledge of anything not *directly observable* was considered impossible. They also believed that the more abstract theories and propositions of social sciences could be reduced to those of more fundamental sciences such as physics – termed *reductionism*. True logical positivism is generally seen as having died out by the 1960s, although tragically for Schlick this happened much earlier. In direct contrast to Pythagoras, Schlick was killed by one of his students – something I am sure my own students dream of sometimes.

While positivism, in one form or another, has been argued as the 'standard view' of Western philosophy of science in the 20th century, its reliance on pure empiricism means that it is not really the foundation of modern science that it is often mistaken for. In fact, another member of the Vienna Circle – Herbert Feigl (1902–1988), who was a student of Schlick – began as a positivist, but eventually became the first to move beyond positivism when he developed and promulgated a **logical empiricist** philosophy of science, which can also be described in general terms as a **realist** position. Feigl became the first of the positivists to settle in the US when he moved to Iowa in 1931, having spent time at Harvard in 1930. In fact, in 1931 he published a paper with Albert Blumberg in the *Journal of Philosophy* which is generally credited with introducing logical positivism to America. Feigl was appointed Professor at the University of Minnesota in 1940, and in 1953 he established the Minnesota Centre for Philosophy of Science, which was probably the first such institution in the world. This Centre became a hotbed of philosophical development and discourse, and many of the contributors to 20th century philosophy of science which are mentioned in this book have passed through it, including Bill Rozeboom and Paul Meehl.

Feigl differentiated his logical empiricist position from logical positivism primarily by his disagreement with the idea that theoretical terms or concepts are solely defined by their empirical observations, or are just 'useful fictions'. Instead, Feigl argued that such terms (e.g. 'motivation', 'electron', 'force', etc.) are almost never defined by their observations (this may be most simply understood as their being 'unobservable'), yet still refer to entities which are 'real'. Thus, in contrast to positivism, realism holds that while many things scientists are interested in, such as internal human processes, cannot be directly observed, one can usefully measure them and study them in the context of theoretical explanations.

In a more general sense, the positivist claim that all knowledge must rely on empirical observation has also been discredited. Observations are instead *theory-laden.*

Observers are not passive receptors of data, but instead interpret it using concepts from, for example, language, culture, or our previous expectations. But, this is not the same as saying that a single reality does not exist (I'll deal with that idea in the next chapter), just that our empirical observations of this reality may be more or less representative due to their theory-laden nature. Similarly, realists have also criticised positivism for not being concerned with causality, only with association. Since only association can truly be observed, positivists contend that causality is an irrelevant concept. However, realists argue that scientific discovery must attempt to uncover the complexity of causal relations, or *why* an association is observed. It is realism, rather than positivism, which should probably be considered as the 'received view' of Western science in the 20th century and especially social science. In fact, even most natural sciences, such as modern physics, can also be argued as fundamentally realist due to their reliance on unobservables (e.g. subatomic particles). Nevertheless, there are of course alternative viewpoints one could take regarding the philosophy of science, many of which fundamentally oppose realism. While a coherent alternative to realism is presented in the next chapter, Alternative View 2.2 presents some additional discussion of this issue.

Alternative View 2.1: Positivism or Realism?

The term 'positivism' is often used to refer to what could be termed the 'standard view' of Western science, by both its supporters and opponents. So much so in fact that the true meaning of positivism seems to have been obscured. However, true positivism itself depends on a number of assertions which have been criticised and ultimately discredited. In particular, positivist conceptions of science only consider things to exist if they are directly observable. And any proposition which cannot be directly empirically tested is nonsense. Positivists called this *verifiability*. This rules out consideration of many theories and concepts which have become fundamental to modern social sciences such as psychology. For example, one cannot directly observe a student's motivation to attend class, only the result (actual attendance). However, motivation as an unobservable construct (which will be discussed more fully in Chapter 6) is a vital part of psychological theory, as are many other 'unobservables'. Even modern physical sciences depend on unobservable particles and forces for their explanations of the universe (read Hawking's *A Brief History of Time* if you want to know more). Positivist philosophy of science must consider any of these things to not actually exist. Nevertheless, few psychologists would consider motivation to not actually exist, nor a physicist consider a quark to be non-existent. Furthermore, causality is a huge problem to positivism. Strictly speaking, one can never observe one thing causing another, only their superficial correlation (try thinking about what you *really* observe when you see two snooker or pool balls collide, for example). But questions of one thing causing another are fundamental to the goals of most modern science. Ultimately, verifiability as a principle is untenable for modern science – since so much modern science is conceptual and not directly testable. For example, Einstein's theory of relativity was not testable from its inception, and even now not all of its empirical consequences are observable (e.g. gravitational waves).

Realist philosophies (or what Feigl introduced with his logical empiricism) share positivism's belief in an objective world which we can observe and measure. However, realist philosophy also contends that there are some things beyond our ability to confirm their existence directly, but yet still have independent existence. In other words, just because we can't see something, doesn't mean it does not exist.

Furthermore, realist philosophies accept the fact that there may be error in observing the objective world. The implications of accepting realism over positivism are manifold for the scientist. Essentially, we are now allowed to postulate abstract, unobservable entities in our theories. These entities can be related to empirically observable effects, and then if we do observe those effects, we can consider our abstract entities to actually 'exist'. So if I hypothesise some effects of motivation (e.g. class attendance) which I can observe, then my observation of high attendance will imply that motivation exists. As already mentioned in the main text, realism can be seen to place theory at the centre of scientific study. Causality is now possible in our theories as well, since the impossibility of directly observing anything more than correlation is irrelevant.

Another criticism of positivism was its contention that observation could 'prove' theory. Instead, Karl Popper (1902–1994) argued along similar lines to Hume before him, that we should never rely on empirical observation to prove our theories. In fact, this is such a compelling idea to most modern social scientists that it is difficult to conceive of anything else. Popper suggested that true scientists should look to *falsify* their theories with observations that contradict them. In this way, theories can never be proved, but only provisionally accepted in lieu of contradictory observations. It is this idea which can be argued to be at the heart of modern scientific methods, and we will see it in many concepts throughout this book, such as hypothesis testing.

The issues discussed above are all evident in the description of the **scientific method** which will be presented later. However, it should not be ignored that the very concept of a single scientific method has been heavily criticised by philosophers such as Paul Feyerabend (1924–1994), who considered that science can never be directed by a single set of procedures and rules. This will be discussed later in Alternative View 2.3, but in essence Feyerabend argued that progress is really made by radical scientists who actually *break* established rules, and that there is nothing which suggests that scientific knowledge is any better than any other. Thomas Kuhn's (1922–1996) theory of scientific progress is similarly concerned with the importance of radical change – or *paradigm shifts* – rather than the incremental progress science is often thought of as making. Interestingly, if you look at the history of scientific progress, you will see that Feyerabend and Kuhn may have had a point. In fact, many of the truly great discoveries have been made by radicals such as Copernicus, Galileo, Darwin, Einstein and Hawking. They and others like them were mavericks, who faced scorn, ridicule and even imprisonment or death for their discoveries, only later to have them become part of established knowledge (sometimes posthumously which is rather unfortunate). I will try to deal with some of these issues, particularly those concerning a single method, later. But first it would seem appropriate to try to cover some key questions which I asked myself as a doctoral student, and continue to ask today.

Alternative View 2.2: Anti-realism and Pragmatism

It should not be of any great surprise that the *anti-realist* position would deny the real existence of theoretical concepts. There have been many different 'flavours' of anti-realist philosophies of science in the 20th century, but here I will focus on **pragmatism**, which is both interesting in a general sense, and has some specific resonance for the researcher in applied social science disciplines. Pragmatism can be considered to have developed in the US in the late 19th century, with the work of Charles Sanders Peirce, William James, and John Dewey. Peirce in particular was a brilliant polymath and fascinating individual. Pragmatism acknowledges an external reality, but considers theoretical concepts to simply be fictions which help solve particular problems. In fact pragmatism's key tenet is that meaning and truth are only defined in relation to how useful they are in action. This is not quite the same as the common mischaracterisation that 'anything which works is true'. Further, pragmatists tend not to believe that truth is absolute and objective, but that it is co-created by us and the reality we are working within. In other words, only when a theory proves useful does it become true. So, theory and practice are not independent, they are inextricably interlinked. A large number of key thinkers in the latter half of the 20th century have been influenced by pragmatism's concepts, including Donald Davidson (who will appear in Chapter 15).

Echoes of the pragmatic view can be found in many of the other theories discussed in this chapter and the rest of the book. It is also something which will likely chime with those among you who study organisational and managerial topics, and particularly those who may have come from a commercial research background. However, pragmatism is not an 'anything goes' philosophy, it is still concerned with theory and reality. It is not a licence to avoid engaging with wider theories or rigorous methodologies.

What is 'science', and who are 'scientists'?

It is at this point I am reminded of a situation when I had been to a rather good party, and (somewhat the worse for wear) was having a few quiet drinks back at the hotel with Ian Lings, Ian's mum and a number of other colleagues from our faculty at the time. While Ian's mum is a wonderful woman, she made something of a *faux pas* when she asked whether any of us ever dreamed of being '*real* scientists' like a close friend of ours, who is a geneticist, 'and discovering important things which help people'. While it is fair to say we were quite insulted by this, and let her know in various loud, drunken and offensive ways (actually, mainly me to be fair since I was as usual the loudest, drunkest, and most offensive), I should really thank her since it did begin the thought processes from which much of the content of this chapter resulted. It should not be news to you that I consider myself to be a 'scientist'. However, at no point in my career as an academic have I ever worn a white lab coat (at work anyway, what I do in private is my own business). Nor have I so far conducted an experiment in a laboratory, dissected anything, or blown anything up in the course of my work. Ian, however, did begin a Ph.D. in chemistry many years ago. Does this make Ian more of a scientist than me, since he at least has a degree in 'real science'? It should by now be quite clear to you that I think not (Ian's mum probably still does though).

So what then is a scientist? Does one wake up in the morning and all of a sudden realise that he or she is a scientist? Does it give me a warm glow as I sit down at my desk for another day of 'doing science'? Not really, to be honest. However, I still have not answered the question of what a scientist is. If you sense I am beating around the bush a little, you are very perceptive. It's because I am rather nervous about the answer since it seems too simple, and I fear you may ask for your money back. *Scientists are people who do science!* Nothing more and nothing less. Of course, this begs the question: what then, is science?

Science and social science

The question of what science is does not exist purely for the interest of philosophers with too much spare time (like the Milesians), or authors who need to fill a few pages (like me). It is a question of great importance to what my non-academic friends refer to as 'the real world' (as in 'why don't you get a job in ...'). For example, at the end of the 20th century, debate raged in many American states as to whether theories of 'creationism' were equally scientific to those of evolution by natural selection. The answer to this question had major implications on how these subjects were taught in schools. The question even came to court in one American state. This case actually resulted in the judge, one William R. Overton, giving a set of criteria as to what makes a 'scientific theory', which seems as good a place as any to start at with a description of science. Judge Overton considered five features to be central to a scientific theory (see Bird, 1998 for some more details and an in-depth discussion).

1. It must be guided by natural law.
2. It has to be explanatory by reference to natural law.
3. It is testable against the empirical world.
4. Its conclusions are tentative (i.e. not necessarily the final word).
5. It is falsifiable.

You may have already come across some of these terms, and some you may not have. Beginning with the idea of 'natural law', this refers to the idea that there are underlying uniformities and general relationships between phenomena which explain the behaviour of things. Most of us can quote a number of scientific laws, or are at least aware of concepts such as 'the laws of physics' – even if it is only from old Star-Trek reruns. The first two criteria essentially mean that claims can be considered scientific if they refer to natural laws, or to facts which rely on natural laws. If not, then any claim is purely conjecture, or opinion. The third criteria means that any claims you make must be testable – i.e. detailed enough to have consequences which can be observed in some way, thus evidence for a claim can be found. Furthermore, no matter how much evidence we have found for our scientific theory, we must always be open to the idea that it may be wrong, and that new evidence may disprove it. Science is full of theories which appeared to be completely correct, only for new evidence to show them completely false (do any of you still think the Earth is flat or that the Sun revolves around the Earth?) Finally, theories should be stated in such a way that we *can* find evidence against them. Thus, scientific claims are never final, and always open to amendment if additional evidence is found.

One can look at what have been called the 'natural sciences', such as physics and chemistry, and quite clearly see that their theories and claims fulfil the above criteria. But what about the social sciences, such as psychology, sociology, economics, management, and my own field, marketing? Claims by most of the social sciences quite easily fulfil the final three of Judge Overton's criteria, but what about the criteria relating to 'natural laws'? Have the social sciences really come up with any genuine laws yet? The law of supply and demand? The expectancy theory of motivation? Are these truly laws? In fact, social sciences such as marketing have sometimes had their scientific status questioned due to the lack of discovery of universal laws (e.g. Buzzell, 1963).

However, if we consider the concept of natural laws in some more detail we find that the question of whether a social science has actually *found* any laws is not really a key issue. In fact, we need to separate the *outcome* of science from the characteristics of science. A natural law is there to be *discovered* not created by science. Thus, the discovery of such laws is the outcome of scientific research. The fact that underlying uniformities and relationships among phenomena are expected to exist in the subject matter of concern for any social science is surely more important than whether or not they have actually yet been discovered. Most of us would argue that social sciences such as marketing and sociology are indeed likely to have underlying regularities and relationships which are there to be conceptualised and subsequently discovered – even if we haven't yet to discovered them. Furthermore, most social sciences are far younger than the natural sciences such as chemistry and physics. Why then should we expect, for example, organisational psychology to have a fully formed set of universal laws for say, motivation? Did physics have such a set of laws 100 years after its inception (if one could pinpoint this time of inception of course)?

The previous discussion also has some implications for organisationally oriented social sciences (such as strategy, marketing, or organisational behaviour) which are not quite as relevant to the natural sciences. In particular, as mentioned in Chapter 1, it is important to distinguish between **normative** and **positive** aspects of fields such as strategy and marketing. This is in some ways analogous to the common debate over science and practice. Normative aspects of a discipline focus on what a manager (for example) *should* do, such as how a firm should plan its long-term strategy, or implement an incentive scheme. By contrast, positive aspects are concerned with 'attempting to describe, explain, predict and understand' the phenomena a discipline is concerned with (Hunt, 1991, p. 10). It is vitally important to avoid confusion between these two approaches to knowledge, especially in the social and organisational science disciplines. Specifically, it is the *positive* aspects of the various organisational study fields that define them as scientific, i.e. the seeking of knowledge to describe, explain, predict and understand organisational and management processes. This is the difference between, for example, marketing science, and the practice of marketing itself. To take another example, the practice of medicine depends on sciences such as biology, physics and chemistry (sometimes, the mix of sciences related to subjects like medicine is called 'life sciences'). The practice of marketing in companies is based around theories and knowledge gained from (among others) *marketing science*. This is one of the reasons I get so angry when people refer to me as a 'marketer' (well to be honest I get angry about a *lot* of things). As I once said 'do you call someone who studies insects an insect?' Of course not, they are called entomologists. I suspect that because the business and management oriented sciences relate so strongly to practical and observable phenomena, the positive, scientific study of these phenomena gets confused with the normative, practical application of scientific knowledge. Clearly understanding the distinction helps in illuminating exactly what it is that social scientists do.

So, you now have an appreciation of what science means in terms of the characteristics of a given discipline. But 'science' is also a term for what people *do*, as well as a type of knowledge. What makes a method of generating knowledge 'scientific', or indeed what makes a type of knowledge 'scientific'? I discuss these issues and others in the next section, which introduces the **scientific method**.

Scientific knowledge and the scientific method

The term 'knowledge' is one which has – like many others introduced in this book so far – caused considerable controversy throughout history. Just what is knowledge? Are there different types of knowledge? Is one type of knowledge different from another? Must knowledge be the 'truth' even? These are interesting questions, and ones which can receive contrasting answers, depending on your viewpoint. Some of these alternative viewpoints will be considered briefly here, and covered in more depth in subsequent chapters. However, I am primarily concerned here with the idea of **scientific knowledge** and its characteristics. It seems plausible to imagine that the basic output of science is knowledge, but when pushed, most laypeople (indeed most scientists) struggle to define exactly what this knowledge actually consists of. One helpful way of looking at this is to consider that this scientific knowledge, the output of science, consists essentially of a body of *declarative sentences or statements* about the world around us, that have some credibility or plausibility which allows us to trust them to some extent. Without evidence of this credibility, you could characterise a statement as simply a 'knowledge claim'. Therefore, we of course wish to provide some evidence which will drive us to either believe or disbelieve these claims.

But the question then becomes one of how exactly do we provide evidence which can assure one of the credibility of these so-called 'scientific' statements, or knowledge claims. In other words, what makes knowledge scientific in nature? While I would not claim to offer any particularly new insight to this debate, it seems to me that the 'scientific-ness' of a particular knowledge claim depends on a few things. Firstly, a given claim should have been confronted with empirical data which could reveal flaws or weaknesses. Yet, this is not always possible for knowledge which claims scientific status. For example, many of the most cutting-edge physical theories, and the knowledge claims which result from them, appear untestable with our current technological abilities, such as claims regarding the nature of black holes in space. Nevertheless, these knowledge claims *are* testable in principle in the future, in the same way that many of Einstein's theories have become testable as technology advanced in the 20th century. Another criterion for scientific knowledge also seems pertinent, that it should explain the relevant phenomena better than any credible rival explanations. Thus, scientific knowledge must be able to survive the occurrence of any data which becomes available. While we cannot, for example, directly observe what goes on inside black holes yet (and maybe we never will) theories regarding the process must be able to explain any relevant occurrences better than other credible theories for them to be regarded as scientific knowledge. Thus, at no point should 'faith' be required to accept scientific knowledge. Any method for generating scientific knowledge should therefore take into account the necessity of confronting knowledge claims with empirical information in an attempt to reveal its weakness.

Furthermore, scientific endeavour should not just be about gathering facts and observations about the world. Science should instead be concerned with creating **theory**. In other words, we should try to develop explanations of what happens in the world, not just observe what is happening. This of course is in direct contrast to empiricist (and by association positivist) standpoints. In my opinion, observation without explanation is not particularly useful. Furthermore, theory gives us reason to expect certain observations. In fact, the agreement between theoretically based expectation and actual empirical observation is one of the cornerstones of the scientific method. From this it can also be seen that science proceeds in a generally incremental fashion. Theories give us reason to expect some things, and combined with creative thinking and observation can suggest new angles on problems. Scientific research can then suggest solutions to these problems which then extend and add to the theory, and the cycle begins again.

Alternative View 2.3: Controversies in Method and Progress

In this chapter I will soon explain what has been termed by many authors the 'scientific method'. However, a radical alternative – most famously and compellingly asserted by Paul Feyerabend in his book *Against Method* – is that there can be no single 'scientific' method. His basic thesis is that for every possible candidate for the 'scientific method', there has been a situation where scientific knowledge has advanced by going *against* its principles. In fact, he argues that the only possible universal principle of the scientific method is 'anything goes' (Feyerabend, 1993, p. 28). While many philosophers of science consider acceptance of this view as a death-knell to traditional notions of science, it is not necessarily so. Specifically, it can be argued that no one method has a monopoly on knowledge; in fact, methods themselves are the products of science and are constantly being improved. Furthermore, one can take Feyerabend's famous example of Voodoo witchdoctors – which he (to his credit) was known to frequent as demonstration of his commitment to the pluralistic standpoint. If such a witchdoctor has developed a reliable method for diagnosing illness, should this not be considered 'knowledge'? Whether or not the witchdoctor attributes his success to metaphysical sources (when it may in fact be due to a physiological reason) is surely immaterial. However, orthodox advocates of the single scientific method would reject this knowledge outright. In fact, one can imagine that much knowledge has in the past been lost or ignored because of such strict adherence to the principles of 'science'.

Related to this is Kuhn's thesis of scientific revolutions. While the traditional view is that scientific progress is made in incremental fashion, Kuhn in his famous book *The Structure of Scientific Revolutions* argued that science also progressed in occasional 'revolutions' where existing ideas and methods were rejected and new ones took their place. Kuhn termed this revolution process a *paradigm shift*, where paradigm refers to a set of ideas, theories and methods used in a science. Both Kuhn and Feyerabend considered that theories and ideas from one paradigm were *incommensurable* with those from another – i.e. one cannot judge the utility of theories and findings from one paradigm from the standpoint of another (see Chapter 15 for some more information). Again then, we move into a situation where 'anything goes' – and one cannot judge work from outside one's paradigm. There is no viewpoint which is independent of all paradigms, and thus no way of comparing knowledge from one paradigm against another. It seems that a full acceptance of this is similar to claims made by postmodernists, that one can never judge the 'quality' of such research by referring to existing scientific standards (see Chapter 3). However, it can also be argued that arguments such as this ultimately lead to nihilism and the irrelevance of the very idea of knowledge itself.

While as Alternative View 2.3 shows, some have argued against the idea of a single scientific method, claims for a 'multiplicity' of scientific methods can be argued as somewhat flawed. Firstly, it is vital to separate the *techniques* used in a given scientific discipline from the *methodology* of the discipline. Techniques are the tools used to conduct scientific research. It is clear that social sciences such as psychology, organisational behaviour and marketing, use considerably different tools from natural sciences such as physics or chemistry. For example, the natural sciences often employ equipment such as Bunsen burners, particle accelerators, radio telescopes and other items. In the social sciences we rely more commonly on questionnaires, measurement scales, content analysis and the like. Nevertheless, these differences have no bearing on whether or not a discipline can be considered a science or not. As Hunt (1991, p. 20) points out 'the scientific method is not restricted to certain kinds of hardware ... or to techniques of gathering data ... or to techniques of measuring phenomena ... or, most certainly, to techniques of analyzing data'. Of course different sciences use different techniques – take astrophysics and biology for example.

The methodology of science is the manner in which a science accepts or rejects the truth of the knowledge created by the techniques it uses. In other words, it is concerned with *justification* of knowledge, not its *discovery*. While we have seen above that different sciences use different methods to discover knowledge, are there multiple ways in which to justify the knowledge created by a science? I will deal with alternative perspectives to some of these issues in the next chapter, however, many scholars have thoroughly discredited the notion that there are multiple ways to assess the truth of knowledge claims. Thus, the single scientific method is concerned with finding evidence to support claims, by using them to generate implications which are testable (such as hypotheses). These implications can then be checked by any investigator and evidence to support the knowledge claim is thus generated. How the knowledge claims are discovered is immaterial to how evidence is generated to support, corroborate and validate them. To take the witchdoctor example in Alternative View 2.3, whether the witchdoctor simply stumbled upon a reliable diagnostic method is immaterial to his *knowledge claim*, but it is the characteristics of the search for justification and explanation of that knowledge claim which makes such knowledge ultimately *scientific*. So, to go right back to the beginning of this discussion, a 'declarative statement' claiming some knowledge is only considered scientific knowledge if it has been subjected to some rigorous search for evidence and justification. It is this method of justification that will be the focus of the remainder of this chapter.

The scientific method

You should recall the previous section, where I argued that the intended output of science was in the first instance a set of declarative sentences about the world, which have a high credibility. However, the plausibility of these statements must somehow be assessed in order for us to rate their credibility. I touched on some of these issues above, but here we will cover the **scientific method** in more depth. The scientific method can be thought of in basic terms as *a set of techniques about collecting and interpreting evidence which are generally considered* *likely to illuminate differences in the plausibility of these declarative statements*, which recommends activities which help to drive us to either believe or disbelieve a given statement. In other words, the scientific method is how we find evidence to either accept (for the moment) or reject our knowledge claims.

The 'scientific method' is really quite a vague term – furthermore it can sometimes raise criticism from those who conduct research within other frameworks that it implies that their type of research is not 'scientific' and thus less useful. Although I would tend to agree with the former (if it doesn't use the scientific method, then by definition it can't be scientific), I would not like to imply that other types of research are less useful, and in this I make some small concession to Feyerabend's arguments. Thus I will avoid the use of the term 'scientific method' from now on, and call it the **hypothetico-deductive** method. This also has the advantage of sounding very clever and impressive, which can sometimes prove very useful in academic circles (some may say that I have built my whole career on it so far). The hypothetico-deductive method was articulated by Karl Popper, who I have discussed earlier, and rests on a very famous problem in philosophy of science which you are about to realise that you didn't bother to remember, even after I told you to. Now, go back to the brief discussion of David Hume and his ideas on observation as a way of proving scientific ideas. Karl Popper built on this idea and provided a very nice example which almost all of us who teach research methods have surely borrowed at one time or another. Specifically, Popper described the situation where you propose that all swans are white (a *hypothesis*). If you count all the white swans you can find, not finding any black ones, does this prove your hypothesis? The answer of course is no, because there is no way of knowing whether the very next swan you see may be black! This emphasises the tentative nature of scientific conclusions as I mentioned above – we can never prove our claims, merely find support for them until conflicting evidence comes along. The hypothetico-deductive approach systemises the search for conflicting (or *falsifying*) information.

Figure 2.2 graphically represents the hypothetico-deductive approach. One of course must first come up with some kind of research question, and define what it is that you are interested in, in a general sense (step 1). Following this is step 2, a search for ideas about that question, perhaps through a literature review or exploratory research, or an examination of prior experience in the area. Here the scientist should begin to think about the important concepts of variables which are relevant, and how they are interrelated with each other. Even more importantly, are there key issues that previous work has missed out? Many of the strategies and methods involved in this section are detailed in Chapter 4. Subsequent to a general search for ideas is step 3, a more formal process of hypothesis development. Hypotheses must be testable, and you should also make them clear and simple. For example, a hypothesis out of one of my own pieces of work (Pankhania *et al.*, 2007) is:

H_2: *The UK Indian ethnic minority will place different levels of importance on the features offered in a product than the UK Caucasian majority.*

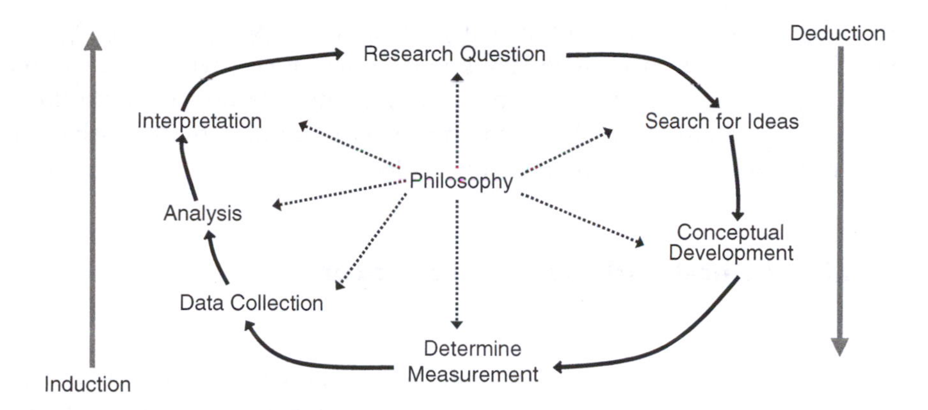

Figure 2.2 The hypothetico-deductive method

Remember, a hypothesis is simply something you expect to see in the data – it has no theoretical content. Hypotheses are just statements, which are *based* on theory, usually presented above the hypothesis. For example, for the hypothesis above, I spent half a page arguing why we should expect to see that in the data. Have a look at the paper if you want to get a feel for this (reference it in your own work too – that should help my citation scores!). Ian will discuss many of these issues in Chapter 5.

Following the theoretical development of concepts, hypotheses and models, we need to determine how to *measure* our variables (step 4). This is the subject in parts of Chapters 6 and 7. Suffice it to say here that measurement is a critical and underdeveloped part of social science, when compared with other methodological subjects, and these chapters may just be one of the most important things you ever read (other than *The Hitchhiker's Guide to the Galaxy* of course). After deciding how to measure our concepts, also called *operationalising* them, we need to collect data on those measurements (step 5). This subject has received massive attention from social scientists, and I cover much of this in Chapters 8, 9 and 11. Of course, once we have the data, we need to analyse it (step 6), which is the subject of Chapters 10, and 12–14. This subject holds more fear for students than any other – especially the quantitative side of it. But really, it's the easiest of all the stages! It's far harder to come to terms with the philosophy of science, design a good study, and collect good data than it is to analyse it. And honestly I'm not just saying it because I know how to do it – my own supervisor will relate to you many hilarious stories of my analysis incompetence at the beginning of my own dissertation work, and my colleagues can tell you of some after its completion! A far harder task is the final one (step 7), that of interpreting your analysis and drawing some conclusions. Here you must decide whether your hypotheses have been supported (remember, *never* proven) or not, and bring your work back to the original theory. Importantly, you should never forget that even if your hypotheses are not supported, this is still interesting news if you have conducted your study with solid methods. You need to relate your findings back to what is already known – and discuss why it is that you think you did not support your hypothesis. I'll be discussing interpretation at length throughout the rest of the book. Remember, the raw numbers mean nothing by themselves, it is *you* the researcher that gives them meaning for the reader.

The scientific method and the social sciences

As you should already be aware, the hypothetico-deductive method was developed in the context of the natural sciences, i.e. physics and the like. However, this book is concerned with social science, not natural science. It is not in question that the social world is different from the natural world – the real question is whether those differences necessitate a different way of investigating the social world. This chapter is aimed at explaining the viewpoint that we do not necessarily need to employ a different method to investigate social phenomena. However, Chapter 3 will present a viewpoint based around the idea that we do need a different way of exploring the social world.

The idea that the approaches and methods of the natural sciences are equally applicable to investigating the social world is termed *naturalism*, or more specifically scientific naturalism. Naturalist viewpoints range from the extreme that all things are reducible to physical properties (*reductionism* – if you recall the logical positivists), to a more gentle viewpoint which simply considers that the social world arises from the physical world, and thus natural science methods can be used to investigate the social world. It can be seen then that underpinning the philosophies of empiricism, positivism and realism within the social sciences is the idea of naturalism. However, it is important to realise that this does not mean that specific natural science techniques must be used, only that the general methodology (i.e. the search for explanation and generalisation, and the hypothetico-deductive method) is appropriate to both natural and social science. For example, Hunt's (1991) quote above specifically referred to the idea that different sciences necessarily use different specific techniques.

There have been numerous objections to the naturalist viewpoint which have been aired throughout the 20th century, by philosophers and social scientists. Chapter 3 will discuss many of these objections, and advance an alternative viewpoint as a contrast to that discussed herein. However, while I may not be so quick these days to nail my flag to the naturalist mast (I like to maintain my mystery nowadays) I was most definitely a committed naturalist (no, *not* a naturist) when I was doing my Ph.D. The next section will discuss some specifics of scientific projects.

Typical examples of 'scientific' dissertations

Of course, I can point to my own dissertation as a typical exemplar of a 'scientific' (or realist) approach to the dissertation, based on the naturalist viewpoint. In essence, it was an attempt to determine how sales managers resolved problems caused by their salespeople, and whether different problem resolution methods led to more positive sales force outcomes than others. Thus, the aim was to first uncover consistent factors generally used by sales managers, then to measure them (and their potential consequences), and then to analyse the relationships evident in the data. In order to do this, multiple methods were employed, beginning with literature reviewing, then qualitative exploratory research with sales force members, and then quantitative surveying of many more sales organisations. Thus, it can be seen that at no point can we define the scientific status of a project by its choice of methods (as was discussed above). I used both qualitative and quantitative methods to explore the research area. However, I utilised the hypothetico-deductive method as a guide to my study, and my aims and assumptions were consistent with a scientific realist approach. In other words, I believed that there was an underlying reality to be discovered, which contained regular and consistent patterns which could ultimately be generalised. Furthermore, I also believed that I could measure unobservable factors like motivation and satisfaction in a systematic and reliable way (which makes the research realist *not* positivist).

Other examples of scientific dissertations I have seen or been involved with in some way are an investigation into the effects of salesperson stereotypes on consumers' information processing, a cross-cultural study of factors impacting on sales force unethical behaviour, a study of the effects of internal marketing on firm performance, and an examination of the interpersonal factors influencing business-to-business relationship quality. Many of these projects were quantitative in nature; however almost all contained some qualitative work, and some were entirely qualitative. Nevertheless, they all fundamentally had as their base the belief that the world could ultimately be objectively measured and the knowledge gained through this research could reflect 'reality'. However, as you shall see in the next chapter, the realist position is by no means the only one available to the organisational researcher, and neither is the hypothetico-deductive the only method of enquiry into organisational phenomena.

Interestingly, from my perspective, I can't really pinpoint a particular time where I made a decision to be a 'realist', or 'naturalist'. In fact, I suspect this is the same for most researchers at the beginning of their careers. By the time you get to the stage of doing a Ph.D. for example, you normally have some solid ideas about how you feel the world works, which can be influenced by all kinds of things, such as your colleagues. I'll address this in some more depth at the end of the next chapter, but I think it's enough to say now that in order to make an informed decision, you need to have a good picture of both sides of the debate about what science is. For most novice researchers such as myself at the time, this is a considerable weakness. I certainly had no real idea of what a non-realist position on science would be, I was just drawn to the ideas collected under the realist heading – even though I didn't really know what this was. Certainly, if you cover the material in this and the next chapter well, you'll have far more information available to you to classify where you stand than I did.

Summary

This chapter is kind of 'twinned' with the next, so now is not the time to offer any final points. Nevertheless, some key points to take from this chapter are:

- The nature of science is a question that has exercised the minds of the great philosophers for thousands of years, and is still a matter of debate.
- Science is done by *people* not machines, and as it is subject to the vagaries of human behaviour and interaction, it's a sociological process as much as anything else.
- An understanding of the development of the philosophy of science over the last 2,500 years is important because it allows a student to place their own efforts into context, and to define their standpoint on research. An *interest* in the area is even better!
- The nature of scientific knowledge is not just a question for dusty academics in their ivory towers. It affects all of us in everyday life – and especially dissertation students!
- What a discipline has *actually discovered* so far does not define it as science. Instead, it is the *possible existence* of, for example, natural laws (i.e. regularities and general relationships between phenomena) which should define a discipline as scientific.
- It is important not to confuse the positive and normative aspects of organisational science. It is the positive aspects (seeking to explain and understand phenomena) which should be considered areas of scientific study, not necessarily the normative application of such knowledge.
- Scientific knowledge should in principle be testable, and also look to create theory which builds on existing theory – not just discover isolated facts.
- The techniques used to *discover* knowledge do not define that knowledge as scientific. Instead it is the logic of *justification* of those knowledge claims which is the distinction between the scientific and non-scientific methods.
- Finally, there has been considerable controversy regarding the scientific method and the incremental progress of science. However, one can usefully systemise the *hypothetico-deductive* method as a logic of discovery and justification of scientific knowledge.

Further reading

- *Sophie's World* by Jostein Gaarder: This is probably the single best book about philosophy that a beginning researcher can read, which justifies its best-seller status (16 million copies and counting). It's interesting, easy to follow and, more importantly, fun. Read it, even if you do nothing else I ever suggest.
- *Foundations of Marketing Theory* and *Controversy in Marketing Theory* by Shelby D. Hunt: Professor Hunt is probably the pre-eminent philosopher of science within my field (marketing). His thoughts have influenced so much of my own, particularly about the nature of science. I recommend reading these two books to get a great picture of a committed realist coming to terms with the nature of social science and his field of study.
- *Popper* by Brian Magee: Popper again has been a major influence on my thinking, and he is the architect of the modern scientific method. This little book is a great introduction to his thoughts on philosophy of science, but there are doubtless many others to choose

from – including more in-depth discussions of the key ideas introduced in this book. Popper also did a lot of work on political philosophy, and some is included here, but I thought that stuff was a bit boring.

- *Realism, Rationalism, and Scientific Method* by Paul Feyerabend: A true original and iconoclast. Whether or not you agree with Feyerabend's thoughts, it's worth trying to get a handle on him just to understand how fearless a thinker he was, and how committed to following through his ideas. A model of a true intellectual we can all aspire to in my opinion. That said, reading his work in the original is somewhat difficult.
- *Philosophy of Science* by Alexander Bird: This book is a great introduction to the philosophy of science. It can get a bit hard going, but that's the nature of the subject after all. This book also contains a much fuller discussion of the nature of science controversy, including all the details of the Judge William Overton court case I briefly touched upon earlier in this chapter.
- *A Historical Introduction to the Philosophy of Science* by John Losee: This book is again a fantastic introduction to the philosophy of science, and is quite easy to read for the beginner. I wish I had found this book *before* writing this chapter!

EXERCISES

1. Create a timeline of the development of thought regarding the nature of science and scientific knowledge from the Milesians to Feyerabend and Kuhn. Note the major developments discussed in this chapter on the line.
2. Now, go beyond the material given in this chapter and fill in any extra ideas and philosophers you feel are also important. Try to justify why their contributions are important.
3. Finally, place at the appropriate points on the timeline important discoveries and theories such as those made by Copernicus, Galileo, Newton and Einstein (and others you feel are important). Can you make any link between the prevailing opinion on scientific knowledge at the time, and the nature of the discovery?
4. Write down a set of typical 'scientific' study topics related to your own research area. What are the factors that make them scientific? What would be the best way to study these topics?
5. Is your supervisor (or potential supervisor) likely to be an advocate of the scientific approach or not? Write 500 words justifying why or why not. One good starting point might be to look at their previous work (e.g. journal articles).
6. Go to the gym. It is not good for you to read books all day!

Chapter 3
The interpretive approach to research

SUPERVISOR'S VIEW: PROFESSOR STEWART CLEGG

Fire! That the world is 'real' and has a material facticity, such that fire will burn you whether you believe it or not, is often seen as the basis for the scientifically realist point of view. However, that something has an innate capacity to do one thing or other, while it is interesting, is not a complete account of that phenomenon. Fire, for instance, has long had a distinct cultural role. When Captain Cook sailed up the coast of what we now know as Australia he noticed a great many fires burning on the landscape. What he did *not* know, and could not have known, was that these fires were set by the indigenous peoples of this vast land, who used fire to shape the landscape, generate fresh growth, and drive food out of the bush so it might go on their camp fires. In short, fire was socially constructed and had a key role to play in the life of the indigenous people.

The Australian continent, as a landscape, appeared to the early European settlers as a *terra nullus*, an empty land. In Europe, there were vast cathedrals, castles, and palaces, sea ports and industrial works, as well as ploughed and cultivated fields. None of these were to be found in Australia. Hence, the land appeared empty and untouched. From a strictly observational viewpoint this would seem correct: no evident modification of the landscape or anything built on it could be seen. However, it would have been incorrect. The landscape had been shaped by fire and that fire had been shaped by human society. Hence, what was important about fire in this instance was its social construction as an instrument of human development rather than merely its objective capacity to burn.

The important point for students is not just to know the 'objective truth' of things but to appreciate the ways in which what is known as members' knowledge shapes what people who belong to different organisations, societies and other collective bodies actually do in their everyday lives. It is important to realise that both Cook, as an objective observer of the landscape, and the indigenous people, as the subjects of his observation, were practical scientists. Each was acting to interpret and control their world. Cook had his compass and instruments, including the telescope with which he saw the fires burning, while the indigenous peoples had fire. Each had a complex knowledge of what their instruments could do. Each was acting on their interpretive understandings. Where one saw fire raging out of control the others could see dinner in the evening, fresh growth in the future, and regeneration of the landscape (some native plant life only germinates after it has been scorched by fire).

The power of interpretive understanding is in coming to terms with the ways in which the subjects themselves construct their own understanding and being in the world. What people know enables them to do that. In that respect, there is no real difference between the scientist and the layperson: each is trying to make sense of the phenomena they relate to by using whatever concepts and tools are available. When the scientist is safe within the laboratory dealing with phenomena like atoms that themselves have no understanding of their being, the scientists' views can go unchallenged except by other scientists. When the laboratory is human life and society it is as well to take into account the views of the lived experiences that constitute the laboratory. And, as might be expected, where there are multiple people their will be multiple views about what is going on. To say that one of these is correct and the others false is to take sides. What is important to good interpretive work is accounting for the diversity of 'truths' that one finds in any community of practice – including science. Science is itself an evolving community of practices. For instance, until relatively recently fire had a privileged place in scientific discourse as one of the four elements. To understand what fire meant for scientists 250 years ago would have meant coming to terms with the truths of that era, when it was widely believed that burning had specific scientific properties. The theory held that all flammable materials contained phlogiston, a tasteless, colourless, odourless, and weightless substance liberated by burning. Although now regarded as false, phlogiston theory allowed chemists to bring explanation of apparently different phenomena into a coherent structure: combustion, metabolism, and formation of rust.

Scientific truths are merely codified and agreed knowledge of the phenomenon that members of specific communities of practices constitute. Sometimes they constitute knowledge of self-evident realist phenomena such as fire. But the 'realism' of the phenomenon is no guarantee of the 'truth' of knowledge about it. So the proper object of research is to grasp how such understandings as are accorded truthful status are constituted and reproduced, whether in science or everyday life. In fact, from this perspective, there is no axiological difference.

VIEW FROM THE TRENCHES: DR ANNA SANDFIELD

There are a lot of rumours about interpretive research work that just won't go away, so let me clear them up right now. Interpretive work is not easy, it is not the best thing for people who find stats a bit scary (a good stats book is) and it is not an excuse for people with no self control to ramble on in an unstructured way. It is not just about chatting to people then presenting it as academic material. No, interpretive work is *real research*, it is academically credible and you can get a first class degree or a Ph.D. doing it. It is demanding, challenging, structured and rigorous. Interpretive work also provides an opportunity to get involved in a subject and with producing your research material, which can be both rewarding and unnerving.

Much of what is written around the actual philosophy of interpretive research is inaccessible and so challenging to apply that it is always easier to ignore the issue and focus on the literature, the data, the analysis (or just about anything else really). A lot of good students fall down here – it is essential to present your own work, both what you've done and why you've done it, in the context of the theory, traditions and principles it stems from and is allied with. Often students undertaking interpretive work are drawn to the approach and proceed to research by heart rather than conscious choice, as a result of their personal worldview and experiences. These things can lead us to relevant research questions and insightful analyses, but need to be supported by a thorough and visible understanding of the theoretical context of our research if it is to withstand academic scrutiny.

Researchers from interpretive traditions are often called upon to defend their research philosophy and need to be sure that their feet are on sound ground. The reasons we are doing our work and the 'point' of our work are, in my experience, more apt to be challenged than that of empiricist researchers. Consequently we need always to be clear about the applications of our findings and ready for the 'what's the point' question. Interestingly, I have never heard an empiricist researcher anxiously comparing their work to interpretive research, saying things like 'they may demonstrate cause and effect but do my results really help us understand what it's really like to be a salesperson?', worrying about whether the discourse analysts in their department will hold any truck with ANOVA, or whether they will be laughed out of their degree/viva for not giving a valid picture of participant experiences. For various reasons the reverse of these anxieties is much more commonly found among researchers doing interpretive work. Now that I am an academic myself, on a disappointingly regular basis students pop in to my office, half way through their dissertations, wondering whether they will get an automatic third class mark for using an interpretive approach, and worrying about whether their research, which they think is interesting and important, is really either. Please take it from me – if you're doing the work then there is a reason for doing it and don't be vague about that. Remember, there are sound practical reasons for conducting interpretive work. If your reasons periodically escape you make sure you write them down somewhere in case of ambush.

It tends to be the case that people are 'drawn' towards particular approaches to research, as discussed here, and it tends to be the case that interpretive researchers are often led towards particular analytical approaches and topic areas because this form of research allows them to get involved, to follow their convictions and use their subjective standpoints within their analyses. It can be a challenging situation for students and supervisors to find a way of translating passionately held beliefs into academic writing. These convictions, which in experimental work need to be put aside in favour of objectivity, can actually be a strength in interpretive work. They can help us find, get access to, and connect with, participants; they can tell us where to look for literature and give us our own unique standpoint from which to construct our analysis and conclude. I would argue for learning to *use* our righteous indignation,which I suspect guides all researchers (whether they admit it or not), with some degree of measure, and making sure that we write everything down, just in case the rhetoric inspired by the indignation leaves at write-up time.

This chapter will deal with a subject that has caused more controversy than probably any other in social science over the last 50 years – that of alternatives to the traditional scientific method (as was discussed in Chapter 2). Almost every field of social science has had to deal with the emergence of strong criticism of the hypothetico-deductive methodology, both from philosophers of science, as well as those within each field who conduct research itself. Now, even if after reading the previous chapter you have decided you are a total hard-core positivist, I still think you need to read this chapter as well. Is that 'why' I hear you say? Well, apart from various other reasons that I will touch on subsequently, one of the major difficulties inherent in this debate has been the general lack of in-depth knowledge of concepts of philosophy of science, and especially among proponents of the 'traditional view'. It has always seemed to me that traditional social scientists have both (a) been far more interested in actually *doing* research than arguing about philosophy, and (b) grown up within a 'comfort zone', or environment where they were exposed to very little criticism of their methods and underlying philosophy from their colleagues and supervisors. Furthermore, it has been very difficult for non-philosophers and practising social researchers to sift through the mass of philosophical discourse to actually determine *what* the argument is about and why it has had such profound impact on social science. Thus, most social scientists (both the traditional and non-traditional sort) are fundamentally under-equipped to deal with criticism of their methods. This leads to the propagation of misinformation, incorrect assumptions, and even personal attacks by those who disagree with one's position (trust me, I've been there and it isn't pretty). In fact, you should already be aware that one of the key aims of this book is to set out some key philosophical ideas and how they relate to the actual practice of research.

This chapter should be seen as a counterpoint to the previous chapter, both historically and philosophically. It sets out the development of alternative perspectives on philosophy of science which developed from around 1600, but reached their fruition in the 20th century. In fact, some of the names you'll see have already been mentioned, yet their key ideas are interpreted in a completely different way in this chapter (that's actually an important lesson to keep in mind here). That said, this chapter should certainly not be seen as 'the final word' on alternative philosophies of science, but merely an introduction and contrast. I would urge those interested to consult the readings given at the end of the chapter, so you can gain a really deep appreciation of the ideas I am going to introduce here.

Anyway, at the end of this chapter I really hope you have come to terms with these key ideas:

- Why the scientific methods and views from the Enlightenment came to be criticised, and the essence of those criticisms.
- The key characteristics of the interpretive worldview.
- How these characteristics impact on the conduct of research in a basic sense.
- The implications of the interpretive stance for you and your research.

Why is it Important to Know This Stuff?

By now you should have a good grounding in the basic concepts of the philosophy of science, and also the traditional scientific approach to research, from Chapter 2. You should also have discovered that my promise of good jokes was somewhat optimistic. There's no point repeating why it's important to understand the general concepts of philosophy of science and how they relate to the success of your project. But why is it important to explore and understand *alternatives* to the traditional scientific method – especially if you already 'know' you are not going to utilise these in your project? I'll deal with these questions on a number of levels.

Firstly, I think everyone should have a grasp of the radical and fundamental changes that have been wrought in the way contemporary philosophy thinks about science and knowledge. Most of us in the social sciences are not really aware of quite how serious the challenge to the traditional scientific method has been – even within the natural sciences. Many of us (for a long time I would have included myself) have tended to treat such terms as interpretivism, phenomenology, or postmodernism with a dismissive wave of the hand, as 'fads', or refuges for those who are 'scared of numbers and rigour'. This has led to some very destructive disagreements within social science fields. However, when one begins to explore the background to such alternatives, it can be seen that the underlying concepts are very hard to dismiss in such a blasé manner – and really deserve to be understood by all practising researchers and research students. *But* I personally find it very difficult to understand these ideas in isolation from an understanding of how they developed, which is why I've included some historical background.

Understanding alternative positions should also make you critically evaluate your *own* position. This should make you more confident in where you stand, what you believe in, and what you think knowledge is and can be. In turn, this should make your own research far more rigorous and resistant to criticism. This applies equally to the material in Chapters 2 and 3 – whatever your own philosophical standpoint is. It's a fact that researchers *do* get criticised about the philosophical foundations of their work – and if this happens to you I'd like to think that a sound knowledge of both these chapters will allow you to defend yourself with some style, and even dare I hope with some panache.

Also, even if you are a hardcore positivist (if there are any left), in the course of a literature review (wait for Chapters 4 and 5) you will inevitably come across studies which are not conducted from a traditional scientific standpoint. In order to evaluate and take account of such work, you will really need to have a grounding in the content of this chapter. If not, you will risk dismissing potentially important information – or even worse, misusing it.

Finally, again this is fundamentally a *human* story like that in Chapter 2. Even more so, the social issues and reactions to them should have genuine resonance to you now as contemporary members of society – so it should actually interest you on that level. And again, learning about these thinkers is important to *anyone* who wants genuinely to think for themselves. Most importantly, if you aspire to be any kind of intellectual at all, you should at the very least be able to pull out a Nietzsche quote at a party (although do be careful who you are talking to – I don't want to be responsible for you looking like a geek).

Science, society (and philosophy) at a crisis point

By the beginning of the 20th century, science was in a golden age of progress. The industrial revolution had totally changed society as we know it, Newton had 'explained' how the universe worked, and Darwin had correspondingly explained how we humans had evolved – quite by chance – from mere single-celled organisms. None of these explanations required the presence or contribution of an unexplained 'creator' or 'prime mover' such as God. It therefore seemed at the time that religion had become irrelevant in explaining how the world worked. One can see then, that this is in complete contrast to the Dark Ages, where philosophy and science were subservient to religion. In fact, could it be argued that *science* was a new kind of religion, supplanting society's reliance on faith and God? Interestingly, this question is still raised directly and indirectly today at the beginning of the 21st century – and can be seen in the popular science writings of authors such as Daniel Dennett (e.g. *Darwin's Dangerous Idea*) and in fiction such as that by Dan Brown (e.g. *Angels and Demons*), the popularity of which speaks for the resonance of these ideas.

However, while scientific progress seemed superficially to be an unarguable good for society, dissenting voices could be heard. For example, the industrial revolution may have had many benefits, but its consequences for the environment began to be seen as negative (and as I live in Birmingham in the UK, the home of the industrial revolution, I should know!) Furthermore, had society lost some of its traditional values, with many leaving the land for big cities, and losing touch with each other in a dehumanised industrial environment? And while it was seductive to 'know' so much about the universe and ourselves in a scientific sense, what place did 'faith' or even 'hope' have in such a world? All these building critiques of science (which I am unable to cover in depth here) came to a head with the creation of what was one of science's greatest achievements, and simultaneously one of its greatest follies, the atomic bomb. Science – and indeed scientists – could no longer be considered morally neutral and always beneficial to the world. Neither could society persist in assuming a continuous programme of incremental benefit from scientific progress. As a result, philosophers, scientists, and many other members of society were forced to reconsider knowledge and knowledge creation itself – and both the natural and social sciences are still reeling today.

There have been many 'alternatives' to traditional science which have emerged in the latter half of the 20th century. In fact, Feyerabend's relativism as discussed in the previous chapter would suggest that they were all equally useful in knowledge creation. Perhaps the ultimate antithesis to traditional science has become known as 'postmodernism' (see Alternative View 3.1). However, in this chapter and indeed the balance of the book, I will confine my discussion to what can be called 'interpretivism' as an alternative to the traditional scientific method. Interpretivism is not really a single 'method' but more of a term for a number of different traditions, which share some common features and underlying philosophical ideas that will be covered as we proceed. The next section will try to give a flavour of the philosophical developments from around 1600, which seem to build towards the emergence of the interpretive framework for social science methodology.

Alternative View 3.1: Postmodernism and its Critics

Postmodernism as a term is used by many people in many different ways, and to offer a definitive explanation of what it is would be pretty much impossible – some would say it is a defining characteristic of postmodernism to be undefinable! Which isn't very helpful but has kept a number of people in jobs for a few years anyway. This little viewpoint should be read as a tentative introduction, and certainly *not* the canonical definition of postmodernism (that should deflect most criticism from the postmodern attack dogs …).

Perhaps a good appreciation of postmodernism can be gained by considering its roots in the 1970s as an architectural movement characterised by mixing of styles and rejection of pure functionalism, as well as a 'de-differentiation' or breaking down of elitism and the difference between 'high' and 'low' (i.e. popular) culture. Later, the idea of postmodernism entered social sciences, often being characterised as a rejection of traditional enlightenment models of rationalism and empiricism. In fact, many postmodern intellectuals would not consider themselves social scientists at all. That said, one could perhaps bring together five main ideas which together seem to characterise postmodern social science and researchers (see Smart, 2000):

1. Language (discourse) is the key force in constructing reality, no object or situation is independent of the language used to describe it.
2. Identity is fragmented, individuals are constructed as a result of their discourse at a given point in time.
3. There is no way to represent and describe objective reality, the description *is* the reality.
4. The idea of grand theories and general laws is rejected, knowledge is local, multiple, and context-dependent.
5. Knowledge is not neutral, it gives power and itself produces certain versions of reality.

You'll see these ideas echoed throughout the rest of this chapter in many ways, but postmodernism itself has been criticised by a number of theorists for being unnecessarily nihilistic – i.e. implying that our previous knowledge is irretrievably flawed and that we can never generate knowledge which has any use outside its specific context, or even that there is no such thing as knowledge. Taken too far, postmodernism essentially rejects the idea of any empirical research and focuses only on deconstructing texts to show their contradictory meanings and suchlike. It is this side of postmodernism – almost a caricature – which has inspired so much vitriol by more traditional social scientists. However, postmodernism can also inspire new ways of looking at the world, incorporating methodological pluralism, and a playful, humorous and ironic spirit to research (indeed, one could in some ways characterise this very book as somewhat postmodern in spirit). Nevertheless, the fundamental rejection of abstract general knowledge inherent to postmodern philosophy makes it difficult to see how postmodernism and realist scientific philosophies can co-exist happily.

The emergence of alternatives to 'science'

You should remember the Empiricist manifesto from the previous chapter – assuming you read it. Essentially, Empiricists (and later, Positivists) believed that scientific knowledge came only from direct sensory experiences, not rational reasoning of the mind. You've already come across Locke, one of the key empiricists. However, one who hasn't appeared in these pages already is Bishop Berkeley (1685–1753), who followed Locke (no it wasn't his nickname, he was an actual Bishop). Berkeley argued that you could never actually get outside your own mind, and therefore how were you to compare an actual 'real' object with the representation of it in your own mind? In fact, Berkeley contended that *all* human experience was phenomenal, i.e. only experiences in the mind (remember the term *phenomenology*, as you'll come across it later). Following from this, Berkeley suggested that the existence of an external 'real world' was in fact an assumption, and an unsafe one at that – all that we know to exist in certainty is our own minds. Actually, if you watch the 'Matrix' movies you should be able to perceive a considerable overlap with their 'pop-philosophy' here (although try not to keep interrupting the action with impromptu philosophy lessons – I'm told that it tends to irritate some people). This idea that 'reality' is merely our individual mental *interpretations* of the world will find its ultimate expression in the interpretive methodology we will discuss later. For now it is enough to understand the seminal roots of such a worldview.

Even more interesting is to consider the role of Kant in this. Kant is usually thought of as a father of modern science, hence his place in Chapter 2. But his work can also be interpreted as another step towards an interpretive worldview as articulated in Berkeley's ideas. Firstly, one must understand that Kant fully believed in the triumph of science in discovering the truth of the world, and was heavily influenced by Newton's achievements in uncovering the 'laws of physics'. In fact he made a modest contribution to Newtonian cosmology himself. However, Kant tried desperately to reconcile the 'truth' of science with Hume's (who followed Berkeley) thesis that causal laws were untenable and we could only ever know phenomena themselves – not laws relating them. Kant's solution (which we touched upon in Chapter 2) was that the mind does not just *receive* sensory perceptions, but that it actively structures them according to its own innate principles. Thus, one can never know reality objectively and independent of the mind itself – only in relation to our own mental processes. All our observations are intimately bound up with our internal knowledge and interpretations. While Kant would probably not approve (and is indeed likely to be spinning on his axis as I write this) this idea can be viewed as the fundamental base for interpretive methodologies. However, it would be well over 200 years before the implications would be taken to their logical extremes and begin to cause waves in social science – when Kant's beloved Newtonian laws began themselves to fall apart.

Much of the next few hundred years of philosophy of science has already been covered in Chapter 2. But in the wake of the 19th and 20th century crises of society and science introduced earlier in this chapter, art and philosophy seemed to take a drastically different course. Naturally, this was associated with radical ideas towards knowledge creation and knowledge itself. In fact, many of these ideas were founded on the *Romantic* worldview rather than the empiricist scientific one (see IDE 3.1). Romanticism emerged at the same time as the Enlightenment and shared its fundamental belief in the power of humans. However, while the scientific model introduced by the Enlightenment focused on reducing the single reality of the objective world to laws and facts, the Romantic movement was more concerned with multiple subjective realities, feelings, and interpretations. Famous romantics included Coleridge, Wordsworth, Blake, and A Flock of Seagulls (no, actually they were New Romantics...[1]).

IDE 3.1: Romanticism

Romanticism (and it is the early German Romantic movement which is generally considered quintessential in philosophical terms) was a social/political movement reacting against alienation created by the modern world. The romantics wished to go back to a situation where there was unity between oneself, others, and nature, and ethics were concerned with love and self-realisation. This was in contrast to the modern separation of man from nature, and the Kantian ideas of duty. Romantics were concerned with community, not the individual, and nature rather than mechanics.

[1] And if you don't understand that joke, you're too young!

One of the key thinkers for my purposes is Frederick Nietzsche (1844–1900). Nietzsche wasn't just a philosopher in truth, but also something of an author or social commentator. His thoughts as expressed in such books as *Beyond Good and Evil,* and *Thus Spake Zarathustra* have formed a hugely influential body of work for philosophy. Instead of accepting a single objectively 'true' way of viewing the world (whether this be religious or scientific), Nietzsche considered that there was a multiplicity of different perspectives through which individuals could interpret the world. Furthermore, he also argued that there was no single 'overarching' standpoint or criterion from which one could judge whether any single perspective was more 'true' than another. These ideas have led to Nietzsche being considered as the spiritual father of postmodern thought. You can also see echoes of these ideas in Kuhn's work on paradigms in Chapter 2.

Nietzsche was fundamentally convinced that individuals had the will to change their realities, but that this invariably necessitated a destruction of their previous selves. One of Nietzsche's most famous quotes is 'God is dead', which probably concerns the idea that humans themselves should be considered the true gods, rather than there being an all-powerful God beyond human comprehension. In other words, Nietzsche argued that not even 'God' was in an overarching position to judge the truth. In any case, Nietzsche believed that we could never prove or disprove the truth, but instead that the truth was in fact *created.* If you compare this idea to the traditional theories of empirical science explored in Chapter 2 you should see serious differences. Thus were new ideas about epistemology, and knowledge itself, germinated. As the 20th century proceeded others took these ideas on and developed them; people such as Foucault, Wittgenstein and Derrida challenged existing models of knowledge in their work – looking to deconstruct the very essence of truth. The 20th century is replete with contrasting and often conflicting epistemologies. That said, for the purposes of the rest of this chapter, one could perhaps take a couple of key points out of this melange of perspectives. Firstly, the role of *language and text* in the creation of knowledge has been a topic of considerable interest. Secondly is the recognition that no one viewpoint or methodology has a monopoly on discovering the 'truth', but that *multiple interpretations of reality exist.* As Nietzsche said: 'Against positivism, which halts at phenomena – 'There are only facts' – I would say: No, facts are precisely what there are not, only interpretations.' [2]

The interpretive approach to research

It is extremely difficult to distil a single methodological 'approach' from the many different strands of methodology, epistemology and general philosophy which could be argued to be 'interpretive'. Even in exploring research articles that claim to take an 'interpretive' approach,

[2] That's the quote you should use at a party – the 'God is dead' one is *such* a cliché.

one will uncover ambiguities, contrasts, and even what seem like downright contradictions. There are many different traditions of interpretive research that have evolved in organisational studies, and general social research itself, and we will cover some of these specific approaches later in the chapter. However, while different traditions are indeed distinct in some important ways, they do tend to blend with each other, and appear to share some important foundations, which this section will set out in some detail.

Hermeneutics as an underpinning

Hermeneutics can be seen as the foundation stone of interpretive approaches to methodology (e.g. Hackley, 2003) – in fact hermeneutics can be translated as 'to interpret' according to the Penguin Dictionary of Philosophy (2000). Hermeneutics began in 17th century Germany, as the study of Bible interpretations (isn't it surprising how tightly religion is interlinked with what we have talked about in this book so far?!) However, the work of Friedrich Schleiermacher[3] (1768–1834) and then Wilhelm Dilthey (1833–1911) developed hermeneutics into the study of understanding all human experience. Key to this development was the rejection of the naturalist viewpoint that the methodology of the natural sciences was appropriate to understanding the human experience. However, Dilthey did not appear to be influenced by the Romantic worldview explored above, instead he was interested in creating a methodology which would allow *objective* understanding of the social world. It seems therefore that he still believed in an objective social reality.

Dilthey considered that to understand the world of human phenomena and experience, one had to understand the socially constructed meanings that made up human life, but that one could never understand this system without understanding its products. This is the basis of the *hermeneutic circle*, a key foundation of interpretive methodology which will become obvious later. The hermeneutic circle is the process of understanding individual phenomena in light of the larger 'whole' from which they derive, and understanding that the whole is itself given meaning by its parts. This is a difficult idea, and a couple of examples of how it works in practice are given in IDE 3.2.

IDE 3.2: The Hermeneutic Circle

Imagine one is trying to interpret the transcript from an interview with a salesperson. The hermeneutic circle concept is relevant on two levels here. Firstly, one can consider the transcript as an individual part of the 'whole' of the organisational context, and thus it should be interpreted in light of all the information one

[3] One of the early German romantics in fact.

has about that organisation. Furthermore, the thoughts of employees as presented in your transcript are themselves part of the whole organisational context and help construct it. Secondly, taking the interview transcript itself as another type of 'whole', one can see how the individual ideas and concepts in the interview content give the interview whole its meaning, but that each concept is impossible to interpret in isolation from the whole transcript. Some practical applications of the hermeneutic circle approach are given later in the book, especially Chapter 9 – but the concept can be used to underpin the entire research process if one wishes.

Dilthey, whose ideas were further developed by Martin Heidegger (1889–1976), did not regard the study of human experience to be separate from that experience itself – unlike many of the thinkers I introduced in Chapter 2. That said, Dilthey regarded experience as providing the *means to understand* experience, but that one could stand apart from that experience in actually analysing it (similar to the ideas of objectivity discussed in Chapter 2). However, Heidegger argued that one was in fact unable to separate oneself from the social context, thus all understanding of human experience is unavoidably influenced by the social context – and therefore an objective interpretation and understanding of any human experience is in fact impossible.

This divergence of opinion on whether objective interpretation is possible (Dilthey's position) or not (Heidegger's position) has resulted in two traditions of hermeneutics. Nevertheless, the Heideggerian tradition appears to be the one which has dominated, and is the underlying position taken by most interpretive methodologies. Thus, for our purposes we can regard the key ideas of hermeneutics to be as follows:

- Methods of the natural sciences are inappropriate to study the social world.
- To interpret a phenomenon one must look at its parts in terms of the whole, and the whole in terms of its parts.
- Understanding of phenomena is based on socially constructed meanings, therefore ...
- The key to understanding human experience is in living that experience, not in rationalisations or philosophical theories.
- However, one can never 'stand outside' that experience to understand it objectively.

Phenomenology, interpretivism and social constructionism

Building on the tradition of hermeneutics, Max Weber (1864–1920) and Alfred Schutz (1899–1959) were also concerned with developing an objective way in which to develop knowledge about the subjective social world. Weber's work can be considered as a further expression of hermeneutics. However, while Schutz was strongly influenced by Weber and hermeneutics, he is generally credited with developing *phenomenology*, which, combined with hermeneutic concepts, is the basis of interpretive social science (e.g. Blaikie, 2004; Bryman, 2004).

Phenomenology as a term is now used in many different ways – sometimes correctly and sometimes not – but it essentially refers to the study of human experiences and of the structures within which humans experience the world (e.g. Hammersley, 2004). Later in this chapter I will examine phenomenology as a specific *method* of interpretive research, but here I am discussing it in a philosophical sense. The key thesis of phenomenology is that the subject and object are inextricably connected. In other words, one who is experiencing something can never stand apart from that experience. Compared to traditional scientific ideas, phenomenology is not concerned with evaluating that experience for its 'truth', only with understanding the experience itself.

This emphasis on *understanding* rather than explaining can be seen as a major difference between interpretive viewpoints and traditional scientific ones. If you remember Chapter 1, you should be able to realise that the difference between aiming to understand and aiming to explain concerns the *axiology* of the approach. Axiology refers to the overriding goal of the approach. Furthermore, interpretive approaches view this understanding as constantly in flux. Any stated interpretation (i.e. an understanding of an experience) is interlinked with the historical context – i.e. the point in time which that interpretation is stated. Drawing from the hermeneutic circle, interpretive approaches view an interpretation at *one* point as both being influenced by *past* interpretations, and in turn influencing *future* interpretations. So understanding is never 'complete'. You will probably come across the term *verstehen,* which is German for 'to understand', if you read more about interpretive approaches. *Verstehen* is a term from hermeneutics originally, but it is now commonly used to designate the concept of the interpretive 'understanding' of an experience. It can be a pretty impressive word to drop if you are talking to the right audience – but make sure to pronounce it right (fehr-SHTEH-ehn), or you'll end up looking like an idiot (like I did).

Furthermore, because interpretive approaches view phenomena as inextricably bound up with time and context, one is unable to separate knowledge of a phenomena from its context. Reality should be viewed as a whole, and individual phenomena viewed in relation to that whole (the hermeneutic circle again). Knowledge is therefore primarily descriptive and ideographic rather than abstract from the specific context (as knowledge is assumed to be in the traditional scientific approach). Furthermore, one must immerse oneself in the context in order to truly understand the meanings and experiences which one is attempting to study (the influence of phenomenology is clear here). These points are concerned with the *epistemology* of interpretive approaches, or the type of knowledge which they aim to generate.

I've left the *ontology* of interpretive approaches until last, because it could be seen as the source of some debate. You will remember that ontology refers to the belief about the nature of reality itself – which is a pretty tough idea to come to terms with. It should be clear already that traditional scientific ontology views reality as being 'out there', a single, objective world which we can measure and explain if we had the tools to do so. It should be equally clear that interpretive approaches do *not* concur, and instead take the view that there are multiple realities. Of course, this seems to open something of a can of worms in terms of the nature of reality. I mean, is there anything specific which actually defines what reality is? One way of closing the lid on this can is to take the viewpoint that reality exists within the minds of social actors, individuals and groups within different sociohistorical contexts. This would seem to work pretty well, and can be considered to be a *social constructionist* ontology – which appears to underlie most major interpretive approaches (Hackley, 2003).

The social constructionist ontology would view reality as being collaboratively constructed between social actors as they interact with each other. Thus reality is unstable, constantly changing, and unavoidably subjective. This implies that one can not really develop an understanding of reality by standing apart from it. Indeed the researcher is unavoidably involved with the reality they are studying (the influence of phenomenology comes through here). As we shall see later, such an ontology has serious implications for what one aims to discover, how one discovers it, and ultimately what kind of knowledge is created. For now, however, it's enough to recap the main tenets of the interpretive approach to research:

- They aim to understand the social world, not explain or predict it.
- Reality is not objective, but rather is a social construction, created within the minds of individuals interacting.
- One can never separate an individual experience from the holistic sociohistorical context it is part of.
- Interpretation, and thus knowledge, is never 'final'.
- Knowledge consists of rich, ideographic description of experiences within their contexts.

Interpretive research traditions

If the previous section uncovered some general principles of an interpretive approach to research, it is also enlightening to examine more closely some of the more common 'traditions' of interpretive research. This is because, as already stated, interpretivism is something of an umbrella term, capturing a multiplicity of traditions which have developed throughout the 20th century. These traditions share common features such as those discussed above, but also have their own unique character. Furthermore, there are many others which I don't mention here, such as semiotics, literary theory, narrative analysis and many others. I encourage interested readers to seek out more information (as always!) One way to use this section is to employ it in interpreting the rest of the book. If you take a phenomenological viewpoint forwards, say, you can evaluate the appropriateness of the methodologies and techniques I will present later in light of the basic worldview discussed below. For example, what does a phenomenological tradition imply about how one should conduct a qualitative interview and analyse it?

Phenomenology and existentialism

A key interpretive tradition in social research has developed from the influence of the phenomenological philosophy discussed above. As we've seen already, phenomenology is concerned with the lived experience of humans – a concern which it shares with the philosophical movement of **existentialism** (see IDE 3.3). Phenomenological research can often be seen to be influenced by existentialist philosophy – which is concerned with the human experience of existing (hence the name).

IDE 3.3: Existentialism

Existentialism in the popular mindset is often associated with three things: (a) the French, (b) black rollneck sweaters, and (c) students in their rooms moping about how bad life is. I myself have great experience of (c), and I once owned a black rollneck (however I was never French). Nevertheless, existentialism is not necessarily synonymous with the pointlessness of existing. In fact, existentialism is really about the importance of the individual's experience of life, rather than society – a recognition of the centrality of the individual. Within this, a great number of philosophers have made their own personal mark – Kirkegaard was concerned with religion, Satre with free choice, Camus with the absurdity of life. But it is Camus' concerns which have wrongly come to represent existentialism (to its detriment). In fact, almost all of the existentialists focused in some way on the positive side of existence, with Satre considering 'existential *angst*' to be essential to freedom and self awareness.

Phenomenological research begins with the direct, lived experience as a starting point, not just the 'articulation' of that experience. This is because phenomenological viewpoints consider much of our experience to be 'intuitive'. Furthermore, people are considered to be active in experiencing the world, and that they collaboratively produce social reality, rather than have reality 'happen' to them.

These assumptions clearly impact on the conduct of phenomenological research. Firstly, topics for phenomenologists tend to focus on understanding experiences of social actors, and the meaning of these experiences – not explaining why things happen. A phenomenological approach to sales force discipline would not look at the causal influences on sales managers' use of punishment, for example, but on the first-hand subjective experience of sales managers (or salespeople) when involved in the discipline process. What are the meanings bound up in the social process of punishment?

In order to access this kind of information, research methods would tend towards qualitative interviews – because in order to access inner subjective experiential information from individuals, I must get them to describe it. One can never access experience from outside it – remember? However, this means the phenomenological researcher should not actively structure the interview too much, as this may prejudice the interviewee's reflections. As reality is a collaborative construction, the interviewer is themselves part of the experience, and this should be taken into account as well. In terms of analysis, I would be looking for description of the experience, but also to interpret that in a non-judgemental way – with empathy for the interviewee. This usually involves heavy use of direct quotes, and particular interest in the interviewee's use of metaphor in describing their unique experience.

Ethnographic research

Ethnography is also a major interpretive research tradition, which shares some overlap with phenomenological traditions, but is quite distinct in its own right.[4] Whereas phenomenology can be seen to be based around a depth psychology tradition, ethnography is rooted in an anthropological tradition – i.e. the study of indigenous cultures. Over the course of the 20th century, ethnographic approaches have found much favour in organisational and social research circles.

Ethnographic research is based on the idea that first-hand experience of culture is a better basis for understanding it than looking in from 'the outside'. Thus, ethnography is concerned with immersing oneself inside a social situation to understand and describe the norms, values, behaviours and rituals of that situation. In contrast to the phenomenological tradition, ethnography could be considered to treat experience as less of a collaborative construction where the researcher is involved, but more of a source of empirical data from which the researcher can make interpretations and descriptions. Thus, while the researcher must involve themselves first hand in an ethnographic study, they should not influence that situation themselves. If you think about this, it actually seems to have a little in common with more empiricist traditions, as well as interpretive ones.

Ethnographic traditions have much use in organisational research, even if one is not taking an interpretive approach to a study. The concept of immersing oneself in a situation is a natural way to begin studying any topic which one has little knowledge of. It is also vital in beginning to interpret the *context* of any situation from the point of view of the participants in that situation. This can have major influences on the interpretation of all types of research data – and especially interviews. The idea of *indexicality* is relevant here – which refers to the contextual meaning of the things we do and say. If you don't understand the indexicality of a statement then you are unable to interpret it in the same way the person who made that statement does.

---

[4] It should also be noted that 'ethnography' is really a term for a certain type of *output* of an ethnographic study, not a term for the methodology itself. Ethnographic approaches need not necessarily result in an ethnography of a culture as their output.

True ethnographic studies normally result in rich, 'thick' descriptions of a social context, involving creative interpretations of the data. Furthermore, the focus is not on generalising to other contexts, but simply on the particular context as an end in itself. This should convey some kind of feeling of what it is like to be a part of that social situation or culture to the reader. In order to gather data for such a study, multiple methods are utilised. However, participant observation is particularly favoured as a way of immersing oneself in a culture. From here, the researcher can utilise formal interviews and informal conversations. Ethnographers also often begin with a wide-ranging review of secondary data about that social situation, in order to gain some kind of basic knowledge.

Critical research and feminist traditions

The term 'critical' as applied to research methodology in the present sense refers to a distinct theoretical position and a corresponding tradition. Essentially, the 'critical' research tradition is founded on Marxist theorists such as Adorno and Horkheimer ([1944] 1997) – although Marx himself seems to have been rather more of an empiricist. Feminist viewpoints have also played a major role in the development of critical research perspectives, and it could be argued that they have supplanted Marxism as the main influence on critical research. Critical research is concerned with the idea that 'truth' as constructed in the social sciences may actually serve the interests of some groups – usually the white, male, ruling classes, or whoever is generally most powerful in a given context – more than others. Critical research aims to uncover the implicit assumptions and ideologies which underlie accepted ideas of the 'truth' in a given social situation.

There is a rich tradition of critical research which has developed in social psychology and most management fields such as industrial relations, organisational behaviour and more recently consumer research. Critical research considers language not as a simple referral to an object, but to actively construct the meaning of an object – which of course you should recognise as a social constructionist ontology. Thus, critical approaches to research consider how language is used to construct what is legitimate, accepted, and indeed 'normal'. Feminist research was one of the major influences on this tradition, with its interest in understanding how our language and cultural artefacts construct the social world as patriarchal, and that traditional social science practice masks numerous assumptions and power relations which in turn privilege one gender over another.

Critical perspectives can offer much to organisational research, although in my experience they can be a bit too seductive to many beginning researchers, and especially those with strong opinions and ideas (ironically, often the best researchers). Critical research is difficult for researchers to conduct,[5] but can often result in exciting and intriguing results if done correctly. For example, some fascinating student projects I have supervised

[5] One reason for this is that relatively few academic supervisors are immersed in the critical tradition.

included critical perspectives on patriarchal power within advertising agencies and its impact on advertising strategy, and also critical analysis of gender representations in marketing communications. That said, from my own perspective, a common fault in student research from the critical perspective is that it sometimes lets the key critical perspective (say Feminism) overwhelm the need to do solid research, and students need to carefully guard against letting their righteous indignation at the world take over! Of course, these points are relevant to all researchers, but those just starting their research career should take particular note.

Like ethnography, critical research does not have a fundamental 'method' of data collection, but tends to mix and match things such as interviews, observation, as well as include a major role for secondary data such as documents (e.g. company and marketing communications). However, data collection does tend to be qualitative. In fact some critical theorists have argued that quantitative data by its very nature reinforces the idea of patriarchal control over society and nature, by way of for example its reliance on taking information without giving anything back (an exploitative strategy), or the necessarily hierarchical relationship between researcher and subject in experimental methodology. In terms of analysis, critical research is fundamentally concerned with language and how it helps to construct the reality of power and control. Thus, specific analysis methodologies have been developed, the most influential of which has been *discourse analysis* which is a set of methods aimed at drawing meaning from language (see Chapter 9 for an introduction to discourse analysis).

Implications of taking an interpretive approach

In this section I'm going to take a look at exactly what it means to take an interpretive approach to a project. Specifically, I often see people at the early stages of their dissertations or academic careers who talk to me about wanting to take interpretive approaches. This is, of course, fine as long as they are sure of two things – firstly, exactly *why* they want to take those approaches, and secondly exactly *what* it means to do so, especially in terms of methods of data collection, the relationship of those methods to the data they can collect, exactly what they can say about the world, and the importance of rigour. More specifically, at this point of the book, if any one of you is thinking slyly to themselves something like 'if I take an interpretive approach then I can avoid numbers, which will make my life easier' then I advise you to do two things:

- Hang your head in shame, because avoidance of something you find difficult, or don't like, is the *single worst* reason for choosing a path.
- Keep reading this book (and if you are in a bookstore, buy it – go on, NOW) and you will discover that interpretive or otherwise non-numerical research is *not* by any means the easy way out.

Now I don't want to generalise (despite my realist leanings), but I've met too many students who wanted to do interpretive work (they normally call it 'qualitative') because they thought it was the easy way out. This attitude is usually a sure sign of a project which is going to get a poor mark, or a piece of research which is going to be rejected for publication. As you are about to see, interpretivist work should not be an excuse for a lack of rigour – just a different approach to it. You should use this next section as a brief guide to the rest of the book in some ways, helping you to pick and choose appropriate methods and strategies for your interpretive project.

Data collection for interpretive research

It should come as no surprise to you that in general interpretive approaches use qualitative data as their main source of insight. This is for a number of reasons. First of all, the interpretive epistemology is generally concerned with understanding the world from the perspective of participants in that world. Usually, if we *quantify* the world (i.e. map it onto numbers as discussed in Chapters 6 and 7) we are placing our own perspective on to it and trying to map that perspective on to all participants. In this way, individual interpretations of the world are ignored – which is completely opposite to the fundamental idea of the interpretive approach. Secondly, the social constructionist ontology necessitates gaining data on how individuals construct reality. Again, quantifying the social world means imposing a worldview upon reality, since the social world is constructed of language and meaning – the nuances of which are lost if they are quantified. As a result, it should be clear that qualitative approaches such as interviews and observation are naturally most appropriate for an interpretive approach.

Furthermore, it can be seen that interpretive approaches are most concerned with understanding social reality as a construction of the individual participants. Thus, if you look back to Chapter 1 you should see that their essential orientation is *inductive*, in that they are trying to generate theory from the data, not impose existing theory on data. In order to quantify the social world, we need first to theorise about it in order to place numbers on key aspects (we'll discuss this in depth in Chapter 6, but for now, just trust me). Without theory, we do not know how to put numbers on to social concepts. Thus, the inductive nature of interpretive approaches is naturally consistent with qualitative data, which does not necessarily require existing theory to structure its conduct.

However, this is not to say that interpretive research can never use numbers. As we've already touched on, certain quantitative data can be very useful to interpretive researchers. In particular, critical theorists often employ national statistical data on demographics (such as census data). Furthermore, numbers are useful in many other cases, such as counting the occurrence of a key term or suchlike. This is why it is so important to never confuse *interpretive* with *qualitative*, as is often done. Simply saying a piece of research is qualitative does not imply it is also interpretive, and conversely saying you are an interpretive researcher is not the same as saying you use only qualitative data. Never make that mistake; you might get away with it for a while, but eventually you are going to look silly. Even worse, you will cut yourself off from many vital avenues of data. In later chapters I will go into a lot more depth about specific methods of collecting data appropriate to interpretive projects, but it's important that you first understand what makes a type of data appropriate before you run off and collect it.

The 'Three Rs' of interpretive projects

If you are anything like me, you'll remember the '3 Rs' from school – Reading, Writing and Arithmetic. Personally, I always thought it was a bit of a mixed message to kids that two of the so-called 'Rs' started with other letters, but that's another story. These 3 Rs (which are directly inspired by Chris Hackley's approach in his 2003 book) are in fact better because they do *all* start with R – Reductionism, Reflexivity, and Representation (and to think they said I'd never amount to anything in school ...).

Anyway, interpretivism isn't just about collecting certain types of data, as I'm sure you now understand; it's a worldview which impacts on the project as a whole, including how you present it in the end. Reductionism refers to simplification (from an interpretive viewpoint, *over*-simplification). Interpretive research rejects outright the goal of reducing complex social phenomena to simple cause and effect relationships, often characterised by the boxes and arrows seen in journal articles. Instead, interpretive projects – as has already been mentioned – focus on rich descriptions of social situations, incorporating alternative viewpoints and factors unique to the context, not on simplifying the reality to an elegant diagram with little relation to the specific context.

Reflexivity is concerned with the role of the researcher in the project. You've already been introduced to the term in the context of data collection, but it can also refer to other aspects of interpretive research. For example, once you've read a wide range of academic articles, you'll probably notice that the 'scientific style' is to write in a very detached and formal way, which follows from the underlying realist/naturalist viewpoint of much social science, where the researcher is an independent observer of the objective reality. By contrast, interpretive studies are often written in a less formal style, which acknowledges the interpretation of the researcher themselves. This reflexive style allows recognition of the role the researcher plays in actively constructing an interpretation of the social context, and how this deepens understanding of the specific situation.

Finally, representation is all about understanding exactly what an interpretive research report actually is. While more traditional scientific studies tend to take the view that their findings accurately reflect a single reality, interpretive research considers its findings to be one of many possible representations of a specific social context. Therefore, it fundamentally depends not only on the data generated, but also on the inherent characteristics (e.g. biases, interests) of the researcher. Interpretive researchers need to take care that they do not fall into the trap of letting their own interests inappropriately colour their representation of the social reality they are studying. Thus, they should maintain some kind of distance from both existing theoretical representations of that context, as well as from the representations of the participants in their research – bearing in mind the requirements of their specific project or tradition (e.g. phenomenology, critical theory or such like).

Generalisability and rigour

The concepts of generalisability and rigour are two which can be seen to be at the heart of debates between interpretive and naturalist/realist research traditions. Unfortunately, misunderstandings and misinformation about the nature of generalisability and rigour can often lead to unfortunate consequences (like being told 'your research is rubbish' by some guy at a bar – I'm not kidding, it does happen!)

I'll deal with some of the practicalities of these concepts in later chapters (e.g. 9 and 10), but for now, generalisability is basically concerned with the idea that the results you have found can be transferred to other situations. In a scientific realist sense, the idea normally refers to an attempt to ultimately generate general laws about something, be it the behaviour of atoms or managers. So if my Ph.D. found that there was a relationship between aggressiveness of sales managers and burnout of salespeople in my sample, how safe am I in saying that this relationship will hold in all cases? In a quantitative sense we can often gain at least a vague answer to this question (which will be covered in later chapters 11 and 12), but in interpretive research it is far more difficult due to the nature of the methodology. However, the real debate comes when you discuss whether the concept of generalisability is even *relevant* in an interpretive context.

Most realist researchers will tell you that considering the generalisability of findings is vital to good research. We can see why; it's because of their fundamental beliefs about objective reality, and their aim to explain it. If I believe there to be an objective reality, then if I determine the truth in one situation, I should be able to generalise this truth to other situations (within some limits). But as an interpretivist, this belief is not the same – nor is the aim of the research. In fact, go back up and write down the basic axiology, epistemology and ontology of interpretive approaches (go on, DO IT!) Back? Good. Right, so interpretive research is of course concerned with individual interpretations, meanings and experiences of the subjective world. It would seem likely then, that findings from interpretive research are context-dependent in many ways – they depend on the social situation at the time, the participants, and also the researcher themselves. So there is really no objective reality to generalise about, and interpretive research by definition is not aimed at creating general laws which can be applied across different situations.

One of the key questions which can be asked of interpretive research is therefore 'what's the point?' If research findings are only applicable to one specific historical and social context, what can I personally get out of them? This is where the debate can get nasty. One way of dealing with it from an interpretive perspective is to ignore it and say it is not relevant to judge interpretive research on standards of empiricist or realist viewpoints. I personally don't think this is overly helpful, and tends to perpetuate the idea among some that interpretive research is an 'avoidance' tactic for second-class researchers. More helpful is to refer to the idea of 'rigour' – which is essentially the concept of showing people clearly that your research was carried out in a way that is appropriate and technically sound from theorisation to final analysis.

The concept of rigour is often one which is used to criticise interpretive work as idiosyncratic and biased when compared to traditional scientific and quantitative work. However, as you should already realise, there are indeed philosophical, theoretical, data collection and analysis techniques which are rigorous and transparent when conducting interpretive research. Furthermore, this is not incompatible with the interpretive view of the world. Presenting your work in a way which assures readers that you have used appropriate strategies and methods, as well as recognising and explaining your own part in creating the interpretation (remember reflexivity) should allow you to enhance perceptions of the rigour of your work. Readers who are confident in your rigour can then judge for themselves whether your findings are applicable to other situations, and also whether they can carry out a similar study. As an interpretive researcher, it is quite possible to make some attempt to consider how likely it is that your results could occur in similar or different situations, and whether there are key issues which could affect the occurrence of similar events. Thus, there can be concern for generalisability and rigour in interpretive research, and the relevance of its results is not necessarily completely bound to a time, place and situation – even though the interpretation is.

What's important for YOUR project?

This section can be considered to be something of a 'conclusion' to the last two chapters. Specifically, philosophy and all that is interesting in itself (well I think so), but if you're like most of my students and colleagues, you're more interested in what it means for the conduct of your research. So what I want to do here is to briefly sum up and discuss the key issues about realist and interpretivist approaches which are of importance to actually *doing* social science research.

I think the first and maybe most important thing is a realisation that understanding philosophy and how it relates to research practice *is actually important!* Without a philosophical foundation, your project is always floating on water – it might keep floating, or it might sink, you just don't know. Understanding your philosophical worldview and how it relates to the practice of research (i.e. the material in the previous two chapters) means you are in a great position to evaluate your research, how to do it, and ultimately how to present it. It also lets you look at other pieces of research in an informed manner, to gain knowledge from them without bias. Understanding different positions and worldviews is also important in being able to relate to other researchers and really see where they are coming from, which should hopefully play a role in reducing conflict between advocates of different traditions.

That said, it's extremely important at an early stage that you get a strong sense for which path you are likely to be drawn to. There are a number of ways of looking at this question, which I'll move on to now.

Choosing an approach

'Choosing an approach' is kind of a misnomer for this bit really – but I used it because, well, basically because everything else sounded stupid. Anyway, it's a misnomer because I actually think an approach *chooses you!* That's pretty mystical and spooky, but what I mean is that through the course of reading the previous two chapters, I think you will have discovered yourself being drawn more to either the ideas presented in Chapter 2 or to this chapter. I know when I was at the very early stages of (what turned out to be) my research career, I seemed to be drawn to empiricist and realist sorts of ideas, without really knowing what they were, and to disagree with ideas of subjective reality and social construction, again without really understanding them.

There are many reasons for this in my opinion. For one thing, I reckon it has a lot to do with who the significant people are in your own initiation into research. Naturally, there will be some you like and agree with more than others (say lecturers or colleagues), and you often find yourself agreeing with their views – which begin to have a major influence on how you believe the world works. Also, research you find interesting and exciting can be influential. Perhaps you like this book, and the fact that I set my stall out as a realist will be influential (that would be really nice by the way). But ultimately it is a combination of factors that draw you to one or another viewpoint. Simply put, I consider that most thinking people – once they learn the tools to express it – can define how they believe the world works, and therefore how we should research it. This is the first way of 'choosing an approach'.

The other way is a bit more pragmatic, and I am somewhat cautious about it. Specifically, most books will give you a table of contrasts between realist (often, they call it positivist, which we already know is a not strictly correct) and interpretivist characteristics. You look at them, and see which ones seem to fit your project ideas, and then go with that. To be honest I really hate these tables, for loads of reasons. Firstly I think that you should consider your project ideas to flow from your philosophical worldview, not the other way round. That's what *really* happens, so why try to cover it up? A project is only 'interpretivist' if you as a researcher are 'interpretivist', not if it fulfils some characteristics on a table. I also think these tables can be used as an excuse for lazy thinking – and avoidance of really engaging with the material in the text. In fact, I want you to read these chapters so much that I'm not even going to put one of those tables in. No really, I'm not.

OK, OK, I will bow to demand and do one. Table 3.1 presents some common characteristics of interpretive research and researchers, contrasted with those of realist researchers and research. I'm not going to tell you how to use it, but I am going to demand

Table 3.1 Characteristics of realist and interpretive research

	Realist	**Interpretive**
What is reality?	Objectively measurable, knowable, separate from those looking at it.	Subjective, interpreted by participants.
What is knowledge?	Singular body of knowledge, agreed upon by scientists, generalisable.	Multiple types and bodies exist, collaboratively constructed, context-specific.
The status of language.	Describes reality as it is, but is independent of what it describes.	Actively constructs reality, and is itself part of what it signifies.
What's the focus on?	Deduction, explanation, prediction, creating general laws.	Induction, description, understanding, generating local understanding.
General approach to research.	Abstract, reductionist, hypothesis testing.	Participatory, reflexive, theory-generating.
Useful characteristics for a researcher[1].	Creativity, rigour, analytical skill, interest in topic, capacity for hard work, tolerance for ambiguity, able to interpret a mass of data, sense of humour ...	Creativity, rigour, analytical skill, interest in topic, capacity for hard work, tolerance for ambiguity, able to interpret a mass of data, sense of humour ...

[1]Can you see what I did there? There is no necessary difference between the type of person who can make a great researcher – whatever type of framework you work with. I *hate* those clichés about interpretive people being more 'creative', or less 'rigorous' and all that.

that you don't look at it until you have properly read the last two chapters. Honest, I'll find out if you don't. I know where you live.

So what am I saying? Well, firstly I am saying that you don't *choose* to be interpretivist or realist – these are just labels for the way in which you think about the world. I simply won't decide tomorrow to do an interpretive project, because at the moment I fundamentally believe the world to be objective and that I can measure it if I try hard enough.[6] However, you can change and modify your worldview – but that's another story. For example, perhaps you've never really looked at interpretive philosophies until now, and you find them compelling so you have moved towards them. That's fine, wonderful even! But you don't do an interpretive *project*, your projects are interpretive because *you* are interpretive. I can utilise *methods* which are often associated with interpretivists, but it doesn't mean I am doing an interpretive project. So think about what you believe the world to be like, in light of the previous two chapters, and whether that viewpoint is compatible with the kinds of

[6]Note that whether I currently have sophisticated enough *tools* to measure it is not relevant, it is the goal which is important (go back to Chapter 2 if you don't get where I am coming from here).

things you want to discover about the world – only *then* can you really determine how you and your project are positioned philosophically.

Of course, there is *another* way of looking at the choice between interpretive and realist viewpoints …

The politics of organisational research

I've touched on political issues before. As you now know, there are debates and fights all the time over which is the 'correct' viewpoint, or even if there is one. So one way of looking at how to determine which worldview you could take is a political one. For example, are you mad keen on a particular supervisor for your project for whatever reason? Maybe they are really important in the field, maybe you know some of their other students who speak highly of them, maybe you just have a crush on them (I get this last one all the time of course). Anyway, if that's the way you want to play it, then it is very likely that you should also share (or at least pretend to) a similar worldview with them. This will of course override all of the *good* things I have talked about above – but I won't deny that it does happen.

Furthermore, in some fields one particular worldview – e.g. realism or interpretivism – is dominant, rising, or subsiding in importance. For example, in the 1970s and 80s, consumer psychology was dominated by a very naturalist, objective viewpoint. Over the last 10 years or so, interpretive viewpoints have begun to rise in importance. Some people tend to 'jump on the bandwagon' of dominant or rising worldviews, to take advantage of these trends even if they are not convinced by them. Again, I would not advise it as a good course of action, because eventually the trend will finish, and you will be left high and dry.

That said, while I would strongly suggest that politics is a very bad *reason* to choose a viewpoint and philosophical tradition to follow, it can be an important *consideration*. Specifically, you should be very well aware of the dominant philosophical approach taken in your field, and also in your own department. This will tip you off to potential hurdles you will have to face. For example, if your department is dominated by realist researchers and you are working within the interpretive tradition, you will have to address different questions when you present your work to them than if you were presenting to interpretivists. Similarly, if you wish to publish your work in journals and conferences, you need to be well aware of how likely it is that they will concur or accept your viewpoint. Also, it is important to recognise how your potential supervisor thinks, both in terms of relating to them and also in terms of whether they are likely to want to supervise your project. The previous two chapters should have given you the tools with which to achieve this task.

Interpretive projects

Finally, I am going to give some examples of interpretive projects. However, I am again going to bow to popular demand and do a table. Table 3.2 shows how the same topics could be approached from either realist or interpretive standpoints, and also suggests different interpretive traditions if you look carefully. It should help you understand the key differences between the traditions, viewpoints, and philosophies we have talked about so far.

Table 3.2 Examples of projects

	Realist	Interpretive
Management discipline.	Identify, measure and model the factors which influence the success of disciplinary action by managers.	Explore the subjective experience of punishment from the perspective of the managers and/or employees of an organisation.
Sales ethics.	Develop and test a set of hypotheses regarding the factors which cause salespeople to behave unethically.	Examine how a culture of unethicality can evolve in an organisation and how salespeople are socialised into such a prevailing orthodoxy.
Fear-inducing advertising.	What characteristics of advertising execution cause viewers to feel negative emotions such as fear?	How do different people experience and react to fear induced by advertising?

Relating this to the rest of the book

So we've reached the end of our little journey through the history of Western philosophy of science and research methods. I'm not sure how you found it, but I thought it was quite fun. If you have digested the material in these chapters you're already well on the way to becoming an excellent researcher.

The rest of this book is more often concerned with technical issues than philosophical ones, but it's vital that you try always to consider the philosophical content of techniques and methods. If the techniques you are using aren't appropriate to the worldview you are employing at the time, then your findings won't really be relevant. A great example was given in the section above on critical research and feminist approaches – remember the implicit assumptions of quantitative experiments and how they relate to the power structure beliefs of feminist researchers? In fact, understanding of these philosophical concepts should ultimately make it completely obvious why different methodologies are preferred by research of different worldviews. Never, *ever* forget Figure 2.1 in Chapter 2, and always understand that the ultimate quality of your findings depends on how well they relate to the methods and worldview you operate within.

So you should now have a tentative grasp of the interpretive worldview as well as the more traditional scientific realist/naturalist one. From here you are in a great position to go forward to looking at literature and actually getting into the field to do some research eventually. That said, an interesting question which often arises here is 'can I mix the approaches'? This often comes up when people misunderstand the difference between qualitative or quantitative *methodologies*, and realist or interpretive *philosophies*. Sure, as we'll see later in Chapter 15, you can mix and match methods where appropriate, but you should now understand that the philosophical viewpoints are somewhat contradictory in many ways. Thus, I find it difficult to see how a single project can genuinely mix and match interpretive and realist philosophical worldviews if they are both expressed to their fullest. Of course, like any good researcher I am willing to be convinced otherwise, but I haven't been so far.

Moving forward from here, think about your own beliefs about the world, and how these impact on the things you want to study. If you have already started research, think about what you are doing and the implicit assumptions it makes about how the world works. Try to relate this to the actual techniques and methods I will discuss as the book goes on. Finally, you should all leave here knowing a bunch of interesting and useful stuff that you didn't know before, and hopefully a feeling for how your own work will fit in to the vast spread of research that has gone before.

Good luck, this is where it really starts to get interesting …

Key points to take from this chapter:

- By the end of the 19th and throughout the 20th century society, science and philosophy was undergoing radical changes.
- From this, new ideas about reality and our place in it developed, leading to fundamental challenges to the enlightenment model of scientific progress.
- Interpretivism was advanced as a key alternative to traditional realist approaches, based around hermeneutics and phenomenology.
- The interpretivist worldview is chatacterised by an axiology of understanding rather than explaining/predicting, an epistemology of subjectivity, and a social constructionist ontology.
- Interpretivist methodologies (such as phenomenology, ethnography and critical research) tend to use qualitative, participatory approaches to data collection.
- The three 'R's of reductionism, reflexivity and representation are crucial concerns in conducting and especially reporting interpretive research.
- *Interpretive research is not an easy way out!*
- Generalisability is a key battleground between interpretive and realist approaches, but it should not be ignored by interpretivists; the concept of rigour can be useful in assuring readers of the value of interpretive research.
- In choosing a philosophical perspective, it is best to go with your feelings rather than trying to jump on a bandwagon or play political games.

Further reading

- *Doing Research Projects in Marketing, Management and Consumer Research* by Chris Hackley: I worked with Professor Hackley for a year, and to be honest he has been one of the major influences on my thinking around interpretive methods and philosophies. This book is a great introduction to doing research from an interpretive perspective, and I would recommend it highly to anyone who wants to learn more detail than I have been able to provide.

- *Social Constructionism* by Vivien Burr: a great introduction to social constructionism within psychology and the social sciences. Again, I would recommend this book to anyone who wants a fuller grasp of social constructionism.
- *Interpretive Consumer Research* edited by Elizabeth C. Hirschman: It's out of print, so I suspect this book will be hard to get hold of (perhaps an interlibrary loan will be necessary), but it is worth the effort. It contains some outstanding chapters on the practicalities of interpretive research, but also most interestingly a set of chapters debating interpretivism and scientific methods. These are fascinating, and it gets a bit heated in places (I love that stuff!).
- *Postmodern Marketing*, and *Postmodern Marketing 2* by Stephen Brown: the high priest of postmodernism in marketing. I would say that his stuff is some of the best written from a postmodern perspective, but he would doubtless say that this is inconsistent with a postmodern perspective.
- *The Passion of the Western Mind* by Richard Tarnas: Once you've read *Sophie's World*, move on to this. It's essentially the entire history of Western philosophy squashed into book form. Almost like one of those 'power-bars' you eat before going to the gym – but I wouldn't eat this book, obviously. Whatever, this book is fantastic and just having it on your shelf is guaranteed to make you more intelligent by osmosis. Or at least impress people you bring back to your house/room.
- *Introducing Nietzsche* by Laurence Gane with illustrations by Kitty Chan: Nietzsche of course was one of the key architects of many of the ideas introduced here – so an understanding of the man is A Good Thing. This is a nice little introduction, and contains lots of pictures. Nietzsche also did some pretty weird and interesting things in his life, so he's worth reading about on that level purely for entertainment!

EXERCISES

1. Go back to the timeline you did for Exercise 1 in Chapter 2. Now place the key thinkers I've discussed in Chapter 3 on it, as well as any others you consider important. Then try again to place key scientific discoveries there and think how they relate to changes in the prevailing mood in philosophy of science (tip, I bet you have to expand the 20th century bit here!).
2. Go and find the lyrics to 'Bruce's Philosopher's Song' by Monty Python, after each line relate the material in the last two chapters to the philosophers in the song.
3. Afterwards, try to link in other philosophers and thinkers I have talked about to the ones mentioned in the song.
4. Write down a set of interpretive research ideas related to your own study area.
5. Now be more specific, write down projects within the phenomenological, ethnographic, and critical traditions.
6. Explain why you consider yourself an interpretive researcher, or conversely why you *don't*: 500 words at least please!

7. Finally, go and listen to some records made by New Romantic bands (e.g. Spandau Ballet, the Human League, A Flock of Seagulls, and especially Japan[7]). Go and find out why the term 'new romantic' was applied to this music scene – does it have any relevance to Romanticism as a philosophy discussed here? Honestly, this is a serious question!

---

[7] Mainly because they were the best of the bunch.

Chapter 4
Reviewing existing literature

Ian Lings

SUPERVISOR'S VIEW: DR ANNE SOUCHON 

Many research students approach their study with some degree of anxiety over data collection and/or analysis, blissfully unaware that what will cause them grief is, in fact, the rather innocuous-sounding '*literature review*'. There are two reasons why the literature review is often a major stumbling block.

First, it is a common belief that the literature should be thoroughly reviewed in a bid to identify a suitable topic (and by suitable, of course, I mean one which will make a contribution to knowledge and be deserving of a Ph.D.). Your supervisor may insist on it, even if this process takes you well over a year; even if it delays your study so much that your funding runs out before you've completed your thesis; even if after reviewing 'your' literature, you decide that there is no theoretical gap there after all, and want to start reviewing an entirely different research stream.

Second, intimate knowledge of the literature is essential in order to position the study within its broader area (otherwise, researchers would forever be reinventing the wheel), develop propositions or hypotheses if this is what the study requires, and explain the findings uncovered in the empirical phase of the project. Thus, as Ian Lings explains below, the literature review is the backbone of the project; it supports the entire study. Its importance is so ingrained that I battle on a daily basis with Doctoral students who are so paralysed by the fear of not knowing the literature well enough that they are stuck at reviewing literature and refuse to move on.

So, here are a few hints to reduce your literature review stress:

(A) Choose a *supervisor*, not a topic. A good supervisor will know the literature already and could (I want to say should) steer you towards a worthy topic.

(B) Learn to let go of the literature. Do not get trapped into thinking that you need to keep collecting/reading/assimilating more and more papers *before* you start conceptualising and/or collecting data yourself. If you do, you are simply procrastinating and using the literature as a security blanket, not as a means-to-an-end. And you run the risk of losing focus and getting lost.

(C) Start multi-tasking: keep abreast of new papers coming out *as you embark on other stages of your research*.

And remember that the literature review is an ongoing activity. It is only finished when the thesis has been successfully defended, hard leather-bound (at some considerable expense), and distributed (for free) to friends and family who will never read it!

VIEW FROM THE TRENCHES: JOOBEE YEOW

If there are two words that would appear in the worst nightmares of the perfectionists of this world, especially the perfectionist researchers, they would be *literature review!* I am in the third year of my Ph.D. and even now one of my greatest fears is that I do not know anything and everything regarding my research topic. What if my supervisors ask me this? Or what if my peers ask me that? Or worse, what if someone in the audience when I am presenting my research asks me: 'Why is the moon round in shape'? Shouldn't I know that too? My research is supposed to earth-shattering, it is supposed to solve all the problems of the world! With this in mind, at the start of my research, I combed through every journal paper and book – in fact, anything that was readable, anything that bore even the slightest resemblance to the keywords of my topic. To my bitter discovery, it was not only resource inefficient, but I ended up *lost in reviewing,* torn in all directions.

If I were to offer some advice from my own experience; first and foremost, structure is *very important* in literature review. Secondly, a crucial point is to have structure, and thirdly, you must have guessed, is **structure.** Start by identifying the most relevant authors, journals, databases and other sources that publish work that is most relevant to your topic. By doing this groundwork, you begin to create a boundary in your mind for your literature review, preventing the temptation to go astray – bear in mind that one needs to actually *complete* the Ph.D. at some stage!

Imagine the literature review is in the shape of a diamond. You start at the tip, broaden your knowledge of the topic and eventually come back again to the tip, where now you have gained your focus and pinpointed the gap in the literature. To know when to stop, when you have exhausted most of the literature relevant to your research, is vital as one needs eventually to derive hypotheses and collect data to be able to produce a piece of work to advance knowledge or inform practice. I am not suggesting that you should limit your literature review, but it is impossible for one to know absolutely everything, thus it is important to know in *depth* what you are doing and in *breath* what is relevant to what you are doing.

Last, but not least, a piece of advice from my supervisor at the beginning of my Ph.D. that I still find very useful: 'Your Ph.D. is not supposed to solve the problems of the world, but to make enough of a significant contribution (even as small as it is in the vast sea of knowledge) that you or future researchers will continue and snowball from it to make greater contributions and *eventually*, change the world of knowledge.'

Many beginning researchers have significant problems with reviewing the literature. This might be due to the fact that there just isn't much information out there on how to do it. In fact, many research students are simply given the instruction to 'go away and review the literature on topic x', closely followed by 'see me in a few months'. Learning how to do a good literature review is therefore often done via trial and error. However, it doesn't have to be that way, and in this chapter I hope to give you a good head-start on doing your literature review, and ensuring you end up with a solid piece of work.

The aims of your literature review are to show that you have studied existing work in your field and to provide insights into this work. An effective review critically analyses material, synthesises it, and will be relevant, appropriate, and useful for the reader. Your literature review presents the case and context for the rest of your thesis. For this reason it is important to demonstrate the relationship of your work to previous research in the area. This chapter is written from a deductive perspective; recommending that you should review the literature *before* starting your project. You will probably have an idea of the domain of the literature that you wish to examine and possibly even a more specific and focused area, however, I am assuming that one of your aims in reviewing the literature is to decide on the specific research that you will undertake. An alternative to this view is presented in Alternative View 9.3 which presents a 'grounded' approach in which the literature is not reviewed until after the project has started.

At the end of this chapter I really hope you have come to terms with these key ideas:

- What literature is.
- Where you can find it.
- What a literature review is, and what it does.

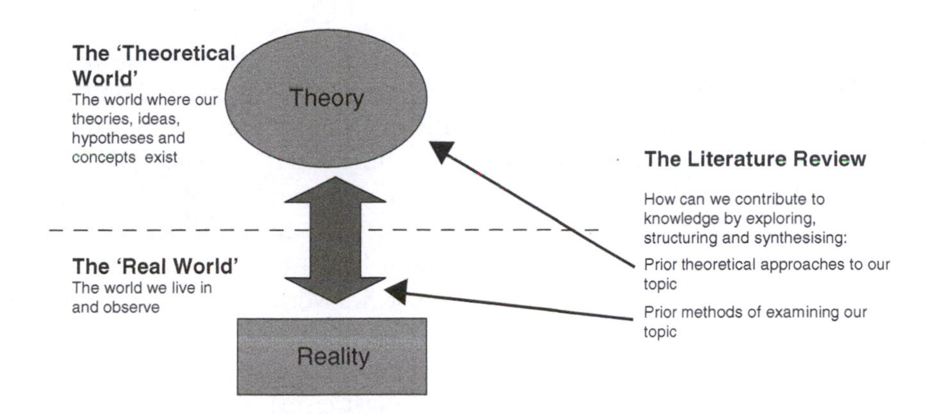

Figure 4.1 The place of literature reviewing

- What critiquing the literature means.
- How you can organise your thoughts.
- How you can structure your literature review.
- How you can organise your sources.

Why is it Important to Know This Stuff?

Understanding the basics of reviewing the literature is essential for anyone who wishes to undertake research and contribute to an existing body of knowledge. It's really about uncovering and exploring how prior researchers have explored the theoretical issues in your topic, and also to some extent which methods they have used to collect data and examine those theories, as shown in Figure 4.1. Becoming comfortable with how to locate, understand and critically analyse literature is necessary for you to build your work on top of that which has been done previously. A thorough review of the literature serves several purposes; it helps you to better understand the field in which you are working, it identifies work that has already been conducted and knowledge that has already been developed, it helps you to identify, and often explicitly suggests, areas in which new contributions can be made, and it will illustrate methodologies that have been applied to your particular field of research. In short, the literature review helps you to ensure that you do not simply repeat what has already been done, and to have more confidence that the contribution to knowledge that you wish to make is *indeed* a contribution.

Familiarity with the literature is essential if you are to be able to defend your ideas and arguments in peer-reviewed written work, or even more daunting, when you are standing in front of your peers, be it in front of a class, at a degree viva or at a conference. However, familiarity is not sufficient for a successful literature review, *critical appraisal* is also necessary. Critical evaluation of others' work is a particularly difficult task for many researchers, especially those who feel relatively junior or who are not yet qualified. I have often heard research students and new colleagues comment 'How can I criticise Professor X's work, she is a famous professor and knows so much more than me'. While this is undoubtedly true (professors do usually know more than those just embarking on a research career) the art of the literature review is in the **critique** (not the criticism), and *all work is open to critique.*

As you will see in the following chapters, there are many different ways to approach a given research question. Previous literature will perhaps indicate that different philosophies have been followed, different conceptualisations constructed and different models created. Each of the approaches that you find in published works will present some benefits to answering a particular research question and some inherent limitations to answering the question. It is a discussion of these philosophies, conceptualisations, methods and findings, and their benefits and limitations that forms the basis of the critique of the literature.

Of course, you will also come across some research that is just weak, and can be criticised as being so (sometimes even in the best journals). In order to criticise research as weak, you will need to not only understand how to conduct your review and critique of the literature, you will also need to know about the research designs, methods and analytical techniques discussed in the later chapters of this book.

What is a 'literature review'?

The literature review is literally that, a *re-view* (or look again) at what has already been written about a topic. The literature review is where you demonstrate that you *understand* that which has been done before, and can point to where this existing research is *deficient* in some way. It's important to realise that you are not trying to 'insult' prior research and researchers here, but to point out where existing work needs some supplementing, which maybe because the world has changed since prior work was conducted, or maybe because such work doesn't address important issues that are now relevant – in fact often the authors will indicate this themselves. Further, you need to explain how your work adds to existing knowledge, by overcoming the problems with the existing literature, maybe by bringing together disparate fields of research and extending them, or developing new theory. You also have to show why your work is *important*, *relevant* and *interesting*. Unfortunately, none of these tasks is easy.

As I mentioned earlier, if you are a research student, it's very likely that one of the first things you will be asked to do on commencing your research degree will be something like 'go away and read the literature' that is relevant to your topic (assuming that you know what your topic will be in more specific terms than just something like 'consumer behaviour' or 'motivation'). Now, it's not that your supervisor doesn't like you and wants to avoid you – although I guess sometimes that's the case. No; at this stage you are actually trying to achieve two simultaneous aims with your reading. You will almost certainly still be trying to tightly define your research problem or thesis (something that you will probably be doing for quite some time in an iterative fashion) and, at the same time, you will be trying to identify, read, understand and assimilate every source of information relevant to your thesis. Therein lies the difficulty. Essentially, you don't know exactly *what* you are going to research until you have read the relevant literature (so everything seems relevant) and you don't know if what you are reading is really relevant until you have decided exactly what you are going to research (which could be many things, as there is more that we don't know than which we do).

If you are in this situation, try to take comfort in two pieces of advice: 'all reading is good',[1] and 'everyone is in the same boat at this stage of their research'. This advice I offer readily, in the knowledge it failed to impress me, assuage my fears and insecurities, or in fact comfort me in any way at all when offered to me by my thesis supervisor. Typically, subsequent experience has shown that he was absolutely right (don't you just hate it when that happens?).

Whatever your situation, one thing is for certain, you have to start somewhere, and, believe it or not, many potential researchers fall at this first hurdle; deciding to start (not deciding *where to* start but just deciding to start *somewhere*). Many of you will have a research topic which is relatively tightly defined. If this is so you will know pretty specifically what you are looking for in relation to unexplained phenomena or theory that is in need of updating or re-examining in the light of a changed world. A **directed** literature review strategy is appropriate in such circumstances. You should write out the research question(s) and analyse it for assumptions (these are what questions you must also answer in order to answer the research question). Write out all of these associated research questions and direct your reading to be able to answers these. IDE 4.1 shows how a research question has assumptions on which it is based, and how further assumptions are made at other stages of the research process. Most often these are not explicitly stated by researchers, but it is useful for you to be aware of the assumptions that you are making in developing your research question and the associated research methods that you wish to adopt to explore your question.

---

[1] Well, this is not strictly always true, but at this point it is a useful rule to live by.

IDE 4.1: Assumptions of a Research Question

A research question is a statement that identifies the phenomenon to be studied. For example, 'What influence do performance bonuses have on employee behaviour?' There are several assumptions that underlie this research question. Firstly, this research question assumes that employee behaviour is something that can be observed by you as a researcher. Underlying this assumption is a realist view of the world, i.e. that there is an observable world to be researched. Depending on the approach that you wish to adopt and the theory on which you base your research, you may have to make further assumptions. If you decide that performance bonuses are one facet of a person's job, along with many other facets, you may wish to adopt a utility framework to analyse the research question. This would require an assumption of 'rational behaviour' and possibly an assumption of utility maximisation by the employee. The question could also be approached using a psychology framework such as the theory of planned behaviour, which also assumes rational behaviour but does not assume utility maximising. Both of these frameworks could direct you to collect quantitative data, which in turn would be based on an assumption that there is a 'real' world and that this can be measured. Further assumptions would then be made in the development of the questionnaire (if one were used) and these will be discussed later in the book. If you were to conduct observational research, then you would make assumptions about the validity and meaning of the observations. You would need to assume that you are observing real behaviour and that your observation is an accurate reflection of what is happening; that you are attributing the correct meaning to the behaviour that you are observing.

If you do not have a very specific research topic, your very first aim should be to try to tightly define your thesis or research question. Most likely, this task will involve coming up with a tentative, working definition. But how on earth do you do this? In this case, an **emergent** literature review strategy works best. Such a strategy involves reading everything, and looking for similarities and contradictions in ideas, methods, theories, assumptions and definitions. From this you can identify interesting research topics that you wish to explore. With the emergent approach, you have the benefit of being able to define the scope of your topic for yourself. Although on the surface this can seem daunting, it has the advantage of allowing you more opportunity to bring your experiences, beliefs and interests to bear on your research. For example, if you are interested in researching 'branding', one starting point is to think about what it is about 'branding' that particularly interests you, and which is not already explained in the literature? Of course, at this point, you don't know if it has already been explained in the literature until you look, but at least you know where to start looking.

Another useful starting point is to think about your observations of the world that suggest to you that existing theory isn't up to explaining the nuances of what you see in the real world. For example, can existing theory explain the fine details of your own experiences of human behaviour, concerning individuals such as customers, employees or managers, or groups such as segments, organisations, industries, or countries? This approach may seem rather 'unscientific' to many (although I hope that reading Chapters 2 and 3 should have given you some pointers on that issue), but it is not a bad place to start developing your research question, provided that you are aware of the purely natural tendency of human beings to confirm our beliefs rather than challenge them; try not to let this bias your readings of the literature.

Furthermore, it is important to remember that you are almost certainly not going to provide a general theory of your field, solve all of the problems that organisations or institutions face and explain all of employee/customer/government or other entities' behaviour (or whatever it is you are interested in). Your research problem will need to be much more focused on a specific issue. Until you have tightly defined your topic, hundreds of sources will seem relevant. However, you cannot define your topic until you read around your research area. Consequently, defining your research question (or thesis) is an iterative process; as you read you refine your thesis, and as you refine your thesis you can decide more easily on what to read and what to ignore.

Finally – and this can be a long and involving process for many – after defining the topic (however tentatively) you are in the position of being able to commence your **directed** reading. But be aware that *directed* is the important adjective here, if you are not directed in your reading you run the risk of becoming lost in the literature, constantly finding exciting avenues to follow but never actually doing anything. You will never complete your research unless you do something. Research requires both *thought* and *action*. Just thinking about your research will not get your thesis written. Please remember that!

Deciding what 'literature' is

It is very common for research students to ask me questions concerning exactly 'what' is literature. It's hard to answer this conclusively, but there are some basic pointers which can help. In general, information for your literature review may be gathered from many sources, and the basic term 'literature' here means the works that you consult to investigate your research problem. That said, while there are many sources of information available, the merits of each must be considered very carefully, and you need to decide how much confidence you wish to place in the information that you find in each of the sources. Should you judge an article from the top journal in your field to be as valuable as one from the local newspaper, or a company report? How do you decide which information is appropriate to include in your literature review? To my mind, there are four main questions that need to be answered for all information in your literature review:

- Is it relevant?
- Does it come from a reputable source?
- Does it present a compelling theoretical argument, and/or rigorous empirical results (i.e. is it any good?)
- What were the motives of the author?

I'll deal with the last question later in the chapter, because it is more concerned with analysing literature, and what you include when you write up your literature review. However, the first two issues are concerned with deciding what types of information to gather for review. To address the question of relevance; there are several decisions that need to be made. Your literature review will need to be sufficiently broad to explain your research area in the context of other research, perhaps in other areas of interest or even other disciplines. Simultaneously, it will have to be focused on your particular research topic, and comprehensive within your own field of enquiry. This means that you will need to be very clear about the definition of your *field* of research; for example, are you doing research in 'marketing' or 'organisational psychology'? Your field should be closely related to your research question or thesis. However, it should not be too close and restrictive, or you run the risk of missing other important literature from adjacent fields, and other disciplines. Actually, you should be adventurous in deciding where contributions to your understanding may come from. Many projects do not restrict themselves to just one body of knowledge, such as marketing, or economics. In fact, some of the best advances in thinking have been as a result of bringing together two or more, apparently disparate, bodies of knowledge to advance in our understanding of the world – which could be termed 'horizontal thinking', as I'll talk about in IDE 4.2.

IDE 4.2: 'Horizontal Thinking'

Horizontal thinking is an interesting term I came across recently when I was reading about creativity, and interestingly enough it recalls a conversation I had with Nick when we were thinking about this book. The idea of horizontal thinking is simply taking ideas and concepts from other fields and disciplines and applying them to your own research problem. It is another great example of how it is useful to read widely and be interested in many different fields. In fact, it's amazing how many ideas you can get from areas which might seem totally unrelated to your own. If you never venture outside your own discipline, you will never be exposed to this kind of thing. There are all kinds of examples of this happening in research, but some of the clearest are the use of Darwinian evolution theory in the social and applied business disciplines, for instance: 'Which automobiles will be here tomorrow?' by Robert J. Holloway, in the *Journal of Marketing*, Vol. 25, Issue 3, p. 35; 'Social Darwinism and the Taylor system: A missing link in the evolution of management?' by Roland E. Kidwell Jr, in the *International Journal of Public Administration*, Vol. 18, Issue 5, p. 767; 'It's Darwinism – survival of the fittest: How markets and reputations shape the ways in which plaintiffs' lawyers obtain clients' by Stephen Daniels and Joanne Martin, in *Law & Policy*, Vol. 21, Issue 4.

Having decided on your topic, and set the scope of your literature search, it is time to start looking for appropriate sources of information. This addresses the second of the two main questions about the confidence of the information and the quality of the source. Where should you get your information about theories, concepts, methods and philosophies that you are interested in? Different types of literature can be grouped in various ways, but for our purposes it is useful to group things according to their intended audience.

Academic literature

Academic (also called 'scholarly') literature can be thought of as work that is written and reported primarily for an academic audience, i.e. scholars who will be using this published work to inform future research in this area. As such, academic literature has certain requirements that are sometimes not met in other types of literature. Academic work should be reported in a scientific manner, such that it is possible for someone reading it to be able to evaluate the theories on which is it based, the research methods used, analyses conducted and conclusions drawn. The need to include lots of information in a very exact manner has the advantage that exactly what the researcher(s) has done should be clear and unambiguous. This means it is easier to identify the limitations of the work, and often this is done for you. However, it can also make academic work dry and tedious to read. The flowery and descriptive language, by its nature often imprecise, which makes normal prose quite interesting to read, often has to be removed to fit to publishing page limits and to make the reporting of the research exact and the work undertaken replicable. Despite the challenge of staying awake while reading academic literature, this is generally the most relevant type of literature for your review. The main sources of academic literature are detailed below, along with some discussion of the usefulness in the critical literature review.

Peer Reviewed Journal articles are works that have been 'refereed' or 'quality assured' by scholars working in the field of inquiry discussed in the paper. If the article is published, then these 'peers' and the journal editor consider that the article has advanced the body of knowledge in some way. In other words, the arguments presented should be well researched and discussed, the research undertaken should have been done in an appropriate manner, the data analysed correctly, and any results should follow logically from the information presented in the article.

As a general rule, peer reviewed articles should be the main source of information for your literature review. Journal articles provide concise information regarding theories, methodologies, applications and interpretations relevant to your thesis. However, not all journals have the same academic standing and it is important to have a feel for the relative importance of each journal in your own field. This is not to say that top-quality work does not appear in lower-standing journals, nor that sometimes average or (frankly) poor work does not appear in top journals. Nevertheless, many people do use the idea of 'journal standing' as a guide to the quality of articles in those journals. Those journals that are the most important tend to have the highest reputation and standing in your field (often called the 'A list'). Many universities have rankings of journals and, although they rarely agree completely, these can be useful in deciding which journals are the most important in your field of study. Table 4.1 is an excerpt from a report which discussed perceptions of different marketing journals, and gives a good example of how different journals are ranked within a field. The *social science citation index* (SSCI) can also be a guide, but not all journals within many fields are ranked by SSCI.

Table 4.1 Example journal quality rankings

Rank	Quality	Name of journal
1	1.867	Journal of Marketing
2	1.837	Journal of Marketing Research
3	1.753	Journal of Consumer Research
4	1.749	Journal of the Academy of Marketing Science
5	1.729	Marketing Science
6	1.608	Journal of Retailing
7	1.587	Journal of Business Research
8	1.544	Journal of Consumer Psychology
9	1.540	International Journal of Research in Marketing
10	1.493	Journal of Advertising
11	1.461	Journal of Advertising Research
12	1.457	European Journal of Marketing
13	1.424	Journal of Service Research
14	1.423	Psychology and Marketing
15	1.380	Marketing Letters

Source: From an unpublished (to date) ranking study, Jordan Louviere, Siggi Gudergan and Ian Lings (University of Technology Sydney).

Note: Quality rankings were determined through a study of marketing academics.

Top-ranking journals can, generally, be thought of as having the most impact in your field, and therefore you can generally have more confidence in the results and findings of any study reported in them. Having said this, it is important not to restrict yourself to just those journals with high quality rankings. There is a whole range of research that is reported in other journals, some are specialist journals and do not always appear high on the list of journal rankings because of their specialist nature, some are journals targeting audiences other than academics. This does not mean that these journals are irrelevant or 'low' quality, just that in the general scheme of things they do not have as much overall impact as others. As Webster and Watson (2002, pp. xiii) report in their discussion of writing a literature review:

> Studies ... have consistently been limited by drawing from a small sample of journals. Even though the [ones] investigated here may have reputations as our top journals, this does not excuse an author from investigating 'all' published articles in a field.

As a final note on journal articles, it is extremely important not to assume that 'just because it is in the journal it must be perfect'. There are many examples of work that has some pretty significant flaws appearing even in top journals. Be aware that time moves on, research standards change, and articles may be published which fall short on some criteria because they are very strong in another. In particular, articles which deal with 'hot topics' may get published even though they are not as strong as they might be. So be careful not to simply assume the quality of the literature, wherever it may appear!

Conference proceedings are articles or abstracts that are published by the organisers of the many academic conferences that occur annually in each field and specialist area. In case you didn't know, academics are always attending conferences (especially those in far-flung locations), and these conferences are ostensibly aimed at disseminating leading-edge research as quickly as possible. They are definitely *not* excuses to visit exotic places and have fun – honest! Many of those who attend conferences go to present their work in front of peers and colleagues, and this work is also generally published in the 'proceedings' of the conference. A lot of conference proceedings are also peer reviewed and have to meet minimum standards of scientific rigour. The main strength of conference proceedings as opposed to peer-reviewed journal articles is that they are often the first place that research is published and tested in front of peer audiences. For this reason, conference proceedings are useful in providing information about the latest research, which often has not yet been published in peer reviewed journals. Conference proceedings are also a useful source of information about who is working in a particular research area, and what they are doing. You can then search to find out what else they have published in other outlets.

Conference proceedings tend not to be a main source of information for a literature review for many reasons. Firstly, there is a general perception in some fields that they are of a 'lower' quality than peer-reviewed journals (although this is not always the case, and not for all conferences in a field either). Further, there is also the idea that most of the high-quality work will eventually reach the journals (academics are rarely happy with 'just' a conference paper). That is not to say that good quality work cannot be expected in a conference paper. Sometimes, conference proceedings can be the only place to get really radical, new, or esoteric work. However, one of the major drawbacks of conference proceedings is the increasing tendency of conference organisers to restrict the size of conference papers to just a few pages. This means that, often, the paper does not provide as rich an indication of the background and scope of the research. Similarly, conference proceedings are often hard to locate and gain access to, unless you know someone who has attended the conference and has the proceedings. Nevertheless, they are a useful resource and are worth pursuing.

Previous research theses and dissertations are also a possible source of information. All UK Ph.D. theses should be published in the British Library and can be requested by inter-library loan. In other countries Ph.Ds may or may not be published; it is often necessary to contact the author to request a copy of their work. However, it is important to remember that they are of uncertain quality (yes, even including mine and Nick's!).[2] For example, you do not know if the student who wrote the thesis did a good job or not; after all, you don't get the examiner's reports on it. Also, most research degrees are seen as an apprenticeship piece, they will often contain mistakes that the researcher would be expected to rectify in subsequent work. As a consequence, you should treat the contents of student theses with some caution. Furthermore, it can be a big task to search through the huge store of theses without any direction. Nevertheless, it's important to realise that they are available to those who are interested.

As a final note, you should be careful about drawing too much from other theses – it can be tempting to use them too much, especially if they are in similar areas. This would seem an opportune moment to mention **plagiarism**: something that should be avoided at all costs. If you don't know what plagiarism is, ask your supervisor or any other academic. They will explain to you what it is, why it is bad and what happens if you get caught[3] – probably at great length.

Teaching literature

Teaching literature is also a type of academic literature; however, its primary purpose is usually to provide a general description of a field, rather than a detailed and scientific description of specific theories and models. This type of literature is generally aimed at students and lecturers who teach or take courses in a field. Teaching literature has many advantages over the academic literature described previously. It is usually much more accessible in

---

[2]Actually, if he ever reads that he might have something to say!

[3]Hint: it's not good!

terms of being easy to read and understand. This makes it a great resource for learning about ideas that are new to you. This accessibility of teaching literature comes at a price though; this type of literature is generally much less comprehensive in its discussion of all aspects of the scientific investigation that underpins what is discussed. This makes it virtually impossible to critique teaching literature in a scientific manner, because essentially what is being presented is '*the accepted wisdom of the day*'. Although teaching literature is a very useful resource to you as a researcher, it should not form a major part of your critical literature review. Two types of teaching literature are discussed below. Hopefully, you will see the merits of both, and also their limitations for inclusion in your literature review.

Textbooks are generally less detailed and less up-to-date than journal articles. By the time that a model or theory has entered the pages of a textbook it is generally seen as the 'accepted wisdom' in a field. This is why it has been included in a book designed for teaching rather than research. Consequently, textbooks are less useful for including in your literature review. But, this does not mean that they are less useful to you. Quite the contrary; as the content of a textbook has been well examined, often simplified and is generally presented in such a way as to facilitate understanding, they make an excellent place to start. This is especially true if the scope of your research takes you into new and unfamiliar disciplines. Textbooks are useful to bring you up to speed on the basic theories quickly and effectively. However, they will not generally provide you with cutting-edge research findings. One thing textbooks are very useful for, though, is for methodology and research techniques (just like this one in fact). The peer-reviewed journal literature on methodology can be a pretty scary place. To write about leading-edge developments in methodology requires that the authors assume those reading the article already know the basics, and often more advanced theories, up to the point at which the paper makes contribution. This may not be the case. It often takes book authors to integrate such material in such a way as to reach a more general research audience.

Finally, as I am becoming aware, the textbook is often the place where authors are able to put down their thoughts without too much censure from reviewers, so you should be aware that not all textbooks have had the same rigorous reviewing as a typical scholarly journal article. Of course, this particular one has.

Case studies

There are two common types of case study that you will come across. These are: (1) Journal articles that describe and report on 'case study research' and which belong in the academic literature category; and (2) Case studies used in teaching, that describe a company situation and provide (or require) some degree of analysis and interpretation.

Adopting a scientific view, the case study can be thought of as a neutral description of a situation, subject to objective analysis. From an artistic perspective, it can be viewed as an incomplete narrative, open to multiple interpretations. Whichever view is adopted, teaching case studies aim for students to gain depth in both problem-solving and problem-posing skills. Most commonly, the scientific view leads you to analyse the facts and to propose a specific answer to a real business problem. The literary view leads you to consider the interpretation of words, to select evidence based on values, and to reflect on the case as a parable. Both of these are laudable aims but they do not address the needs of your research literature review.

Practitioner-oriented literature

We use the term 'practitioner-oriented' to refer to literature who's primary target is those who actually have 'real' jobs in the field you study, if you see what I mean. For example, if you are a marketing researcher, 'practitioner-oriented' literature includes trade journals aimed at retail store managers, advertising executives, human resource managers, rather than journals aimed at academics studying those fields. Several types of practitioner oriented journals are available and some are discussed below.

Magazines and trade journals. The definition of magazines for our purposes is somewhat ambiguous. The Oxford Dictionary lists a magazine as 'a periodical publication containing articles and illustrations'. However, it should be clear at this point that we do not mean magazines like *Woman's Weekly*, *Hot Celebrity Gossip*, or the *NME* (although we know many academics who do read such august publications[4] for non-research purposes in general). We are assuming that the type of magazine you may consider reading for your research would address issues relevant to your research. Among academic circles I have heard the term '*magazine*' used to describe non-peer-reviewed publications and publications intended for a more managerial audience. These could be quite specialist, such as *The Economist, Marketing Week* or *New Scientist;* or they may be more general in nature,such as *Newsweek, National Interest* or *Time.* These publications can also provide a good starting point for justifying your research and demonstrating that it is both current and topical. General information about new discoveries, policies, etc. can provide a useful way to explain to your reader the impact of your work on the business environment.

As are textbooks, magazines are unlikely to be useful for inclusion in your literature review. However, like textbooks they can be a great resource to help you to understand your research domain. They can also be brilliant to 'set the scene' of your research in the real world, and give it a nice foundation. Typically, articles written in this type of publication are less technically difficult than peer reviewed articles and so can aid in developing your understanding of a particular area, prior to getting into more technical content in peer reviewed journal. It is worth remembering, though, that these articles are often journalistic and may be politically motivated, so it is always worth taking the time to try to understand the motives of the author before using information from them.

---

[4]And many others far too embarrassing to list here!

Government reports and business reports are also a good source of general information. The government and many businesses undertake research into areas of particular importance for them. These published reports can be a useful source of secondary information, depending on your field of study. However, many business reports are confidential, or at least embargoed for a period of time, so those that paid for them can get the best advantage. If you are lucky enough to get hold of one of these before it is released to the public domain, you should be careful about how you use it – or you could get someone (including yourself) into a lot of trouble. However, all publicly listed companies have to produce a public report at the end of each financial year, and these can be very useful for research purposes. A cautionary note with government reports is to remember that there is the potential for them to contain political bias, which may result in reporting of selective 'facts' to support a particular view; they should be interpreted with care!

Newspapers are not usually that useful. Information in newspapers is often only of note as 'background'. For example you may want to refer to particular pieces to illustrate trends, discoveries or changes, in much the same way as you might refer to general magazines, discussed above. Nevertheless, they can give an indication of what the public considers important at the time, which in some fields (especially those which are policy-related) is very important. As with magazines, trade journals, government and business reports, newspaper articles are subject to bias, both from the journalistic nature of the piece and the political affiliations of the source. Depending on the publication, they may also only have a passing acquaintance with the truth, and so caution is advised when using them.

The Internet

The Internet is the fastest-growing source of information on the planet, and it has revolutionised the life of an academic. For example I can't even imagine what it must have been like to have to physically search through hard copies of journals to find an article of use. But while the Internet is a great resource to connect you directly to the sources of literature I have just talked about, what about the information you can also get from the Internet such as on websites and the like? Do not be fooled into thinking that just because information is available on the Internet that it will be useful to you, or should be included in your research. My personal feeling is that you should avoid using the Internet as a direct source of information about theories, models, methodologies and such like. This information will also be available in peer reviewed journals and this should be your first port of call. Anyone with access to a computer can post information on the Internet (I could give you some examples, but the Internet changes so fast that they would be out-of-date immediately).

When you find information on the Internet, you have no way of knowing if this information is true, scientific or motivated by things other than the advancement of knowledge. For example, many individuals have grudges against some corporations, and they have Internet sites as a forum for their bitterness.

If you do search the Internet and find useful models and theories, try to confirm what you have found in scientific publications to see if the theory has been tested. As a great professor (who shall remain anonymous) once said to me 'theory without evidence is just opinion, and opinions are like a★★★holes,[5] everybody has one'.

As a general rule, if you find useful information on the Internet, make sure a reputable source is cited, and then find that study for yourself. If you intend to cite this source, make sure that you have, and can, read the original source yourself.

In suggesting that you avoid using information from the Internet I do not mean avoiding accessing peer reviewed journals available on, or via the Internet. Most academic libraries now have fantastic sets of electronic resources, and there are many databases which collate and index journal articles. These databases are constantly growing, and it is good advice to consult with your librarians to see what you have access to. You may even be able to help out your supervisor – who, if they are anything like me, have no idea of the full range of resources! Furthermore, some academic journals are what can be called 'e-journals', meaning they are published solely on the Internet, and not in hard copy at all. If an e-journal is peer reviewed the quality should be just as rigorous as a typical 'off-line' peer-reviewed journal (depending on the reputation of the journal).

Evaluating the 'quality' of literature

Once you have found the literature, you need to make some kind of 'first-cut' to work out what is worth spending more time on, and what can be discarded immediately. As shown above, there are many different sources of literature and it is easy to get overwhelmed and confused. The following checklist can be used to help you to decide the 'quality' of the research that you have found:

- *Provenance:* What are the author's credentials, qualifications and affiliations? Affiliations can point to alternative motives and so are important. Are the author's arguments supported by some kind of evidence?
- *Objectivity:* Is the author's perspective unbiased or prejudiced? Are contrary views and data considered in the piece or is certain pertinent information ignored to prove the author's point? Typically, journalistic reports do not consider alternative perspectives; often government reports also fail to incorporate alternative views.
- *Persuasiveness:* Which of the author's arguments are the most and least compelling? The peer review process should identify incorrect arguments, but subsequent work may challenge some assumptions and may invalidate the arguments on which the work is based.
- *Value:* Are the author's conclusions convincing? Does the work ultimately contribute in any significant way to an understanding of the subject? Many papers present replications of previous work in new contexts; although this is important to establish the generalisability of a theory, many

[5] If you're American, please remove one star.

journals will not publish straight-forward replications. This has the disadvantage that theories may go unchallenged or unconfirmed as replication studies may not get published.

However, remember that there is far more to analysing and reviewing a piece of work than just these few pointers (I'll discuss this soon). In particular, the last two points can be quite a difficult task, and if you are unsure of them at this early stage, it's best to keep the literature for now and make your mind up later, when you come back to read it again (which you will do many times).

Remember that when you are conducting your literature search, you have access to some great resources. Most librarians are also skilled researchers; they can help you identify reputable sources. They have more experience of searching for, and within, these sources and so can save you a lot of time by showing you how it is done most effectively. Your supervisor should be able to guide you towards journal rankings and provide you with a feeling for which are the better journals in your field of enquiry, other research students will have developed research strategies that you could consider adopting, they may have accessed journal databases that you are unaware of, and will almost certainly have made many of the mistakes that you are about to make. Try to minimise your effort by learning from their experiences.

How do you turn 'literature' into a 'literature review'?

As stated earlier, the aims of the literature review are to demonstrate that you understand that which has been done before, explain why your work is important, relevant and interesting, and how it adds to existing knowledge, either by bringing together disparate fields of research and extending them or developing new theory. Before describing what a literature review is, it is worth mentioning the most commonly encountered examples of what a literature review is *not*. The following issues are all very common with new researchers, so you shouldn't feel bad about them. However, if you do find yourself prone to these problems, you should make strenuous efforts to overcome them – and the best way of doing this is to write, write, and write some more. Then get your supervisor to read it. Then write again (and so on ...). If you are a research student, one point worth making here is that your supervisor is a useful resource for you,[6] but one which may quickly wear out. Supervisors have many conflicting demands on their time; teaching, writing and reviewing articles and books, administration, supervising other research students. If you put poor work to your supervisors they will be unhappy, and may well tell you so (never a nice experience). If you ask your supervisor to comment on your work, please make sure that it is as good as you can make it. Most importantly, don't be afraid to get feedback, but also please

---

[6]If you are not a research student, your academic colleagues can often perform the same function.

do your utmost to *learn* from that feedback for next time. Most supervisors don't expect fantastic work at first, but it rapidly grates when students repeat the same mistakes over and over.

How not to do it

First, a literature review is not a list or summary of one piece of literature followed by another. It's usually a bad sign to find a series of paragraphs beginning with the name of a researcher, describing what they did and then moving on to the next researcher on the list. The aim of the literature review is not to simply list all the material published, without any consideration regarding how it fits together and how it can be synthesised into your research question. If all you are providing is a list of information then the reader has to do all the work. They have to interpret, synthesise and come to a conclusion about what they have read. They will soon tire and – worse – may come to a conclusion different from the one you hold. After putting in all that mental effort to come to their own conclusions they are unlikely to change their mind just because you wish them to, and you may then experience resistance to your views, making it harder to convince the reader of the 'worth' of your work. IDE 4.3 presents a *laundry list* of relevant facts regarding strategy, resources and capabilities. This example (and IDE 4.4) are not meant to reflect the work of the authors cited, just some inappropriate ways of presenting their work in the context of a literature review. Although the information itself is OK, there is no attempt to *interpret* the information presented and the reader is left to work out for themselves what is important and what is not; also the reader has to try to work out how these different pieces of information fit together. This is really the job of the author, not the reader.

IDE 4.3: A 'Laundry List'

Topic: 'Dynamic capabilities and organisational strategy'
Strategy is a pattern in a stream of decisions that gives guidance to organisations when dealing with its environment, it shapes internal policies and procedures (Hambrick, 1983; Mintzberg, 1978). It is a relative phenomenon; business level strategy can only be analysed substantively in relation to competitors' strategies (Hambrick, 1983).

Porter (1985) states that there are two main strategies that companies can follow in order to increase performance and gain competitive advantage: cost leadership or differentiation. Both strategic options are applicable to a mass market or segmented market approach. In an alternative framework, Miles and Snow (1986) identify four strategic types: Prospectors, defenders, analysers, and reactors.

Gruber and Harhoff (2001) consider resources to be the starting point of strategic deliberations and argue that resources are the main drivers of organisational performance. This view can be traced back to Penrose (1959) who stated that 'The business firm [...] is both an administrative organisation and a collection of productive resources; its general purpose is to organise the use of its "own" resources together with other resources acquired from outside the firm.'

Organisational capabilities are intangible assets or resources, based on skills, learning, and knowledge in deploying resources (Amit and Schoemaker, 1993; Combe and Greenley, 2004). Helfat and Peteraf (2003) differentiate between operational and dynamic capabilities. Operational capabilities are high-level routines (or collections of routines) that offer management a set of decision alternatives for the production of significant outputs. Routines represent repetitive patterns of activities (Nelson and Winter, 1982). Dynamic capabilities do not directly aim at the production of a product or a service (Helfat and Peteraf, 2003; Teece *et al.*, 1997); they build, integrate, or reconfigure operational capabilities and concern change (Helfat *et al.*, 2007).

Eisenhardt and Martin (2000) describe dynamic capabilities as specific organisational and strategic processes that contribute to the value creation of the organisation. They define dynamic capabilities as: 'The firm's processes that use resources – specifically the processes to integrate, reconfigure, gain and release resources – to match and even create market change. Dynamic capabilities thus are the organisational and strategic routines by which firms achieve new resource configurations as markets emerge, collide, split, evolve, and die' (p. 1107).

Teece *et al.*(1997) emphasise the development of management capabilities and combinations of organisational, functional, and technological resources, and define dynamic capabilities as 'the firm's ability to integrate, build, and reconfigure internal and external competences to address rapidly changing environments. Dynamic capabilities thus reflect an organisation's ability to achieve new and innovative forms of competitive advantage given path dependencies and market positions' (p. 516).

Secondly, a literature review is not the same as a *literary* review. The purpose of your review is not to identify the merits and weaknesses of the literary style of the article (whatever you may think about how well it is written or otherwise). Unlike a literary review, which is typically concerned with poems, plays, short stories, novels, or books as a finished piece of writing, a literature review is an extensive search of the information available on a topic and its evaluation. IDE 4.4 shows how a literary review of the literature may look, based on similar content to that in the previous example. You can see that, although a conclusion is

IDE 4.4: A 'Literary Review'

Topic: Dynamic capabilities and organisational strategy

Mintzberg (1978) discussed strategy as a pattern in a stream of decisions that gives guidance to organisations when dealing with its environment, it shapes internal policies and procedures. The article is somewhat technical and the logic of the conclusions was not clear to me, consequently, it is difficult to establish if the definition of strategy is appropriate or not. In contrast, the work of Hambrick (1983) is much easier to read and the suggestion that strategy is a relative phenomenon because any strategy at the business level can only be analysed in relation to competitors' strategies seems reasonable based on the information in the article.

When looking at different types of strategy two main views were available via ABI Inform. One article by Porter (1985) discusses the possibility of two main strategies that companies can follow in order to increase performance and gain competitive advantage. These are cost leadership and differentiation. Porter's suggestion that these options are equally applicable to segmented or mass markets is an elegant solution to the generalisability problem that plagues so much work of this type. An alternative view is discussed by Miles and Snow (1986), but this article was much more technical and did not communicate the basic ideas as well as Porter's work. Consequently, the dual strategy framework proposed by Porter will be used in my study.

presented about the best framework to use, this is based on the literary merit of the article and not the theoretical soundness of the work.

Reading the literature

Let's not make any bones about this, reading academic articles, especially when you are starting your research career, and the area is new to you, is difficult. Not only is it difficult, it's boring a lot of the time. Space in academic publications is expensive, so journal articles have to make maximum contribution for minimum words. This, and the need to be clear and unambiguous, gives rise to a dense, and very exact writing style, with much of the padding which we take for granted removed. This style can be difficult to read because it is generally not entertaining; every sentence contains relevant information that should be important. Don't worry though, reading academic writings should become easier the more you read in your area. From the outset it is worth being purposeful in your reading (and writing).

This will help you to avoid becoming too bogged down with trivia, or by being distracted by new 'shiny' ideas that you will regularly come across.

1. In your reading, remember that you want to précis the work you read, but you have to decide: (a) what information is important to your research, and emphasise it, and (b) what is peripheral, and can be omitted from your review. One way of doing this is to focus on the major concepts, conclusions, theories, arguments, etc. in the article you are reading and look for similarities and differences with other related work, including your own. Before you can do this though, you need to know exactly what problem or research question you are looking at. Try asking yourself: 'What is the *specific thesis, problem, or research question* that my literature review helps to define?' Can you answer it? Once you can, you can then work out which parts of the papers you are reading are important and which are peripheral to your literature review.
2. Related to deciding what is important or not are questions regarding the area of your literature review that you are focusing on. It is unlikely that you will read the papers that form your literature only once; typically, you will need to read them many times, each time looking for something specific and different. Your literature review may have sections looking at issues of theory, methodological issues, quantitative studies and evidence, qualitative studies and evidence, and more. In most cases it is not possible to examine all of these issues at once. Typically at the start of a research project or degree, you don't have the know-how in the area to analyse the literature for methodological issues. If you are a student, training in philosophy and methodology will help you to develop these skills, but you will probably have to wait until you have completed these classes before you can fully analyse the literature for these issues. Try not to worry about this; most people are in the same boat, and don't let them tell you that they are not.
3. Initially you will probably want to review the literature to identify themes, theories, patterns and ideas related to your central thesis. There are many ways of organising information that you find in the literature to help you to identify patterns that arise. For a thematic structure (which is one of the most common structures found in academic wiring of this type) I prefer to use a kind of mind map (see Figure 4.2 overleaf).

Other people use different techniques to organise their thinking; there is no right and wrong way, just the one that suits you the best. Some other techniques for organising information include spider maps, clustering organisers, interaction outline organisers and Venn diagrams. There is some quite sophisticated software available to help you to do this, but I have always found that a piece of flip chart paper and some coloured pens work just as well (but perhaps this is a function of my age and technological ability).

Structure and synthesis: Adding something to what's there

It's important to realise that the literature review should have its own value and intellectual contribution to your research project. As I have already stated, simply listing something does not provide anything that the reader could not do themselves, if they could be bothered. You need to provide some kind of added value to the literature, which proves you know

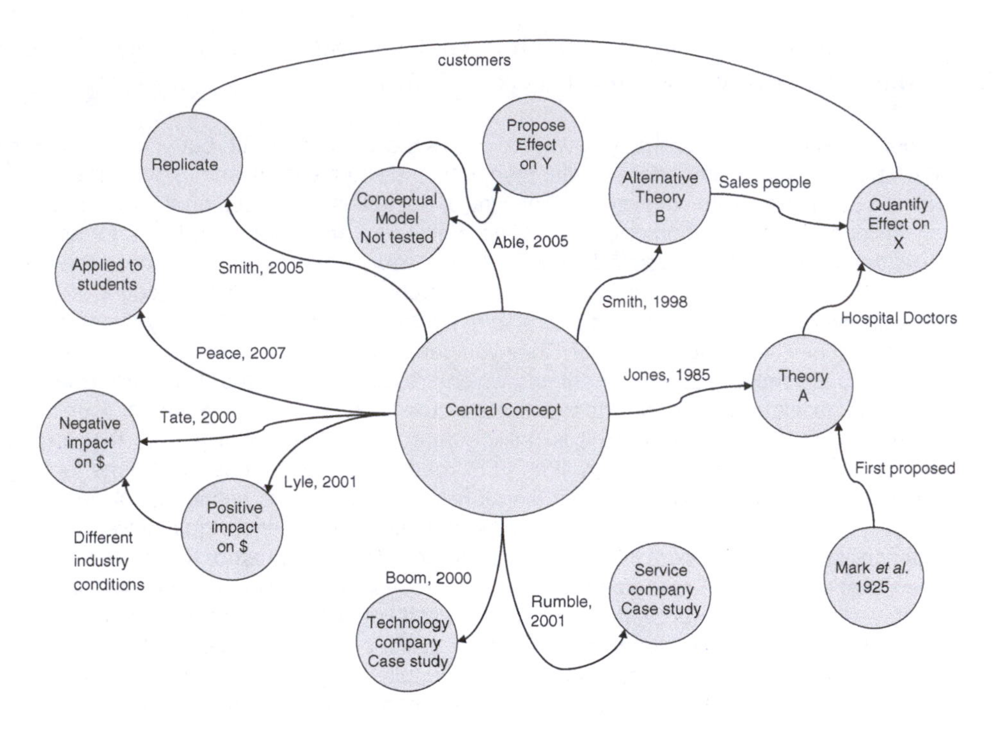

Figure 4.2 A mind map of literature
Note: References are fictitious

the field, as well as have added something. I find that considering the literature review as another component of your theoretical contribution really helps you clarify what you need to do. There are two main ways which a literature review could contribute to our existing knowledge. First is by organising the wide-ranging body of literature in such a way that new perspectives are given, leading to your own research questions. Second is by synthesising and drawing from the literature to create a new and original theory about your topic area. I'll discuss both of these as the chapter moves on.

Structuring your literature review

Rather than simply listing works that have been conducted in your research area, as shown in IDE 4.4, your literature review should be structured around your thesis or research question. The literature should be evaluated and its contribution to your research identified. You will need to consolidate this literature into meaningful 'themes', explaining what is known and what is not, what is controversial and what has already been identified as interesting areas for future research. You will then need to synthesise all this into a new/advanced/modified theory, which I'll discuss in Chapter 5.

Chronological structure: For some studies, organising your literature review chronologically is an appropriate structure. Such chronological literature reviews may be useful if you wish to explore the evolution of a particular theory or body of knowledge. Typically though, a purely chorological structure to your literature review is not appropriate. It is more commonly used to structure sections of the literature review that are organised along other lines. An example of a chronological structure is given in Table 4.2.

Table 4.2 Example of chronological structure

Time period 1	Time period 2	Time period 3
Concepts discussed in this time period. Qualitative work regarding these concepts. Quantitative work examining constructs and their nomological network.	Concepts discussed in this time period – how they evolved from those in the previous time period. Qualitative work regarding these concepts – how does it confirm or challenge previous work? Quantitative work examining constructs and their nomological network – how does it confirm or challenge previous work?	Concepts discussed in this time period – how they evolved from those in the previous time period. Qualitative work regarding these concepts – how does it confirm or challenge previous work? Quantitative work examining constructs and their nomological network – how does it confirm or challenge previous work?

Conceptual and thematic structures: Many literature reviews are organised by the concepts studied. This can be a useful way to organise your writing. Once this broad structure has been adopted, a different structure can be adopted for the discussion of each of the concepts in your review (such as chronological, methodological or contextual.) Organising your literature into meaningful 'themes', and developing an appropriate structure for your literature review can be achieved in many ways. Thematic reviews of the literature are organised around the topic under investigation, rather than chronologically, although the chronology of the literature may also be important. The choice of how to organise your literature review will ultimately depend on your preference, the literature that you are reviewing and the research question that you are addressing. Whatever the structure of your literature review, you will have to illustrate how previous research relates to your research question and how it relates to other works which you include in your review. (Remember, these must also be clearly relevant to your research question.) An example of a thematic structure is given in Table 4.3.

Methodological structure: A methodological review of the literature differs from the above in that the focus usually is not the content of the material; rather it is the 'methods' of the researcher. Typically for first research projects a methodological literature review is not appropriate, as the aim here is generally to understand the concepts, models and

Table 4.3 Example of thematic structure

Construct 1	Construct 2	Construct 3
Definitions of the construct, commonalities and differences in conceptualisations. How it evolved and how it has been applied. Empirical studies (qualitative and quantitative) explaining the role of the construct in a nomological network. Operationalisations of the construct in previous work, strengths and weaknesses of these, etc.	Definitions of the construct, commonalities and differences in conceptualisations. How it is related to Construct 1. Theories that explain these relationships. Empirical studies (qualitative and quantitative) examining the relationships between Construct 1 and 2. Operationalisations of Construct 2 in previous work, strengths and weaknesses of these, etc.	Definitions of the construct, commonalities and differences in conceptualisations. How it is related to Construct 1 and 2. Theories that explain these relationships. Empirical studies (qualitative and quantitative) examining the relationships between Construct 1, 2 and 3. Operationalisations of Construct 3 in previous work, strengths and weaknesses of these, etc.

frameworks used to describe and explore your area of interests. A methodological review of the literature may come later in your project, when you better understand and can critique the methods used by various researchers. At this stage you may wish to revisit your draft literature review and discuss methodology in more detail. This will be dealt with later in the book when methods are discussed. Unless absolutely necessary for your research, I would recommend using a methodological structure only as a sub-structure for a conceptual or thematically organised literature review. In this way, previous research examining the concepts in your conceptual model can be organised according to the methods that were used to conduct the research, but the overall arguments in your literature review remain centred around the relationships between the constructs of interest to you.

Writing within your structure

Once you've decided on how to organise your review, the sections you need to include in the chapter should be easy to figure out. They should arise out of your organisation. In other words, a chronological review would have subsections for each vital time period. A thematic review would have subtopics based upon factors that relate to the theme or issue and a methodological review would have sections reviewing the various methods. However, other sections may be necessary for your literature review but may not fit in the organisation of your work. You will have to decide what other sections to include in your literature review, but remember, put in *only what is necessary*.

In the following discussion, I am assuming a conceptual or thematic structure as this appears to be the most prevalent in social science research. When examining your concepts, you will need to address some common areas that an informed reader will be looking for:

- What do we know about the key concepts or variables?
- What are their characteristics?
- What are the potential relationships between concepts (researchable hypotheses)?
- What existing theories explain the relationships between these key concepts or variables?
- What research has been conducted to explore all of the above?
- Where is this research inconsistent, are variables always viewed as the same thing, or do some authors call different things by the same name, or the same thing by different names?
- What are the overriding characteristics of the concepts?
- Is empirical evidence available to confirm the existence of the concepts, and the relationships between them? If so, how have researchers defined and measured key concepts?
- Is the empirical evidence consistent, inconclusive, contradictory or limited in some way? If so, Why?
- What methodologies have been used?
- Where have data been collected?
- Are these satisfactory?
- How are they similar to what you propose? How are they different?
- Are there views in the literature that need to be examined in more detail?
- Why study (further) the research problem?
- What contribution can the present study be expected to make?

Once you have decided your central research question or thesis, and have identified appropriate sources of information and have started to organise the ideas in these sources of information into some coherent structure, you can start to communicate your *story*.

Remember (and this is a hugely important point), *you are not writing a literature review just to tell your reader what other researchers have done*. Your aim should be to show why your research needs to be carried out, how you came to choose certain methodologies or theories to work with, how your work adds to the research already carried out, and that sort of thing. I always say to students that the literature review is not a history of everything they read, it is an argument.

This raises another, and often painful, point. You have to *edit out information that is not relevant to your argument*. I know that this may be painful for you. After all, you have read the information, internalised it, made notes on it, typed it up and incorporated it into your document – it must be relevant, you took weeks to do all that! Don't delude yourself, examine every sentence critically and ask yourself how does it contribute to the argument that you literature review presents. If it doesn't then cut it out, be ruthless and your review will be much more focused and relevant.

Some final thoughts and tips

Your literature review should aim to critically evaluate previous research, comparing and contrasting what has been done and what hasn't, showing relationships between published works (e.g. is Smith's theory more convincing than Jones'? Why? Did Smith build on the work of Jones?), and demonstrating how this relates to your research. Some tips to help you achieve this are:

- Follow through a set of concepts and questions, comparing papers to each other in the ways they deal with these concepts and questions.
- Among other things you can look at are:
  - What research questions do the authors pose?
  - Do authors define the concepts in the same way?
  - Do they use the same underlying rationale or theory to discuss the concepts? (The next chapter may help you to decide this.)
  - If comparing quantitative research papers; do different authors operationalise constructs in the same way?
  - Are data drawn from similar or different contexts?
  - How are the data analysed?
  - Are the data and analysis appropriate for the study? Can they answer the research question?
  - What are the major conclusions made by the authors in terms of the research questions that the authors pose?
  - Are the data sufficient to draw the conclusions that the authors present?
  - Do authors come to similar conclusions about the nature and impact of the constructs that you are interested in?
  - If not, why not? (The previous questions should allow you to answer this.)
  - What limitations does each of these authors present about their own work?
  - Do they also give you insights into the limitations of previous work? (Often this forms part of the justification that is presented for their work.)

Also, it is vitally important to *keep all your bibliographic information* in an easily retrievable format. One day, possibly quite a long way into in the future, you will have to write your references pages (whether you are writing a thesis, or an article). You do not want to find that you didn't keep the information you need to do this, and consequently have to spend days or weeks finding the references for the citations in your thesis.[7] You will spend a lot of time in the library or on the Internet tracking down the sources that you read, going through your writing to find which information came from which source. Most likely, you will not be able to find all your sources and will then have to remove the ones that you can't find, hoping that they are not critical to your argument. If they are, there is nothing for it but to continue to search for them or a replacement. It is far better to avoid this by keeping

[7] As Nick did, and still does! In fact, I bet he is doing it when writing this very book!

this information in your notes from the outset. Always put citations into your writing and immediately into the reference list for your work. Software packages such as Endnote and ProCite can help greatly in this process. However, they don't do it for you; you will have to develop the discipline to remember for each citation to make sure there is a reference. Do you have a piece of work that you are writing at the moment? How many times have you written 'insert ref here' or something similar? If you have, make sure you go back now to find out and insert that reference, you will thank me later (well actually if you do it you will probably not even think about it, if you don't, you may just remember me telling you to and regret ignoring me).

Some things to avoid

Perhaps just as important as the tips about things you need to *do* to help you be successful, are the things you need to *avoid* in order to make a good job of the literature review. So here are a few which may help your cause when you are conducting your review.

Using only those papers that support your view: A common weakness of a literature review is one-sided reporting. It is tempting to report only those studies that support your view of the world and how the constructs within it should relate to each other. This is unscientific and should be avoided. You need to ensure that you review and present papers that both support your view and contradict it (if they exist).

Trying to read everything: If you try this you will never be able to finish reading. The idea of the literature review is to provide a survey of the most relevant and significant work, not to provide a census of all the published work that relates even in the tiniest way to your research. There will also come a time when you have to **stop reading**. This does not mean stop completely but stop for the moment and consolidate your knowledge. Typically, once you have conceptualised your theoretical framework, tested it mentally against your peers, supervisors and perhaps at a presentation, the time has come to nail your colours to the mast and adopt your model as the one that you will use and test further. Stop adding new information from more extensive reading, this will just continue to confuse you and prevent you from progressing. It's time to move on the next stage of your research.

Reading without writing: Even given the often intractable nature of academic journals, it's much easier to read than to write. Not writing is one of the most common mistakes that research students fall into. Many excuses abound, and I have heard a lot of them: 'It's all in my head and I am sorting it out before writing it down', 'I don't need to write because I am much more of a thinker than a writer', 'I'm going to write it all down when I have finished reviewing the relevant literature'. Interestingly enough, Nick used all of these, and still does in fact.

It's all just excuses for putting off what we don't want to do. As a supervisor, no matter how inventive the excuse, I can generally tell when a student is procrastinating for some reason, maybe because they do not understand what they are doing, and are avoiding challenging their understanding by refusing to commit what they know to paper. The discipline of writing helps you to understand what you have read, and highlights what you do and don't know for you and your supervisor. It will help you to identify relationships between the works that you have reviewed, and highlight inconsistencies in the literature and a whole range of other important stuff. By refusing to write you are denying yourself the chance to learn what you know and what you don't. In my experience, persistent refusal to write generally leads to disaster. The student either does not progress their thinking, or the supervisor gives up and decides that the student is not working and cannot meet the research deadlines imposed on them. Either way, a common consequence of failure to write regularly is failure to complete the research project.

It's very important to recognise that what you write will *not* be a final or near-final version, and you should not expect it to be. It will evolve and change as your understanding grows, as you discover new things, as your writing style becomes more 'academic' and as you incorporate your methodology, results and conclusions. Writing is a way of thinking, so allow yourself to write as many drafts as you need, change your ideas and information as you learn more about your research problem. If you are passing these drafts to a supervisor, or colleague, remember my earlier comments and please make sure you don't wear out your supervisors' patience by passing interminable rough drafts to them for comment.

Summary

Remember that the aim of your literature review is to show that you have studied existing work in your field and provide insights into this work. An effective review analyses and synthesises material, and will be relevant, appropriate, and useful for the reader. Your literature review presents the case and context for the rest of your research. For this reason it is important to demonstrate the relationship of your work to previous research in the area. Without a good literature review, your work will never be able to assure the reader that it makes a solid contribution to knowledge, so you should *never* ignore the importance of the literature review stage. Key points to take from this chapter:

- The most important stage in a literature review is **starting**. Do not spend an age agonising over *where* to start, just start somewhere. The path will become clear after a while.
- The second most important stage of the literature review is **stopping**. Eventually you will need to decide that it is time to move onto the next stage of your research, even though you may have missed one or two articles that may be relevant to your research question. If you don't stop you won't progress and consequently won't finish. Don't worry about the one or two articles that you may have missed. If you have conducted a thorough review, there is a vanishing small chance that one or two missed articles will answer your research question for you and spoil your thesis.
- The aims of your research and the research question are important; they help to focus and direct your reading.
- Reviewing academic literature is an iterative process; you will need to read papers several times, each time focusing on different aspects of the paper.

- You will use the literature to explain what is known in the field in which you are working and what is not known.
- What is not known forms part of the rationale for your thesis and motivates the work that you will be doing in your research project.
- Critiquing literature is not the same as criticising it, and in fact authors often critique their own work when they discuss the limitations of their research.
- Your literature can be organised in several different ways, although thematic organisation is often used.

Further reading

There aren't too many sources for information on reviewing the literature, but in more recent times a few interesting pieces of work have arrived.

- *Doing a Literature Review: Releasing the Social Science Research Imagination* by Chris Hart: One of the very few books entirely dedicated to the literature review. As such it is a vital source of information for beginning researchers, and even those more experienced are likely to pick up a few useful tips.
- *Critical Reading and Writing for Postgraduates* by Mike Wallace and Alison Wray: A good introduction for the actual process of reading and critiquing academic literature.
- *Doing Your Research Project: A Guide for First-Time Researchers in Education, Health and Social Science* by Judith Bell: This book is highly rated by many of my students, and gives some good information on how to get out there and review the literature.

Recent work on systematic literature reviewing in the social sciences (drawing from evidence-based medical research) also provides a useful starting point. For an introduction you can check out a 2003 paper in the *British Journal of Management* by David Tranfield *et al.* entitled 'Towards a methodology for developing evidence-informed management knowledge by means of systematic review'.

EXERCISES

1. Write down your area or field of research.
   - Is it too broad? Can you narrow it down?
   - What *specifically* do you want to look at?
2. List the constructs that you are interested in.
   - Which of these is the central construct of your thesis?
3. Create a mind map with your central construct taking the dominant position and other constructs surrounding it.
   - What does the literature tell you about the relationships between your central construct and the other constructs in your mind map?
   - Does the literature tell you anything about relationships among the other constructs in you mind map?

4. Look in your literature and identify several different definitions for each of your constructs. (There will be more than one, even if they are somewhat similar.)
   - How do these definitions differ? Are the differences important?
5. For each of the definitions can you identify different operationalisations of the construct?
   - If you identified three different definitions in Q4 and three different operationalisations for these definitions in Q5 you now have nine operationalisations of the same thing. This is where it gets interesting. Now you can start to put together a bit of a critique of the literature.
6. How have these operationalisations (or operational definitions) been used? Are they applied qualitatively or quantitatively? Why were they applied in this way and what has the author used them for?
7. Comment on the suitability of the research using the information that you have collected in the previous exercises.
8. Do you have a bibliographic database? If not, set one up today. Go on, just do it. If you already have one, is it up to date?

Chapter 5
Theory, conceptualisation and hypotheses

Ian Lings

SUPERVISOR'S VIEW: DR NICK LEE

I got a bit antsy not saying anything for two whole chapters, so I thought I would put my two cents in here. Seriously, theory has been one of the major thorns in my side since I graduated with my Doctorate and began publishing my work – or more accurately trying to. I remember getting many rejection letters from top level journals with the same criticism each time; 'this work has no theory'. For a very long time I couldn't understand this criticism – 'after all', I thought 'this manuscript has about 10 theories in it, one for each hypothesis!' The more experienced among you will already have seen my naive error. However, it took me a long time to come to grips with the idea that having a strong theoretical foundation for your work is not the same as throwing as many theories as possible together without any logic behind *why* those theories are linked. Basically, and I admit I am still working on really becoming comfortable with this, your work should have some kind of overall coherence linking the various concepts together. There are many general theories of social behaviour (or whatever it is that you study) which you could use as fundamental foundations of your work. In turn this will inform the development of your more specific theory – perhaps by adding new ideas and theories to extend its explanatory power, or solve a weakness in it. In other words, most of the time social scientists are working at the margins of existing theory, but not creating completely new theories.

Unfortunately, this kind of thing takes a while for a keen researcher with visions of changing the world to come to grips with! It's very easy to go into a research career thinking that in order to make a contribution and become famous (or whatever drives you) you must create or discover something entirely new. After all, that's what all the scientists you've ever heard of did, isn't it? But eventually, you'll come to realise that virtually no researcher has *ever* come up with something completely new. In fact, you can probably trace back the lineage of almost all of the major discoveries or theories to earlier theories and ideas. The famous researchers who discovered something 'new' usually did so by working at extending, or solving a problem with, an existing theory. Or, perhaps, they were looking for an explanation for something which they saw or experienced, and then discovered that none existed. Another common way which seemingly 'new' theories get developed is the application of ideas from outside the relevant field. This kind of thing can happen through pure luck, you may meet a fascinating colleague from another department over coffee, or something stronger, and get talking. Most of my best work has started in this way actually. So, I guess if I were to conclude, I would say that the best way to do something original is *not to try to*! What I mean is; don't go into your career specifically trying to come up with something new. Go in with the goal of answering important questions, and if you need to create something new to do this, then you will do so. My other advice would be to keep an open mind in *all* respects. Expose yourself to as many different ideas, people, and situations as possible, read anything that interests you – as well as the stuff specifically related to your area. But before you go off creating new things, make *absolutely certain* you are completely well-versed on the theory which is already out there!

VIEW FROM THE TRENCHES: DR JOHN RUDD

The process of conceptualising a theoretical model and developing sound hypotheses is fraught with opportunities for you to get ahead of yourself. Try to avoid this as it will only cause a great wringing of the hands further down the line. Focus on the theory, and develop your model and your hypotheses from this. Remember, while you may be very clear on why your overall model looks the way it does, where is the supporting theory/ evidence that says that hypotheses 'x' may be worth further investigation? Why does factor 'a' impact on factor 'b' positively? Why not the other way? Why not negatively? If you do not know then how do you expect a reader, or a reviewer, of your work to believe in it?

A theoretical model is not a process diagram! This is bad! Let me explain. Coming from a background in industry, I was very much used to buzzwords like 'brainstorming', 'blue skies thinking' and 'imagineering'. These techniques allow teams of managers to, very quickly, consolidate the complexities of the competitive environment into a process diagram on a couple of well-thumbed flip charts. Usually there are various arrows and feedback loops, accompanied by a smattering of exclamation marks and well-placed smiley faces and cash signs; presumably signifying success of some kind. While these have proven to be extremely valuable in applied circumstances, they will be of little, or no, use to those of you interested in an academic career. 'Why'? I hear you cry. 'They are woolly', I reply. Also, and more importantly within a research framework, they are based on experience and 'gut feel', not on theory. While an arrow here and an arrow there (dotted or otherwise) may convey to the drawer, and his immediate audience, a very specific nuance of management action, to anyone else they may very well be interpreted as the daubings of a lunatic. In developing a theoretical model it is important to avoid the trap of the process diagram! Make me happy, don't do it.

Theory is the foundation on which much academic research is based. Without it, researchers are in the dark about **how** phenomena relate to each other and **why** they relate to each other in the way that they do. Think about some of the common statistics that we see reported by firms and governments: 'socially deprived individuals engage in more crime than socially advantaged individuals'; 'young people drive faster and are more reckless on the road than older people'; people in certain parts of the country are 'happier than others'. These reported relationships are often presented just so, especially in the tabloid press. Although they may make an interesting topic of discussion, the fact that crime is related to social deprivation, speeding related to age or happiness related to location, does not offer us any insights into *why this may be so*. Without an understanding of why, it is impossible to make any meaningful recommendations to manage these issues (a particularly relevant issue in the applied social sciences). The role of theory is bound up with the 'why' question. Without theory all we can say are things like: 'maybe young people shouldn't drive', or 'social deprivation needs to be addressed if we want to manage crime'. However, if we have an underlying theory to explain *why* such relationships between factors like age and reckless driving are observed, then we can say so much more. For example, if we theorise and later find support for the idea that young people drive fast because they believe that nothing bad can happen to them – that they are invincible – then we can address this underlying perception of invincibility to manage the problem, maybe through education. In research, we can interrogate the theory, and other competing theories that explain the same thing, and conduct research projects to see if it is really perceptions of invincibility that are driving this behaviour or if it is something else. In other words, we test the theories to see which is the better at explaining what is happening.

One thing is for certain, if you do not understand what theory is and what it does, you cannot conduct credible research. Furthermore, it becomes difficult for you to articulate your contribution to academic knowledge. With this in mind, read on, this chapter will hopefully answer your questions about theory and its role in research. At the end of this chapter I really hope you have come to terms with these key ideas:

1. What theory is and its role in social science.
2. The philosophical underpinnings of theory.
3. The difference between laws, theories, concepts, models, measures and hypotheses.
4. How to construct and recognise a theory, extend it, and contribute to the theoretical foundations of your subject.
5. How to represent your theory in a conceptual model, and how to develop hypotheses from it.

Why is it Important to Know This Stuff?

Theory is the foundation of science, both the natural sciences like chemistry and physics, and social sciences like business, sociology, and political science. Many people view the natural sciences as 'better' at developing and testing theory than the social sciences. However, this is not really true. Certainly, natural sciences are often better at defining and controlling the conditions under which a theory applies, and typically inanimate matter behaves more consistently than do people (this links back to what Professor Clegg said at the beginning of Chapter 3). Theory helps us to explain what has happened and to predict what will happen. When an apple fell from the tree, supposedly on Sir Isaac Newton's head, he theorised from the observation that the earth attracted the apple towards it, his head just happened to be in the way. From this observation (and many more I suspect) Sir Isaac eventually developed a theory which argued that all objects with mass attract each other. This eventually, after a great deal of work, became his *Universal Law of Gravitation.* It is important to note the difference between a law and a theory, which will be discussed in depth later. In common usage, most people consider laws to relate primarily to the natural sciences, and to always hold under the right conditions. Theories however, are more provisional. Of course, interesting as it is to have an explanation for why the apple fell on his head, Newton's theory serves a more important role. Having developed his theory and repeatedly tested it, leading to the Law of Gravitation, Sir Isaac could now *apply* the Law to *predict* the behaviour of any object in relation to another object; such as which will move the furthest, how fast, at what point will the objects collide, and how much energy is needed to make sure that the force of attraction is overcome. Pretty useful if you want to put a satellite in orbit around the earth, for example. In other words, theory itself exists (obviously) in the theoretical world, as Figure 5.1 shows. However, scientists and others use theories and laws to predict events in the 'real world'. If we observe those events, then our theories have support.

In the social sciences theories serve the same purpose. They are used to explain events, like behaviours, and perhaps to predict them. Unfortunately for social scientists, people do not always behave as predictably as apples. If a planet has enough mass to also have gravity, the apple will always fall towards the ground at a given rate, the apple cannot decide that it doesn't like the ground and so will decide to fall towards the stars. This inherent awkwardness of the human race poses several challenges for social scientists, but more of this later in the book. Unfortunately, beginning researchers commonly have difficulty when developing theory. In fact it is hard for many to even come to grips with what theory actually is. Even worse, there are few resources available to help the confused researcher understand what theory is, and for many it is therefore a process of trial and error (and reams of criticism) before something finally 'clicks'. This chapter is aimed at giving you a broad introduction to the idea of theory in social science, and from then on you should be able to build on it using your own experiences. So needless to say, I think that everyone should read this, because without theory, science is merely a technical exercise with questionable relevance.

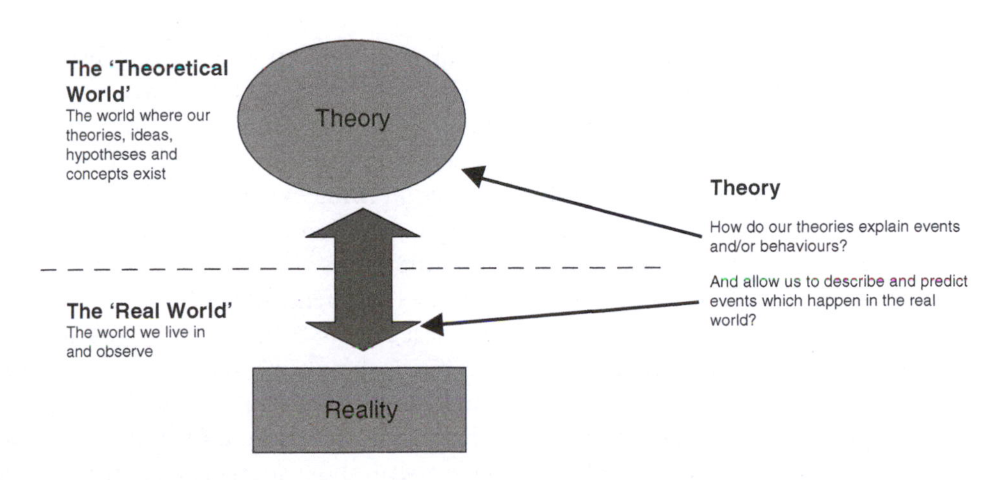

Figure 5.1 The place of theory

Some philosophical assumptions

Before we together embark on the voyage of discovery that will hopefully illuminate the nature of theories to you, it is important to explore the underlying assumptions of theory in general, and the basic philosophical approach that is a prerequisite to theory development and testing in the social sciences. Science is an important label here. The word *science* derives from the Latin verb *scire*, 'to know'. Although it is possible to 'know' through faith or intuition, the scientific method (as described in Chapter 2 for example) requires that it should be possible for other investigators to establish the credibility of any knowledge claims we make. This credibility is typically approached, although never finally 'proved', through empirical replication of work, and comparison of the observations of different researchers studying the same phenomena. However, pure logic and mathematics can also be used to provide evidence of knowledge claims (for example, many cutting-edge physical theories have never been directly tested using real-world data). But the ultimate test of any theory is whether the events it predicts in the 'real world' are actually observed.

This brings me to the next assumption of the scientific method. That there is an objective 'truth' to be observed. An objective truth is something that, no matter what we believe to be the case, will always be true. It is related to the idea of an objective reality, one which exists independent of us. Remember questions like: 'Do you see the same colour orange as I do?'; 'Does a tree falling in a forest make a noise, even if there is no one there to hear it?' These are questions to do with the objective reality of the world, whether it exists independently of us or is a construct of our minds. Objective truth is contingent on a philosophy that suggests that our beliefs, whatever they are, have no bearing on the facts of the world around us. That which is true is always true – even if we stop believing it and even if we stop existing at all. This is a notion of *epistemological objectivity*; truth can be determined inter-subjectively by generally agreed methods or procedures.

Contrast this to a purely subjective view of the world, which would suggest that there is no reality independent of people's perceptions. This extreme view is known as *metaphysical idealism*, and suggests that so-called 'physical' things don't really exist at all, in fact nothing exists independently of our experiences, which are in our minds, and therefore nothing exists independently of our minds and reality depends on being experienced. This leads us to the notion of a subjective truth or *epistemological subjectivity*. Somewhere towards the middle of these two extreme philosophical standpoints lie the views of critical realists and critical relativists. Your views about theory and the role of the scientific method in developing knowledge will depend on where you stand. Critical realists believe that we must *assume* the existence of an objective reality so that we can make claims about cause and effect relationships; even though these claims will be imperfect, while critical relativists argue that there is no single knowable reality waiting 'out there' to be discovered. Even though critical relativists accede that there may well be a single social and natural reality, they do not believe that science can reveal it. The critical relativist view has given rise to criticisms of the scientific method and the development of other approaches to knowledge creation, such as postmodernism, discussed elsewhere in the book. However, in this chapter, as in most of the rest of the book, I have taken an objective view of reality and adopt a predominantly critical realist view of the world. This will become important later. For the relativistic researcher, however, the concept of theory as an explanation for events is still important, although not all relativists will consider it necessary to have any *a priori* theory behind their work at all.

Laws and theories: What they are and what they are not

In your readings for the literature review, you will need to decide what constitutes laws, theories, frameworks, conceptual models, hypotheses and arguments; and which of these are theoretic or not, logical or not, or both or neither. The first stage in being able to do this is to understand what each of these is. This is much easier said than done! Definitions, especially of theories, laws and conceptualisations, are somewhat confused and confusing in the literature. Here, I will try to make sense of the different opinions about just what these things are, and importantly, what they are not.

Laws

In scientific research, laws are most commonly encountered in the natural sciences and consequently I won't spend too long discussing them here. However, it is important to consider the differences between what most laypeople think of as 'laws', and what a law is in actual practice. To the average person, natural laws have several characteristics, among which are:

1. They are true; there have never been repeatable contradicting observations.
2. They are universal; they appear to apply everywhere in the universe.
3. They are simple; typically expressed in terms of a single mathematical equation.
4. They are stable, and have not changed since first discovered.

In this sense then, laws are considered to be universal truths, things that are *always true*. However, let's take, for example, a very simple law, which most people would recognise at least in some way: Newton's Universal Law of Gravitation. Newton's theory (briefly) states that every object in the universe attracts every other object by a force pointing along a straight line combining the two. This can be represented by a law in the form of an equation:

$$F_g = G\frac{M_1 M_2}{R^2}$$

F_g = the force of gravity, M_1 and M_2 are the masses of the objects and R is their separation. G is a constant.

The equation translates as the force of gravity is a function of the masses of the two objects and the distance between them. From Newton's first publication of *Philosophiae Naturalis Principia Mathematica* in 1687 until Einstein's development of general relativity, this was generally considered a law. At that time, Newton's theory had the characteristics of a law to most people, in that there had never been repeatable contradicting observations, it appeared to apply everywhere in the universe, it was expressed in terms of a single mathematical equation, and it was stable, and had not changed since it was first discovered. However, as science and measuring technology moved on (Nick will discuss measurement in the next two chapters), Newton's description of gravity began to exhibit some inconsistencies. In fact, Newton's 'law' is *not* accurate under certain conditions (e.g. approaching the speed of light). Instead, Einstein's general relativity is a much better expression of gravity. Even so, Newton's description is accurate for many 'practical' purposes, and therefore is widely used. So, from being considered to be a universal 'law', Newton's equation has really become more of a practical tool – and is not really considered to be a good explanation of how the universe 'works' today. In fact, this is a great example of how scientific progress works. Most of the time, a law is only a law until something better comes along which shows that the existing law does not hold. Nevertheless, Newton's equation is still generally considered a 'law' as it does predict accurately under a specific set of conditions. This example also illuminates another characteristic of laws – they are not an explanation of *why* or *how* things happen, they are just descriptions of *what* happens. Newton's law by itself does not explain anything about why or how bodies attract each other, it just describes what actually happens. One needs more than just this law for a theory of *why*.

So, you have seen that even in the realm of non-sentient entities like apples and planets, it is extremely difficult to formulate natural laws that are always true. What hope then do we have in the messy social world, where the players in our laws have consciousness and free will? Unsurprisingly, laws are not generally encountered in the social sciences, perhaps reflecting this difficulty of identifying universal truths within human phenomena. But also, it should not be forgotten that most social sciences are far younger than the natural sciences. That said, many social disciplines do tend to use the *language* of laws, such as economics (e.g. the law of supply and demand). It is a common assumption among social scientists though, that laws are not able to be formulated about the social world. It would seem that this argument may often be founded on a naive idea of what a law actually is. As you saw above, a scientific law is *not* necessarily something which holds absolutely and always, and almost all natural scientific laws have exceptions, and tend to hold only under distinct, defined, conditions.

If one accepts this more realistic definition of what a law can be, then the idea of laws in the social sciences becomes less fanciful. A law can be an expression of a theoretical principle – such as the laws of supply and demand – or they can be mathematical formulae such as Newton's above. Laws can also be regularities which have been established through repeated empirical replications (these are often called *empirical generalisations*). So, if you accept the idea that there are at least *some* regularities (which are not purely accidental) in the social world, it seems to be unavoidable to accept that it is at minimum *possible* in principle to create laws in social sciences. Remember, a law does not have to be something which is **always true**, all laws have defined exceptions. However, this brings up what may be the real problem with the idea of social laws. More specifically, the exceptions to physical laws are well defined and regular (e.g. Newton's law does not hold at velocities nearing the speed of light), but the exceptions to social laws are far more dependent on the unique social context in existence at the time of observation (Kincaid, 1994). So when a social law does not hold under empirical observation, is it possible to clearly define the local conditions which caused this failure? If not, then it is impossible to determine whether the exception to the law was caused by local conditions, or a fault of the law itself.

In fact, one wonders whether the question of whether there can be social laws is even of particular importance. Certainly, we have evidence that indicates that there do exist non-accidental regularities in the social world, and perhaps this is the closest social scientists can ever get to a 'law'. Instead, social scientists tend to couch their statements about regularities in the language of **theory**. In contrast to laws, theories are generally characterised by being more complex. Theories generally have several component parts, and are more likely to be changed as the body of available experimental data and analysis develops. Most importantly, unlike physical laws, which summarise and describe empirical events, theories *account for events, explain them and relate them to other events*, often making predictions which may subsequently be tested. To finalise this point, **a law simply describes what happens (e.g. apples fall to the earth); a theory explains why it happens.**

Theories (Origin Greek theoria 'contemplation, speculation')

What then, is a theory? This question is more difficult to answer than one might think. The word theory has several meanings, depending on which field you are working in and what philosophical viewpoint you favour. A definition of theory is made even more difficult by the fact that its common usage is different to its scientific usage; worse still, usage in the natural sciences also differs from usage in the social sciences; and to cap the whole thing off, usage within the social sciences differs between individuals! These confusions about the nature of theory can be seen in definitions offered by both the Oxford and Cambridge English dictionaries.

The Cambridge Advanced Learner's Dictionary has this to say:

Theory: noun

1. *a formal statement of the rules on which a subject of study is based.*
2. *or of ideas which are suggested to explain a fact or event .*
3. *or, more generally, an opinion or explanation.*

The Oxford English dictionary:

Theory: noun (pl. theories)

1. *A supposition or a system of ideas intended to explain something, especially one based on general principles independent of the thing to be explained.*
2. *An idea accounting for or justifying something.*
3. *A set of principles on which an activity is based.*

In common usage (i.e. conversations between non-scientists), many people use 'theory' to mean 'opinion' or 'conjecture', suggesting that a theory is not necessarily based on facts; in other words, it is not required to be consistent with descriptions of reality. However, this usage is not what I mean when I talk about 'theory' in the social sciences. When a social researcher talks of a theory, he or she is not referring to a guess or hunch, as might be the case in everyday speech. For a scholar, a theory is a logically self-consistent model or framework that describes and explains how related phenomena behave; it is generally based on, and may be supported by, some kind of observations. A defining characteristic of a *scientific* theory is that it makes falsifiable or testable predictions about things not yet observed. According to Stephen Hawking in *A Brief History of Time,* 'theory is always provisional', in this sense one can never prove a theory. No matter how many observations agree with the theory, one can never be sure that the next observation will not contradict it. To disprove a theory, only a single repeatable observation that disagrees with the predictions of the theory is necessary. You should remember this basic concept from Chapter 2, when Nick talked about Karl Popper and the black swans.

Using existing theory to explain behaviour

In most social science research we are trying to explain some aspect of behaviour; the behaviour of individuals (customers, employees, politicians, individual team members, fanatics, etc.); or the behaviour of groups (teams, families, companies, nations, societies, political or religious parties); sometimes we are exploring the behaviour of systems of management, such as manufacturing systems, HR practices or government policies. Most commonly, in the applied fields of social research (like business), general theories explaining these phenomena are drawn from disciplines like psychology or economics, but occasionally theories from other disciplines such as physics, philosophy or mathematics are also relevant. It is important when examining your research topic to understand those theories that explain what is going on in the small aspect of the world that you are interested in. For example, if you are trying to explain and understand how people behave in response to certain stimuli, you may wish to explore some of the theories discussed in psychology (e.g. the theory of planned behaviour, game theory, expectancy theory), and you may also wish to explore the economic theories that attempt to explain the same phenomena (such as utility theory). Of course, there are other general theories that also attempt to explain human behaviours in different contexts, and these should also be explored fully.

This is one of the key areas where beginning researchers get confused. In particular, the novice researcher will often not actually build their work on an existing general theory at all – as Nick related at the start of this chapter. In fact, even many more experienced researchers (especially in the applied social research disciplines) fail to solidly ground their work in an existing theory, and then are often confused when they are criticised for not doing so. The difficulty is that grounding your work in existing theory is *not the same* as picking and choosing a cornucopia of theories from all over the place to justify your work. Unfortunately for me, this is a very hard concept to get across right now. Many research students especially, assume that they should create some kind of new grand theory rather than base their work on existing theory, but this is not usually the case. Perhaps an example will help. Imagine your research is looking to examine the relationship or interaction between a buyer and a seller, which is quite common in many different fields of research. In a general sense, one can explore this in various different ways, each based on a different general theory. One way is *social exchange* theory, which considers that relationships between people are essentially exchanges of various resources. People stay in relationships because the benefits they get exceed the benefits they would get if they left the relationship. Another way of exploring relationships is *social network theory*. In the present context, this perspective would conceptualise individual buyers and sellers as being part of a 'web' of relationships of various types, some stronger than others. One could also explore *transaction cost* theory, which would consider the various costs to the buyer of purchasing from a given seller. Of course, there are many other ways of looking at relationships, and each one of these general theories would influence you to look at a different set of concepts and ideas. Within your general theory you would probably look to add something new or original somewhere, to make a contribution to knowledge. There are many ways of doing this, and it is something you need to think about very carefully in the early stages of any piece of scholarly research. In other words, **where does your work make a contribution to existing theory**?

What you should *not* do is simply toss a whole bunch of concepts and ideas together, mixing and matching theories without an overall framework. As I have already said though, it is quite common for new researchers to do this, and I have made the same mistake myself (and you can see Nick has too from the beginning of this chapter). The problem is that, without an overall theoretical framework, there is no reason for those concepts and ideas to all appear in your model, and to be related to each other, apart from your own 'intuition'. While intuition can be a major help to a researcher, it should not really be the whole basis for a theory. The common retort I hear to this is 'so how am I supposed to contribute to theory without adding new theories to it?' Indeed this is a fair question, and deserves an answer. Simply put, you can modify and change existing theories using ideas from other theories, but this has to be clearly and logically justified. Using additional theoretical ideas to *add to* existing theory is not the same as throwing loads of different theories into some kind of witch's brew without an overall structure.

This is not to say that all research must follow existing theory. Certainly there is room for researchers to create entirely new theories. However, creating a new theory is not for the faint-hearted, and is never a risk-free proposition. This means it is rarely a good choice for a research student or inexperienced researcher.[1] Again though, creating a new theory is not the same as throwing together a bunch of others. A new theory must be self-contained and consistent with itself, it must offer a general explanation for the phenomena at hand. Furthermore, it must explain things **better than previous theories**. Going back to the buyer–seller relationship example, a new theory must either: (a) be a general theory of relationships (not just buyer–seller), or (b) show why existing general theories are not adequate to explain the unique situation of buyer–seller relationships. From here, your new theory must *then* go on to show how it explains the phenomena in some kind of materially superior way to existing theories. Needless to say, it is usually easier to show how existing theory should be **augmented** by new ideas, rather than thrown out completely. However, this is not always the case – sometimes existing theory is just plain wrong (do you still believe the Earth is flat?), and if you are truly convinced of this, then I, and I trust Nick, would say *go for it.* But don't expect an easy life (in fact, Nick will touch on this in Chapter 15).

So moving on, assuming you have an overarching theoretical perspective, it's time to see how it relates to your research. One of the defining characteristics of a scientific theory is that it *makes falsifiable or testable predictions about things which can be observed.* It is these predictions that allow the theory to be tested over and over in different contexts. With continual testing, the body of evidence supporting the theory builds up, and the theory gets modified (by the contributions of newer research) to overcome the limitations identified by such repeated testing in different contexts. Also, the existence of several theories that explain similar phenomena in different ways, based on differing assumptions and sometimes different underlying philosophical views, allows for comparisons of the explanatory and predictive ability of these competing theories to be made, essentially testing them against each other in different contexts. Of course, sometimes contradictory evidence builds up to such a stage that a given theory is discredited, and this can be a long and painful process for adherents to that theory. More on this in Chapter 15.

Developing theory

As I touched on above, in most instances scholarly research aims to make some contribution to theory, not necessarily a large contribution, but some advancement of the theory in

[1] On the other hand, it could be argued that only research students and inexperienced researchers have the time to dedicate to creating new theory, and also are not totally immersed in existing theory yet either.

some manner. Of course, different research contexts require different types of contribution. Masters and Doctoral level research certainly needs to make some kind of contribution, and research by full-time academics is often held to very high standards in this regard. Undergraduate research may have a more modest aim (perhaps to apply an existing theory to a new context and provide new information or additional evidence for a theory) but this still requires an understanding of what theory is. Consequently, theory relates to your literature review inasmuch as your theory is a systematic and formalised expression of all previous observations (found from reviewing previous work) that is predictive, logical and testable (I will come to this later). *However*, when conducting the literature review, and looking at previous observations in the field that you are interested in, it is most usually the case that reported observations contradict each other, contradict other theories and generally appear to be inconsistent. But what should you do when this happens?

The art of critical evaluation of these inconsistent findings or observations is for you to evaluate what is going on with the results that previous researchers have reported. Take for example two studies examining a similar situation and reporting different or even conflicting observations. Your job, as a reviewer of these studies, is to try to work out if the conflicting results support, modify, or challenge the existing theory that you are interested in. There are many reasons why conflicting results may be reported (and you will become very knowledgeable about these as you move through this book). The results may be inconsistent because one or other of them is plain wrong; or maybe they are inconsistent because there are other factors at work which have not been accounted for in the explanation of the observations; they could be inconsistent because there is error which is masking what is really being observed, or they could be inconsistent because the researcher is interpreting similar data yet coming to different conclusions. In this instance the observations may actually be the same, just the interpretation different. So how much confidence do you have in the reported results? This will depend on how well you think the researchers have applied particular methods to collect and interpret the data, (remember, no method is perfect), where the data were collected, perhaps the results are sample-specific and not sufficiently generalisable to be considered as either supporting the theory or not. Consider the example of Newton's Law given above: you may read many articles that report that gravitational force always works the same way; this may have been tested in a variety of ways with a variety of objects at many different times and in many different locations. It may be reported by many esteemed researchers. Then you come across a paper that reports that this is not true, that in some instances objects do *not* attract each other in the same way. In fact, this really happened, although it was more that the law did not accurately predict some events than that apples started falling upwards! So, what do you do? Ignore the anomaly? This is a tempting option, and one that many people will engage in when given information that contradicts their view of the world. However, we are scholars so should not allow ourselves to bury our heads and ignore the contradictory information. What then? Well we can examine the research paper; look at the methods, conditions under which the observations were made, methods used to make these observations, and ultimately come to a conclusion about the validity of the observations. Bear in mind that even though we are scholars, we are also human, and humans have a tendency to place more importance on information that supports their existing views than information which challenges those views. Even if we do not allow ourselves the comfort of ignoring contradictory advice, we must ensure that we do not find ways of dismissing it simply because we do not know what to do with it. The challenge is to look at the information provided and work out whether: (a) it is justified, and therefore that our universal law or theory is not quite so universal, or (b) the research is flawed in some way and so we can legitimately argue that the observations, although contradictory, probably do not challenge the validity of our theory. Our third option is to accept (a), but to argue that it is not really that important a departure. This is kind of what has happened with Newton's example. We know that it is not accurate near the speed of light, but we also accept that it remains a useful predictive device within its strictly defined conditions.

Another explanation of the existence of contradictory evidence is the possibility that the theory is *based on an incorrect assumption*. All theories are based to some degree on assumptions, at the most philosophical level these may be to do with the nature of reality as discussed at the start of this chapter. Other assumptions may be included in a theory because they were thought to be 'true' at the time that the theory was developed but have subsequently been shown to be untrue (or at least replaced with an alternative truth). It is worth remembering when you are reading about theories that they *always* contain some assumptions, which, by definition, are accepted without proof. The more assumptions a theory has the more complex it is. In fact, a commonly cited argument for simple theories is known as **Occam's Razor**, which is discussed in IDE 5.1.

IDE 5.1: Occam's Razor

Occam's Razor is a general principle of theoretical development and interpretation that is credited to William of Ockham (1288-1348). Thus, it is sometimes referred to as 'Ockham's Razor'. You can also see the basic idea of Occam's Razor echoed in many other areas of methodology, particularly statistical methods. Occam's Razor is essentially the principle that a theory should rely on as few assumptions, and propose as few hypothetical entities, as possible. It is often expressed as the maxim that 'the simplest explanation is usually the best'. Or at least that's how Lisa Simpson referred to it in episode 6 of 'The Simpsons' season 7. Occam's Razor is a way of choosing between competing theories, as long as they are all equally 'good'. This, of course, depends on what you define as good. Some theorists use the criteria of 'correctness', so, for example, Newton's Law is simpler than Einstein's General Relativity – but we shouldn't prefer it since we know it to be incorrect. The problem occurs when we don't know whether theories are correct or not – commonly the case when we are developing theories! In this case we should use Occam's Razor as a general principle to guide our theoretical development. In other words, we should certainly never make our theories unnecessarily complicated, but nonetheless, we should never over-simplify them to the point where they are obviously not accurate. Speaking of Newton, he stated it nicely when he said that, 'we are to admit no more causes of natural things than such as are both true and sufficient to explain their appearances'. In other words, our theories should first be aimed at providing an accurate and realistic explanation, but should never be *unnecessarily* complex. When you are developing your own models and theories, you would do well to take this advice to heart.

An illustration of how theories are based on assumptions, and also of how **models** can be derived from theories, can be found in early astronomy. The Greek astronomer Ptolemy created a planetary model based on the prevailing astronomy theory, and its assumptions, at the time. Some of these assumptions were based on the idea that the Earth, being God's creation, was naturally at the centre of the entire universe. So, the observed motion of the stars and Sun were explained by assuming that the Earth was at the centre of the planetary and solar system, and theorising that the planets and the Sun made circular orbits around the Earth, and the stars were on a sphere outside of these orbits. Retrograde motion of the planets was explained by smaller circular orbits of individual planets. This astronomical theory could be illustrated as a mathematical model, and could even be built into a physical model, an *orrery*. In fact, even today mathematical calculations based on Ptolemy's model can predict, to a great degree of accuracy, where the planets will be at a given time. All this evidence suggests that the theory and the model are good representations of the real world. This example also illustrates the idea that a theory is a *model of reality*, one that describes and predicts certain measurable occurrences, yet may not be a good description of what the world is actually like (just like Newton's so-called Law). Another, more accurate, theory can later replace the previous model, just as this model of the planetary system was replaced 1,500 years later at the time of Copernicus, although not without much wailing and gnashing of teeth (being as it destroyed the assumption that the Earth was necessarily the centre of the Universe).

Assumptions are the weak points in any theory, as they have to be accepted on faith, which is quite contrary to most philosophies of science. However, a given theory can never explain absolutely everything down to the finest detail, so it must to some greater or lesser extent rely on assumptions about those parts of the world which it does not directly relate to. Thus, assumptions are essential in the development of theory, but while they cannot be removed completely, we can at least aim to base our theories on as few assumptions as possible. When examining the assumptions upon which a theory is based, it is important to remember that *assumptions* themselves can be neither true nor false, since there is no way of proving them to be either. If there were a way, they would no longer be assumptions. For example, the assumption of Earth being the centre of the Universe was no longer an assumption once it was discovered to be untrue. Nevertheless, we can comment on the usefulness or uselessness of assumptions, depending on whether deductions made from them correspond to actual events. To take a more social scientific example, many classical economic theories depend on the assumption that the decision maker in any situation is both (a) rational (i.e. always makes the best decision to maximise benefit) and (b) has access to perfect information about every situation. It is up to you to judge whether these assumptions are realistic, or more importantly whether models relying on them are still able to usefully predict or explain economic behaviour.

Doubtless you have noticed that so far I have focused mostly on the natural sciences to explore the notion of theory. This is because, in the physical world, it is often easier to see the relationship between physical events and theory, to show how theories can be incorrect, and how the assumptions on which the theory is based can be wrong. Within the social sciences, understanding the nature of theory is complicated by the fact that the behaviour of people is generally less predictable than objects in the physical world and the factors that influence behaviour are more varied, often less measurable and less well understood. This gives rise to an interesting debate in the field of social science about what theory is, and there is considerable disagreement. When does an 'idea' become a theory, and then when does a theory become a law. If ever?

Despite this, there seems to be more agreement about what theory isn't. Most importantly, when reading a theoretical work (maybe a literature review, an article, a research monograph, etc.) there are many different components which might be confused with theory by the unwary. For example, in such work you will probably see lots of *references*, *variables*, *data*, *conceptual definitions*, *models* and *hypotheses*. While all of these may be relevant to theory in a supporting role, they should not be thought of as actually *being* theory. Instead, as Sutton and Staw (2003) show in their excellent book chapter, theory is that part of the work which shows the patterns of interconnectedness between phenomena; providing details about the mechanisms of causality in these relationships; and answering questions about **why** these phenomena are related, and **why** the relationships operate as they do. Furthermore, a strong theory should be more than an explanation of historical events (typically your observations), it should also be able to predict future events and outcomes.

If theory is not references, variables, data, conceptual definitions, models or hypotheses, this is probably a good place to have a look at these to see what they are and how they relate to theory. References, variables, data and concepts are the topic of later chapters in the book so I won't deal with these in detail here. In the next paragraphs we will deal with models and hypotheses, since they are very often confused with theory itself.

Models

Like so much in the academic literature examining theory, the distinction between a theory and a model is not always clear. Often the two terms are used synonymously. I will draw a distinction between theories and models here which I hope will help you to think about the theories that you are working with, and may wish to develop. Theories attempt to **explain** phenomena, whereas models by themselves are like laws in that they can only **describe**. Both can be used to predict future phenomena, but in slightly different ways. A good model should be *based on* a solid theory, but the model is just a descriptive representation of the theory, and by itself offers no explanatory power. Think about Newton's Law – which can also be considered to be a mathematical model describing the behaviour of bodies. It offers no description or explanation of why those bodies are attracted, just a mathematical description of what does happen, allowing you to predict what might happen in the future. The theoretical component would be a detailed thesis on *how* bodies attract each other according to their mass and distance. Of course, as we now 'know', theoretical explanations of gravity are elusive.

In many instances, when we create a theory we are also constructing a model of reality. A model is a representation (literally, 're-presentation') of the real world; but it is not the real world. For instance, a scale model of a Ferrari, no matter how detailed and intricate, is clearly not the Ferrari itself; the aspects of the car represented in the scale model are, only in certain limited ways, representative of the actual entity. However, in most ways that matter, the scale model of the car is not an actual car. It *describes a car* to a greater or lesser extent. But to explain how a car actually worked, you would need to refer to a detailed theoretical description of the internal combustion engine, electronic control systems, transmissions, aerodynamics, and many other things. Take a look at Figures 5.2a and 5.2b, which both represent the same model of the relationship between consumer satisfaction and behaviour. One is a graphical model, and the other is the same thing represented in mathematical form.

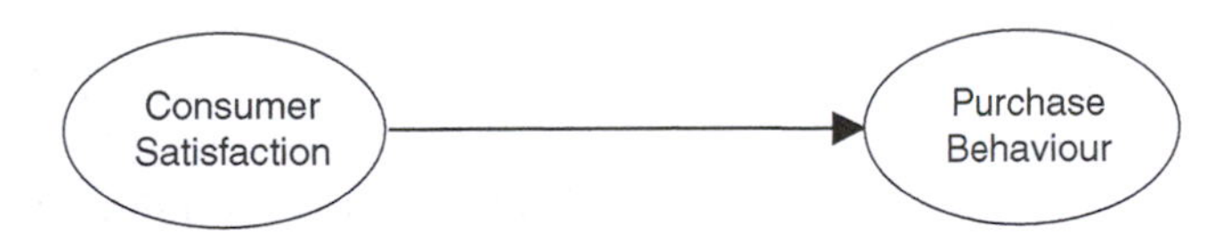

Figure 5.2a A graphical model

P = *f*(CS)

(purchase behaviour = a function of consumer satisfaction)

Figure 5.2b A mathematical model

Both these models are only representations of the real world. Such models are **based on** corresponding underlying theories, of which there are several. Different theories give rise to different models, each of which may be able to describe the same phenomenon to a greater or lesser extent. As a representation of behaviour in consumer markets such competing models and theories are useful, but all of them are incomplete. They are based on their own sets of assumptions, which may be different, and these assumptions may or may not be true (we do not know if they are or not).

For example, let us look at two competing theories that predict the behaviour of consumers. I have grossly simplified these theories to illustrate the point and apologise to both economists and psychologists who may well cringe at the lack of detail in the explanations of these two theories. The first theory has its foundations in economics (utility theory), the second in psychology (theory of reasoned action). From economics, utility theory states that an individual's utility is a measure of the relative satisfaction gained from engaging in a behaviour (perhaps buying a car) to satisfy their wants and needs. Accordingly, utility (relative satisfaction with the car) can increase or decrease. Utility theory explains people's behaviour in terms of their attempts to increase their utility (relative satisfaction) with the behaviour (car purchase) given the economic constraints which they endure (buy the car that provides the most satisfaction, given limitations on the amount of money one can spend). It is also generally accepted that products have several salient attributes (the car's colour, brand, power and fuel economy). Utility theory would predict that the individual would weigh up the cost of each of these attributes against the satisfaction gained by having different levels of each. Their choice of car will be the one that provides the most overall satisfaction. This utility maximising behaviour is based on the assumptions of rationality and perfect information, which I touched on above. Assumptions such as this dominate classical theories in microeconomics. Yet they are still assumptions because they cannot be directly tested, so have to be taken on faith.

Clearly an assumption such as rationality may be incorrect in certain circumstance, most notably where the preferences of the individual are not stable, such as when they are not sure of the consequences of making a particular choice. A competing model of human behaviour derived from a psychological perspective is the Theory of Reasoned Action. The Theory of Reasoned Action suggests that a person's behaviour is determined by their intention to perform the behaviour and that this intention is, in turn, a function of their attitude toward the behaviour and their subjective norms. According to the theory of reasoned action the behaviour of an individual can be predicted by understanding the beliefs that they hold about themselves and their environment. These beliefs are thought to underlie the person's attitudes and subjective norms, and ultimately determine their intentions and their behaviour. Simply put, the Theory of Reasoned Action suggests that a person's intention to perform a behaviour is predicted by their attitude toward that behaviour and how they think other people would view them if they performed the behaviour. This intention to perform a behaviour then predicts the actual behaviour itself. The Theory of Reasoned Action has its own set of assumptions, most notably that the behaviour of the individual is voluntary and decision making is a conscious activity. In certain circumstances these assumptions may be incorrect, such as when the decision is not a conscious one, perhaps because it is impulsive or habitual, or the behaviour is not voluntary, perhaps because it is determined by a third party such as an employer.

Proponents of both these theories concede that the assumptions made are not a totally accurate description of reality, but would argue that both theories are good inasmuch as they help researchers to reason, and provide help in formulating falsifiable hypotheses. In other words, theories do not necessarily have to be perfectly accurate explanations of what happens in the world. Instead, the criteria for the usefulness of a theory is whether those departures from reality invalidate the theory. Of course this is a thorny question, and leads to significant disagreement because different researchers have different criteria for what makes a theory valid. For some, to assume that individuals have perfect information and are rational is so patently incorrect that any theories drawn from such assumptions can not be of any use at all. For others, the fact that such theories give us the basic mental tools to explore a lot of human decision-making, and allow the development of models which *do* seem to describe human behaviour with a reasonable level of accuracy, is enough to retain such theories. Many critics of social science theories do tend to make the error of assuming that to be useful, a theory has to be a perfect representation of what happens. This is of course not really the case, and scientific progress has to start somewhere. It is up to the individual to determine whether they consider a theory to be useful, even though it may contain some unrealistic assumptions. If we had to ignore theories unless they were perfect representations of the world, would we have any theories at all?

Moving on, from these different theories it is possible to develop different conceptual models. A conceptual model is one which is based on theory, in this instance we have two competing conceptual models because we have two competing theories to explain and predict behaviour. The conceptual model represents the theory as applied to the real world; it consists of a set of variables and a set of logical and quantitative relationships between them. Typically the conceptual model refers to only some aspects of the phenomenon in question (in the Utility Theory and Theory of Reasoned Action examples, these aspects are a small set of determinants of an individual's behaviour). This means that two models of the same phenomenon may be fundamentally different, as they are based on different theoretical backgrounds and underlying assumptions. This is illustrated in Figure 5.3.

Remember from the previous discussion that models by their very nature are incomplete and, like theory, are based on some explicit assumptions, which are also often incomplete (or even false). It is nearly always necessary to make assumptions in order to simplify the real world into a theory and then further into a model; however, we also need to make sure that we don't include so many assumptions that acceptably accurate solutions are not produced. Other reasons why conceptual models may differ, even if they are based on the

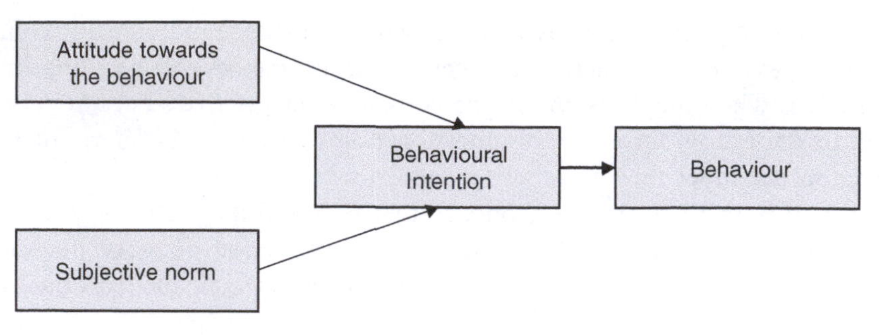

(a) A conceptual model of the theory of planned behaviour

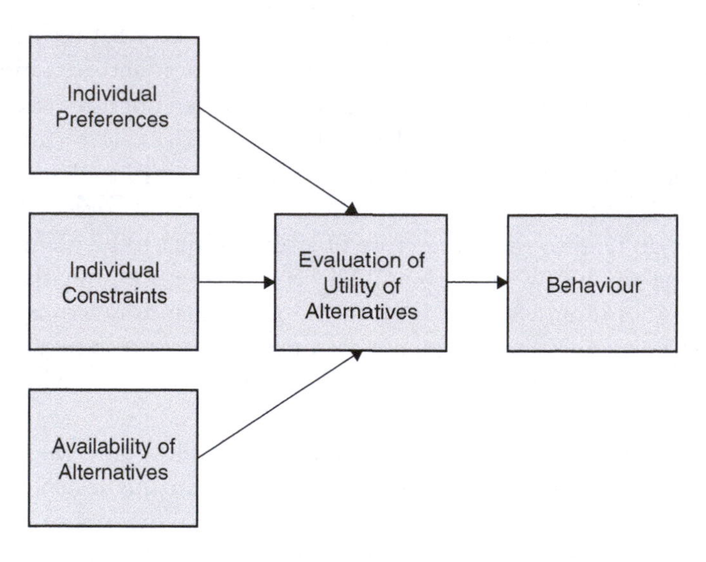

(b) A conceptual model of utility theory

Figure 5.3 Different theoretical models

same theoretical background, include the preferences of the person developing the model, the use to which they want to put it and the other assumptions that they have made regarding the nature of the world. For example, a researcher using a utility framework to examine satisfaction may decide to use a general framework such as the one in Figure! 5.2 shown earlier, or alternatively they may decide that they have sufficient information to 'know' what the alternatives are and the attributes that the individual uses to evaluate these alternatives, as shown in Figure 5.4. This could than be represented as a more specific conceptual model describing the influence of the satisfaction with each attribute with the overall utility of the product chosen.

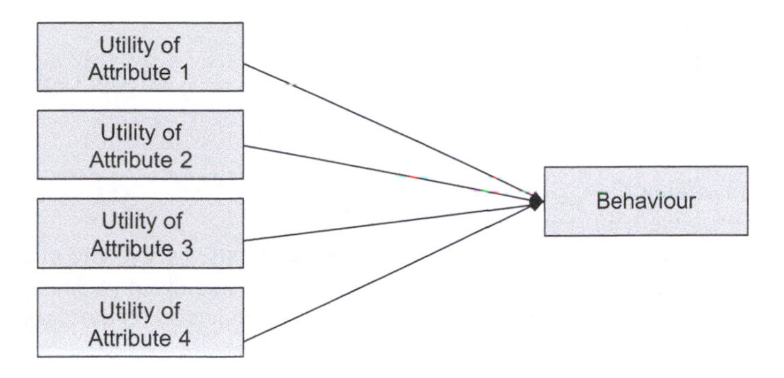

Figure 5.4 A more detailed model

The fact that two models attempting to represent the same element of reality may be essentially different, presents opportunities and challenges to the researcher. First, it means that if you wish to use a model you need to understand its original purpose and the assumptions that it is based on. This is particularly important when putting the critical literature review together. Examining, and explaining, the assumptions of the underlying theory that a model is based on is an essential element of commenting on the applicability of certain theories and their associated models to different contexts and for different purposes. When critiquing the work of one researcher in comparison to others, comparing the assumptions and simplifications that have been made to create the conceptual models used, is an effective way in which to comment on the applicability of different research to the context in which it has been applied and its suitability for the context in which you are interested.

Hypotheses and propositions

But once you have developed a model, this is only half the job. It is now possible to derive formal hypotheses or propositions from it. For example, you could think of every 'link' in the models presented in Figures 5.3 and 5.4 as needing a formal hypothesis or proposition linked to it. Many people get hypotheses and propositions confused with theory, which is understandable, so let me clear this up right from the start. First, it is necessary to differentiate between the terms **hypothesis** and **proposition**, which often get confused.

The Oxford English Dictionary defines hypotheses and propositions as follows.

hypothesis n. (pl. hypotheses)

1. a proposition made as a basis for reasoning, without the assumption of its truth.
2. a supposition made as a starting-point for further investigation from known facts (cf. THEORY).

3. a groundless assumption.
   [LL f. Gk hypothesis foundation (as HYPO-, THESIS)]

proposition noun

1. a statement or assertion.
2. a scheme proposed; a proposal.
3. Logic a statement consisting of subject and predicate that is subject to proof or disproof.
4. colloq. a problem, opponent, prospect, etc. that is to be dealt with (a difficult proposition).
5. Math. a formal statement of a theorem or problem, often including the demonstration.

On first reading, hypotheses and propositions appear to be very similar, and they are in many ways. But there are some important differences too. Yet in the social sciences confusion abounds about the exact usage of the two terms. A proposition is, strictly speaking, a **statement that predicts a relationship between two or more variables**, one that answers research questions and makes predictions. These predictions are of the type: *A **causes** B*, or *an increase in the amount of A will **lead to** an increase/decrease the amount of B*. Important to note here, is that if the statement does not offer any causality, and merely indicates that A and B are correlated, then it should technically be called a hypothesis. However, in common social scientific usage, a *hypothesis* is used to describe a proposition that will be tested in the study being reported, irrespective of whether there is causality inferred, and *proposition* is used when there will not be a test of the relationship between the constructs. Nevertheless, this is not strictly correct.

A more correct and useful distinction would define a hypothesis as simply **a statement which predicts what you expect to observe in your empirical data**. By itself, it has no theoretical content.[2] Of course, hypotheses should be *supported* by detailed theoretical arguments and logic, but the hypothesis itself is just a prediction of what you will observe in your data. This is the source of the distinction between correlation (hypothesis) and causality (proposition) made above. Causality is actually a theoretical concept, and as you can never actually *see* causation in your data, a hypothesis should never state it. A proposition, on the other hand, is kind of like a summary statement about a given theoretical idea, which may or may not relate to actual empirical data or tests.

Hypotheses are derived from the theory on which your research is based. This theory will usually provide an indication of the direction of causality; for example, A causes B, or B causes A, and the size and sign of the causality A increases or decreases B and by how much. Hypotheses should be closely related to your conceptual model, inasmuch as they typically describe the arrows in the model. The scientific method, specifically the hypothetico-deductive method, requires that hypotheses be **falsifiable**. This means that they must be written in such a way that other researchers can show them to be false (usually by

[2]There will be more about hypotheses in Chapter 14 about quantitative testing.

using empirical data, but sometimes from pure logic). For this reason, hypotheses predicting a relationship between two variables are accompanied by a **null hypothesis** which predicts *no* relationship between the variables. Normally the null hypothesis is not stated in journal articles as it can easily be derived from the hypothesis that is presented.

Using the example of the Theory of Reasoned Action above, it is possible to derive several hypotheses about the relationships between the constructs in the study. For instance, the theory tells us that the *more positive the person's attitude* towards a behaviour, the *more they will intend to perform* that behaviour. Similarly, the *more the person's subjective norms support* the behaviour the *more the person will intend to perform* the behaviour; and finally the *more the person intends to perform* a behaviour; the *more they will display* the behaviour.

These statements may be written as formal hypotheses:

H_1: A person's attitude towards a given behaviour will be positively associated with their intention to undertake that behaviour.

And the associated null hypothesis:

H_0: A person's attitude towards a given behaviour will have no association with their intention to undertake that behaviour.

Similarly the relationship between subjective norms and intentions to behave can be written as a formal hypothesis thus:

H_2: A person's subjective norms about a given behaviour will be positively associated with their intention to undertake that behaviour.

And the associated null hypothesis:

H_0: A person's subjective norms about a given behaviour will have no association with their intention to undertake that behaviour.

For the relationship between behavioural intentions and behaviour the formal hypotheses would be:

H_3: A person's intention to perform a given behaviour will be positively associated with their behaviour.

H_0: A person's intention to perform a given behaviour will have no association with their behaviour.

Note that the hypotheses only state an *association*, not any causal relationship or effect. Your theoretical logic which leads up to your hypotheses may well propose causal influences (indeed we tend to think in this manner all the time), but since you cannot ever observe causality, your hypotheses should not make any predictions regarding it. Remember, stick to exactly what tests of your empirical data can provide evidence of. Once the hypotheses, and the associated null hypotheses, have been formally stated they can be tested. Typically this is done by collecting and analysing empirical data to establish support for either the hypothesis or the null hypothesis. You will get to looking at what data are and how to collect and analyse them later in this book.

Supporting a hypothesis

Once tested, retested and further tested, a supported hypothesis may become a well-accepted part of a theory, or occasionally may grow to become a theory itself. It may be tempting to think of such well-validated hypotheses as laws. They are not! One should more accurately refer to repeatedly supported hypotheses simply as adequately verified, or as dependable. However, even dependable hypotheses remain provisional, as by their very nature hypotheses cannot be proven to be true. Observations which support a hypothesis *fail to falsify* it rather than prove it to be true. As both myself and Nick have mentioned already at various points, a single, non-confirming observation can prove a hypothesis to be false.

An appropriate example of the provisional nature of hypotheses would be my first visit to what is in my opinion[3] the most beautiful place on Earth, New Zealand. New Zealand is famous for having more sheep than people, and on my first visit, I noticed that all the sheep I saw were white. From this I could have formed the hypothesis that *all sheep in New Zealand are white*. Even though it does not predict any association, this is still a hypothesis, as it predicts *something* I could test, and it is falsifiable. In fact, anyone could falsify my hypothesis by observing a single black sheep. If someone with nothing better to do were to try to do this though, there are some considerations that are required for good science to be conducted.

Firstly, I myself have to correctly define and communicate the statement of my hypothesis and define the variables in my hypothesis. Without this, it is impossible for any other researcher to examine my hypothesis in a meaningful way. What exactly do I mean by 'sheep'? Does this include lambs and rams? What do I mean by New Zealand? Does this include only the two main islands, or the smaller offshore islands as well? Provided that I have clearly and unambiguously defined my variables (more about this in later chapters) and clearly stated my hypothesis, any researcher can come along and test my hypothesis. Some researchers will be better at this than others, and much of that depends on the methods that they use to make the observations, and therefore how confident we can be in the observations that they make. In order to have confidence in the findings of these imaginary researchers that wish to examine my hypothesis, we need to be assured that measurement errors are sufficiently small. Have they adequately distinguished black sheep from goats or llamas, or

[3]Honestly, I am not just putting this in here for Nick's benefit!

the many other animals that look like black sheep but are not really black sheep? If we are confident that the method was suitable and the error sufficiently small, then finding a black sheep falsifies the 'white sheep only' hypothesis.

There are other types of hypothesis which are more common in social sciences research than the type used in the sheep example above. For example, many of the hypotheses I've already given you assert associations between variables, such as *A is positively associated with B*. For example, if one observes a particular independent variable change, then one will also observe a certain dependent variable change. This formulation, also known as an **if-then** statement, applies whether or not a proposition or theory asserts a direct cause-and-effect relationship (remember, hypotheses can only state what can be observed).

Beware! Not all if-then statements are hypotheses. For example, 'If you warm yeast, then more gas will be produced' is not a hypothesis. It is instead a simple prediction. The problem with this statement is that there is no theoretical proposition to test. What is related to what? Is temperature a variable? Is yeast a variable? Is gas production a variable? Which gas? A better hypothesis along these lines would be 'The temperature of yeast is positively associated with the amount of carbon dioxide produced'. This hypothesis clearly states what we expect to observe, and the key variables. However, it does not make clear the assumptions – which in this case are that the yeast is present in a mixture of flour, salt, water and milk, which provide the fermentable sugars which are converted to carbon dioxide. This context would be discussed fully in the theory which preceded the hypothesis.

Hypotheses about possible correlation do not stipulate the cause and effect *per se,* they only state that A is related to B. Among other key philosophical and technical issues, verifying causal relationships is complicated by *intervening variables*. Observations may give the appearance of a direct cause-and-effect relationship between A and B, but further investigation may reveal other factors not mentioned in the proposition. Also, observing that changes in A are correlated with changes in B, does not provide any information about the cause and effect. In such circumstances it is possible, and often common, to mistake the effect for the cause, and vice versa (i.e. potentially get the hypothesised cause and effect backwards).

Summary

At various points throughout this chapter I have characterised laws, theories, models and hypotheses. This discussion was based on a critical realist philosophical view of the world. This is not to suggest that critical relativism is not 'as good' or that metaphysical idealism is not valid though, just that the idea of developing theory is most easily discussed from the critical realist (or positivistic) viewpoint. This is the first challenge that you will have to face. You need to decide which philosophical standpoint you intend to take (this will also be influenced by your supervisors' views of the world too). You have also seen the relationship between laws, models, and theories: laws are supposedly always true (in their context), theories are always tentative, models describe, theories explain. You have seen how the same theory can give rise to different models and how different theories can give rise to competing models to explain the same phenomena. These differences arise, in part, from the assumptions that researchers make in developing and adopting a theory to a particular problem.

You have also seen how the hypothetico-deductive method can be used to develop and test hypotheses (and associated null hypotheses) and have explored the nation of proving a hypothesis correct (or more specifically we have noted that this is not possible). Finally, one of the aims of this chapter was to illustrate the need for strong theory and the need to understand what theories are (and what they are not) if you are to do this. Most academic research projects aim to make a contribution to knowledge in some way, and one way of doing this is to contribute to theory. This does not mean developing a whole new theory, but more usually means examining existing theories and making an incremental advancement to them, maybe by challenging some of the underlying assumptions or by developing alternative conceptualisations of the theory and testing these.

Key points to take from this chapter:

- Strong theory provides a foundation on which to build your research and is the cornerstone of a well-considered project.
- There may be several different theories that attempt to explain the same phenomena, typically these will be based on different assumptions and may derive from different areas of social science.
- Understanding the assumptions of a theory is important to evaluate the usefulness of that theory.
- Theories can often be represented in conceptual models; competing conceptual models arise from competing theories explaining the same phenomena.
- Theories, and the scientific method, are by definition based on a philosophy of epistemological objectivity.
- In the Hypothetico-Deductive Method, it is impossible to prove a scientific theory true by means of induction, because no amount of evidence assures us that contrary evidence will not be found. Instead, a process of deduction involving the process of falsification is used.

Further reading

There aren't too many sources specifically about theory, but a book I have always found helpful is *Evaluating Social Science Research* by Paul C. Stern and Linda Kalof. This book gives a lot of attention to theory, and how to evaluate it. One can move from here (with the help of other sources) to come to terms with actually creating theory.

There are also some great articles on theory, and doubtless you will come across many in your own fields. In marketing, some great works are:

- Hunt. S (1990), 'Truth in marketing theory and research.' *Journal of Marketing,* 54 (July), 1–15.
- Zinkhan, G. M., and Hirschheim, R. (1992), 'Truth in marketing theory and research: An alternative perspective'. *Journal of Marketing,* 56 (April), 80–88.
- Stewart, D. W. and Zinkhan, G. M. (2006), 'Enhancing marketing theory in academic research' *Journal of the Academy of Marketing Science,* 34 (4), 477–480.

EXERCISES

1. What are epistemological objectivity, and metaphysical idealism? How do these concepts influence theory development in the scientific method?
2. What is the difference between a law, a theory, a model and a hypothesis?
3. For your research project:

   a. What phenomena are you interested in?
   b. Think about different theories that aim to explain the relationships between the phenomena that you are interested in.
   c. What are the assumptions of these theories?

4. Identify two or three journal articles that describe the relationships between the phenomena that you are interested in.

   a. Can you identify conceptual models that are presented in these papers?
   b. How well do these conceptual models relate to the underlying theory?
   c. Do the authors explicitly state what theoretical foundations they are basing their work on?

Chapter 6
Concepts, constructs and measurement

SUPERVISOR'S VIEW: PROFESSOR DENNY BORSBOOM

Stuck in Psychometrics: I work in a psychometrics department, and I guess many people think of me as some sort of statistician – but I really don't feel that way. As far as I'm concerned, I am a psychologist who has gotten stuck in psychometrics. Why? Because, even though I am more interested in psychology than in psychometric models *per se*, I do not think that you can do much in the way of worthwhile science if you haven't found out how to connect theoretical terms – intelligence, extraversion, self-efficacy, etc. – to empirical observations. To do that properly, you have to solve the measurement problem. And psychology (and many related or similar disciplines), in my personal view, hasn't so far done a very convincing job in this respect.

Now, the fact that the measurement problem, in most areas of psychology, is basically unsolved is not widely recognised. People – researchers as well as laypersons – are often quite uncritical in accepting statements like 'IQ-tests measure intelligence'; often they will even equate 'intelligence' (the theoretical concept) with 'IQ' (the score that you get from an IQ-test). Researchers do this because they are interested primarily in relations between variables (e.g. 'does breast feeding increase a child's intelligence?'). They don't want to spend their whole life figuring out the measurement issues (and learning all the difficult mathematical models) before they can get to what they perceive as the really interesting stuff. So they just substitute IQ for intelligence when it comes to statistically analysing their data. However, the commingling of, say, IQ and intelligence, is a little too quick for my taste, and the same holds for most other important variables in psychology. For instance, IQ is a single number. To substitute 'IQ-score' for 'intelligence' in empirical research one therefore has to assume that intelligence can also be represented as a single number. Why should we believe that? How should we investigate whether this assumption is justified?

What, by the way, is intelligence? How does it relate to IQ-scores? How do we mathematically formalise such a relation, and how do we test whether we are on the right track? These issues, to me, are not problems that merely need to be solved before we can do the really interesting work. They *are* the really interesting work. And that's why I'm happy to be stuck in psychometrics.

VIEW FROM THE TRENCHES: WALTER HERZOG

I have just completed my Ph.D. in consumer behaviour at the University of St. Gallen (Switzerland). My dissertation manuscript comprises papers on topics in consumer psychology and psychometric theory. However, a question I often had to deal with was: 'Why are psychometric or measurement issues relevant for 'applied' researchers?' Let me begin with the following story: I will probably never forget a comment of a reviewer of one of my conference papers. About one-third of the paper consisted of an appendix with statistical results. Although the reviewer was quite positive and highlighted the 'practical relevance' of my findings, (s)he closed the review with the following sentence: 'It would have been desirable to empirically test the proposed model'. The reviewer obviously did not recognise any of the numbers in the appendix, even though I referred to it throughout the manuscript! So, how could (s)he then conclude that my model was of practical value or 'relevance'?

Now, the point that I want to make here is not that reading reviews can be quite funny (although they can be). It is about the relation of 'relevance' and 'rigour'. Most applied researchers would agree (especially after two or three pints of beer in a relaxed atmosphere at a conference dinner) that a nice 'story' (i.e. theory) brings you through the review process of almost any journal – despite methodological weaknesses. In other words, 'relevance compensates rigour'. However, how can a result be relevant *without* rigour in testing the hypothesised relations among the variables under study? In my view, rigour is a **necessary condition** for the relevance of research findings. Of course, rigour itself cannot produce relevant results, but a good idea or an interesting research topic without rigour in theory-testing is of limited worth.

In this perspective, the role of measurement becomes immediately clear. Measurement of the variables under study is not just a 'bonus', or something you have to do to get your research published. It is the central step in the research process that gives you access to the concepts, and relations among the concepts, under study – thereby translating good ideas into relevant results, and identifying bad ideas as such. Without measurement, good ideas will remain merely ideas, and will not be differentiable from bad ideas. I always conceived this important function of measurement theory for applied research as a motivation to deal with psychometric issues. And after a while, when you realise the immense value of psychometrics for your applied research, this seemingly nerdy stuff gets more and more exciting.

However, during your studies you are likely to come across people (maybe reviewers) who are less excited about measuring variables or statistical issues, and might be of the opinion that fooling around with statistics is wasting time that could be invested in more interesting 'applied' issues. I remember several such encounters during the last three years, and sometimes I thought that it might be the case that these people are much more clever than I am and therefore, they do not need to test their theories in a proper way since their hypotheses are correct anyway. Such people must be very impressive applied scientists!

Measurement is completely ubiquitous in today's world, whether you know it or not. In order to get to the stage of your education where you are reading this book, you have almost certainly been subjected to a battery of measures, from your IQ, your reading ability, perhaps SATs (standard aptitude tests), the GMAT (graduate management admission test), or various other exams. Perhaps you learnt a music instrument when you were younger, or danced; if so, you would have probably been measured on your ability to do such things, and given various gradings. If you're ill, you'll be taking some kind of carefully measured amount (or dose) of medicine; if you are not ill, you might be going out to a bar tonight for a carefully measured pint of beer. Furthermore, measurement properties and theories impact our lives almost constantly. Virtually none of the technology used to write this book, for example, would be possible without measurement. Recipes for dishes are, of course, full of measurements as well. However, we hardly ever think about measurement until something goes wrong. I once had a flatmate who misread teaspoons for tablespoons of salt when making guacamole. Fortunately, there was a large supply of drinks on hand. Speaking of drinks, I remember learning the hard way that English beer was in rather larger 'pints' than those I used to drink in New Zealand. If you are thinking of petrol consumption, you better work out the units you are concerned with (how many litres are in a gallon?), and many London market-traders are still working out how to use grams and kilos instead of ounces and pounds. Although we survived for thousands of years without formalised measurement theories, the advent of measurement was one of the key factors in the rise of technology and science. In a social science context, the massive advances made since the beginning of the 20th century would have been impossible without accompanying advances in measurement theory.

By now you should be well aware of my fetish for the theory that lies behind the methods we use to do research (trust me, there are worse fetishes to have), as well as the historical development of these theories. I'm hoping that by now you are beginning to realise how an appreciation of these things can help us better understand how and why we do research. I'm hoping this because this chapter contains some pretty difficult concepts to grasp if it's your first time thinking about them, and I really want you to make the effort to become comfortable with them. If you do this, then you'll be able to use the practical sections of this and the next chapter much more effectively – if not, you will become (yet) another automaton, plugging numbers into a formula and not realising why or even how you are getting it wrong. In reading this chapter I want you to get a flavour of the importance of measurement theory, and perhaps be inspired to find out more. But even if you don't get interested in measurement itself, I want you to take away a real appreciation for the importance of good measurement to your research, and a commitment to actually doing it properly as much as possible. Because in the past, have I *ever* seen some bad measurement. Please, don't contribute to this yourself, especially after reading this and the next chapter (boy that would make me mad!)

At the end of this chapter I really hope you have come to terms with these key ideas:

- What measurement is, and the importance of rigorous measurement.
- The different rules by which we assign numbers to qualities.
- The difference between direct and indirect measurement, and what a 'latent construct' is.
- The difference between constructs and concepts, and the importance of defining your constructs very clearly.
- What a dimension is, and how to decide whether your constructs are 'multidimensional'.

Why is it Important to Know This Stuff?

At this point, I am hoping that you are beginning to understand many of the ideas relating to the 'theoretical side' of research. Many of you will also have actually got a tentative idea of the theoretical model you may wish to examine. However, this model is exactly that – theoretical. It doesn't exist in the real world. In order to investigate it, we need somehow to collect data which allows us to detect the presence and amount of the concepts which make up our model. In fact, this process is critical to the success of your project. Unfortunately it is also a process which is often little understood and poorly managed by researchers.

So far, we've been talking about developing the theoretical side of our research – the philosophies, concepts, and arguments which make up our theories. However, we now need to think about how to link that theory to the real world, which is what now need to think about how to link that theory to the real world, which is what we can actually observe. This chapter marks the first point where we really look at **how** to link theory and reality. We've been building up to this throughout the first five chapters of this book, but here we begin to put together both sides of the coin, theoretical and real. Understanding this link will put you in a great position to conduct good research, as well as to evaluate the quality of your and others' research. Figure 6.1 should look quite familiar to you.

The material in this chapter should also help you critically analyse other research, such as that you are reviewing in the conceptual development of your own research. In doing so, you may save yourself a lot of heartache later on in the process of research, and may actually help yourself do considerably better research. It will also allow you to have a ready source of questions when you view presentations of research, say in your faculty or at a conference – which can really help you look clever (or irritating, take your pick).

Plus, I think it's really interesting – honest!

Measurement and the theory behind it

Before we take a look at some of the major concepts of measurement, it's a good idea to have a think about exactly *why* we measure things, or even *what* measurement actually means. One thing which may surprise you is that measurement as a formal area of study is quite a recent idea, in fact Savage and Ehrlich (1992) seem to imply that it was less than 30 years

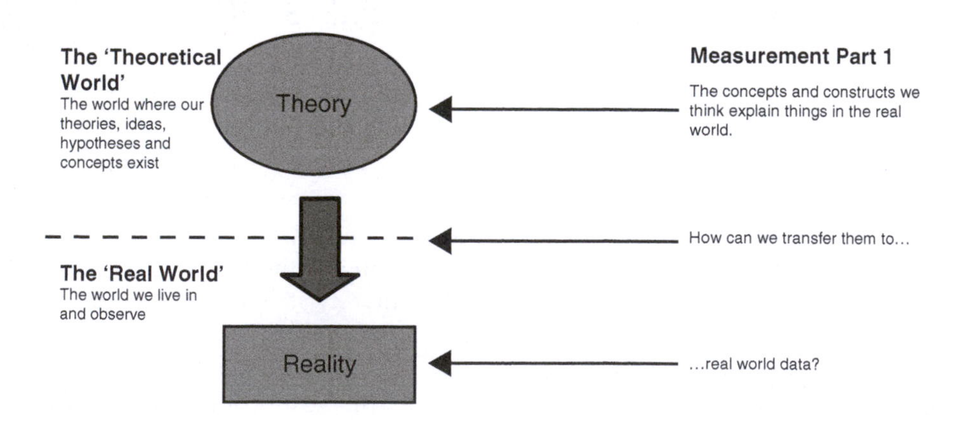

Figure 6.1 The place of measurement

old at the time of their writing.[1] Of course, concepts relating to measurement itself have appeared throughout human history, and both the Bible and the Koran include references to measurement, particularly as they relate to commerce (see Hand, 2004). Interestingly, many of the great philosophers you've already met in these pages (if you are reading the book in order) have been contributors to measurement theory. Aristotle wrote about quantities in his work, and the ancient Greeks were often concerned with such matters. Furthermore, Descartes was one of the first to theorise that one could assign a numerical value to length, area, and volume by counting how many standard units most closely approximated the object. In other words, to measure the length of a line segment, for example, you could count the amount of standard units (i.e. of the same standard length) which end-on-end came closest to the length of the line segment. I'm not sure about you, but it seems almost unbelievable that we could be well into the Enlightenment before someone came up with this idea. Related to this, while you're reading this chapter, remember that measurement theory is still evolving and by no means 'set in stone', no matter what your colleagues think.

With that in mind, let's begin by exploring just what the purpose of measurement is, or even what measurement itself it. First and foremost, measurement can be thought of as the business of quantifying attributes, i.e., *assigning numbers to represent their magnitude*. For example, you as an individual possess many qualities or attributes. Some of these are easily observable and obvious, such as your height, your weight, the length of your hair, the size of your feet and the like. However, you also possess many more subtle attributes, such as intelligence, extraversion, motivation, self-esteem and such. Many of these latter attributes have been developed by social scientists from theory and can't actually be 'seen' by us. Measurement is the process of assigning numbers to represent the amount of any given attribute which is present. Note that I said we measure the *attribute*, not the person (or organisation, or whatever). You don't measure a person, you measure their height, or their self-esteem.

Try to remember the points made above as you move through this chapter, as they imply some interesting and important things which I will point out subsequently. Firstly, measurement is fundamentally *quantitative* as opposed to qualitative. What I mean by this is that measurement is explicitly concerned with numbers. If you read various other chapters of this book you should be clear that there is something of a divide between qualitative (which focuses on gaining direct access to words, thoughts, and feelings, and immersion in the research context) and quantitative (which tends to focus on abstracting oneself from the research context, and converting qualities into numbers to standardise them) research. Chapters 2 and 3 looked at some of the philosophical backgrounds to such approaches. While qualitative data have some unique benefits which will be discussed in later chapters

[1] I'm not so sure I agree with this, but they are definitely a lot smarter than me, so I will just go with it.

(Chapter 9 and 10 especially), they are fundamentally inappropriate for manipulation using many of the tools which have been developed in or adopted by the social sciences, such as mathematics and statistics. For one thing, qualitative attributes are difficult to standardise, and easy to confuse. Take height, for example. Due to some great cosmic joke, I am a mere 5 feet 7 inches tall, but does this mean I am 'tall' or 'short' – well that depends whether you compare me to Snow White, or the Seven Dwarfs, doesn't it? But I am 5′7″ whoever you compare me to. This allows a consistent interpretation of my height, whatever the context I find myself in – be it Lilliput or the Land of the Giants. Using the qualitative terms 'tall' and 'short' can lead to confusion, for example in my family I am actually one of the tallest; if we lived in a small village where average height was quite low, I may in fact come across as quite tall. Now if I were to be set up by my mum on a blind date with a girl who liked 'tall men' from a neighbouring village where average height was much greater, things would clearly not work out well (although my charming personality may carry the day). The use of standard quantitative measures would avoid such confusion and heartache.

Similarly, think of 'numerical ability' – many students of mine over the years have insisted they were 'rubbish with numbers'. In my experience this tends to be a function of the fact they compare themselves with people who are very very good. Essentially, in a University environment, average levels of numerical ability (and most intelligence-related factors) are clearly higher than the general population. Furthermore, a student also is commonly exposed to those who are numeric experts – the tutors who are teaching the course, and the top students as well. This tends to lead the less numerically-strong students to think they are far worse than they actually are in relation to the general population. In fact, in a quantitative test, most of these students would be far above the norm for the population in quantitative ability, not 'rubbish' at all. One perspective on measurement is that quantifying attributes allows us to place them in an artificial, numerical, objective world, where the mess and subjectivity of the 'real' world is removed. And once attributes are mapped on to numerical values, we are able to manipulate the numbers with mathematical and statistical tools – which is incredibly useful. However, this mapping of 'real to artificial' is a concept which seems to fit best with the idea of measuring things which are 'real' and 'observable' themselves – such as height. Height is a real, objective, observable attribute, which we map onto numbers. But as we shall see later, when we come to think about the things we measure most often in the social sciences (self-esteem, personality traits, etc.), the *opposite* is a more helpful way of thinking. But hold that thought for now, that's just a heads-up.

Either way though, **measurement is the process of mapping the magnitude of an attribute to a numerical value – or transferring the amount of a *quality* to a *quantity*.** It is this mapping process that measurement theory is concerned with. The idea of quantifying qualities (which has a nice ring to it) also relies on some key assumptions – many of which have been criticised from certain perspectives. First of all, once we quantify these qualities, our numerical operations are performed on *them* and not the qualities themselves. For example, when you translate two people's heights to numbers, you may get 172 cm and 186 cm.

These two numbers are just that, numbers. It is only in our heads that we know they represent the heights of two people (say me and my tall blind date from above). I can technically do anything I want to mathematically to those numbers, and nothing will of course happen to my actual height itself. For example, if I divide 172 in half and get 86, it doesn't mean that all of a sudden I become even shorter (God forbid!) We must always maintain the link between the attribute and the number which represents it – this requires a set of rules to make sure we are doing it right. Firstly, if the mapping of the attributes on to the numbers is done poorly, or is somehow defective, then any conclusions we draw from our numerical manipulations are also defective. For example, I would usually measure height with some kind of solid ruler, but what if I used a rubber rope? This would mean that according to the tension on the rope, I would get a different number each time I measured the same object! This would of course mean my measurement was meaningless – one day I would be 179 cm tall (brilliant!) and another day 168 cm tall (awful!) In that case I might as well just give up trying to measure things and go back to saying 'short'. In a nutshell, this is the challenge of measurement, and the more complex the attribute we are trying to measure, the more complex and debatable the rules of measurement are. This is important because, once we manipulate our numbers and come up with some answers, we must then map these answers *back* to the things we were trying to measure. Poor measurement means we have no basis with which to map our numerical results back to the things we were trying to measure – so our results are meaningless. Secondly, we must have rules by which we can manipulate the numbers which are appropriate to the attribute we are trying to measure. Basically, numbers themselves have mathematical properties of their own. Sometimes these properties are not held by the attribute in question, and sometimes the numbers are unable to fully represent some quality of the attribute. If you look at IDE 6.1, you'll see what I mean, and we'll fully discuss this when we talk about **scales of measurement** later on.

IDE 6.1: Numerical Representations of Qualities

By this stage of your education, I assume you have some knowledge of numbers themselves – even if you don't *think* you do. For example, you know that numbers have certain properties – e.g. '10' is a bigger number than '9', and is 10 times bigger than '1'. But many of the qualities we want to map to numbers do not even share this basic 'order of magnitude' attribute. Take gender for example. If we allocate '1' to represent males and '2' to represent females this should not be taken to mean that females are twice as 'big', or 'good', or whatever, as males – even though their numerical representation is. In this case the number is just a label for each gender. So in this particular case, the raw number is *more powerful* in terms of properties than the attribute it is measuring. We have created different **scales** to deal with this problem, which I'll discuss very soon.

More interesting to me (and less often talked about) is that many attributes we wish to measure are *more powerful than the numbers we use*. For example, one property of most number systems is that they are discrete. In other words each numerical value is separate from the one below and the one above. Many attributes we may wish to measure are instead *continuous* – there is no demarcation between one value and the next. Think of a bar graph (discrete) versus a line graph (continuous). We could divide a line up into five segments, for example, and number them 1–5. But each of these five segments would therefore represent a **range** of values of the line. This would mean that our numerical measure of 1–5 was less powerful than the actual attribute we were trying to measure – we've lost some information. I like to think of this in terms of music (as usual). I remember when CDs came out, there was (and still is) a lot of controversy over whether they sounded better than vinyl LPs (ask your parents – or maybe your grandparents – if you are wondering what an LP is). CDs represent the sound by cutting it up into thousands (around 16,000 per second in fact) of tiny bits (discrete), whereas on an LP there is a groove cut which is a direct representation of the original sound wave (continuous). CDs are more convenient, and sound really good in most situations, but if you have the correct equipment and the right situation, most audiophiles agree that LPs actually sound better.

Bringing it back to a social science context, a variable like 'satisfaction' is theoretically continuous, but we usually measure it with a range of numerical values (say 1–5). In cutting it up into these discrete segments, we have lost some of the information in the actual variable. It is our job as researchers to work out the appropriate trade-off between information lost, and the need for numerical representation. What this also means, is that – like CDs' representation of music – measures are almost always only an *approximation* of the actual value of the quality or attribute within our subject. In other words, there is always some kind of error involved. The concept of **measurement error** is a vital consideration in measurement theory, and research in general.

Measurement theory is complex and substantial in size, and it is a difficult task to even give a short introduction without raising more questions than answers. Nevertheless, some important distinctions can be made which should serve to provide a theoretical context to the rest of this chapter. This should in turn allow you to (a) gain a fuller understanding of what you are doing, and why, when you measure, and (b) impress the uninitiated – which I find is surprisingly important in life. First, it should be clear that *counting* is different from *measuring* – although both are essentially concerned with quantities and numbers.[2] Whereas it is simple to count the amount of observable, discrete objects (such as students in a class, or phone numbers in your address book), how do you count attributes like time, area or – even more obscurely – attitude and satisfaction? Some attributes, like time or area, can be divided into standard units, and we can then count how many of these units (or *quanta*) which most closely approximate the size/amount of the attribute you want to measure (see IDE 6.1 for a discussion of measurement as approximation). When you are a child at school, you learn measurement by actually physically doing this, laying short rods end-on-end next to a longer rod to measure length, for example. Normally as adults though, we are able to do this automatically, or I guess we would have to carry around rather a lot of small rods and other stuff with us just in case we ever needed to measure something.

Of course, this measurement process depends on a number of things. Firstly, we must have discrete, standardised quanta to use. Even such a basic concept as this is subject to international debate. For example, the US uses imperial quanta such as miles, pounds and gallons, while Europe (supposedly) uses kilometres, kilograms, and litres. Even worse, when it *is* used, a UK gallon is different from a US gallon! Fundamentally, we must also recognise that measurement is necessary, that more than one quanta must be used to measure the extent of our attribute. Finally, we must have rules for *concatenation*. This basically means how we 'add up' the quanta to represent the quantity of the attribute. When measuring length, would you lay your standard length quanta end-on-end or in parallel? In practical terms, if you had 10 standard quanta rods (say they were a foot long each), how would you use them to measure a 5 foot length of rope? Of course, you would lay the rope down, and lay the rods next to it until you reached 5. What about a 5 and a half foot length of rope? What about a 15 foot length? Concatenation rules seem simple in this context, but as we go on to measure more and more complex attributes they become correspondingly complex and also highly important (plus, the word makes you sound really clever). For example, how do you 'add up' the various elements which make up a measure of the 'quality of life' in a particular country? Is average salary more important than levels of pollution?

The discussion above also brings into relief one of the absolutely key concepts of this chapter (and the next one) – the distinction between **direct** and **indirect** measurement. Direct measurement is essentially what I have been referring to so far – i.e. giving numbers to the actual attributes we wish to measure, like weight or height. We can only directly measure things that we can actually observe in some way (e.g., age, speed, etc.). Nevertheless, many of the things that are of interest to psychological, organisational or social researchers are not observable at all. Now, before I go on, turn off the stereo or TV and prepare to think about

---

[2]The history of numbers and mathematics is far too long and complex to even begin to detail here, but it is certainly interesting enough for me to recommend you investigating it. Some references are given at the end of this chapter, and Hand (2004) has a nice introduction in the context of measurement.

this concept carefully, as the rest of this chapter, and the next, is based on it. Think back to the previous chapters about theory development and conceptual models. Such models often consist of concepts such as intelligence, customer satisfaction, love, commitment, trust, motivation and the like. How do we observe such things? Even if I were to cut your head open and spoon around in it, I would be unable to find the bit in there marked 'motivation', and measure its size.[3] What about intelligence, as mentioned in Professor Borsboom's viewpoint at the beginning of this chapter? 'IQ' you say? Well, it is a mistake to think of your IQ score as a direct measure of your intelligence (which is a shame if yours is really big). Instead, theorists have argued that IQ (which is the ability to answer certain types of questions to a time frame) should be related in some way to intelligence. But this is definitely not the same thing as saying IQ *is* intelligence. We can't measure things like intelligence, motivation, or other attitudes and psychological factors directly, so we must use **indirect** measurement. In other words, we need a model to relate the amount of intelligence, or motivation, or whatever, to the *measures* we are using, and therefore we derive the score for motivation from the scores of our subject on these measures. As you move through this chapter, you'll often see references to these latter measures – which are combined in some way to get the measure of our actual attribute – as **observed variables**, although in other work you may find them referred to as 'manifest' variables, 'items', 'indicators', or similar things. The thing we are actually interested in (e.g. motivation) will be termed a **construct** for the most part, and in other work you may find it called a 'concept', a 'latent construct', an 'unobservable', or various other combinations.[4] But the important thing to remember from this paragraph is that *a measurement of an attribute is not the attribute itself.* This will become highly relevant in a few pages, but for now, look at Figure 6.2 for an example.

Scales of measurement

The previous section introduced the idea of 'models' of measurement, which are essentially rules as to how measures can represent unobservable attributes. However, even in direct measurement applications, we need rules to help us decide how to assign numbers to attributes. Remember the earlier discussion, and also IDE 6.1, where I talked about how numbers may possess properties that the attributes we are trying to measure do not? **Scales of measurement** can be thought of as the basic rules which tell us what properties we can allow our measurements to have, due to the properties they are trying to measure, and what

[3] Of course, as science marches on, brain imaging techniques such as functional Magnetic Resonance Imaging may be able to help us begin to directly measure things such as emotions or attitudes (assuming they do in fact exist physically, which is far from agreed-upon), but we are a long way from this right now. Nevertheless, if you are interested in measurement, I suggest keeping your eye on this over the next decade or so!

[4] I actually believe there should be distinctions made between these terms, but now is not the place to go into that.

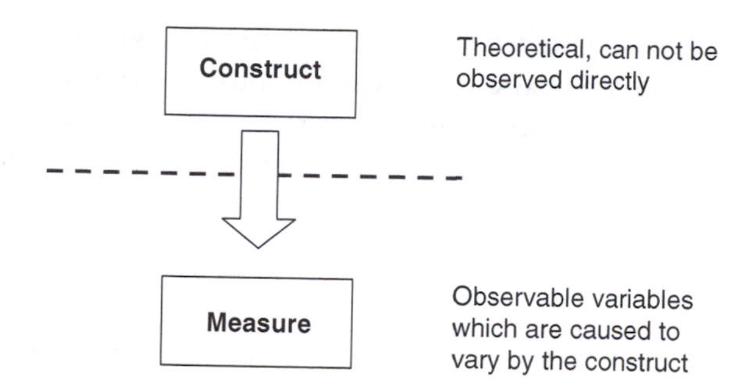

Figure 6.2 Constructs and measures

analysis we can therefore perform. There are four different scales, each of which is more 'powerful' than the last. By 'power' I mean that the scale gets closer and closer to having the properties of the real number system. If you don't quite get this, then read on and it should all make sense in the end. Either way, the four scales are called in ascending power order; **nominal**, **ordinal**, **interval**, and **ratio**. A little trick to remember these is to think of *NOIR* as an acronym, which of course is French for black (I think this is quite clever, but to be honest all my students seem to think it's a bit lame).

Nominal scales

Nominal scales simply represent categories with numeric labels. For example, the variable 'gender' could be labelled as '1' for male and '2' for female, or vice versa. It could just as well be labelled '0.111' for male and 'π' for female. The numbers themselves are solely labels. This means the order of the numbers means absolutely nothing in terms of the attribute you are measuring. Another good example of a nominal scale could be for the variable 'country of birth', with a number assigned to the country given by the respondent. Nominal scales are used when the variable we wish to measure has no order of magnitude. For example, one gender is not bigger or better than another. So we must use nominal rules when analysing the measurement. Nominal rules tell us that the only thing we can do is to count the occurrence of each value (how many are in each group). So we can say 'there were 20 males and 10 females'. We can also take the 'mode' of the variable – the most common value. So if males are '1' and females are '2' we can say '1' is the mode. It makes no sense to do anything else (such as take the mean or median), as there is no order to the values under nominal rules. If we find the mean to be around '1.25', this value means nothing of any sense to us does it? Is the typical value therefore some kind of part male-part female super-creature? Nominal scales are of course the least powerful, but for variables like gender, country of origin, industry, and others where there is no order of magnitude to the categories, they are all we have. Nominal scales tend to be generally ignored or quickly passed over in many situations. However, they are actually quite important and understanding them can save you a bit of time and trouble when you first learn how to use statistics packages like SPSS. Basically, never get into the habit of giving your nominal variables non-numeric labels (e.g. **m** for male and **f** for female, or **y** for yes and **n** for no), learning how to use numbers to label such things is a great exercise in beginning measurement and statistics.

Ordinal scales

Ordinal scales add the idea of 'order' to the categories of a nominal scale – hence the name. They are very commonly used in social research. To use them, your variable must have some kind of order of magnitude. For example, we could measure wealth with the scale 'poor = 1, average = 2, rich = 3'. This variable clearly has some kind of order, but what is the difference between 1 and 2, or 2 and 3? In this case we can't really tell, other than the fact that 'rich' is more wealthy than 'poor' and 'average', but we have no way of telling how much, or whether the difference between 'rich' and 'average' is the same as between 'average' and 'poor'. Ordinal rules do, however, let us take the median – or the middle value – since the order of numbers does make some sense. The property of order also allows us to use ranking techniques on the data – which opens up a whole range of statistical tests (covered in later chapters). We still can't take the mean though, since the gaps between the numbers in an ordinal scale have no meaning. But remember, to use an ordinal scale, your attribute must posses the order of magnitude quality – wealth does have order, gender does not.

Interval scales

Interval scales add a consideration of the 'interval' between the numeric values to ordinal rules. A classic example of an interval scale is that of the Celsius temperature scale. For example, the difference between 10 and 20 degrees C is the same as the difference between 30 and 40. In other words – the *gaps between the numbers* finally represent something. This has major implications for interval rules, because at last we are able to take the mean of an interval scale, which opens up huge vistas of statistical testing, which you'll be delighted to know are coming up in a few chapters. Because the leap in usefulness between ordinal and interval rules is so big, social scientists are very keen to argue that their scales are interval at least. However, it's not always as simple as all that. You must be able to argue that the difference between the points of your scale is equal across the whole range of the scale. When we measure temperature in Celsius this is easy, but when we measure say self-esteem on a 5-point 'Likert-type' scale such as that shown in Figure 6.3, it's arguable at best. My advice here is to consult some additional sources (like those at the end of this chapter) and come to your own conclusions about this issue. In most practical situations, however, researchers tend to go with the assumption that such scales are interval, unless it is very obvious that the gaps are not equidistant.

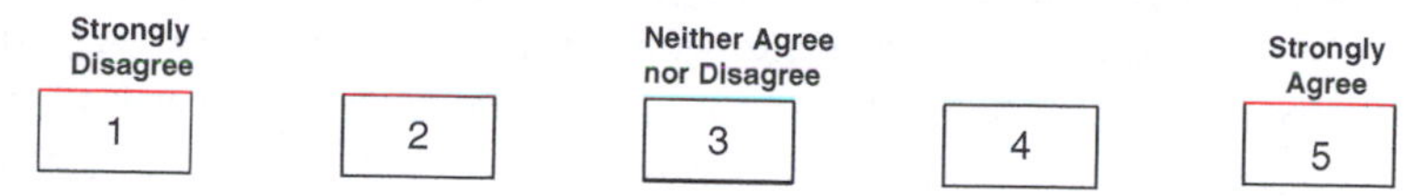

Figure 6.3 A 5-point Likert-type scale

Ratio scales

Finally, we come to ratio scales. Ratio scales have all the properties of interval scales plus the idea of an absolute zero. For example, what does zero in the Celsius scale mean? It doesn't mean 'no temperature', it means 'water freezes'. It's certainly possible to get colder than this. A ratio scale of temperature would have a zero which occurred at the complete absence of temperature. In fact, this is termed the 'Kelvin' scale of temperature, where 0 K is the coldest temperature possible (for fact fans, that's –273.15 degrees Celsius). In order to use a ratio scale, your quality or attribute must possess an absolute zero; attributes such as age, wealth, and company sales do so, but it's harder to argue that many psychological attributes do. The advantages of the ratio scale over the interval one to social scientists are not as great as the advantages of interval over ordinal though. You can perform proportional transformations (feet to centimetres, for example), and you can take the geometric and harmonic means of the variable. And anyone who finds a use for the latter should drop me a line.[5]

There are a few things to remember about scaling which are quite important. Firstly, remember that the attribute you are measuring determines the most powerful scale you can use (remember, I defined 'power' at the beginning of this section). Gender possesses no order, therefore you can only use a nominal scale. Self-esteem does possess order, and it is probably continuous, therefore you could divide it up into equally spaced intervals and use an interval scale. Or you could use an ordinal scale if you weren't confident in designing equal intervals. Company sales has an absolute zero, therefore you could use a ratio scale if you wanted, or you could use interval or ordinal if you would rather. Why would you use a less powerful scale? Well it's usually the case that more powerful scales are harder for respondents to fill in, and sometimes you just don't need that extra information. The extra information you get from a ratio scale is not often going to be that important, compared with the information you could get anyway from an interval scale. This also suggests a need to understand what you are going to do with your data *before* you collect it! You'll be glad you paid attention to that sentence one day in the future, trust me!

---

[5]Well, I am being facetious here. The geometric and harmonic means are used in a number of situations, it's just that *I* haven't had a use for them so far.

What is a 'construct'?

I have to apologise, for that last section on scales was somewhat dry, I hope you haven't given up on me. Nonetheless, those ideas are pretty important because they show us how we govern measurement using rules with which to assign numbers to measures of attributes. This section also covers that, but in a slightly different way. What I'm interested in here is rules which show us how we should assign measures to the sort of unobservable concepts social scientists like us are usually interested in, such as motivation, attitudes, and the like. Theoretically speaking, it's the key section of the chapter. So pay attention.

Remember above, when I talked about measuring things like motivation and IQ, which we couldn't actually observe, and therefore couldn't measure directly (say by putting a measuring device next to them)? Well, unfortunately these sorts of things appear to be the ideas which most interest us in the organisational and social sciences. If you go and read almost any article in a relevant journal, you'll find that it will usually be concerned with the relationships between **unobservable**, also called **latent**, **constructs**. We call these things latent or unobservable precisely because we cannot see them directly. We call them 'constructs' because they are exactly that – they are *constructed* within the minds of researchers because they appear likely to be a useful explanatory device in some theory which is being examined. What do I mean here? Well I think a little history will help (sound familiar yet?)

The idea of constructs can probably best be traced back to psychological research in the early part of the 20th century. At this point psychological researchers were developing many theories with which to explain human behaviours, or *why* people do certain things. Now of course, the only thing we can directly measure is the behaviour itself, but this does not often help explain why it happened. Theoretical psychologists looked to explain why behaviours occurred, by constructing hypothetical variables such as 'motivation', which were theorised to influence your performance of some behaviour. Figure 6.4 shows this idea in diagrammatic form. What you have here is a latent, unobservable construct of 'motivation', which is considered to influence a number of behavioural consequences, which we *can* observe. Also, have a glance at Alternative View 6.1 for a brief picture of the debates which went on at this time.

Alternative View 6.1: Are Constructs 'Real'?

During the early part of the 20th century, you will remember that the positivist/empiricist philosophy was having a large impact on science, and psychology was no exception. Factor analysis (you'll hear about this later) was being developed as well, and statistically inclined psychologists were using this to explore whether underlying concepts could explain our behaviour. Some of this work still influences psychology today. At the same time, psychoanalysts were explaining behaviour using concepts such as *libido*, *ego*, and *superego*.

Empiricist psychologists were vocal on the subject that nothing which is not directly measurable can exist, and that entities must be reducible to empirical equations in order to have value (this position is called **operationalism** which you'll also briefly hear about at the beginning of the next chapter). However, other theoretical psychologists argued that certain constructs could never be reduced simply to observed data. Much of this debate is summarised and explored in MacCorquodale and Meehl's (1948) brilliant (but difficult for the beginner) paper in the *Psychological Review*, which argues that unobservable constructs can indeed be `real', even though they are not directly observable. Nevertheless, they make the point that no unobservable construct should specify something which is `impossible' in light of what we already know. For example, libido could be considered as a term for a set of sexual needs – which is the type of construct which is indeed reducible to empirical observation (e.g. need1 + need2...). However, one could *not* specify an unobservable construct of libido as some kind of liquid which `flows', or becomes `dammed' (as was being implied by psychoanalysts at the time), since existing knowledge of physiology suggested that the nervous system did not consist of a set of tubes with various liquids in them (see MacCorquodale and Meehl, 1948).

So it is quite acceptable to think of constructs as `real', even though we can not observe them directly, but we must be careful as to exactly what properties we specify our constructs as having.

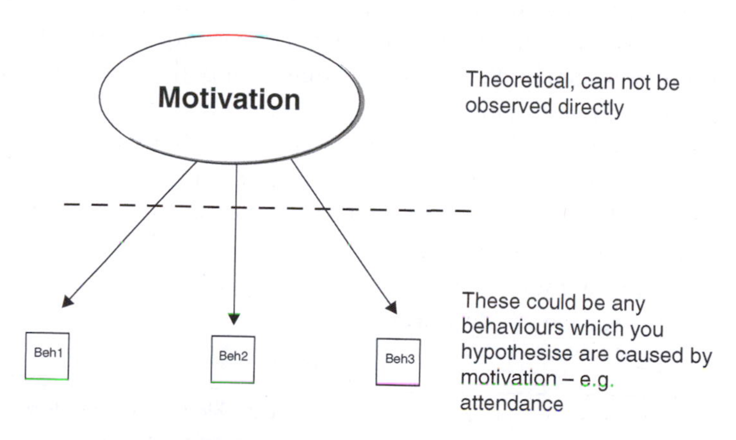

Figure 6.4 Hypothetical construct

The idea of unobservable variables – essentially 'inside our minds'[6] – which have observable impacts, quickly caught on in the social sciences. Much of this had to do with Nunnally's (1967) seminal book on the theory of how to measure these concepts. But even more so, the idea of constructs is extremely appealing to most social researchers, since we are ultimately looking to explain why things happen, yet we can't see inside the mind of individuals. However, instead of using actual behaviours as observable items, researchers now commonly use questions or statements on a questionnaire. You've probably already come across many such measures (sometimes they are called 'multi-item scales' or just 'scales') in your work. While the theory is called 'psychometric' theory, and was originally used to measure psychological constructs, it has also caught on as a way of measuring organisational variables and the like, such as a firm's 'market orientation'. Although I don't want to start a debate on the rights and wrongs of this, I do want to clearly make the point that theories of latent constructs were originally designed solely to measure unobservable psychological factors.

Concepts and constructs

All of the previous theory in this chapter has been building up to this small section. We've been talking about the basics of measurement, and then trying to transfer those concepts to the situation which is most common in social research – measuring unobservable concepts. This section will explicitly define exactly what such unobservable concepts actually are, and give you a consistent language to use for the next chapter, where we talk about the practicalities of developing measures of such concepts, and also hopefully when you conduct your own research. It's important to clarify a set of terms, or language for these purposes, because there are all kinds of terms bandied around in the literature, which tends to confuse things somewhat. This section therefore puts a little cap on the theory presented so far. Firstly, let's define the term **concept** as meaning a general idea in our heads about a variable which has a part to play in one of our theories about human behaviour, organisational performance, or whatever it is we are interested in. For example, I might think that an employee's satisfaction with their job will have an important influence on their absenteeism. But then I need to ask myself; 'just *what is* this concept of satisfaction with one's job?' It is when I start putting words to that concept, and defining what it means, that I *construct* its meaning within the framework of my theory, and also therefore within the wider context of other relevant theories. I will also give this concept a more formal name – say 'job satisfaction'. The concept is no longer a vague idea, but it is now more formally defined, i.e. 'job satisfaction' means something consistent and specific, it is now a **construct**.

---

[6]Note I said minds not brains – if these variables are simply reducible to brain signals then we will be able eventually to directly measure them with new technology. The *mind*, however, now that is a more interesting concept!

Interestingly, some theorists don't make the distinction between concept and construct, considering them to be pretty much the same thing (e.g. Bryman, 2004). However, I like to clearly separate out the vague ideas we have in our heads about things (concepts) from the more formalised definitions of them (constructs). Perhaps this is because I tend to walk around this world with my head full of vague ideas which need defining, but I think its valuable to delineate between mere 'ideas' and the things that are actually components of our theories. I base my distinction on a great example that my Ph.D. supervisor once gave me; you can think of a concept as sort of like an invisible idea in the air in front of you – you basically know what it is, and that it's 'there', but you can't really pin it down – nor can you explain it to anyone else. However, what you could do was throw a tin of paint in the air, and it would cover the concept and make it visible, and it then becomes easy to see and describe. The concept becomes a *construct*. Think of the paint as the words you use to pin down the concept and make it easy to see, and so others can see the same thing as you.[7]

Anyway, once we have a construct, everyone knows what we are talking about, and also how it relates to existing work in the area. Because of this, *the construct definition process is the most important step in measure development.* Get this right, and the rest will almost always work out (if you do it properly). In fact assuming the data and technical side are OK, I can usually trace almost all problems with measures 'not working' back to a flawed construct definition and conceptualisation process. Most commonly, researchers do a poor job of working out just where their construct differs from other already existing constructs, or whether there are separate and distinct aspects of the construct which need to be treated separately. In fact, we'll take a special look at the latter aspect in the next section. This doesn't just apply to constructs you develop, but existing ones as well – most of the problems you'll find with existing constructs and measures are because they were defined and conceptualised poorly, and the next chapter will provide some good advice as to how you might avoid such things.

A note on dimensionality

As a final note on the idea of construct definition, I think it's important to talk about an issue in the construct definition process which you will almost definitely have to grapple with in some way, be it for your own new constructs, or evaluating other people's. This is the issue of **dimensionality**. Or more specifically, **multidimensionality**. I'll say more about the technical side of dimensionality in the next chapter on developing measures of constructs, but here I want to talk about it in a more theoretical sense.

When you are developing a construct definition, you often come up against the idea that your construct is actually very complex. And the more you think about it, the more

[7]Credit of course goes to Prof. John Cadogan for this example.

complex it seems. As an example, think about the concept of 'job satisfaction'; what does it really mean? It could be argued that it is in fact made up of many different aspects, such as 'satisfaction with working conditions', 'satisfaction with management style', 'satisfaction with promotion prospects' and many others. Your first decision in this case is to be absolutely certain in what you are interested in, and what job satisfaction really is. If you continue to think all these aspects are important (and it seems that many people do tend to think in this way when they define constructs), what often happens is that you will tend to say 'job satisfaction is multidimensional, and I need to measure all these dimensions and combine them'. Before I go further, I would just like to say that *this almost never works well in a technical sense*. In my experience most multidimensional scales have major problems when they are being developed. But this is by-the-by, I want to talk in conceptual terms. There are plenty of good articles on the technical side (e.g. Law *et al.*, 1998), but not much on the conceptual side.

Conceptually, there are three ways of representing a construct, such as job satisfaction which you have decided has multiple 'aspects'. They are shown in Figure 6.5a–c: 6.5a shows an individual item capturing each aspect, 6.5b shows a classic 'multidimensional' measure, and 6.5c shows each dimension represented as a completely separate construct. My personal feeling is that most of the time what people decide to represent as multidimensional constructs could much more effectively be represented by separate constructs for each dimension. However, for some reason, students (and researchers in general) appear to be very easily seduced by the multidimensional model. Who knows why? Maybe it just looks cooler? And of course, everyone knows a cool-looking model is half the battle (I wish I were joking).

Although there is not much theory available on how you should choose which model (a–c) to use, I as usual have a few thoughts. Firstly, Model a should be your primary one, which you should find conceptual reasons to reject. For example, when you think in more depth and you decide the construct which you thought was just one 'thing' actually has multiple aspects, you will need to decide between b and c. One thing you should think about is the relationship between your 'second order' construct, and the 'first-order' dimensions. Specifically, what does the 'second-order' construct actually mean? According to model b[8] morale is a 'real' thing, which influences the dimensions' occurrence. The dimensions also can not occur independently of each other since they are caused by the same common source, so we are expecting them to be intercorrelated in some way. As the second-order factor increases or decreases, the first-order ones must necessarily also move. Can your theory support these assertions? Most of the time it cannot! If not, you can look for other models of multidimensional constructs (e.g. Law *et al.*, 1998), or you could consider the dimensions as

[8]There are other models which are covered in the references I have given, but this one is a good illustration, and my point here still stands as key. Furthermore, this model is the one implicitly used by most researchers when they create multidimensional constructs.

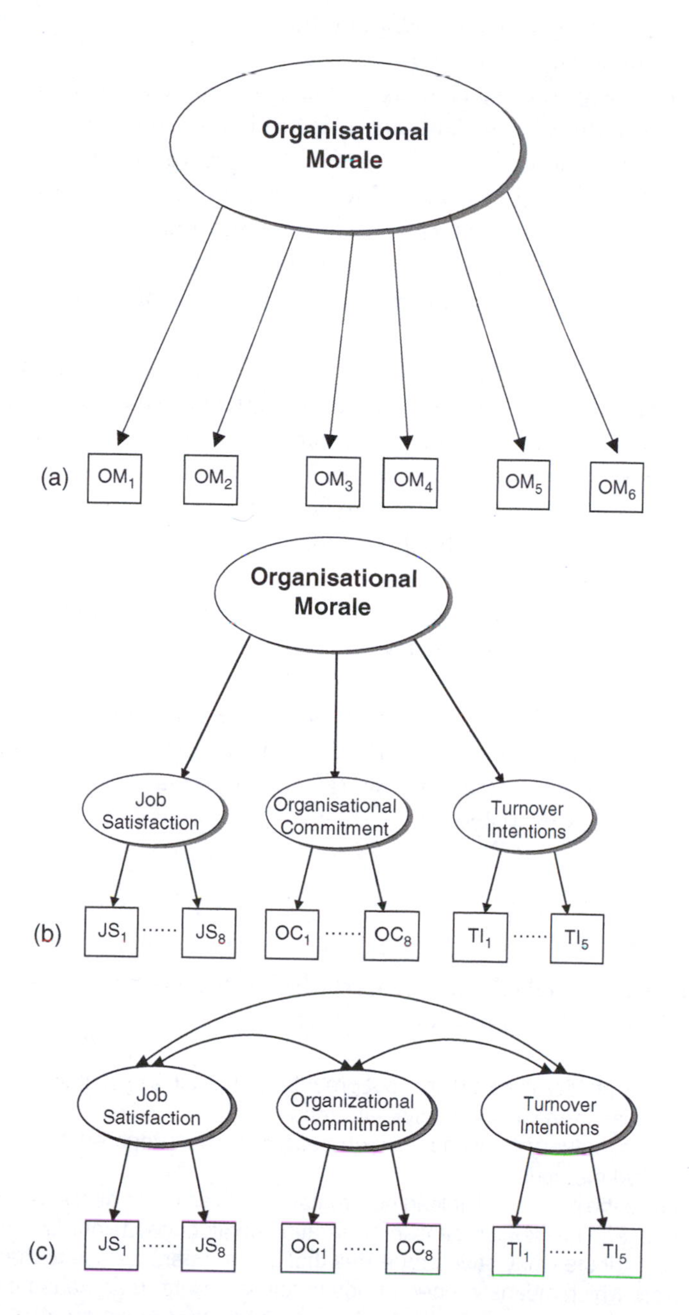

Figure 6.5 (a) A single construct; (b) A multidimensional measure; (c) Three separate constructs

separate constructs (6.5c) since you could argue they have their own conceptual 'meaning' and deserve to be individual constructs.

The other common issue (I hesitate to say mistake, because it is very common and I can see that it's easy to slip into this way of thinking) is that individual relationships are hypothesised from each dimension to various consequences. For example, thinking about Figure 6.5b, one could hypothesise that 'job satisfaction' influences citizenship behaviours, while 'turnover intentions' cause absenteeism, and 'morale' influences performance. If you find yourself doing this, it is almost always a good sign that you should be going with model 6.5c rather than b. Why? Well it seems to me logically difficult to argue that individual dimensions can have their own relationships with consequences according to model 6.5b. For example, if second-order morale influences all dimensions (which it should) then how can one dimension but not another have an individual influence on a consequence? And how can the dimensions have different influences than the main construct? Remember, the dimensions are merely aspects of the construct, *not constructs in their own right*. It's like saying that individual manifest items used to measure a construct can have relationships with consequences. This kind of thinking is normally indicative that the dimensions are in fact separate constructs, with their own relationships.

Now, it should be clear that this section is not a set of rules regarding multidimensionality. Better thinkers than me have grappled with this issue. And besides, there is a lot more thinking to be done here. What I want you to do is take this section as a set of tools to help you *think* about dimensionality, and a caution to be very careful what you want to do, because I commonly see problems where Ph.D. students (for example) have conceptualised multidimensional constructs that do not work well after they have collected their data – causing endless difficulties in analysis.

Summary

As this chapter is critically linked with the next, there's not much point in summarising now, but some key points to take from this chapter are:

- Measurement as an idea is an old one, but probably not as old as you think, and the formalisation and study of measurement is actually quite recent.
- Measurement is actually evolving as you read this, be prepared to keep modifying your assumptions and methods.
- Measurement is the process of linking numerical quantities to the attributes we want to examine in our theories, and is a key process in generating confidence in your findings.
- However, the attributes may have properties that the numbers we use to measure them do not, and vice versa, which means we need rules to tell us how to treat measurement.
- There are many key assumptions and rules which tell us how we are able to link numbers to the attributes we want to measure. Scales of measurement are one such set of rules, which tell us how we can manipulate the numbers we have used to measure an attribute.

- In a social science context, we are usually concerned with the *indirect* measurement of *latent constructs*. Constructs are formal definitions of ideas we have in our minds about key concepts which make up our theories.
- Construct definition is extremely important, and it will be one of the major influences on the success of your research.

Further reading

- *Measurement: Theory and Practice* by David Hand: This is a great book on measurement in general. It's not really a textbook or instruction manual, but more of an overview of measurement from its beginnings to the current state-of-the-art. I think it's absolutely fascinating and very useful. It will definitely help you understand the importance of measurement, and the theory and philosophy behind it.
- *Conceptualization and Measurement in the Social Sciences* by Hubert M. Blalock: One of the key texts on defining constructs – especially the first two chapters. It doesn't often get read too much these days but I think it is still highly relevant for all researchers who wish to measure 'stuff' somehow.
- *Measuring the Mind* by Denny Borsboom: You should remember Professor Borsboom from the start of this chapter. Once you have got the hang of the theory I've introduced here, you should go on to this book, which is a really excellent consideration of measuring latent constructs in psychology.

There are also a number of great journal articles which have appeared over the last 50 or 60 years on constructs and the like, such as:

- Bagozzi, Richard P. and Edwards, Jeffrey R. (1998) A general approach for representing constructs in organisational research, *Organisational Research Methods* 1 (1): 45–87.
- Bollen, Kenneth A. (2002) Latent variables in psychology and the social sciences. *Annual Review of Psychology* 53: 605–634.
- MacCorquodale Kenneth and Meehl, Paul E. (1948) 'On a distinction between hypothetical constructs and intervening variables,' *Psychological Review* 55: 95–107.

EXERCISES

1. What is measurement?
2. Think about the last time measurement caused some kind of problem or confusion to you in everyday life. What was it? Why did this confusion arise? Can you relate it to any of the concepts in this chapter?
3. Thinking now about scales of measurement (remember – NOIR), explain the most powerful scale which can be used to measure the following attributes and why:

    a. Market share
    b. Motivation
    c. Country of birth
    d. Attraction
    e. Relationship quality

4. In fact, if you have some time, why don't you try to define a construct of relationship quality from the existing literature?[9]
5. Is measurement as discussed in this chapter incompatible with any of the various schools of thought explored in Chapter 3? Why?
6. Finally, don't you think you should get out into the fresh air and enjoy yourself a little?

---

[9]Not as easy as you thought was it?

Chapter 7

The process of measure development

SUPERVISOR'S VIEW: PROFESSOR JOHN CADOGAN

Like many academics, I first experienced the joys of measure development during my Ph.D. In fact, a major contribution of my Doctoral work was the development of a new measurement scale to capture 'export market orientation'. Strange as it sounds, the process really was good fun, and I enjoyed it.

It relies on you being able to develop one or more 'item banks' (basically, bunches of questions that will constitute the new measures). You do this using a variety of sources, including your own imagination, other published scales, and qualitative enquiry, perhaps by speaking to potential respondents for clues. At this stage, there is a strong element of creativity involved in the process. You have to develop the wording carefully to ensure that the meaning of the questions is just right, that you nuance things so that you direct people to provide the right kind of information. Consequently, the initial stages of the measure development process are certainly more art than science. I remember thinking that perhaps I was going over the top, developing item banks that were far too large: 'How would I fit all these questions on a questionnaire? Wouldn't it be too long and too repetitive?' I needn't have worried. Some students find this part of the measure development process easy (perhaps because it involves playing with words, not numbers) and dread the bit that will follow (because that involves 'doing statistics').

And yes, once you've created the questionnaire, and collected the data, you get to spend hours and hours poring over descriptive statistics (e.g., means and variances), correlation tables, factor analysis tables and reliability analysis tables. The thing is, you are looking for elegant solutions to measure development problems – and when you get it right, exploratory factor analysis can produce tabular outputs that show off these solutions quite nicely. Likewise, confirmatory factor analysis packages can produce path diagrams that look quite impressive. So you find yourself proudly showing off your 'elegant' factor analysis results to fellow students and family members (who usually put up with you the first few times). It is also at this stage that it begins to dawn on most novice measure developers that it would have been useful if they had made their item banks even bigger. About now, when measures have started to emerge, I tend to find that students who were once nervous of 'statistics' begin to blossom. Statistical approaches that once were unfathomable, and statistical language that once was gibberish, are both used freely. The students have unknowingly become statisticians.

VIEW FROM THE TRENCHES: DR AARTI SOOD

Developing a measure can be extremely tempting and, almost, exciting – as it virtually guarantees that your Ph.D. will make a significant contribution. However, it is vital for you to understand exactly what you are trying to measure before you embark upon this process, otherwise it can be an extremely stressful and time-wasting experience. It sounds obvious but you can only measure something once you know exactly what it is that you are trying to measure. Thus, take you time when specifying and defining your construct as it is arguably the most important step. A starting point for me was to look at how previous researchers had operationalised constructs that were similar to what I wanted to develop a measure for. This not only helped me define my construct but was also useful for generating an initial pool of items for my measure as well.

Although adding to your item pool, as there is some debate in the literature about this, I think it is a good idea to include negatively worded items at this stage. Hopefully these will go towards strengthening your measure, and giving you one line of defence against the dreaded 'common method bias' criticism. This will prove to be a great plus point for you in your viva! Trust me. Following generation of your item pool, it is extremely important to carefully choose expert judges to evaluate your measure. Remember, you want to end up with a set of items that best reflect the construct you want to measure. Therefore it is preferable to choose experts who are from your area of research. They will also be helpful in assessing any problem items such as ambiguous or double-barrelled items.

If you are in the position to be able to collect a separate set of data to evaluate your measure then that is great and you are very lucky. However, seeing that many of us have both time and financial restrictions, the best piece of advice I can offer you is to **make sure you include a 'back-up' measure in your questionnaire.** What I mean is, include a measure that is the closest to what you want to measure. It is perfectly possible that – even after all the blood, sweat and (yes) tears that have gone into developing your measure – it simply will not work. I say with some understatement (since Nick told me I couldn't swear in this) that this will be frustrating and somewhat depressing, but at least you will have *something* to work with! So, in a nutshell be extremely patient in understanding what you want to measure and ALWAYS include a back-up measure!

The previous chapter dealt with a lot of the foundational ideas about measurement. After reading it you should have a good idea about what measurement actually is, and the types of things social scientists often measure. Also, you should be comfortable with the idea that we need rules to connect our constructs to our measures of them, and tell us how we are able to manipulate those numbers.

This chapter, on the other hand, is where you'll start looking at the theory and practice of actually connecting numbers to your constructs. It's all very well having very elegant and well-defined constructs, but how should you actually go about designing measures of them? It is this part of measurement theory which has received the most attention from scholars in the last 50 years, which has resulted in a proliferation of different ideas and theories about how to construct measures. I'll focus on arguably the most influential of these theories throughout this chapter, but will also introduce some other ideas towards the end. But remember, measurement theories are always evolving, so it pays to keep up with the relevant literature to make sure you are always knowledgeable about current thinking.

Moving on, at the end of this chapter I really hope you have come to terms with these key ideas:

- What an 'auxiliary theory' is, and how it connects real world data to theoretical concepts.
- What validity is, and why it is important.
- 'Psychometric' theory as a key example of auxiliary theory.
- How you should go about developing a measure of a latent construct using the psychometric approach.
- Some examples of alternative theories of measurement, such as Item Response Theory.

Why is it Important to Know This Stuff?

By now I expect you all to understand what measurement is and why we need to measure things. You should also know about latent constructs, and how they are unobservable, even though we need somehow to measure them to transfer them into the real world. You also know that – because constructs are unobservable – it's really important to define your constructs clearly. But what do you do now?

What you need to do is work out how to transfer that theoretical latent construct into real-world measures. We covered the concepts behind that in the last chapter, but now we talk about the technical side of things. This of course then has implications for what the real world results you find (i.e. the 'numbers') mean in relation to the theoretical world concepts you are trying to measure. Figure 7.1 expresses this key idea. Try to think about measurement as a whole in terms of combining Figures 6.1 and 7.1.

Without understanding this key link, between theoretical concepts and real world data (expressed here in terms of measurement) it's no exaggeration to say that you will never really be able to do good research, and you will certainly never be able to measure anything well. If you can't be confident about how you measure your concepts, you will never be able to be confident in what your findings mean for your theory. Needless to say, this is A Bad Thing. How can you conclude your research project if you are unsure of what you have actually found? For example, if your theory argues that compliments from the manager influence employee self-esteem, you are unable to find any support for this theory unless you are confident you have measured self-esteem correctly.

Thus (and I don't want to labour the point), without good measurement, no one can ever take your findings seriously; not your supervisor, your colleagues, journal reviewers, or even yourself.

I think that makes it pretty important.

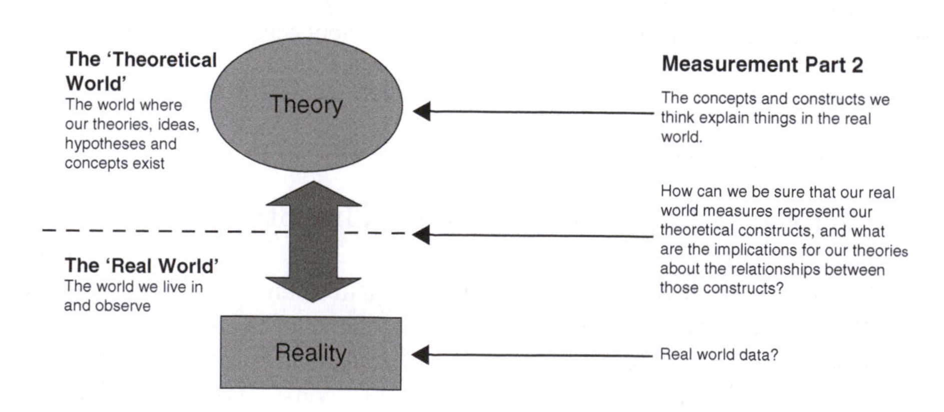

Figure 7.1 The importance of measurement, part II

Moving from the theoretical to the real world

In the previous chapter, we talked a lot about what constructs were, and how to define them. That said, however well you describe your construct, you should be aware that it is still only *theoretical*, that is it is located in what we've so far called the 'theoretical world'. In other words, you have defined something which you think has an important place in a theory of some kind. We've introduced this idea before in the book, when we talked about theory construction and in other places, but until now we've solely been located in the theoretical world. For the purposes of this book, the measurement of latent constructs can be thought of as the process of moving our theoretical constructs into the 'real world' – i.e. collecting data about them.[1] Remember, we can't *see* these constructs, that's why we must 'construct' them! Unfortunately the theoretical world is just that, theoretical. Instead, we live and operate in the real world (well most of us do), and therefore must somehow transfer our constructs into things we can actually work with. Once we work out exactly how we can represent our construct in the real world, we have what can be called an **operational definition**. There are actually multiple theories which propose to explain how we can link real world data to theoretical constructs. Blalock (1982) termed this 'auxiliary theory' to distinguish it from theories which link theoretical constructs to other theoretical constructs. We're usually most interested in the latter theory (which could be called structural theory), but without the auxiliary theory, our real-world measurements may bear no relation to our theoretical world constructs. In case you're *still* wondering, this would be A Bad Thing. Remember back to the previous chapter, when I talked about indirect measurement. No matter how elegant our measure may be numerically, we must still be able to justify *why* it represents the theoretical construct we say it does.

The operational definition is the outward manifestation of our auxiliary theory. It defines exactly what in the real world we say represents our theoretical construct. I say it is a manifestation of the auxiliary theory because (whether you realise it or not) it rests upon some idea or theory of how to connect real-world data to theoretical world latent constructs. The auxiliary theory I have been implicitly referring to so far, and will continue to do so for the most part, is called 'psychometric' theory,[2] which was mentioned in the previous chapter (take a refresher look at Figures 6.2 and 6.4 as well), and it developed from the roots introduced in Alternative View 6.1 in the previous chapter.

[1]You'll remember from the previous chapter that when we are measuring observable things like height and weight, it pays to think about measurement as moving them on to a more abstract mathematical plane. However, when we talk about measuring latent constructs, it helps to consider measurement as moving our consideration to a more 'real', empirical, world.

[2]You might see it – or parts of it – termed 'classical test theory' sometimes, or even 'domain sampling theory', depending on what other books you read.

However, it's important that you realise this theory is not the only one available, nor is it unquestioned among social scientists. I'll briefly cover some alternatives towards the end of the chapter. Nevertheless, it is very widely used in the social sciences, and provides a solid base from which to work. Indeed, most alternative theories have psychometrics as their fundamental roots – even if it is only as something to react against.

Although a full discussion of psychometric theory is outside the scope of this book (some good references are given at the end of the chapter), it is appropriate to cover some key points. Firstly, psychometrics makes the underlying assumption that latent constructs actually exist, but are unobservable. This is kind of a weird idea, but it is quite intuitive to most of us that a construct like 'motivation' actually exists somehow, so let's just go with it for now. Of course, those who were paying attention earlier will note that this must therefore be a realist sort of theory, rather than an empiricist or positivist theory (if you're unsure why, go back and hit Chapter 2 again).

The next key thing is that psychometric theory makes the assumption that the 'real' thing, which we call a construct, influences some things which we can actually observe. We could argue, for example, that university students' motivation influences their classroom attendance (see Figure 6.2). We therefore could take attendance as a manifest or observable **indicator** of the unobservable motivation construct. However, this kind of indicator would have some problems. For example, your attendance may be influenced by many things other than motivation – such as your health, the weather, the traffic, your alcohol consumption the night before and all kinds of other things. Thus, should I take low attendance levels as indicating low levels of motivation, or that the traffic on the way to school was heavier? A good indicator should be influenced primarily by the construct we are trying to measure, not anything else. Furthermore, attendance would need to be recorded by actual physical observation at the time, so what if I can't be there then? Instead of using that type of measuring instrument, we should think of something which is a little easier to administer if possible. Whereas there are many different ways of doing this, what normally happens is that we define a *set of multiple questions* which can be filled out on a questionnaire, varying answers to which we argue are directly caused by the level of motivation of a student. One example could be asking a student their level of agreement with the statement 'I attend class because I enjoy it', or something like that. IDE 7.1 shows how in my Doctoral research, I moved from theoretical construct to a set of manifest indicators for the construct 'sales manager caring'. We use multiple indicators (rather than just asking a single question) for many reasons. Arguably the most important reason is that we can get an idea of how 'well' the indicators represent a common construct (which they should) by examining their inter-correlations. On a more practical level, multiple items 'average out' errors by respondents, and allow us to capture more of the full 'meaning' of the construct in our measure.

IDE 7.1: Developing the Construct of Sales Manager Caring

After extensive qualitative research, the construct of sales manager caring was defined as concerning **the degree to which sales managers invest *emotional* and *affective* resources into the social process of problem resolution**.

From here, it was decided to measure the construct by tapping the perceptions of salespeople – the subject of the caring, rather than those who were displaying the caring. Conceptually speaking, this was because it was felt that caring was a construct which at its heart was concerned with the subject, and that the giver may have inaccurate estimations of how they were perceived by the subject of their activities. For example, you may think you are being very caring to a friend, but they in fact may not think that at all.

The construct was operationalised by way of a number of items which were given to salespeople. Salespeople were asked to rate how strongly they agreed with the items on a 1–5 scale, which is displayed in Figure 6.3 in the previous chapter.

The original set of items numbered 13; after the process detailed in Figure 7.2, the items finally settled upon (presented here in shortened form) included items such as:

Manager is friendly
Manager is empathetic
Manager can put himself in others' shoes
Manager is something of a counsellor

So, moving to a slightly wider frame of reference, the term **operational definition** can be thought of as referring to exactly what manner in which we mean to measure the construct. In other words, referring to IDE 7.1, the operational definition of sales manager caring concerns the items, but also how they are used to create the final measure. Are they summed? Averaged? Or something more complicated? If you think back to the early sections of Chapter 6, we are in the general area of rules of concatenation here. At this point, dealing with actual numbers, we are now fully in the real world, and must be extremely careful not to lose touch with what we really want to do – that is look at relationships between constructs in the theoretical world. Interestingly, as a side note, the term operational definition has been co-opted from an empiricist auxiliary theory called *operationalism*. According to this theory, a construct is nothing more than its measurement (see Alternative View 6.1 in the previous chapter). This throws psychometrics into nice relief, being as psychometrics defines the latent construct to be something independent of its measurement – with the items merely being caused by the latent construct. Operationalism has been generally discredited, so I won't

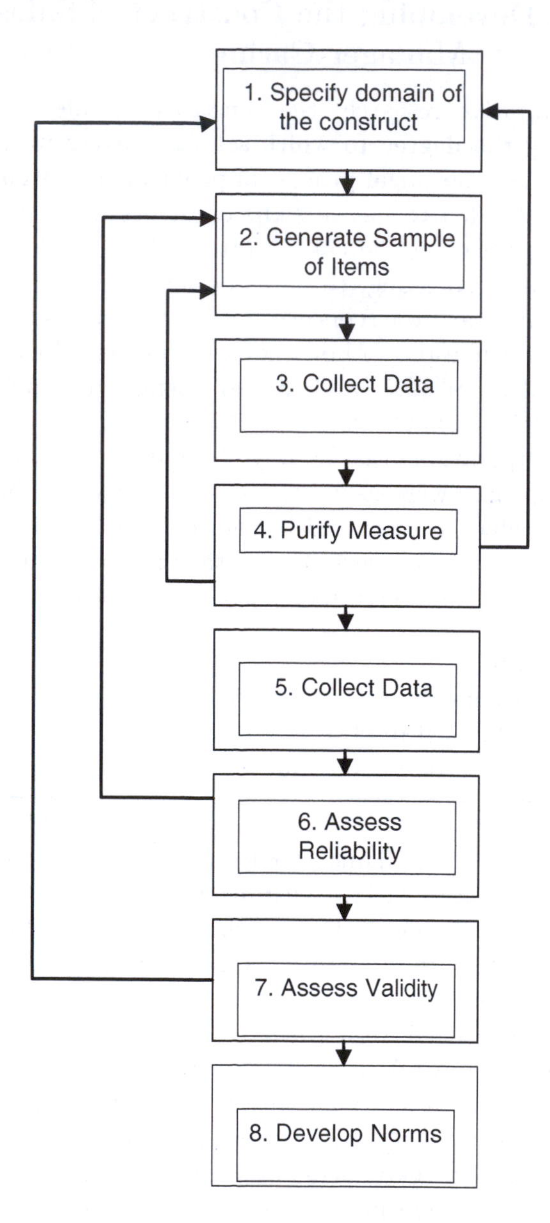

Figure 7.2 A traditional process of measure development
Source: Lee and Hooley (2005), adapted from Churchill (1979).

spend any more time on it right now, but it is probably worth your keeping it in mind, even if it is just as a counterpoint to other theories.

Developing a measure

This section is designed to give you a brief introduction to the process of developing a new measure for an unobservable construct, according to what could be called 'traditional' theory (i.e. psychometric). Of course, it is impossible within the context of such a book to give you fine details of the process – and in fact there are many great books on the subject which will be referenced throughout. Use this section as an overview, a basic source from which you can go into more detail when required using other sources. Figure 7.2 shows a diagram of this process, which I will use to structure the following discussion. What can be seen here is that the process is a technical one – in that you are assumed to understand the relevant auxiliary theory prior to beginning, which should drive how you do the stages. Unfortunately, many have and continue to use such models as this without thinking about the theory of measurement (see Lee and Hooley, 2005 for a discussion of this).

We've already talked a lot about the first stage; *specify the domain of the construct*, so I won't repeat myself other than to say it is arguably the most important stage, so please take note of the earlier discussions in Chapter 6. Once you've done this, you must develop indicators from which to make up your measure. Remember that earlier, I briefly mentioned that you generally need to use multiple items to measure a latent construct? Well these items have to come from somewhere! There are many sources of items, such as existing theory and academic experts. However, it is also common to use qualitative exploratory research to discover key aspects of constructs which you can use to develop items from – like interviews, focus groups, observations, etc. For example, you might want to interview managers and employees in a wide variety of contexts in order to develop items about a type of leadership. Of course, you don't simply ask your respondents 'so, how should I measure leadership then?' It's a little more complicated than that. Chapters 9 and 10 are good introductions to qualitative research, but on a very basic level getting respondents to relate key stories and incidents which relate to leadership, and just talk about their feelings, observations and opinions on leadership is a great start. You could also spend some time within an organisation, observing how managers lead their employees, and how employees react to that. Reviewing the existing literature on leadership is also a great way of developing items. What you normally get from this process is a large set of items, which may or may not be good measures of your construct. This is a good thing, because the rest of the process is essentially one of reducing that large pool to the smaller set of 'best' indicators of your construct, through a number of stages.

The first thing I like to do is 'ask the experts'. Basically, what I mean here is to find a bunch of academic experts in your area (say six or seven professors and lecturers who know a bit about the field you are working in) and ask them to look at your items to see if they think they could represent the relevant construct. I use a worksheet which contains the construct definitions, and a table where the experts can rate how well they think a given indicator represents a given construct. Usually, you are developing more than one measure, so the experts should do them all at the same time which means they can compare how well each item measures different constructs. You can see part of such a worksheet in Figure 7.3, which I actually designed for my Doctoral work. If you are developing only a single measure, it might be an idea to include 'dummy' items which you *don't* think measure the construct, to check whether your experts are paying attention. Interestingly, I tend to find that this process is nearly as accurate as statistical procedures in detecting 'good' or 'bad' items.

Once you've done this, you'll find a few of your items are clearly poor indicators, so drop them from your consideration. For example if you look at Figure 7.3, I found that some of the items which I thought were pretty clear indicators of 'aggressiveness' were actually rated as indicators of 'responsiveness'. Now, although you might think your 'experts' either made some mistakes, or are simply stupid, this is not often the case. In fact it's more likely that things

Sales Person Item Bank:

Please place a number (1–5) in the relevant column if you think an item relates to that construct.

Item	Responsiveness	Aggressiveness	Caring
In general, when a problem needs dealing with, my manager deals with it quickly.			
My manager can often see the reason for a problem, and is very concerned with helping the sales person correct it .			
My manager could be described as 'fiery'.			
My manager doesn't accept excuses for causing problems.			
My manager doesn't seem to have the confidence to take the necessary action to solve a problem.			
My manager doesn't seem to take the initiative when dealing with a problem.			
My manager doesn't waste any time when dealing with a problem.			

Figure 7.3 A section of an expert analysis form

you thought were good indicators in fact weren't. On the other hand, you might find that some items are questionable, for example perhaps one or two experts thought they indicated the 'wrong' construct, but others didn't. I think it's normally best to keep these items at this stage – you can always drop them later. That said, keep an eye on them, and I bet you find they are the first ones to fail subsequent tests. Strictly speaking, we should then go out and collect data to see how good our measure is (stages 3 and 4). However, in a lot of social research we skip to stage 5 for various (usually pragmatic – like time) reasons.[3] What this means is that you move directly to a test of your measure and the theory associated with it – so you do both tests together, using the same data. However, this is frankly poor practice, and we should really collect preliminary data and evaluate the measure before including it in our full questionnaires. Also, if it *is* done, stage 3 often uses student samples. But unless you are looking to measure a general population, or student, sample with your final measure, this is *also* poor practice, and pretty much a waste of time. For example, if your measure is designed to measure sales manager performance – what valid information can a student sample tell you about it? Alternative View 7.1 discusses the relevant issues concerning sampling for measure development. Either way, the technical process of purification in stage 4 is the same as stage 6, so there is no reason to repeat the discussion.

Alternative View 7.1: Sampling in Measure Development

I'll be covering the issue of sampling and representativeness in much more detail in Chapter 11, but it's appropriate here to look at a few key issues. If you look at a lot of psychological research, you'll find that much measure development (essentially stage 3 and 4 of Figure 7.2) is done by collecting data from student samples. For example, I could hand out a set of items to one of my undergraduate classes and get 150 sets of data back, which I could then analyse and purify. Of course, this would be very easy in practical terms. Furthermore, because a lot of organisational researchers have psychology backgrounds, you can also find quite a lot of this practice throughout organisational research.

Nevertheless the question must be asked as to whether this is in fact good practice. Any potential criticism is based around the idea that students may be inappropriate because they have little knowledge of the construct in question. For example, if you wish to develop a measure of salesperson role conflict, students are essentially unable to answer questions on such a construct from a position of knowledge. In such cases

[3] That said, some fields have more tradition of using the 'full' process, such as psychology, and this is unarguably a superior and more rigorous methodology.

they will either not answer or simply put random answers down. This is likely to lead to biased data and thus any statistical purification you do will be meaningless. Any measure development for such constructs (which most organisational research uses) must be done on a sample of the intended final population – one reason which separate measure development samples are not often taken in organisational research.

However, if you are developing a measure designed to be used on a general population – such as self-esteem or many other general psychological characteristics – students may be just as good as any other segment of the population. In such a case, you need to consider whether students may be systematically different from other groups of the population, and whether this may influence your data. If not, there is little reason to avoid student samples in measure development. The issue of using student samples in organisational research is covered in a general sense by Calder *et al.* (1982) in their interesting paper, which will be discussed in more depth in Chapter 11, and this has plenty of implications in the present context too.

If we aren't taking a separate measure development sample (which we really *should*), what normally happens is that after the expert analysis stage, we include the measure in a questionnaire with all the other measures we are using to test our theoretical model (see Chapter 5 for more discussion of models). We then send out the sample and wait with bated breath for it to return (see Chapter 11 for information on collecting quantitative data).

After the few weeks of stress about whether you will ever get enough responses, and the inevitable panic when none arrive in the first week, you'll probably end up with a bunch of responses. How many responses you need is an interesting question, most authors recommend that you need around 150–250 responses to be confident in any measure development activity. There are many reasons for this, though. Firstly, many of the analysis techniques we need to use to assess the measure rely on large samples for confidence in their findings (you'll learn more about this in Chapters 13 and 14). The more items you have in your measures, the more responses you will need of course. This is a key consideration. Also, the larger your sample, the more confident you can be that it is not overly influenced by chance fluctuations, such as over-large representation of small sub-groups. Once you have your data, you can then spend a long and boring week entering them into your analysis package of choice (although I discuss software in Chapter 13, since no one is paying me, I won't recommend one way or the other!). Now you have some data, and you should do some preliminary analysis along the lines of that discussed in Chapter 13 – i.e. cleaning your data, and descriptive analysis.

Moving on, we usually at this stage want to assess the 'quality' of our measurement. This process is usually concerned with assessing the *reliability* and *validity* of our measures.

Validity is covered in the next section, but reliability basically refers to how consistent your measurement is. For example, if you were to measure the same person twice, one week apart, would the measurement be pretty much the same (assuming their level of the latent construct remained the same)? If not, then it could be argued that the measure captures some kind of random error rather than what you want it to catch. The difference between reliability and validity can be summed up by the classic example of the faulty measuring scales which weigh every person 5 kg too heavy (nightmare, I know). These scales always give a weight which is exactly 5 kg too heavy, so they are reliable in that they are consistent and not randomly incorrect. However, they are not valid as they do not give the 'correct' measurement. For something like weight and height this is easy to understand and discover, because there are pre-existing standards of weight which we can test our measuring instruments against. But what about a latent construct like job satisfaction? It's an altogether more difficult question.

Although there is some debate about how to measure reliability for latent constructs, we usually capture it by measuring the *internal consistency* of the items in our measure. In other words, if all the items are caused by a latent construct, they should also be inter-correlated to some extent. Theoretically speaking, therefore, the less random error there is in our measure, the more inter-correlated our items should be. There are many measures of internal consistency, but the most popular one has been Cronbach's coefficient *alpha* (see DeVellis 1991 for example). Cronbach's alpha essentially measures the proportion of variation within a set of items which can be attributed to some kind of common cause. Theoretically, of course, we think this 'common cause' is our construct, but we have no real proof of that. If you are really unlucky you could be developing a great measure of something completely different! At this point, it's really important that you never lose touch with the fact that you are trying to work out whether your set of items is a good measure of some construct which you defined previously. Never get lost in the statistics to the extent that you forget the construct itself! Going back to Cronbach's alpha, its popularity can probably be attributed to the fact that Nunnally (1967) gave some 'cut-off' values which he suggested indicated reliable measures. And we all know how much researchers love stuff like that. Although this approach has been vastly popular since the 1970s, there have been some concerns, which I would advise you to check out (see Cattell and Kline, 1977; Kline, 2000).

Validity of measures

Validity is an interesting idea, it's essentially the most important characteristic of any measure, yet misconceptions abound about it. It's primarily a conceptual issue, yet we tend to assess it using statistical tools and rules of thumb, some of which actually detract from validity (see Lee and Hooley, 2005). Ultimately, a measure of a construct is valid if it accurately measures the construct (Carmines and Zeller, 1979). But what does this actually mean?

For most situations, in practical terms this means that variation on the latent construct should be accurately captured by the measure. So if my level of 'motivation' is lower than yours, my score on a valid measure of motivation should be lower than yours. The more accurately the measure tracks variation in the construct, the more valid it is. One step further on is to actually map point values of the measure to point values of the construct. For example, what does a score of '4' on a 1–7 scale of motivation mean in terms of your actual level of motivation? This is a whole other issue, but one which we are not often concerned with in theoretical research.[4] Nevertheless, if you are a clinical psychologist, for example, or someone else who uses indirect measures to assess individuals, it will be important to you.

However, as you should be aware, we can never actually measure the latent construct directly – so how do we ascertain whether our indirect measure accurately reflects variation in the true latent construct? This question has occupied the minds of many over the last century. Firstly, in order to be valid, a measure also has to be reliable – which we must also assess (see above). Secondly, we should also realise that we can never get a perfectly valid measure, and even if we did we would never actually know this because we can't see the latent construct. Also, consider that validity is essentially a property of the purpose you are putting your measure to. In other words, a measure of motivation may be a valid measure of an underlying trait of motivation, but not of their work performance. Again, construct definition is highly important here!

There are various different 'types' of validity which have been discussed over the years, of which I will introduce a few. Firstly, *criterion-related* validity is a test of whether your measure accurately estimates or predicts the value of some criterion (it could also be termed *predictive* validity). It really is as simple as that and is actually quite an intuitive concept to most of us. It's very useful when we are looking to develop scales to test individuals (like the psychologist example above). For example, does the GMAT (Graduate Management Admission Test) accurately predict how well an MBA student will perform on the course? Or how well does a pregnancy test predict actual pregnancy? In situations like this, criterion-related validity is of huge importance! The correlation between the measure and the criterion is the only thing relevant to criterion-related validity, and selection and measurement of the criterion is obviously key. Also, this should suggest to you that criterion-related validity is highly empirical, rather than theoretical. However, a limitation is that for most situations in the theoretical social sciences, there is no criterion with which to assess validity. We could assess, say, motivation with the criterion of 'class attendance', but is this really a good criterion? I suppose it may be if we want to measure motivation for the purpose solely of predicting attendance, but this is not often the case in theoretical research. Remember, validity is about

---

[4]This is because theoretical research tends to look at relationships between theoretical constructs, not individual scores on measures. In order to explore the former, we must be confident in how close the variation in a construct maps to the measure, but not the individual point score.

the purpose of the measure, so if we want to measure an underlying latent construct of role ambiguity, or organisational loyalty, criterion-related validity may not be the best approach.

Another type of validity is *content validity*. This is essentially how well a measure represents a specific area of content. Of course, this is bound up with your construct definition. This is easy if you are trying to measure something simple like mathematical ability of nine-year-olds, or in an organisational context something like share price performance. We just work out what the construct consists of, and construct a test which covers all, or a sufficient sample of, these issues (obviously this is a simplification). But what about Self-Esteem? Satisfaction? Relationship Quality? Unfortunately, in the social sciences we rarely have exact and agreed-upon definitions of content for our constructs to draw from. Thus, content validity usually relies on some kind of judgement that we have got the 'right stuff' in our measure, or whether it 'looks right'. In my opinion this process would be better called *face validity*, and is similar to the expert judgement process I talked about earlier. That said, sometimes face and content validity are considered the same. So content validity in this sense is a great idea, but not one which can be rigorously assessed in general (although a dissenting voice will be heard later in this chapter).

Finally, we come to *construct validity*. It is similar to, but should never be confused with, criterion-related validity. Construct validity essentially requires you to specify theoretical relationships between your latent construct and other things which you think are related to it (e.g. antecedents and/or consequences). Sometimes this is called 'nomological' validity (how's that for a word?) Basically, what you do is specify some theoretical hypotheses around your latent construct, and assess these relationships with your data. So if you think motivation will have a positive impact on class participation, you can collect data on both, assess the results of your analysis, and if you find a positive relationship, then a small piece of evidence exists for the validity of your motivation measure. The more elaborate your network of hypotheses, the more rigorous the test of construct validity. Furthermore, the more repeated studies support the predictions, then the stronger the evidence of construct validity. However, we must be pretty confident in our theoretical hypotheses, and in the measures of our other constructs – not to mention the quality of our data and analysis – in order to be confident in the strength of this method of testing.

As you can see, assessing validity for the type of latent constructs we normally want to measure in the social sciences is not an easy task. You should take the previous discussion as a set of pointers from which to investigate the issue of validity in some more depth, as well as to help you in assessing prior work and guiding your own.

Other approaches and models

This section is aimed at giving a very brief flavour of some other models of measurement – or 'auxiliary theories' as they were termed previously – which have developed in the latter part of the 20th century. In general they are adaptations of psychometrics, and were designed to counter specific criticisms of the psychometric model. Although it is beyond the scope of this book to give full details on each theory, I hope to give you an idea of their strengths and how they relate to the general approach given earlier, as well as some directions to shape your future reading. You will then be in a better position to judge how you should measure the constructs in your own research.

Formative and causal models[5]

You should have noticed that the psychometric model we have discussed so far considers variations in the underlying latent construct to cause the variation in the indicators. However, in recent times, social scientists – including many in the organisational and management sciences – have argued that this direction of causality may in fact be reversed in some cases. In other words, it seems that in some cases indicators can be argued to cause the presence of constructs. A classic example (see Diamantopoulos and Winklhofer, 2001 for an excellent introduction) is socioeconomic status (SES). If one considers SES to be a combination of measures like education, income, employment and place of residence, then the presence of these items *causes* your level of SES. If any single item was to change, SES would also change, even if the others remained the same. Variation in the indicators therefore drives variation in the construct. By contrast, the psychometric (called 'reflective' in this type of discussion) model assumes that the indicators are driven by the construct, and thus if the level of the construct changes, then all the indicators must also change. Deciding between formative and reflective models is a conceptual decision based on a number of criteria. Firstly, think about your construct; is it something in existence (although unobservable) which you consider to cause the appearance of certain items (e.g. a personality trait)? If this is the case, your model should be reflective. However, if the individual items are in fact separate components which together cause the existence of the construct (e.g. SES, or Advertising Expenditure), then you should explore the formative model. This decision is becoming more and more important in social science as the formative model becomes more accepted. The downside is technical, it is in fact rather difficult to create and assess formative measures. But this should not stop you if formative measurement is the right conceptual decision.

The C-OAR-SE method

The C-OAR-SE method (it stands for Construct definition, Object classification, Attribute classification, Rater identification, Scale formation, and Enumeration) was developed by Professor John Rossiter (e.g. 2002) as a reaction against what he saw as increasing reliance on the blind application of statistics to the process of measurement. This model does illuminate

[5]Note, there can be argument about whether there is a difference between formative and causal measurement. However, at present the literature seems to treat them as synonymous.

some interesting issues and problems within measure development, and is thus well worth a look. It's certainly been the source of some interesting and fun debates between myself and Professor Rossiter. The C-OAR-SE model is based around the idea that not all constructs can be captured by traditional psychometric, or formative, models, and in fact some do not need to. Instead, C-OAR-SE argues that the only type of validity of use is 'content validity', which can not be assessed statistically, only by agreement of experts on whether or not the measure is valid. While the C-OAR-SE procedure itself is long and involved, it can be summarised by a concern for construct definition (which in fact is similar in spirit at least to what I have said in this, and especially the previous, chapters). However, C-OAR-SE splits construct definition into a number of sections, including the object (e.g. Coca-Cola), the attribute (e.g. quality), and the rater (e.g. consumer). All three of these can vary, implying different models of measurement. Prof. Rossiter considers this to be a rationalist rather than empiricist (which he considers psychometrics to be) theory, in that it relies on judgement not empirical validation. However, it seems to me that it is strongly pragmatist as well.[6] While C-OAR-SE makes some important points, it hasn't really caught on. This is probably because many of the constructs we measure do fit within the psychometric or formative models, and we already have theories which deal with them – and what's more these theories provide us with tools to assess the quality of our measures independent of expert judgement. However, it is unarguable that C-OAR-SE provides a strong critique of existing measurement, and is worth investigating.

Item response theory

Item response theory (IRT) appears superficially very similar to the psychometric model explored in the main part of this chapter. It shares the assumption that items are caused by underlying constructs (although IRT terms them 'latent traits'), but where psychometric theory focuses on the construct level in the main, IRT focuses on the individual properties of the items in more depth. Furthermore, the properties of an individual item are not dependent on the respondent or on the group of items used. This is in contrast to psychometrics, where item properties depend on the group of people who are tested as well as the collection of items themselves. The upshot of this is that IRT allows a more rigorous test of measurement across different groups – e.g. cross-cultural – since the item statistics are independent of the group. In addition, IRT allows one to select items which are most accurate to each individual's ability and level of the latent trait – so conceivably each person could fill in a different test which is customised to most accurately measure their level of the latent trait. The downside of all of this is complexity for one thing. IRT models are much more complex than traditional psychometric models. Also, it has always struck me that for many social science research purposes, customising tests to individual populations is not as important as

---

[6] And of course, as you will know by now, psychometric theory is in fact Realist not Empiricist, but now is not the time to get into that.

being able to send out a consistent 'pretty good' scale to many respondents – for example, on mail-out surveys. So sometimes IRT may be a little impractical. Nevertheless, I think it is definitely worth investigating in situations where you are measuring multiple different sub-groups, testing individuals (such as in a clinical or educational context), or in other face-to-face measurement contexts.

Final words and summary

To cap off the end of my discussion on measurement, which I have to admit has grown somewhat longer than I'd hoped, I just want to make a few notes from my own experience about measurement. These notes are primarily to do with practicalities of measurement, especially where Ph.D. and other dissertations are concerned. First I want to deal with the issue of 'other people's measures'. If you are developing your own measures for new constructs, then you should go through the most thorough process possible – drawing from this chapter. However, for most projects, you will be using measures which have been developed by others for at least some of the constructs. Here I think you can take a slightly different approach. In particular, most existing measures should have gone through a process similar to that suggested herein already (well you would hope so if they have been published in reputable journals). That said, I still feel it is necessary to look at the reliability and validity of these measures along with your own new ones. It could be the case that prior work has not been able to use techniques as sophisticated as those available to you, and it is also necessary to assess how well these measures work with your sample. The major confusion occurs when (as is often the case) these existing measures don't actually work as well as they did in the past. What do you do? Well the first thing to *not* do is panic. If you have done your research well (i.e. collected good data, used good analyses), then it can hardly be argued as your fault that these measures don't work. In many cases, if you look closely at the existing measure and construct, you may find it wasn't conceptualised or developed in the past as rigorously as you hoped. Therefore, to some extent you are fighting a losing battle and can only do your best with what you have. My advice is really to try to anticipate such issues, by including alternative measures of key constructs, just in case the existing measures do not work so well.

Also, one should consider that individuals who answer questionnaires may not be telling the whole truth, and may in fact be biased. One key bias which has received plenty of attention is *social desirability* bias (e.g. King and Bruner, 2000). This refers to the idea that individuals to a greater or lesser extent tend to try to present themselves in the best light possible. Therefore they may answer some questions in a way which makes them look smarter, nicer, kinder, or whatever. This can be a major problem if you are measuring many psychological constructs. The first thing to do is try to avoid it at the source, assure respondents that their answers are anonymous if possible, or confidential at minimum.

Make it clear that they are not being 'assessed', and that there are no 'right or wrong' answers. Even so, there are measures of socially desirable response tendencies, and I recommend including one in your questionnaire. You can then correlate items and scales with this measure, to see whether social desirability bias is a problem. More recent research has explored many other types of bias, and I would advise any researcher becoming familiar with such literature (e.g. Baumgartner and Steenkamp, 2001; Podsakoff *et al.*, 2003).

Cross-cultural measurement is also a key issue. My main point here is that it is not as simple as merely translating your measures into the language of another culture and expecting them to work. Many researchers actually recommend going through the concept and measure development process anew when you wish to transfer one measure to a new culture. However, in many cases researchers need to measure the same thing in multiple cultures, which necessitates some kind of comparability of the measurements. In this case, there is substantial advice on how to develop measures which are what is called *invariant* across cultures (e.g. Steenkamp and Baumgartner, 1998). Whereas much of this literature is quite technical, it is very important that researchers consult it very early in the development process.

So, by now you should have a pretty good grasp of the key ideas of measurement as they have developed within the social sciences, and particularly organisational research. However, what's probably even more important is that you recognise that measurement is a vital process in itself, and should never be treated as an afterthought. Without good measurement you will never be able to be confident that your findings bear any relationship to the theories you so dearly wish to explore. You should leave this chapter with an appreciation of the importance of measurement, as well as hopefully some level of interest in what is a really interesting (and under-rated) area of methodology. Finally, try to take Figure 7.1 as a model in some way for the whole research process. The idea of linking the theoretical world to the real world is a key one, and upon it depends the validity of the whole social research process. The rest of the chapters will to a greater or lesser extent be concerned with this process in one way or the other – whether it be linking theoretical concepts to real-world data, or real-world findings back to theoretical world concepts and relationships.

The key things to take from this specific chapter are:

- The operational definition of a construct is the set of rules which link your theoretical-world construct to the real-world measurement of it.
- An auxiliary theory is one which sets out exactly how constructs relate to measures. Without solid auxiliary theory, our structural theories (i.e. those which relate constructs to each other) can not be tested with real-world data.
- In order to generate a good measure of a construct, you must define that construct very clearly. You can then follow a process to generate and assess the validity of that construct's measure.
- Validity refers to how well your measure captures variation in the latent construct. You can assess this in a number of ways, including exploring your measure's relationships with other measures.

- Alternative measurement (also termed auxiliary) theories are formative measurement and IRT, these can be appropriate in certain situations.
- There are differences between developing entirely new measures and assessing existing ones. You should also make yourself aware of the chances of response biases, and various cross-cultural issues if they are relevant to your research.

Further reading

- *Scale Development: Theory and Applications* by Robert DeVellis (1991), and *Summated Rating Scale Construction: An Introduction* by Paul Spector (1992). These two little books were my own introduction to the practicalities of developing measures. I still consult them from time to time, and I think they are a great introduction to measurement.
- *Psychometric Theory* (3edn) by Jum Nunnally and Ira Bernstein: The 1967 first edition (written solely by Nunnally) is generally considered 'the' classic text on psychometric scale development, but it's pretty hard to get hold of now. Being the weird obsessive I am, I hunted high and low for mine (well, on the Internet anyway). If you can't get hold of the original, or don't have my strange desire for such things, this third edition is updated and revised, and pretty much just as good. However, to be totally honest, I do rather like the original version since I feel a few key ideas have changed a bit in this latest revision. I also just love old books like that.
- *Reliability and Validity* by Edward Carmines and Richard Zeller. This is an excellent introduction to validity, and really helps in understanding what can be quite difficult concepts. You can buy it separately, but it also available as part of a single-volume collection of four measurement titles (including the Spector one above). What a great idea for a birthday present!

There are many other sources of information on measurement available, lots of which are articles in the academic literature. Below is a selection I think are really good which cover the psychometric approach:

- Churchill, Gilbert A., Jr. (1979) 'A paradigm for developing better measures of marketing constructs', *Journal of Marketing Research*, XVI (February), 64–73.
- Gerbing, David W. and Anderson, Janet C. (1988) 'An updated paradigm for scale development incorporating unidimensionality and its assessment'. *Journal of Marketing Research*, XXV (May), 186–192.
- Gerbing, David W. and Hamilton, Janet G. (1996) 'Viability of exploratory factor analysis as a precursor to confirmatory factor analysis', *Structural Equation Modeling*, 3 (1), 62–72.
- Lee, Nick and Hooley, Graham (2005) 'The evolution of "classical mythology" within marketing measure development'. *European Journal of Marketing*, Vol. 39 (3/4) (if I do say so myself!)

And here's a few which look at alternatives:

- Diamantopoulos, Adamantios and Winklhofer, Heidi M. (2001) 'Index construction with formative indicators: An alternative to scale development', *Journal of Marketing Research*, 38 (2), 269–277.

- Rossiter, John R. (2002) 'The C-OAR-SE procedure for scale development in marketing', *International Journal of Research in Marketing*, 305–336.

EXERCISES

1. Going back to question 3 in Chapter 6 about defining relationship quality, explain the process you would go through to create a measure of relationship quality.
2. Explain what 'auxiliary theory' is, how it relates to 'structural theory', and why it is so important.
3. For the following constructs, explain whether (or in what situation) a student sample would be appropriate to develop their measures, and why or why not[7]:

    a. Self-esteem
    b. Attitude towards an advertisement
    c. Sales manager caring (see IDE 7.1)
    d. Brand loyalty
    e. Job satisfaction

4. What is reliability, how can something be reliable but not valid?
5. Explain what construct validity is, how it differs from criterion-related validity.
6. What is social-desirability bias and how could it influence your measures?
7. Put this book down and go read a work of fiction for a while.

---

[7] Have a look for research on these topics if you want to get some examples.

Chapter 8
Research design

SUPERVISOR'S VIEW: PROFESSOR MICHAEL WEST

Before starting to cook a wonderful new meal, it is vital to have the recipe clearly laid out before you, even if you have to extemporise a little during the process. The research design is the recipe for your meal. Start with a poor recipe and the result will be bland or worse – inedible. Start with a superbly thought-through recipe and the result could be the best meal you have ever made. Moreover, many others will find it delicious, satisfying and nourishing. In designing research do the best you can do. Your research aims to advance human knowledge, nothing less, nothing more. That is an ambitious undertaking and it is therefore vital to take a careful, methodical, thoughtful and thorough approach to produce an outstanding design. Try to design the research to offer new understandings or new methodologies. Research design is craft work; you are a skilled sculptor, painter, chef or poet. You should approach the design of your research with an attitude of commitment to the highest quality, to superb craft work and with a determination to feel pride in the quality of your research design. The more carefully, completely and thoroughly you plan your research the better it will be. The more that your design is informed by theory, the more likely will your research make a real contribution and the less likely it is that your research ends up with no or only uninteresting findings. Weaknesses in research design are inevitable but the more thought you put in at the beginning, developing the most robust and innovative methodologies, the more likely it is that your research will produce findings that are richer than you anticipated. Be ambitious, but also be realistic. If you have never cooked a meal for ten do not try to cook a meal for 200. Ensure the recipe is as detailed as you can possibly make it and ask as many master chefs as you can to advise on your recipe. Remember that research design is about ensuring that your research makes a contribution to knowledge. Treat research design as the most important stage of your research.

VIEW FROM THE TRENCHES: LAURA CHAMBERLAIN

Designing research is not an easy task, and can often be overlooked or rushed in order to get to what seems like the all-important data collection phase. I think the key to the research design stage is *balance*. Some researchers do not place much emphasis on research design, concentrating on obtaining any data possible, and then fitting it to the model or theory later. However, this is not an advisable approach because (particularly with experimental design) if some key factor is overlooked, or the most appropriate data is not collected, it can be a fatal flaw in your research. On the other hand (if you are a perfectionist like me) you can get a little, shall we say, *focused*, on having the perfect research design. This leads to spending too much time on the designing stage and not actually getting to the data collection as quickly as perhaps you could have.

In order to develop a balanced approach to research design it is important to make sure you know at the outset what data you are trying to generate with the research design and how to account for reliability and validity issues. In fact, it's a good idea to make a checklist of every key component of good research design (e.g. reliability, validity, etc.) and working out how your design covers all these bases, just to make sure you don't miss anything out. In addition, even if you are being led in a particular direction, there is no harm spending a little time thinking about all the methodological options available to you. In fact, try to get as much advice from as wide a range of colleagues as possible. However, be wary of those who recommend that you use a particular design if they have never used it themselves, and always get further advice from those who have actually implemented designs in practice, before you go ahead and commit.

Of course, all that advice may get a little confusing, but the broader your exposure to different designs, the better the position you are to choose the best one. Remember the old saying, 'if all you have is a hammer, everything looks like a nail', as it is highly appropriate here. If nothing else, at some point someone is bound to casually say to you: 'Wouldn't it have been better to do xyz design?' At least if you have already thought about it, you can justify why you *didn't* use xyz and, more importantly, why you have developed the research design you are using!

So, by now I imagine your heads are almost completely full of abstract theories, philosophy, conceptual models, and measurement ideas. If that is the case, I have some bad news for you. You better start clearing a hole in your brain, as now we are going to begin to talk about the actual *practicalities* of doing research. If you have studied and taken in the material so far, you'll be in an excellent position to understand the rest of the book. If not, you might be able to understand the basic practical tasks you need to undertake to do good research, but you'll have trouble understanding *why* you would do these things, and how it all fits together into a coherent piece of work. So make sure you are at least comfortable with the first seven chapters before you move on to this one, and the rest of the book.

Research design is an interesting part of the overall research process, and it's one of those things that you'll probably see many different opinions on if you read around the subject a bit. In particular, different disciplines have tended to develop different traditions of design, which can sometimes lead to students and beginning researchers not being exposed to the basic overall principles of research design before conducting their projects, and instead just being told to 'follow my lead' by their supervisors or mentors. Rather than this approach, in this chapter I am going to go right back to the basic principles of research design, independent of the actual method that is used to conduct the research (e.g. a sample survey, or an experimental manipulation or a qualitative study), and try to explain the key ideas behind all good research designs. From there we can move together towards discussions of some specific different methods and their characteristics. More importantly, you will then be able to relate these methods back to the general concepts of research design, and make your own decision as to what the most appropriate design and method is for any project.

The view I take is that research design is first and foremost concerned with finding answers to your research questions. This is of course rather obvious I would hope. However, it's vital that you never let the overall research questions move far from your mind. Research design itself can be a rather technical and detailed process, and if you forget exactly why you are designing your research, it is easy to lose sight of the forest (the research question) for the trees (the details of your design). This sometimes leads to beautiful, technically elegant, but theoretically sterile designs. Ultimately, the purpose of your design is to outline how you can generate empirical evidence to examine your research question. This is often a hypothesis testing approach, but does not have to be. However, within whatever philosophical perspective you utilise, the idea is to generate some kind of useful answers to your questions. The criteria for usefulness are often the generalisability, validity and reliability of your conclusions. The design doesn't tell you exactly what to do, but rather is the 'framework' for your study.

The concepts of design in this chapter are generally underpinned by an idea that our research questions are concerned with *relationships* between variables. Ultimately, most serious research is concerned with studying whether variables or concepts are related, even if those variables do not always have to be the kinds of 'quantitatively oriented' theoretical concepts I talked about in the last few chapters. This concern for relationships is the fundamental base for the principles of good research design, and you need to keep that in mind throughout the chapter. It is also an excellent exercise in learning how to think rigorously about your own research. However, you shouldn't expect this chapter to go into fine detail about all the various research designs that could be used. There are better and more appropriate sources for that kind of information. Furthermore, these designs are not the 'only' designs possible. In particular qualitative designs can be amazingly diverse and flexible (even though most quantitative designs tend to fit nicely into the categories I discuss here). But almost all research designs follow one or the other of the various logics which underlie the research designs. Here what I really want to do is give some more abstract information, to help you decide which general type of design you need, and to arm you with the thought process needed to design your own research, in conjunction with other sources.

At the end of this chapter I really hope you have come to terms with these key ideas:

- That much of research design is concerned with the control or observance of the variation of concepts/variables, and that it is important to determine exactly what type of variation you are interested in.
- That we can partition variation into theoretical, extraneous, and error variance.
- The basic principles behind experimental design and why it is seen as the 'best' design by many researchers.
- The difference between external and internal validity.
- The basic characteristics of cross-sectional, longitudinal, and case-based research.

Why is it Important to Know This Stuff?

Research design is something that many beginning researchers don't really think about seriously. This is a strange statement to make, but I think it is pretty accurate. In many cases, what happens is that you are so focused on a certain project that in your head you already have a fair idea of what 'type' of research you are going to do before you do it. For research students the situation is often even more pronounced, in that few supervisors are expert on multiple research designs. I think this situation has the potential to lead to disaster. In particular, if you wish to publish work in respected scholarly outlets, your work will always be subject to a careful analysis of the underlying design. Without a good appreciation of why your design was the most appropriate one, you will be unlikely to get past the first hurdle.

Research design is important because it is essentially the stage where you design how you are going to collect data from the real world to explore or test your theory. If you look at Figure 8.1 you can see that the arrow has two heads. This is because your theory should drive your research design, but your design is really about how to transfer 'stuff' from the real world (i.e. data) back to the theoretical world to allow you to examine your theories. However, it is important not to confuse the basic principles of research design with the 'methods' of data collection, which will be dealt with in later chapters. In fact, research design is about different underlying logics to collecting data and how that data is related to theory. Of course, some designs are more suited to certain data collection methods than others. But each one of the research design logics presented here has something valuable to add to your consideration of how to conduct research effectively.

Therefore, one important point is that this chapter is *independent* of any method you might be intending to use. If you are intending to do qualitative or quantitative work, the principles I will outline here will be useful. Admittedly, it may look to some like many of these designs are only for quantitative researchers, but this is not really the case. I'll be making reference where appropriate to how qualitatively focused researchers can use this information. Another key point is that research design is a practical process as well. I am going to begin with basic principles, what we are trying to do with research design. But of course this has to be balanced with practical considerations as well, for example financial and time resources. But, and I can't stress this highly enough, understanding the principles of research design will have a major impact on the success of your project, and also on the likelihood of your being able to publish it in a well-respected outlet. Trust me, I know, and once you've done something, you can never go back and change it (as I am sure my mother thinks sometimes!)

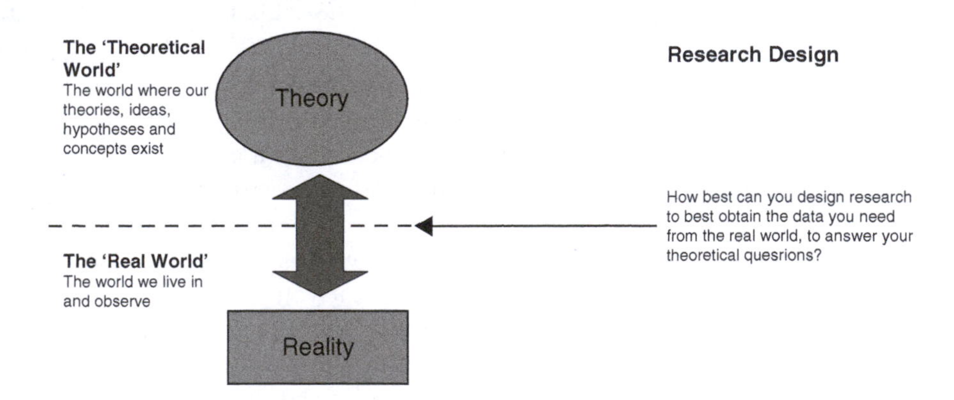

Figure 8.1 The place of research design

Research design and the control/observance of variation

I said earlier that the primary task of research design was about providing answers to your research questions. That's true, but over the top of this is overlaid the main technical task of research design; **the need to control or at least observe variation** in your empirical data (I'll also use the term **variance**). So far now we have mainly talked in abstract terms about theories and models, but now we need to start thinking about what kinds of data we need to actually *test* a model. Now, don't get the idea that I am only talking about certain types of projects here (e.g. quantitative realist ones), the principles I am going to elaborate on are relevant to all research – even though the language I am going to use will probably be more familiar to a realist researcher. Alternative View 8.1 later provides some thoughts on the application of this thinking to the interpretive types of research discussed in Chapter 3, so if you are confused then have a read of that and my thinking should become clearer.

Anyway, imagine a very simple research question regarding what factors influence students to attend my lectures on Research Methods. Over the course of my career I have been interested in this on a practical level, and sometimes wonder if there is anything at all which is a reliable predictor of attendance! Imagine you looked at some previous research, and developed some theory (see Chapters 4 and 5) which suggested the idea that higher levels of students' 'motivation to learn' influenced a higher attendance. A model of this theory is in Figure 8.2. There are many specific methods in which we could gather information to test this model, and provide some answer to the research question, such as surveys, experiments, observations, even qualitative interviews. However, there are some key research design principles which apply to all the specific methods, to ensure we have the right kind of data to answer our research question. These principles are independent of the specific method, and you need to understand *them* as well as your research question before you can decide which method is best suited to your goal.

First, let's look at the two concepts in Figure 8.2; motivation (the independent variable) and attendance (the dependent variable).[1] Our first concern is how these two concepts – which are concerned with the substantive hypothesis in our research – **vary** in level. Most crucially, we need to be able somehow to actually see variation in the dependent variable. If every single student has the same level of attendance across the term, for example, how can we see what factors influence attendance? This is a key factor to take into account, but to be perfectly honest, it seems that most researchers simply assume their dependent variable will

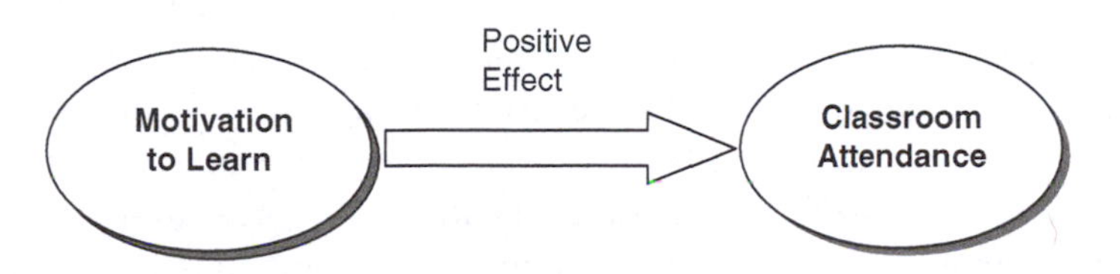

Figure 8.2 A theoretical relationship

[1] I am making the big assumption here that you have worked out the best way to measure these concepts if you need to (see Chapters 6 and 7 for more discussion of measurement).

have a sufficient level of variation. It's something you can't really 'control', as that would bias your results (this will make sense later), but you should at the very least make sure that there aren't any factors which will stop your dependent from varying. For example, if the class you intended to study had a mandatory attendance requirement, it would probably be a poor research design to study that class if you were interested in how motivation influenced attendance.[2] More under the control of the researcher is the variation in the independent variable – in the case of Figure 8.2 this is motivation. In our research design, this variable must vary substantially across the people we are studying, or it will be hard to separate out the effect of motivation from the total variation of the dependent variable. In other words, if your independent variable doesn't vary much, its effect on the dependent variable will be very hard to see when you analyse the data. This principle is sometimes relevant to our sample selection (later in this chapter I will talk about the 'level of analysis'), our measurement design, and our experimental design (if you are using experiments). A basic rule is to make sure the independent variable has as wide a range as possible in your sample, in whichever way is appropriate to your specific method. The variance of the independent variable is sometimes referred to as *experimental* variance. I have also heard the term *systematic* variance used. I actually like to use the term *theoretical variance* to refer to the variance of all concepts in your model that relate to your substantive theory. This sums up the need to be aware of (if not explicitly control) how all the key concepts vary.

Unfortunately, theoretical variance is not the only thing you need to worry about. There are almost definitely many, many other extraneous factors which are likely to influence attendance of my Research Methods classes, which you are not really interested in for your theory, but will still have an impact. For example, higher rainfall levels tend to decrease lecture attendance, as do morning start times, the presence of attractive alternatives (personal and situational!), and myriad more factors. None of these factors is part of our substantive theory, but in order to determine more accurately the contribution motivation makes to attendance, we need somehow to 'get rid of' this *extraneous variance.* There are a number of problems which extraneous variance can cause. The worst problem is when there is an extraneous variable which you don't know about, which might even mean your research ends up with wrong conclusions. For example, what if in the real world there was a third concept (which I will term here 'work ethic') which had a positive effect on *both* motivation to learn and classroom attendance, and in reality there was no influence of motivation on attendance? This is shown in Figure 8.3. Of course, your research is not concerned with work ethic, so it's not part of your theoretical model. Unfortunately, if you didn't take into account this variable in your research design, you might still see a positive influence of motivation on attendance in your research. However, in actual fact what you would

[2] If you don't understand this, consider the fact that even a student with low motivation will be forced to attend the class in that situation – which means the true effect of motivation on attendance will be obscured by the 'forced' nature of attendance.

be observing was a **spurious** relationship. A spurious relationship is the name given to a relationship which you see in your data, but is not really existent in the real world, and it's caused by your failure to take account of a factor which is *not in your substantive theory*, but has an important effect nonetheless.[3] This situation, shown in Figure 8.3, is a worst-case scenario, and basically would mean that your research results bore no relation to reality at all. What is more normally the case is that there are many possible extraneous factors, and it is your job to somehow design research which allows for the removal or control of the variation of the most important of these factors, while still allowing the variance of your theoretical concepts to be observed. There are many ways of taking into account extraneous variation, and IDE 8.1 is a brief discussion of them in the context of different methods.

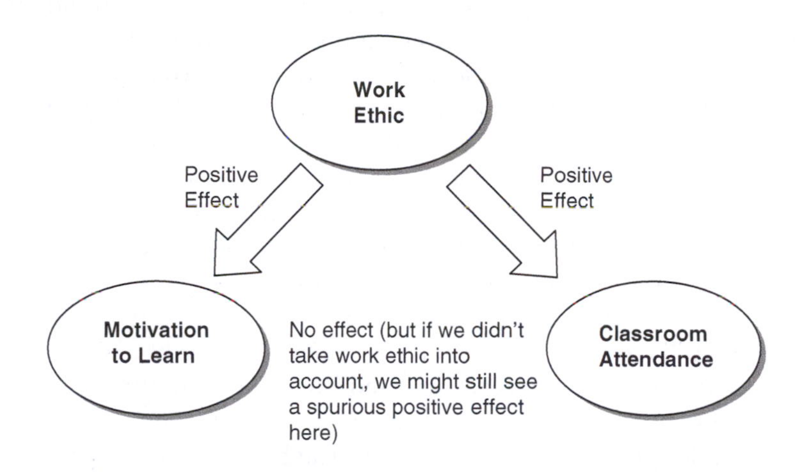

Figure 8.3 A possible spurious relationship

IDE 8.1: Controlling Extraneous Variation

The most effective way of controlling extraneous variation due to a specific factor is simply to remove that factor. For example, if you think that gender has an influence on motivation (extraneous to your theory) then you could collect data on only one gender. Or if firm size has an impact on performance which is extraneous to

[3] Of course, for other researchers, this work ethic factor might be exactly what they are theoretically interested in, and your 'motivation' factor (or any number of others) will be extraneous.

your theory, you might only collect data from firms employing 500–1,000 people for example. The rule here is that to remove the effect of a possible extraneous variable, you make your sample as homogeneous as possible on that variable. The important downside of this is that you are restricted in the conclusions you can draw from your research. For example, if your study includes only males, you are unable to say anything about females in your conclusion. Or if you included only small firms, you can only draw conclusions about this small range of firm size. In fact, any relationship you discover could be very different in large firms, but you can only guess this as you have no information. So you should be careful when using this method to control extraneous variation.

The second method is useful in experimental designs, and is called **randomisation**. Experimental researchers tend to think that this is the best way. Randomisation is the process of randomly allocating subjects into your different experimental groups. So if you have 100 subjects to allocate into two groups (one which will receive an experimental treatment and one which will not), you should randomly assign your subjects to those groups. Theoretically, this should 'even out' the extraneous variation, leaving both groups statistically equal on all possible extraneous factors – meaning the only difference between the groups will be whether they receive the treatment or not (i.e. your theoretical variance). Of course, in reality the groups are unlikely to be completely equal in all possible extraneous factors, but randomisation means that the probability of them being statistically equal is far higher than with any other method. The rule here is that you should randomly assign subjects into groups, and randomly assign treatments and conditions to experimental groups, whenever it is possible. The downside of this method is that it is only really usable for experimental designs, which are not always the best or most appropriate way of getting data.

A third way of controlling extraneous variance is to simply build in that factor to your research design. So, for example, if gender or firm size were potential sources of extraneous variance, you could measure them *as well as* the theoretical concepts you were interested in. You can then use this data to remove the variance of gender and firm size from the total variance of the dependent variable. Because randomisation is so effective, this method is less often used in experimental research, unless the researcher is interested in that particular variable for some reason. However, in survey research it is perhaps the most important way of controlling extraneous variance, as it does not influence your generalisability in the same way as if you were to remove the extraneous factor as suggested above. You often find these extraneous factors which are built into the design termed **control factors** in research reports. If you are a survey researcher then it is vital that you take account of major control factors which are likely to influence your dependent variable. The downside of this is that one can always think of 'one more' control factor to include in the research design – so where do you stop? This issue can lead to very long and unwieldy data collection instruments. The trade-off the researcher must make is to somehow include the control factors most likely to influence the results, while still keeping the data collection tool efficient. This is pretty much a judgement call.

The final type of variation we need to be aware of is *error variance*. Error variance essentially refers to variations of 'stuff which you can't really see or measure', and is generally considered to be random, as one factor may go up while another goes down. So when taken across all the possible factors, we consider it to be random. It can be quite confusing to get a handle on, but you can think of it in a number of ways. First of all, the less control you have over your research, the more chance that random, unpredictable factors will impact on your data. For example, if you run a questionnaire survey and mail it out for people to fill in at home, you run the risk of its getting lost in the post, going to the wrong address, or if it is received the respondent may get distracted while filling it in and make mistakes, as well as various other transient factors influencing their answers. However, if you herd everyone into a room and watch them as they fill in the questionnaire, you have removed many possible random error factors. This concept is relevant to all kinds of method. However, sometimes, it is very difficult to have a large degree of control over your research. I also spoke about error variance in the chapters on measurement. In essence, the more rigorously designed your measures are, the less chance they are to be influenced by random error factors (e.g. misunderstandings, biases and the like). Finally, there are many individual difference factors (e.g. personality) which may influence our dependent variables. Often these factors can be considered to be extraneous variation (see above), but when we can't identify, observe, or control them we consider them to be error variation. The best way to minimise error variance is firstly to design as much control as possible into your research method, and secondly to design your data collection devices and measures as rigorously as possible. But of course, random error will always be present to some extent in your research.

Level of analysis and theoretical variation

The 'level of analysis' is an issue which should concern almost all social researchers, and especially those who – like me – investigate organisational issues. Unfortunately, in my experience this idea has generally not been considered often enough by research students and beginning researchers. I, as usual, say this from bitter experience, having made what I consider to be some rather nasty mistakes in my early work (but let's not go into detail here ...). To help explain the concept of levels of analysis, think about almost any situation which a social

Alternative View 8.1: The Logic of Comparison and Qualitative Research Design

It is pretty unarguable that many of the concepts discussed in this chapter are associated with a more quantitative approach to research, and this is especially so with experimental design. Indeed, many qualitative research texts will tell you that designs for qualitative research can not be 'pigeonholed' into boxes like quantitative ones can. I'm not so sure about this, but one thing I do agree with is that qualitative research design has – if not a greater flexibility – a little more creative freedom possible in its design. So one thing I would recommend is to avoid focusing on the 'quantitative versus qualitative' divide when you read this chapter, and try to stay focused on the key logics of the research designs. Then you will be able to apply these key concepts to your work, whatever the methodology you wish to use.

One great example is what Bryman (2004) calls the *logic of comparison* which underlies the experimental design. As you will clearly see below, experiments always rely on some kind of comparison. This comparison can be before and after treatments, or between experimental and control groups. This logic either explicitly or implicitly underlies many other forms of research. In a qualitative context, we are often very interested in comparing different types of situation. In fact, you'll see in Chapter 10 (especially IDE 10.1) that much qualitative analysis relies on this logic of comparison to justify its findings. Without comparison between different cases, you are reduced to making purely descriptive conclusions about your data. Of course, this may be exactly what you want to do (for example in some case study research). But even underlying that is often an implicit desire to draw some kind of conclusion about how that case illuminates some aspect of a theory, or tells us something we don't already know. Without even an implied comparison against anything else (for example how a case is somehow different to the 'regular' social world), it is often hard to justify why such research contributes to knowledge in an original way. It is hard to imagine research which at minimum does not compare the knowledge gained from study against the knowledge we already have – and in doing so invokes the logic of comparison.

researcher is likely to study,[4] such as a business organisation, an educational establishment, or the like. Such situations, institutions and (especially) organisations naturally consist of a number of levels, which are **nested** within each other. For example, students are nested into class groups under teachers, these class groups are nested into year cohort groups under

[4] Of course, this may not apply to *all* possible situations we may wish to study, but it certainly applies to many of them.

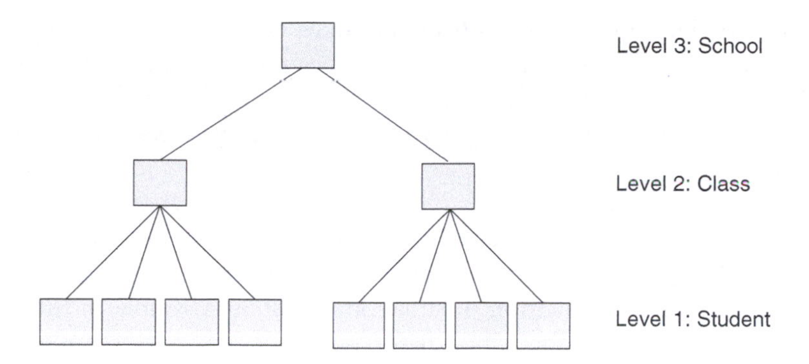

Figure 8.4 Nested structure example

'deans', these cohort groups are nested into (say) school groups under headmasters, these school groups are nested into geographic regions under a regional coordinator or something like that, and so on. A business organisation is similar. Figure 8.4 gives a representation of this, which should make things clearer.

Now, this nested, multi-level, characteristic leaves the researcher with a number of key decisions to make. The most important decision is a theoretical one; you must decide at an early stage whether your theory or key constructs operate at the *group* or the *individual* level. This decision is very important for almost all researchers, and it is absolutely *vital* for all researchers who are studying theories which work 'across' levels – for example the influence of managers on employees, or the influence of organisational strategy on employee behaviour, or regional initiatives on school performance, and so on. **Group level** (also called 'homogeneous') theories essentially predict that the higher level concept will operate the same for all members of the lower-level groups. So, if you are examining a manager's leadership style, a group level theory would predict that *all* of that manager's employees would perceive basically the same thing about their manager's leadership. Or if you were looking at the influence of organisational culture, a group level theory would predict that all members of the organisation perceived the same culture. By contrast, **individual level** (also known as 'independent') theories predict that the lower-level group members are free of any group-level influences. So for the leadership example, an individual level theory would predict that each subordinate perceives their manager's leadership style differently somehow.[5] Furthermore, theories can be independent at one level, and homogeneous at another. Consider a multi-national firm with many branches around the world (maybe a bank). If you are interested in the internal culture of the bank, this may be homogeneous

[5] There is a 'middle ground' here, which is termed **heterogeneous**, where the individual lower-level group members are predicted to have some group-level similarities but also some differences. However, for the purposes of clarity I won't discuss this at length.

at the level of individual employees of a bank, but independent across different banks in the same company (if the branch management has a major impact on the culture development). Or it may be homogeneous across branches of one country (if the national management has the major influence) but independent across countries (if management policies and styles differ across countries).

This of course has major impacts on the way you theorise about your concepts, but here I will be talking about the research design issues it brings up. The most important impact it has (and the one which causes constant confusion) is on your decision about exactly what units of the organisation or situation you should sample in order to achieve a good level of theoretical variance. The classic mistake I see is the sampling of multiple units (say employees) from one group (say an organisation), when the theory clearly refers to constructs which are homogeneous at that level (say internal management policies). Imagine that you are interested in how organisational culture influences individual employee satisfaction. You need to first work out at which level your independent variable varies. According to most accepted theories, it will be hard to justify that culture is a factor which will primarily vary at the individual level. Instead, corporate culture by definition varies across different organisations.[6] The impact on your research design at this point is on your sampling. If you sample 150 employees from one organisation, then your theory actually predicts that those employees should not vary much on their corporate culture, as it is a *group-level* variable! Thus, any variation you do see should be due to random error, and therefore any changes in your dependent variable (job satisfaction) can not be attributed to your hypothesis, but to extraneous or random factors. Instead, you should sample employees from 150 *organisations*, as this is the level your independent variable operates on. This decision is one of those things which can 'make-or-break' your project. If you go out and collect data which does not tap variation at the correct level of analysis, you simply can not do your project. It's what we in the business call a **'fatal flaw'**. You will basically have to collect more data, which, as you will see later, is pretty much the worst thing that can (realistically) happen. Have I made it seem important enough yet? No? OK then, how about you imagine I am standing in front of you shouting this last paragraph right at you (to help you imagine what I look like, I have been confused with the famous actor Brad Pitt before).[7]

Furthermore, if your theory works at the group level, you need to make another important decision. This decision regards whether or not you need to collect data from *multiple* members of the group. For example, in the organisational example above, should you collect data from one member of each of 150 organisations, or 5, 10, or 150 members? There are practical and

[6]This is not to say that one can not go against existing theory. However, if you wish to you will need to provide some strong and rigorous alternative theories.

[7]This is actually the truth, but admittedly the lady in question was two years old at the time, and Brad was looking a bit rough in the photo.

theoretical reasons to think about this, and it is in fact subject to some debate. Alternative View 8.2 gives some pointers to think about.

Alternative View 8.2: How Much Data to Collect?

There are a number of things you should think about when you decide how much data to collect in 'nested-group' situations. However, one key practical thing to think about is what your options are if you get it wrong. For example, if you collect 10 members per group and it turns out later you needed less, this is far less of a problem than if you collect one member per group and later you decide you needed more. So one rule of thumb in this kind of situation is 'when in doubt, collect more not less'. I know you probably expected that to rhyme. Sorry!

Anyway, the first theoretical thing you should think about is whether what you are investigating *needs* multiple team members. I was at a recent presentation where the speaker explained how she had rejected data from any groups which had fewer than three members. When I asked why, she replied that her theory was concerned with social influence (or some such) and therefore she thought that theoretically she needed the views of at least three people in order to capture this sort of thing. Good answer I thought. Certainly put me in my place!

Another thing to consider is how 'unique' each team member will be on the concepts you are interested in. What I mean here is that for teams who will be very homogeneous on your key concepts (e.g. if you think they will all see the same leadership style from their manager) you need to collect fewer members than if you think they will be very heterogeneous on those concepts. At its extreme, if you think they will be identical (imagine you were collecting data from teams of 'clones') you would need only one.

Finally, you need to think about the technical requirements of your analysis.[8] Some analysis methods need more team members than others to work effectively. However, this is something which is a little outside the scope of this chapter.

Level of analysis and measurement

The ideas of levels of analysis presented above also raise another related issue, which is strongly related to the measurement theories I talked about in the last couple of chapters. More specifically, a lot of social and organisational research actually deals with theories

[8]Again, a great example of how you need to think about your analysis *before* you collect your data!

which 'cross levels', as some of my examples above do. For example, a study on how organisational culture influences employee job satisfaction contains concepts which are at both the organisational level (culture) and the employee level (job satisfaction). A study on the effects of leadership style (often at the manager level) will usually be concerned with employee-level effects. So the decision you need to make is; **how do you collect data at these multiple levels?**

There are two main ways to approach this issue. First, you could collect data at all levels your theory is concerned with. So if your research is investigating the impact of teacher behaviour on student learning, you collect data from teachers about some factors, and students about others. You may also wish to go to another source for your final dependent learning variable (e.g. objective test scores). In this case, you need to consider the information in Alternative View 8.2, to determine how many cases you should sample at the lower level. The other approach is to collect data from one source. For example, you could simply ask students about their teachers to collect teacher-related data, as well as asking the same students about student-related factors, and their own learning. Of course, the advantage of this latter method is efficiency. You only need to tap one source of information (students), which leaves you free of complex matching of students to teachers, and designing different instruments and data collection activities.

However, before you can do this, you need to consider some vital issues. One is that of measurement. Basically, can you use subjects at one level to measure concepts at another? So if you are measuring firm performance, are you justified in asking employees to judge this? This question is actually two questions (stay with me here, it's important). Firstly **do the subjects at your chosen level actually have access to that information**? Can you justify that employees can rate the overall performance of their firm? This is a question you have to answer on a case-by-case basis. For some concepts (e.g. student evaluations of their teacher's behaviour) it is easier to justify than others. But it is harder to justify that a front-line retail store employee will be able to provide very accurate information on the financial and market share performance of individual parent company divisions. The second measurement issue concerns **what you are measuring** in this case – is it the *actual concept* (e.g. teacher behaviour) or is it the rater's (e.g. the student) *perceptions of that concept*? Of course, in most cases it is the latter, and you then need to justify why these perceptions are likely to be valid measures of the concept you are actually interested in. One good way of doing this is to look at previous academic research in that and related areas, which should help you get a picture of what is and isn't accepted.[9]

The other issue which you need to think about is that of **common method bias**, which is again something that few researchers consider until it is too late (and they get a manuscript rejected). This is a complex issue, and in fact is generally misunderstood by

[9]Of course, being accepted in the literature is not necessarily a good indicator of whether something is methodologically appropriate or not, but it is a good start.

many people (including some academic journal manuscript reviewers!). Common method bias occurs when the method of data collection (e.g. using a single source for all your data) you use somehow influences the scores of respondents on the measures or instruments you are using. In other words, when you collect independent and dependent variables from the same source, this may influence how closely they are related in your data set. But there are many different factors at play here, of which I can give only a basic introduction: for example, if you ask a consumer about whether a new product is likely to be useful, and then ask them whether or not they intend to purchase the product. It could be argued that the consumer will give an answer to the purchase intention measure which is highly correlated to their answer to the usefulness question to avoid cognitive dissonance – whatever their 'true' purchase intention is. In order to avoid this possibility, one should collect these data from different sources (e.g. ask the consumer about usefulness, and then measure actual purchasing from another source). However, you should remember that common method bias itself is really only a problem when there is a reason to expect some characteristic of the method to influence your results. In my experience, though, the term 'common method bias' sometimes gets used as a criticism for any research where the dependent and independent variables are measured using the same source. This is not the case, and in some situations it is not even possible to collect independent and dependent variables from difference sources (e.g. if you are investigating individual psychological theories). In fact, in my view there is no reason to make a blanket criticism of such research, unless you have some theoretical reason to expect either the common method bias mechanism above, or that there is extraneous variance not taken account of which may positively bias any relationship. Such variance could be due to an individual difference factor (e.g. a personality trait which influences both usefulness perceptions and purchase intentions scores). However, this latter case is not 'common method bias', but instead a failure to take account of extraneous factors (see above).

The experimental approach

Now we have those hugely important and often misunderstood concepts under our belts, it's time to move on to an introduction to the various different 'types' of research design available to you. For a number of reasons, I'm going to begin with the experimental approach. Most importantly, I think the logic behind this approach very nicely illustrates a number of key issues about research and research design, which will allow you to understand why other designs are like they are (along with their strengths and weaknesses). Secondly, it is also important to understand that for many in the social sciences, experimental designs are the 'gold standard' of research. Whether you agree or not that they are the 'best', you need to understand why they hold such an exalted position. However, you shouldn't get the idea that the only useful designs are experimental in nature. In fact, in many social research settings, true experimental designs are rare, so you may have little experience of them at the moment. Nevertheless, experiments are a key part of social research, and one piece of advice I would offer is that you should clearly understand why an experimental approach is *not* appropriate to your research, before discounting it.

Experiments are highly valued by many because of their very strong **internal validity**, which is explained – along with its counterpoint, **external validity** – in IDE 8.2. However, the converse of this strength is that they are also very difficult to conduct in many applied social research projects.[10] One reason for this is that true experiments require the *manipulation* of your independent variable(s). To understand this, look at Figure 8.5, which is a classic experimental design.

IDE 8.2: Internal and External Validity

Questions of validity are dealt with in various ways throughout the book, but they are also appropriate here. The question of internal validity is tied in inextricably to an understanding of the control group in an experiment. Simply put, without a control group (which differs from the experimental group solely in that it does not receive the treatment) one is unable to rule out all alternative explanations for any change in the dependent variable before and after the treatment in the experimental group. What this means is that with a proper control group (a key component of which is random assignment, see IDE 8.1) you can be more confident that any change in the dependent variable is caused by the independent variable you manipulated. I say 'cause' here because this is exactly what the theory means to imply. *Internal validity is about ruling out alternative explanations for your hypothesised causal effect.*

But – and the clue is in the name – internal validity is only concerned with factors 'within' the research design. A researcher should also be concerned with *external validity*. External validity is concerned with whether your results are generalisable to other situations or not. For example, do the characteristics of the individuals you have studied, or the situational context you are working within, reduce the generalisability of your findings? This is in fact a common criticism of experimental work, particularly that which uses student samples (again this will be dealt with in later chapters too). How far is one able to generalise findings from

[10] In social and organisational psychology this is not so much of a problem, and they are used far more commonly. However IDE 8.2 should also give you some food for thought regarding some of the approaches used by many psychological researchers.

a sample of undergraduates in a tightly controlled laboratory setting, to a hospitality worker in a restaurant service setting, for example? Furthermore, will the very fact that the participants realise they are taking part in an experiment influence how they behave? A highly internally valid study which has low external validity is a perfect example of what detractors would term a 'sterile' study, i.e. one with little practical implications even though it is a technically beautiful design.

EG: (R) O_1 X O_2
CG: (R) O_3 O_4

Figure 8.5 Classic experimental design

There are a number of key features to this diagram which I will explain. **EG** refers to the *experimental group*, i.e. those who will receive some treatment or other manipulation of the independent variable, while **CG** refers to the *control group* who will not. The **(R)** indicates that the groups are *randomised*, which was explained in IDE 8.1. The various **O**s indicate the observations you make, which basically means your data collection activity. So here it shows that you collected data at two time periods – before and after the experimental manipulation or treatment, which is marked as an **X**. What this means is that between the two observation periods, you did something to change the levels of your independent variable. Maybe if you were looking at the influence of expected rewards on classroom attendance, the **X** could refer to the experimental group getting a flyer which informed them that high attenders would receive a prize. So what this means is that one group has had the level of your independent variable increased, and the other – the control group – has not. Of course, it is the researcher's job to design an effective manipulation, and in many cases this is not as easy as I just made it sound!

So why is this design considered to be so great? Well, in order to explain it, recall what you are actually trying to do: work out whether *the independent variable has some effect on the dependent variable*. In order to do that, we need first to see some variation in the dependent variable, which we hope is associated with the independent variable. But how can we be sure? Let's take another look at the things which could influence the dependent variable. First, there are all kinds of individual difference factors, like personality and other things unique to the individual. Well, in the experimental design we consider that *randomisation* evens these out across the groups (see IDE 8.1). Second, there could be some external factors that could influence things. Examples of these are what are called *history* factors, which refer to changes in the situation (e.g. a very cold and rainy winter reducing attendance), or *maturation* factors, which refer to changes in the actual participants (e.g. becoming more 'responsible' as they move through university, and thus more likely to attend class). We consider these types of

$$
\begin{array}{ll}
O_2 - O_1 & = E + U \\
O_4 - O_3 & = \quad U \\
\hline
(O_2 - O_1) - (O_4 - O_3) & = E
\end{array}
$$

Figure 8.6 Error in the classic experimental design

factors to influence both groups pretty much the same, all things considered – although we should always take care that there are no obvious differences between the group situations for example (e.g. different physical environments may lead to different exposure to history effects). So in the grand scheme of things, we can argue that virtually the only thing which is *unique* to the experimental group is the treatment itself. Thus, if we see a difference in levels of the dependent variable between the control and experimental groups, we consider that the independent variable has probably had an influence.

Figure 8.6 shows this as a kind of formula. The top line shows that the difference in the dependent variable between the first and second observations of the experimental group consists of changes which are theoretically caused by the independent variable **I** and also the various extraneous factors **E** I've already discussed. However, the bottom line shows that the difference in the dependent variable between the first and second observations of the control group are *only* caused by the extraneous factors. Subtracting the bottom line from the top line should leave us with the effect of the independent variable **I**, which is what we wanted to find out. That said, it is absolutely vital to ensure you have taken into account the possible extraneous factors discussed earlier in this chapter, or you won't be sure of what is really influencing your dependent.

However, experimental designs are certainly not a universal panacea. For one thing, as IDE 8.2 shows, you often need to balance internal validity with external validity. A key distinction here is between **field** and **laboratory** experiments. Lab experiments are more internally valid, as you have more control over measurement, situational, and other factors, and usually they are easier to design as you can control all aspects of the setting. However, field experiments tend to have somewhat more external validity as they occur in natural settings which are less likely to bias your results. That said they are often very hard to design, and ultimately it may in fact prove impossible to design any kind of 'true' experiment for many social research projects.

Another major issue with experimental designs for social research is that they are ill-suited for examining theories with many independent and dependent variables. Each additional independent variable you include adds significant extra practical and technical difficulty to your design. Although it is not feasible at this point to explain the practicalities of the various designs in detail here, you should examine very closely the literature on experimental designs (start with the 'further reading' at the end of this chapter) before committing yourself. Unfortunately, most social research theories do tend to have many different variables, all linked in a complex network of variables and interactions. Such models are difficult to test experimentally.

If a true experiment is not feasible, there are other options. One interesting option is termed the **quasi-experiment**, of which much has been written (see the further reading of this chapter for more information). There are many different types of quasi-experiment, but the common factor is that they share some, but not all, of the *internal validity* requirements of true experiments. Even so, the results of such studies can prove to be very strong if they are conducted and evaluated in the right way.

Cross-sectional designs

The experimental approach above is usually considered strong as it allows us to *control* variation in our independent variable(s), and then observe variation in the dependent variable. This variation in the dependent is observed in two ways: (a) between the control and experimental group, and (b) between the pre- and post-treatment time periods. Naturally, **cross-sectional** designs are also concerned with variation, but the method of observing variation in the independent and dependent variables is very different. Firstly, cross-sectional designs collect data on all the variables in the study *at a single point in time*. So there is no opportunity to examine 'before and after' effects. Therefore cross-sectional research must observe variation in the relevant variables by studying *multiple cases*. In practical terms, this often means collecting data on all your variables in one 'sweep' of a large sample of cases. For example, I may wish to approach the question of whether motivation influences class attendance by performing a one-shot survey of 1,000 randomly selected students at my university. I might create measures of motivation and attendance using the theory in Chapters 6 and 7[11] and then look for an association between the two variables across my whole sample. The logic behind this approach is that those students who scored higher on motivation should also score higher on attendance. So what you are taking here is essentially a 'snapshot' of a situation, and hoping that you can observe the relevant variation. Of course, the survey is not the only cross-sectional design, although it is a popular one.

Cross-sectional designs are common in social and organisational research for many reasons (some more justifiable than others). For one thing, not all research questions are amenable to the experimental design. Not all independent variables are able to be manipulated, and not all situations are controllable. But, whether or not cross-sectional designs are necessary in a given situation, it can not be denied that they suffer from some key internal validity-related disadvantages. In particular, it is often very difficult to control all possible sources of extraneous variation (see IDE 8.1), and of course it is impossible to observe any time ordering to the associations between variables. This means that you have difficulty making

[11] Of course, I might want to think about common method variance here ...

an argument for any causal relationship between your variables. They are also dependent on strong instrument and measure design, as cross-sectional designs generally require systematic and standardised measurement of variables across the multiple cases, in order to observe the variation. In many cases, this makes the material in the last two chapters very important.

However, cross-sectional designs can have some advantages over experimental methods. In particular they can achieve higher levels of external validity, especially if you select an appropriate sample (see Chapter 11). Furthermore, they also offer the opportunity to collect data on far more variables than is usually practical with an experimental design. This makes them ideally suited to examining the complex models often evident in organisational and social research. Also, although technically speaking we are only able to observe patterns of *association* between variables (not causal relationships), there are some ways in which we can be more confident in making tentative conclusions about causality from cross-sectional research designs. First and most importantly, your underlying **theory** is of critical value. In order to argue that your observed associations support a theory that *x* causes *y*, rather than *y* causing *x*, you must have developed a very strong *a priori* theory regarding exactly why this should be the case. In fact, the central role of theory in cross-sectional research is to my mind a bit of an advantage – since right from the beginning the researcher should be very clear about the importance of strong theory. Sometimes one can also make inferences about the temporal order of variables, even in a cross-sectional design. For example, if your theory is that gender influences attitude towards football, it is highly unlikely that an observed association would correspond to attitude towards football influencing gender! That said, even though in that case the temporal precedence condition was almost certainly met, it is unlikely that all other sources of extraneous variation have been accounted for.

Longitudinal designs

Longitudinal designs are far less common than cross-sectional designs in social research, as they are generally considered expensive, time-consuming, and difficult. However, as we shall see, this is not always the case. A longitudinal design is distinguished from a cross-sectional design by the fact that the same sample is measured at multiple points in time. The classic types of longitudinal designs in social research are the *panel* and *cohort* studies, both of which usually rely on multiple administrations to a sample of a questionnaire of some type. The difference between the two types is that a panel study relies on a general sample, while a cohort study uses an entire cohort of people (or a sample of a single cohort). A cohort is a group of people who share some characteristic, usually something like birth week, or the sharing of some experience. You are right in thinking that they are quite similar in general design, and for most social projects the panel design is more useful – as it contains elements from multiple cohorts (e.g. people born at many different times). Therefore, a panel study can look at the influence of cohort membership, as well as many other variables. The cohort study, on the other hand, can only look at non-cohort effects, as there is no variation of cohort membership. That said, large-scale cohort studies such as the 1970 British Cohort Study, or the newer Millennium Cohort Study,[12] can offer valuable insight into how cohort members develop over time. That said, most small-scale[13] academic social research projects which use longitudinal designs would not really be considered by researchers as either a panel or a cohort study, even though they are probably one of either (just at a smaller scale).

Both these types of longitudinal study tend to rely on similar methods to cross-sectional studies (e.g. questionnaires). So don't forget that therefore they are subject to the same internal validity issues as cross-sectional research. That said, the longitudinal design does allow insight into the temporal order of variables, allowing stronger causal inferences to be made. However, there are some unique problems with longitudinal designs which need to be mentioned. Perhaps most critical is that of *sample attrition*. In other words, between measurement periods members of the sample do inconvenient things like move house, decide they don't want to participate any more, or even die. The main issue with this is whether or not those who leave the sample are in some important way different from those who do not. If so, your results will be biased. Also, in a social research context there is not actually a lot of information on how best to conduct longitudinal work. For example, how does one decide the time period to leave between waves of data collection? And of course – just like experimental research – longitudinal designs may suffer from history and maturation effects which may unduly influence your results. Furthermore, simply participating in on a wave of the research may somehow influence or condition responses to the next wave of data collection. This is actually similar in spirit to the common method bias mentioned earlier (although it is not called that in this case), where response on one measure may influence responses to other measures (in this case over time periods).[14]

While longitudinal research is not commonly used in most social and business research fields, in econometrically based research it holds a prominent place. However, this type of research is usually very different from the panel and cohort-type studies discussed above. Much econometric work involves the collection of what we would traditionally call **secondary data**, such as stock price indices over multiple years. This type of research could be called **historical modelling**, since rather than beginning your research and then moving forwards, you are in fact collecting data from the past. One area which is proving very popular at present within my own field of marketing is the modelling of influences on product purchasing through the use of supermarket scanner data. In this case many of the disadvantages

[12]Visit http://www.esds.ac.uk/longitudinal/access/introduction.asp for information on these studies, and also on some panel studies run by the UK Government.

[13]By this I mean ones which are not at the national government level, or run by large market research firms with huge resources.

[14]Experimental research suffers from this as well, due to the 'before' and 'after' treatment measures, and in that context it is called the **testing effect**.

discussed above are not so prominent. The data is not collected by administering measures to individuals, and therefore the conditioning effect is not a problem. However, sample attrition can be a problem still, but in a different way. In the case of collecting secondary data, it may be the case that you are restricted in the data you can collect for each time period. For example, you may wish to collect data on the exact day a company first published its website, but instead only the week or month of that site's first appearance may be recorded. Or you may wish to collect daily commodity price fluctuations, but some records may not be available for certain time periods for one of many possible reasons. Nevertheless, this type of historical modelling can be highly useful and a fruitful source of research ideas.

Case study designs and action research

The case study is a design that seems to cause a lot of confusion in research students and even more experienced researchers. In simple terms, a case study is exactly as it sounds – the detailed analysis of a single case. It is a popular topic in many social research fields, and also in the managerial disciplines. It's also quite common in medical research contexts, and much of what is now accepted as medical knowledge (especially in the brain sciences) was generated by the in-depth study of particular patient cases. However, the source of the confusion seems to lie somewhere around exactly how one defines a 'case'. This is a surprisingly complex issue, and there are a great variety of approaches here. Most commonly, a case is defined as a single social setting. For example, it could be an organisation, a school, or some other kind of social context. Very often, the case is further delineated as a specific situation within that social setting. For example, it could be a case of mass redundancy in an organisation, or the implementation of a new policy in a school. However, a case can really be anything you want it to be, as long as there is a clear definition of what the case consists of, and a clear demarcation between what is 'in' the case and what is not.

The problem arises when one considers where to draw the line between a case study design, and a cross-sectional or longitudinal design based in a single context. For example, if you collect data in a single organisation, does this mean you are automatically doing case-study research? I, and other far more eminent scholars (e.g. Bryman, 2004) would argue not. To me, a piece of research can only be defined as a case study if the object of interest of the study in some way concerns the case itself, and not just what is going on within the single situation you are collecting data from. For example, much organisational research is conducted within a single firm. In most of these projects, the single firm is used in order to increase the likelihood of high-quality data, not as an object of interest in its own right.

The citations given above also raise the interesting question of whether case study research is necessarily qualitative or quantitative. I would think that you know me well enough by now to know what I would say to this. Certainly, there seems to be a common misconception that case study work is qualitative, but this is not really accurate. It is almost certain that most case studies will at the very least employ a mix of data collection methods, and even the most avowedly qualitative approach may include secondary quantitative data (like firm performance records, school exam results, and the like). And case studies *can* be entirely quantitative, but this is not often the situation. In particular, the logic behind case study research – the intensive examination of a single situation, and the focus on unique features of one setting – do not lend themselves exclusively to qualitative designs.

Furthermore, by now you should be able to quickly grasp that the underlying logic of case study research is thus not necessarily based on generalising findings to other situations. In fact, it is a source of debate as to whether one should be concerned with issues of validity, reliability or generalisability (which are dealt with in various ways throughout this book) within case study research. Here, there is little chance of a 'right' or 'wrong' answer, as it really does depend on your own philosophical background. However, it is important to realise that for many case study researchers, the aim of their work is *not* to generalise to other settings, but to deeply understand a single setting. It is the reader's choice as to whether that is a valuable outcome or not.

Possibly the key decision in a case study design is the choice of case itself. The case should be chosen for a solid theoretical reason, most commonly because it will in some way provide the necessary information to answer your research questions. This is of course a subjective judgement, and one which needs plenty of thought. Something else which needs thought is whether or not you need to select multiple cases. In particular, you should carefully consider whether you need cases with different characteristics in order to answer your research questions. For example, if your theory involved the idea that a programme of redundancies would result in lower levels of motivation for those employees not made redundant in a bureaucratic organisational culture than in an innovative organisational culture, a single organisational case would not allow you to answer this question. Here, you would probably need to find at least two cases, one organisation of each culture. This type of design is often known as a **comparative design**.

Strongly related to the case study approach is **action research**, which is an influential methodology in some of the more applied social and organisational fields. Action research is basically the idea that the researcher actually acts as an agent for change in a particular situation (e.g. a company, or a school). In this sense, the researcher is clearly part of the research itself, not standing apart from it. There are many different varieties of action research which have been developed, but they all share this basic characteristic. Another key feature is that theories which are developed through action research are tested by intervention in the research context. So if you develop a theory of classroom attendance, this theory is tested by putting the theory *into action*. The research is thus a collaboration between the researcher and the researched in many ways. In the first instance then, any theory coming from action research is somewhat context-specific, although in the long term (over a series of different projects) more general theories can be the result. This makes action research somewhat at odds with the traditional scientific model as presented in Chapter 2, and more consistent with the interpretive ideas of Chapter 3. Of course, like all of the other methods presented here, it is beyond the scope of this book to give full information on action research, but I recommend you look at this chapter's further reading list to learn more. Also, check out Professor Evert Gummesson's book which is referred to at the end of the next chapter.

Tying it all together

As you've probably worked out, different research designs tend to be associated with different methods of data collection. But remember, one of the key messages of this book is that saying such a thing is not the same as saying that one can *only* use certain methods with certain designs. However, it is unarguable that certain methods of data collection lend themselves better to achieving the goals of certain designs. It should also be quite clear from which philosophical perspective each of the designs developed (another reason for the methodological differences).

What is interesting about the different designs is that the logic behind them is generally similar, except where it isn't of course! What I mean by this slightly baffling statement is that most of the approaches are concerned with somehow observing *variation* in key variables, but stopping variation in extraneous ones. However, the case study approach is not necessarily interested in variation at all, but instead with deeply examining a single issue.

That said, there are quite a few overlaps between the methods when you think about it carefully. For example, if you conduct a study within a single industry to try to remove industry variation, you are incorporating some characteristics of the case study approach. Or when you collect data before and after a natural[15] event (e.g. the introduction of a price reduction) you are incorporating some of the logic of experimental design. So how do you decide what design to use? Of course, it depends on the best way to answer your research questions. One thing you should clearly understand is that one design is not inherently 'better' than another, whatever you may be told. But most certainly some designs are more appropriate for certain research questions than others.

Of course, in some fields certain designs hold more sway than others. In disciplines where the 'scientific' approach discussed in Chapter 2 holds sway, experimental methods tend to be seen as the 'top of the tree' to aim for. Case study approaches are often relegated to 'exploratory' status either implicitly or explicitly. In such disciplines, even cross-sectional work can often be considered a poor relation to the experiment. Yet in other disciplines, case study approaches are considered the norm, and other designs are far less popular. As a beginning researcher, you need to take into account these more 'political' issues – even though you shouldn't be driven too strongly by them. But it is definitely important to understand the political realities of your discipline.

---

[15]In this context, 'natural' means that it was not directly controlled by the researcher.

Summary

Research design is one of those subjects which can be as complex or as simple as you wish. For each one of the different types of designs I've written about above, entire books have been written. Yet as I noted at the beginning of the chapter, many researchers go through much of their careers with only a rudimentary appreciation of the broad sweep of research designs. Instead, such researchers tend to use the design they picked up during their formative years for most of their work, only looking to engage with the deeper issues of research design when they reach a road-block somewhere along the line (maybe a manuscript rejection, or an argument with another researcher!)

While this can lead to a long and successful research career, it does depend on the assumption that you learnt it the 'right' way at the start, and that all research questions you might ever want to answer can be approached the same way. To me, that kind of career would be a little boring for one thing. But it can also lead to a situation where, if someone from another research 'school-of-thought' criticises you, you have little defence other than saying: 'I did it this way because it's the only way I know'. Not a very convincing argument, and the kind of thing which leads to further entrenchment in your own methods and less appreciation for other options. So I hope you have picked up a broad appreciation of the key characteristics of various research designs, and where they may or may not be appropriate.

Key points to take from this chapter:

- That research designs are not necessarily bound to certain research methods, and that the principles inherent in the design can be captured with various methods.
- That variation is of critical importance for many research tasks, and that it can be split into three different types; theoretical, extraneous, and error.
- The concept of level of analysis, and how it relates to research design.
- That experimental research is often considered the bedrock on which other forms of research are built, and that it is also fundamentally based on the logic of comparison.
- How internal and external validity can influence the usefulness of your findings.
- That cross-sectional, longitudinal, and case-based research also have useful strengths, which can make them more appropriate to certain research tasks.

Further reading

- *Foundations of Behavioral Research* by Fred N. Kerlinger and Howard Lee. An excellent and in-depth introduction to research design (and many other aspects of research) from a traditional behavioural science perspective. This means it is great for experimental designs in particular.
- *Marketing Research: Methodological Foundations* by Gilbert A. Churchill and Dawn Iacobucci. Currently in at least its 9th edition (the older editions were solely authored by Churchill), this is another classic text on general research methods, but from a more applied research

perspective. This means it is a little broader than the Kerlinger and Lee book above, and devotes more attention to different research designs.

- *Qualitative Inquiry and Research Design* by John W. Creswell. A great discussion of various different traditions and designs for qualitative researchers. Yet again, though, I think the principles in this book can be of use to all researchers.
- *Experimental and Quasi-Experimental Designs for Generalised Causal Infererence*, by William R. Shadish, Thomas D. Cook, and Donald T. Campbell. This is the latest edition of a truly classic book (earlier editions were authored by just Cook and Campbell), which deals with how to design experiments in the most valid way for various situations.
- *Case Study Research: Design and Methods* by Robert K. Yin. Another classic text dealing with a specific type of research design mentioned here. If you are interested in designing case studies in a rigorous manner, start here.

EXERCISES

1. Imagine a research question regarding the causes of absenteeism within the workplace (the question is deliberately broad):

   a. First think about what the key independent variable(s) might be for your theory (i.e. theoretical variation), and at what level of analysis they might be.
   b. Secondly, what kinds of extraneous variation could you face?
   c. Thirdly, how will you maximise your ability to see theoretical variation, and minimise extraneous variation?
   d. From here, you should get a good picture of which of the general research designs is most appropriate for your research question. So which is it – experimental, cross-sectional, longitudinal, or case – and why?
   e. Once you have decided this, try to design research questions which would be appropriate for examination using the three research designs *other* than the one you decided on for part d.

2. Think clearly and carefully about the differences between internal and external validity. How might these be linked together? Is there a necessary trade-off between internal and external validity? Or is it possible to design a research study which is very high on both? What might such a study look like?
3. I think you should at this point make a list of your 10 favourite songs, and play them in order from lowest to highest. Then justify why you chose Number 1.

Chapter 9
Collecting qualitative data

SUPERVISOR'S VIEW: PROFESSOR EVERT GUMMESSON

There remains a lot to be done in developing our skills of collecting higher quality qualitative data. Quantitative researchers have the same quality problem but they live under the illusion that numbers are precise and objective. It's a snug life in the best of all worlds. 'No worries', to quote Crocodile Dundee.

Qualitative researchers live messier lives. One disturbing observation is that our ability to collect – or rather generate data, because data are primarily socially constructed – does not seem to improve. Case studies today are not built on higher data quality than 20 years ago. Where is the progress? The techniques that are presented in handbooks are the same, except that the Internet has opened up new opportunities.

However, business reality (my field of research) is risky, ambiguous, fuzzy, chaotic and unpredictable. I have advocated that we should start with the basic issue, that of access, and then do our best to get close to the phenomenon we are chasing. Although we can't do without it, the research ritual is not the real thing; it's the validity and relevance of results that count. Advice from books and classes is a great starting point, but to match professional explorers – Columbus, Sherlock Holmes, Einstein, investigative journalists like Mike Wallace of '60 Minutes', or businesspeople breaking new ground like Richard Branson – researchers have to: (a) practice; (b) use all senses, intuition, experience, wisdom, insights, judgement, creativity and audacity; and (c) be systematic and reflective, swing between involvement and detachment and between being law-and-order bureaucrats and free-wheeling entrepreneurs.

Research techniques have no life of their own – they only come alive through the researcher's persona.

VIEW FROM THE TRENCHES: JENNIFER WALKER

Start early and expect setbacks! My advice to anyone embarking on qualitative research is never to underestimate the difficulty and time-consuming nature of this form of data collection. As soon as you know what your methodology is, get going! It will take you longer than you think! I remember realising the enormity of the task that lay before me as I watched with jealousy my quantitative data-collecting friends receiving their questionnaires within hours of whipping up a quick group email. Qualitative research usually relies on a relatively small number of people giving up a significant amount of time, often for little or no reward. To convince anyone to participate is a challenge in itself, but it can be done!

I conducted three focus groups for my M.Sc. dissertation, and struggled to get committed people who could attend the sessions all at the same time. I found that if someone sounded slightly non-committal, then they almost always eventually dropped out. It's practically impossible to coerce people into giving up their time, so only add a participant to your list if they sound genuinely interested in attending. I was tempted on occasions to put off my focus group sessions for certain potential participants who I thought would be excellent respondents, but who had limited spare time. This isn't a good idea as it can just lead to deadlines being pushed back and other respondents losing interest. It can sometimes be frustrating and demoralising, but if you always assume that there will be a few no-shows, you can compensate for it. It is useful to have some back-up participants ready to step in if necessary as a depleted focus group can limit the flow of conversation and reduce the strength of your results.

All-in-all though, if you're determined and organised, collecting qualitative data can give you a real sense of achievement and can provide fantastically interesting results for analysis.

Qualitative research is an interesting area (do you notice I keep saying that about everything?). I remember a few years ago when I was still a bright young (and good-looking) lecturer asking a class whether they felt that they preferred qualitative to quantitative research. When a vote was called for, at least 70 per cent of the class voted that yes they did indeed prefer doing qualitative to quantitative work. Intrigued, I picked on one of the students as to a reason why: 'Because you can like, blag it can't you?' was the answer. Of course, this student was referring to the idea that you could simply make qualitative results up, rather than be forced to use objective formulae and procedures as in quantitative approaches. That moment permanently shaped my own personal approach to qualitative work, and teaching it. No, not towards 'blagging it', but towards demonstrating how qualitative work can be just as rigorous as many think quantitative work is – from whatever philosophical perspective one comes from.

In fact, depending on how experienced a researcher you are, you may have already come across the manifestations of the 'qualitative-quantitative divide' in your career. In fact, the various disagreements touched on in Chapter 3 are in some ways related to this. As I have already mentioned, arguments between researchers who are committed to qualitative and/or quantitative methodologies have been heated and destructive throughout the last 50 years in various social science fields. However, if you remember back to Chapter 3, I suggested that these arguments should not be conducted at the methodological level, but are instead mainly concerned with alternative ways of looking at the world. Once you become clear about your philosophical standpoint, methodological decisions are (or should be) in fact mainly technical – i.e. which type of data can answer your research question most effectively? It is from this perspective that the following chapter (and in fact the next six chapters) should be read.

More specifically, I hope that as a researcher you will decide on the appropriate methodology for each part of your research project in light of your needs, not dependent on any prejudices of yourself or your colleagues/supervisor. As a result, this chapter is mainly concerned with the practicalities of qualitative data collection. Nevertheless, where different philosophical standpoints would suggest contrasting or alternative techniques, I spend time noting these, and their implications for doing good research. However, one thing you should be immediately aware of is that – despite the 'blagging' image – doing good qualitative research is just as (if not more) difficult than doing good quantitative work. Even though there are no complex formulae or numbers, there are many other difficult ideas to come to terms with.

My ultimate aim here is to provide an overview of qualitative data collection which can be used by all researchers, not just those who are committed interpretivists. At the same time, I want to show how good qualitative work can be useful even in the most hard-core scientific research projects. Anyway, at the end of this chapter I really hope you have come to terms with these key ideas:

- What 'rigour' is in qualitative research.
- The importance of sampling to the quality of your research.
- The range of different qualitative data sources and collection methods.
- How important decisions on transcribing and recording your data are.

Why is it Important to Know This Stuff?

This chapter will be read by two types of people, those who are thinking about taking a qualitative approach to their project, and a few interested readers who wish to gain a basic understanding of qualitative data collection, but have little intention of ever actually doing it. I think this is a sad situation. As I have said and will repeatedly stress, methodology decisions should not be based on prior prejudices, but on what is the best way of getting data and analysing it *for the issue in question.* There are so many researchers who consider themselves as 'quantitative' or 'qualitative', without a real understanding of either why or what the 'other' methodology actually entails. Inaccuracy and dogma are rife in social science!

The enlightened researcher (which will be everyone who reads this book cover to cover, I hope) can make the appropriate methodological decision in light of their research question – which will of course also depend on their philosophical standpoint. Therefore, a good researcher will have at the very least a basic grounding in both quantitative and qualitative data collection and analysis issues. Fundamentally, we are dealing with the same issues as in many of the later chapters – i.e. how do we actually obtain data from the real world? This is shown in Figure 9.1, which by now I imagine is looking kind of familiar.

A repeated theme of mine is the idea of critical self-evaluation. Understanding about different research methods will allow you to see exactly where your own position is, and why you are holding it. This allows you to clearly defend yourself when you are challenged. If an examiner (or reviewer) asks you 'why did (or didn't) you use a qualitative approach)' you will need a good answer. The material in this chapter is a good start on how to answer a question like that.

On a pragmatic level, the material in this chapter should be useful to everyone. Firstly, of course, it provides an introduction to how to get out into the field and collect data. It also distils a number of unfortunate mistakes and other experiences I have had out there myself – hopefully you won't repeat them after reading it! But, even if you never get out into the wide world and collect qualitative data, you will almost certainly need to evaluate other projects (e.g. articles) which have done so – without a grounding in the area you may not be able to do so effectively. Even worse, you may never read any qualitative research, and miss out on a rich and fascinating section of your own theoretical literature. And of course, if all you want to do is criticise qualitative research, well you are going to need to know about it somewhat aren't you?

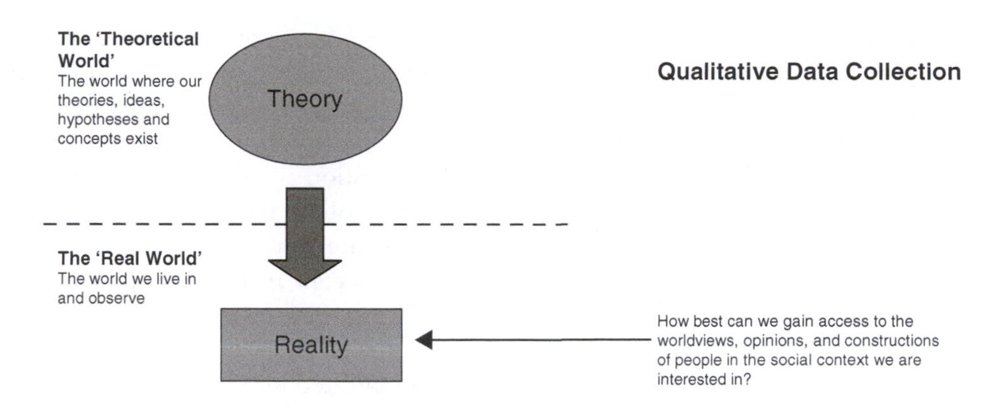

Figure 9.1 The place of qualitative data collection

Rigour in qualitative research

The concept of 'rigour' is not one which most quantitatively oriented researchers would associate with qualitative research. Normally, such researchers assume qualitative work to be 'soft', 'subjective', and maybe a little bit 'flaky'. Certainly, the subjectivity of qualitative work can be one of its prime strengths, in particular when we consider the contextually situated nature of qualitative work (see Chapter 3 for some more information on context and subjectivity). In fact, some philosophical perspectives actually 'play up' to this soft and subjective image, inherently disagreeing with the very idea that research itself can ever be objective (again, have a look at Chapter 3 if this isn't that clear to you). However, for the beginning researcher, I feel that it isn't really necessary to get into these debates. In fact, many researchers who use or want to use qualitative work are not fundamentally committed to an interpretivist philosophical framework. For those researchers, the idea of rigour is a key one. That said, if one wishes to evaluate rigour, surely one needs to have some criteria to do so? Of course, as usual, this has been the source of some debate.

Rigour is a slippery notion. It can be taken in a broad sense to refer to the 'quality' of your research methods – are they consistent with good practice in your particular context? Or in an even more general sense, is there *any* kind of coherent strategy behind your research efforts at all? In qualitative research there are many different ways of approaching the idea of rigour. Perhaps a good place to start are concepts of reliability and validity. You should remember these two ideas from the couple of chapters about measurement, and how they can be used to help judge the quality of your measurement (and thus your research). However, in a qualitative context we don't really 'measure' things in the same way as in a quantitative one. So are reliability and validity still relevant? Well, as is the case with most things in this book, there are different ways to approach the issue.

Some qualitative methodologists have tried to transfer notions of reliability and validity directly to qualitative research (without the measurement connotations of course). Judging by the references that appear in assignments, one book which is quite popular with my students is by Mason (1996), which clearly appropriates validity from quantitative research, describing it as essentially being about answering the question of whether you are actually observing or measuring what you say you are. Or in other words, is what you 'say' is happening in your research actually happening? Or are you in fact deluded (say by your inherent biases). We'll look at this in a lot more detail in the next chapter about analysis. Others have looked at *external* and *internal* concepts of validity and reliability (e.g. LeCompte *et al.*, 1993). External reliability essentially refers to whether your study can be replicated by another researcher, which is a complicated idea in qualitative research, being as it depends so heavily on the context and the researcher. Internal reliability is not really relevant to single-researcher studies, as it refers to whether different researchers agree about the same piece of data. Internal validity is quite similar to the approach to validity mentioned above, and concerns whether your theoretical ideas match up to the data. External validity is similar to notions of 'generalisability' which you have no doubt heard of before. Here we are talking about whether your findings can be applied to other social contexts apart from the one you have studied. In qualitative terms this can be a difficult question as the logic behind qualitative work is quite different from the statistical logic behind quantitative generalisation. Of course, the approaches to validity and reliability mentioned above are not the only way of looking at the concept of rigour in qualitative research. Alternative View 9.1 covers some different ways of exploring the issues.

Alternative View 9.1: Alternative Approaches to the Rigour Issue

Not all qualitative researchers have been happy to simply appropriate ideas of reliability and validity from traditional quantitative research. Instead, authors such as Guba and Lincoln (e.g. 1994) suggest using **trustworthiness** as a criterion for evaluating qualitative research. In turn, trustworthiness consists of four main components. Firstly, *credibility* refers to whether your findings bear any relationship to the data you drew them from. *Transferability* is about whether you can justifiably transfer your findings to any other contexts. *Dependability* is similar to reliability in that it's about how well you can assure people of your findings and the way you got to them from the raw social context. Finally, *confirmability* refers to whether you can show people that you acted appropriately in your research, in terms of not being influenced by biases (either from your own personal values, or theoretical background).

There are even more extreme approaches to rigour, which in fact seem to reject the very concept itself. For example, Lather (1993) draws from postmodern theory to create something she calls 'ironic validity', which appears to consider traditional concepts of validity mere rhetorical devices.

The interpretive philosophical standpoint of course considers reality to be a social construction between actors (e.g. the researcher and the subject), so how can we ever assess the 'accuracy' of our representations in relation to some objective standard? Thus, it seems that some authors have replaced a concern for such standards with notions of whether a research project provides any 'benefit' to its constituency. That said, Seale (2004) strongly criticises such approaches to evaluating the rigour of qualitative research, which 'substitute moral values and political positions as guarantors of standards', calling them 'frighteningly weak' (p. 409). Instead, he argues for – rather than objective criteria – a recognition of 'the value of careful scholarship, commitment to rigorous argument, attending to the links between claims and evidence, consideration of all viewpoints before taking a stance, [and] asking and answering important rather than trivial research questions' (pp. 409–410). These ideas would appear to be a useful guide to research practice for most scholars

Of course, it can be seen that these ideas of how to approach the question of rigour are inextricably bound up with how you view the world, the existence of an objective truth, and the possibility of a researcher ever uncovering it. If one believes one is trying to uncover the essential 'truth' of a social situation by doing research, then of course, traditional notions of 'validity' are appropriate when evaluating the quality of your representation of that reality. However, if one believes that there is no such thing as a truth (remember Chapter 3?) then it seems somewhat futile to attempt to see how close our research has come to uncovering it. Instead, researchers from this (non-realist) perspective tend to reject the concepts of reliability and validity, and focus on the characteristics of the representation, almost as an end in itself (see Alternative View 9.1).

Personally, I tend to take something of a middle ground here. As you are no doubt aware by now, I do believe that there is an external reality which I am investigating, but also recognise that in a qualitative context this reality may be represented in different ways. It is the researcher's job to convince their audience that their own representation is somehow valuable, and in my opinion this means it should somehow bear some credible relation to the data and situation which I drew it from. In other words, is my interpretation of that social situation **justifiable**? It is the process of convincing the audience of that justifiability which I believe is the key task of the researcher. I flatly reject the Feyerabendian[1] notion that any conclusion is useful if it somehow provides benefit, whether or not it is based on any kind of justifiable interpretation of data. Conclusions should always be in some way justified in relation to the data and the way it was collected and analysed or interpreted, whether this be quantitative or qualitative. In a qualitative context one can take many approaches to this justification process, as hopefully, I have already shown. However, as you move through this and the next chapter, you'll come across related ideas of validity and reliability very regularly. In fact, whatever approach you take, an appreciation for the various concepts of validity and reliability should permeate all of your qualitative research, from design to analysis to the write-up. Hopefully, the tools in these chapters will help you come to terms with assessing the rigour of your qualitative work, since without assuring the reader of the rigour of your findings, how can a reader be sure of the value of those findings to them?

Qualitative sampling

Sampling is an issue which often causes students and researchers some confusion within a qualitative context. More specifically, most of us are brought up on the logic of statistical sampling (see Chapter 11 for this), and then when we learn about qualitative sampling we have considerable trouble fitting it into that model. At worst, we assume that either (a) we should try to achieve the ideal of 'probability sampling' for qualitative research, or (b) all qualitative sampling is 'convenience'. Neither of these assumptions is particularly helpful, and lead to some considerable misperceptions about qualitative work.

The key issue to consider is that qualitative sampling actually relies on a completely different logic to quantitative sampling. In fact, it can be argued that one isn't actually collecting data at all, but instead *generating* it in conjunction with your participants. Alternative View 9.2 discusses this idea. In terms of 'ideals', while the quantitative approach is based around the ideal of a random selection of a (usually large) sample of cases from a given population, to my mind good qualitative work is based around the ideal of a 'purposive' selection of a small number of cases from the population – which is about as far away from 'random' sampling as you can get. There are many ways of exploring why this is the case, but I want to try to get away from philosophical arguments and make this point relevant to all researchers. The simple practical reasons we can't rely on the standard statistical logic of sampling in qualitative research are due to its reliance on small samples, and the necessity to generate rich information about your research questions (if we aren't doing the latter, then why use qualitative research at all?) Therefore, we need a sampling

---

[1] I think I just made that word up, but if you don't know what I mean, go back to Chapter 2 and look at Alternative View 2.2 to brush up on your philosophy.

method that helps us select cases that are likely to be able to provide us with this rich information.

Alternative View 9.2: Data Collection or Data *Generation*?

There are two alternative ways of looking at data – which you can probably work out for yourself from close reading of Chapters 2 and 3. However, now is probably a good time to revisit them in the context of practicalities. First of all, the traditional positivistic/realist approach would consider data to simply 'exist' in the world, waiting for you to collect it. In this framework, the method you use to collect it should be the appropriate one of course, but the researcher themselves should have no influence on the research subjects or the data. Moreover, many research theorists who take a more interpretive approach to research would consider this unrealistic, particularly in the case of qualitative research. Instead, a researcher could consider that they *generate* the data in conjunction with the participants or data sources. In other words, the very interaction of the researcher with the respondent, context, data source, and situation act together with the researcher's own perceptions to co-create the actual corpus of data. Furthermore, the researcher is usually at least implicitly analysing the data at the same time. In this framework, data does not exist independent of the research itself. This subjective and interactionist framework is repeatedly referred to in other chapters of this book, and many of the further readings given at the end of this chapter develop it more fully.

Without a knowledge of the qualitative sampling logic, researchers can make the mistake of assuming their qualitative sampling must be 'convenience', as most general research texts discuss this method (in their chapters on 'sampling'), and convenience sampling looks quite similar to what one may have to do in a qualitative project. Unfortunately, this leads to the misperception that qualitative methods are not based on a rigorous sampling methodology, which then impacts on perceptions of the validity of qualitative work – and especially the external validity. In fact, good qualitative work should have a systematic and well-defined sampling plan, which allows the researcher to define exactly why each case is selected, rather than simply grabbing the first few people on the street, your flatmates, or whoever responds first to your request for participants.[2]

Along these lines, a good base to build from in learning about qualitative sampling is the idea of **purposive sampling**. Purposive sampling is exactly what it sounds like, sampling with a *purpose*. Most of the time the purpose here is to sample cases or people who are *relevant*

[2]Indeed, these last three would be classic 'convenience' samples.

to your research questions. This could of course mean pretty much whatever you want it to mean, but I like to think of it as looking for the cases which are likely to provide information regarding your key research objectives and theoretical questions. Of course, you'll note that you should therefore have some kind of idea regarding your theory before you go out into the field. I think this is a good idea, but you should be aware that some researchers do not agree (see Alternative View 9.3). Also, you should not forget that cases which are relevant to your research are not restricted to those which you think will support your theory; *deviant cases* are ones which you think have characteristics which mean they may contradict your theory. A very strong test of the theory is therefore whether it holds in such deviant cases.

Alternative View 9.3: To Theorise or not to Theorise?

There is a school of thought among qualitative researchers which advocates beginning a qualitative project with no appreciation of existing theory. This kind of thinking probably comes from the grounded theory perspective of Glaser and Strauss (1967). They argued in their seminal book that the researcher should be *tabula rasa*, a blank slate, before going into the field. Those of you with good memories should recall this phrase from Chapter 2, as it was used by John Locke in his argument for pure Empiricism (and thus I find the use of it somewhat ironic in this context). The argument against prior theorising seems to be based on the idea that an awareness of previous theory might bias your ability to let the data truly speak to you, and your interpretation will be contaminated by your pre-existing mental models.

Of course, it is a little naive to imagine that a researcher is ever able to completely cut himself or herself off from theory about their subject for all kinds of practical reasons. I mean, it's not as if researchers start off on research projects without first being interested in them, and looking around for information. Most of us get our ideas from reading theory anyway! In fact, the use of prior theory appears to have caused something of a bust-up between Glaser and Strauss in later years. Strauss' subsequent work (e.g. Strauss and Corbin, 1998) actually advocates some appreciation of prior literature before going into the field, while Glaser (1992) remains committed to the idea of letting theory 'emerge' from data with no prior knowledge.

Whether or not you go along with the possibility that one can ever be completely *tabula rasa*, this argument has an important upshot. Basically, as a researcher you should be very careful as to how you let your appreciation of existing theory influence your research, and be sure that you are not being overly biased.

Purposive sampling has considerable overlap with **theoretical sampling**, which is a specific term introduced by Glaser and Strauss (1967) in their work on *grounded theory*.

Grounded theory is a complicated and specific qualitative method, but concepts from it have found their way into many qualitative research methods, including the ones I like to use. Theoretical sampling is, I think, a very good structure to base your qualitative sampling strategy on. You can think of it as beginning with purposive sampling as above (although there is disagreement on how much theory you should have before you go into the field for the first time, see Alternative View 9.3), but then continuing as an iterative process, by letting the theories and findings which emerge from your data influence the next round of sampling. In other words, the theory controls the data collection. IDE 9.1 provides an example of how theoretical sampling could work in the context of a practical research project.

IDE 9.1: Theoretical Sampling

When I conducted my own Ph.D. research, I began with a qualitative study of sales force members. My preliminary reading of the relevant literature had suggested that it was going to be important to tap both sides of the manager–employee dyad. So this was my first theoretical criteria. Furthermore, early theoretical ideas had emerged regarding the likely influence of other characteristics, such as gender, job experience, and industry type. Selecting cases which varied on these characteristics was also an important criteria for my sample.

An important component of theoretical sampling is to look for 'deviant cases'. Such cases are ones which seem likely to provide information that might contradict your theory, and you are usually better able to select such cases the more time you have spent on the project. For example, after a few interviews, it became clear that certain industries (e.g. photocopiers) seemed to be populated by highly aggressive managers, some of whom commented that other industries were less so. As a result, I moved on to select some cases from the health care industry, as this was one which had been specifically mentioned by respondents as being 'softer'. If I could still uncover similar behavioural styles in industries such as machine tools or photocopiers, I could be more certain of my theory.

Another key way I worked was to use 'snowballing' methods. More specifically, I asked each respondent at the end of the interview to suggest managers (or salespeople) they knew who would (a) be interested in participating, and (b) provide either similar or contradictory information. Combining this with the theoretical criteria, I was able to develop a very comprehensive sampling strategy. Furthermore, using an iterative and continuous process of transcribing and analysis (i.e. not waiting until the end to start) I was able to judge the point when I began to reach 'theoretical saturation', and therefore stop collecting data.

One thing theoretical sampling has much to say on is sample size, a concept that is often used as a stick to beat qualitative work with. Specifically, as already mentioned, qualitative work tends to use small samples, which goes against the traditional statistical logic of large, random samples. Theoretical sampling takes the actual size of the sample to be less than relevant. Instead, since theoretical sampling is an iterative process, you should continue sampling until you reach what is called *theoretical saturation*. Although this concept can be difficult to grasp, you can think of theoretical saturation for a particular idea or concept as being reached when no new information about that concept comes to light in repeated cases, you are very clear about what that concept actually is and how it varies, and that the relationships between it and other concepts are well defined (Strauss and Corbin, 1998). Of course, this means that one does not select a sample size prior to research design, but that it develops somewhat organically as the research proceeds.

That said, as a rule of thumb, it is unlikely that you will gain enough information on a reasonably complex theory from fewer than 20 interviews, and the more complex your theory is, the more interviews will be needed. This complexity can be concerned with how many sub-groups you need to sample (men and women, different social classes, many different industrial groups, etc.), or the number of theoretical concepts in your study, or many other things. One useful way of describing this to yourself, to aid in selecting your final sample size, is detailed in Figure 9.2, with reference to a study of sales manager problem resolution I conducted for my Ph.D. dissertation.

However, although it is easy to do, you shouldn't fall into the trap of automatically thinking that 'people' are the only sampling units. In fact in qualitative research many other units may be relevant. For example, in research on customer complaints, the appropriate sampling unit may be an incident of poor service – and each single person may have multiple instances of this. In organisational psychology the relevant unit may be managerial

	Industry Type					
	Capital Equipment		**Office Products**		**Health Care**	
			Gender			
Position	*M*	*F*	*M*	*F*	*M*	*F*
Sales Manager						
Salesperson						

Figure 9.2 A sample matrix

punishment interactions, again an individual manager may have many of these to draw from. In relationship research the best unit may be failed relationships, and I can imagine that most people have a string of such sampling units! In situations like this your sample may consist of 20 *people*, but many more relevant units, and you should think in terms of this when you do your sampling. For example, no matter how many actual people you sample, you can never reach theoretical saturation unless you sample enough variety in the appropriate unit.

Of course, there are times when convenience sampling is all we can do. However, it is vital we are aware of what kind of respondents we need, and where to find them. One way of doing this is to use snowball sampling. In such situations, you can use one informant to suggest others who may have useful information on your research topic. Or you can use personal contacts to help you find the right people or cases to sample. Again though, you are looking for people who have the right kind of information for your study, not just anyone. For example, for the type of study suggested in Figure 9.2 there was no point in asking my fellow-student flatmates for interviews as they would have virtually no information of relevance. However, I could have asked them for some contacts of people they knew in business who would have been useful.

The key point to take away here is that sampling is an extremely important part of qualitative research, and should be treated as such. In my opinion, the entire usefulness (call it validity if you want) of your study rests on the appropriate selection of sampling units. If you can not justify to the reader why your sample is appropriate, why should they place any worth in your findings? Of course, once you decide on your sampling method, you then need to decide on how you will actually access your data, which is what the next sections deal with.

Interviewing

Interviewing is probably the most popular technique in academic qualitative research. It's also a very useful base to build from in looking at other qualitative techniques, so you should take the material in this section as relevant to other qualitative data collection methods as well. Interviewing is useful because it's very flexible, both in terms of content and time, and can be tailored to suit your research questions, respondents, and your own lifestyle much more effectively than many other qualitative methods. However, you should not get *qualitative* interviewing confused with the structured interviewing you might do in quantitative research – where you may get a respondent to fill in a structured questionnaire face-to-face or over the telephone. A good way to make this distinction is to think of qualitative interviews as **in-depth interviews**, which also gives a nice flavour of their roots in depth psychology and psychoanalysis. In-depth interviews are of course far less structured than quantitative interviews, and to a greater or lesser extent are driven by the interviewee, not the interviewer. Furthermore, in-depth interviews commonly go off-track to pursue interesting angles and examples, and this freewheeling, flexible approach is usually encouraged by the interviewer to some extent. The key difference however is that in an in-depth interview we are looking for *rich*, *in-depth* answers which tap deeply into the respondents own experiences, feelings, and opinions.

That said, in-depth interviews can be split into two main types, the **unstructured** and the **semi-structured**. While these are essentially two ends of a continuum (and thus rarely used in their purest form) they provide a useful contrast. In a totally unstructured interview, the interviewer will at the most use a few brief topics (sometimes just one) to prompt the interviewee, who is then allowed to respond however they want. Probing by the interviewer is only done to follow up points of interest, or to keep things going along smoothly. Conversely, the semi-structured interview is guided by a more detailed *topic guide* which will contain some fairly specific questions to ask, and likely ways of probing, examples to ask for and so on. There remains a lot of flexibility to follow up individual points, but in general the same questions will be asked of each interviewee.

Unstructured interviews are usually used when the researcher feels that even a basic structure will 'impose' a particular worldview on interviewees, and prejudice access to their internal views, feelings and experiences. You should make the link here back to Chapter 3, and be thinking that this kind of opinion is likely to be held most strongly by the committed phenomenologist. My own feelings are that using unstructured interviews can make it very difficult in pragmatic terms to generate useful data, since there is no guarantee that the respondent will talk about anything relevant! However, the philosophical point is well-made, and unstructured interviews can be very useful in the right circumstances. Semi-structured interviews, on the other, hand are particularly useful if you already have a clear theoretical appreciation of your topic (e.g. from a literature review), which allows you to structure a good topic guide. Also, in multi-person data collection teams, or multiple-site (or case) investigations some structure is needed to make sure all the interviews are comparable. Nevertheless, the choice of structure is dependent both on philosophical and practical considerations. The more committed to a social constructivist, non-realist viewpoint, the lesser degree of structure you are likely to desire, although you should balance this against practical considerations.

I referred above to something called a topic guide, which can also be called an interview guide. It's your key document, and a good one will ensure that your interviews go well. It is essentially a memory prompt, and schedule for your interview. Of course, it will contain different degrees of detail depending on how structured you wish to make your interview, but I will discuss here a guide for a typical semi-structured interview. You need to think very carefully about how you will get the information you want – how will you ask questions to access the internal worldviews and experiences of your respondents, which will enable you to answer your research questions? Without a guide, your interview can quickly descend into either (a) chaos, when the interviewee goes off on completely irrelevant tangents (such as relating stories of their last birthday party, which has happened to me), or (b) awkward silence when you have no idea what to say next. Some parts of an example interview guide are provided in Figure 9.3, from my own doctoral research. You should in particular try to order your topics in some consistent way, which will help the flow of the interview. For example, start with broad topics followed by more detailed probing. Furthermore, if there are particular questions you tend to forget, or sound awkward asking, write these down to help you out. Also, if you have trouble linking sections of the interview together, write down some link phrases to help.

Of course, the key part to your interview is the actual questions you ask. They are the way that you access the internal world of your respondents, so they had better be good. While

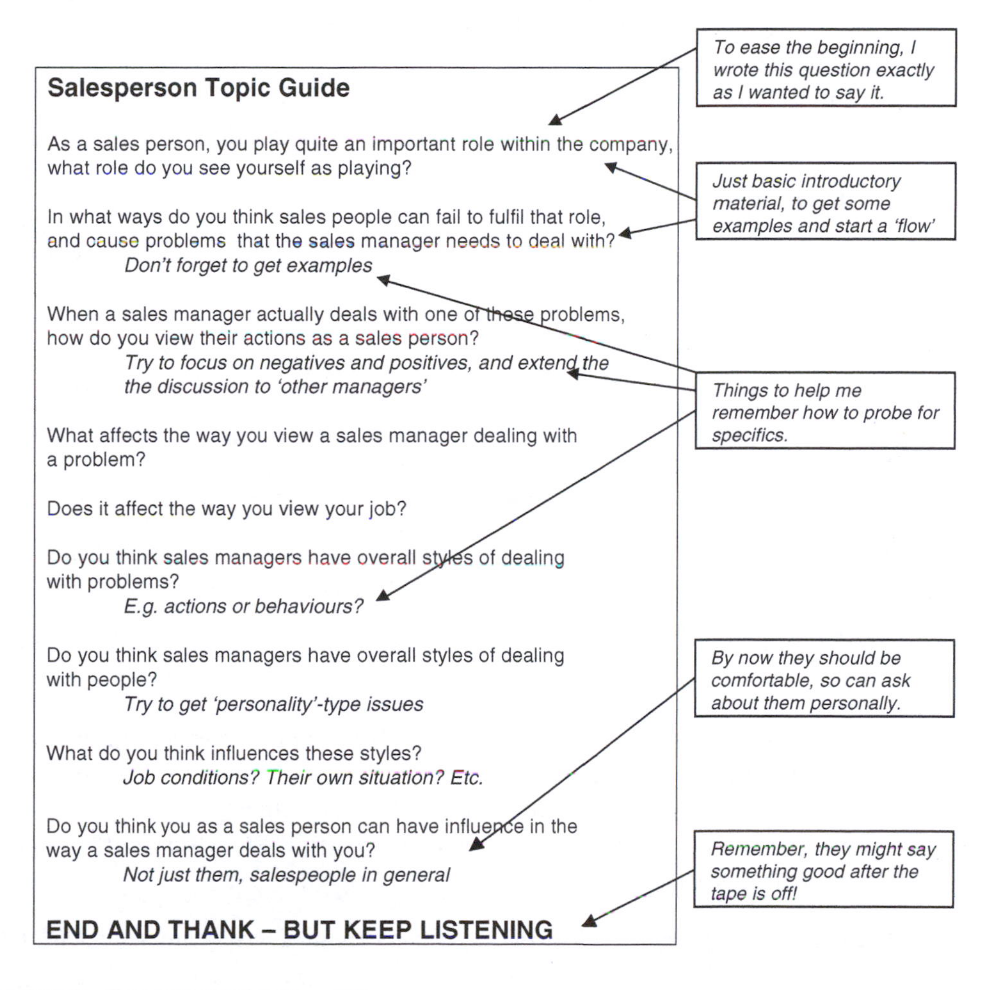

Figure 9.3 Example brief topic guide

good interviewing is a skill (simply watch a variety of TV talk shows for an illustration of how skill is important), there are a number of key different types of questions which you can learn which should help you develop into a great interviewer. There are also some questions you need to avoid at all costs. IDE 9.2 shows the different types of questions you should know about.

Finally, there are some practicalities (which are also relevant to other types of qualitative data collection) which should stand you in good stead. Most of these are based on my own experience (i.e. mistakes) so trust me, they are important. First, make sure you are prepared, that you know the topic, as well as the interviewee's own situational context, to help you understand the interview better. Prepare by *practising* interviewing, perhaps interviewing your friends, getting videoed and watching yourself (painful, I know), to find out where you tend to go wrong or right. You would be stunned just how helpful this is. If possible make sure the setting is quiet and private. I have interviewed people in restaurants, canteens, and all kinds of noisy places; it's not ideal let me tell you.

IDE 9.2: Different Types of Questions

Questioning techniques are vital to qualitative interviewing, you need to understand how to use questions to get the rich data you want. The worst type of question in a qualitative interview is one that results in a closed 'yes' or 'no' answer – you might as well get them to tick a box! Here are some more useful types of questions:

Introductory	*'Can you tell me about...?'*
Follow-up	*Use active listening, repeating,reflections*
Probing	*'Can you expand on...?'*
Specifying	*What, 'why, when, how much of...?'*
Structuring	*'Can we move to...?'*
Interpreting	*'Does that mean...?'*

For some more sensitive topics, you need to be a little more creative. For example, when I was doing research on sales manager problem resolution, I came to realise (eventually), that people were often more comfortable talking about 'other' people than themselves or their employees. I used some of the following techniques to gain information in that context:

Hypothetical	*'Suppose your manager was to sack me, what would that be like?'*

Devil's Advocate	*'Some say problem employees bring it on themselves, what do you say?'*
Ideal Position	*'How would an ideal manager deal with this problem?'*
Interpretive	*'Would you say that dealing with problem employees is more difficult than you expected?'*

Also, make sure you have your equipment completely sorted, and you know how it works! I'll be talking more about tape recording later on. Finally, make sure you get to the location nice and early, so you are not late, panicky and sweaty, which is never a good look, and tends to get things off to a bad start.

During the interview, I usually begin by getting a basic record of key data on each respondent, such as demographics and the like, which is really useful later on when you may wish to make comparisons across different groups, or get a feel for the context of the interview. When questioning, try not to get over-excited and lead the respondent down paths you particularly want them to go; let them get there themselves. Conversely, you must be interested in the respondent and what they have to say; at all costs try not to look bored! When you have finished the interview, it's also often useful to switch off the tape recorder, or use some other obvious 'close' (like 'thanks' or the like), and just keep chatting a little while. You will find that many fascinating points come up here, so keep your ears open. After the interview, as soon as possible make a few basic notes on what happened, and the key points were, as well as your own first thoughts on the information. This summary can be really useful later on when you analyse, and just to get clear in your head lessons for the next interview.

Focus groups

Focus groups are a form of qualitative data collection which involves the simultaneous participation of a number (usually around five to eight) of respondents, along with a moderator or facilitator. They have been common for many years in commercial market research, but only recently have they made inroads into academic social and organisational research. Even in academic marketing research their use is relatively infrequent. Focus groups should not be thought of as simply a way of saving resources by getting more respondents at the same time (i.e. 'simultaneous individual interviews'), but as a specific method in their own right. By definition, a focus group is *focused* on a particular topic, and should be used because the researcher wishes to explore the way that topic is discussed or constructed *by the group*, not as a set of individuals. As a result, group dynamics and processes are of key importance to a researcher who wishes to use focus groups. This means that a moderator should spend some time learning about group dynamics (hopefully with some practice before the first group). In particular, watch for participants who either (a) try to take over the group, or (b) avoid expressing any opinions at all. Such participants need to managed carefully.

Focus groups are especially useful for topics which are of common public concern to the group you wish to study, such as advertising, consumption, politics, or health. Within an organisational research context, focus groups are useful to explore many kinds of issues, such as change management, organisational policies, and the like. They can also be useful in a highly exploratory context when you wish to gain a basic grounding in a social setting, or particular topic, since they allow the researcher to observe how social actors interact, use language, and provide a wide range of viewpoints. Focus groups also mean the moderator has less power to direct the group than in an individual interview, which allows participants more scope to bring issues of importance to them out. As well as this, the group setting provides more scope for participants to be challenged and have their views argued with. While this can be a challenge for the moderator, it has the advantage of providing a more genuine picture of how issues are discussed and thought about in the social world. Thus, a well-run focus group can give more opportunity to study how the social world is constructed by participants – as we do not experience the world in isolation, but construct it together with other actors.

Nevertheless, focus groups are not always the appropriate choice. First of all, for the inexperienced researcher it can be a major challenge to moderate a focus group. This can be exacerbated by the type of respondents you wish to use. For example, you should be very careful about the make-up of your focus group in terms of the mix of demographics and their relation to your research topic. Sometimes you may wish to bring opposing viewpoints together for a specific purpose, but in many cases this can cause major problems to the moderator. In such situations, professional moderators may be required. For example, for one particular study, I and a colleague wished to examine young children's opinions and attitudes to Fair Trade products (see Nicholls and Lee, 2006). As children are notoriously difficult to control in group situations, we used a trained moderator to collect the data. Furthermore, some types of people are very difficult to organise into a focus group, often simply because of scheduling problems. Table 9.1 provides a very basic comparison of the kinds of topics and respondents which are most ideally suited to either individual or focus group interviews. However, this table is not a set of 'rules', just a set of things to consider when selecting your method. Any topic or respondent can be appropriate to any method, depending on specific contextual considerations.

When designing a focus group study, it is of course necessary to consider the number of groups needed, and how many participants should be in each group. In terms of the number of groups, there is no set figure that automatically means the research is 'done'. I think that the **theoretical saturation** concept introduced above is a useful guide to this decision. However, it does depend on exactly how complex your study is, and in particular how much it depends on respondent differences such as gender, age, and other demographics.

Table 9.1 Focus groups and interviews

Focus groups ideally suited to:	**Interviews ideally suited to:**
Research Objectives	
• Orient yourself to a field or language • Explore a range of attitudes, opinions • Observe consensus, etc. • Add context to quant work	• Explore the world of the individual in depth • Do case studies with repeated interviews over time • Test an instrument or questionnaire
Types of topic	
• Issues of public interest or common concern, e.g. politics, media, new tech. • Issues of an unfamiliar or hypothetical nature	• Detailed individual experiences, choices, or personal biography • Issues of sensitivity which may provoke anxiety, embarrassment, etc.
Types of respondent	
• Must not be from different backgrounds, which may inhibit discussion or cause problems	• Difficult to recruit • Elite or high status • Business people (usually) • Children under 7

In such situations you may wish to stratify your sample to include as many different features are represented. In terms of the number of participants per group, this decision depends on both practical and theoretical considerations. Firstly, without a reasonable number (I think five) of participants, a focus group will not exhibit enough social interaction, making it a bit pointless. However, beyond a certain point (I think about eight to ten) the interaction is just too complex, factions develop, some people become dominant, and things can easily get out of hand. Some say that smaller groups should be used in situations where topics are complex and involving, and larger groups when topics are less involving and you want a wide range of opinions (e.g. Morgan, 1998a). My own feeling is that a group size of six to eight is pretty good for almost all purposes. However, make sure to take into account the possibility that some participants may not show up on the day – this is surprisingly common, as Jennifer related at the very start of this chapter.

At the beginning of the focus group, make sure to introduce yourself, and give a basic appreciation for the topic. As well as this, get agreement on the some basic 'ground rules' such as only one person talking at a time, confidentiality, impartiality, and that all opinions are welcome and the necessity for disagreement (while acceptable) must only be constructive and not personal. While questioning techniques can be similar to individual interviews, focus groups often require a bit more structuring to get the group interaction going effectively.

In particular, you should not expect too much out of the group at the start, and instead focus on 'ice-breaking' activities (hopefully of general relevance to your topic) to get everyone comfortable interacting and participating. It is also important to remember to take advantage of the social situation of a focus group, and build in activities and questioning techniques which are designed to involve all participants and encourage them to interact among themselves. One common mistake made by inexperienced moderators is simply to ask questions of everyone one-by-one, without encouraging any interaction. It is of course essential to have a topic guide, and also to remember to continue to probe for more specific examples from your respondents, as sometimes focus groups can rely on 'shared knowledge' which the moderator or analyst does not have access to. At the end of the session, make sure to end things on a positive note, thank everybody, and explain what will happen to the information you have just gained.

Observation

Perhaps the other major method of qualitative data collection is observation. While the interviewing techniques described above come mainly from a depth-psychology background, observational techniques are mainly drawn from anthropological research, where it was common for researchers to actually enter and participate in a culture they wished to study. While there are some general concepts of observation which can be applied to most situation, beginning researchers need to realise that almost every social situation is different, and in most cases they will need to rely as much on improvisation or even luck as much as knowledge gleaned from textbooks. Also, going into a social setting to observe it – especially covertly – can be an intimidating, scary, and even dangerous experience (imagine being exposed as a social researcher studying football-hooligan or drug-dealing culture). And the emotional difficulties don't stop once you are finished, many observational researchers have to grapple with feelings of betrayal while writing up and publishing their work, after having spent so much time in that social situation. I've even known some researchers to 'go native', and disappear into the culture they were studying! So observational research is not for the faint-hearted, but it can offer incredible insights.

The first issue to deal with is gaining access to the situation you wish to study, which is not an easy task. In 'closed' settings (e.g. schools, firms or other formally organised situations like cults, etc.) you will usually need boundless determination to get the chance to enter the organisation for research purposes. Useful avenues can be friends, contacts within the setting, or academic supporters who may have some influence. Of course, you will almost always need the support of gatekeepers such as leaders or managers. To get this you generally need to be willing to negotiate exactly what you want (in terms of time and access) and often need to offer something in return (like a report). But be careful that in your enthusiasm to gain access, you don't end up in a situation where you are effectively paralysed (low access, lack of ability to publish your work, or becoming a cheap consultant for the firm). Gaining actual *physical* access to 'public' situations (e.g. communities, gangs, clubs) can be easier, but in almost every social situation even if you can gain physical access, you will need some way 'in' to the social side of that situation. In such cases finding a respected member of the situation who will take you 'under their wing' is really useful, as is having contacts inside the group. However, in situations where neither of these is available, it can sometimes come down to simply 'hanging around' the setting until you gain some kind of interaction with the actors. Of course, you will almost always have to make sure you look like you might 'fit in' with that group, so try not to dress in a suit and tie if you want to study an illegal motorbike gang, unless they are called 'The Devil's Accountants' perhaps.

Of course, the access problem can be eased a little if you become a 'covert' observer, and enter that situation without telling anyone you are a researcher. Although this does not ease the task of getting 'social' access always, it can help gaining access to the physical situation. But such techniques are fraught with difficulties and ethical concerns. Is it right to gain information from people without their knowing you are 'studying' them? What happens if you get found out? Can you even bring yourself to write up the research without feeling as if you have betrayed the people who have likely become your friends? Covert access can have major benefits though, allowing you to access parts of the context never available to overt researchers (especially in situations where a public 'front' is presented). However, it can actually make it very difficult to do your job. For example, it is not really acceptable to pull out a notebook while you are having what everyone else thinks is a normal conversation!

But just getting into the context is not the end of it. You still need to somehow gain the trust of those people within the organisation or setting. Many will think you are some kind of official 'inspector' at first, and your actions in the early part of your research (particularly if you see inappropriate activities) will determine the trust you gain. A simple way of getting a picture of this is to watch virtually any movie about undercover cops, or when a 'new guy' joins some army unit or police force (even better if it is a 'geek', a 'woman' or some other 'different' person). Focus on allaying people suspicions, playing up your knowledge and expertise, demonstrating your trustworthiness, and looking for any tests that participants might give you. Also, within the observation, you will also likely want to interview people, and similar issues concerning sampling as those already discussed will then come into play. That said, you will need to take into account the social context, your own 'overtness' and other specific issues when you are conducting interviews within an observational study.

Documentary sources of data

There are a vast amounts of other types of data that qualitative researchers can collect. In particular, while the previous discussion focuses on generating data from 'real' situations and face-to-face interactions, qualitative research can just as well utilise pre-existing data such as documents, or other textual data. One fast-growing source of data for qualitative analysis is of course the Internet. The Internet provides a vast resource of textual data for qualitative research. Much of this data can be treated similarly to any other document (as I will introduce below). However, the Internet is not just a document repository, it is also a hub for genuine social interaction. More specifically, there are thousands of 'virtual communities' on the Internet, where interested participants share experiences and information. These communities can be an amazingly rich source of data for the qualitative researcher. In fact, they can allow you quite easily to track the history of a particular topic, as well as the social network which underlies a given community, because all messages are usually kept online. Of course, if one wishes to research within an online community, it is good practice to ask permission from the moderator, as well as the participants where possible. The observation and analysis of interaction on the Internet is currently a very recent development, but it is likely that with the increasing use of the Internet in contemporary society, it will become more and more important to the qualitative researcher.

There are many other types of documents and textual data existing that the qualitative researcher can access. The government produces many official documents, such as policies, enquiry reports, White Papers and the like. These can prove to be of great importance to many qualitative research projects in social science. As well as official documents, private sources also produce masses of documentary data rich in meaning and insight. For example, companies produce annual reports, mission statements, product literature, catalogues, press releases and advertisements – to name but a few. Organisations also tend to produce a lot of 'private' material such as minutes of meetings, internal policy documents, memos and the like. Social and organisational researchers often find that this kind of material (when it is accessible) is a goldmine of information. And of course, in today's world no mention of documentary data would be complete without mentioning the mass media. Newspapers, television, magazines, and many other media sources can provide substantial information to the qualitative researcher. In fact, my first ever piece of published research was a qualitative analysis of how the word 'ruthless' was used in mass-media descriptions of managers (Lee and Cadogan, 1998[3]).

Individuals also create masses of documentary data and other information throughout their lives that can be used in qualitative analysis. For example, historical and political researchers commonly use personal letters and diaries as sources of data in their research, although social and organisational researchers have not utilised these as often. That said, it is more common for social researchers to actually collect data by asking potential respondents to write a diary, or letters, for the specific purposes of the research. For example, consumption and purchase diaries are a reasonably common way for consumer researchers to collect data. E-mails can

[3] This paper was published at a conference, so it will be hard to get hold of. Not to worry, you aren't missing much!

also be a useful source of information, where they are recorded. Narratives and life stories (e.g. autobiographies) can also be useful sources of data, whether they are generated expressly for the research or collected by a researcher.

However, when we are collecting data not generated specifically for the purposes of our research project, we need to spend some time evaluating how useful that data can be. There are many different criteria which could be used, but Scott (1990) provides a rigorous yet simple set of very useful things to think about. First, you should question the *authenticity* of the data. Is the data 'real'? Are you absolutely sure of who wrote it, or where it came from? *Credibility* is also an issue, and you must be sure that the information is free from bias or error, or at the very least be aware of the likely biases in that information. Scott also suggests that you must have an awareness of how *representative* your data is – is it typical, or if not how idiosyncratic is it? Finally, you must also assess how *meaningful* the information is, or in other words can you actually understand it. While these are difficult criteria to pass with flying colours, or even to evaluate in many pieces of data, it is very important that you spend time considering them when you are working with documentary data. In fact, you can consider this as an extension to the rigour discussion right at the beginning of this chapter.

Recording your data

Of course, gaining access to a social situation, or individual, or group, is not the final piece in the data collection puzzle. Once this is done, you need to have some way of recording your data. Probably the key decision is whether you take notes, or use some kind of electronic device such as a tape recorder, video recorder, or in today's high-tech world, some kind of digital recording device (I've even seen some people recording my lectures on an Ipod – or maybe they were listening to music!). Where at all possible, in interview or focus group contexts (observation will be discussed later) I recommend using a recording device. However, not all researchers recommend this, and some feel that it can unnecessarily restrict the information you actually retain for analysis (see Gummesson 2000, for example). That said, to my mind at least, not worrying about writing notes frees your mind to concentrate on the progress of the interview, enhancing your ability to build rapport, and react to interesting information. Also, I have found that sometimes respondents can see you writing down some things and start second-guessing what they are going to say next, either trying to avoid saying controversial things, or keep saying what is clearly the 'right' thing. Furthermore, in a focus group I always advise where possible to video record the group. This is because it can get very hard to tell who is speaking at any point in time using only audio recordings, especially if multiple people speak simultaneously. Of course, transcribing a video tape can get messy, with all the fast forwarding and rewinding, but with the increasing use of digital video this is less of a problem. When using some kind of audio tape recorder, I always make sure to use two things: (a) full-size 90 minute tapes, and (b) an external microphone.

Smaller 'dictaphone'-style tapes are dependent on having a transcribing machine (and they can get very expensive), and longer than 90 minute tapes have very thin tape that breaks easily with all the use they get in transcribing. That said, if your tape does break, don't panic, because with a bit of ingenuity you can actually stick it back together with thin tape. Just make sure to copy it as soon as you possibly can afterwards! Also, when you set up in an interview or focus group, make sure you test the equipment first with the respondent. There's nothing worse than running a 90 minute interview, getting back and finding that the microphone was in the wrong place and all you can hear is your own voice!

Sometimes you will have to take notes. This is particularly relevant for observational research. Even if you were able to tape a whole day, imagine transcribing it! Field notes are the method of choice in recording observational research. One key rule I have always lived by (after learning the hard way) is *never assume you will remember something*, no matter how important it may be. The human mind forgets quickly, and massively. A useful strategy, inspired by Bryman (2004), is to take notes in three ways. First are what I call **mental notes**. As soon as something happens which you need to record, make a mental note of it. This simple act can help a lot. Then, as soon as practical, make a **brief note** in your notebook. It's normally best to do this discreetly, rather than in front of everybody – this can make people feel very self-conscious (which is why I recommend the mental notes above). Then, at the end of the day spend some time writing up **full field notes** of the day with as much detail as possible, including context, time, date and the like. Again, never assume you will remember the details later on. If in doubt, write it down. Remember that these notes are in fact the raw material for your analysis, so if you don't have any data, you don't have a project.

Transcribing interview and focus group recordings is a thorny issue for many researchers. One decision which needs to be made is *who* will do the transcribing. Unfortunately, transcribing is in many cases both time consuming and boring. Thus, researchers often like to employ professional transcribers. I do not recommend this myself, which tends to make me unpopular with my students. Transcribing interviews yourself has so many advantages that I think where possible it should be the method of choice. Firstly it gets you intimately connected with your data, and allows your mind to begin thinking about the issues immediately. Secondly, your presence at the interview should minimise mistakes and misunderstandings in the transcription. Also, I strongly advocate transcribing interviews as soon as possible, not waiting until the end of the research programme. Since you can guarantee over four hours transcribing for each hour of interview, spreading this out is beneficial. It also allows you to take into account any issues which arise in an interview prior to the next one. The other major question in transcribing is *what* to transcribe. My own personal feeling is to transcribe everything, even things you think right now are irrelevant. This is because you never know at the beginning of a project exactly what will be the outcome at the end. Missing out swathes of data runs the risk of prejudicing what you come out with, which in my opinion kind of misses the point of a qualitative approach. Related to this is the question of whether you should transcribe just words, or other utterances, gestures, and the like. Of course, if you are using a specific analysis method like discourse analysis (see Chapter 10), you will probably utilise a more detailed transcription scheme, but I tend to focus on the words and the pauses and utterances ('um', 'ah', and the like) primarily.

Summary

Understanding how to collect qualitative data is a vital part of becoming a well-rounded researcher. Even more so, it is important to break down the prejudices which exist in many field of social science, that qualitative data can be 'easy' to collect, or even reliant on random chance and being in the right place at the right time. A qualitative data collection programme can be as detailed and rigorous as any quantitative study. Indeed, unless you have philosophical disagreements with the very concept of rigour and truth in research, qualitative research should always be done with concern for these concepts. As has already (and will be repeatedly) said in this book, without high-quality data, none of your conclusions are trustworthy, and assuring readers of this is one of your most important tasks as a researcher.

Key points to take from this chapter:

- Rigour in qualitative research is associated with the 'quality' of your research methods.
- Validity is an important concept in qualitative research; however, there have been various different approaches to it from different researchers.
- Thinking about whether the claims you make from your findings are **justifiable** is a good way of thinking about concepts of validity and reliability.
- Sampling is a key part of your research design, and will have major impacts on your conclusions.
- There are various ways a qualitative researcher can collect data: 'in person', such as interviews, focus groups, and observation.
- There are also vast amounts of documentary evidence available to the qualitative researcher, some of which are relatively untapped by social scientists.
- Recording and transcribing your data are also a very important parts of the process, and should not be treated as an 'afterthought'.

Further reading

There are many general sources on qualitative methods for social and organisational researchers. However, original ideas can also be found in literature dedicated to management research. A selection of both of these sources would include:

- *Qualitative Methods in Management Research* by Evert Gummesson: The concepts in this book were touched upon in the previous chapter when I wrote about 'action research'. This book (and much of Professor Gummesson's other work) is an original and useful contribution to qualitative methods from a specifically 'management research' viewpoint, which stands apart from the more 'traditional' sociological sources given below.

- *Doing Qualitative Research* by David Silverman: An excellent introduction to the field, and Silverman has a great perspective on qualitative research. This book has been a pretty big influence on my own thinking about qualitative methods.
- *An Introduction to Qualitative Research* by Uwe Flick: A more 'theoretical' book than Silverman's, but includes some excellent information about the philosophical background and development of qualitative research.
- *Basics of Qualitative Research: Techniques and Procedures for Developing Grounded Theory* by Anselm Strauss and Juliet Corbin. Grounded theory has also been a big influence in many ways on my qualitative research techniques (although I would never say my work was 'true' grounded theory), and I think all budding researchers should explore it. Strauss' perspective is to my mind more pragmatic and useful than Glaser's, and I like this book a lot.
- *Qualitative Research Practice* edited by Clive Seale, Giampetro Gobo, Jaber F. Gubrium and David Silverman. This is a big book with many different chapters by different authors. I have found it a very useful resource of perspectives and techniques about qualitative research. If you can't afford it yourself, try to get your library to get it so you can look at it.

EXERCISES

1. What makes qualitative research 'qualitative'?
2. Does your answer to question 1 mean that all numeric measures are fundamentally incompatible with qualitative research?
3. Which philosophical perspective (see Chapters 2 and 3) do you think could be best considered as the base for qualitative research methods? Why is this?
4. If you have previously been considering a quantitative research project, think about how your project could be addressed using qualitative research:

   a. Would qualitative work add anything to your existing methodology?
   b. Could your existing methodology be replaced by a totally qualitative approach?
   c. Is your topic fundamentally inappropriate to qualitative research, and if so, why do you think this is?

5. Do you think the Logical Positivists would be keen on qualitative methods? Why or why not?

   a. Another angle – is qualitative research compatible with empiricist philosophy?

6. Hey, it's pretty much halfway through now – why don't you give yourself a pat on the back and take the night off – go out to a club and do some dancing.

Chapter 10
Qualitative data analysis

SUPERVISOR'S VIEW: PROFESSOR CHRIS HACKLEY

Dr Nick Lee's chapter on qualitative research is powerfully well-informed and exceptionally well-written. Reading it with enthusiasm, it stimulated two recurring thoughts. The first was 'Where are the citations to my publications which Lee promised?[1]' I read thousands of words a week, all with a finely honed sense of literary appreciation, yet no word in the incomparable lexicon of Western literature gives me the satisfaction of 'Hackley' followed by 2005, 1998 or whatever. I'm not soliciting undeserved praise, you understand. Someone could write: 'There have been many outstanding studies in this field, with the deplorable exception of Hackley (200X), quite the most inept, scurrilous and fraudulent piece of "work" ever published', and I'd still feel the same glow of existential affirmation. The second thing which kept occurring to me as I read this chapter was 'Should we be talking about *qualitative* research or *interpretive* research?' What I mean is this: research needs data sets (empirical research anyway). Qualitative or quantitative, and usually both in some degree. What separates research paradigms, if you will, is whether the findings are presented as facts or interpretations. My own Ph.D. was based on my version of discourse analysis, and I offered a number of 'interpretive repertoires' induced from my interview data. To my great relief, my examiner didn't ask me to thoroughly explain this inductive process. He didn't ask questions like 'why those interpretive repertoires, and not others?' He didn't ask because he knew the answer. I was explaining my interpretation of these data sets, not claiming to have discovered some new facts. As you'd expect, I had to offer some philosophical arguments as justification. As is made clear in this very chapter, using, and most importantly, justifying qualitative data findings can be far more difficult than it looks. But my examiner understood the interpretive research approach well so he was receptive to those kinds of arguments. And in case you were wondering, the story of my Ph.D. research was published as Hackley (2000). There, got one in.

---

[1]Note from Nick: They're actually in Chapter 3!

VIEW FROM THE TRENCHES: DR JANE MATTHIESEN

'You *don't* want me to do a questionnaire?!' That was my first reaction when my supervisor first proposed using *only* qualitative methods in my Ph.D. After shock came fear. First of all, I didn't know anything about qualitative methodology, apart from the very superficial stuff they teach in most research degrees, and had no idea *how* to do qualitative work. Secondly, I came from a strongly positivistic quantitative discipline (psychology) and was very aware that most people in my field didn't think much of qualitative work, so I also had no idea why I would *want* to do qualitative work. I was in denial. This quickly turned into anger and frustration. Why would my supervisor want me to use this methodology if he knows it would undermine the quality of my work? Is he trying to sabotage me? The next stage was bargaining. I agreed to do some qualitative work but only if I could 'validate' it using quantitative methods. We had a deal: I'd do 100 interviews and 1,000 questionnaires. I started interviewing people and loved the work. It was exciting to deal with real people instead of pieces of paper, being able to push and probe rather than just taking everything at face value. Seeing when people were unsure, deceitful, sad or angry. It was a fantastic experience. Then came depression – I had to analyse all these beautiful rich words and turn them into useful data (and in my mind, that still meant numbers). The qualitative analysis was extremely difficult and time-consuming, the frequency counts painful. It was undoubtedly much more intense than any quantitative analysis I would have been able to concoct, but the beautiful thing was that, in the end, I had meaning and not just numbers. And all of a sudden I understood why my supervisor had told me that qualitative work was 'enough'. The interviews offered plenty of data to fill two Ph.D.s. That was the moment of insight and the moment I stopped grieving for quantitative methods!

Qualitative data analysis tends to suffer from a rather unfortunate image problem, as you can see from Jane's story above. This problem causes those who have never tried to do 'proper' qualitative analysis to assume it is *ad hoc,* lacking in rigour, and biased (remember 'blagging it'?) This problem also causes the ill-informed beginning researcher to gravitate towards qualitative approaches because they think they are 'easier'. Sometimes this leads to poor research. A vicious circle then ensues which perpetuates the negative image of qualitative analysis. More often it leads to the researcher 'drowning' in masses of data, with absolutely no idea what to do with it, and a rather sheepish realisation that indeed, qualitative research was not as easy as it looked.

It should come as no surprise to you then when I say that for many people qualitative research has the unhealthy image of being 'easy'. This is caused by a few things. Firstly is the fact that many social scientists remain dogmatically wedded to the traditional quantitative model of scientific research, and mistrust qualitative research in general. But hopefully the fact that you are reading Chapter 10 (well done by the way) of this book should mean that you are not entirely one of those. More pressing a concern to my mind is the general lack of information about qualitative analysis available. I look up to the shelves of my study and see literally over 50 books about quantitative analysis, I then look to the left and see but a solitary volume entitled *Qualitative Data Analysis*. While this is not to say information is not available from other sources,[2] the point remains valid. For many researchers, particularly in the past, qualitative analysis was like a 'black box' – some data went in, and some findings came out. There was no real concern as to how the researcher arrived at those findings.

The aim of this chapter is to provide a solid platform for you to conduct rigorous qualitative analysis, which will allow the various constituencies of your work to have confidence in your findings. Of course, this chapter is by no means the final word on analysis, but it should provide a good jumping-off point for you to go forward into the sometimes rather deep waters of qualitative analysis. Again, like the previous chapter, I aim to avoid where possible philosophical discussion, as I feel those decisions need to be made independently, prior to methodological ones. But of course where philosophy is unavoidable it will without fail raise its head! Thus, this chapter should be read in a pragmatic manner, not an ideological one, and also as relevant to *all* researchers in the social sciences.

Either way, at the end of this chapter I really hope you have come to terms with these key ideas:

- That qualitative data is data which in a general sense is or can be transformed into *words* rather than numbers.
- That such data can be very rich, and analysis can be helped by *reducing* it to key ideas and concepts.
- Qualitative analysis can be described as a process of extracting and presenting these key ideas, themes and concepts in various ways.
- Key tasks in this process are coding, data displaying, and drawing conclusions.
- Concern for reliability and validity should pervade this process.

---

[2]After all, I don't own *every* analysis book in existence (and if you keep it quiet, I'll let you in on the secret that I haven't read all the books on my shelves either!)

Why is it Important to Know This Stuff?

Many of the points I raised in the corresponding section of Chapter 9 of course remain relevant here, so there seems little point repeating them (go back and read them if you must!) Naturally, this chapter will hopefully be extremely useful to those students setting out on a path of qualitative research. In particular, I think the concepts in this chapter provide a solid 'framework' to the researcher, helping to ensure they do not get lost in the data, or become seduced by its richness into anecdotalism. Remember, we are dealing with many of the same issues as we will be in later chapters – how do we go about looking at data from the real world and drawing conclusions relating back to the theoretical world (see Figure 10.1).

However, knowledge of qualitative analysis methods is particularly important to all researchers who wish to become strong, well-rounded contributors to their discipline. First of all, to the quantitatively oriented researcher, looking at things from a qualitative perspective takes you out of your 'comfort-zone' extremely effectively. It allows you to see possible new ways of looking at a problem, which will almost definitely lead to interesting and useful viewpoints and solutions. It also exercises your mind. Furthermore, I always find the flexibility and scope for originality in qualitative analysis extremely refreshing, especially after a long session of adhering to a quantitative methodological framework. Essentially, for me at least, they seem to exercise different parts of my mind, which always leads to new and often useful approaches to a given problem.

If you want to be an effective member of your discipline you will need to have the confidence and competence to fairly evaluate qualitative analysis – whether this is in existing research articles, ones you have been asked to review, grant proposals, theses, or anything else. Without a knowledge of what makes 'good' qualitative analysis, you will either tend to consider all qualitative analysis 'bad' or be unable to recognise when it is good – or worse when it really *is* bad!

Finally, I have found a solid understanding of qualitative analysis has opened up huge vistas of projects that I have been lucky enough to work on, and collaborators who I have been blessed to work with. Without that knowledge (and my usual tendency to let everyone know about it) I would never had participated in many of the interesting research projects and teams that I have.

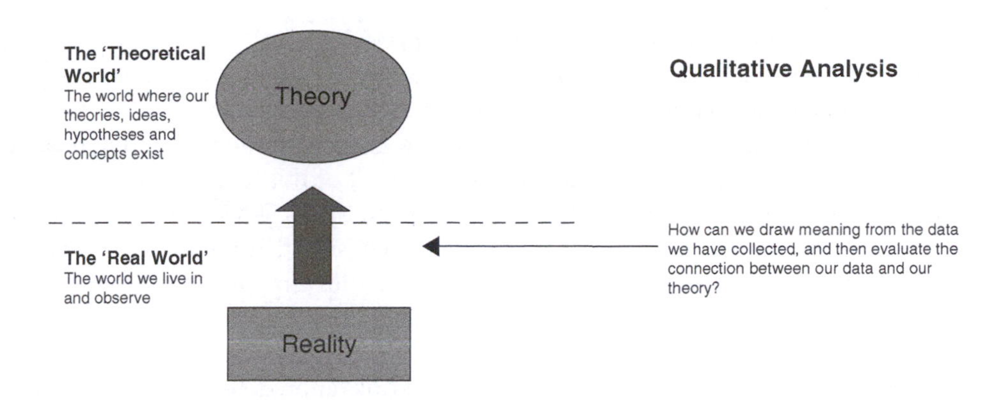

Figure 10.1 The Place of quallitative analysis

A perspective on qualitative analysis

When considering how to analyse 'qualitative' data, the first question that needs to be answered is 'exactly what is it that defines a set of data as qualitative?' In fact, in the social sciences it can be argued that *all* data begins as qualitative – as one of Locke's or Berkeley's sensory experiences[3] – and is subsequently transformed into words, images, sounds or numbers. An interesting question is exactly who this transformation is done by. On one level, it can be argued that in qualitative research the subject of the research (e.g. the interviewee) transforms their experience into words which are then uttered to the interviewer. By contrast one can suggest that quantitative research *imposes* the transformation onto subjects (say the respondents to your questionnaires) by asking them to express their experiences by way of working out which rigid box they fall into, or how much they agree or disagree with an 'objective' statement. However, the very act of transforming a raw set of qualitative data (e.g. transcribing an interview recording) can also impose the researcher's own conceptualisations on to that data. This is particularly relevant when recording observational data; separating out pure recording of the experience from the researcher's own interpretation of that experience can be a key issue to keep in mind when collecting qualitative data to analyse.

A very simple way of looking at the nature of qualitative data is to consider it as data in the form of words or, more pertinently, meaningful collections of words. Admittedly, this excludes things like visual data, but if we extend the definition to include data that can be transformed into words, that problem is solved for the moment. Qualitative data has some key strengths which have a major impact on the way in which qualitative analysis methods have evolved, and for the way you should think about qualitative analysis. We've covered

[3]If you don't recognise these names, you probably need to read Chapters 2 and 3.

many of these strengths in previous chapters, but let's recap a little, especially as they are more useful than rigid definitions of what qualitative data is. Firstly, remember how a lot of qualitative work is focused on exploring events as they occur naturally, and is grounded within the context? This allows analysis to really get to grips with the underlying meanings and layers of the social world. We should try not to strip all of this 'context' away when we analyse the data. Of course, qualitative data is also 'rich and thick'. This again means that our analysis methods should play to this strength, while recognising that the richer the data, the easier it can be to get lost in it – even though it can make our findings really compelling to the reader. And perhaps my favourite strength is the flexibility of qualitative data – there are literally limitless ways you can design analysis methods for qualitative data. This of course makes it difficult for the beginner as there are few 'textbook' approaches available. But when you take advantage of this strength, you can create fantastic and enlightening analysis tools which allow you to see the world in entirely different ways.

A general approach to qualitative data analysis

Although there are many and varied approaches to qualitative analysis available to the researcher, there are few that are actually set down clearly, allowing the novice researcher a good starting point from which to move forwards. The approach set out here is indebted to that of Miles and Huberman (1994), who's work provided my own initiation into qualitative analysis. Much of the balance of this chapter will be devoted to providing detail on this general process.

The first step in analysis occurs even before the collection of data is started, in a pre-planning process involving a theoretical appreciation; which questions to ask, how to ask them and the like. These issues were covered in the previous chapter, and they have an important impact on the analysis you can do later. Immediately following the data collection should come a brief process of summarising the interaction, which can be a key influence on your more detailed analysis. The first major part of post-collection analysis is concerned with data reduction. Miles and Huberman (1994, p. 10) define data reduction as 'the process of selecting, focusing, simplifying, abstracting, and transforming the data', and I am yet to find a better definition. I tend to explain it to my students as trying to reduce the rich data set down to its core ideas, although we will go into this in more detail later. Following and concurrent (at least in part) with reduction is what I consider to be the fun part of qualitative analysis – data displays. While displays can simply be selections of text (like quotes), it is often helpful to draw a parallel with quantitative information. Not all quantitative data is displayed in numbers, often charts and other visual displays are used to help understanding of the data. The concept is exactly the same with qualitative data. Finally, and again this often occurs along with reduction and displaying, is the drawing of conclusions. I often find students have problems with this stage. This is basically the process of deciding what your data 'means', and can be difficult for all researchers. For example, a problem that one of my students is having as I write this is exactly where to stop; the data is so interesting that she is tempted to keep adding to the conclusions.

One key point to keep in mind here is that you shouldn't think of this as necessarily a sequential process. In particular, I generally advocate where possible the beginning of preliminary analysis during the data collection. For many people, waiting until after all the data is collected can result in an intimidating and demotivating pile of thousands of pages of text to analyse. Analysis during collection can also help modify later data collection efforts (the iterative process mentioned in the previous chapter). Furthermore, in the process of reduction the analyst often develops ideas for displays, and begins to get tentative ideas for conclusions as well. These things should never be ignored simply because you are 'not at that stage yet'.

Reliability and validity in qualitative analysis

You'll remember that notions of reliability and validity were raised early on in the previous chapter – and you were warned that they would occur again. Indeed, the analysis of your data is yet another key point in a piece of qualitative research where questions of reliability, validity (I used the term *justifiability* as well) raise their heads. Silverman (2005, pp. 209–210) sums up the importance of these concepts to analysis with the strongly worded statement that 'short of reliable methods and valid conclusions, research descends into a bedlam where the only battles that are won are by those who shout the loudest'. Although it was suggested in the previous chapter that qualitative data collection was not inherently unreliable or invalid, concern still needs to be given to how that data is analysed, and whether we can justify the conclusions we draw from that data.[4] However, there are, of course, dissenters, and some opposing views are presented in Alternative View 10.1.

Beginning with reliability, in analysis this can generally be considered to concern the manner in which the raw data is transformed into 'analysable form'. This can involve things like transcribing, but also issues such as coding. In particular, how much of the researchers' own inference has gone into, say, summarising or transforming that raw data into a transcript, and that transcript into a set of codes? In fact, a number of scholars argue that extended swathes of raw data be included in research write-ups, including such things as the interviewer's questions and prompts (Bryman, 1988; Silverman, 2005). This allows readers to get a better picture of the respondents' own concepts and categories, without relying solely on the interpretation of the researcher. It also helps readers determine whether the researcher's interpretation is able to be relied upon. When transcribing or otherwise transforming the raw data, it is important to have consistent methods (especially when multiple team members are working with the data) and notation styles. For instance, do you transcribe all utterances,

[4]Of course, you've already seen in Chapter 6 and 7 (and it will be covered again later) that qualitative researchers do not have the monopoly on reliability and validity problems – these are relevant to quantitative research too.

even things like 'mm', 'um', and other various tics and pauses? In fact, there are many more details involved in conversation which you could record, and newer developments in *conversation analysis* (a variant of discourse analysis, which will be discussed later) are good examples of this approach. The way in which you record your raw data will have a major impact on your ability to reliably represent the perspectives of your respondents.

Validity, on the other hand, is an altogether more nebulous concept in this context. Drawing from the previous chapter, we can consider it to be concerned with how well your conclusions reflect the data you drew them from – how justifiable are your conclusions? Of course, whether these conclusions reflect some kind of underlying truth or reliability (external validity) is a philosophical question which may or may not have relevance to you; but it is my view that the concern for internal validity or what Guba and Lincoln (1994) called **credibility** is important to all qualitative analysts. Although we covered many of these issues in Chapter 9, there are specific concerns for the qualitative analyst. Most pertinent is the issue of **anecdotalism**, which refers to the temptation to base your conclusions on a small number of quotes or examples which epitomise key points, rather than a thorough investigation of the data. As you are about to discover, qualitative analysis is *not* about simply extracting a good quote which exemplifies a theoretical idea. For example, why was one quote included and another not? Were there alternative interpretations of the same material? Was there data which contradicted your chosen example? If so, how common was it? How much were your interpretations and selections influenced by prior theory? Answers and reassurances about these issues provide the real meat on the bones of the validity concept as it refers to qualitative research.

Alternative View 10.1: A Counterpoint to Reliability and Validity Concerns

A full discussion of those viewpoints which essentially reject the notions of validity explored in this chapter is of course far beyond my remit (and my capability – I've already tied myself in knots trying to explain postmodernism in Chapter 3!) However, if we consider the social world to be constantly in flux and ever-changing, it has been said that it's somewhat nonsensical to spend time worrying whether our methods are reliable, since they can never truly be replicated (e.g. Marshall and Rossman, 1999). In terms of validity, postmodern thinkers would argue that the very nature of qualitative research renders any criteria for judging it irrelevant (Hammersley, 1992). Postmodern thought rejects the idea that there is a set of privileged criteria which can be used to judge one piece of research as 'better' than another; all representations are equal. Poststructuralist positions (such as feminism, ethnic and other critical studies) would also argue that our existing notions of validity are not relevant. Oftentimes, the criteria for such work involves concepts such as whether it is somehow emancipatory, or otherwise helpful to its subjects and wider constituents; does it break down existing barriers, or raise awareness of problems? Is it humane and socially informed? Of course, criticism from traditional quarters stresses the inherent impossibility of then telling whether such research is in fact 'good or bad'. This is rebutted by poststructuralists, with the argument that the very concept of 'good and bad science' is the problem, as it has been used in the past as a way of maintaining control on knowledge and progress by a minority, and that traditional scientific criticism is irrelevant as poststructuralism is concerned with a completely different set of aims and objectives. It is usually at this point when I am inclined to refer to the quote by Silverman that I gave earlier.

There are many ways of providing information which can reassure readers that your conclusions are valid. **Triangulation** is one way in which you can try to enhance validity. It involves looking at the issue from different angles (maybe using different types of method, or different analysis techniques, and the like). Whereas this works well if you assume there is some kind of external reality which you can get a 'fix' on, it is quite incompatible with the more interpretive ideas presented in Chapter 3. If there is no 'truth', then how can looking at different perspectives get you closer to it? Triangulation can certainly be useful to enhance the richness of your data set, but you do need to be careful when you employ it to enhance validity. Another commonly advocated method is that of **respondent validation**, which involves taking your early results back to the people you studied, and asking basically whether you are on the right track. Although I have always been a bit of a fan of this method, others are not so sure (e.g. Bryman, 1988). Of course, it is not really in question that respondents can provide interesting insights; the crux of the objection relates to whether you give the views of the respondents more weight than any other view. Why should their interpretation be more valuable than yours, for example? Nevertheless, I still feel respondent validation can be useful if you wish to make sure you have recorded respondents' perspectives accurately – if that was your goal. While I have poured a little cold water on some oft-cited bulwarks to validity, there are some other ways of thinking about validity which may be used with more confidence, and these are presented in IDE 10.1.

IDE 10.1: Refutability

Silverman (2005) develops the concept of **refutability**, which draws from Popper's ideas of falsification (see Chapter 2) as a defence against charges of anecdotalism. While it should be clear to you that this kind of approach may be anathema to some of the philosophical standpoints expressed in Chapter 3 (and in Alternative

View 10.1), it does provide a very solid set of principles for thinking about how valid your conclusions are. Basically, the principle of refutability implies that you should always seek to *refute* your initial assumptions about the data. You will undoubtedly recognise this principle from the Popperian emphasis on hypothesis falsification (if not, Chapter 2 is calling you). Of course, we are usually hoping that we *won't be able to* refute our original ideas, but equally, we cannot accept them as 'knowledge' unless we have done our utmost to do so. There are a number of more specific techniques which can be drawn from qualitative methodology which can help us do this. For example, researchers should always look to explore their ideas by comparing their findings from one case to those for another. In my Doctoral work, I studied sales managers, and then took those tentative theories to a set of salespeople. Within the data set, it is also useful to begin with a small part (say one transcript), and then slowly snowball out until you have incorporated and compared your findings with all parts of the set, constantly flipping between the various parts of your data, and modifying your conclusions as new insights emerge. This *constant comparative method* is similar to that advocated in the Grounded Theory approach I have already mentioned. It also involves what Silverman (2005) calls *comprehensive data treatment*, or making sure every single piece of data is somehow analysed. More specific is the search for *deviant cases*, or cases which seem to exhibit relevant characteristics at odds with the rest of your data set. For example, in my Doctoral study of sales manager problem resolution, I was aware that existing knowledge suggested that disciplinary activities were emotionally stressful and difficult for managers to carry out, and this was borne out in many of my interviews. However, I made concerted efforts to interview managers who admitted that they *didn't* have any problems carrying out such activity. The principles of refutability incorporated into the qualitative work allowed me to have more confidence in the validity of my conclusions regarding the antecedents to and consequences of sales managers' problem resolution.

Preparatory steps in analysis

The first step in analysis can be considered to be the design of the study – before you even get out into the field, let alone collect data. Although we considered many of these issues in the previous chapter on data collection, they still have relevance here. One key decision you need to make is how to bound your efforts. Do you go into the field with virtually no preconceptions or do you have a tightly structured framework? Of course, there are pros and cons to both sides of this debate. A pre-existing conceptual framework or set of categories allows you to 'see' more clearly what is useful or not to your study; but then again it could also restrict you from developing any new insights inductively. Of course, if you are studying something completely new, then you will not be able to develop too much of an existing framework anyway, but this is not often the case. In fact, as Miles and Huberman (1994) point out, we are almost always furnished with some kind of pre-existing knowledge, and it is somewhat silly to try to deny this. At a minimum, our skills as researchers influence us to interpret events in different ways from others. On the other hand, having some kind of framework allows you to structure your later analysis methods more easily – you have a good idea of what concepts and categories are going to be there, but you have to be careful to 'let the data speak' for itself, and not bend it to fit your existing model. If this sounds like a trade-off, that's because it is, and you need to be careful to find the right balance (which can be influenced by such mundane political things as your funder or supervisor).

Your research questions and sampling methods will also influence later analysis. You need to make certain at a minimum that your sampling strategy will give you enough data to answer those research questions, and the notions of refutability presented in IDE 10.1 are also relevant here. For example, if you don't look for deviant cases, you will not be able to take that particular approach to validity. Also, the instruments you use to collect data have a major influence on the data you collect. If you go in with few prepared instruments (e.g. interview questions, observation log books and schedules, and the like) you run the risk of not being able to differentiate between useful data and irrelevance – leading to data overload at minimum. However, again too much structure can leave you blind to the situational context and overly influenced by previous models. It's usually best to settle somewhere in the middle; the more exploratory your study, the less instrumentation you will be able to create. If you are looking to compare multiple cases or situations, however, instrumentation will be of considerable help in comparative analysis.

Your decisions on how to manage your data will also have a major bearing on analysis. When I began qualitative work, in 1998, I used no special qualitative software, but I did maintain all my work on computer. Others I know managed their data by hand, using sticky labels and card files. As I moved on, I incorporated qualitative data analysis (QDA) software such as QSR NUD*IST[5] and its updated version, called NVIVO. Interestingly, I think my approach to analysis has been quite strongly influenced by the ease of coding and retrieving information in these packages. Some would undoubtedly argue that this is A Bad Thing, perhaps removing the ultimate creativity from qualitative analysis. However, tools are not the reason for such a problem. In fact, a lack of creativity is the researcher's fault, not the fault of the tools. What is not in doubt is that in a qualitative project of any reasonable scale (say over five to ten interviews), the use of QDA software at a minimum to organise and manage your data can make your life a lot easier. There are a number of key issues you need to think about regarding data management, and these are summarised in IDE 10.2.

---

[5] I'll be honest, it was mainly the name that attracted me first, and the fact that my institution paid money to send me on a 'NUD*IST Course', which wasn't as much fun as I was expecting!

IDE 10.2: Data Management

The first thing you need to think about is how you will gain access to your data. This may seem easy at first, but when you have a large project which goes on for an extended time period this is not so easy. Also, it's not just about gaining access to the entire transcript or case notes. What about specific parts within that unit? You'll also need to record what analysis you did and how it developed. This can be incredibly important for later writing up – especially in light of the iterative process of qualitative work, and the need to document your methods for validity and reliability purposes.

Finally, it's necessary to think about what you will do with the data and records after you are finished – you will at minimum need to keep them for some period of time. This could be because you are going to write up your dissertation into some articles, or to have the data on hand for examiners or funders to look at for themselves. It is for all these reasons that having your data in electronic format, with the use of some kind of QDA package, is probably the most helpful in the contemporary environment.

Lastly, one piece of advice. **Back up your data regularly!!!!** I say this from bitter experience!

The first thing I usually do after a piece of qualitative data collection (say an interview, or maybe a key event in an observation), after spending some time reflecting on it, is write up a short **contact summary**. The contact summary form I often use is shown in Figure 10.2, and as you can see it is a pretty simplistic sheet of paper. The detail you go into on this form is up to you, but you should always try to keep it to one page. It is meant to be a simple sheet which allows you to focus on the key issues which came out of the contact. It can be drawn from your conceptual framework (e.g. which key concepts were mentioned), be more exploratory (e.g. what were the main overall themes), or more usually both. It should be driven by the research questions you are trying to answer. Another useful idea is to leave some space for writing down ideas for future data collection efforts which were suggested by this contact (e.g. did some questions prove difficult, can they be rephrased?)

The contact summary should be done as soon as practical after the contact; its aim is to record those overarching observations and feelings about the contact, which can prove of immense help in later analysis. A set of these sheets can give you a good impression of what was going on in your data, and help you design a further scheme of data reduction. It can also be used as part of a hermeneutic type of analysis (see IDE 3.2 and related material), as a good way of getting a first impression of 'the whole' of your contact. That said, Miles and Huberman (1994, p. 52) suggest that you shouldn't do a contact summary immediately after

Interview details: *Here, record things like name, position, time and date*

Salient Points	Themes
Here, write down any interesting points you can remember	*Here, try to think about what overall themes they could represent.*

Figure 10.2 Example contact summary sheet

the contact, as you can be overwhelmed by what they call 'vivid incidents', and that you should always write-up first. As implied above, my personal feeling is that this misses the point a little, as it seems to me that a contact summary should get the *first impressions* of a contact, before anything else. However, my opinion is based on interview research, where you have a verbatim record of the contact available (the tape). In an observational context, Miles and Huberman's concerns are very relevant, in that a pre-write-up contact summary can influence your later write-up of the field notes.

Coding and data reduction

It is not overstating things to say that **coding** is at the very core of the analysis approach I usually utilise. Strangely, it is also the idea which I have found most difficult to explain to students. I have always suspected that this may be because I am just not very good at explaining it, but I imagine we are all about to find out whether or not this is the case. In essence, coding begins as data preparation, and moves you forward into truly beginning to analyse your data. First, imagine the amount of information you might begin to build up in a typical qualitative study: interview transcripts, field notes, miscellaneous documents, and the like. This can get rather difficult to handle; for example, how can you retain all that information in your head in order to compare various parts of it? Or how are you to quickly retrieve important pieces of data from the pile? Even worse, the words in your data will often have different meanings across different people, or people will say different words when they mean the same thing. What we need is a way of encoding the key ideas of the data, as well as reducing the sheer amount of it, and allowing it to be quickly retrieved and rearranged. Coding helps us do this, and then builds from there to draw meaningful conclusions about our data.

A code is simply a *label* which you attach to a bit of text, whether it be a single word, a whole paragraph, or even an entire document (e.g. a transcript). They are designed to capture the *meaning* of that unit of text – not just the words (remember, different people use different words for the same underlying meanings). Once raw data is coded, it can be retrieved, compared, and used to answer the research questions – and if QDA software is used this process is almost ridiculously easy, although the *thinking and interpretation* behind it is still complex. There are many different styles of coding, ranging from very unstructured right up to extremely structured. It's probably best to begin with a somewhat structured approach to help you understand the basic process of coding, and to this end, IDE 10.3 demonstrates some different types of codes, but these are not the 'only' way of coding. In a qualitative project, you should feel free to be creative, once you understand the basics. Figure 10.3 is a screenshot of a coded paragraph from QSR NVIVO, which demonstrates the basic coding idea.

IDE 10.3: Four Types of Code

Miles and Huberman (1994) give good examples of three types of codes, *descriptive, interpretive, and pattern,* to which I add another, *organisational.* They operate in a rather nice hierarchical structure. I think it's a good idea to begin with 'big' or high-level codes which describe the whole interview and help you organise your data, which I term 'organisational' codes. You can see one in Figure 10.3 which is called 'Sales Manager', which told me the whole interview was with a sales manager. Such things are often concerned with demographics, e.g. the interview was done with a 'sales manager', who was 'female'.[6] These codes are of course driven by your objectives and likely analysis. For example, I anticipated comparing sales managers with salespeople, and males with females, thus I needed an easy way of retrieving relevant data from these groups. It may sound

[6]My 'actual' codes were simply those words, since from the beginning I used software to do my qualitative analysis. In the past a code such as 'sales manager' would often be expressed by something like 'SM' – which is of course where the name 'coding' comes from.

trivial, but if you are doing a large-scale study with many interviews over a year or more, let me assure you these things are necessary. A descriptive code simply describes what's going on in a piece of text – e.g. is the sales manager talking about her salespeople's prior performance? A code of 'prior-perf' may be used here. Interpretive codes are used when you have gone beyond merely describing what's happening to making your interpretation of what's going on 'behind the words'. They are often used more in research which allows you to get deeply involved in a context, such as observation or case study. For example, was the sales manager using poor prior performance to justify disciplinary activities for salespeople she in fact had personal problems with? The code in this case could be 'ext-just' for external justification. Pattern codes are used when (usually through continued iterative readings and data collection) you are able to detect underlying patterns, themes, and links in the data. For example, sales manager's disciplinary activities within a firm may in fact be part of an underlying political struggle between different teams, notated by the code 'pol-strug'.

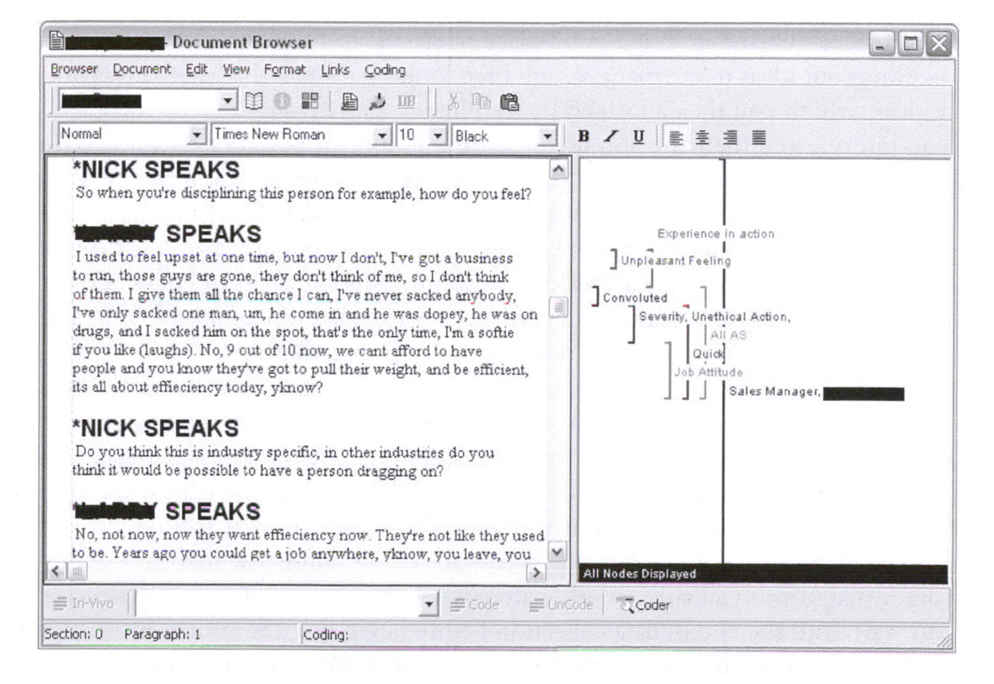

Figure 10.3 Example coded paragraph from QSR NVIVO
Source: Used with kind permission of QSR International: www.qsrinternational.com.

Coding is quite a complex process, and one thing which should be mentioned is that it is iterative just like many other aspects of the qualitative process. You often start by simply describing the data with codes, and then as you get more of a holistic picture of what's going on underneath, you recognise patterns, concepts and links between them. This then necessitates you returning to previously coded sections and re-evaluating them, adding interpretive layers on top of the basic description. You should recognise this concept as somewhat hermeneutic. There is some disagreement (of course) over how much of a pre-structure of codes you should begin with. For most people, their conceptual work will have suggested at least a preliminary set of concepts and categories to work with. For example, in my study of sales manager problem resolution I began with the idea that disciplinary activity comprised the actual 'action' and also the 'interpersonal style' with which it was delivered. Thus, I created two master codes ('action style' and 'interpersonal style), which had subcodes, such as 'AS-fast' or 'IP-aggressive'. There were also codes for antecedents and consequences, such as 'prior-perf' and 'team-respect'. Thus, I had a starting list of maybe 40 codes, which is quite possible to keep in memory. Of course, I had it stuck up on my computer monitor, and it got modified as the coding process proceeded. That said, it is important not to generate too complex a scheme, as in the end you will not really be reducing the data too much. A more inductive approach, such as true grounded theory, for example, would not start with such a list, but instead try to generate codes from the data. This can be difficult for the inexperienced researcher, but a good place to start is to look at a piece of data in great detail, marking out ideas in the margins, and then looking to combine those ideas into more abstract ideas, which you then attach codes to. Phrases which were used by the respondents when you interviewed them are also useful starting points for codes (which is called *in-vivo* coding). I think most researchers fall somewhere in the middle, beginning with a tentative structure, but allowing it to evolve in ways suggested by the data.

You'll probably find as I did, that once you actually start coding, you'll get the hang of it pretty quickly and at first your list will snowball into silly numbers of codes. Try to avoid this. Use the benchmark of keeping your structure on a single piece of paper if possible. Also, try to work with an overall structure, not just a set of unrelated codes – this is one of the reasons a theoretical appreciation can help your analysis. One of you main aims is usually to find some kind of structure in the data, so it makes good sense to keep this in mind. Also, try to make the code labels 'sensitising', by which I mean give them easy-to-understand names, not numbers. This helps you to think about things, and also eases the teamworking process if that's relevant. Speaking of which, it can also be useful to have a second analyst check your coding once in a while, just to see if you are being consistent in your coding. Also, don't forget that good qualitative work is iterative and evolving, not rigidly structured, so try not to wait until the end of data collection before beginning the coding process. Finally, do try to keep in mind that the coding process can be argued as one of placing your own interpretation on the data, and therefore you should be very careful that you 'let the data speak', rather than get drawn in to 'making it fit' your earlier theoretical ideas.

Data displays

A data display is another central pillar of qualitative analysis. It's another concept which many have trouble understanding. It is however, quite simple when you think about it. Think about a set of numbers about people's preferences, you can display this in any number of forms, for example as a spreadsheet. However, it is more insightful usually to display it as a graph. Qualitative data is in the same boat here. Simply displaying large swathes of textual data is not often insightful (although can provide compelling context when used appropriately), nor is simply lifting out a few quotes (running the risk of anecdotalism). Also, the qualitative research report (another large body of text) can be difficult for readers to comprehend, especially if they are pressed for time. Combined and done well, these things can comprise a fairly useful piece of research analysis. But is there a way of doing what quantitative analysts do as a matter of course, creating those pretty diagrams, models, graphs and charts? In this section the concept of qualitative data displays will be introduced, and some examples given. However, you should always keep in mind that qualitative displays are a forum for creativity in analysis; design them in the way you think helps understand the data best, not by slavishly following examples.

One way I have found useful to think of data displays is as small lamps. Imagine a statue in a museum, your data is the statue, and the data displays are the lamps that let the public see the key parts of interest of that statue. If you have a set of qualitative data, it can be lit up in a number of ways. Each different way helps the reader to understand the findings differently. So our task is to illuminate the data set with lamps (i.e. displays) in such a way that the reader can see it more clearly. Sometimes certain aspects are so important they need multiple lamps, and other times we need a single lamp to illuminate a part of the data. Of course, if you extend the metaphor, lamps can also cast interesting shadows, and be used to point out some parts and hide others; but this kind of thing is not what we will talk about here.

There are a number of ways of classifying data displays. Firstly, there is the display which is focused on a single case (be it an interview, focus group, observational site or the like), which are termed **within-case** displays. But we also like to compare across different cases, perhaps in an attempt to increase generalisability, or to deepen our understanding of the situation, which is called **cross-case** analysis. We can also think about the aims of the displays. Some displays are focused on **describing** the data, while others are focused on **explaining** what is happening, which usually involves some kind of causality-based thinking. We'll focus here on the actual displays, as they are often applicable to many of the various classifications given above. If you want to know more, it would be a good idea to look at the references given at the end of this chapter.

The design of a display can usually be considered to fall into one of two main camps: the *matrix* or the *network*; although you can possibly think of the network as the *diagram* as well. There are other types of display, such as the poem (yes really), but there isn't enough space to go into them here. You should always think about the purpose of your display.

Is it for your purposes, to let you get a picture of the data set as a whole, or challenge your assumptions? Or is it for the final reader, to actually illuminate or justify some aspect of your conclusions? For example, sometimes you just want to create a matrix which pulls all the relevant data together and compares it, say, by gender. If you are doing this for yourself, it can be as detailed as you want, but for a final display you need to work out whether it is going to provide the reader with any additional 'illumination power' when condensed into a format suitable for publication.

A matrix is exactly what it sounds like, one concept crossed over with another. Figure 10.4 shows a matrix of 'action speed' crossed over with 'locus of comments', where I was trying to figure out whether my respondents were only describing *others* as quick to punish salespeople, not themselves. Doing this for each individual helped me begin to infer that quick punishment could be seen as a negative characteristic by many. Matrices can be even more ordered than this, for example, you could order them by time, or key events, such as in a purchase decision process. One decision to make is what to put in the cells – direct

	Personal Comments	**'Other Managers'**
General		
Responsive	23-29: 'if they don't suit then they're out, you with me?...we cant afford to have people...linger on'. 63-64: 'I can tell within a week whether they're going to be any good' 165-167: 'if I'm going to get rid of someone [then I do it], but I prefer to try and coax them to do a better job, but you can only go so far' 237-238: 'if they don't pull their weight they're gone, its that simple, no matter how well they get on with the others' 242: 'if I notice I put my foot on it straight away, you can't be everywhere' 327-328: 'give me a week and I'll sort him out and he's gone if he's no good' 352-357: 'I asked them for all the help I could...[and]...they couldn't care that much so I closed it down' 489-490: 'I got rid of him, I didn't want to but I had to'	138-140: 'other people wouldn't give the lad the chances I gave him, they'd have had him out quicker' 167: 'a lot of managers...have got no mercy' 190-191: 'if they don't pull their weight they're gone' 301-302: 'if they don't pull their weight then they have to go' 467-469: 'are [managers] sympathetic today? No...my son is nothing like me, if he's got to get rid of someone he does it'.
Non-responsive	40-41: we give him about 4 chances and in the end...I just kicked him out, we were wasting our time' 111: 'I give him that many chances, he'd upset a few of the personnel'. 177-178: 'I'm a softie if you like' 271-272: 'I said you come back in 6 months and [if] you're alright I'll give you your job back' 330-331: 'if I think he's got potential I'll extend his...trial' 371-374: 'I'd do anything to keep these [employees], put my own house up for mortgage...these blokes are good blokes, they've worked for me a long time'.	

Figure 10.4 Example within-case matrix

quotes, descriptions, inferences or something else? You'll note in Figure 10.4 that I have described what's going on, and then put line numbers for the transcript. This wouldn't have been useful for a published display, where no transcripts are available. Nevertheless, you should be careful not to over-infer when constructing matrices, nor to taking small quotes out of context. Doing so can divorce you from your data rather effectively.

I always seem to find diagrams more interesting than matrices, perhaps it's because I am a frustrated artist, or not. Probably it's because I think in very visual terms, as most of my students will tell you. There is an almost infinite variety of diagrams which can be drawn which help illuminate what's going on in your data. It's difficult to really overstate the variety of diagrams that are possible in qualitative analysis. In fact, what you can do is driven purely by your research objectives and the data you have collected. So, of course, it is surely needless to say that you have to be very clear about your objectives, and what data you need, *before* you go and collect it!

A classic example of a data display, which I haven't had the chance to use yet, is the time line, say of a consumer decision process for a new car. Time could be on a horizontal axis, and another key variable (perhaps 'amount of information searched') on a vertical axis. Another interesting format is exemplified in Figure 10.5, which was developed by one of my students (Jennifer Walker, who appeared at the start of Chapter 9). It shows the evaluation process of consumers to information about a company's ethical behaviour. This display came from a single focus group of highly ethically aware consumers. It helped illuminate a number of things, most specifically the key importance of a concept termed the 'moment of scepticism', where individuals doubted the authenticity of the information.

Displays play a hugely important role. They can allow you to see things in the data which are not obvious simply by examining the text, they can help readers understand the conclusions more easily, and they can condense huge amounts of data into manageable and illuminating formats. You should be thinking about how to display the data very early on, drawing tentative diagrams, designing matrices and the like. However, take care not to become wedded to certain displays too early. Displays are always evolving, and if you remove yourself from the raw data too early your thinking is then going to be basically driven by what you put in your display. Remember, the data should drive the display, don't try to force the data to fit a display which you really like.

The displays above were essentially *descriptive*, but we can also use displays to begin to develop explanatory links in our findings. Now is not the time and the place to discuss causality, but it should not be in question that displays can help us get a handle on the concepts which seem to be influencing other concepts in our data. While matrices can be used in this context, I have always found diagrams to be more intuitive – probably because I tend to draw them myself to explain theories to others. Figure 10.6 shows a within-case diagram designed to illuminate the set of antecedents and consequences to a sales manager's speed to punish a problem salesperson. It was based on the coding and other processes already explored above. Such diagrams can be very simple, or very complex, depending on

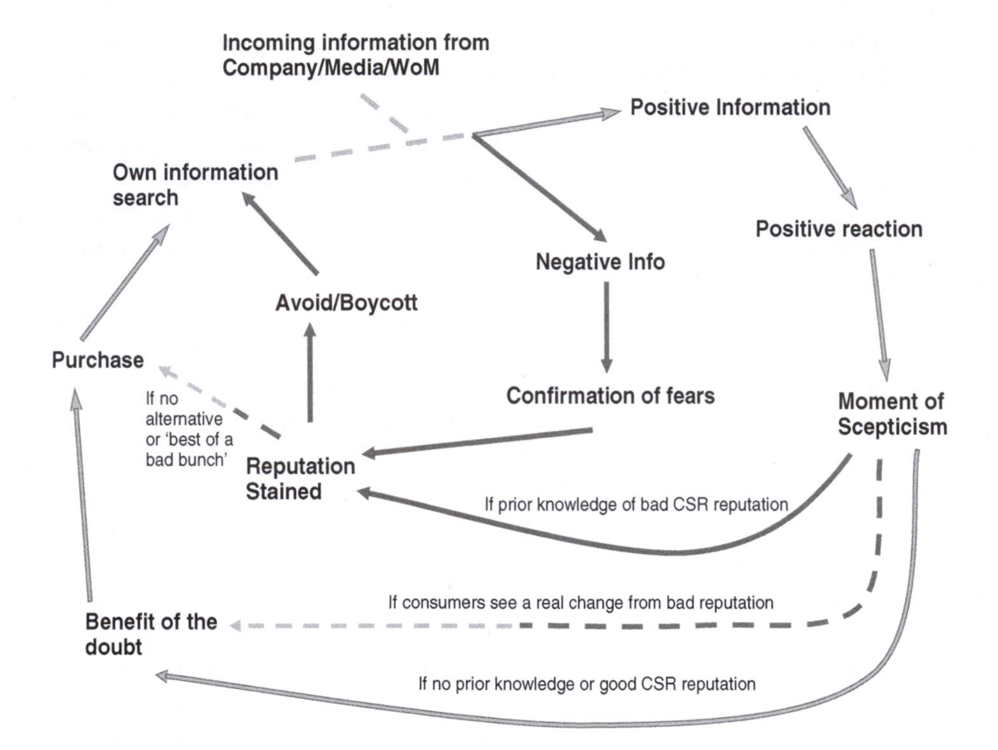

Figure 10.5 Example cyclical diagram
Source: Used with kind permission of Jennifer Walker, from an unpublished Msc Dissertation (Aston Business School, 2006).

the complexity of the situation itself, as well as the amount of information in the case. I also expect that I could have made the diagram more complex myself, by incorporating more of my own inference rather than relying as I did on descriptive coding. You can develop these diagrams by beginning with a theoretical conceptual framework, or purely from the data itself. Of course, most people fall somewhere in the middle, such as in Figure 10.6. But it does depend on your data collection – if you are basing your data collection on theoretical frameworks, you are more likely to end up with a diagram that looks like an existing theoretical model.

All of the concepts referred to above can be applied to a cross-case situation as well. Here, we are usually looking for patterns across cases. Are there uniform antecedents to quick punishment, for example? If there are differences, what are the specific aspects of those cases which may be influencing differences? You can see that yet again these kinds of conclusions are bound up inextricably with data collection. If you don't have the right kind of cases, you can't draw conclusions about their similarities or differences. One way of doing cross-case

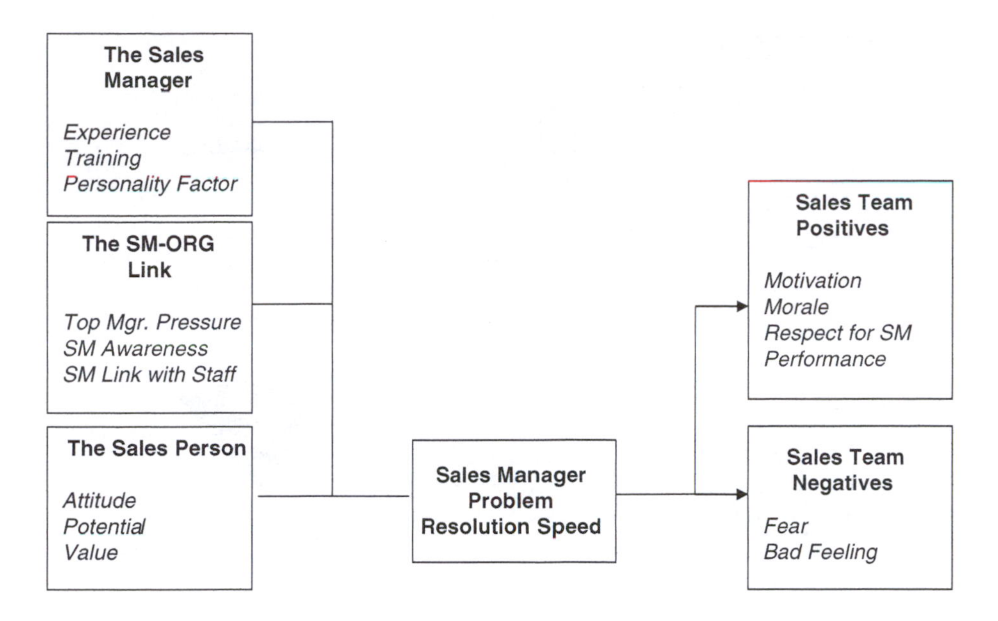

Figure 10.6 Example within-case conceptual framework

analysis is to develop a framework from one case, and then examine subsequent cases to see whether they 'fit the pattern' or not. Or you could look for key themes or variables which occur repeatedly across many cases. I combined these approaches when generating a cross-case model from multiple within-case diagrams like Figure 10.6.

Another common approach is the 'meta-matrix', where one can directly compare, say, different types of respondent (e.g. males versus females) on various factors. It could be expected that such matrices can be unwieldy, and this is indeed the case. In fact, Miles and Huberman (1994) refer to them as 'monster-dogs' for this reason. But when used properly, they can be a powerful way of exploring your data.

An example of a cross-case diagram is given in Figure 10.7, where the designers were looking to explain why consumers chose to resist adopting innovations. You can see the numbers refer to the proportions of times respondents from the eight focus groups discussed each concept. This display led to a rethink on how different factors may influence different types of resistance, from passive to active.

Beginning to draw conclusions

As you begin to code and display your data, you will naturally begin to draw some conclusions, and think about what your data 'means'. It is here we start to get to the nub

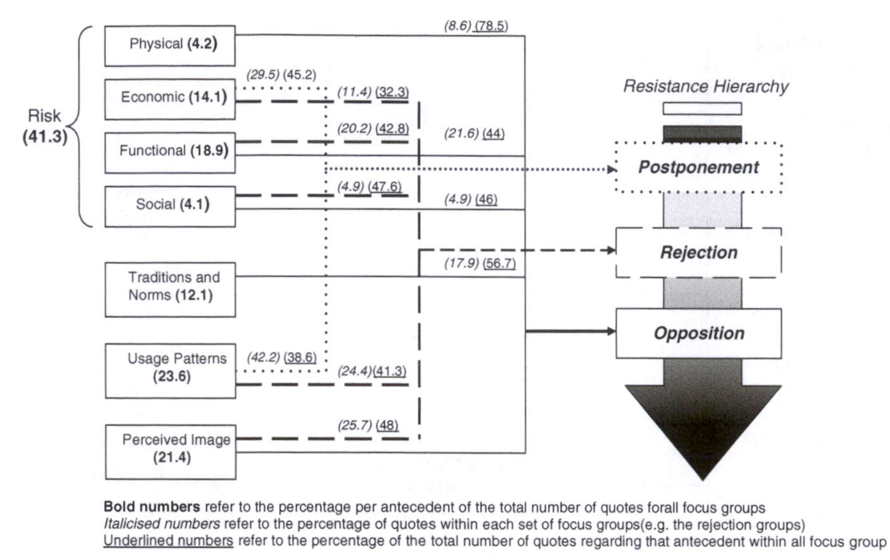

Figure 10.7 Example of cross-case conceptual framework

of qualitative analysis; how do we know what that data means? However, it's vital to avoid 'over-interpreting' your data. What I mean is that you should guard very carefully against putting your own ideas 'on to' the data and not letting the data speak for itself. There's a fine line between interpreting data in light of prior theory and your ideas, and biasing your conclusions. Qualitative analysts generally present their conclusions in the third major component of good qualitative research, extended text – the first part being appropriate selection of quotes and raw data to exemplify your points, and the second being good displays. I sometimes call this section of the analysis *creating a narrative* for your research, as you are essentially telling a story. However, this term can be a bit confusing for those who are in fact conducting the specific form of narrative research (which none of my students do) so I won't use it again here. In creating the text, you should understand that your displays don't stand alone for the reader, you need to explain them, pick out key points and patterns, and ultimately build a convincing evidence-based argument as to what you are trying to say.

There are various approaches to generating conclusions and meaning from your data and its displays, but I will focus on one particular higher-level issue you need to keep in mind; **plausibility**. In other words, do your conclusions intuitively feel right? This is dangerous ground. Most of us can almost always pick out some plausible explanation for even the most random events – as the continuing attention paid to astrology demonstrates so clearly (I'm a Leo if you're interested). If the only justification for a finding you can give is that it seems intuitively correct, you are in trouble. Similarly, do not dismiss potential conclusions simply because they are implausible, or fly in the face of existing wisdom. Some of the world's greatest discoveries were made after researchers closely investigated their implausible original findings.

Essentially, rather than thinking solely in terms of intuition, which was the 'black box' at the heart of qualitative analysis for far too long, start looking at your data for patterns, and explaining those patterns. Maybe these patterns are across multiple sites, people, or multiple examples given by a single participant. Compare these patterns, look for situations where they do and do not hold – which could be called *boundary conditions*. Some people like to use numbers to represent the comparative importance of ideas and variables, which was done in Figure 10.7. While coding has taken you right down into the data, try to raise your level of abstraction to one which takes in all of the data. Think in terms of general concepts or variables and their relationships, not always individual people or cases.

Verifying your conclusions and their validity

Of course, anyone can draw some conclusions from a set of data, the real task is to convince yourself and your readers of the 'goodness' of those conclusions. Validity is something which has cast a long shadow over the last two chapters, and it remains a key concept here. But first we will consider a few areas which you need to examine to convince *yourself* of your work, which you should find intimately bound with all of the issues we've covered so far.

First is you as the research instrument. How can you be sure that you were an unbiased tool? In the previous chapter we spoke at length about the inherent *reflexivity* of qualitative work, in that the researcher can influence the respondents, and the respondents can influence the way the researcher works. There are few solutions which can be offered at the analysis stage though – you can't 'remove' many of these influences here. It is simply a case of good research design and careful practice. Nevertheless, it is relevant to the analyst, as you really want to be clear on the likelihood of bias in your work, especially when writing it up. Look for feelings of 'betrayal' of your respondents, and try to maintain an ethical stance throughout.

We've already spoken about tools for exploring validity earlier in the chapter, such as the refutability concept. But overall you need to be concerned with looking at whether you are being overly anecdotal in your conclusions. Do your patterns really explain *all* the data? Sometimes, it can be useful to get an outside party to comment on your findings, a colleague or supervisor, for example. This can help you step back a little. But remember, these people may be even more likely to be seduced by the 'plausibility' issue, as they are less inclined to look at the whole data set.

As already mentioned, looking for extreme or contradictory examples of your conclusions can help. Can you find reasons for why they did not agree? Were they special cases, are they ignorable reasons, or do they necessitate re-evaluation of your conclusions? Try really hard to look for contradictory explanations, and see whether your conclusions still hold more water than them. Sometimes, this can actually necessitate collecting more data which is specifically targeted at deviant cases or contradictory explanations. Of course, I realise that very few people ever want to do this at the 'end' of a project. But remember you should not think about a qualitative project in stages, but as iterative and cyclical. In this context it therefore makes perfect sense to collect some more data late in the day, to provide some confirmatory evidence.

Finally, we come to the question of validity, which ties pretty much everything together which has been mentioned in the past two chapters. By now you should have a good understanding of the concept, and it is unnecessary to go through it here yet again. Suffice it to say that simply doing 'good' research may not lead to valid conclusions. Your research doesn't operate in a vacuum, if that were the case you would conduct it, write it up and then spend the rest of your life reading it in your bedroom, never showing it to anyone else (rather like Gollum with his 'precious' ring)[7]. If we wish it to be read, and possibly used, by other parties, we owe it to them and ourselves to consider criteria for its quality. I remember Eddie Vedder, lead singer of the band Pearl Jam, petulantly accepting a Grammy Award with the simple speech 'you can't judge art'. Unfortunately for us, while Pearl Jam's Grammy-winning song 'Spin the Black Circle' may be a work of art, research is not,[8] and it needs to be judged as to its quality. Whatever those quality criteria are – and there are many as the previous chapters have shown – the qualitative analyst needs to consider them when conducting their work and presenting it to the outside world. With specific relevance to the processes discussed here, you need to be concerned with the **internal validity**, or credibility, or justifiability (whatever you want to call it) of your conclusions. How well do they reflect the social situation or issue which you examined and collected data about? Ignoring data collection issues, *how well does your analysis reflect the data?* Whatever you believe about the eternal flux of the social world, how it is constructed between actors, or the existence of an underlying 'truth' and our likelihood of gaining access to it, this question **must** be answered convincingly.

A brief introduction to some other issues

This section will contain some brief 'sketches' of a number of other qualitative issues. Some of these issues are specific types of methodology, others are more conceptual, but I think it is useful for all researchers to realise that the methods presented above are not the 'only' methods, nor are they necessarily the 'best'. They have certainly worked well for me, resulting

---

[7] If you don't know what I am talking about, stop reading this book and go and read *The Lord of the Rings*. If you don't own a copy swap this – actually, swap another book – for a copy.

[8] Although doubtless many postmodernists and poststructuralists will disagree.

in quite a lot of good work, but there are others. This section should give you a set of directions to go in if you wish to expand your knowledge of qualitative approaches.

Content analysis

Content analysis is something which I've always found a little confusing. On the one hand, it is often considered a qualitative technique, probably because it primarily works with textual data. On the other hand, it can be considered as quantitative in essence, as you are counting the occurrence of certain distinct phrases. Nevertheless, in contrast to most qualitative techniques, the focus of content analysis is on objectively identifying and usually counting given features of the data. You can use content analysis on all kinds of data, from text (e.g. newspapers, advertising, transcripts) to visual data (perhaps TV programmes, advertising again). It can be particularly useful in analysing published text, such as studying trends in media reactions to a key issue, or in exploring advertising content. A good introduction to content analysis is in Franzosi (2004). Altheide (1996) proposed a more 'qualitative' content analysis (which I employed myself in my first ever 'real' research project), where the analyst takes a less structured approach, allowing the categories to emerge more inductively and recognising context – rather than imposing a rigid 'objective' structure on the data.

Semiotics

In contrast with the structured approach of content analysis is semiotics, which is the study of 'signs'. It can be somewhat arcane, but the basics are reasonably simple. Semiotics is essentially concerned with the analysis of documents – although it can be applied to other data as it considers everything to be a 'text' – and explicitly recognises that that most signs have underlying meaning. It is the researcher's task to uncover this meaning. By way of explanation, semiotics considers every *sign* to be made up of a *signifier* (something which points to an underlying or hidden meaning), and the *signified* (the hidden meaning). A strength of semiotics is that it encourages us to look beyond the obvious in analysis, but it could be argued that the results can be somewhat analyst-dependent. It has been employed in many situations, wherever the interest is in looking beyond surface manifestations (e.g. advertising research). A useful introduction is given by Manning (2004).

Discourse analysis

Discourse analysis (often referred to as DA) is heavily based on some of the 20th century philosophers who appeared in Chapter 3, particularly Michel Foucault (1926–1984), who considered discourse to essentially create the ways in which we look at objects and phenomena. Like many such qualitative methods, it can be impenetrable for the uninitiated – as attendance at a DA-focused conference will show – and really refers to a set of different approaches. DA is fundamentally opposed to the idea of independent reality, and is wedded to the idea of social constructionism. In this framework, DA looks to explore the underlying objectives of a discourse – what are the parties trying to achieve and how? DA treats almost everything as a discourse, so it can be applied to most data sources. In contrast to my own feelings, DA researchers seem to be somewhat shy of documenting their exact methods, preferring to consider it a 'craft' (e.g. Potter, 1997). DA is also related to conversation analysis (CA) in some ways. However, CA is focused on 'naturally-occurring' conversations (i.e. not really interviews), and also employs detailed analysis techniques to uncover the structure of interaction in talk. These methods can be usefully employed in many situations, and it really does depend on your research objectives and (to some extent) philosophical assumptions, particularly in the case of DA. Useful introductions to DA and CA are Potter (2004) and Clayman and Gill (2004) respectively.

Narrative analysis

Narrative analysis is really a set of different methods, which all share a concern for the 'stories' that we and others use to describe, understand and explain the world and their place in it. Therefore, it can be seen that it is not so much interested in the objective 'facts' of the situation, but how people interpreted it and their position/role within it. Of course, this necessitates a natural concern with temporal order, as well as an interest in the social construction of meaning. It is naturally suited to research about people's lives and biographies, but it is not difficult to see how 'smaller' events can be approached in this way – such as purchase decisions, disciplinary activities (I'm always talking about that aren't I?) or other organisation and consumer topics. Data is often collected through dedicated narrative interviews, the approach can be applied to other interview data or data from observations. The approach can be criticised as potentially subject to biases from the respondent – for example they may wish to present themselves in a positive light rather than tell their 'real' story. But by now you should be capable of rebutting that argument with some of the concepts in Chapter 3, and this one too. In fact, try it as a little thought experiment.[9] A useful introduction to narrative methods is in Andrews *et al.* (2004).

Feminism: An example of the political influence in qualitative research

I debated for some time whether or not to write this brief section. I don't want to imply that feminism is either (a) some kind of special set of techniques and methods (although some will disagree), or (b) that feminism is the most important of the 'critical' traditions of qualitative research. However, it does provide a nice example of how political positions can be used as bases for research traditions – so I am willing to risk it. In brief, feminist research could be considered to be subsumed within general critical and poststructuralist traditions. Here, as I mentioned earlier, our cherished notions of validity are called into question. However, the point I want to make here is that not all research traditions are in

---

[9] Hint: start by thinking about (a) who is doing the defining of 'real' here anyway, and (b) are such biases interesting in their own right regardless?

fact aimed at uncovering 'the truth' (in realist terms), or even 'a truth'. In fact, many critical research traditions (of which feminism is one) have the goal of bringing about some kind of positive or emancipatory change in the context, or society as a whole. Within the research tasks themselves, the focus would be on allowing respondents' own voices to be heard without imposing control, and in reciprocating during fieldwork (giving as well as taking data). While this is a gross simplification, it is easy to see how considerations such as this would influence the research questions, data collection, analysis, conclusions and ultimate reporting of feminist research. For example, such traditions are clearly very amenable to an 'action research' methodology, where you participate in the context while researching it, with the aim of 'changing' the context for the better as the research outcome. The goals here are very different from what we might implicitly expect from a 'research project'. More information can be found in Kitzinger (2004).

The Internet

In putting this section at the end, I don't mean to imply that the Internet should be treated as an afterthought. Indeed, a consideration of the Internet as an environment to study and utilise to collect data should pervade your thinking. The Internet does offer some interesting advantages and opportunities that deserve special mention though. One thing I have found fascinating is the prevalence of interpersonal contact on the Internet – for example there are masses of social networks based around things like TV shows, computer games, music and products. People use these as hubs for their own social interaction in some ways – not just sad people with no 'real' friends, but regular people like you. Even better, this interaction is generally archived, so you can track it. Also, today there is a rising trend for 'virtual worlds' where you can even purchase 'land' to 'build' on using real money. The possibilities for ethnography and other types of qualitative research here are endless. The Internet is also a useful medium for more 'traditional' research. For example, it can be used to enhance your ability to contact geographically diverse respondents, using email, live messaging, audio, or even video. A useful introduction to the issues involved in online qualitative research is Mann and Stewart (2000), although bear in mind the evolution of the Internet means such material often dates quickly.

Summary

At various points throughout this chapter I have characterised qualitative analysis as being traditionally a 'black-box'. This may be fine for experienced qualitative researchers who are comfortable with their interpretive philosophical standpoints, and readers who share the same views and are willing to take on faith any conclusions of a research project. However, it is of precisely zero value to a beginning researcher, or the analyst who wishes to engage with the link between research findings and some kind of outside standards of 'quality'. Such a standpoint also runs the risk of leaving qualitative analysis in the hands of an 'elite' who know what they are doing, and who then essentially control the dissemination of that knowledge. In recent times such opinions have become less prevalent, and great books on qualitative analysis are beginning to appear more regularly. This chapter was an attempt primarily to introduce a basic framework for qualitative analysis in the context of a wider appreciation of research in general, linking it where necessary to various philosophical assumptions while also giving solid practical tools. An appreciation of 'quality' in qualitative analysis should also be considered to run as a seam through this chapter. In light of this, I hope that you now have at the very least a respect for qualitative analysis, and something of a springboard from which to investigate it further if necessary.

Key points to take from this chapter:

- All data can be considered as originally 'qualitative' in some ways, but qualitative data for most intents and purposes is that which is or could be transformed into words.
- The qualitative analysis process is generally that of reducing the vast amount of data to themes, ideas and concepts. However there is a tension between this and retaining the fundamental richness of qualitative data.
- Most qualitative analysts should not ignore considerations of reliability and validity, although there are a number of different perspectives on these ideas.
- Coding is the starting point of analysis, allowing you to closely explore the underlying themes and concepts in your data.
- Data displays allow you to see and present the data in many different lights, which provides a far richer and more useful analysis.
- Be careful when drawing conclusions not to be seduced by the 'plausibility' of your findings, nor of relying solely on intuition, researchers should also consider the 'quality' of their findings.

Further reading

There are many great books out there that I've already referred to, in particular the ones in Chapter 3 (especially Chris Hackley's one) and of course Chapter 9, here are a few more specifically about analysis:

- *Qualitative Data Analysis* by Matthew B. Miles and A. Michael Huberman: A wonderful book which goes farther than I ever could. Anyone who wishes to analyse qualitative data and does not fundamentally disagree with the general approach of this chapter should get a copy.
- *Collecting and Interpreting Qualitative Materials* edited by Norman K. Denzin and Yvonna S. Lincoln: A good collection of interesting material, particularly strong on the more interpretive side of things.

EXERCISES

1. What is 'qualitative' data? How can you determine whether data is qualitative or quantitative?
2. Think about and explain some possible uses that numbers can have in a qualitative project.
3. Considering validity, go back to Chapter 3 and try to write a counterpoint to IDE 10.1 from the perspective of Nietzche.
4. Speaking of validity concerns, respond to the argument that 'a concern for validity within qualitative research is nothing more than a cringe towards "traditional" notions of science which is irrelevant in contemporary social science'. Begin by explaining exactly what this argument may mean.
5. Consider how the Internet could have an impact on a qualitative research project, in terms of data collection and data analysis. What are the potential advantages and dangers of this?
6. At this point, I think it would be valuable if you went and learnt a tune on a musical instrument – try an Irish whistle if you don't already play something (I once had a Ph.D. student who could play virtually any tune on that, the show off!).

Chapter 11
Collecting quantitative data

SUPERVISOR'S VIEW: DR IAN LINGS

If you are conducting a quantative study, collecting your data is another major milestone in your research process, and one that can be fraught with anxiety. Generally your data collection resources (time, money and respondents) are limited. This means that often in reality you have only one bite at this cherry, despite what so many research methods books will tell you. You may be anxious as you question yourself; do my models and frameworks adequately reflect the real world? Have I designed my collection instruments appropriately? Have I chosen appropriate respondents that will provide me with the data I require? Will they agree to provide me with this data, either through their own efforts (if you use a self-response method) or if I observe them (using an observational technique)? *Oh my God,* what if I forget to ask a question or make an observation, what if I ask the wrong question, etc? WHAT IF IT DOESN'T WORK? Well, calm down, panic will never help you run a good data collection programme.

The panic of data collection, in my experience, tends to lead first-time researchers down one of two paths. Either a lack of confidence causes them to refuse to move to the data collection stage by procrastinating endlessly over their conceptual frameworks and models, eternally refining them to make sure they haven't missed anything. Or, they are so keen to finish, graduate, get a job and earn some money (at last), that they want to rush into data collection, seeing it as the last major hurdle to finishing the thesis, leading to corners which are cut, and poor data. Unsurprisingly, I would advocate an approach somewhere between these two extremes – and working through the material in the *other* chapters of this book will have just as positive an impact on your data collection as this dedicated one will!

The objective of your quantitative data collection is to provide you with a source of 'evidence' against which you can test your hypotheses. If you never collect the data you cannot test your hypotheses and the project will not progress; if you collect the wrong data, you will have to repeat the exercise once you discover that you have the wrong data. This is one of the main problems that first-time researchers face. You won't truly know if your conceptual framework is missing something important or if you have forgetten to collect an important variable until you have analysed your data. So data collection and analysis are inextricably linked. You *must* have an idea about what you intend to do with the data before you collect it. Both your intended analysis technique and your theoretical framework should give you a good idea of the data you need, but you don't know until you have analysed your data. So what are you to do?

Professor Gummesson highlighted the need for researchers to *practise*, and to use their experience, wisdom, insights and judgement and to reflect on their work. But as a first-time researcher you may not have experiences to reflect on. This is where practise comes in; I cannot emphasise enough the value of *practising your research*. Conduct a small-scale pilot study, collect the data, analyse it and interpret the results. Even a relatively small sample will give you important information about how well your full study will work. *It is not wasted time*, it will not slow down and it will almost definitely prevent you from making easily rectified mistakes that can cost you a lot of time, effort and money to put right.

What I am advocating is, from this point onwards, complete your project on a small scale first; gain some experience of the data collection, analysis and interpretation; reflect on this, and redesign your study if necessary. If you identify some problems you will be glad that you did; if it all works well, you can sleep more soundly in your (or someone else's) bed at night, knowing that you are on the way to a successful project.

VIEW FROM THE TRENCHES: ANDREW FARRELL

Firstly, let me just say that the majority of my comments refer to questionnaires. This is because it's what I mainly employ, and in my experience it's what the majority of people who say they are collecting quantitative data for their research actually mean. Now, I'll begin with something sinister. Quantitative data collection is a daunting process as it remains largely out of your control. You can study your sample with the greatest of precision, you can design the most easily completed, interesting, novel and downright pretty questionnaire ever, but if the respondents don't want to fill it in, they won't. *And there is nothing you can do about it!*

Well, that's not entirely true. There is something you can do. In order to combat respondent inertia, you need to arm yourself with an in-depth understanding of quantitative data collection procedures. It isn't possible to know 'too much' about quantitative data collection. If other people at your institution have been involved in the process before, ask them about it. Ask what went wrong, what went right, what they would do differently the next time. Everyone has at least one piece of advice that you will probably find indispensable.

The hardest part of quantitative data collection is getting the involvement of your participants. Due to the larger sample sizes that are often found (some would say required) in quantitative data collection, you generally don't have the option of personally contacting each participant and building up a rapport with them, as you tend to have when attempting qualitative data collection. Therefore, it is crucial that you are able to 'sell' your project to potential participants. Make them *want* to be involved. Make them worry about what they could miss out on if they are not involved. But, while doing this, don't forget that your participants are doing you a favour, and not the other way around. Participants are busy people. Shorter questionnaires mean more responses. Easy questions mean more responses. It's very tempting when designing a questionnaire to try and measure too much, to sneak a few extra questions in there so you can add another variable to your model that you are interested in. We all dream of being able to test the most comprehensive model ever conceptualised in our particular area, but that's all it normally is, a dream. It's nice to be able to achieve a healthy balance between the amount of data collected and the length of your questionnaire, but sometimes you've just got to be ruthless. Don't forget, a simple model is easier to explain, and easier to sell to your respondents.

Just remember, quantitative data collection can seduce you, with promises that more data means more power and more testing, which means better publications. However, a model, and by association a Ph.D., doesn't need to be complicated to make a contribution, but it does need sufficient data available to test it. If I'm asked if I'd like a complicated model with a small sample size, or a simple model with a large sample size, I know which one I'd choose every time (hint, it's the latter!)

Quantitative data is often what beginning researchers assume they are going to be collecting when they begin a research degree or career in most departments. Nevertheless, there are contrasting traditions and viewpoints towards different types of quantitative data collection, depending on what field you are involved in. In my own field, marketing, as well as a lot of other business disciplines, there is a prevalence of questionnaire survey designs – especially in the UK (Saunders and Lee, 2005). In the psychological disciplines (including consumer psychology) there is a tradition of experimental designs. In many finance, economics, and related disciplines, the approach is often based around collecting longitudinal secondary quantitative data.

These different approaches each offer contrasting strengths and weaknesses, meaning they are more or less appropriate for different research objectives. For example, if you wish to look at the influence of motivation on performance, utilising a longitudinal analysis of secondary data may be less useful than collecting experimental data. Therefore it is of course necessary to understand the basic link between your research question and the data you need to collect. This chapter will begin with the logic of sampling for surveys, as this is probably the fundamental theory of quantitative data collection. Following this, I will outline some key issues which need to be considered if you are using a different data collection method, or research design. Finally, some hints and tips about instrument design will be given.

After the previous few chapters, you're probably under the impression that if you choose to collect quantitative data, you won't have to deal with any criticism of your approach, as it is 'accepted'. Although this is in many ways true, choosing to collect a set of quantitative data poses its own problems. For one thing, you are choosing to be bound by a far more rigid set of principles and guidelines, so you had better spend some serious time learning these principles. In fact, this chapter is designed to provide a springboard into the sometimes deep waters of quantitative data collection, from which you can determine the appropriate methods to employ, and get a basic appreciation of what these methods entail. It is primarily concerned with the theory behind the practice of quantitative data collection – as there are many other excellent resources which tell you 'how' to collect data (e.g. how to design telephone surveys, etc.), and some of these are given at the end of the chapter.

In keeping with this, one important point to make at the outset concerns the Internet. As technology and society evolves, the Internet is becoming a vitally important tool to collect quantitative data. However, the Internet does not make the basic theories and principles outlined here invalid. Instead it augments your options with which to apply them. Consequently, the Internet will receive little explicit attention in this chapter, except where specific pieces of advice need to be given.

At the end of this chapter I really hope you have come to terms with these key ideas:

- That sampling is of key importance to statistics and the generalisability of our findings.
- What representativeness means, and the different ways of looking at the issues involved.
- That while probability sampling is seen as the 'gold standard' of sampling, in practice non-probability samples are more often used.
- The differences between interactive or non-interactive data collection methods.
- The key issues involved in instrument design.

Why is it Important to Know This Stuff?

As I have already mentioned, choosing to collect quantitative data involves an implicit choice to accept the basic principles and assumptions that underlie quantitative research. You are going to need a good appreciation of the underlying theory and its implications before you are capable of doing a good project. For one thing, a lack of understanding about quantitative data collection will make it really hard for you to truly grasp the basic principles of quantitative analysis – which is a common problem I am faced with among so many of my students.

While there are fewer political issues to deal with when compared to qualitative and interpretive approaches, the quantitative researcher will probably still face criticism from others for their stance. Just as the qualitative researcher should have a good knowledge of the reasoning behind their position, so should the quantitative researcher. You owe it to yourself and others to understand the bases of your chosen approach – or else how do you know 'why' you chose to collect quantitative data? Why should qualitative researchers be the only ones who need to justify themselves? As well as this, understanding the theory of quantitative data collection will allow you to determine when criticism of your work is justified, and when it is not.

Basically, what I am saying is that for quantitative researchers, it is important to know and accept the principles behind the approach. Furthermore, you will need to know this kind of information in order to interpret the quality of other pieces of quantitative research – which can have a huge impact on your theoretical work. For example, knowledge of sampling theory can have a big influence on how important you consider a given set of findings are to your own work.

Of course, we are dealing with the same basic issues as in other chapters (such as Chapter 9), the gathering of real-world data with which to examine our theory, and Figure 11.1 is almost identical to Figure 9.1. Finally, for those who truly know without doubt that they will never use quantitative data, they had better work out some reasons why – and this chapter would be a good starting point.

Quantitative sampling

Earlier in this book, I spent some time discussing the logic behind qualitative sampling. If you wanted to characterise this process, you could probably say that it was concerned with selecting 'appropriate' sampling units (or cases), with the benefit of some kind of criteria – whether it be theoretical, practical, or analysis-based. Hopefully, you also saw the link between this kind of approach and the underlying interpretive philosophy, and also the

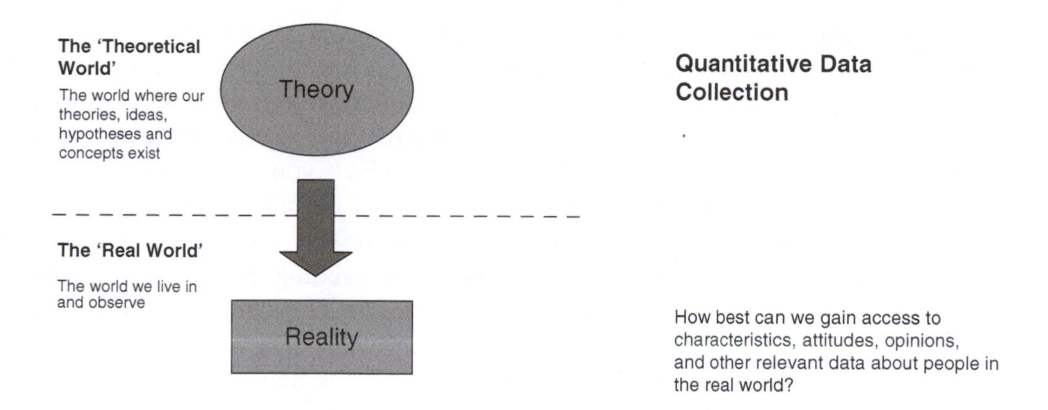

Figure 11.1 The place of quantitative data collection

needs of qualitative analysis techniques. However, the logic behind quantitative sampling is fundamentally different, which is why students often get confused between the two. The logic of quantitative sampling is also absolutely fundamental to statistical analysis, as hopefully you will grasp by the end of the next couple of chapters. So understanding this will give you a great start to learning about statistics – which I imagine you are not looking forward to if you are anything like most of my students.

First, to imagine the following scenario let's go back to the Milesians from Chapter 2 (again, you can use swirling colours and whooshing sounds if you want). If you remember, they wanted to know the answer to the question 'what is reality made of?' Let's pretend that instead of sitting around philosophising about it, they wanted to get the opinions of the Milesian population. Now Miletus was a small city in our modern terms, so it is easy to imagine that our Milesian researcher could feasibly go around the entire place and get the thoughts of every single person – a **census**. Our researcher would then be confident that all opinions were taken into account. However, what if some Milesians were busy when our hero called on them, or couldn't be bothered to reply? Does this introduce some error into the answer? Also, what if we were actually interested in the opinions of the entire population of what is now called Turkey – are the opinions of Miletus an adequate substitute? If not, surely it is impossible to collect opinions from the entirety of 'Turkey', so how would we decide who to collect data from? Perhaps we could go to the biggest city, stand in a central plaza and ask whoever comes past (and whoever will stop and talk to us)? Or maybe our intrepid researcher could get on a horse and ride around 'Turkey', looking for people to ask opinions of? Or instead, maybe we could employ say 1,000 people to each ride off and get the opinion of one person, then come back?

Now, let's make clear that none of these data collection strategies is inherently 'wrong' – they should all result in some data of interest to the researcher. The problem comes when we wish to **generalise** our results to situations and contexts *outside the data*. For example, can the findings from our Milesian census be generalised to the entire population of 'Turkey'? It is unlikely that any of the strategies above will provide what we call a **representative** (see Alternative View 11.1) sample – i.e. one which mirrors the population (within limits). Firstly, those who participated in our Milesian census (which you could also consider to be a sample of the population of 'Turkey') seem likely to be different from the rest of the population – after all, they were a distinct colony, who were interested in philosophy when no one else in the world appeared to be. Both the standing in the plaza and riding around strategies depend on who is around at the time, and who the researcher selects. This is likely to lead to bias. For example, if I were the researcher I might be more likely to select attractive women than men (well, I might as well be honest about it, I would). Also, not all members of the population have an equal chance of being selected in the sample. If all we are interested in is the findings as they apply to the individuals we have questioned (e.g. when we were only interested in Miletus), this is no problem. But when we need to generalise our results to a larger population, how can we know whether this is appropriate?

Alternative View 11.1: Representativeness

Representativeness is a thorny problem in my opinion. The common perception is that to truly generalise your findings to the population, you must have a *representative* sample, but what does this actually mean? Does it mean that if your population is 50 per cent male and 50 per cent female, so should your sample be? Even if this is so, how do you ever know the characteristics of your population in such detail? Calder *et al.*, (1982) provide an interesting perspective on this issue. Essentially they define two types of generalisation: (a) *effects* generalisation, where you are interested in applying your findings directly to some specific population or interest, and (b) *theory* generalisation where you are trying to find basic theories which apply to a variety of real-world contexts, i.e. a general understanding of the real world. According to Calder *et al.*, the latter situation does not require you to be concerned about the specific context you have sampled, nor the actual effects you observe (e.g. correlation sizes), but only in their potential to support or refute your theory (you should recognise Popper's influence here). In an effects generalisation situation however you *are* interested in whether the specific findings are applicable to the specific population – for example the size of the correlation between advertising and sales for a specific target market. It is reasonably clear that in *most* academic research, we are more interested in our theories as a whole rather than their specific effects.

Calder *et al.* consider that one can not be very confident in effects generalisations without a representative sample of the population. However, this is not the case for theory generalisations. In fact, the only criterion is that your sample is able to provide a test of your theory, not whether it is representative of some hypothetical population. Interestingly, they argue that strong tests of theory are *usually* best done with homogeneous samples (those which don't vary on characteristics which may influence your variables of interest), as you are less likely to detect false relationships. The upshot of this is that Calder *et al.* (p. 200) argue that representative samples are not necessarily required for theory generalisation purposes, as 'statistical generalisation of the findings is not the goal. It is the theory that is applied beyond the research setting ... and, any sample within the theory's domain (e.g. any relevant sample), not just a representative one, can provide such a test'. This of course does not excuse one from thinking seriously about the type of sample which is able to provide a good test of your theory – e.g. if your study is about sales managers' actions, a student sample is not necessarily able to provide a good theory test.[1]

In fact, such approaches can lead to various types of **error** in your sample. If you do not use what is called a *probability sample*, then some members of the population are more or less likely to be selected than others, which can cause statistical problems, as we shall see later. However, many (if not most) social science research projects don't use probability samples, even though the very logic of statistical analysis depends on it. I'll talk about this later on. Even if you do manage to use a probability sample, there are still other possible problems. For example, your sample may still not be representative by some unfortunate chance, which is called *sampling error*. The latter is difficult for the researcher to deal with, however, so most time is spent on *non-sampling error,* which concerns things which are caused by problems in your methods. For example, you might have selected your sample from an incomplete sampling frame (e.g. if you use the telephone directory, non-listed numbers have no chance of being selected), or those you do select may not respond (like when someone rings you for a market research survey in the middle of your favourite TV programme), or you may not be able to contact some members of your sample. You can see there are many problems which can arise in the sampling process. But even though it is virtually impossible to get a representative sample in 'real' social research, you need to understand why it is important. It is certainly not adequate just to collect data from 'whoever is around at the time'.

[1] One interesting perspective on this is that it moves quite close to parts of the qualitative sampling logic in Chapter 9, doesn't it?

Probability sampling

The probability sample is the 'gold standard' of quantitative sampling. In fact, this can be considered from two angles. Firstly, quantitative methodologists (i.e. those of us who actually study methods themselves) consider it to be the 'ideal' method of sampling, and the only one which allows you to draw statistical generalisations from your sample to the population. On the other hand, many quantitative researchers (i.e. those of us who actually *conduct* quantitative research) tend to consider it something of an unrealistic ideal in practice, one to aim at but hardly ever achieve.[2] Later, IDE 11.1 will show how the demands of research practice can make it difficult to achieve the perfect probability sample in many contexts.

IDE 11.1: Is Probability Sampling Realistic?

As already mentioned, probability sampling is the 'gold standard' for quantitative data collection. But in practical terms it is extremely difficult to conduct. Of course, if you have a well-defined population and a perfect list of it, then it is actually easy. And if any of you ever find yourselves in such a situation then I would be very surprised! Let's deal with the population issue first. In fact, many researchers don't really even seem to think about the population to which they wish to generalise at all. To test this, go and ask one of your colleagues about a research project they are doing, and then ask what population they are going to generalise to. You'll probably get some kind of vague answer like 'ummm, sales managers'[3] or 'ahhhh, Internet users'. What does this actually mean? All sales managers? Internet users between 25 and 40? Without a good idea of the population, it is impossible to take a probability sample. However, even if we do have a good idea of our population, it is almost never the case that we also have a perfect list of that population! Imagine our population is 'all chocolate consumers in the US', how do we find a list of those people? What about 'all UK small business owners'? We can possibly get a list of those registered companies, but what about those who are not registered – are they included in our theoretical reasoning? Even for as simple a population as 'the entire population of London' it is practically impossible to obtain a list. In most cases – especially in applied social research – we have to do the best we can to generate a useful sample. But we should be under no illusions that we have a 'true' probability sample. Does this mean our work is invalid? In a purely technical sense I guess it does!

---

[2] Those of us who are both methodologists *and* researchers can sometimes get confused over just what we think!

[3] I say this because I have given that very answer in the past!

However, the logic outlined in Alternative View 11.1 is not in agreement here. Furthermore, if we know the rules and theories behind sampling and why it is important, we can be in an informed position to judge the value of our non-probability sample-based conclusions. That's why it's important to read this and the next chapter of course!

The first key issue to be concerned with is deciding exactly what your **population** is. The population is who you wish to generalise your results to. Consider the Milesian example above. Do we wish to generalise to the population of Miletus, or 'Turkey', or the World? This has important implications for your sampling strategy, as well as for your findings and conclusions. Although larger or more general populations can make your theoretical conclusions seem more 'weighty', this is only the case if you are justified in generalising to that population. In other words, generalising our findings to the whole World rather than just Miletus might make us feel we did a more important piece of research, but this generalisation would be untrustworthy or nonsensical without a coherent sampling strategy. For the purposes of illustration, let's imagine we are solely interested in generalising to the population of Miletus at this point. However, before we start, you should never forget that no matter how rigorous your probability sample is, there is still the chance that it is subject to random sampling error. In fact, some form of sampling error is always evident.

The most basic type of probability sample is the **simple random sample**. This is essentially a perfectly random selection from a perfect list of all members of the population (the sampling frame). To conduct this, you must have a perfect sampling frame of all members of the population, and randomly select your sample elements from this list (e.g. numbering each element and selecting via a random number generator). Thus there is no bias, and I can't select just the attractive women, because the random number generator does the selecting for me. However, this necessitates numbering the entire population list, which can be laborious. A slight modification is **systematic sampling**, where you begin at a random point between 1 and n by using a random number generator, then selecting every nth member systematically. You define n by dividing the number in your sampling frame by the sample size you wish to take. But, if your sampling frame is ordered in some way (e.g. alphabetically), this can cause bias, so it's best to somehow rearrange it. Of course, this may be just as laborious as numbering each element!

However, in some cases I might want to make sure I select the right proportions for various groups – say citizens and servants in the Milesian example. This *might* happen in a random sample, but it's not guaranteed. In this case I can use a **stratified random sample**, which involves breaking my population into relevant strata, and then randomly or systematically sampling within these strata to achieve sample proportions which accurately mirror the population. This is useful when you think that the strata might be relevant. For example, whether you are a citizen or a servant might be associated with many personal traits which are relevant to your study of perceptions of reality. However, it's only feasible when you can get the right information about your population.

But what if my rich Milesian sponsor (well, someone has to pay for this research!) actually wants to study the perceptions of the entirety of 'Turkey'? We've already seen how this could involve a lot of travel, and if we just randomly select elements from a (hypothetical) list of the entire population, it will most likely be virtually impossible to get to all these people within a reasonable time frame (quite apart from the practicalities of travel). A **multi-stage cluster sample** can be used in this case. If we decide we want a sample of say 1,000 people (we'll deal with sample size later), we could divide 'Turkey' into an exhaustive set of 'provinces' and randomly sample five provinces, then randomly sample 200 people in each province. There are many other ways of dividing up the overall population, but the key is to maintain the randomness of the sampling method. This method can also be combined with the stratification method above.

Non-probability sampling

As seen in IDE 11.1, the probability sample is more often an ideal than a reality, and as we know, these ideals can be extremely seductive (Hollywood has been trading on that for nearly a century so far). It is far more common to see organisational and other social research projects using non-probability samples than probability ones. While there are many different strategies available, I will focus here on the most common, which is termed the **convenience sample**. Convenience samples have a bad reputation, in fact the very name carries connotations of lazy research and a lack of concern over exactly who you sample. However, I believe convenience sampling can be looked at from at least two perspectives. In fact I think it is important to recognise that convenience samples do not necessarily denote bad research, not least because they are so commonly used! It is far better for researchers to admit they are using a convenience sample and justify why their research remains useful, than to ignore completely this fact and 'pretend' they are using a probability sample.

While I am going to introduce some positive ways of thinking about convenience sampling in this section, I'll begin with the dark side of this practice. Let's go back to Miletus again (I think I am beginning to like it there). Say that I couldn't find a good list of the Milesian population, which naturally causes me some panic. So, like most days I am sitting in the 'Milesian Arms' tavern thinking about my problems,[4] and in a blinding flash of inspiration decide to just collect data from whoever enters the bar during the next week, which turns out to be a sample of 200 people. Because I am a pretty likeable and well-known figure in Miletus, almost everyone answers my survey so I've got a good solid set of data, problem

[4]OK, OK, I admit that I am taking artistic licence here, but just go with the flow. Besides, this story is starting to resemble my life quite closely now.

solved! The problem is with generalisation of course. Those people in the tavern are almost definitely different from the general Milesian population. Even worse, I can think of plenty of reasons why their opinions about reality would be different too! This is purely lazy research, which I could never advocate as a good strategy. That's not to say you can never sample from a tavern, just that in this case it is lazy and inappropriate.

But there are plenty of other sampling strategies which are technically 'convenience' but still allow us to generalise our theoretical results to other contexts – as long as we are comfortable with the logic described in Alternative View 11.1. This is of course very lucky since we are almost never able to generate perfectly representative samples. Essentially, we need to make the best efforts to generate samples which are able to test our theories. Understandably, this kind of approach is only relevant to the theory generalisation task, not the effects generalisation task – so in some contexts we are bound by the representativeness logic detailed above. But most academic projects are theory-based, particularly in the social sciences.

There are two key criteria you need to think about when you are looking to take a non-probability sample for theoretical purposes. Firstly, can your population give you any data of interest in order to test your theory? For example, if you are interested in influences on managerial choices of different punishment activity, many would consider a sample of typical first year just-out-of-school undergraduate students inappropriate. This is simply because I fail to see how they could answer any questions from a perspective which is informed by any experience of the situation you are theorising about. However, if you wish to study the experience of *receiving* managerial punishment, the same typical 18–19-year-old first-year undergraduate sample might be more appropriate, since almost all of them should have worked as subordinates before (and you could screen the others out). Of course, if the typical first-year undergraduate in your institution is more mature, then perhaps this argument may differ. The second issue is whether those you select as your sample should have any systematic differences on any variables or characteristics of interest from the population you are interested in. Or if you are not interested in a specific population (e.g. you might be interested in a general consumer population), does your sample have any specific characteristics which would influence how you interpret your results? Let's take the undergraduate example again, if I am interested in sales executives, will the opinions of undergraduates (who have probably worked primarily in menial jobs) about experiencing punishment be systematically different? Or would they differ from a more general sample of employees on characteristics of interest? For example, undergraduates tend to be younger – is this likely to bias my conclusions?

These questions are also relevant when you make an attempt to collect a more general sample – such as when you stand in the car park of a shopping mall and try to get 250 responses. You need to work out whether your sample is likely to be systematically different from the population you are interested in (in this case probably general consumers). Or when you go through the telephone directory and select companies in an attempt to interview administrative assistants about their motivation. If you follow the theoretical logic of Alternative View 11.1, you are perfectly justified in using such a sample, and also generalising your theoretical conclusions (although not the specific effect sizes). However, this is only justifiable if you can show that the characteristics of your sample are not likely to have biased your results in some way. You can do this by appealing to demographic characteristics – showing you don't have any unusual groupings compared to your theoretical population (e.g. all males, or all over 65, etc.). Also, you should provide theoretical justifications as to why your sample is unlikely to be systematically different on any characteristics of interest.

Nevertheless, this section should not be taken as a *carte blanche* to collect any old data and generalise it to any setting. Instead, my argument is that it is probably better to bring the process of non-probability sampling 'into the open', and admit that it is far more common than probability sampling in practice. It is preferable to base our non-probability samples on some kind of theoretical logic, than blindly ignore them, or even worse desperately try to conceal the fact that we are not using probability sampling. Even more so, it is by far the best strategy in practice to 'try your best' to get a sample as close to probability as possible, and to make it as 'representative' as possible as well. But as already said, if you can't get the perfect sample, this does not necessarily invalidate your research – just make sure you understand why representative probability samples are seen as desirable.

Error in samples

As alluded to earlier, there are two main sources of error in samples: **sampling error** and **non-sampling error**. Sampling error is the difference between the sample and the population (i.e. how 'non-representative' is the sample?), and is something that is present to a greater or lesser extent in all samples. Using a probability sample is no guarantee against sampling error, but a well-designed probability sample does minimise the chances of it occurring to any great extent. Of course, to assess the degree of sampling error, you do need to have a good appreciation of what your population is.

Non-sampling error, on the other hand, is error which arises either because your sampling strategy was inadequate or biased, or your data collection and/or analysis techniques were poor. *Non-response* is one possible source of error here, which is when some of the people you try to contact either refuse to respond, can't be found (e.g. their addresses are wrong) or just can't give you the information you need. You will also have non-sampling error if your sampling frame is not an accurate reflection of the population. Some other sources of error are subsumed within the technical processes of data collection and processing – e.g. poor questionnaire design, incorrect administration (perhaps caused by bias in sample selection), or mistakes in data entry.

Dealing with these problems is not straightforward, nor in some cases is even assessing whether you have a problem. For example, how can you tell whether non-response is a problem? For it to be a problem you need to expect that non-responders are systematically different in some important ways to those who do respond. Of course to do this you would need to somehow get data from non-respondents! One popular way of getting a picture of non-response is to compare those who respond very quickly to those who respond very late to a mail survey, the logic being late responders are likely to be more similar to non-responders (Armstrong and Overton, 1977). But this is only applicable to mail surveys, and has also been criticised on a number of levels, even by its originators! Another way is to try to get a sample of non-responders to answer a very short set of questions in order to compare these answers with those who have responded. But there are no easy answers here. In terms of technical and administrative errors, these need to be minimised by careful data collection and analysis techniques, which are covered in various other chapters throughout this book. This is relatively easy if you are the sole researcher, but you need to be much more careful if you are working with others – say if you are employing people to collect data for you. In this case you have to be very clear in your instructions, and also do at least some monitoring and checking. I always found that paying your research assistants well (and being nice to them) helped too!

How big should a sample be?

This is a common question from students to supervisors, and it's one I have grappled with on many occasions. Some textbooks give calculations for desired sample size with a given level of *precision*, which basically means your sample mean is *more likely* to be closer to the population mean (I'll discuss sample means and stuff a bit more in the next chapter). I will refer to some of these books at the end of this chapter. However, these formulas are arguably rather unrealistic in practice. Firstly, you tend to never focus on one simple value (e.g. the mean), but instead your data set will be trying to get many different estimates of population values at the same time. Also, such considerations ignore non-sampling error, which is often a more major issue. Quite apart from any formulae, a larger sample makes it more likely that your sample will be a better representation of the population (assuming it is a probability sample). The ultimate size of the population has no bearing on this; a sample of 500 people from a population of 1 million is theoretically the same in terms of 'accuracy' as a sample of 500 from a population of 10 million. Strange I know. Just go with it. Thus, in practical research terms there are more important considerations which you need to deal with in terms of sample size than this hypothetical idea of precision.

First is pure practicality – how big can you get your sample to be within the limits of time and resources? This needs to be balanced with the research considerations below, but there comes a point when you just have to settle for your sample and make the best of it (or you will be collecting data forever). Of course, you can only do this as long as you have a good argument as to why your sample is going to give you useful and trustworthy findings. Along the same lines you will need to factor in an expectation of non-response. For example, industrial mail surveys in the UK tend to get response rates between 15 and 30 per cent, so you will need to sample a correspondingly larger number of people to get the same amount of data. To judge this you will need to get into the literature in your field and try to get a picture of the average response to data collections efforts similar to yours. You can boost your response rates in various ways, such as by pre-notifying your sample and getting their agreement (I have found this to be the most effective), offering incentives, sending out repeated waves of questionnaires until you get a response, and the like. That said, this can be rather expensive and time consuming. But I guess it comes down to the question of 'how much do you want the data?'

Another consideration is the intended analysis techniques you want to use. Most quantitative techniques are squarely based around large-sample theories. Thus, if you want to employ such techniques you will need to understand how much data you need to collect. Although there is considerable debate over exactly how large a sample you need for various techniques, in most cases larger is better. For example, if you want to use cross-tabulation tables, you will need to have a certain number of data elements in each cell. Sample size issues are relevant to methods like analysis or variance, multiple regression, correlation, and even more so for iteration-based techniques, such as factor analysis and structural equation modelling. Of course, if those terms mean nothing to you, then you will be looking forward to Chapter 14!

In essence, sample size selection is a combination of all these factors, mixed in with a political understanding of what is expected in your field (we'll look at this issue a bit more later on). It's very unlikely to be the precise and objective business talked about in many research textbooks, simply because research itself is often not the same thing as the idealised models that those books write about. Just like most real research, sample size decisions are practical and sometimes political. But you need to understand the 'rules' even if you want to bend them a little.

Other considerations

The information so far in this chapter has been based on the survey sampling methodology, but this is not the only type of quantitative data one may collect. In particular, the logic behind collecting data for experiments contains some additional concerns. First, it can be seen that most of the concern so far has been on issues of generalisability, or what we could call *external validity*. But we should also be concerned with the *internal validity* of our research, especially in the experimental context. This basically means we need to design our sample so that it can actually provide a good test of our theory (whether or not we can justifiably generalise those results). A great example of this is in the way of data collection for a typical experiment. Imagine we want to test a theory that positive reinforcement increases performance of students. In order to test this, we might use two groups of students, one which was subjected to positive reinforcement, and one which was not (a control group). However, we need to make sure that the groups are equal with regard to any other independent variables which might have an effect on performance, such as intelligence, motivation, and the like. In order to do this we need to assign each student to one of the two groups *at random*.

This process of **randomisation** (discussed in Chapter 8) is key to the logic of experimental research, and in theory it 'spreads out' the varying characteristics of your subjects across the experimental groups so that any possible confounding influences should be approximately equal across the groups. Of course, just like probability sampling can not guarantee zero sampling error, randomisation can not guarantee that all groups are equal on their level of confounding variables, but at least we have given ourselves the best chance. Yet, as you can see, randomisation cares little for the external validity of the population, it is simply a method of avoiding confounds *within* your sample. In order to generalise your findings, you still need to have some concern for the sampling theories discussed above.

Another way of controlling for possible confounding variables in experimental (and other) designs is to simply remove that variable. For example, if you think that gender will have an impact on your dependent variable (and you don't want to test this), then you can use subjects of only one gender. While this removes the chance that gender differences will confound your results, it also means you have lost the ability to generalise to both genders. This is even the case if you work with the logic in Alternative View 11.1. Why is this? Well, you have just told me that you *expect* gender to influence the results, thus the genders are systematically different in some way – so your findings can not really be seen as relevant to both genders. You can't have it both ways! You could also employ this method in a mail survey if you are willing to put up with the lack of generalisability. Nevertheless, in an experimental design, randomisation is usually a superior method.

Another key consideration for experimental data collection is the time factor, and of course this also has relevance for any type of data collection which extends over multiple time periods. In essence, your subjects change over time – just like anyone else does. There are two ways in which these changes can be thought about. First is what is called a **history** effect. Basically, between two measurement periods (say a pre-treatment and post-treatment in an experiment, or two time periods in a longitudinal study) there is a good chance that other variables will have some impact on the subjects. If you are researching the effect of a promotional discount on sales, then if another product also introduces a promotion, this will naturally affect your dependent variable of sales. Of course, the longer between the two measurements (pre- and post-promotion), the more likely that such events will occur. Also, this kind of thing is far more likely if you are in a field setting than a laboratory setting, where many things can be controlled. That said, if your research needs long time periods between measurements, you can hardly keep your experimental subjects locked up for days on end. Well, not since ethics committees started to take an interest in our research!

The other way that time can impact on your dependent variables is through a **maturation** effect. This effect refers to how people (or any other organism) naturally change and grow over time, and there isn't much you can do about it no matter how you try to control for it. For example, people learn over time, and this learning may influence your dependent variable. Cognitive ability increases and then decreases as we age, and you need to take this into account if your research is over a long time period, and if cognitive function is likely to be a confound. Similarly, people's work motivations change naturally as their life situation changes. Many other factors are also subject to such natural growth and change. While it's unlikely that you will be doing studies which last many years, it is not entirely out of the question. Nor is it impossible that some variables may change far quicker than that – especially in some situations. For example, if you are studying students at the start and end of a year of study, their learning will (hopefully) have changed at a far higher rate than a general population. You need to take this effect into account in your research design.

Methods of collecting your data

Of course, all of that stuff about sampling is just so much theory without your own knowledge of how you are going to go about collecting your data. There are many different individual methods, but they can be broken up into two main types – those which are interactive, and those which are not. **Interactive** methods involve the subjects of your research in some way, usually by questioning them and recording their answers. For example, by sending them a questionnaire, or stopping them on the street to ask them questions. By contrast, **non-interactive** methods simply involve the researcher recording information about the subjects, normally by way of observation. For example, you may sit in a shop and count the number of people who look at a given product, then how many subsequently purchase. Of course, each method has its own advantages and disadvantages, and in fact different traditions of research tend to use different methods. For example, in my field (sales management) interactive methods are more common, but in other fields, such as consumer psychology, non-interactive methods play a big role. Figure 11.2 displays examples of the major different methods of each category of research. However, it's important to realise that the decision to use each kind of research is normally taken in light of the characteristics of data you need, and I'll try to give a picture of the considerations you'll need to take into account below.

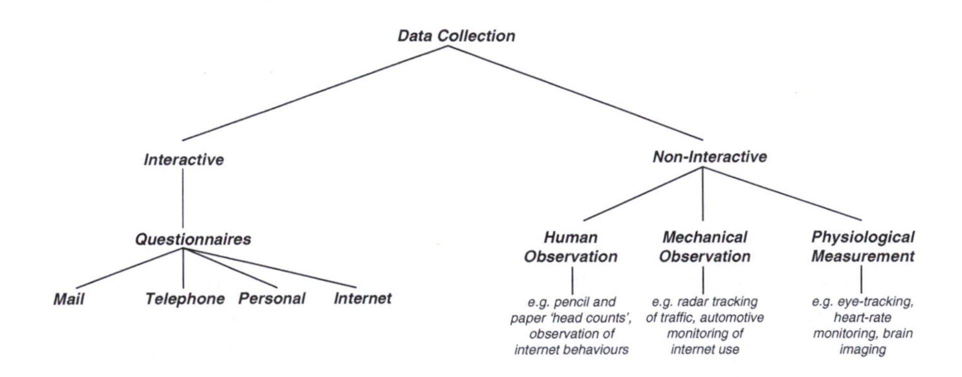

Figure 11.2 Interactive and non-interactive data collection methods

First of all, interactive methods are usually far more flexible. If you can think of a specific question about a piece of information you need, then you can normally collect that information. For example, information on internal constructs such as motivation, purchase intentions, attitudes and the like can be obtained via interactive questioning methods. That said, it's not quite as easy as that, and much of the information in Chapters 6 and 7 deals with how we should measure such concepts. Nevertheless, in terms of flexibility interactive methods are a clear winner, and you could sum them up with the rather snazzy slogan: 'If you want to know, just ask'. By contrast, non-interactive methods are pretty much bound to collect data about those things we can see. Furthermore, we are limited to those things we can see *right now*. There is no way you can get information about what happened in the past, nor what is likely to happen in the future. So basically, you are often stuck with information about observable behaviour, which is fine if you are interested in that, but not so good if you are not. However, technological advancement has led to a grey area here, which is explored in Alternative View 11.2.

Alternative View 11.2: Using Technology in Non-Interactive Research

The inexorable march of technology has allowed researchers to investigate all kinds of issues which in the past would have been incredibly difficult. One area where modern computers have allowed us to look into areas which would have been previously out of bounds concerns the observation of past behaviours. Firstly, the Internet is a goldmine of prior behaviour. In fact, almost every activity that you undertake on the Internet is recorded for posterity, and the well-informed researcher can reconstruct your behaviour with some degree of accuracy. Also, you'll find that people record their own behaviours, in settings like online communities, which the researcher can use to reconstruct the social behaviour of the community grouping. Of course, this type of thing often inhabits the grey area between qualitative and quantitative research. Another area which is proving to be of major utility to researchers is the vast amount of purchase behaviour data collected by retail scanners (like those ones at the supermarket). This data is in essence a record of your purchasing, and when combined with a loyalty card it is possible to reconstruct the patterns of a household over a given time period. Ignoring the somewhat worrying Big Brother connotations here, it is easy to see how fantastic such a set of data could be to a research. In the terms of this chapter, it is essentially a set of non-interactive data that can in fact record past behaviour (although when the behaviour was recorded, it was in the present I suppose). This type of data straddles the boundary between primary and secondary, sharing some characteristics of each. Of course, it is still unable to go beyond the surface-level issues, but for many research projects this is not important. One possible disadvantage is that it may be very difficult for academic researchers to get hold of, being as it is usually proprietary data collected by major research corporations, or retailers.

Interestingly, while interactive methods are by far the most flexible, an argument can be made for non-interactive methods being more objective – when used appropriately. Firstly, interactive methods rely on the willingness of the subject to give you the 'true' information after you have asked for it. In some situations, subjects may not be willing to do this, especially if you are asking them embarrassing questions. Furthermore, I've often found that subjects are desperate to give what they see as the 'right answer', no matter how many times you insist that you are only interested in their opinions. Thus, sometimes, subjects give what they think is the right answer, even if it bears little relation to their own knowledge or opinions. Furthermore, interactive questioning methods rely on the recall of participants if they are to measure past behaviour or opinions, and of course the longer into the past you wish to look, the harder it is for people to remember. The researcher or research instrument may play a role too (remember the idea of reflexivity in qualitative research, it's also relevant here). More specifically, in a personal interview situation a subject's responses may be influenced by the interviewer. This may also be relevant when you use a mail or other self-administered questionnaire; your question design may somehow influence the response (I'll touch on this in the next section). Non-interactive methods suffer less from these problems, they record objective behaviour as it actually happens, and do not depend on subjects to recall it. Furthermore, it may even be the case that subjects don't even realise they are being studied, which of course eliminates the chances of them modifying their behaviour to suit the researcher. Finally, the fact that non-interactive data collection is unable to measure non-observable things means that the data they *can* collect is more objective by definition.

A brief introduction to instrument design

Once you have decided how you are going to collect your data, you will then need to design the data collection instrument. This can be a difficult and frustrating exercise, and it's necessary for you to realise that careful instrument design is a very important part of a good research project. Without a good instrument, your data will never be of high quality, and of course this means that your research will also be less than adequate. Within the context of this book, it is completely impossible to give you all the information you will need to design top-quality data collection instruments, and therefore I am going to restrict this section to some general information about the design of self-administered surveys. The major reason for this is that design is probably *most* important for questionnaire surveys where the subject fills in the questionnaire themselves, as the researcher doesn't have a chance to correct any errors or help the respondent at all. However, at the end of this chapter I will discuss a few books which go into far more detail about design. You really should check these out if you want to be confident in your design.

The first issue to contend with is length. In fact, the length of the questionnaire is probably the single most important factor in influencing how many people are going to respond to your questionnaire. You need to balance out the need to cover everything you require for your research project with your desire to minimise length, and this issue is also bound up with issues of design and structure too. There is no minimum or maximum length of questionnaire, in all honesty, and the type of research you are conducting is also a major factor here. For example, in commercial surveys which are randomly mailed to consumers, length must be very short, but if a commercial research firm is paying the respondents, length can be longer. In an academic context, people will generally try to help you out if you write a good cover letter (i.e. begging them!), so you can get away with a bit of extra length, especially if you stress that you are a student and *really, really* need the data. If you get agreement from your respondents to fill in the questionnaire before sending it to them you can also make it longer – but remember to be (reasonably) honest about how long your questionnaire will take to fill in when you get agreement. It is counterproductive to tell people to expect a 10 minute survey when it is more like a 30 minute one. In fact, the more time you spend with people gaining their agreement, and the more relevant to them the topic is, the longer you can make the survey. I have run surveys of over 30 pages which gained quite good response rates, but the topic was very relevant to a select group of executives, and we spent a very long time with them gaining their agreement and convincing them of the benefits of participation. Most of my academic industrial mail surveys have hovered around 8–10 pages of questions, which is rather long compared to the recommendations of many research textbooks. However, respondents were pre-notified, and I spent a long time drafting good cover letters which stressed how much I needed this data. You should also balance the need to get lots of information which you don't *really* require here. More specifically, you should have some back-up measures and concepts in a survey, just in case your main model doesn't work out. You may also wish to collect data for multiple projects in one instrument. All of these considerations need to be balanced out – not an easy process.

Tied in with this is the issue of design. A better-designed survey can be longer in page terms. In fact, one thing you should *always* avoid is to 'artificially' decrease page length by cramming questions into tiny spaces; your questionnaire needs to be clear and easy to read. It's far better to have an extra page or two than to have a confusing and hard to read questionnaire. Modern word-processors allow you to do really neat things regarding the design of your questionnaire, and you should take advantage of these capabilities as much as possible. Unfortunately, I have seen far too many astoundingly poorly designed questionnaires, which do more to put off respondents than encourage them to complete the questionnaire. In particular, you *must* spend time proof-reading your questionnaire to avoid errors creeping in, like duplicate questions, spelling mistakes, poor wording and the like. Give it to someone else as well, although it can get a bit soul-destroying when it comes back with corrections all over it. However, in design terms try to balance out the need for good design with cost and practicality implications. For example, it might be great in design terms to print your questionnaire in all the colours of the rainbow, but this will cost a huge amount compared to simple black and white. Similarly, it's usually better to have your questionnaires professionally printed in booklet form so they open out flat; but if you can only afford photocopying and a staple in the top corner, that's what you will have to go with.

Another key issue bound up with all of this is the structure of the questionnaire itself. There are various theories on where you should put the different types of questions, which could be considered a bit contradictory (surprise surprise!) So what I will try to do here is give you an overview of the things you need to balance out. First and foremost, try to give your questionnaire a logical structure of some kind. For example, you might want to ask general questions first and then more specific questions later on. This allows the respondent to get their brain 'primed' for your more complex questions. Some theories also suggest you should keep questions on the same topic together, which allows the respondent to focus their mind on one topic at a time. Furthermore, there's nothing worse than filling out questions on one topic, then getting a few pages down the line and the same topic coming up again. I tend to follow this line of reasoning myself, but on the other hand it could be said that respondents can get lazy if they are answering the same topic consistently, leading to them not reading the questions thoroughly, making assumptions, and ultimately leading to poor data. Thus, the other view is to mix up your questions to keep the respondent thinking. Theory also suggests that you should keep more personal questions until the end of the questionnaire. Your respondents are probably more likely to answer personal questions if they've already invested their time to get that far. However, another unavoidable fact of questionnaire surveys is that some people do stop part-way through. If your important questions are at the end of the questionnaire, then this means that more people will miss these out than if they are at the beginning. You therefore need to balance this out with the other considerations. Personally, I tend to put key measures reasonably close to the front, after basic questions which just focus the mind of my respondent. At the end I tend to have a page of demographic questions. For most of my work these questions are not essential, so if a respondent gets bored and ignores them, I can still use the response in some ways as my most important data is usually still there.

Tips on writing good questions

There is a vast body of literature available on the specifics of scaling techniques, different forms of questioning, the appropriate type of response form for each type of information you require, and many other issues. I'm not even going to try to cover all the ground in this area. Instead I am going to discuss a few good and bad ideas when you are designing the actual questions you intend to use to collect your data.

The first thing you need to consider is whether to use open ended or closed questions. An open question such as: 'What is your opinion on advertising legislation in this country?' gives the respondent the chance to answer in their own words, but also has the disadvantage of a lack of comparability and consistency across respondents. Such questions can be useful to start things off, or when you are not sure of your topic right now, but more usually you will use closed questions, where you give the respondent a set of responses, and the respondent will choose the response which most closely matches their position. There are many different types of closed questions (also known as fixed alternative questions), and some of the various types are shown in Figure 11.3.

There are a number of considerations when you design the choices on closed questions. Firstly you must make sure the choices are mutually exclusive and exhaustive. That is, each respondent must be able to choose one and only one alternative, and for every respondent there must be an appropriate alternative. In practice, this means that there must be no overlap between your choices, and you should almost always include an 'other (please specify)' option in your questions when necessary. Another decision you must make regards how many alternatives you will give the respondent. Think about the Likert-type scale example

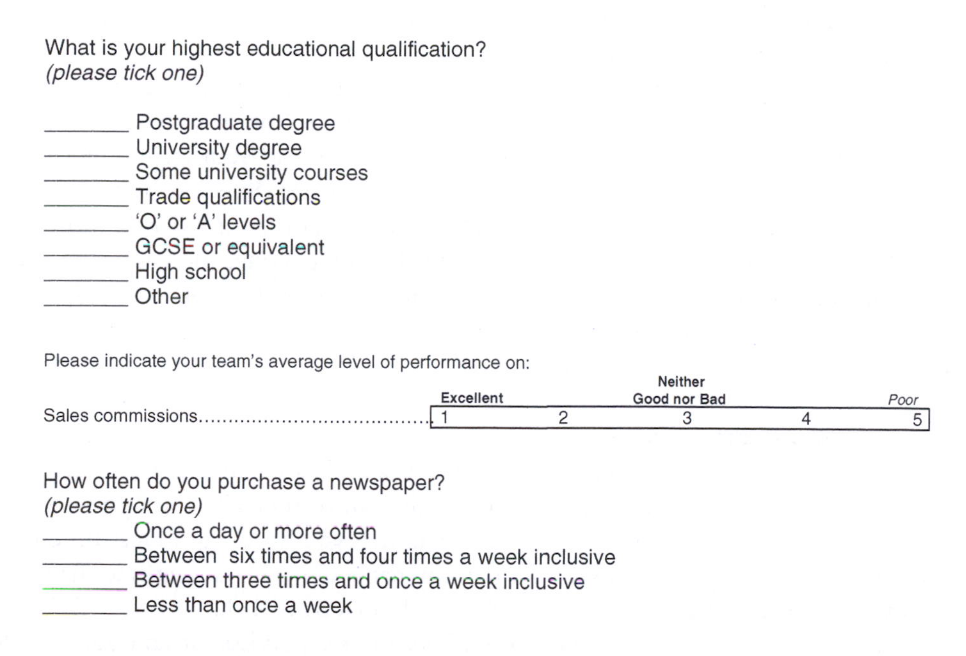

Figure 11.3 Different question response types

in Figure 11.3. Should you use a 5-point scale, or a 9-point scale? A 9-point scale is certainly more fine-grained, but you need to think whether respondents can really distinguish between information at that level. For some concepts they may be, but for other they may not be. Furthermore, the more alternatives there are, the more difficult it is for respondents to answer the question. It has always been my feeling that one should attempt to minimise the effort required by the respondent. Therefore I try to use the least amount of choices necessary to get my information. However, sometimes you need to give a wider range of possible responses. This is particularly relevant if you think your responses will be clustered at the extreme ends of the scales. In this case you need to spread the responses out by giving them more options. For example, if a typical 5-point Likert-type scale has 'strongly disagree' as its extreme end, a 7-point may have 'very strongly disagree', while a 9-point might have 'very, very strongly disagree'. While this may not be an ideal method, it does tend to have some effect on spreading extreme responses out.

The next issue you have to consider is the wording of your questions. This is a key influence on your results, as poor wording is highly likely to result in poor data. First and foremost you need to remember that you are designing your questionnaire for your sample, not to impress your colleagues with big words, or anything like that. You must always remember to write your questions as simply as possible within the bounds of your topic. In fact, if you find that it is impossible to write your questions in such a form as can be understood by the least well-educated of your likely sample, you may wish to reconsider the use of a questionnaire. You also need to avoid accidental ambiguity in the wording – your questions have to be completely clear. Similarly, make sure each question refers to one and only one issue. For example, double-barrelled questions such as 'are you impressed by my wit and intelligence?' are never advisable, as it is impossible to interpret what an answer of 'yes' (or more likely 'no') would mean. You must also never lead your respondents down a particular track with your question wording, keep the wording objective and factual. You should, in addition, avoid making the respondent make difficult estimates or assumptions as well. While an entire chapter could be devoted to this topic alone, the basic rule is to try to make your questions as clear as possible, and reduce the workload on your respondents. This allows them to give you the information you need as easily as possible, which in turn should increase the accuracy of that information.

Testing your draft questionnaire

Once you have designed a questionnaire or other data collection instrument, what should you do next? No, the answer is not 'rush out and collect all your data'! In fact you need to go through a series of tests first before you can be certain that you have a good instrument. This is important, because one of the worst things that can happen to a researcher is to throw away a bunch of data because the questionnaire contained key errors. I think the ideal sequence consists of three main stages. Firstly, you should get your supervisor or colleagues to look at the questionnaire. This usually results in a whole bunch of demoralising questions that make you think your work isn't as good as you thought it was. You need to take all these comments seriously, and if they are helpful take them into account. But don't forget that no one except you knows *exactly* what you are trying to do, so don't be afraid to counter-argue sometimes if you don't think a change is necessary. After this, I think it is useful to take your questionnaire out into the field and test it on the people who are going to answer it for real. The best way of doing this is to run some personal interviews with potential respondents, which have been called 'protocol' interviews (e.g. Diamantopoulos *et al.*, 1994). Sit down with them, and ask them to fill in your questionnaire while you watch. As they go through, ask them to comment on things that they found difficult, and record these comments so you can modify your questionnaire accordingly. This stage often shows up wording and other question design problems. Finally, you should run a **pilot study**, which is a mini version of your full study. Take a small sample of your population, and administer everything exactly as you would in your full study, to see if everything works out well. Please, don't avoid this step, as you can get into heaps of trouble if you do. It's never nice if you send out 1,000 questionnaires in your full study only to find out that some problem with your method results in no one sending them back! Much better to find this out in a small sample of 50 or 100. Furthermore, if your pilot works out Ok, then you can incorporate that data into your main study.

Cross-national instrument design

Cross-national research is becoming increasingly popular for many reasons, not least of which is the realisation that traditional US or Western theories and research may not be able to explain what happens in other societies. However, conducting cross-national research is fraught with difficulties for many reasons. In particular, the design of your questionnaire can be extremely difficult when you try to translate it to another country. In fact, translation itself is not as simple as it sounds. It's usually not enough just to get your questionnaire translated into another language, you should then get it 'back-translated' by someone else into its original language. This is a very basic check on the adequacy of your translation. However, any researcher experienced in translated questionnaires will know that even with the best translation in the world some concepts are unable to be translated accurately. I came across this when I had some of my salesperson questionnaires translated to be used in Thailand, discovering that some of my key concepts simply did not exist in that culture in the same way. In such situations you need to be very careful in making decisions about how to compare the data from different countries. Another line of thinking suggests that you should not even try to transfer concepts and measures from one culture to another, but instead you should go through the development process completely separately for each culture you wish to study. This is fine if you are studying countries in isolation, but it makes things virtually impossible when you want to study and compare multiple cultures, as you no longer have consistent measures. The two contrasting approaches can be considered to be polar extremes of a continuum. The *emic* approach argues that cultures are unique and are thus best studied in isolation, while the *etic* approach counters that there are universal concepts in existence, and thus one should focus on developing measures which can be used in multiple cultural contexts (see Craig and Douglas, 2005). The best position here is probably somewhere in the middle. Certainly, it seems plausible that there are at least some common attitudinal or behavioural factors across cultures. However, researchers should be careful not to assume that *every* concept they are interested in is the same across cultures, nor that one can unthinkingly apply measures developed in one culture to another. Overall, cross-national research can be a minefield, so you should think carefully about conducting it if you are an inexperienced researcher. Those who do wish to conduct such research should begin by consulting some of the specialist books on the subject.

Summary

This chapter was designed for you to use as an introduction into the field of qualitative data collection. Each topic in this chapter is worthy of its own book, and indeed each topic has many books available on it which contain far more detail and should be consulted in addition if you are serious about conducting quantitative research. This chapter presents key issues and decisions which need to be made in the design of a quantitative data collection project, as well as some viewpoints which have sometimes been ignored by other sources. It is also an attempt to put quantitative data collection in the context of a wider appreciation of research in general, rather than just as a technical process. Too often are beginning researchers indoctrinated into the technical process of quantitative research without understanding why they are conducting such work. Hopefully this chapter, when read in conjunction with the rest of this book – will go some way towards helping researchers think about quantitative work in a wider context, rather than just as a process to follow.

Key points to take from this chapter:

- Quantitative sampling is of key importance to statistics.
- It is particularly important to the generalisability of our findings.
- The representativeness of samples is not a straightforward issue, and there are various ways of approaching it.
- Probability sampling is the 'gold standard' of sampling, but in practical terms it is hard to employ perfectly.
- Non-probability samples are not inherently poor, but you do need to think carefully about how you use them.
- Sample size is also a complex issue, and you need to take many factors into account when designing your sample.
- Your data needs determine whether you use interactive or non-interactive data collection methods.
- Questionnaire design is a complex business, with many conflicting issues which need to be balanced out.

Further reading

- *Mail and Internet Surveys: The Tailored Design Method* by Don A. Dillman. This is generally thought of as 'the' book on survey design. The first edition was actually called *The Total Design Method*, but Dillman has extended this approach and renamed it to reflect the changes. All told it is a classic of its kind.
- *Marketing Research: Methodological Foundations* by Gilbert A. Churchill and Dawn Iacobucci. Already mentioned in Chapter 8, this book is also a great introduction to general data collection issues. It contains excellent information on sampling and general research methods and is a fine example of a 'textbook' approach to research methods.
- *International Marketing Research* by C. Samuel Craig and Susan P. Douglas. This is a great starting point for exploring the techniques and concepts relating to doing international and cross-cultural research.

EXERCISES

1. What is the difference between a sample and a population?
   - Why don't we always use the population?
2. What does 'representative' mean in the context of sampling?
   - Do we always have to have a representative sample? Why or why not?
3. Design a method of taking a simple random sample of household shoppers in the UK.
   - What factors would effect your methodology?
   - How could you stratify the population and why might you want to do this?
   - How would a cluster sample help your research method?
4. What are the key factors you need to take into account when you design non-probability samples?
5. What is the difference between sampling and non-sampling error?
6. What factors can influence the internal validity of a quantitative study?
7. Describe a topic ideally suited to interactive data collection methods, and explain why.
8. Describe a topic ideally suited to non-interactive data collection methods and explain why.
9. Imagine I wanted to design a questionnaire with the following sets of questions:
   - Demographic information
   - Job satisfaction
   - Work motivation
   - Opinions on how much of a 'bully' their boss was
   - Work stress

   What would be the 'best' way of arranging these questions, and why?
10. I think now you should go out with your friends (I hope you still have some!) and have a nice meal. Personally, I am always partial to a curry.

Chapter 12
How and why statistics work

SUPERVISOR'S VIEW: DR CARL SENIOR

The joy of stats: I was initially sceptical when asked to contribute this commentary. After all what could I write that my esteemed colleagues have not already supplied? I am a cognitive neuroscientist not a specialised statistician! However, after a long introspection, which was fuelled by several glasses of wine, I came to the conclusion that I did have something to offer!

Many students are scared of statistics and statisticians. This dark world of alpha values, probabilities and ANOVAs seems to terrify people. It's my hunch that statisticians, being a fairly maudlin bunch of people, tend to like the fact that students are scared of 'their trade' and facilitate this fear with impenetrable advice. There can be nothing more damaging to your self-esteem (and the development of your research) when you go to see an advisor with a question and return with pages and pages of formulae and distribution graphs, or worse still a sticky note with scribbled page references to an aged text on multivariate statistics. However, unlike the bogeyman, the fear of statistics, and all related software, is a real thing. Merely reading the comments on the various websites that get returned from a web search with the terms 'I hate SPSS'[1], will quickly convince you that this fear has reached a pathological stage for many. However, the key to unlocking this great mystery and progressing through the darkened quagmire of statistical knowledge is simple and straightforward – don't be scared!

Here the words of Franklin D. Roosevelt, the 32nd President of the United States of America, ring true: 'You have nothing to fear but fear itself'. Statistical science is merely a way of understanding the behaviour of things in the world around us. If A does B what is the probability of C occurring? These tools should not be

[1]SPSS is one of the most popular statistical packages, and will be referred to a lot in the coming chapters. However, reading one of the several hundred comments from the 1,547 members on the '*Let's burn SPSS and dance on its still warm ashes*' group on the facebook.com social networking site it seems that it may not be that easy to understand; '*... i was in the process of doing an avova (whatever that is) and got stuck... screw spss, damn it to hell!!!!!!! bastard spss, i hate hate hate it!!!*'

feared but embraced with fervent joy! The very basic tools allow you to examine a given data set and discover new things about the behaviour of your experimental variables – yes actually discover new things! Once you have conquered your fear of statistics this process of discovery can be quite intoxicating and you may find yourself being swallowed up by the number crunching. So the final caveat here would be to protect yourself with a clearly defined *a priori* hypothesis. With the hypothesis in hand you are free to explore and discover the joys of statistics.

VIEW FROM THE TRENCHES: JEREMY DAWSON

As research students, we tend to be interested not only in the answers to questions, but also in how and why they are the answers. So it seems natural that some of us should want to know why doing a few simple calculations on a sample of data should tell us some 'truths' about the world at large. Well, unfortunately it's not always as simple as that. It's important to realise that statistical tests are based on certain mathematical and probabilistic principles that – well, just are. Take, for example, the fact that so many natural phenomena follow a normal distribution. Why do they? It's as pointless to ask that as it is to ask why the Earth is round, or why oxygen is a gas. It's just the way things occur naturally. Once you accept certain principles like this, it is possible to deduce mathematically why statistics work, but it's not always easy. I come from a mathematical background, and I often find the working difficult to follow. Accepting these facts as a matter of blind faith, though, is hard to accept and often contrary to our inquisitive and rational nature.

I sometimes find it useful, when I'm having difficulty accepting something, to try to see it for myself. Not convinced that a sample of a few dozen will tell you much about a larger population? Try doing some random sampling from some data source, and have a look at the statistics of the sample – you'll be amazed at how accurate they are most of the time. Having difficulty understanding why Type I errors occur? Set up some bogus hypotheses (ones you know to be false), and you'll notice that about 1 in 20 of them come out as statistically significant anyway. By doing this, you'll not only satisfy yourself that these things ARE correct, but you'll notice that you're using evidence you've gathered to convince yourself about some general principles – the very essence of why statistics work.

If you have been reading this book cover-to-cover then you should congratulate yourself for getting this far, so take a moment to do just that. Also, you might want to give yourself a little rest before you start on this next section of three chapters. That's because the next three chapters deal with quantitative data analysis – the dreaded 'numbers' which almost all novice researchers have some trepidation about. If you are feeling a bit scared of the numbers, then perhaps the following story will help you feel more at ease (by now you should be getting good at the swirly colours and whooshing sounds, so go ahead and use them again).

In 1997 a confused 22-year-old entered a programme at Victoria University of Wellington in New Zealand called the Bachelor of Commerce and Administration with Honours in Marketing. This was a one-year postgraduate degree about advanced marketing and research theory. One of the first courses was called MARK 405 Advanced Marketing Research, which basically meant 'statistics and quantitative research'. In the very first lecture our hero was asked a question regarding Type I and Type II error (these concepts will appear later in this chapter), and had absolutely no idea what it meant. At the next lecture he was asked the same question, and he remained unable to understand the concept. Our unfortunate student thus became something of a laughing stock, and was asked a statistics question at the beginning of every lecture – being singularly unable to answer any of them. Ever.

You'll probably not be surprised to know that the 22-year-old was me. I got an A+ in that course, and an A+ in the following dissertation. In 1998 I entered the Ph.D. programme, and nine years later I am a Senior Lecturer, teaching research methods (including statistics) to undergraduate, Masters, and Ph.D. students, and have run advanced workshops on Structural Equation Models for organisations like the UK Academy of Marketing. I do still have a bit of a mental block with Type I and Type II error, as many of my students will confirm! Why do I say this? Well, I cannot stress too highly just how diabolically *awful* I was at statistics when I began in 1997. People don't believe me now, but it's true! The moral of the story is that I believe that absolutely *anyone* can learn how to do good quantitative analysis. I really do. Yes, even you. I am living proof of it, and if I can do it, so can you.

However, one thing it takes is – no, not talent – but *hard work*. Some people have a gift for this kind of thing, I'm not one of them. I learnt how to run structural equation models through necessity; I just had to know how to do it in order to do my Ph.D. And then in my first lecturing job I had to teach Market Research (the new guy always has to!) so I needed to learn a whole lot of foundational things which I had no idea of before: probability theory, data distributions, the central limit theorem, sampling theory (we covered the latter in the previous chapter), all the fundamentals behind the complex statistics I was actually using. Suddenly, all of those more advanced things I had been doing began to fall into place. I wished I had learned this kind of thing before starting my Honours degree![2] That's the kind of stuff that this chapter is concerned with. I really wanted to make the basic foundations of

---

[2]And to be fair to my undergraduate lecturers, I probably *would* have learnt them if I hadn't spent the majority of my undergraduate degree somewhere *other* than my lectures.

statistical analysis accessible to novice researchers like the one I was in 1997, and take the fear away. Hopefully, when *you* get asked about Type I and II error, you will be able to answer.

At the end of this chapter I really hope you have come to terms with these key ideas:

- Statistics requires effort to master, but anyone can do it.
- Statistical inference is how we determine whether or not our sample results support our theoretical hypotheses.
- Probability theory is conceptually and technically the base of statistical theory.
- The normal distribution also holds a central place in statistical theory.
- Statistical and substantive significance are the two key issues to think about when interpreting your results.

Why is it Important to Know This Stuff?

Like I said just before, there are three chapters about quantitative analysis coming up. Yet, I think this chapter is the most important of them all, even though it doesn't contain much mention of 'sexy' stuff like multiple regression, structural equations, conjoint analysis, ANOVA, correlations, or whatever method is currently 'hot' in your discipline. Those are the kinds of things you'll probably be needing to do for your dissertation, so why would you want to waste valuable time reading about: sampling (didn't we already do that anyway?), distributions, and – horror of horrors – probability theory? Well, I think this chapter is the key to understanding the fancy numbers stuff that you will ultimately want to do. And I think you guys should have already worked out that in my opinion it's actually the *understanding* of research methods which allows you to do good research, not knowing how to plug numbers into some complex formula. There are so many researchers who are brilliant at analysing quantitative information with amazingly complex mathematical tools, but who have merely a rudimentary understanding of exactly what is going on in relation to their theory and its link with the real-world data. I am reminded of the old saying about someone who knows the worth of everything but the value of nothing when I speak to those kinds of people. Furthermore, the knowledge in this chapter is transferable to any of the specific analysis methods you might be thinking of using later on, and will really help you understand how they work – consequently improving your work greatly.

In fact, that's what this chapter is really about, the link between the empirical data you collect from the 'real world' and the theory you are trying to test (see Figure 12.1). Without understanding this you run the risk of making some major mistakes in the interpretation of your numbers. I personally remember a time when, as a brash young research student, I sat in a presentation where a senior researcher made such a rudimentary error in interpreting their statistics that I wasn't sure I could believe what I was seeing. While their results technically supported their hypothesis, the researcher had failed to realise that this support was of precisely no practical value! This was all caused by a failure to understand exactly how statistics work (of course this was *after* my 1997 debacle!)

So, if you intend to do quantitative work, this should be the first chapter about analysis that you read, it's really that important. But what if you are not going to do quantitative research? Well there are a few reasons to read this chapter as well. First, I reckon you need to understand the logic behind quantitative analysis so you can decide against it in the full knowledge of it. You never know, it might make a lot of sense to you and you could find yourself having an epiphany and becoming a quantitative researcher! Secondly, if you get into an argument with one of those quantitatively oriented people, you could have a lot of fun by knowing all this stuff!

Plus, I worked really hard on this, so you could at least pay me the respect of reading it!

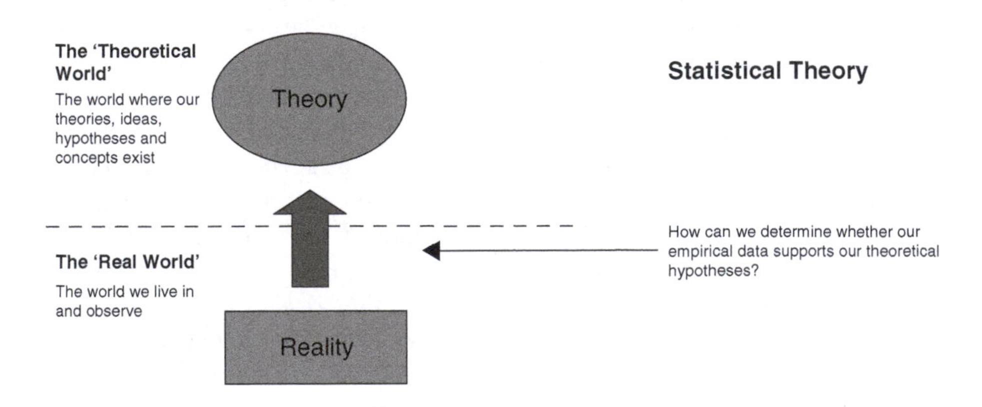

Figure 12.1 The place of statistical theory

What are statistics and why do we use them?

The question of exactly what statistics are is an interesting one, since I have detected a little bit of a 'common-usage' problem in the way many researchers and the general public discuss them, and I think clarifying this is a good place to start any discussion of quantitative analysis. First of all, let's get any misconceptions out of the way though, statistical analysis is *not* inherently difficult. I am not sure why so many students have some kind of irrational fear of numbers, but it is undeniable that for many of us, just the thought of those rows and columns full of numbers is at least slightly unnerving. However, when you think about it, it's not that frightening at all. Remember how in the qualitative chapters I made a big point of how such analysis was very unstructured, lacking concrete frameworks? Well, quantitative analysis is almost diametrically opposed to this. For most situations, there is a limited set of analysis tools you can use, and you will almost always have decided which strategy you are taking before you even go and get your data. Even better, you can then go to a textbook or research article and find *instructions* on exactly how to do it! In fact, I look at statistical analysis as very similar to cooking using a recipe book. You decide what you want to cook, look at the recipe, get the ingredients, and then if you can follow instructions you can cook the dish. Of course, there is always room for some creativity, but you need to have the base of the recipe first. Follow this and you really can't go wrong. Map-reading is a similar example. All the instructions are there right in front of you, you just need to learn the skills to read that map, and once you do, you can read virtually any map! What I mean is not that quantitative analysis is easy. Instead, it requires the learning of a set of well-defined skills to enable you to apply them to different analysis situations, just like reading a cookbook, or any other set of instructions. But of course, we think not in numbers but in words, so when we are faced with a huge spreadsheet of data, or a massive 50 pages of numerical output from a computer analysis, it all gets a bit overwhelming.

First, let's think about why we need statistics. Imagine that we collect quantitative data in some way, say using a mail-out survey. So we have maybe 500 responses, all typed in (carefully) to a spreadsheet in our analysis package of choice (SPSS, SAS, STATA, S-PLUS, Statistica, or whatever). Well, we usually have two main tasks from here. Task one is to discover what is going on in our data set in terms of our research questions. So if we had a hypothesis that one variable was positively related to another, we need to see if our data shows this. There are two ways of doing this. One way is to 'eyeball' the data in some way. Maybe we simply stare at the two variables on the spreadsheet to see if higher values of one are associated with higher values of another? With 10 responses we might be able to do this, but with 500? You'd surely have to be some kind of freak of nature! So maybe we plot one variable against another in a scatterplot. This is OK, you can see all 500 values in one place and get an idea of a relationship, but really in most cases it's your judgement against mine as to whether there is a relationship there. Check out Figure 12.2 – how strong a relationship would you say is in that scatterplot just by eyeballing it? Then go ask a friend. Do you get the same answer? Sure, if your answers were 'pretty strong' or the like, but try expressing that as a number between 0 and 100. Still get exactly the same answer?

So what we need is some kind of summary number, which tells us in simple terms the characteristics of our data set we are interested in. For example, we might want to measure the *average age* of our population. This value, when it is measured using the entire population,

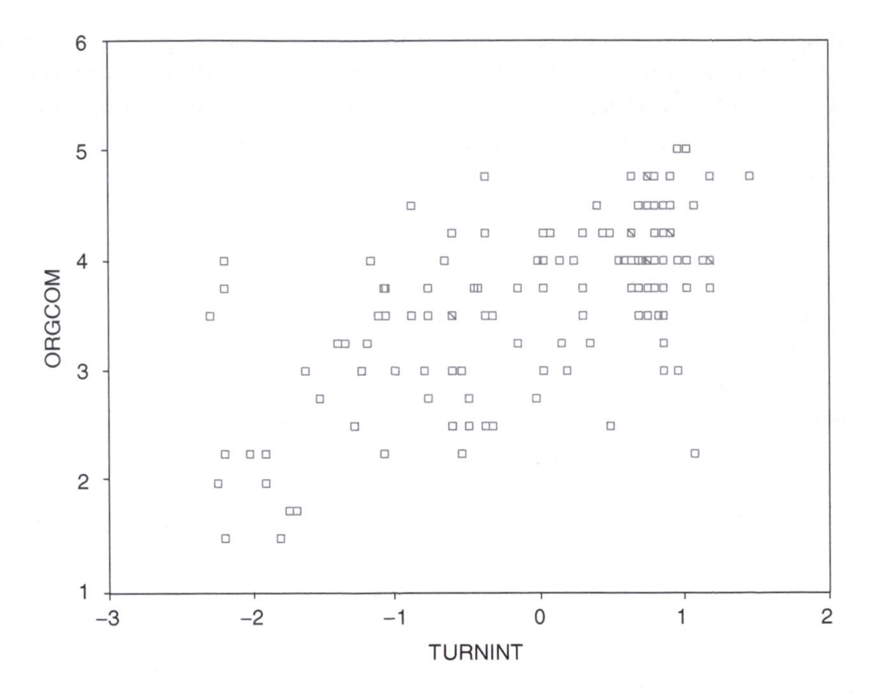

Figure 12.2 A scatter plot

is called a **parameter**. However, when we measure the characteristic using only a sample, it is called a **statistic**. Statistics summarise our data set in simple and consistent terms. This means we don't have to make inconsistent estimates from our raw data. Now, let's think more carefully about the second task we have in data analysis. Remember back to the previous chapter when I introduced the idea of a census versus a sample? Well, if we have collected a census of our entire population our job is done when we get the parameter values. However, if we only have a sample of our population, we need to *estimate the likelihood of the statistic we observed in the sample, being the same as the 'real' parameter in the population.* This is called **statistical inference** – and it's what most people think of when the word statistics comes up. It basically means we are trying to *infer* what is happening in the entire population from our sample (can you now see why sampling theory and generalisability were so important in the last chapter?) There are many different ways of thinking about this question which result in terms you might have already come across, things like **confidence intervals**, **statistical significance**, **significance testing**, and the like. In fact, I think it is this second task which is the most difficult for students to come to terms with. And it's the basic subject of this chapter. I'll work through it from its base in sampling distributions and probability theory right up to the concept of significance testing, and some implications for the conclusions you might draw from your tests.

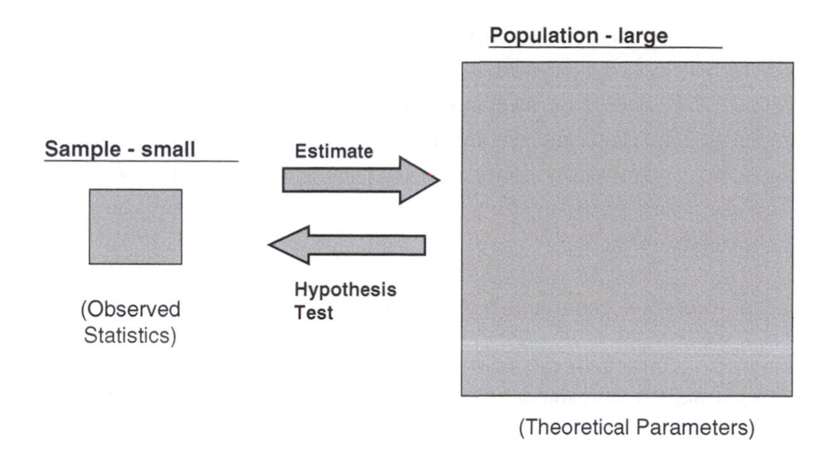

Figure 12.3 Samples and populations

First, let's make completely clear what we are talking about when we mention statistical inference. Figure 12.3 represents our usual situation in social research. We have some kind of (usually rather nebulous) population which we want our results to be of relevance to. However, we can't study the entire population, for various reasons, so we must take a sample of it. Now, remember that most statistical theory rests on the fact that we took a probability sample from the population, but we discussed *those* thorny issues in the previous chapter (we will come back to them later though). For the purposes of this discussion, let's assume we've taken a probability sample. Our first task is to **describe** what's happening in the sample. This can be considered in two ways. First we better check how representative our sample is of the population, or check the characteristics of the sample to make sure that they won't unduly influence our analysis or conclusions in some way. So, for example, if our population is equally split between males and females, what is the split of our sample? This kind of basic descriptive analysis is very important to later analysis, so you should spend some considerable time on it (I'll cover it in the next chapter). The next type of description is to work out the *statistics* which pertain to our hypotheses. For example, we might be running correlational analysis, so we need to work out the *correlation coefficients*, or maybe we are doing analysis of variance, in which case we need to work out the *F-Ratio* and the like. This sort of thing is often scary to the beginner, but to be fair the computer does it in the main. I'll be discussing this kind of thing in more detail in Chapters 13 and 14.

So at this point we have our data set described in such a way that we know its characteristics, and we also know how consistent our sample is with our hypotheses. If we had a census, we would be done. But of course we don't in general. What we *really* want to know is the likelihood that those statistical results we have **observed** in our sample are actually occurring in the population. This is the crux of statistical inference, and is the key to whether or not your theoretical hypotheses are *supported* or *rejected*. For most computer analysis packages, this stuff is done at the same time as computing the statistics. The process is conceptually represented in Figure 12.3, basically we are trying to transfer the empirical results of our data back to the theoretical population (which is what we are really interested in). As statistical inference will be the main point of this chapter, there are a few key ideas to keep in mind here, which should serve you well:

- The statistical values we observe in our sample (assuming we ran the formulae correctly) are *unarguable* – we can see them right in front of us.
- The corresponding parameter values in the population are *theoretical*, we can never completely observe the population data without a census (which is almost always impossible).

Keep these two concepts in mind, because I will be coming back to them when I discuss statistical inference in more detail later. Next, I am going to take you through a couple of highly important concepts which will prove crucial later on.

The normal distribution

The most basic type of statistical analysis is to measure the frequency of occurrence of each value of a given variable among the cases you measure. So say you have a set of 250 questionnaires from individuals, you could count the frequency of each age value (call it a **data point**) for the data set. Collecting these in a table or a chart (like Figure 12.4) would create a **frequency distribution**. The numeric values are on the x axis, and the amount of times each value occurs is on the y axis. This is what is known as an *empirical* frequency distribution, as it is created from observed data.

On the other hand, *theoretical* frequency distributions are based on an *infinite* number of observations. You can imagine what would happen here quite easily. Try making the way we measured age more and more fine-grained (e.g. instead of years, try months, then days, then minutes, and so on). At the same time imagine massively increasing the amount of observations (data points) so that each value still has a lot of observations. Keep going and going and you can imagine that the bars in Figure 12.4 would eventually blend together into a theoretical **continuous** distribution like that in Figure 12.5. Such distributions are vital to statistical theory, and they have a number of characteristics. First, we of course can never know how often any single value occurs because there are an infinite number of them (which means we can't define what a 'single' value actually is). This is one of those irritating features of 'infinity' which is really hard to get a handle on, so let's stop and think for a minute, and take things slowly. First, consider that 'infinity' is pretty much a 'theoretical' idea, so stop thinking about your experience of the real world about now. It's impossible to determine how often a single point occurs in a continuous distribution, because you can never actually define a single point. Think about Figure 12.4; it was easy to define

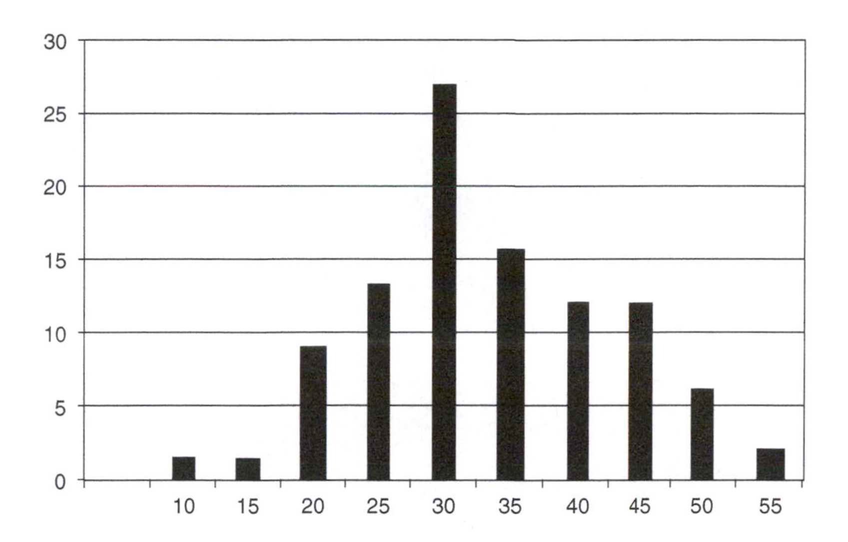

Figure 12.4 A frequency distribution

the single points of '30' and '35' as they are discrete values which we had collected data on. However, we could divide the difference between those more finely, say into '30', '31', '32', '33', '34', and '35'. That's great, still easy to see the discrete points (there would be 6 bars instead of 2). Now keep doing this dividing for a while in your head. Next, imagine *never being able to stop doing that dividing*. Remember, that's infinity! You would never be able to actually settle on a set of discrete points because you could forever keep dividing them even more finely (think about the ideas of 'infinity; and 'forever' seriously for a while, as a lot of mathematical and statistical theories rest on them). Yet, while we can never define a discrete point value for an infinite distribution, one thing we do know is that *every possible* value is represented in the distribution (it's infinite, remember). Therefore, there is a 100 per cent chance of any data point you can imagine (e.g. '30', or '30.00000000000123897') being one of the infinite number of values. So this means that the *area under the curve* of a continuous distribution like that in Figure 12.5 can be taken to represent a *total of 100 per cent*. What this means is that we can find the chances of a given **interval** of values – say between 1.5 and 2.5 – by measuring the area under the curve between 1.5 and 2.5 on the x axis. The mathematics of this kind of thing is what you might have heard of as **calculus**. But before you run screaming, it's not really necessary to know any of that, it's the *concepts* that are important.

There are many different 'shapes' of distribution, but the one in Figure 12.5 is very important. It's called the **normal distribution**, and is a fundamental part of statistical inference. It is *bell-shaped* in that values are more common in the middle of the possible range, and it has a very precise mathematical definition. You will come across this concept

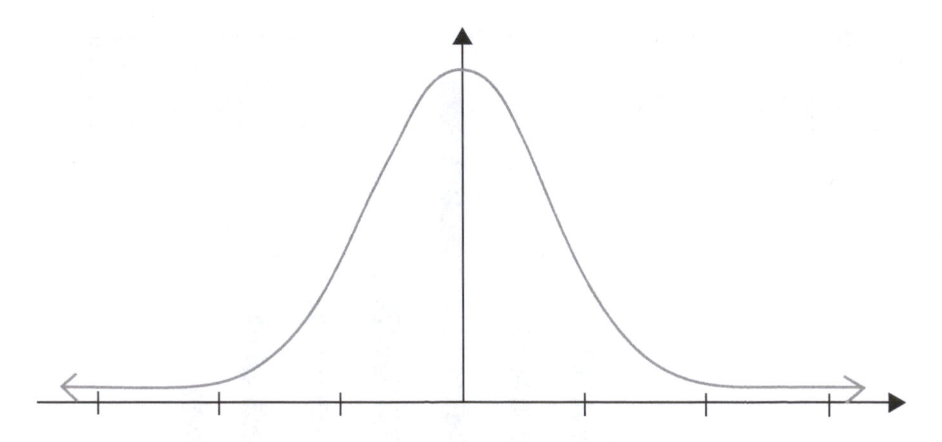

Figure 12.5 A continuous distribution

so many times in your statistical analysis career that you will come to love it like a comfort blanket. Or maybe that's just me? Anyway, before we move on we need to just define a couple of other things. First is the concept of **central tendency**. This number essentially tells us at which point the distribution is 'centred'. But there are many ways of measuring this, which you've probably heard of: the *mode*, the *median*, the *mean*, and many others. For our purposes, the most important measure is the **mean**.[3] If you don't know what a mean is (or the other measures), then I would say that you might want to go back to a slightly more basic statistics text and find out before going on. The mean is another of the basic building blocks of statistical inference. The second key concept here is that of **variation**. This value tells us how much individual observations *differ* from each other. Again, there are many different ways of measuring this, and the *range* is one. The key measure is the **variance** of the data set. In order to find it, you need the mean. The variance is the *sum of the square of every value's deviation from the mean*, divided by the *number of observations*. This basically measures how far each observation is from the mean, as the greater the variation in a data set, the more widely dispersed from the mean each observation will be. Of course, for a theoretical distribution we can't actually physically do this, but the rationale is solid. If you are wondering why we square the deviations, it is in order to remove the problem of positive and negative deviations (i.e. above and below the mean) cancelling each other out. The square root of the variance is known as the **standard deviation**,[4] and we use this on many occasions as the variance is actually in units

[3]One good thing to do would be to go back to the measurement chapters and think about the different types of scales that let us take different measures of central tendency. Is it starting to fit together now?

[4]You might know this as the *root mean square* (RMS), especially if you are from an engineering or physical science background.

which are squared (due to the formula), and for many other reasons which you might work out later.

Now remember the normal distribution is a theoretical frequency distribution, and that thus we could think of the area under the curve as representing a total of 100 per cent of all the possible observations you could make. And that also we could therefore find out the *chances of the occurrence* of any value within a given interval by measuring the area under the graph between two points on the x-axis. So what if, instead of thinking of the points on the graph in absolute terms (e.g. 1.75 and 2.3), we made one of them the *mean* and measured the other one in *standard deviations*. This is useful when we consider what mathematics tells us about the normal distribution. We don't need to know how, but 34 per cent of the area under the normal distribution is contained between the mean and the value which is **one standard deviation** away from the mean. Of course, the normal distribution is symmetrical, so it follows that 68 per cent of the possible values in a normal distribution occur within the interval from one standard deviation below the mean to one standard deviation above. Furthermore, 95 per cent of the observations occur between two standard deviations above and below the mean. In practical terms, this means that if the variable you were examining is normally distributed in the population, with a mean of 100 and a standard deviation of 10, 68 per cent of them should fall between 90 and 110, and 95 per cent between 80 and 120. These facts are so astonishingly useful that you should go and copy them out 20 times. Go on, you'll thank me later.

You'll come across these concepts many, many times in the next few chapters, so please make the effort to understand them before going on. Once you've done that, you can move to the next section. However, it's only fair to warn you that some people might find this next bit a little unpleasant.

Basic probability theory

Probability theory is kind of like medicine. You really hate having to take it, but then later on you are glad you did because you feel much better. It's also one of those things that never seems that useful when you learn it in isolation, a bit like algebra and calculus at school. What this means is that most students don't take any notice of probability theory when it comes up. Unfortunately this means that later concepts of statistical inference are much more difficult to grasp. Probability theory is vital to statistical inference for one reason. When we are trying to estimate the likelihood of population parameters from sample statistics, we are dealing with some degree of uncertainty, therefore we need to talk about them in terms of **probability**. Now a full introduction to probability theory would take an entire chapter itself, so I'm going to try to get the key points across which will help you understand how statistical inference works, but it would be really great if you went away and read some more stuff as well! Also, be aware that there is a lot of terminology coming up in a short space, so take it slowly, take notes, and make sure you understand before going on.

Let's start at the very beginning since, as the song goes, it's a very good place to start. There are all kinds of ways you can think about probability, but one good definition is to consider it *the estimate of the chances of an event occurring in the future.* We can make this estimate in a number of ways. **Theoretical probability** is the type of probability we can estimate based on pure logic – like the changes of getting a '5' on the roll of a fair die, which is 0.167 (i.e. 1/6). We don't need prior observations or experience to estimate this. But more often we are talking about **empirical probability**, where our estimate rests on past observations, without any necessary logic. For example, we can estimate the chances of being struck by lightning based on the frequency of it occurring in the past. This type of estimate is termed *objective* as it is based on prior observations. On the other hand *subjective* empirical probabilities are based on our own estimates, for example when they refer to situations which have happened rarely, or never, in the past, or where we have poor information (e.g. the situation has changed since our empirical information). In these cases, different people may come up with different estimates. Betting odds are good examples of this. For example, you could go to a number of different betting shops (in a country like the UK), or look at an Internet betting exchange, and you will see many (slightly) different odds – which are essentially subjective empirical probabilities – for the same event (such as Sunderland AFC beating Manchester United FC by 4 goals).

A *probability experiment* is an abstract way of talking about any time we do or observe something with an uncertain outcome. For example rolling a die, taking a test, selecting a sample from a population, asking a girl (or boy) out, and the like. We can repeat these many times in theory (sometimes we need to!) and each repetition is called a *trial.* The thing we are measuring in the trial (e.g. the value of the die, the response of the girl/boy, mean age of the sample) is called a *random variable.* We can measure our variable in many ways, depending on our needs, but the key is that it is uncertain, and therefore associated with a probability. The set of all possible outcomes of your experiment is called the *sample space* of the experiment. The sample space of the die roll experiment is 1, 2, 3, 4, 5, 6, since these are all the possible results of the roll. These outcomes must be exhaustive and mutually exclusive, i.e. the set must contain all possible outcomes, and only one of these outcomes can occur in a given trial. These outcomes are called *simple outcomes.* It's not easy in most cases to define the sample space for a probability experiment (e.g. try thinking up all the possible responses to asking a girl out), but it is an important stage of any probability problem.

Once we have done these preliminary tasks, it's time to give actual *probabilities* to the outcomes. We can base these on logic, experience, or even just our own subjective judgement, depending on the situation. But whatever we do, the probabilities must fulfil two rules:

- The probability of any one simple outcome must be represented by a number between 0 and 1.
- The sum of all the probabilities of the simple outcomes in a sample space must be 1.

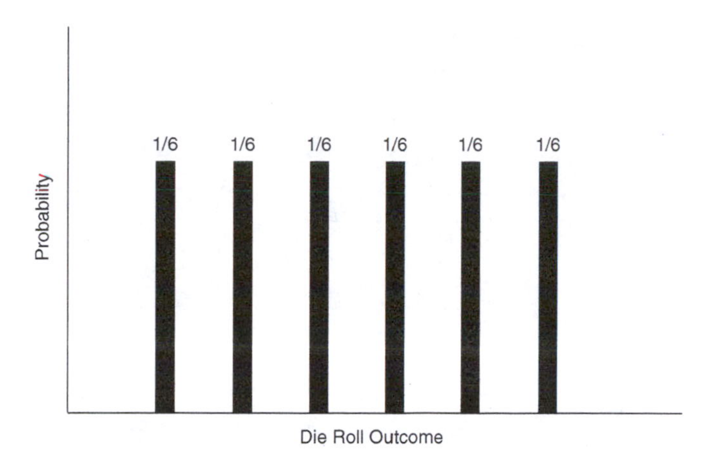

Figure 12.6 Probability distribution for die roll

All the simple outcomes and their probabilities together form a *probability distribution*. This distribution can be displayed in a table, or perhaps you'd prefer it in a graph. Figure 12.6 shows the probability distribution for the die roll experiment. It assumes a fair die, so each outcome is equally likely in theory. You'll note that the bars representing the probabilities are separated, which indicates that we are dealing with *discrete* outcomes – ones where there are no possible intermediate values (i.e. we couldn't have an outcome of 1.5). Most of the time, in statistical inference contexts, we are dealing with *continuous* distributions (like the **normal distribution**). We'll be coming back to this, but just keep it in mind for now.

That said, most of the time in the real world we are not that interested in simple outcomes, but with sets of simple outcomes. In the die roll we might be more interested in getting 'a value less than 5', which would be the set 1, 2, 3, 4. This set is known as a *composite outcome*, and occurs if *any one of the simple outcomes in the set* occurs. The probability of a composite outcome is the sum of the probabilities of the simple outcomes. Unlike simple outcomes, composite outcomes do not have to be exhaustive or mutually exclusive, although they might be. Figure 12.7 represents two composite outcomes, A and B, which are neither exhaustive (there are some simple outcomes outside the composite ones) nor mutually exclusive (the composite outcomes overlap). The composite outcomes are made from a sample space of 10 equally likely simple outcomes $\{o_1 \ldots o_{10}\}$. Imagine rolling a 10-sided die, which should be no problem to those of you who have played 'Dungeons and Dragons'. We'll be using this figure to illustrate a number of relationships among probabilities.

If you look at Figure 12.7, you'll see that the composite outcomes A and B overlap. In this situation, we are often interested in the **conditional probability**, which is the probability of

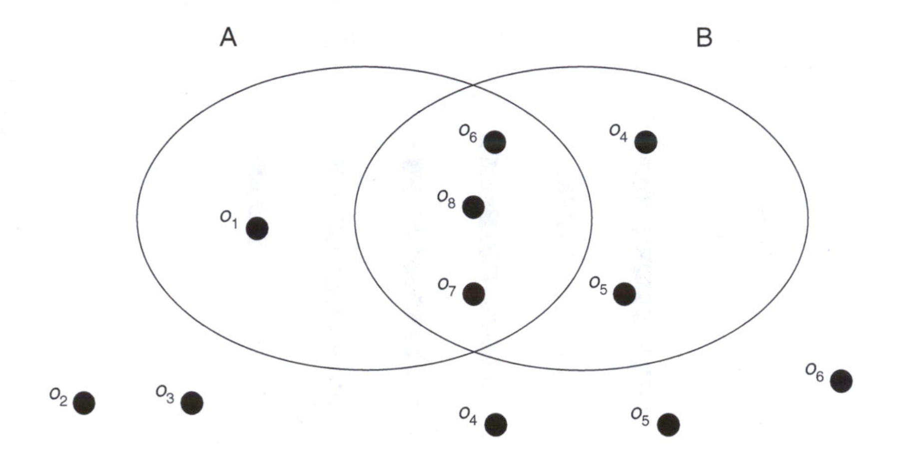

Figure 12.7 Composite outcomes

one composite outcome, given that another composite outcome has occurred. Imagine we are interested in the probability of outcome A, given outcome B. In Figure 12.7, outcome B consists of the simple outcomes $\{o_4, o_5, o_6, o_7, o_8\}$. We need to determine the probability of A given that B has occurred. In Figure 12.7 we can quite easily see that 3 of the 5 outcomes in B are also in A, so the probability of A given B is 3/5 or 0.6. The notation for a conditional probability is P(A|B), and the formula for working them out is:

$$P(A|B) = \frac{P(A \text{ and } B)}{P(B)}$$

Where the top ratio represents the probability of *both* outcomes occurring, and the bottom is just the probability of B occurring. In Figure 12.7 this is easy to see. The probability of both outcomes occurring is just the number of simple outcomes in the overlap between the two composite outcomes (3) divided by the number of total simple outcomes (10). The probability of B is just the number of simple outcomes in B (5) divided by the total number of simple outcomes (10). We need the formula because we don't always have easy diagrams with small sets as in Figure 12.7, and conditional probability is very important to many other probability ideas.

Sometimes, we want to know the probability of both composite outcomes A and B occurring at the same time, which is termed the **joint probability**, and is notated as P(A and B). This of course should be less than the individual probabilities of the outcomes, and is also dependent on the conditional probability. To get the joint probability we use the *multiplication rule* for probabilities, which is:

$$P(A \text{ and } B) = P(A|B)P(B)$$

If you go back to Figure 12.7 you should be able to work it out both by simply reading off the figure, and also by putting relevant numbers in the formula. Give it a go, you'll hopefully get an answer of 0.3. We might also want to know the probability of either A or B occurring, which is given by the *addition rule* for probabilities:

$$P(A \text{ or } B) = P(A) + P(B) - P(A \text{ and } B)$$

Try this on Figure 12.7, and you'll hopefully get an answer of 0.6.

We use the term *independent outcomes* when the probability of A is the same whether or not outcome B has occurred. In our notation this would mean:

$$\text{If } P(A|B) = P(A), \text{ then A and B are independent}$$

Also:

$$P(A \text{ and } B) = P(A)P(B) \text{ if A and B are independent}$$

In Figure 12.7, the outcomes A and B are *not* independent, as $P(A|B)$ is 0.6, but $P(A)$ is 0.4. In other words, A occurs more often when B also occurs. This kind of thing can be extremely useful in all kinds of contexts. Imagine if we are trying to determine whether the probability of a pass score on a final year economics exam is independent of the occurrence of a pass score on a first year statistics exam. Using empirical probability figures, we could provide a good indication of this.

Sampling and probability

Now we have a decent grounding in sampling distributions and probability theory, we can start to apply it to the situation of statistical inference, which is after all what we really want to talk about isn't it? The basic idea here is that, if we want to relate our sample statistics back to population parameters, we need some kind of theory to do so. Now, one thing we do know is that the sample is just a subset of the population, so the sample statistic will differ from the population parameter in some way. But what if we knew how that statistic behaved? For example, if we took an *infinite* number of samples from the population and took the same statistic – say the mean – of all of them. If we knew this, we could use our knowledge of probability to state how confident we were that the sample mean was within some given distance of the population mean. So, what we need is a *probability distribution* for the statistic, in this case the mean. The distribution, which describes the values the statistic can take and the probability of each value, is called a **sampling distribution**. Each different statistic has its own distribution, but we will focus on the mean as both a perfect example, and probably the most important. One thing to remember, though, is that sampling distributions are purely theoretical; we can of course never take an infinite number of samples. But imagine that the sampling distribution is made up of a frequency distribution of all the means from an infinite number of samples – i.e. some means will occur more often, others will occur less often.

This is where the method of sampling comes into play, as it influences the type of inferences you can make from the sample. Simply put, a probability sample underlies almost all of the following theory, but I've covered many of those issues in the previous chapter. For now, just assume that we took a probability sample. Moving forward, the sampling distribution of the mean consists of all the possible alternative values that the sample mean can take, and the probability of each value. We can create this distribution mathematically, using the characteristics of the parent population and the sample size, if we know this information. But it is just like any other distribution in that it has its own mean and standard deviation. We would of course like to know how these figures differ from their corresponding ones in the population. There are a number of different theorems available which tell us this. They have been mathematically proved, but we won't go into that here (which you will doubtless be thankful for). The most important one for our purposes is known as the **central limit theorem**, which relates to the sampling distribution of the mean of a variable drawn from a non-normally distributed population (which is the case for almost any variable). It is in fact rather amazing. The central limit theorem states:

- *If a population variable x is distributed with mean μ and a standard deviation σ, then the sampling distribution of the mean x, based on random samples of size n, will have a mean equal to μ and a standard deviation equal to*

$$\frac{\text{Standard deviation of the population}}{\text{Square root of the sample size}}$$

Further, the distribution will tend to be normal as the sample size n becomes large.

We refer to the standard deviation of the mean given by the formula above by the specific term **standard error of the mean**. Knowledge of this sampling distribution is amazingly useful, because it allows us to make statistical inferences with only one sample, rather than have to draw many independent samples and create a new sampling distribution every time. But never forget that this is just an estimation, and then only when the sample is large.

Now, before we go further, what size is 'large'? Well, while it is impossible to say (as it does depend on the population characteristics), many studies have shown that even samples where *n* is as small as 30 can result in a sampling distribution which comes close to normal.

So, that was a bit scary, but in practical terms what does this mean? Well it means that – since we know a number of important characteristics about the normal distribution, our task of making inferences about population parameters from sample statistics just became a whole lot easier. OK, so what do we know about the normal distribution so far? Well, it's a theoretical continuous distribution. So that means we can determine the probability of a obtaining a sample mean between any two points on the x-axis by simply measuring the area under the graph between the two points. But, most crucially, because we also have some information about the relevant points, we don't necessarily need calculus to work out the area under the graph. Remember that *we know about how much of the area falls between the mean and one and two standard deviations above and below*. If you don't remember, start this chapter again until you do! Don't move on to the next section till you are confident that you understand the material so far.

Statistical inference and hypothesis testing

There are two ways to approach the issue of infering parameters from sample statistics. In elementary statistics courses we usually begin with the concept of defining *confidence intervals* around the sample statistics. While this is a nice exercise, it isn't really what we do in most research contexts, so we won't cover it specifically here. That said, you will probably find this section a bit easier if you have got a handle on confidence intervals in the past. What is far more common in real research contexts is that we use our sample statistics to provide support or otherwise to **hypotheses** that we make about the population parameters. We spent time in previous chapters talking about the theoretical content of hypotheses, but now we are talking about actually testing these hypotheses against empirical data. At last! Our theoretical hypotheses give us grounds to expect our empirical sample data to behave in a certain way. We use our data to test the probability of our hypothesis being true. If our data cannot provide support, we are faced with the choice of either rejecting our empirical data, or rejecting our theoretical hypothesis. In almost all cases, if our data collection and measurement procedures are solid, we are on safer ground rejecting the theory than the empirical data. After all, it's kind of hard arguing against something we can see in front of us (data) in favour of a theoretical hypothesis which we have no real evidence for!

When we test a hypothesis, we are basically working within the Popperian tradition (go back to Chapter 2 if you aren't clear on this). Remember, Popper said you could never *prove* a hypothesis, only *disprove* one. This has important implications for how we should go about testing a hypothesis. Imagine we had a hypothesis that job satisfaction has a positive correlation with performance. According to Popper, no matter how many times we observed this relationship in our various experiments, it would never be proved, all we can do is *disprove* it! Not very helpful. But what if – in our heads – we imagined that we had *another* hypothesis – one which instead stated that job satisfaction did *not* have a positive correlation with performance. Then, we could disprove this hypothesis by observing a positive correlation between job satisfaction and performance, in turn providing implied support for our original hypothesis, which in this sense is termed the **alternative hypothesis**. The hypothesis predicting no relationship is called the **null hypothesis**, and it is basically a philosophical concept. We normally deal with alternative hypotheses in practice, things we are trying to observe. But don't forget that underneath this, in philosophical terms, there is a process of disproving the null hypothesis going on.

Let's look at a simple example. Imagine I am interested in the mean amount of acid drops in a bag (they were my favourite sweet as a child). The shopkeeper tells me that on average I get 20 acid drops to a 50 pence bag (this is a long time ago!) But I am interested in whether or not this is the case. Because I am a trusting child, I believe the shopkeeper, therefore my hypothesis (the alternative hypothesis, or what I am trying to find support for) is:

$$H_1 : \mu = 20$$

The null hypothesis (what I am trying to disprove in order to support my alternative hypothesis) is:

$$H_0 : \mu \neq 20$$

As a convention, null hypotheses are labelled as H_0. Also, note we could have chosen either of these as the null – depending on what it was we were trying to support (alternative) and what it was we were trying to disprove in order to find this support (null). In fact, later in this chapter I will switch these around.

Now, it is both practically and conceptually impossible to measure every bag of acid drops from the shop. I mean, when would I have measured them 'all'? After a year, 10 years? Until the shop closed? Until the shopkeeper died? So of course we need to take a sample of bags. Maybe I get 50 of my friends to each buy a bag and count the number of acid drops. Of course, I would need to apply for a research grant from my Mum for this (I hope she is more generous than most funding bodies). So, what if we got a sample mean of acid drops per bag over the 50 bags as 15? Would I still be confident in my hypothesis of a population mean of 20? What about a sample mean of 26? Or 21? Or 19.5?

Of course, I need some more information here to answer that question. Let's imagine I get a sample mean of 19. From here, I need to know the characteristics of the sampling distribution of the mean. Now I know, because I read the earlier bits of this chapter, that it will depend on the sample size, and also the shape and standard deviation of the population. If I knew all this information my task would be easy. On the other hand, in reality it's unlikely I know anything concrete about the population. So, in this situation you can substitute in the sample standard deviation as a good estimate of the population one. The process is one of working out how far our sample mean deviates from the hypothesised mean – i.e. how many *standard deviations* away from the hypothesised population mean is our sample mean? Once we have done this, (which you could do by hand using a simple formula), you then need to work out *how likely is it that you* ***observe a sample mean*** *that far from the population mean if the* ***hypothesised population mean*** *really was 20*? The less likely, the less inclined you will be to accept the hypothesis. Remember, as long as we are confident in our methods, we can't really quibble with the observed sample mean; our safest choice is to reject the theoretical hypothesis. A worked example will probably help here, and I will show you one soon.

But, what do 'likely' and 'unlikely' really mean? This is where the next major statistical inference concept comes in, the **significance level**. The significance level is the probability we give to an outcome below which we consider it 'unlikely'. What I mean here is that, how unlikely would your observed sample mean have to be before you consider it too unlikely to occur if the hypothesis of 20 were true? Then you would have the choice of either rejecting the hypothesis of 20, or rejecting the observed results as being down to chance. The most common significance level (often given the Greek letter *alpha*[5] or α) is 0.05 which as a percentage is 5 per cent. An alpha of 5 per cent means that the chances of observing your sample mean *if the hypothesis were true* is only 5 per cent. This is justifiably an unlikely situation, so you can feel confident about rejecting the hypothesis. But don't get the idea that 5 per cent is some kind of 'magic number'. In fact it is purely an arbitrary value which has come to signify an acceptable chance of being wrong. However, you need to consider many other factors when exploring the significance of your hypothesis tests which will be discussed later in this chapter and the next. Figure 12.8a shows a standard normal distribution which helps to illuminate these issues. You can see that the x-axis is measured in standard deviations from the mean which means we can use this in all contexts as long I work out how many standard deviations from the hypothesised population mean my sample mean is. You should always decide on your significance level *before* you collect data, not after you analyse the data. In this way the significance level is a test which your hypotheses have to pass.

One final thing to note before I give you an example of this in practice is that Figures 12.8b and 12.8c show how we can split the probability either between the two tails of the distribution, or we can put it all into one tail. These are called *two-tailed* and *one-tailed* tests respectively. We make this choice depending on our hypothesis. Take the acid drops example above. If we have no particular reason to suspect that the mean will be either above or below our null hypothesis, forever we must use a two-tailed test (Figure 12.8b). But if we suspect that it is either solely below or solely above the hypothesis, we can use a one-tailed test (Figure 12.8c). For example, if my **null** hypothesis is that the population mean is 20, but I suspect the shopkeeper is filling the bags with fewer acid drops, and that the possibility of the shopkeeper filling the bags with more is not feasible, my **alternative** hypothesis will be that the mean is *less than* 20. In this case I can use a one-tailed test. The advantage of the one-tailed test is obvious in the figures, my sample mean has to deviate from the hypothesised sample mean by less to pass the 0.05 significance test (1.65 standard deviations versus 1.96).

[5]But just to make things confusing, quite a few other concepts are also called alpha!

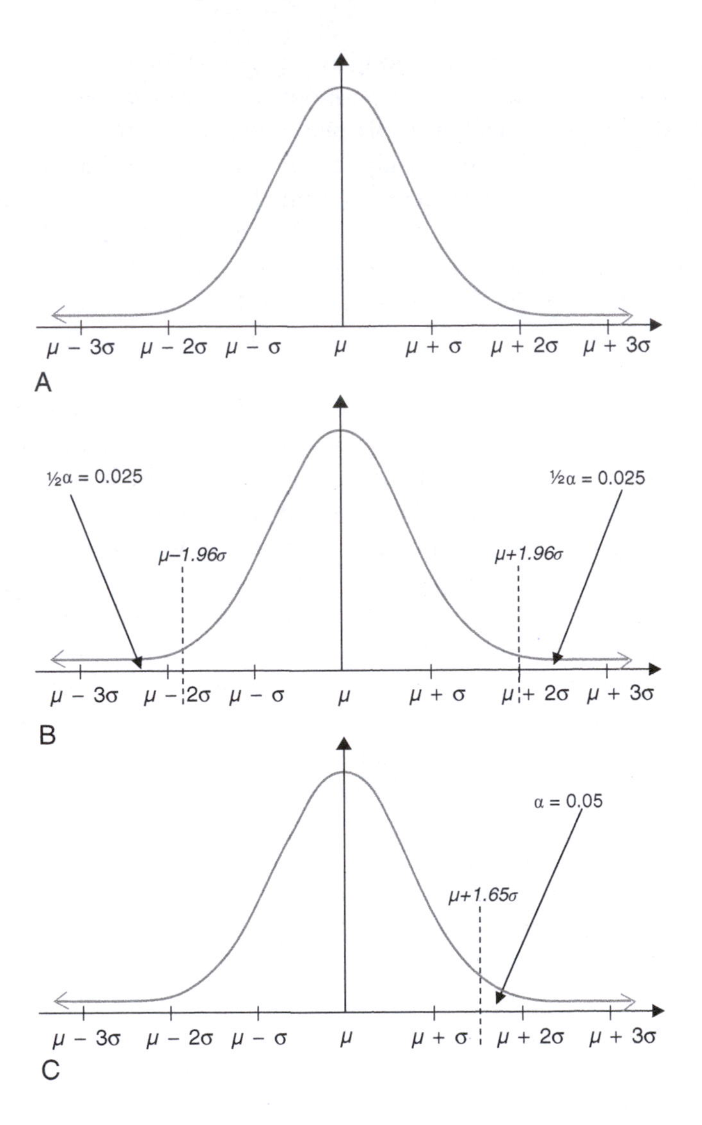

Figure 12.8 (a): The normal distribution (b): α of 0.05 with a two-tailed test (c): α of 0.05 with a one-tailed test

At last, let's go through a worked example to solidify all these concepts. For the acid drops example I will set the significance level at 0.05 prior to doing any analysis. The null H_0 is set at 20, the alternative is two-tailed, in that I don't have any theory or expectation of which way the mean will differ (above or below), just that it will differ somehow. Say I take a sample of 50 bags, and get a sample mean of 19 acid drops per bag with a standard deviation of 2. You need to work out the likelihood of achieving a sample mean of 19 if the null population mean of 20 were true. Since you are unlikely to have the population standard deviation, you need to use the sample standard deviation as an estimate. Technically, this means the results are approximate, but we tend not to worry about this. We first need to work out the standard error of the mean (remember the central limit theorem above) with the formula:

$$\frac{\text{Sample standard deviation}}{\text{Square root of sample size}}$$

Doing this for our example gives us a result of 0.28. Using this value, we can then change the expression of our sample mean from a raw number (19) to a *deviation from the hypothesised mean of 20*. In other words, on a standard normal distribution, how far away from the mean is the sample value in standard deviations? This statistic is called the z statistic. The formula to do this is:

$$\frac{\text{Sample mean} - \text{hypothesised mean}}{\text{Standard error of the mean}}$$

In this example we get −3.57. This means that our sample mean is essentially 3.57 standard deviations below the hypothesised population mean – expressed graphically in Figure 12.9. In fact, we are *way* beyond unlikely here! The critical value of z which you need for a 0.05 level of significance is actually plus or minus 1.96.

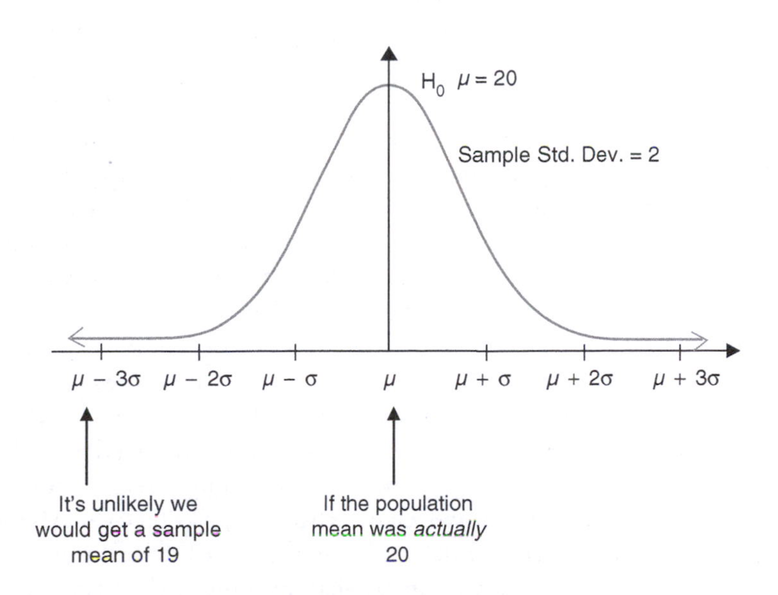

Figure 12.9 Deviation of sample mean from population mean

We can see that, if our null hypothesis of 20 were true, it would be highly unlikely that we would observe the sample mean of 19 in a sample of 50. Whoops, looks like my sweet shop proprietor is stiffing me! This example also illuminates another key point about statistical inference, that your *results depend on sample size*. Look at the formula for the standard error of the mean above; the bigger the sample size, the bigger the denominator, which will mean the smaller the standard error. In turn, the formula for the z value will then have a smaller denominator, increasing the size of z. So for any given difference between sample statistic and hypothesised parameter, a larger sample will be more likely to give you a significant difference. This means that the test has more **power**, which is a concept I will cover soon. It's up to you to decide in some cases whether this is desirable. Normally, we consider it *is* desirable, because we are trying to find a difference which will let us reject the null hypothesis.

What actually happens in practice

The above was a detailed example to illustrate exactly what goes on in the process of statistical inference. It shows a ***z* test** for the difference between a sample mean and population mean. It's a great example, but it's not often what we actually do in practice. One thing you need to understand is that every different type of test has its *own* statistic which is associated with it. For example, one type of correlation test has an ***r*** statistic, and analysis of variance (ANOVA) has an ***F*** statistic. Each of these has different formulae, and many of them are distributed in different ways. You don't need to know this in detail, but what you do need to know is what happens when you get the results of such tests in a programme such as SPSS.

Computer software will normally calculate the statistic, and then give you a **significance** value which will be expressed in a decimal format, like the 0.05 value I gave you earlier. In many cases, the software won't nurse you through by 'telling' you whether or not this is significant, you need to work out what critical value you want from that significance value first. In most cases, you will hope the significance will be equal to or less than 0.05. This signifies you have achieved an alpha of 5 per cent for a two tailed test. But remember, if you are using a one-tailed hypothesis and associated test, you will only need to achieve a value of 0.1. But be aware that in some cases you can 'tell' the program to give you one-tailed or two-tailed results. Make sure you know what you are doing here. For my purposes, I always leave the computer to give me two-tailed significances, which I can then halve if I am using one-tailed tests. If this doesn't make sense, you need to go back and read the last few sections again. Figure 12.10 shows a set of example results from an ANOVA in SPSS, with some annotations to show exactly what I mean (I'll cover ANOVA in more depth in Chapter 14). You can see that the significance is 0.942, which is nowhere near our hoped-for value of 0.05. In this case we can say that our observed statistic does not give us enough evidence to reject the null hypothesis.

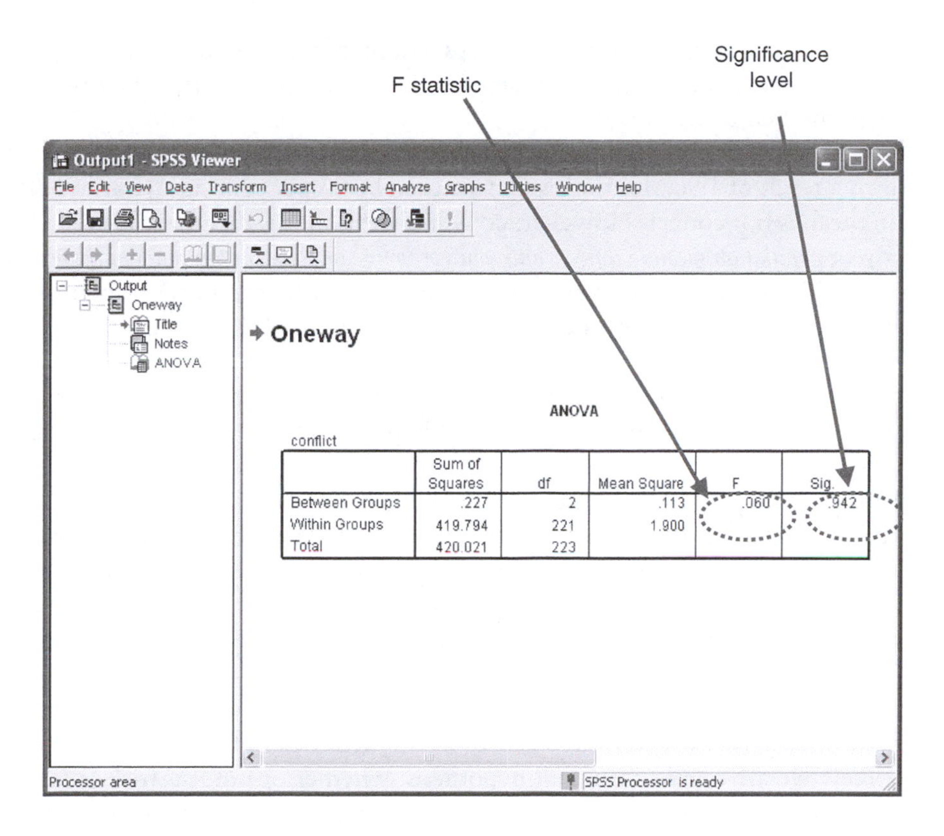

Figure 12.10 SPSS example of ANOVA

Type I and Type II errors

I promised earlier that I would deal with Type I and Type II errors, so here it is at last, and maybe with your help I can lay a few ghosts to rest! The first thing to remember is that when we perform statistical inference, we are dealing with *probabilities*, not exact answers. If you don't get this, you should go back and re-read the chapter from the start. Really, go on …

Anyway, moving back to the acid drops example, when we got our z test result, we decided that it was highly unlikely that we would get a sample mean of 19, if the hypothesised mean was 20. Notice I said **unlikely**, not impossible? This is a key distinction. When we get our statistical results, we have a decision to make. Remember, the sample statistics are there in front of you, it is the hypothesised population parameter which is theoretical. We can either decide to (a) judge the hypothesis unlikely and thus reject it, or (b) decide that our hypothesis is likely enough to accept it. The significance test is a short-cut to doing that, but never forget it is a decision. You could just as well decide that the sample mean of 19 were some kind of bizarre error, and therefore accept the hypothesis of a population mean of 20. But in the case of our acid drops example, we would be going against the balance of probabilities. In that case, it seemed to be a better bet to trust the observed data than the hypothesised mean.

Never forget, however, that there is a chance you can get this wrong. For example, if your z test returns a result of 1.96, this means that you can be 95 per cent sure your hypothesised population mean is not correct. However, conversely this means that there is still *a 5 per cent chance that your population mean is correct, and you got your sample mean by random chance.* In that case, we would be rejecting the hypothesis when it is in fact true for the population, and committing an error. Thus, **Type I error** is the situation where we reject the null hypothesis when it is in fact true in the population. Conversely, **Type II error** occurs when we accept the null hypothesis when it is in fact true in the population. Table 12.1 presents the two different types of error in the context of the null hypothesis testing approach we have been looking at.

The chance of a Type I error is quite a simple thing to work out. It is basically equal to the significance level you decide on before analysis. In the acid drops example, we decided on a level of 0.05. So we had in simple terms a 5 per cent chance of committing a Type I error – i.e. rejecting the hypothesis when it was true in the population. If you wanted to minimise Type I error, you could decide on a more stringent level of significance, like 0.01. You are now less likely to reject the hypothesis in general. On the other hand, the likelihood of committing a Type II error is more complex to determine. In fact, it is often ignored by researchers. We touched on one of the determinants earlier – sample size. The larger the sample size, the more likely we are to reject the null hypothesis, whether or not it is true or false in the population. But Type II error also depends on the parameter value itself, the significance level (in the opposite way to Type I error), and the size of sample standard deviation.[6]

Of course, it should make sense to you that Type I and Type II error are negatively related. As Type I error is reduced, Type II error is increased. So as an analyst, you need to trade-off **power**, which is basically how sensitive your research design is to differences between sample statistics and hypothesised parameters – which reduces Type I error – against the chances of Type II error. Unfortunately, it's not really as simple as plugging things into

Table 12.1 Type I and Type II error

Statistical test result	**True state in the population**	
	H_0 is true	**H_0 is false**
H_0 is true	Correct!	**Type II error**
H_0 is false	**Type I error**	Correct!

[6] As an exercise, go back to the acid drops example and try to work out how the standard deviation could influence Type II error. Hint: the logic is similar to the sample size issue.

a formula to work out the right balance. Instead, you need to make a subjective judgement in most cases. In fact, few applied researchers even consider this balance, and simply go with whatever is 'standard' in their own discipline. But a good researcher will judge this balance by taking into account a number of key considerations. Your considerations need to be sympathetic to your objectives and also the implications of your results. For example, a number of scholars have noted that statistically significant results (i.e. ones that reject the null hypothesis) are more likely to be published.[7] Therefore many researchers focus on reducing Type I error, with the corresponding increase in Type II error. But what if your results are likely to have key impacts on individuals or society? Medical and psychological researchers need to deal with this issue very often. For example, if you are conducting a drug trial, then if you incorrectly reject your null hypothesis (which is likely to be along the lines that 'the drug has no effect') and conclude that a drug has an effect on a condition when it does not, you may cause major problems. In such a situation, Type II error needs to be given serious consideration.

Statistical and substantive significance

Before wrapping this chapter up, it's important to touch on a more conceptual issue to do with significance. What I've given you in the last few sections is an introduction to **statistical significance**. However, hopefully the last part on Type I and Type II error should have placed a seed in your mind along the lines of 'well, is it enough to simply obtain statistical significance?' No, simply put, it is not. You need also to think about the implications of your results. More specifically, do your results have any relevance to the real-world situation you are trying to explore? I'll go through an example which should give you an idea of what I am trying to say here.

Let's go back to the acid drops example. If I take a sample of 50, and find a sample mean of 19.5. Work through the formula and you will get a z of -1.79. As we should all understand by now this does not reach our critical value for 0.05 significance. So we would conclude that we don't have enough evidence to reject the null hypothesis of 20. Our shopkeeper is OK. So, what if I took a sample of 64, again with a standard deviation of 2. Run through the two formulae; (a) calculate standard error of the mean which comes to 0.25, and (b) calculate the z value using this standard error, which now comes to -2. In this case we would conclude that our sample *does* give us reason to reject the null hypothesis of 20. Bad luck for our shopkeeper. This example shows how the higher your sample size, the *smaller* your deviation from the null has to be for you to find it significant. Now this is all well and good, in fact it makes sense. The closer we get to the population, the more likely our sample results are to mirror the population, so even small deviations can contradict our null hypothesis. In fact, if we had a sample of 1,000 bags, our sample mean could be

---

[7] J. Scott Armstrong has been particularly vocal on this in my own field of Marketing.

19.88 acid drops (with a standard deviation of 2) per bag, and we would still find a statistically significant difference! But, what would this *mean* in practical terms? Would we be justified in complaining about it? In my opinion, probably not. How could a shopkeeper be that exact? However, if we were looking at deciding whether or not a key part of an aircraft deviated from a standard size in millimetres, this kind of exactness might be exactly what we need!

I will return to this point in a couple of chapters, when I talk about 'effect sizes', but for now you should understand the key issues here. In essence, you must always try to relate your raw numbers back to the theoretical and practical problems you are trying to answer. You may indeed find statistically significant differences in your data, but do they really mean anything of consequence back in the 'real world'? Hopefully, you should also be beginning to understand that statistics and statistical significance are simple mathematical and probabilistic conventions, not infallible answers to all your problems.

Summary

As a reader (and possibly an absolute beginner), you had a lot of thinking and remembering to do in that chapter. For some of you, that might be the first time you have ever really paid attention to statistical theory. So if nothing else you should be pleased if you have got to this point and feel that you understand the bulk of the material here. Now, I will say it again, if you are not confident you understand it, don't assume it will get better over the next couple of chapters! Go back and work through the chapter until you feel happy you are getting the picture before moving on. It's no exaggeration to say that if you don't understand this basic theory, then statistical analysis will be a mystery to you. You might be able to plug things into formulae, but you won't really know what's going on. Eventually, you will make mistakes. Do you want to risk that those mistakes will be discovered at a key juncture? Your *viva* for example? Or a presentation? If you don't mind looking a fool (and I have seen this happen) then by all means do what you will.

The basic idea of this chapter was to present the key material required for a complete beginner to understand *why* statistical analysis works the way it does, and how we are able to make inferences about a population from a small sample. You should read it in conjunction with the rest of the book, however. The links with the philosophical material in Chapter 2 particularly should be understood, as well as the measurement Chapters 6 and 7, and Chapter 11 too. Equally, try to understand the fundamental reasons that this kind of analysis might disagree with an interpretive philosophy. Think about this material as a guide, and a way of understanding what is going on with numbers. It's probably not been too much fun for you if you had to struggle, but it does actually have its own rather elegant logic when you begin to see how it works.

Anyway, it's not exaggerating the point to say that almost all of the sections in this chapter could be the subject of a book of their own, and at the very least their own chapter in an elementary statistics book. So I would never claim that this was *all* you ever needed to know about basic statistics. However, I can tell you one thing I am sure of; I wish I'd known this stuff when I started my Ph.D.!

Key points to take from this chapter:

- Statistics is not inherently difficult, it just takes time and focused effort to understand the basics first.
- We use statistics to describe our data so we can understand it better than simply looking at it in raw form.
- Statistical inference is the task of determining the chances of the results we observed in our sample, mirroring those in the population.
- The normal distribution is absolutely key to understanding statistical inference.
- Statistical inference deals with probabilities, not exact answers, thus you should understand the key concepts of probability theory as well.
- We can use statistical inference to work out whether or not our theoretical hypotheses are supported by empirical data.
- The level of statistical significance is the probability we give to an outcome below which we consider it 'unlikely'. The most common level is 0.05, or 5 per cent.
- We must always consider the substantive significance of our findings as well as the statistical significance.

Further reading

- *Taking the Fear Out of Data Analysis* by Adamantios Diamantopoulos and Bodo Schlegelmilch: This is a wonderful introduction to quantitative analysis and statistical theory designed for those who are terrified of numbers. I have known both of these individuals for many years now (Diamantopoulos was an external examiner for my own Ph.D. in fact) and can say that they are among the best in the business. I don't think that their jokes are as good as mine though!
- *Multivariate Statistical Analysis: A Conceptual Introduction* by Sam Kash Kachigan: Once you feel confident, you should go on to this book, which is a fantastic introduction to statistical theory and 'how stuff works'. I hope it is not too difficult to get hold of.
- However, there are plenty of viewpoints which tend to disagree with some of the key principles of statistical theory. *J. Scott Armstrong* is always worth reading, and some of his interesting articles (many of which are available on his website) include:
    - J. Scott Armstrong (1995), 'Publication of research on controversial topics: The early acceptance procedure', *International Journal of Forecasting,* 11, Notes: 1–4.
    - Raymond Hubbard and J. Scott Armstrong (1997), 'Publication bias against null results', *Psychological Reports,* 80, 337–338.
    - J. Scott Armstrong, Robert J. Brodie, and Andrew G. Parsons (2001), 'Hypotheses in marketing science: literature review and publication audit', *Marketing Letters,* 12 (2),171–187.

- Probably the most vocal critic of the hypothesis testing methodology was *Paul Meehl,* who made many contributions to a lot of other areas as well. Meehl's thinking is often incandescent in its brilliance, and a great introduction can be found in a paper by *Bill Rozeboom*, another outstanding thinker:[8]
    - Rozeboom William W. (2005), 'Meehl on metatheory'. *Journal of Clinical Psychology,* 61: 1317–1354.

EXERCISES

1. Explain the difference between parameters and statistics. Are there any situations where we would still need a statistic if we had the parameter?
    a. Is statistical inference necessary if one has population data?
2. What type of distribution is the *normal distribution*?
    a. Why is it important to statistical inference?
    b. What percentage of the area of a normal distribution is between −1.96 and 1.96 standard deviations of the mean?
    c. What does this area represent?
3. Draw a diagram of a set of two composite outcomes A and B with the following characteristics:
    a. There are 12 simple outcomes
    b. $P(A) = 4$, $P(B) = 6$
    c. $P(A \text{ and } B) = 2/12$
4. Use the distribution from question 3 to answer the following questions:
    a. What is $P(A|B)$?
    b. What is $P(A \text{ or } B)$
    c. Are A and B independent?
5. Explain how the statistical hypothesis testing approach is linked with Karl Popper's theories on scientific method. Pay particular attention to the characteristics of the normal distribution, significance testing, and null hypotheses.
6. Imagine you are interested in the mean petrol consumption of the new Ford Tippex, which is quoted in advertisements as being 35 mpg. You take a sample of 35 cars and find the mean mileage of the sample to be 34.5 mpg, with a standard deviation of 0.6. You set a significance level of 0.05.
    a. What are your null and alternative hypotheses?
    b. Does your data support the contention that the mean petrol consumption of the new Ford Tippex is 35 mpg?

---

[8]However, if you really want to get into Meehl, check out his *Selected Philosophical and Methodological Papers*.

c. If there is a statistically significant difference, is it substantively significant in your opinion? Don't just think about the magnitude, but also the context and importance of mileage and claims about it.
d. With the same figures of sample mean and size, what would the standard deviation need to be to change the results of your hypothesis test? What does this mean in practical terms?
e. With the same figures of sample size and standard deviation, what would the sample mean need to be to change the results of your hypothesis test? What does this mean in practical terms?
f. With the same figures of sample mean and standard deviation, what would the sample size need to be to change the results of your hypothesis test? What does this mean in practical terms?

7. That was pretty serious stuff, so you deserve a reward. Go and expand your mind in a different way by visiting an art gallery or something like that.

Chapter 13
Quantitative data analysis I

SUPERVISOR'S VIEW: PROFESSOR FELIX BRODBECK

Although this may seem unusual for a scientist, for me the most important stage of data analysis is the one where you develop a 'feeling' for the data at hand. Of course, the more involved you were in data gathering, setting up the data template, data entry, and checking for errors and plausibility of variable values, the better 'feel' you already have. But your data journey does not stop there. After that stage, if not way before, you are usually keen to test your major hypotheses. Feel free to do so, however, and this is not seldom (despite what you might imagine from reading academic journals), it happens that your hypotheses do not come out the way you were hoping for. At that stage, check your data again, but this time, also look at the distributions, and test them, for example, for normality, perform outlier analysis, use histograms, scattergrams, box and whisker plots, and more, in order to understand the characteristics of your variables and how they relate to each other. This activity is called *exploratory data analysis*, and John Wilder Tukey (1915–2000) wrote a pioneering book about it, which by now is a classic. In his own words, 'If we need a short suggestion of what exploratory data analysis is, I would suggest that, first, it is an attitude, AND second, a flexibility, AND, third, some graph paper (or transparencies, or both)' (from his 1986 publication in *American Statistician*). I learned from his book that nature *speaks to you via data*, and it is up to you whether you learn to listen well and learn more about nature – via induction and further hypothesis testing. Let me finish here with another famous quotation from Tukey: 'The combination of some data and an aching desire for an answer does not ensure that a reasonable answer can be extracted from a given body of data.' (Again from his 1986 *American Statistician* article.)

VIEW FROM THE TRENCHES: YVES GUILLAUME

If you look at other Ph.Ds. or (especially) published articles, you will rarely see any of the things Nick talks about in this chapter. So why should you bother, as doing it the quick and dirty way, and starting with the 'real' analysis straight away (the stuff he will talk about in the next chapter), may save you valuable time for the 'more important' things you will be reporting in your Ph.D., and the publications you will get out of it? Well, that you don't see these things reported doesn't mean that others didn't do them. And as research is one of the areas where truth and idealism are still appreciated values, the community assumes that you did do all the things discussed in this chapter. For those among you with a more practical approach to life, doing the things recommended here may help you to save lots of trouble as you go forward to the more sophisticated analysis.

Let's start with cleaning your data. I often work with longitudinal data sets. What I usually do is enter the data for each measurement point into separate files, assigning an identifier based on which you will match the files afterwards. But if the identifier is wrong you will end up with many fewer cases than you have actually collected. This is not only a waste of time, money and energy (you may still remember the trouble you had getting access), but is also a major drawback for your analysis, as you will have less power. On a more general level, not checking your data for errors may bias your results (as the data that are entered is wrong, you may end up with a relationship between two variables in the opposite direction you were hypothesising, or you may not find any significant relationships at all!). Unfortunately, there has hardly been any data file that I have worked with so far that didn't contain any errors that occurred during the data entry process. We are all human after all! Running frequency checks and looking for outliers may help you to detect these cases. You then can go back to the original questionnaires and type in the right values.

Finally, doing the things suggested in this chapter may also help you to get a better feel for you data. Graphing the relationships you are looking at and running inter-correlations and partial correlations will tell you immediately, whether the relationships you have hypothesised are likely to be found in your data or not. Further, some of the statistical procedures require assumptions. If they do not hold in your data you may get biased or non-significant results. Having detected them prior to your real analysis allows you to apply transformations so that your variables satisfy the conditions for the more sophisticated analysis, which in return will help you to find the true relationships, and which may make it more likely that you find significant relationships.

So why should you bother about this chapter? It helps you avoid a lot of trouble!

So, Chapter 13, unlucky for some! Here we arrive at the section you might have been dreading at the start of this book. But you know what? I think you probably feel a little better about things now. If you worked through the previous chapter thoroughly then you will have a pretty good picture of how things are going to work for you, and hopefully the fear factor should have reduced a little. Remember, everyone can master quantitative analysis, it's just a question of effort.

Anyway, this chapter is where you begin to actually look at the quantitative data you have collected. But I really hope you aren't looking at this chapter for the first time sitting next to a big pile of data that you have already collected! In fact I have named a section of this chapter specifically to stop you doing that. This is because it is extremely important that you have a good picture of *what* analysis you are going to perform before you go and collect your data. This is most clear from Chapters 6 and 7 about measurement – if you don't collect the right kinds of measures then you won't be able to perform the analysis you need to. However, this is the kind of stuff you learn through experience and not often from textbooks.

You'll also notice by the end of the chapter that you *still* haven't come across much information on the stuff you've probably heard more advanced students or colleagues discussing in hushed tones. You know, things like correlation, regression, ANOVA and all those arcane formulae. Well, that's because before you can go there, it's tremendously important you understand your data. As you'll see, you need to really know what your data looks like before you can justify which type of analysis you can perform on it. You should already have an inkling of this from the previous chapter, which will continue to grow as you become more comfortable with the underpinnings of statistical inference. *Then* you will be in a position to do quantitative analysis from a position of strength.

In this spirit, at the end of this chapter I really hope you have come to terms with these key ideas:

- The importance of computers in modern data analysis, and also the possible problems they cause.
- Why you need to think about analysing your data before you even think about collecting it.
- What **data cleaning** is, and why it is so important.
- How to describe your data using tables, figures, and numbers.
- What the **assumptions** of most statistical inference methods are, and how to test that your data fulfils them.

Why is it Important to Know This Stuff?

You should already have a good impression of why I believe it is important to understand the fundamentals of statistical inference. In fact by now I expect you to have a good idea as to why I think it is important to understand the theory which lies underneath research in general. And I also think you agree with me too, or else you would probably have given up reading this book. I certainly would have, I mean my jokes by themselves aren't good enough to sustain the book surely? Some people have told me they're not even that funny!

The things in this chapter are important because they support the inferential analysis you will do to test your hypothesis. This stuff isn't particularly 'theoretical' like the previous chapter, it's more practical, but without it your later theory tests don't make much sense. For example, lots of analysis methods (such as regression) rely on **assumptions** about your data. You need to see whether or not your data fulfils these assumptions. As well as this, you need to explore your data for all kinds of mundane things, such as mistakes in entry, or outliers (I'll explain this later). While this kind of thing might seem quite simplistic and not the high-level analysis you really want to be doing, it is essential to good analysis and reliable conclusions.

Perhaps even more importantly, doing the kinds of things I will talk about here will develop your intimate knowledge of your data, helping your confidence in what you have found and also improving your future research efforts. I know it sounds weird, but think of your data like your best friend; get to know it and its characteristics, care for it, try to understand and fix any problems with it. Actually, when you consider that the quality and trustworthiness of your findings and conclusions depends on your data set, it's not so weird after all. Look at Figure 13.1 for a conceptual representation of what you are trying to do here.

So what if you are not going to collect quantitative data? Well, I think it's still important to have a good understanding of this kind of thing. In fact the principles here are the same as those for qualitative data in essence. I also think all researchers need to understand how to treat quantitative data sets in order to evaluate whether or not *other* research has done so rigorously. In fact, qualitative researchers may often find themselves looking at large quantitative data sets such as national statistics and the like. So understanding how such sets should be described is very useful. You might also find that many researchers *don't* spend enough time on the things I am about to cover as they should.

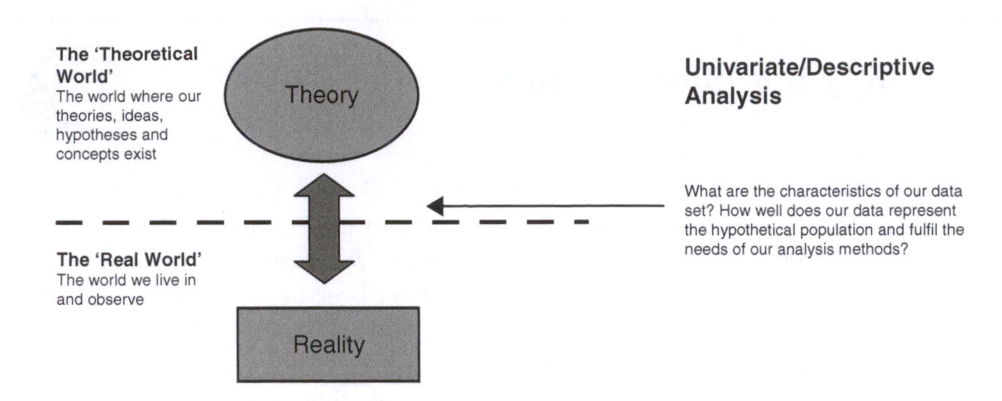

Figure 13.1 The place of preliminary analysis

Quantitative analysis software and 'the dark side'

Before I get into the real business, it's probably going to be useful to give you some words on statistical analysis software. Now I have already alluded to the fact that we hardly ever do analysis by hand anymore, and in fact I would argue that the advent of massive computing power in a package small and affordable enough for every social science researcher to have access to it has done more to improve the quality of social research than almost anything else. Any of us can do things in seconds now that would have taken days of highly technical hand computations only 50 years ago, and access to a mainframe maybe 20 years ago.[1] That said, some branches of science still need access to mainframes and days of analysis, in fact I have a friend who has moved universities primarily to gain regular access to an IBM mainframe (I think he just wants to challenge it at chess). So don't assume that *all* scientific analysis can be done on your average PC!

Unfortunately, there is a dark side to this massive power and ease of analysis. The dark side (just like in the 'Star Wars' movies) is the seductive and easy path, but it will only lead you astray. What I am talking about is that – because analysis is as simple as clicking a button these days – researchers do not spend enough time learning what is going on underneath their data, and inside their analysis methods. Furthermore, many researchers do not know enough about what their analysis results mean, and rely on simplistic 'rules of thumb' to tell them what their results mean. Some examples of this were given in the previous chapter, when I talked about statistical significance testing, and in the section about Type I and Type II error. Remember, you should never rely totally on anyone else to 'tell' you what to do

[1] In fact, some of my bosses still relate stories of doing the analysis for their Ph.D. using a mainframe at night, using punched cards! Actually, maybe not the punched cards part.

when it comes to analysis, and especially how to interpret the numbers. Go and find out for yourself the key issues and you will be a far stronger researcher (and will avoid many embarrassing situations). Even though 50 years ago analysis was much more difficult and time-consuming, you simply couldn't actually do it without really understanding what was happening inside the methods and also the data itself. Today, I could even teach a five-year-old the basic steps to do the same really complicated analyses – but that's not the same as being able to understand and interpret its results. Do not be seduced by the easy path of the 'dark side'! However, if you have got this far into the book, I hope you have learnt to respect and appreciate – maybe even enjoy – the fundamentals of research, what is really going on underneath the data we explore on the surface. If so, analysis software will probably be the most useful tool (outside your own brain) that you can ever learn to use for your career.

So with that out of the way, I feel more comfortable discussing software. One thing you need to understand is that there are many different pieces of software available, and it may be the case that you have to learn various different pieces in your time as a researcher. Some pieces of software are used because they are specialist analysis methods, for example, a program like LISREL can be used to perform a type of analysis called 'Structural Equation Modeling'. There are a number of competitors to this piece of software, but LISREL seems to be the most popular. Of course, with any piece of software, much of its popularity is due to embedded knowledge. For example, I took ages to learn how to use LISREL properly, so I don't have much interest in learning another piece of software unless it can do a lot more interesting stuff. You might find that such mundane factors as these are the main reasons for the use of various types of software in your department.

In terms of 'general' analysis software, I use a piece of software called SPSS, which seems to be quite popular. However, I am told by people (who take more of an interest in such things) that other software like STATA, SAS or S-PLUS is more powerful, and there is also a powerful piece of software called R which is free *and* powerful. So why don't I use them? Well, I have a copy of STATA, and have worked with S-PLUS with colleagues, as well as investigated R. They all look really great, but I've used SPSS since I was a graduate student, learnt how to program it in its own language, most of the people I work with use SPSS, the university has a site licence for SPSS so it costs me nothing – all of those completely humdrum reasons which have little to do with how good the software it. Furthermore, SPSS is very popular, and this means there is a vast variety of 'how-to' books which teach you the basics of analysis using SPSS, so self-teaching is pretty easy for most students. SPSS does what I need it to do (most of my heavy analysis gets done on LISREL) and I know it really well. The only reason I would change is if I needed to do something it could not, which I did do recently when I splurged a large amount of money on a copy of Statistica.

What I am saying is that the *choice* of software for the most part is not important in terms of what you can do. All of the big packages can do virtually everything you will need to do.

Oh, but one thing that I would not recommend is using Microsoft EXCEL for much. Admittedly, it can do some very pretty charts, but in terms of statistical analysis it is not that useful, and it seems to work in a very different way to most of the specialised statistical packages like SPSS. So I tend to avoid it for doing analysis. In my opinion, you should choose a piece of analysis software on one important criterion, once you know which software can do what you need to do. That criterion is *whether or not it is used by your department or supervisor*. Learning a new piece of software by yourself at the same time you are learning how to do analysis itself is a really hard thing to do. I think that if you have never used analysis software before then you should always look to begin with software which is known very well by your close colleagues or supervisor. Then you have a ready body of expertise to help you out. For example, my Ph.D. supervisor was (and is) an expert on LISREL, so if I had gone to him and asked to use EQS or AMOS (which do broadly the same thing) he couldn't have helped me with the software. Trying to learn that at the same time as learning how to do structural equation modelling would have been incredibly difficult.

The other key point to make about software is that you should be able to do almost everything I am mentioning in this book with *any* of the basic analysis packages – even though I talk in terms of SPSS and use those figures as examples. If something needs a specific package then I will mention this.

Preparing your data

Now, once you have your gleaming super-powerful new computer and a big fat pile of data next to you, what should you do? Well, if you are at that stage I can only hope that you have a lot of luck, because there are a few things you should have thought about **before collecting your data**. Now, a lot of the foundational and measurement things have already been discussed, so here I am going to deal with more practical issues.

The key thing you need to think about is how to enter your data into your analysis package in such a way that you can perform the analysis you need to. It's not really possible to give you examples of every situation you might find, so I am going to try to show you the basic principles of how to do this, and from there you can work things out for yourself more effectively. Your first task in this is to learn how to 'code' your data. Coding is the process of assigning each answer to your questionnaire a number.[2] Remember, quantitative research works with numbers, so you need to convert all of your data to numbers. In some cases, as in the example given in Figure 13.2, you can get your respondents to put numbers in for you. But more often you will get them to tick boxes or something similar. In this case you will have to 'code' the questionnaire yourself. Figure 13.3a shows a section of one of my

[2] I will use the term 'questionnaire' to refer to any type of quantitative data collection instrument you might be using – but this information is not just applicable to mail-out questionnaires, etc.

SECTION 1: YOUR FEELINGS ABOUT YOUR ORGANISATION AND YOUR JOB

1. Please use the following scale to indicate the extent to which the statements below describe how you feel (place the appropriate number in the relevant box). Please remember there are no right or wrong answers, and all data is confidential.

Strongly Disagree		Neither Agree nor Disagree		Strongly Agree
1	2	3	4	5

Your Role within the Firm

I feel certain about how much authority I have in my selling position ☐

I have clear, planned goals and objectives for my selling position ☐

I know that I have divided my time properly while performing the tasks connected with my selling ☐

I know what my responsibilities are in my selling position ☐

I know exactly what is expected of me in my selling position ☐

I receive clear explanations of what has to be done in my selling position ☐

Feelings about your job

When I perform well, I know it's because of my own desire to achieve ☐

I don't need a reason to sell; I sell because I want to ☐

Becoming successful in sales is something that I want to do for me ☐

If I were independently wealthy, I would still sell for the challenge of it ☐

I wish I didn't have to retire someday so I could always continue selling for the pleasure of it ☐

I sell because I cherish the feeling of performing a useful service ☐

If it weren't for the money, I would not be in a selling job ☐

I sell because I get paid to sell ☐

After a long, hard day, I realise that if it weren't for the money, I wouldn't put up with this job ☐

Feelings about your firm

I am willing to put in a great deal of effort beyond that normally expected in order to help this organisation be successful ☐

I talk up this organisation to my friends as a great organisation to work for ☐

I feel very little loyalty to this organisation

I would accept almost any type of job assignment in order to keep working for this organisation ☐

I find that my values and the organisation's values are very similar ☐

Figure 13.2 Example questionnaire

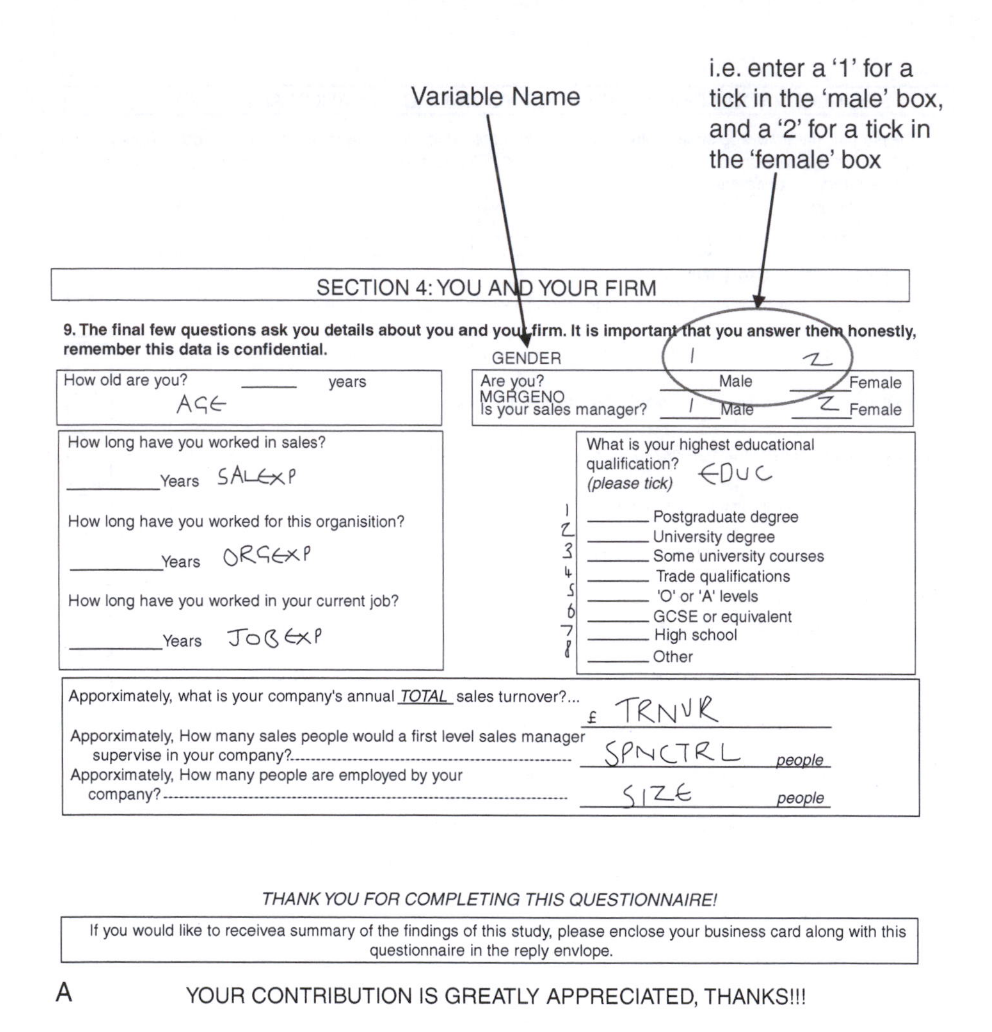

Figure 13.3a Section of a coded 'master' questionnaire

questionnaires which has been 'coded' by me, while Figure 13.3b shows the same sections which has been filled in by a respondent. One thing you should understand is that you don't need to code every questionnaire that comes back. That would be somewhat laborious! You simply have one 'master' questionnaire with the codes on it which you can refer to when you enter the data.

The next thing you need to think about is entering the data into your analysis package. Figure 13.4 shows a screenshot of SPSS with the section of data from Figure 13.3 entered into it. You'll notice a few things. Each questionnaire (called a **case)** runs *along a row* of the

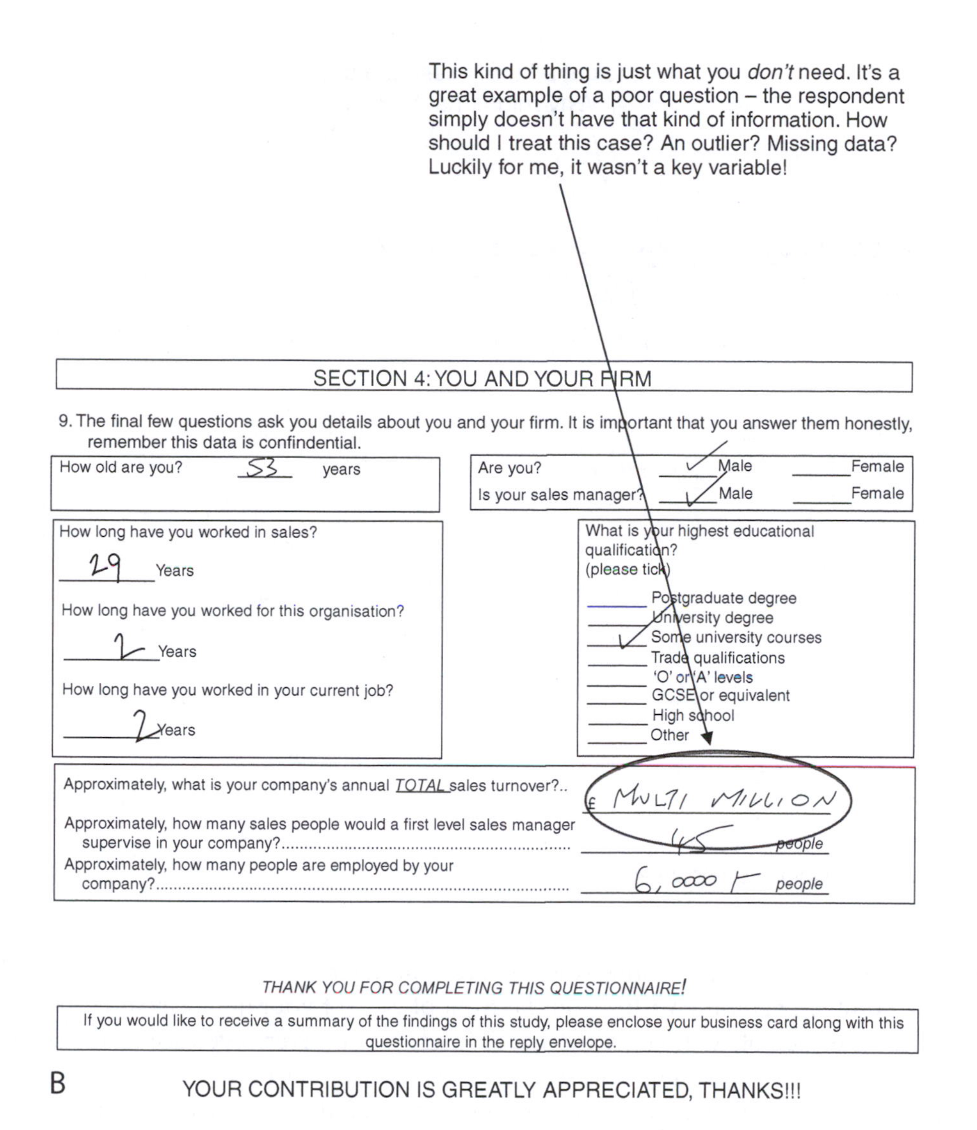
This kind of thing is just what you *don't* need. It's a great example of a poor question – the respondent simply doesn't have that kind of information. How should I treat this case? An outlier? Missing data? Luckily for me, it wasn't a key variable!

SECTION 4: YOU AND YOUR FIRM

9. The final few questions ask you details about you and your firm. It is important that you answer them honestly, remember this data is confindential.

How old are you? 53 years

Are you? ✓ Male ____ Female
Is your sales manager? ✓ Male ____ Female

How long have you worked in sales? 29 Years

How long have you worked for this organisation? 2 Years

How long have you worked in your current job? 2 Years

What is your highest educational qualification? (please tick)
____ Postgraduate degree
____ University degree
✓ Some university courses
____ Trade qualifications
____ 'O' or 'A' levels
____ GCSE or equivalent
____ High school
____ Other

Approximately, what is your company's annual *TOTAL* sales turnover?.. £ MULTI MILLION

Approximately, how many sales people would a first level sales manager supervise in your company?.................. 45 people

Approximately, how many people are employed by your company?.................. 6,0000 + people

THANK YOU FOR COMPLETING THIS QUESTIONNAIRE!

If you would like to receive a summary of the findings of this study, please enclose your business card along with this questionnaire in the reply envelope.

B

YOUR CONTRIBUTION IS GREATLY APPRECIATED, THANKS!!!

Figure 13.3b A filled-in questionnaire

spreadsheet, with the answers to each question running *down a column* of the spreadsheet. You should notice that the top of each column has been labelled with the same name as that in the master coded questionnaire.

You'll also notice an *extra* variable to the left of the spreadsheet, called **code**. This is a number of key importance, and something that many novice researchers forget about. Basically, this variable is a unique code number you give to every single questionnaire

Look at all that missing data!
Why might that be?

example data.sav - SPSS Data Editor

File Edit View Data Transform Analyze Graphs Utilities Window Help

8 : code 80.00

	code	age	gender	mgrgend	salexp	orgexp	jobexp	educ	trnvr	spnctrl	size	var
1	35.00	28.00	2.00	.	1.00	1.00	1.00	4.00	3303000.00	5.00	30.00	
2	68.00	24.00	2.00	.	3.50	2.00	2.00	2.00	.	9.00	.	
3	70.00	23.00	1.00	.	2.00	1.50	1.50	2.00	.	10.00	.	
4	79.00	24.00	1.00	.	2.00	2.00	2.00	2.00	300000000.0	9.00	2500.00	
5	81.00	54.00	1.00	.	30.00	20.00	20.00	7.00	.	8.00	.	
6	82.00	23.00	2.00	.	1.50	1.50	.50	2.00	.	10.00	.	
7	49.00	34.00	2.00	.	4.00	4.00	4.00	4.00	.	2.00	250.00	
8	80.00	24.00	1.00	.	3.00	1.00	1.00	2.00	100000000.0	9.00	.	
9	59.00	24.00	2.00	.	3.00	2.50	.50	2.00	.	8.00	.	
10	53.00	41.00	1.00	.	24.00	4.00	4.00	5.00	.	2.00	100.00	
11	52.00	30.00	1.00	.	5.00	2.50	2.50	5.00	.	2.00	.	
12	48.00	31.00	1.00	.	7.00	3.00	3.00	2.00	30000000.00	2.00	240.00	
13	54.00	28.00	2.00	.	1.00	2.00	2.00	5.00	.	2.00	.	
14	77.00	43.00	1.00	.	12.00	10.00	10.00	5.00	.	8.00	2000.00	
15	58.00	25.00	1.00	.	2.00	1.50	.50	2.00	70000000.00	9.00	1000.00	
16	47.00	45.00	1.00	.	10.00	7.00	4.00	2.00	.	2.00	.	
17	40.00	42.00	2.00	.	14.00	.50	.50	6.00	9000000.00	12.00	40.00	
18	11.00	38.00	1.00	.	16.00	1.00	1.00	2.00	10000000.00	12.00	48.00	
19	34.00	33.00	2.00	.	9.00	2.00	2.00	2.00	4000000.00	5.00	20.00	
20	37.00	26.00	2.00	.	7.00	7.00	7.00	3.00	5000000.00	10.00	32.00	
21	31.00	42.00	2.00	.	10.00	3.00	3.00	6.00	400000.00	2.00	6.00	
22	18.00	39.00	.	.	15.00	4.00	4.00	3.00	10000000.00	12.00	48.00	
23	15.00	30.00	1.00	.	2.00	12.00	2.00	6.00	10000000.00	12.00	48.00	
24	14.00	29.00	1.00	.	4.00	6.00	4.00	5.00	10000000.00	12.00	48.00	
25	16.00	62.00	1.00	.	26.00	18.00	18.00	4.00	10000000.00	12.00	48.00	

Data View / Variable View

SPSS Processor is ready

Figure 13.4 Example spreadsheet

before you send it out, for various reasons. Now in practical terms it can be as simple as writing a number beginning with '1' on the front of each of your questionnaires, but I have toyed with the idea of writing on the back, inside front cover, even using invisible ink! I'll explain why. The code number serves two very important purposes. The first purpose is only really relevant to mail-out surveys, and is to record who has and has not returned your questionnaires. Specifically, if you put the code number next to the individual you send the questionnaire out to, you can tick them off as they come back. Therefore, if you want to send out reminder cards, or another wave of questionnaires, to non-responders to increase the response rate, you know exactly who to send them to instead of having to send them to everyone again. However, in my experience, respondents sometimes see code numbers as some kind of suspicious way of finding out who they are. This can reduce their likelihood of response, which is why I toyed with the idea of 'hiding' the code number. That said, I have come to the conclusion that it is better to be upfront about it, and I now put it on the front cover with a small note which explains that it is only used for determining response numbers or something similar. However, since your data is now not truly 'anonymous' you should not pretend that it is. Instead you should be clear that your data is *confidential* and will remain so. In fact this is highly important to the ethics of your work.

But the code number is also highly useful for another reason. Basically, it allows you to match the actual physical questionnaire to the case in your spreadsheet. This is vital if you find some mistakes in data entry later on, and need to go back to the originals. Without some way of matching the case to the original questionnaire you have no way of checking what the actual value in the questionnaire is, so no way of reliably correcting your error. So, even if you don't need the code number for reasons of non-response analysis, you should code all your entered questionnaires at the very least before you enter them into the analysis package. As a final note regarding preparation, you should also make plans to *keep* your questionnaires for some time. My own motto is to keep the original data (not just the spreadsheet) until the publications which I planned to write from that data have been accepted (so far this means that I have boxes of data stretching back over six years now!) At the *very* least a research student needs to keep the original data until their exam, as the examiners have every right to ask to see it.[3] Also, you should **not** just chuck it in the bin when you are finished, especially if it is not anonymous. You should find some way of destroying it. This brings up the issue of data protection and ethics. In contemporary times, individuals and states have become considerably more careful about regulating the use of personal data. Once you collect data from individuals and institutions, you are entering this minefield. Therefore, make sure you make yourself knowledgeable about your legal and ethical responsibilities regarding the use of personal data in your institution and your country.

Cleaning your data and dealing with missing data

Of course, once your data is entered into the spreadsheet, the preparatory job is only half done (sometimes not even that). What you need to do is **clean** that data. What cleaning means is exploring the data for mistakes and errors, which can be made both by you and by the people that filled in the questionnaire. You will also need to decide what to do when a respondent has missed answering some of your questions.

The first stage of this will be done usually while you are entering the data. You might find that a respondent has made an error in their response when you are entering the data. This is very seldom easy to deal with, and you basically have two choices. You could either leave that piece of data out (treat it as missing), or try to make an assumption about what the respondent 'meant' to say. The safest option is to treat that piece of data as missing. However, in our constant quest for more data, we usually want to somehow include as

[3]They hardly ever do, but you never know.

much data as possible. In this case you need to decide whether it is reasonably justifiable to make an assumption about the data. For example, if on a 5-point scale a respondent has entered '7', is this a piece of poor writing and they wanted to enter a '1', or are they making a point that their opinion is even more strong than '5', or did they just make an error? Each one of those conclusions implies a different intended response, and thus a different way of 'correcting' the error. Usually, the best way of dealing with this is to use your judgement at first, rejecting all those data points which are impossible to interpret. After this, you should make a decision in conjunction with someone like your supervisor or a colleague who has a more impartial point of view.

Once you have entered your data, you need to check it for errors in entry. Now I know that if you are anything like me, you will think that you are so great that you couldn't *possibly* have made an error in your data entry. Nevertheless, unless you entered something like 10 questionnaires of 10 items each, I guarantee that you will have made an error. In fact I am so sure of this that, if you can prove you haven't made an error, I will give you your money back on this book.[4] The process of checking for errors and the like is called **data cleaning**. I used to absolutely hate data cleaning, and to be honest it is still one of my least favourite parts of analysis. In fact, I tried to avoid it as much as possible, particularly as I rose through the ranks of academia, thinking it was a mundane task which I was *far* too busy and important to do. However, when I worked on a project with an internationally renowned professor (Felix Brodbeck in fact, who wrote the introductory viewpoint for this very chapter), I was amazed to be invited to his house for the evening, along with one of his Ph.D. students (Yves Guilliaume, who wrote the corresponding 'View from the trenches' here) who was also working with us, to sit around his computer and clean the entire data set! This involved about five hours, two packets of cigarettes, and almost four pots of coffee, as we all sat there, going through the data set in minute detail. *Wow*, that really gave me a wake-up call: if even this really important guy took data cleaning so seriously then I better do so as well. Of course, this makes perfect sense, and I alluded to it earlier. Your data is one of the key impacts on your success, so treat it as such. Cleaning the data allows you to firstly get all those errors out of the data, but it also lets you get to know the data – remember, like your best friend. So why would you ignore this stage, or leave it to a research assistant?

The actual process of data cleaning is pretty simple. Go through the data looking for mistakes in entry. One good way of doing this is to do frequency tables of each question (see below). In fact, you can combine the data cleaning process with the descriptive analysis process I talk about below. For example, if you tabulate a 5-point scale, and there is one item with a '33' in it, you know you have a problem of some kind. You then need to look through the data set to work out which case the mistake is in. Most software has a

[4] Not really.

'find' function, which simplifies the process. So it's usually easy to find the mistakes, the problem is what to do about them. You need to decide whether it is a genuine error that you made in entry, or something else (e.g. some of the other errors I talked about above). Sometimes this is easy – e.g. you see a '33' entered on a 5-point scale. Most of the time this means that you hit 3 twice. So go back to the original questionnaires and see if this is the case. It's at about this point that you will regret not giving your questionnaires a code number, meaning it's impossible to find the questionnaire and be sure of what error you have made.

Describing your data

Once we have cleaned the data, we can begin to analyse it. The first stage of analysis is sometimes called **univariate** analysis, because it deals with the variables one-by-one. I tend to call it **descriptive** analysis, because it is used to describe the characteristics of your data. You will probably use some of these techniques in the data cleaning process above – particularly the tables in the next section. Descriptive analysis is a vital part of getting to know your data, and understanding how it might behave in later analysis, as well as deciding whether or not your data is of 'good quality' or not. I'll be discussing some of the uses of these techniques at the end of the chapter, but for now lets focus on the 'hows', not the 'whys'.

Describing your data with tables

The most basic form of descriptive analysis is the frequency table. Figure 13.5 shows a frequency table for one of the variables in the questionnaire I presented in Figure 13.3. You can see that this table describes the education level of the respondents. The 'frequency' column shows the raw amounts of cases in each valid category (e.g. Seven people's highest qualification was high school), as well as the amount of people who did not answer the question, in the 'missing' section (there are 10 here). There are three columns which describe the percentages. The first 'per cent' column includes the missing values in the 100 per cent, while the 'valid per cent' does not. So as you can see there are slightly different values here. The 'cumulative per cent' works with the valid percentages to show the contribution each category makes to the whole. It's not really that useful unless you are dealing with 'ordered' data. Sometimes you might want to group categories however. For example, imagine that you had asked people to write their age down in years. In this case you might have 50 or 60 unique categories, each with only a few cases in it. This wouldn't provide much information for you. Instead you might want to **group** your data into fewer categories (e.g. 10–20, 21–30, 31–40, etc.) You must be careful though that your categories do not overlap, and are also exhaustive in that they are able to collect every possible value in the questionnaire. IDE 13.1 discusses this in some more depth.

Level of Education

		Frequency	Per cent	Valid Per cent	Cumulative Per cent
Valid	University Degree	24	16.9	18.2	18.2
	Some University	8	5.6	6.1	24.2
	Trade Quals	25	17.6	18.9	43.2
	O or A-levels	36	25.4	27.3	70.5
	GCSE/equivalent	21	14.8	15.9	86.4
	High School	7	4.9	5.3	91.7
	Other	11	7.7	8.3	100.0
	Total	132	93.0	100.0	
Missing	System	10	7.0		
Total		142	100.0		

Figure 13.5 Frequency table

IDE 13.1: Thinking About Data Before Collecting it

The example about asking people to give you their age in years, and then grouping it for analysis, is a perfect example of why you should carefully consider what you are going to do with your data before collecting it. Let me explain. We know that people are less likely to answer a personal question such as 'what is your age' if we ask them to give the actual number. So asking for this will reduce our response rate. Fact. On the other hand, we get more detailed and precise information about the proportion of the sample that does respond. *However*, when grouping the data we throw out that extra information. This implies we never needed to ask for it in the first place! So we could instead have designed a question which actually asked the respondents to indicate which *age group* they were a part of. This would have given us as much information as we needed, *and* increased our response rate when compared to asking a respondent their actual age. If we had realised that later on we were just going to group the data, *before* we designed the questionnaire, we would have avoided unnecessarily reducing the response rate by asking for detailed information which we wouldn't even be using. We would also have made our later analysis task easier as the groups would have been pre-designed for us. The point I am making here is that you need to have a decent picture of how you are going to use your data before collecting it, or you may collect at best unnecessary data, and at worst not collect something you need. In fact, a worse situation would be to collect grouped age data when you really needed raw age data. There is no way of converting grouped age data to raw age data at all.

There are of course many other options for creating tables of your data, but Figure 13.5 shows the key information that you need to be aware of.

Describing your data with pictures

Although frequency tables are useful for some purposes, most people find it easier to comprehend a data set in visual terms – i.e. by using some form of picture. However, different types of data require us to use different types of pictorial representation. If you think back to Chapter 6, I talked about different scales of measurement (nominal, ordinal, interval, ratio). For nominal data, there is no order to the numbers, so a graph can only represent the relative sizes of each of the groups. In this case we would use a pie chart (Figure 13.6a) or a bar chart (Figure 13.6b) to represent them – as has been done here in the case of gender. We should also use these types of charts to display ordinal variables. Notice that for the bar chart in Figure 13.6b, there is a *gap* between the bars. I'll discuss this in a short while.

If you move to displaying data which is measured in interval or ratio format, you can instead use a **histogram** to display it, as in Figure 13.7, which displays some scale data from a single item of a 1–5 Likert scale to measure job satisfaction.[5] Now it took me a very long

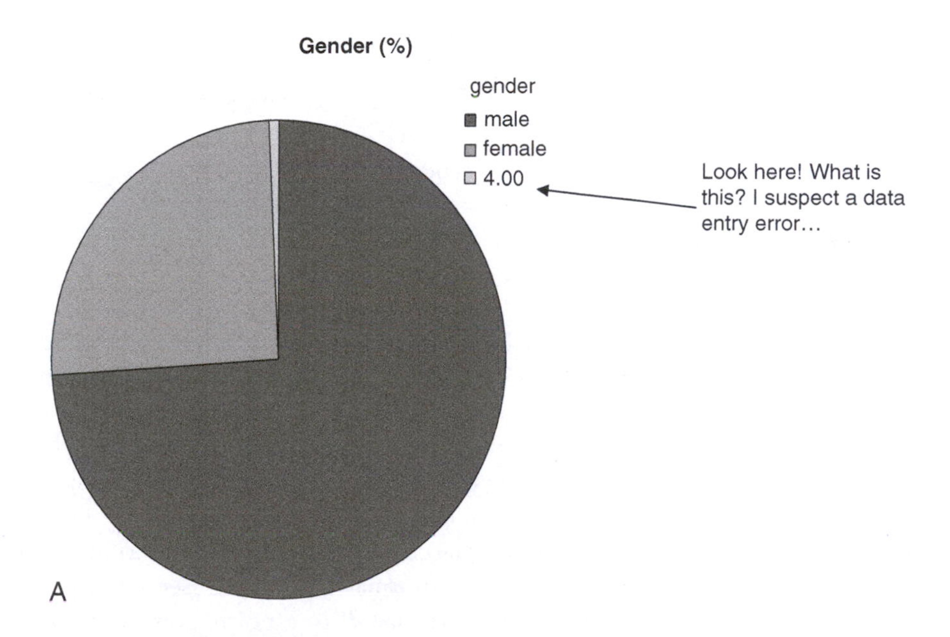

Figure 13.6a Pie chart of gender

[5]The concepts discussed in Chapters 6 and 7 are highly relevant here, so go back and study them if you don't clearly understand what is happening.

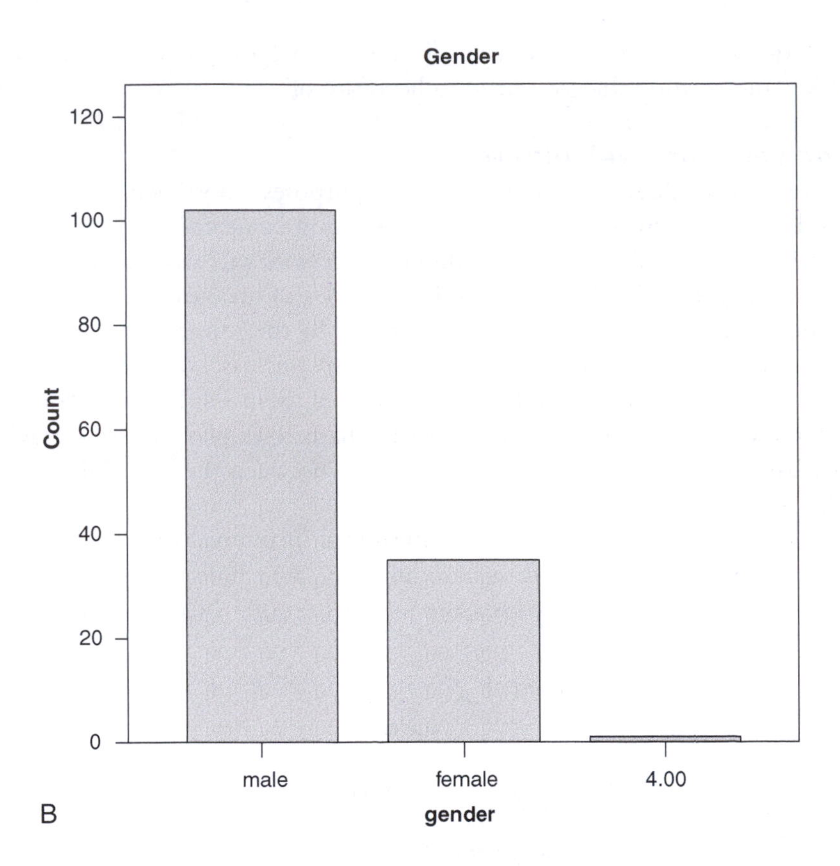

Figure 13.6b Bar chart of gender

time to work out the difference between a bar chart and a histogram, but you should be able to see it quite clearly – the bars on a histogram have no gaps between them. This implies that the discrete scale values are just categories of an underlying continuous variable (go back to the previous chapter if you don't understand the idea of a continuous variable). This makes sense, as in this case we are artificially cutting the underlying concept of job satisfaction into five 'slices' to both ease the task of the respondent, and our own analysis job. This is made even clearer by the fact that the software has placed a continuous distribution over the top of the histogram. This distribution is essentially a normal distribution (see Chapter 12), and gives you a quick picture of how close your own data is to a normal distribution. I'll talk about why this is important later on (although I imagine you already have an inkling), but in this case we can see that the data isn't too far away apart from being a little skewed towards the higher values.

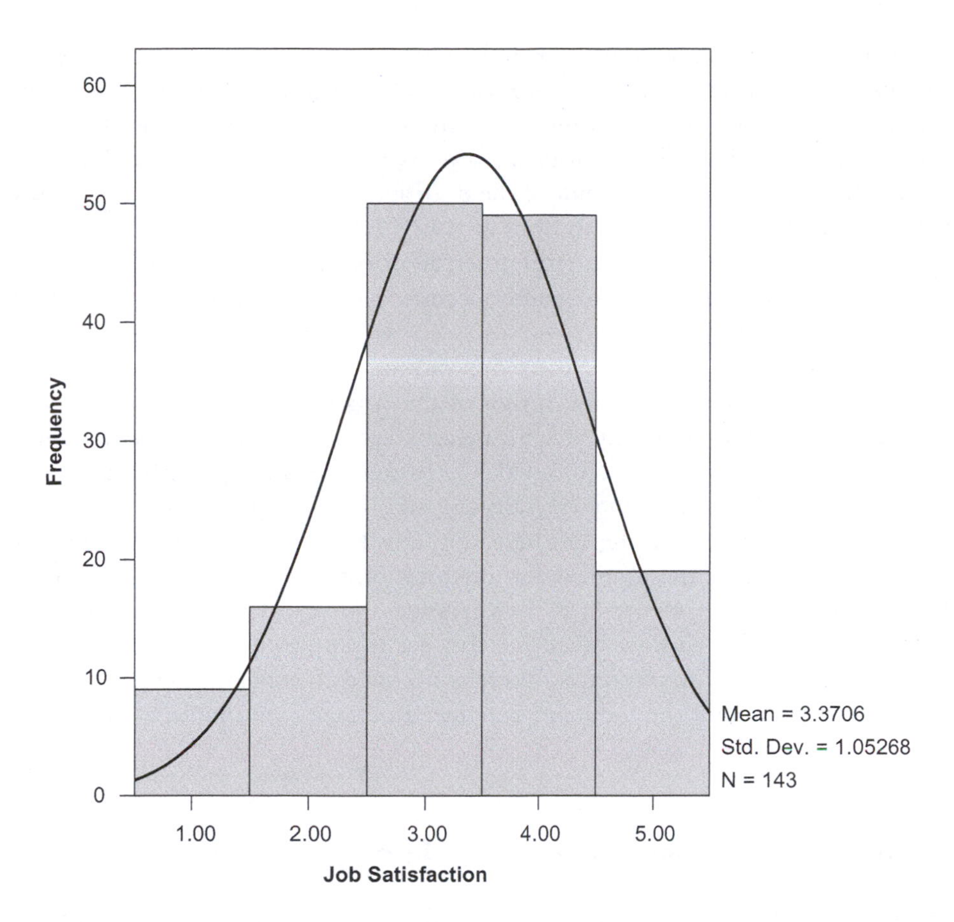

Figure 13.7 Histogram of job satisfaction item

Describing your data with summary numbers

As well as pictures and tables, we also use numbers to describe the characteristics of our data. In the previous chapter, I talked about the importance of measures of central tendency and variation to later analysis. So it should come as no surprise that these two measures are key in the present context.

In terms of central tendency, three main different values are relevant. Of course, you should already know that different scales of measurement restrict us to using some types of measures here. The **arithmetic mean** is the sum of all the values, divided by the number of cases. We usually refer to this as simply the **mean**, but we should really specify the 'arithmetic' part, as there are other types of means, such as the *geometric*, and *harmonic*. Sometimes it is referred to as the 'average', but this term could mean anything, so let's not use it, OK? You can only use the mean on interval or ratio data.[6] While the arithmetic mean is a powerful value, it is rather vulnerable to **outliers**, or extreme values of the variable. I'll talk about outliers more later on, but if it is a problem, you might want to use the **median** instead of the mean. The median is the midpoint of the distribution. Imagine if you lay all the values out in order from highest to lowest in front of you. Finding the centre of this would be the median. You can use the median on ratio, interval, or ordinal data. Finally we come to the **mode**, which is simply the most frequently occurring value. It's not much, but it's all we can do with nominal data.

Moving to variation in the data, there are various different ways of getting a picture of this. The most obvious one is the **range** of the data – or the difference between the highest and lowest values. Unfortunately, it is easy to see how the range can be influenced by outliers. One way of getting around this is to use the **interquartile range**. This is created by dividing the data set into quarters and taking the range between the start of the second quarter, and the end of the third quarter. This then ignores outliers. However, we don't often use either of these ranges for anything other than getting a basic picture of the data. What's far more important is the **variance** and **standard deviation** of the data set. These basically tell you how much the data set varies around the mean, and both of them were discussed in Chapter 12, so there is no need to repeat it here. They are both influenced by outliers, but the influence is reduced because you divide by the number of cases.

Assessing the characteristics of your data

Already, I have given you some ideas of how you use the information you get from descriptive analysis. First of all you can use it to help clean the data. Secondly, it is useful to get a 'feel' for the data set, and develop your knowledge of it. But most importantly is a third task, that of assessing whether your data is appropriate to the analysis tasks you have in mind for it. More specifically, most analysis techniques rely on certain **assumptions** about the data you are feeding into it, as well as the underlying variables in the population. These assumptions have been alluded to quite often so far. For example, in Chapter 6 I talked about levels of measurement, and in Chapter 12 I talked about the normal distribution. This section will detail the key things you need to think about when you do many common forms of analysis. Of course, it is impossible to set out the key assumptions of *every* type of analysis, but you should be able to gain a good working knowledge of the basics here.

[6]That said, sometimes you will see it used on what is strictly ordinal data – like the Likert-type scale data we have already talked about.

Assumptions to consider

When you perform quantitative analysis, you implicitly accept a number of things. I have talked about a number of these things in previous chapters; philosophical things like our beliefs about reality and knowledge. But that's not really what I mean when I talk here about 'assumptions' of quantitative analysis. No, here I am talking about the assumptions about your data that you must make when you want to conduct statistical inference itself. The basic ideas behind many of these were discussed in the previous chapter, such as the central limit theorem (remember what that is?). Without assuming the sampling distribution of statistics like the mean, the idea of statistical inference simply doesn't make sense. However, drawing from this, there are some other overarching assumptions about the data itself which you need to consider before you even go forward to further analysis. These assumptions apply to what are called **parametric tests**, which are the main thing we are dealing with for the rest of this chapter and the next. The difference between parametric and **non-parametric** tests caused me no end of confusion when I began to learn about statistics (almost as much as Type I and Type II error), so IDE 13.2 provides a brief discussion of the differences.

IDE 13.2: Parametric and Non-Parametric Statistics

The concept of 'parametric' statistical tests refers to our assumptions about the underlying distribution of a given variable in the population. The key concept here is the normal distribution. If you go back and review Chapter 12, you should get the idea that we ideally need to know the population distribution of any given variable in order to make judgements as to how likely or unlikely a given statistic is to occur in a sample. For example, we know that if our variable is normally distributed in the underlying population, then if we draw a number of samples (say 100) of equal size from that population, and compute the means of each of those samples, the distribution of the sample means will be close to a normal distribution. If you remember Chapter 12, you'll also realise that this allows us to calculate the probability that the mean of any single sample is different from our hypothesised population mean. Furthermore, even if we are unable to assume the variable is normally distributed in the sample, the central limit theorem allows us to assume that the sampling distribution of the variable is normal even if we suspect that the population distribution is not – but only if our sample is large enough. Furthermore, if we wish to estimate the mean of any given variable, it must be measured at least at an interval level (see Chapter 6).

But if you are unable to make these assumptions (which are discussed in more detail in the main text), you are unable to utilise either any information about the underlying population distribution, the sampling distribution, or take the mean. One such situation may be where you have a small sample of a variable which you do not expect to be normally distributed in the population. In such a case the central limit theorem falls down. Or you may have only ordinal or nominal data for your variable(s) of interest. In fact, it is surprisingly common to be in some of these situations. To deal with them, statisticians developed what are called non-parametric, or **distribution-free** methods. You'll usually find that there is a non-parametric method for almost every parametric method. You might be wondering why we don't use non-parametric methods as a rule – and avoid having to make these (sometimes less-than-entirely-plausible) assumptions. Well, as a rule, non-parametric methods are less powerful than parametric ones (that's the trade-off you see). Furthermore, different non-parametric tests tend to be sensitive to different quirks of your data, so in some cases you would need to use multiple tests to try to understand what's going on. Also, it's ironic (to me at least) that non-parametric methods – which have relatively simple requirements for the data – seem to be generally more complex to perform and interpret.

First and absolutely foremost is that your data is **normally distributed**. By now you should be pretty comfortable with the idea of normal distribution, and are probably totally bored with it. Nevertheless, you should also have an appreciation as to why it is so important. First, we need to check that every single one of our variables is normally distributed, or at least close to it. Many researchers simply use the histogram with the normal distribution (like Figure 13.7), if they even do anything, and check roughly whether it 'looks' normal. This is not really good enough by itself – although it's a good start. You should also at a minimum check the values of **skewness** and **kurtosis**. Skewness is a measure which shows how far to the left or right of the middle the mean of your variable is, and kurtosis measures how flat or pointed (compared to the normal) your distribution is. For a perfect normal distribution, both should be 0. The further from 0 you get (positive or negative), the worse your distribution is. But how far is too far? Well, one way of working this out is to convert the scores into standardised z-scores. Remember we did this with means in the previous chapter? We can do it with skewness and kurtosis in exactly the same way – the sample value minus the hypothesised population value, all divided by the sample standard error.[7] So, you should already have worked out that if we return a z value of above or below 1.96, then we need to reject our null hypothesis (at a 95 per cent level of significance) that the population is normally distributed. This would be bad. However, if you have a small sample size, you might want to increase your level of significance as you have less

[7]Think about what the hypothesised population value should be – in this case, it's 0 as we hypothesise a normal population distribution.

power to detect differences. Conversely, if you have a very large sample size, you may wish to place more emphasis on judgement than statistical testing (as the increased power may result in trivial divergence from a normal distribution being found to be statistically significant).[8]

You also need to check the **variance** of your data. The first thing to do is purely descriptive. Simply put, each one of the variables you are going to employ in your analysis actually needs to vary! This seems a bit of a no-brainer, but you would be surprised that it can be a problem quite often. Imagine the question regarding 'education' in Figure 13.3. So what I want to do is see whether higher values of this variable (i.e. more education) might be associated with higher levels of performance. So what if every single respondent has ticked the lowest level? There is utterly no way of seeing whether performance is associated with variation in the education variable, as there *is* no variation in the education variable – whatever respondents score on performance, they have all scored the same on education. I realise this is an extreme example, but it does happen. For example, you can often find that poorly designed Likert-type scales can have almost all responses clustered at one extreme or the other. I have actually seen this happen in real data, collected at some expense by a close friend. Again, you can check this by simply looking at the histograms of each variable, at the same time as you look at the skewness and kurtosis. However, you also need to check a statistical assumption regarding variance, the **homogeneity of variance**. This means that the variance of your data needs to be the same throughout your data – however you divide it up. For example, if you are testing different groups (e.g. males and females) you need to test the assumption that each of these samples comes from populations of equal variance. Or if you are running correlations, the variance of one variable must be the same at all levels of the other variable. This is quite a confusing thing to come to grips with, and to make things more confusing the different types of tests tend to have different ways of looking for it. As a consequence, we will leave further discussion of this until the next chapter.

There are two or three (depending on your intended analysis method) more assumptions you need to check out if you are using parametric statistical methods. Unfortunately, there are no numerical 'hard and fast' ways of checking these assumptions, you have to use judgement. Firstly, you need to ensure that your data is measured at least at the **interval** scale of measurement (go back to Chapter 6 if this isn't making sense). Whether you need all of your data measured at interval level, or only the dependent variable is determined by the specific analysis tool you are using, so it will be covered in the next chapter. You also need to judge whether your data fulfils the **independence** assumption. In other words, data from each participant should be independent, in that respondents are unable to influence the responses of others in the study. This is a research design issue which you needed to think about

[8] If you don't understand the concept of power, go back to the previous chapter where it is introduced.

before collecting your data, though (what, you're reading this *after* collecting your data?!) Finally, you need to determine whether your analysis technique relies on an assumption of **linearity**. This means that the relationship between the variables in your model can be represented by a straight line, rather than a curved one. If you have hypothesised a curved relationship (for example as stress increases, performance increases up to a point, beyond which increased stress results in a decrease in performance), then a technique which relies on the linearity assumption will at best underestimate any relationship. At worst, it won't even detect a relationship. Again, this will be covered in a bit more detail in the next chapter.

As a final note on assumptions, you should also be aware of how **robust** your chosen analysis method is to what are called **departures** from the assumptions. A departure from an assumption means that the data doesn't fulfil the assumption to some degree, which could be greater or lesser (e.g. the distribution could be non-normal to a high degree, or a lower degree). The robustness of a given method is a judgement regarding how much the departure from the assumption is likely to influence the results of that technique. So for example, if your data is non-normally distributed, is this likely to seriously bias your results? Some techniques are quite robust, so you don't necessarily need your data to be perfect, but others are not robust, and need you to feed in data of a very high quality. Each method has its own unique characteristics, and you should find these out before using it.

Outliers

You should also check your data set for **outliers**. Outliers are extreme values of a variable, and we already know that they bias the mean and variance scores of your data set. However, there are two types of outlier. Type one is a simple mistake in entry. For example, we saw earlier that you might inadvertently enter a '33' when you meant to enter a '3' for a 5-point scale. There's no debate about what to do here, just somehow fix it! In fact, where your variables have defined ranges (e.g. 1–5), outliers are always mistakes of some kind.

However, sometimes we have variables without explicit ranges. Go back to Figure 13.3a and b. You can see that some of the variables are open-ended in terms of their range. For example, it is feasible that one or two respondents may be much younger or much older than others – these would be outliers. Much more likely is that a few respondents will have either very large or very small values of a variable such as 'firm turnover'. In fact you can see that the respondent in Figure 13.3b has put 'multi million' down here. If all my other respondents are from small business then we have a rather problematic outlier, which will influence any analysis of that variable. In such a situation you need to make some decisions about what to do with this case.

First of all, are you going to specifically use that variable? In the case of the particular research project which the questionnaire from Figure 13.3 comes from, the turnover variable was simply for descriptive purposes, to see what the sample characteristics were. I didn't intend to actually use it in my hypotheses. So the outlier wasn't an analytic problem. However, if one of my hypotheses included firm turnover, it would have become a problem. In this case I have two choices – delete the entire case which the outlier occurs in, or do not. Many sources recommend deletion, on the grounds that outliers unduly influence the results of analysis. However, you then give yourself a conceptual problem. Are your results now generalisable to companies with very large turnover? It could be argued that you have reduced the generalisability of your findings by deleting some genuine data (remember, the outlier is not a mistake, it is real data). My own feeling is that you should be very careful about deleting outliers which are not obvious mistakes, and you should *always* consider the conceptual implications of deletion as well as the statistical ones. Ultimately, the nicest, cleanest statistical results are meaningless if they bear no relation to the real world. And unfortunately, the real world is a messy place.

Summary

Your enjoyment of this chapter was probably directly related to whether or not you understood the material covered in Chapter 12. If you did, then most of this should have made perfect sense. If not, then I imagine that you understood the words, but couldn't work out *why* we would want to do these things. As I have repeatedly stressed, understanding why is the key to performing good analysis consistently, and also being able to work out for yourself what to do and why. Remember, it's no good relying on somebody else to tell you what to do – what if they are wrong?[9] Or what if you get asked to explain what you did? I shudder to think. I repeat, if you aren't comfortable, go back and work through the last two chapters until you *are* comfortable. Ask your colleagues as well, sometimes they can help you understand.

The material in this chapter is usually thought of as the most tedious and boring part of analysis. This is not surprising, since normally you are excited about testing your hypotheses and things like that, so you want to get to *that* stage as quickly as possible. I have certainly been guilty of that in the past. But it's a big mistake to ignore data cleaning and descriptive analysis, and I have tried very hard to show this. On a purely practical level, you need to be certain that the results of your hypothesis tests are not due to strange characteristics in your data (e.g. outliers). Thoroughly cleaning and describing your data set is the only way you can be sure of this. Furthermore, for the uninitiated, these kinds of analyses actually provide a very 'friendly' introduction to the numbers game – which is quantitative analysis. But remember, this chapter is but an introduction, and I could never say that it was the last word on this kind of thing, so go and read more if you need to.

---

[9] And yes, even your supervisor, or articles published in top journals, can be wrong.

Key points to take from this chapter:

- Computers have made quantitative data analysis many times easier in recent times. Most software packages do similar things, so choose one where there is ready expertise around your department (but not Excel[10]).
- However, don't rely on the software too much, you need to understand what is going on underneath to make sure you are doing the right things.
- Make sure you think about your analysis *before* collecting your data, particularly in terms of how you will enter it into the spreadsheet.
- **Always** make sure you spend time thoroughly cleaning your data before analysing it.
- Following this, you should describe your data. You can use tables, graphs, and summary numbers to do this, depending on what is appropriate.
- Most statistical analyses rely on a set of assumptions about your data, such as normality, independence, and homogeneity of variance. You need to use descriptive analysis to check for these assumptions before going further.
- Outliers are a thorny issue. Sometimes it is appropriate to delete them, but you need to make sure you know the implications of doing so – both in a conceptual and statistical sense.

Further reading

Most of the books I referred to in the previous chapter are also highly useful here, so I won't repeat them, but one additional book which you might find helpful is:

- *Discovering Statistics Using SPSS* by Andy Field: This book is huge! But it is also an excellent introduction into the world of quantitative data analysis, and also takes you step-by-step through the required processes on SPSS to get results. What's more, Field has an engaging writing style which is full of humour (you can judge for yourself whether he is funnier than me ...).

EXERCISES

1. Go and do a small survey of your departmental colleagues. Ask them what statistical analysis software they use, and why. Try to decide which is the most commonly used package. Also, determine the general reasons why people use that package. Are they practical, statistical, political, or otherwise?
2. Look at Figure 13.8, it is a page of a questionnaire. Decide how you would code and enter that data into an analysis package like SPSS.
3. What effects are outliers likely to have on your descriptive analyses?
4. What are the key considerations you need to take account of when deciding whether or not to remove outliers?
5. Explain clearly the difference between parametric and non-parametric statistical analysis.

[10] Sorry Mr Gates, but I just don't think Excel is designed for this kind of thing. Please don't sue me.

1. What is your age?____________________ years

2. What is your gender? *Please tick.* Y Male Y Female

3. How much do you enjoy MARK 203? *Please tick one box.*

It sucks! 1	2	3	4	It's average 5	6	7	8	It's superb! 9

4. On average, how much have you enjoyed/are enjoying the other Marketing options you have taken or are taking? *Please tick one box.*

They sucked! 1	2	3	4	They were average 5	6	7	8	They were superb! 9

Figure 13.8 MARK 203 Course satisfaction questionnaire

6. Imagine you have a set of data from the questionnaire in Figure 13.8 containing 65 cases. You want to see whether the value for Question 3 is suitable for later statistical analysis. Your sample data has a mean of 4.5, and a standard deviation of 0.3. Your first check is for normality. You get values of 1.5 for kurtosis, and 1.9 for skewness. Do these values suggest that the distribution for Q3 is significantly non-normal (with a 95 per cent significance level)? How would you interpret these results?
7. Now you have begun to delve into the wonders of playing with quantitative data, I can imagine you are quite excited. I think you should go outside for a bit, play a sport for example. Analysis can get addicting, so make sure to get outside once in a while!

Chapter 14
Quantitative data analysis II

SUPERVISOR'S VIEW: PROFESSOR MARNIK G. DEKIMPE

I'm a marketing professor, so when using my own experience to shed some light on the general ideas in this chapter, I may be biased somewhat by recent developments in that field. However, having published also in other areas (such as finance, human resource management, and public policy), I feel these developments are not unlike those in many other business domains. As such, my insights may also be of (some) relevance to readers outside the marketing discipline. At the very least, we all think we know something about marketing. Indeed, we are all consumers, we are all bombarded with advertising messages, and we all have seen hundreds of promotions during our supermarket visits. Likewise, we are all used to applying models. Indeed, we all have a mental model of how the world works, we use an implicit model to anticipate how others will react to what we are communicating, we have a mental model on what would be a reasonable price to pay for a given good or service, and we are upset (or pleasantly surprised) if the actual price deviates from this expectation. Yet, if we put the two words together to form ***Marketing Models***, many people (whether they are managers, students or just interested customers) tune out, and argue that this is something for marketing academics working from their ivory tower, or for marketing consultants trying to make some extra money by using incomprehensible jargon. However, before tuning out, it is important to keep the following things in mind:

- As this chapter shows: *it does not take long to take the fear out of quantitative analysis.* Just try it, and before long, you will have great fun 'playing' with data.
- *Don't try to run before you can walk*: don't start out with the most complicated Bayesian learning or structural equation models you can find in the recent academic literature. Oftentimes, simple correlations and regression models will already get you many (if not most) insights. As you become more experienced, you will automatically start to appreciate the added benefits of more complicated models.

- The need for quantitative analysis will only increase in the years to come: more and more marketing data become available (on more and more products, from more and more competitors, in more and more markets), making it harder to comprehend what is really going on in the marketplace based just on gut feeling or intuition. Hence, you may as well jump on this train (which will not stop, I can assure you) early on, rather than being left behind by your competitors.
- Indeed, just as there is a digital divide, there will be a *data modelling divide* (which will only become wider) between those that benefit from the added advantages careful data analysis provides, and those left in the dark. What side do you want to be on?
- However, if you are a manager, don't fear that you will become redundant. *Models are not meant to replace managers.* They are there to help managers make better-informed decisions. Managers should identify the problem and keep a strong input in how the model is developed (you don't want modellers to get carried away and solve the wrong problem), and (most importantly) should be the ones to put the model to good use. Even if you don't have the time, energy, or interest to develop models yourself, it pays to know some basics, and to know how to communicate with hard-core modellers.

The recent data explosion in marketing (just think of the wealth of data becoming available through consumer panels, or of the richness of retail scanner data) will create numerous opportunities for the modern marketing manager and researcher, and the situation is similar in many other fields of study. Quantitative analysis and marketing models help to seize these opportunities to the fullest. Nowadays is a good time to be in marketing (or business in general), especially if you know your numbers!

VIEW FROM THE TRENCHES: DR. ERIK MOOI

There's no such thing as doing a 'quantitative analysis'! There are many types of quantitative analysis including techniques like regression analysis and principal components analysis, which all serve a different purpose. During my own Ph.D. I had to do about a year of coursework – learning about all kinds of different quantitative techniques – before I really started with my own research. During this period I probably thought this was a waste of time as I would only use one or two techniques at most. Well, in retrospect I can probably see the point much better.

One important benefit is that having a reasonable overview of many of the techniques that are out there helps you pick the right method for the task. It also helps hugely when you read articles to be able to understand what they have done, even if you don't have all the details. Also, it can help you in writing a more balanced thesis that uses multiple methods to cover the same, or different, questions. That should help in starting an academic career successfully, as under the pressure of publishing afterwards you'll have little time to read up on your methods skills after finishing your Ph.D. So perhaps, it wasn't a waste of time after all!

So, we are racing at great speed towards the end of this book now, and if you are reading it cover-to-cover (well done by the way) you should be seeing the light at the end of the tunnel. But, just to continue the cliché, you know that it is always darkest just before the dawn.[1] For many of you, this chapter will cover the stuff you've really been dreading. In fact, I guess if I am honest I have been dreading writing it too! But really, it's not that scary when you think about it. In fact, this chapter will stay away from the complex formulae and mathematics of analysis, and focus very much on the underlying logic and use of these techniques.

I reason that most of you will be using a computer to do the 'leg work' of analysis, and that if you need to know the formulae, you can go and find far better sources than this to go through them (written by people who actually know them, unlike me). You may think that this is inconsistent with the discussion in the previous chapter about the dangers of software, but that's not quite the case. In fact, it's the logic and theory behind the analysis methods which is most important to learn about and understand, not the actual mathematical formulae. Knowing when and how to use different analysis techniques, and why, is vital to your success in my opinion.

The chapter will be structured in such a way as to help you understand the two main traditions of quantitative analysis. We'll begin with some very basic concepts, and then split into two approaches: (a) the search for associations, and (b) the search for differences. As I will discuss, both these traditions are more or less popular in different fields of research, meaning that sometimes a student does not get a lot of information on one or the other.[2] Following this, I'll go through some important concepts in the interpretation of your results (where a lot of mistakes get made!). Finally, I'll introduce some more advanced methods of analysis you might come across.

However, one thing to keep in mind is that the rationale for these tests and – especially – their significance level, is based around the material in Chapters 11 and 12, so you should

[1] But you know, is it really? I mean, where did that saying actually come from? Answers on a postcard (or email) please.

[2] For example, as my background is in marketing management, I learnt virtually nothing about ANOVA until I had to teach it to grad students!

be pretty clear on that before moving on. Thus, at the end of this chapter I really hope you have come to terms with these key ideas:

- There are two main branches of analysis, the associations between variables approach, and the differences between groups approach.
- These approaches have developed apart from one another, and they tend to be associated with different research designs.
- The main method of analysis for the associations approach is multiple regression, and for the differences approach it is ANOVA. But both approaches are essentially the same thing underneath.
- Both regression and ANOVA are flexible and powerful, and can be extended to analyse very complex designs.
- However, you should always remember that your analysis should relate back to the real world. Therefore, remember that your results can never prove causality. You should also consider the implications of your sample strategy, and the real-world substantive significance of your findings.

Why is it Important to Know This Stuff?

All of the basic issues covered in this section of the previous chapter also apply here. Naturally, Figure 14.1 is virtually identical to Figure 13.1. But in this chapter we at last start to cover the things you might have read about in articles and books on your research topic. I suppose you might wonder why something you probably built up to be the 'most important' thing you need to learn about (i.e. analysis) only consists of a few chapters in this book. Well that's because – despite what some people will say to you – analysis is actually the *least important* part of any research project. Of course, I don't mean that you should just ignore it and do any old thing with your data. Instead, what I mean is that a great piece of analysis should not be able to save a poorly conceptualised, poorly designed and/or poorly conducted piece of research. Unfortunately it is all too common for researchers (and not just beginners either) to get 'dazzled' by some fancy analysis, and forget that without the underlying theory, design, and data being solid, the analysis is meaningless.

Analysis is also held in such exalted status by many, because a lot of people think it is hard to do. And in some ways they are right. Many of the complex techniques in vogue today are quite complex and involving. Also, any form of analysis tends to have its own language. So anyone who can 'speak the language' or actually conduct some of these fancy forms of analysis is often perceived as some kind of genius, whether or not they actually know what they are doing! This is because a lot of working scholars feel that they: (a) just don't have time to learn a new analysis technique, (b) are not smart enough to, or (c) simply can't be bothered, and will just find someone who *can* do it to work with if needed. This leads to the 'mystification' of analysis (which is something I criticised in Chapter 10 about qualitative analysis). However, almost all quantitative analysis methods are fundamentally based on some basic frameworks of analysis, which are reasonably simple to understand if you put some effort in. From there, you should be confident in going further to demystify quantitative analysis for yourself.

This means that this chapter is relevant even to students who do not wish to conduct any quantitative analysis ever. Is it not important to learn how to interpret the findings of research which may have used quantitative analysis? I certainly think so. Also, understanding the basic concepts underlying quantitative analysis will allow you to see more clearly the reasons why or why not you might want to use it. As an aside, it will also give you some tools with which to spot the charlatans who ply their trade by over-complicating their analyses, and who confuse everyone by spouting lots of jargon while saying little of any consequence. By the end of this chapter you should at least be confident enough to ask the question 'but what does that really mean?' of anyone, and to understand a good answer. Of course, I don't expect any of you to ask that of *me* any time!

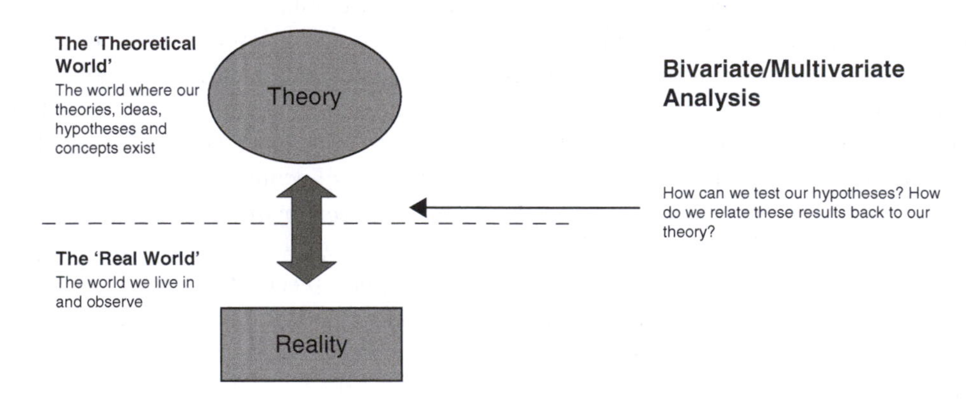

Figure 14.1 The place of quantitative analysis

Theory testing, research design and quantitative analysis

This is an important little section of the chapter, because (in some ways) it ties together a lot of different sections of the research process, and should allow you to clearly see the importance of taking a holistic approach to your research project, instead of just doing things *ad hoc*. Anyway, consider the conceptual model in Figure 14.2, which depicts a theoretical

Figure 14.2 A theoretical model

relationship between teaching style and learning outcomes. From a quantitative perspective, there are two main strategies we could use to empirically examine this theory, and each of these is associated with a different 'tradition' of analysis. I call it tradition, because to me a lot of science seems to be driven by embedded traditions regarding what methods, paradigms and procedures are 'appropriate' within any given academic field;[3] however, you could also call them 'analysis frameworks'. It's important that you are clear about the tradition or framework you are going to use to analyse your data *before* you design your research and collect your data, because the data you need for one framework is often not ideal for the other – even though you will find later that they are actually quite similar below the surface.

The first main framework I will discuss I call the **associations between variables** approach. This tradition of analysis covers the methods which look to compare different variables to see whether or not they are related. The discussion begins with basic bivariate correlation, and moves on to simple and multiple regression. If you studied economics, finance, or many of the other management disciplines (such as marketing, like me) you will probably be more familiar with regression-based methods than you are with ANOVA. This analysis tradition is based around cross-sectional and longitudinal research designs rather than experimental ones. Again, in Chapter 8 the strengths and weaknesses of such designs were discussed, but in this chapter the focus will be on the key features of the analysis methods.

The second analysis framework we are going to deal with I call the **differences between groups** framework. This analysis framework takes in the methods which look to compare different groups of respondents to see how they differ on key dependent variables. It begins with simple *t*-tests and moves on to the Analysis of Variance (ANOVA) method. This tradition is strongly based around the analysis of experimental data, and if you are studying (or have studied) some form of psychology then you will most likely have been trained to think in this way. That said, as I will show later, the ANOVA model is actually pretty much the same as the regression one, and it is really historical factors which have created the perception that they are fundamentally different. In Chapter 8 the advantages and disadvantages of

[3]One of the first people really to get to grips with this issue was Thomas Kuhn in his book *The Structure of Scientific Revolutions*, and from then on quite a lot of people got interested in what could be called the 'sociology' of scientific practice.

experimental designs were discussed, and of course no method of analysis can escape these issues, but in the coming sections I will outline the differences approach and some additional things you need to keep in mind, specific to the analysis methods.

If you look back to Figure 14.2, it can be seen that it is a theory which can be tested using either of the frameworks. This is because teaching style[4] is the kind of thing we could feasibly manipulate in an experiment (e.g. two groups of teachers, each trained to use one style only), but it is also the kind of thing that is likely to vary among the population anyway (e.g. different teachers should exhibit variation in their teaching style, if they are not trained to use only a certain one), allowing us to collect a large cross-sectional sample and still see enough variation in the independent variable to test whether it is associated with variation in our dependent variable. Of course, you would have to determine which of these designs was most appropriate depending on the characteristics of the independent variable in this case. You can go back to Chapter 8 to see the details of the different research designs, and I won't go into them too much again here. Suffice it to say that each tradition of analysis would at heart be looking to discover information as to whether teaching style causes or influences learning outcomes. Now, before you leap up in indignation, let me just say that whether or not we can ever *prove* causality is not the issue. But deep down under our veneer of scientific respectability this is what we are usually looking for. Our research of course can only ever give us indications of causality, and I have and will continue throughout this book to caution you about the over-interpretation of your work in this regard. The different research designs each have strengths and weaknesses in terms of what evidence they can give us regarding causality, and these naturally flow through to the associated analysis methods. In particular, each tradition will begin by positing a different form of hypothesis for the relationship. The differences tradition will likely develop a hypothesis something like this:

H_1: *The experimental group (exposed to higher levels of a given teaching style) will exhibit higher levels of learning than the control group*

Whereas the associations approach will most likely postulate a hypothesis similar to:

H_2: *There will be a positive association between teaching style and learning.*

Remember from Chapter 5 that a hypothesis is simply a statement which you expect your data to support. All the theoretical logic for these hypotheses will be in the text of the project (or manuscript, or thesis, etc.). And in fact, for each of the analysis traditions, you would expect the theory to be broadly similar. However, because the data you collect for each tradition will be different, and subject to different types of analysis, the hypotheses will also differ.

---

[4]The exact teaching style variable would of course be defined in your study much more clearly.

So the final thing to talk about, and doubtless this is an issue which you are champing at the bit to read about, is exactly how should you choose between traditions? Well, the choice is mainly a research design one, so the key decisions are made there. The analysis methods are subservient to the research design. Although that's not to say that one for example *must* have experimental data to use the differences approach. In fact, the analysis method is really subservient to the data. If your data falls naturally into groups (say if the independent variable were gender) then the differences approach is probably the natural one, even if the data is collected with a cross-sectional survey design – although later I'll discuss some ways to use this kind of data with an associations approach. So it's not really very easy to answer the question of why one would choose one analysis approach over another, apart from saying that 'it depends on your data, which depended on your research design, which probably depended in part on your research objectives, and in part on the tradition you are working within'. Sorry about that.

Analysing associations between variables

Let's begin by exploring the idea of associations between the variables in your data set. While there are many different techniques which can be used for analysing the associations in your data set, the more common ones are based in one way or another around the methods of correlation and/or regression, with more or less modification. The overall goal of these techniques is to look whether variables are *associated* with each other, that is, are changes in one variable associated with changes in another? In the context of a cross-sectional survey to examine the relationship between advertising exposure and purchase behaviour (for example), we would be interested in whether subjects who deviated from the overall mean of our hypothesised independent variable also exhibited associated deviations from the mean of the hypothesised dependent variable. So do those who report higher advertising exposure also report higher purchase behaviour (a positive association), or lower purchase behaviour (a negative association). I'll discuss this kind of thing in light of two different methods of searching for association, correlation and regression.

Correlation

The first thing we could do if we wish to look at the association between two variables is look at their **covariation**, which is taken by comparing the deviations from the mean of each variable for each person, and multiplying them. So, if one person deviates from the sample mean advertising exposure by 1.5, and from the sample mean purchase behaviour by 2.5, we would multiply these together. If you take the average of these **cross-product deviations** you get the *covariance*. The covariance is useful for a number of more advanced statistical techniques, but for our purposes here it has a problem, this being that it is depends on the scale that each variable is measured on. This makes it hard to compare covariances to each other, and therefore to differentiate between 'large' and 'small' covariances. Fortunately, the great Karl Pearson invented what is known as the **Pearson product-moment correlation coefficient**, which is often known simply as the 'Pearson correlation', or the 'Pearson *r*'. This is simply a standardised form of the covariance, which ranges between −1 and +1. A Pearson *r* of +1 indicates a perfect positive association, and −1 a perfect negative one. A value of 0 indicates no association between the variables in the sample.

It is important to note that for the purposes of testing associations, Pearson correlations can only be used with interval or ratio data. 'Why?' I hear you ask. Well, remember that to take a covariance (which the Pearson correlation is a standardised version of), we need to take the mean of our variables. As you should recall from Chapter 6, only interval or ratio data allows us to take the mean. However, there is a non-parametric alternative called **Spearman's rho**, which does not require interval data, as it works on the rankings of your data (e.g. is the person ranked highest on advertising exposure also ranked highly on purchase behaviour in the sample?) The interpretations of both correlations are pretty much the same, so from now we will just deal with Pearson correlations. If you are using SPSS, and you run a set of Pearson correlations, you will hopefully get data in a matrix form such as that in Figure 14.3. The variables used here are respondent age, and three measures of their work experience (how long they have been in the sales profession, how long they have been in their current company, and how long they have been in their current job).

It is reasonably simple to interpret such a matrix. First, consider that it is a diagonal matrix, in that the above and below diagonal elements are the same. Now, SPSS actually highlights

Correlations

		salexp	orgexp	jobexp	age
salexp	Pearson Correlation	1	0.602**	0.547**	0.819**
	Sig. (1-tailed)		0.000	0.000	0.000
	N	138	138	138	137
orgexp	Pearson Correlation	0.602**	1	0.861**	0.555**
	Sig. (1-tailed)	0.000		0.000	0.000
	N	138	140	140	139
jobexp	Pearson Correlation	0.547**	0.861**	1	0.510**
	Sig. (1-tailed)	0.000	0.000		0.000
	N	138	140	140	139
age	Pearson Correlation	0.819**	0.555**	0.510**	1
	Sig. (1-tailed)	0.000	0.000	0.000	
	N	137	139	139	139

**Correlation is significant at the 0.01 level (1-tailed).

Figure 14.3 Pearson correlation output from SPSS

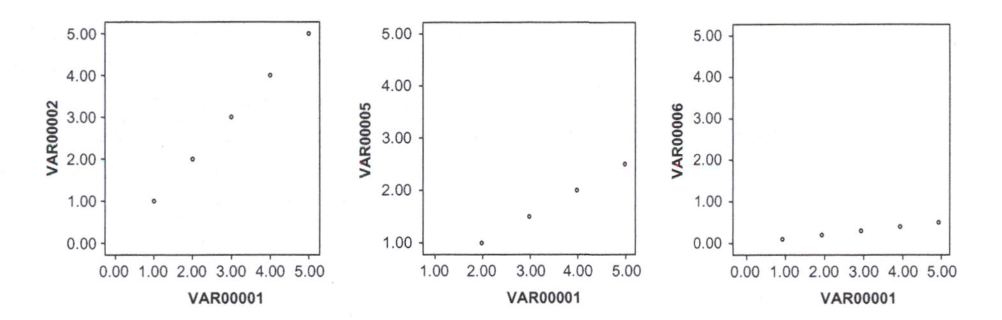

Figure 14.4 Perfect correlation lines

with asterisks the statistically significant correlations, but you shouldn't rely on this, [5] as it rests on the significance level you tell SPSS to flag up. Of course, the significance you are looking for will be dependent on the level you set for your hypotheses, and whether or not it is one or two-tailed. In this case, we can see the one-tailed significance is less than 0.05, which is significant for a 95 per cent level of confidence.

Interpreting the correlation coefficient can be a little confusing. First and foremost, this is not a measure of causality, just association. Secondly, and this is the bit many find confusing, the r does not allow you to predict values of one variable from the other, it is simply a measure of how closely they are related. If you look at Figure 14.4, you will see that a perfect correlation of 1 can be returned from almost any set of two variables which lie on a perfectly straight line, whatever the gradient of that line is (unless it is perfectly horizontal or vertical[6]). In order to move beyond simple association and towards prediction of one variable from values of another, we need to discuss **regression**.

Regression

Regression is an amazingly useful tool in its own right, as well as being the basis for many different methods of modelling the relationships between variables. So understanding it is very useful. We'll begin by discussing **simple regression**, which is simply the idea of predicting the value of a given **outcome** variable from another one. There are various and different names that are given to these variables in different research traditions. The outcome variable is sometimes called a *dependent*, *endogenous*, or *criterion* variable, while the **predictor** variable is sometimes called an *independent* or *exogenous* variable. To avoid confusion, let's stick to predictor and outcome, OK?

[5] I got into trouble as a grad student for cutting short a statistics tutorial by telling the class to 'just look for the stars' (meaning the asterisks of course)! So I probably should go into some more depth here!

[6] In this case, you can't compute the correlation, as one of the variables is constant.

The basic idea of regression is that a straight line can summarise the association between an outcome and a predictor. The question is, how do we know where to draw the line? At school you probably used your judgement to eyeball a line, but how do we *know* that line is the most accurate one? Instead, regression uses a mathematical method called the *least squares* method to define the line. This method is pretty simple in concept. Basically, for almost any practical situation, there will be a greater or lesser proportion of values which either lie above or below the line. If you measure vertically from each point to the line, this should give you an indication of how well the line fits. These distances from each point to the line are called **residuals**, and the criteria we use to determine the best line, is minimising the total size of the squared residuals.[7] This 'line-of-best-fit' (aka a regression line) can be summarised by the following equation:

$$Y_i = (b_0 + b_1 X_i) + e_i$$

Where Y_i is the predicted value of the outcome variable for subject i, b_0 is the **intercept** of the line (i.e. where the line cuts the vertical axis of the graph), and b_1 is the **gradient** of the line (i.e. the amount that Y changes with a one unit increase in X). X_i is the value of the predictor variable for subject i, and e_i represents the difference between the predicted value of Y for subject i and the actual value of Y that subject i scored. This term is basically there to tell you that the regression line isn't perfect, and there will be a difference of more or less between what you predict and what the actual real world value would be. The b values are generally called **regression coefficients**, and are one of the things we are looking for in the output from our statistical package.

The other thing we are interested in is how well the line fits our data. It may be a 'line-of-best-fit', but if your data is very scattered, it *still* won't fit very well. The R^2 represents the amount of variation in the outcome variable that your regression line explains. For a simple regression, you can take the square root of it and get back to the Pearson correlation. Of course, this also means that for a Pearson correlation you can square it and get an R^2 just like for simple regression! Cool huh? Another way of assessing the regression model is to use the F ratio, which basically compares how well the best-fit model explains the data with how 'inaccurate' the best-fit model is. You hope that this F ratio is large, at least over 1. I'll come back to the F ratio later though.

I am not going to show you any output for simple regression, instead, I am going to move straight on to multiple regression, since it is much more likely you will be using it. I think you can work the interpretation of simple regression out for yourself, as it's pretty much the same but less complex. So, imagine you had an outcome variable which you theorised was actually effected by *more than* one predictor? How would you produce a regression

[7] Why are they squared? Because if we didn't square them, the above and below-the-line residuals (i.e. positive and negative) would cancel each other out.

model here? You could use many different simple regression lines, but this would mean you wouldn't be taking into account each predictor at the same time, which will lead to very misleading results. Instead, we use a slight extension of simple regression, which predicts Y_i from a combination of all the predictors, in the form:

$$Y_i = (b_0 + b_1X_1 + b_2X_2 + \ldots b_nX_n) + e_i$$

Here, b_1 represents the coefficient of the first predictor (X_1), b_2 the coefficient of the second (X_2), and b_n the coefficient of the nth predictor (X_n). So what this means is that for every predictor, you have a separate b coefficient. The principle of the multiple regression model is pretty much the same as the simple one, although of course instead of a two-dimensional plot, you would have to visualise an $n + 1$-dimensional one (which can get messy if you have more than two predictors). But the principle is the same. Furthermore, you also get an R^2 value, which can be interpreted just the same as before, although of course it is not based on the simple correlations.

There are a *lot* of things you need to take into account when you do multiple regression, far too many to go through here in detail, so I am going to mention some critical things you should learn about before setting about analysing your data. For more information I *highly recommend* checking out some more in-depth sources such as those mentioned in the 'Further reading' sections. Firstly, you should never just throw in a bunch of variables in the blind hope that some of them will predict your outcome. Regression predictors should always be chosen from theoretical logic and research. In fact, you should have a model in mind before you even collect your data. You should also look for outliers in your data, as these can have a major impact on the regression coefficients. That said, the discussion of outliers in Chapter 13 holds here, so be careful about justifying your deletion. Most regression software gives you many different **diagnostics**, which are measures helping you interpret whether a given case is an outlier. Always check the diagnostics!

Furthermore, you need to examine the possibility that your predictor variables suffer from what is known as **multicollinearity**, which occurs when your predictor variables are correlated with each other. High multicollinearity is a major problem with your data, since this means it is very hard to separate out the influences of each individual variable on the outcome variable. But the key question is what is a high level? Well, the first thing to do is examine the simple Pearson correlations between all your predictor variables. If any correlate higher than around 0.8 then you may have a problem. However, most regression software gives you the option of some other diagnostics which allow you to go a bit deeper than that.

So, once you run your regression, you might get something like that in Figure 14.5 although this will depend on what diagnostics you select, and how you enter your variables into the regression model. Here, I am only going to talk about interpreting the basic stuff. First, you can look at the Model Summary, which gives you the R^2 and the 'adjusted R^2,

Model Summary

Model	R	R Square	Adjusted R Square	Std. Error of the Estimate
1	0.724[a]	0.524	0.514	0.85246

a. Predictors: (Constant), roleamb, jobsat, orgcom

ANOVA[b]

Model		Sum of Squares	df	Mean Square	F	Sig.
1	Regression	108.990	3	36.330	49.995	0.000[a]
	Residual	98.829	136	0.727		
	Total	207.819	139			

a. Predictors: (Constant), roleamb, jobsat, orgcom

b. Dependent Variable: turnint

Coefficients[a]

		Unstandardised Coefficients		Standardised Coefficients		
Model		B	Std. Error	Beta	t	Sig.
1	(Constant)	−2.302	0.473		−4.869	0.000
	jobsat	0.314	0.111	0.233	2.830	0.005
	orgcom	0.816	0.129	0.522	6.320	0.000
	roleamb	−0.085	0.114	−0.049	−0.748	0.456

a. Dependent Variable: turnint

Figure 14.5 Regression output from SPSS

which – without going into too much detail – indicates how well your model generalises. Ideally we want the adjusted to be close to the basic R^2. Of course, higher R^2s are better, but we'll come back to this later in the chapter. As it stands, this is a nice model, indicating that over 50 per cent of the variance in 'turnover intentions' (i.e. intention to leave the firm) is explained by my predictors (job satisfaction, organisational commitment, and role ambiguity). Following this, we can look at the ANOVA table, where we want the F ratio to be large and significant. Next, let's look at the individual b values. The 'constant' represents b_0, but unless we want to draw the line (or predict values of our outcome) we don't usually look at this much. The other b values are found in the column headed 'B', but these are difficult to interpret as they are not standardised (just like covariances). Instead, we normally look at the values in the 'Beta' column, which are standardised. The b values tell us how much that predictor would influence the outcome variable if the effects of all the other predictor variables were held constant. This brings us back to a research design point. If you don't include all the relevant predictors, the *b* will not be an accurate indicator. But I digress. Each *b* also has an associated *t*-value and significance, which show us whether or not each *b* is significantly different from zero. While it's your choice to decide on a relevant value of significance (see Chapter 12), for a typical two-tailed 95 per cent level of confidence, the significance should be <0.05. In this case, we can see that role ambiguity does not have a significant beta, meaning that the other two variables are doing the work of explaining turnover intentions.[8]

Regression is very flexible, and I can't go into all of the permutations here. But I will briefly mention a couple of very useful extensions. The previous discussion has focused on the case of regression using interval or ratio data, as a natural extension of the correlation discussion. However, you can also use regression if you have categorical or group variables, like gender (two groups) or nationality (many groups). You can do this in regression by using what is called **dummy coding**. In brief, you can use this to represent grouped data by creating variables which take on the value of 0 and 1. For example, males could be coded 0 and females 1.[9] With more than two groups, you need to create multiple dummy variables, each coded 0 and 1. It's rather too involved to go any further than this, but it is important to know that it is possible to incorporate grouped data into regression models. If you need to do so, I would advise looking at the sources mentioned later on in this chapter.

Also, you can use the regression approach to examine the influence of variables on categorical (i.e. group) outcome variables. For example, you might be interested in the factors which predict choice, e.g. purchase/not purchase, the factors which predict whether someone passes or fails a test, or whether someone survives an accident or not. The technique of **logistic regression** allows us to predict such categorical outcomes from either continuous or categorical predictors. In essence, logistic regression looks to predict the probability of the occurrence of an outcome, given the values of your predictor variables. You can't use normal regression for this task, as the assumption of linearity would be violated. So logistic regression is based on the idea or transforming the data using a logarithmic transformation. Hence the name. Logistic regression is the base for a whole host of different modelling techniques, which are very influential in various branches of social science.

So that is a basic introduction to regression. Remember that there is lot more to it than that. But you should now have a good picture of how regression works, and how to use it. So let's move on to a slightly different perspective on data analysis.

---

[8]The sharper among you may have noted that the influences seem to be in the wrong direction – I mean why would high levels of organisational commitment actually *increase* turnover intentions? The trick here is that the measure of turnover intentions is actually reversed in wording, so that higher scores indicate *lower* intention to leave the firm.

[9]See Chapter 13 for more information about coding.

Analysing differences between groups

There are two main methods of analysing differences between groups of your sample, the ***t*-test** and **ANOVA**, which stands for 'ANalysis Of VAriance'. Both methods on the surface compare the mean values of different groups of your sample, but underneath they work slightly differently, as you shall see. Also, there are some conditions you should be aware of before you collect your data. Firstly, both these methods require that the *dependent* variable be measured at least at an interval level. That said, many research applications actually use what are truly ordinal level measures – such as Likert-type scale data, and this is generally accepted. However, you should at least be aware of the need to take the *mean* of your dependent variable, and if this makes no sense in a given application, you should not use such tests (as in many other situations such as the Pearson correlation, there are non-parametric alternatives). Furthermore, like many analysis tools, these techniques also assume that your data come from a normally distributed population.

The t-test

The *t*-test works by comparing the means of two groups of your data. There are two types of *t*-test, and it's vital you choose the right one for your data. This was something I had a lot of trouble with myself when I was learning about analysis! The **independent samples** *t*-test works with two groups of *different* people (say men and women), although you would probably think of them as being the 'same' sample. The **dependent samples** (aka **paired measures**) works with two groups of the same people, say measured on two different time periods. Just to clarify this, take Figure 14.6, a repeat of the classic experimental design from Chapter 8. To test differences in the mean score of the dependent variable on the measures taken from the post-treatment experimental and control groups, we would use the independent samples *t*-test. However, to test the difference between pre- and post-treatment levels of the dependent variable on the experimental *or* the control group, you would use the dependent samples *t*-test. Does that make sense?

The basic idea of the *t*-test is that, if the two groups (often called samples) come from the same population (i.e. there is no difference between them in the population), you'd naturally expect them to have the same mean value for your dependent. If the mean *was* different, this would be by chance. In such a case, a big mean difference is very unlikely. This is the

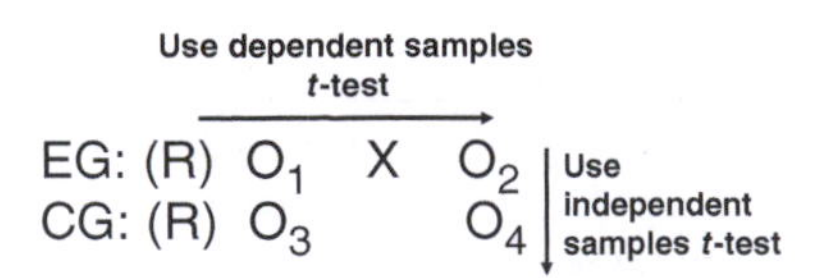

Figure 14.6 Classic experimental design

null hypothesis. The larger the difference between the two group means (and the larger the sample size), the less chance there is that it is merely a random fluctuation, and the more chance there is that there is some difference between the groups on the dependent variable. Remember, in most cases we *want* to find a difference between the groups, as it implies our independent variable has some effect.

Beginning with the independent samples *t*-test, in this case we need an independent variable which either naturally or by design divides the overall sample into two groups. For example, gender is a 'natural' divider, whereas experimental/control group is a 'by design' variable. But each divides the sample into two groups, of which each subject can only be in one (i.e. *independent groups*). Once you decide on your variables – hopefully at the research design stage – you can quickly and easily run the test in SPSS,[10] and you'll get some output like that in Figure 14.7.

The first part of the analysis is the 'group statistics'. I mainly look here at the difference between group means, and the size of the two groups. Moving down to the actual test results, this table is split into two parts. On the left of the table is *Levene's Test* for equality of variances across the two groups. This is important, as one of the assumptions of the *t*-test is that both groups have the same variance, so if the variances are not equal, the *t*-test needs to be adjusted. If the Levene's test results are significant, then we conclude that the variances of the two groups are different. This result then tells you which row of the *t*-test results you should read. The bottom row is used when equality of variance can not be assumed,

Group Statistics

	gender	N	Mean	Std. Deviation	Std. Error Mean
answer	male	36	5.39	2.533	0.422
	female	33	4.58	2.136	0.372

Independent Samples Test

		Levene's Test for Equality of Variances		*t*-test for Equality of Means						
									95% Confidence Interval of the Difference	
		F	Sig.	t	df	Sig. (2-tailed)	Mean Difference	Std. Error Difference	Lower	Upper
answer	Equal variances assumed	0.408	0.525	1.435	67	0.156	0.813	0.567	−0.318	1.944
	Equal variances not assumed			1.445	66.559	0.153	0.813	0.563	−0.310	1.936

Figure 14.7 Independent samples *t*-test output from SPSS

[10]Remember, this book is not about the technical details of how to conduct the analysis, but the conceptual thinking behind choosing certain methods, and interpreting the results. There are many books in the 'Further reading' sections which will show you step-by-step how to actually do the analysis. Personally, I recommend that the first book about statistical analysis you read after this is the one by Andy Field *(Discovering Statistics Using SPSS)*.

Paired Samples Statistics

		Mean	N	Std. Deviation	Std. Error Mean
Pair 1	stress1	2.1277	141	0.44483	0.03746
	stress2	2.8227	141	0.84755	0.07138

Paired Samples Correlations

		N	Correlation	Sig.
Pair 1	stress1 & stress2	141	0.155	0.066

Paired Samples Test

		Paired Differences					t	df	Sig. (2-tailed)
					95% Confidence Interval of the Difference				
		Mean	Std. Deviation	Std. Error Mean	Lower	Upper			
Pair 1	stress1 - stress2	–0.69504	0.89397	0.07529	–0.84388	–0.54619	-9.232	140	0.000

Figure 14.8 Paired samples *t*-test output from SPSS

and the top row when it can. From here, you would look at the relevant *t*-value and its associated significance level, to determine whether your hypothesis is supported or not. In Figure 14.7 the *t*-value is 1.435 and significance is 0.156 (we use the top row as Levene's test is non-significant). From here we can conclude that there appears no significance between males and females on the 'answer' variable. This is not surprising given the small difference in means evident in the group statistics table.

In a situation where we have two non-independent samples (say before and after measures of an experimental group), we need to use the *dependent (paired) samples t*-test. If so, you will get output like that in Figure 14.8. The first table is essentially the same as what you would get for the independent samples test. But the second table is a correlation table, between the two groups. Because the samples are paired (i.e. from the same people), there may be some consistency in the responses, so we need to know whether or not this is the case.

The third table is the most important one, however. You'll note it is similar to the independent samples *t*-test results. Here, you'll want to look at the boxes on the right which show the *t*-value and the associated significance. In this case we can see there is a significant difference between stress measured at time periods 1 and 2. The tables show us that stress at time 2 is higher than at time 1. If we had administered some kind of treatment between the two time periods, this would be an important result.

ANOVA

Like regression, ANOVA isn't really one technique, it's more of a family. Furthermore, ANOVA is actually – conceptually-speaking at least – the same thing as regression (think about the idea of dummy-coding grouped data in regression). However, because there has historically been something of a split between those researchers who were interested in the experimental approach (e.g. psychologists) and those who were interested in cross-sectional or longitudinal designs (e.g. economists), ANOVA and regression have essentially developed separately with little overlap. This is, of course, as many of the more 'social' aspects of scientific research are, rather silly. Anyway, ANOVA is basically the technique of comparing the *ratio* of systematic (i.e. caused by an experimental variable) variance to that of unsystematic (i.e. error) variance. This ratio is called the *F* ratio, and at this point the overlap with regression should start to become clearer. ANOVA is amazingly flexible, and in fact the various 'flavours' of ANOVA can be collected together under the heading of the **general linear model** or GLM (e.g. you'll find this on SPSS, and it confused me mightily until I worked out what it was). That said, ANOVA is not always taught in terms of the regression model (it is often taught and written about in terms of variance ratios[11]), so your own experience might be somewhat different.

We'll talk about some more complex ANOVA variants later, but the basic idea of ANOVA is to compare more than two means together. For example, there might be more than two levels of the experimental treatment, or we might want to compare multiple nationalities, or many other situations. The *t*-test only lets us compare two means. So why not do lots of *t*-tests to compare all the combinations of groups? The basic reason for this is that it *increases the Type I error rate* (remember Chapter 12?) ANOVA does not compare the combinations of means, but is instead an overall or *omnibus* test, which tests the null hypothesis that all group means are equal. Thus, ANOVA simply tells us whether there is some difference between the means, not where that difference specifically is. For example, in a three-group situation, ANOVA can't tell us whether the difference is between all the group means, between group 1 and 2, or 1 and 3, or 3 and 2, etc. I'll cover this later on.

ANOVA uses the *F*-ratio to compare the amount of systematic variance in the data to the amount of unsystematic variance. Thus, larger *F*-ratios are better. As we saw in the discussion of regression, the *F*-ratio can also be thought of as a comparison of the explained variance compared to the unexplained (i.e. error) variance. Although I have already stated that it should be more than 1, in ANOVA analysis we are very concerned that it reaches statistical significance, which is done in exactly the same way as for everything else. An example of the basic ANOVA output is in Figure 14.9, which should look broadly familiar by now. This simplest type of ANOVA is called **one-way ANOVA**, which tests independent groups of data (analogous to the independent samples *t*-test but allowing for more than two groups). First we have the descriptive analysis, where we can 'eyeball' the difference in means. Next is a

[11] This is a fine way of thinking about ANOVA, and makes good sense. However, once you start talking about more complex designs it becomes very unwieldy. Nevertheless, in the context of this book it doesn't really matter which approach is taken, as I won't be going into the details too much. I mention ANOVA in the context of regression simply because I think the dummy variable and *F*-ratio overlaps are cool, and also because modern statistical software tends to be based on the GLM framework.

Descriptives

answer

	N	Mean	Std. Deviation	Std. Error	95% Confidence Interval for Mean		Minimum	Maximum
					Lower Bound	Upper Bound		
high school	20	4.80	2.397	0.536	3.68	5.92	1	9
some college	20	4.75	2.468	0.552	3.59	5.91	1	8
degree or postgraduate	20	5.50	2.013	0.450	4.56	6.44	2	10
Total	60	5.02	2.288	0.295	4.43	5.61	1	10

Test of Homogeneity of Variances

answer

Levene Statistic	df1	df2	Sig.
2.145	2	57	0.126

ANOVA

answer

	Sum of Squares	df	Mean Square	F	Sig.
Between Groups	7.033	2	3.517	0.664	0.519
Within Groups	301.950	57	5.297		
Total	308.983	59			

Figure 14.9 Oneway ANOVA output from SPSS

dedicated box for the equality of variances test, which we want to be non-significant. And following that is the ANOVA test proper. Here we are interested in the *F*-statistic and its associated significance.[12]

But as we mentioned earlier, we don't know between which specific groups the difference lies. There are two ways of dealing with this. First, if we have theoretical reasons to expect differences between particular groups, we can set up **planned comparisons** between these groups. However, it is more usual that we see a significant *F* and then decide to see where the specific differences lie. In this case we use ***post-hoc*** tests, which basically boils down to multiple *t*-tests, but using a stricter criterion for significance to avoid inflating the Type I error rate. There are many varieties of *post-hoc* comparisons, so if you want to use them you'll need to make sure you are using the right ones – although few researchers actually do this and just go with the default on their analysis package! Of course, I wouldn't recommend that myself.

As I said before, the coolest thing about ANOVA is its flexibility. First, we can include additional predictor variables which we hypothesise will have an impact on the outcome. For example, remember from Chapter 8 when I discussed how additional non-experimental

[12]As an aside, the 'between groups variance' refers to systematic variation, and the 'within groups variance' to unsystematic. These labels are a holdover from the variance-ratio method of conceptualising ANOVA, since SPSS doesn't use the GLM method for simple one-way ANOVAs like this, although it does use GLM for the other ANOVAs it offers.

factors could influence the dependent variable? Well, if we measure them as continuous variables (i.e. don't split them into groups), we can include them as *covariates* in an ANOVA, which then becomes an Analysis of COVAriation, or ANCOVA. In other situations, we might have multiple experimental treatments (i.e. independent variables) which we manipulate. We can incorporate these using a *factorial* ANOVA, which is really flexible. Finally, we can also incorporate *repeated measures* ANOVA designs (analogous to the paired samples *t*-test), and ultimately can mix things together to analyse what can be some very complicated research designs. That said, one caution I would make here is to be very careful about including too many independent variables in your designs, as they can get very complex to analyse. There's no point in reporting a magnificently complex four-way interaction if you can't explain what it actually means in the real world. Remember this!

Interpretation of statistical results

I think it is probably useful at this point to return to the real world applications of statistics after all that theory. Remember, as I have previously stated, that there is a big difference between statistical significance and substantive significance, or what could be called the 'real-world' usefulness of your results. If you just randomly chuck a bunch of data into a statistical analysis package, you'll get some results, and even some significant ones too! Remember, the Type I error concept implies that you'll get a significant result purely at random sometimes! So you should always take your statistical results back to your research objectives, and determine what they actually say in terms of the real world.

First of all is the danger of over-interpreting your results with regard to causality. In particular, no amount of fancy analysis methods can ever 'prove' causality. Some philosophers would even tell you there is no such thing as causality at all. All we can do with analysis is show some empirical association within our data (e.g. a regression coefficient), and judge the chances of that occurring by chance if there was none in the population (i.e. the significance test). An experimental design gives us some more confidence, but remember it is the design that helps here, not the fact that we use ANOVA rather than regression (recall earlier, when we said they were pretty much the same). Sure, if you design a research project where you can observe the time-order of your independent and dependent variables, then include *every single possible influence* that could ever effect the dependent variable, then you could say to me you are reasonably confident that the independent causes the dependent. And of course, if you actually ever do design a social scientific study with these characteristics, then please give me a call!

The concept of the **effect size** is also important. As I mentioned in Chapter 12 it is important to consider the substantive significance of our findings. The effect size is a standard measure of how 'strong' the effect you have observed is. For each statistical test value (e.g. the t or F values), we can convert them into an r value, i.e. a Pearson correlation coefficient. We already know this is a standardised measure of the strength of a relationship, so it makes a nice standard measure of the effect size. I won't go into the details of how to calculate r from each different statistic, but rest assured it isn't that hard. Of course, the issue is then what makes a strong effect? This is dependent on your research context, and research task. While many researchers don't consider rs of 0.1 or 0.2 to be very large (and technically they'd be right), in some contexts they can actually be quite substantive. For example, if you told the manager of a multi-million pound business that s/he could improve profit by 10 per cent by incorporating a different management style, I imagine they would consider that of some substantive importance. Similarly, reducing mortality rates by even a small amount can be of major importance. So it's not always necessary to look for 'big' effect sizes. Also, the effect size calculation is of use even if your statistic has not been found to be significant. For example, in some situations (e.g. small samples) even large effects may not be statistically significant, so the effect size can be a useful angle from which to describe your results. Finally, it's also important to note that not all researchers report effect sizes, although they probably should. In fact, you might find your colleagues in need of your righteous 'assistance' in utilising effect sizes in their research. In addition, some critics of significance testing argue that it should be thrown out, and only effect sizes used.

Finally, it's probably important to bring this all back to the idea of generalisation. For most situations, we are interested in generalising the results of our analysis back to the hypothetical population. That's the role of the significance test after all. Remember, without solid sampling methodologies (see Chapter 11 for more on this), you run the risk of making incorrect generalisations. This is known as the **inductive fallacy**. If your sample is unlike your population in some relevant way, [13] then your inductive conclusions from the data back to the population will be incorrect – whatever the fancy analysis tools you use. There are many different types of inductive fallacy, but they are all based on the idea of incorrectly generalising an observation.

Going further: A magical mystery tour

The bulk of this chapter has dealt with two basic approaches to data analysis: regression and ANOVA. These methods are powerful and flexible, but in many cases there are things we need to do which the basic techniques above are not suited to. That said, it is surprising just how much you can do with regression or ANOVA, and I sometimes despair at the convoluted analysis reported in academic journal articles, where simpler approaches would

[13] Most people say that your sample should be 'representative', but if you recall in Alternative View 11.1 I showed that it wasn't quite as simple as that.

have been just as (or more) appropriate. In this section I will briefly introduce some other techniques which you might come across. But remember, this is only a brief introduction, kind of like 'speed dating' for analysis methods. Have a quick chat, check whether or not you see anything you like, and make a note to learn more later. Perhaps over coffee, or dinner, maybe have a nice bottle of wine, and let's see where things end up.[14]

Sometimes, we are interested in seeing whether a number of variables group together naturally. For example, if we develop a multi-item scale (see Chapters 6 and 7), our theory suggests that the items will tend to covary with each other, since they are caused by a single underlying factor. In this situation we can use something called **factor analysis**, which examines exactly that. Or, I might be interested in whether a large set of variables can be 'combined' into fewer ones which capture the 'essence' of the larger set. Such variables could be used in multiple regression for example. In this case I could use **principal components analysis**. Now there is actually some confusion between these two methods, and many researchers consider them interchangeable. However, I seem to have been put on this Earth, in part at least, to repeatedly explain that they are *not* the same thing.[15] Factor analysis is a tool which assumes that there is a structure of latent factors underlying your data set, which gives rise to the variation in the observed variables. This variation is considered to be in part caused by the factor, and in part by random error (just as in the classical measurement theory in Chapters 6 and 7). Principal components analysis, on the other hand, creates components as simple linear combinations of the observed variables. While the results are often similar, they do not have to be, and one shouldn't use components analysis when factor analysis is the appropriate tool.

Conceptually similar is **cluster analysis**. However, in this case we are trying to group our cases, or respondents, rather than the variables. For example, maybe you think that one can segment a given market using demographics like age, income, and education. Cluster analysis is a tool which allows you to see whether your sample falls into groups which tend to share similar values on a set of variables (e.g. one group high on income and education, but low on age, one group with medium income and education, but higher age, etc.). This method is very popular in business research. However, it is very reliant on the data, and also the interpretation of the researcher, and can be hard to understand for the beginner. Conceptually similar is **discriminant analysis**, which looks to see whether certain variables discriminate between respondents who fall into groups.[16] For example, which factors discriminate between those who have a university degree and those who don't? Or between those who recover from a certain medical condition versus those who don't? Again, it can be hard to understand for the beginner, and very reliant on the data you use.

---

[14]Can you tell that I often write late at night?

[15]Sometimes I feel like Bill Murray in the movie *Groundhog Day*.

[16]In fact, discriminant analysis can be used to validate cluster analysis results.

Finally, you might have noticed that both ANOVA and regression only seem to be able to cope with a single dependent variable. But what about complex models with multiple outcomes? Well, the ANOVA/GLM approach can be extended into Multivariate ANOVA (**MANOVA**), which allows multiple dependent variables. This is a very flexible approach, but can be extremely complex to understand and interpret. The regression model can be extended into **path analysis**, which in turn can be extended into something which is called **structural equation modelling** (SEM). SEM combines the principles of factor analysis with that of path analysis to form a very powerful general model for analysing all kinds of theories. Since its introduction, it has become one of the most influential and popular methods of data analysis for non-experimental research designs, within social science especially.

Summary

Well, that wasn't so bad was it? I hope you've come away from this chapter with a certain confidence that you will eventually be quite capable of either (a) conducting effective quantitative analysis, and/or (b) interpreting the results of the analysis which you might see in articles and books. Taken together with the previous three chapters, you should have the basic tools with which to develop your quantitative analysis and interpretation skills to a high level. But don't forget that – even though you might have thought the material was complex and involving – I have only really scratched the surface of analysis. For almost all analysis tasks, you should use this material as a 'springboard' from which to learn more.

My most cherished goal in this and all of the last few chapters has been to demystify the analysis process, to help beginner and more experienced researchers to feel more comfortable with data analysis procedures and results. It really bugs me when I see researchers ignoring the fundamentals of analysis because they are 'too hard', or because researchers are more interested in 'real-world applications, not ivory-tower models'. It bugs me even more when blatantly incorrect analysis methods are reported, but these errors are not picked up because reviewers and assessors haven't taken the time to learn the fundamentals. As researchers and scholars you have a duty to your discipline (and scholarship as a whole) to be competent and knowledgeable about all things which may affect the validity and applicability of research results. Even though analysis methods (both qualitative and qualitative) may look daunting, it is important to develop the required knowledge to allow you to conduct and evaluate rigorous research. With this in mind, I hope you have taken the following main points from the chapter:

- There are two main 'branches' of quantitative analysis, aimed at either testing differences between groups, or associations between variables.

- It is important to recognise the differences between the branches, as they are based on different research design traditions.
- However, there is actually substantial overlap between the two approaches.
- The associations approach is based around correlational analysis, which extends to regression. Regression is concerned with predicting the value of an outcome variable from one or more predictor variables.
- The differences approach is based around the *t*-test and ANOVA methods. They essentially look to compare the differences in mean levels of a dependent variable across two (*t*-test) or more (ANOVA) groups, which can represent natural groupings (e.g. gender) or experimental treatments (e.g. high, medium, low reinforcement levels).
- Both regression and ANOVA methods are the basis for many more complex analysis tools, and are flexible and powerful models to base your analysis around.

Further reading

As you are no doubt aware by now, quantitative analysis is a massive field, and each section of this chapter (maybe even each paragraph!) has multiple books written about it. Again, there is plenty of useful information in the books I have already referred to in the corresponding sections of previous chapters. In particular, the first place I would go to after this would be Andy Field's *Discovering Statistics Using SPSS*. Also, Kerlinger and Lee's *Foundations of Behavioral Research* has some great information, although it isn't as approachable as Field's. After that there are some great resources on the various analysis methods I have discussed.

- *Multivariate Data Analysis* by Joseph Hair, *et al.* This is a great introduction to the theory and techniques of many of the complex analysis I have presented above.
- *Applied Multiple Regression/Correlation Analysis for the Behavioral Sciences* by Jacob Cohen *et al.* A huge and comprehensive introduction to the associations between variables approach.
- *A Student's Guide to Analysis of Variance* by Maxwell J. Roberts and Riccardo Russo. This book is a nice comprehensive yet approachable introduction to ANOVA, although it doesn't really focus on the regression approach to ANOVA. I include it because, along with Kerlinger and Lee, it was what I used to teach myself ANOVA. So it can't be that bad.

EXERCISES

1. In the same spirit as Exercise 1 in Chapter 13, go and ask your colleagues which analysis framework they are more confident in – regression or ANOVA? Ask them whether they prefer experimental or correlational research designs. Then, go further and probe their background. Which analysis technique do you think they would have learnt first? Is there any link between these factors?
2. Look at Figure 14.2, and design two total programmes of quantitative research to examine this model. You should now be able to incorporate issues of research design, measurement, data collection, and analysis. Design a research project from an experimental perspective *and*

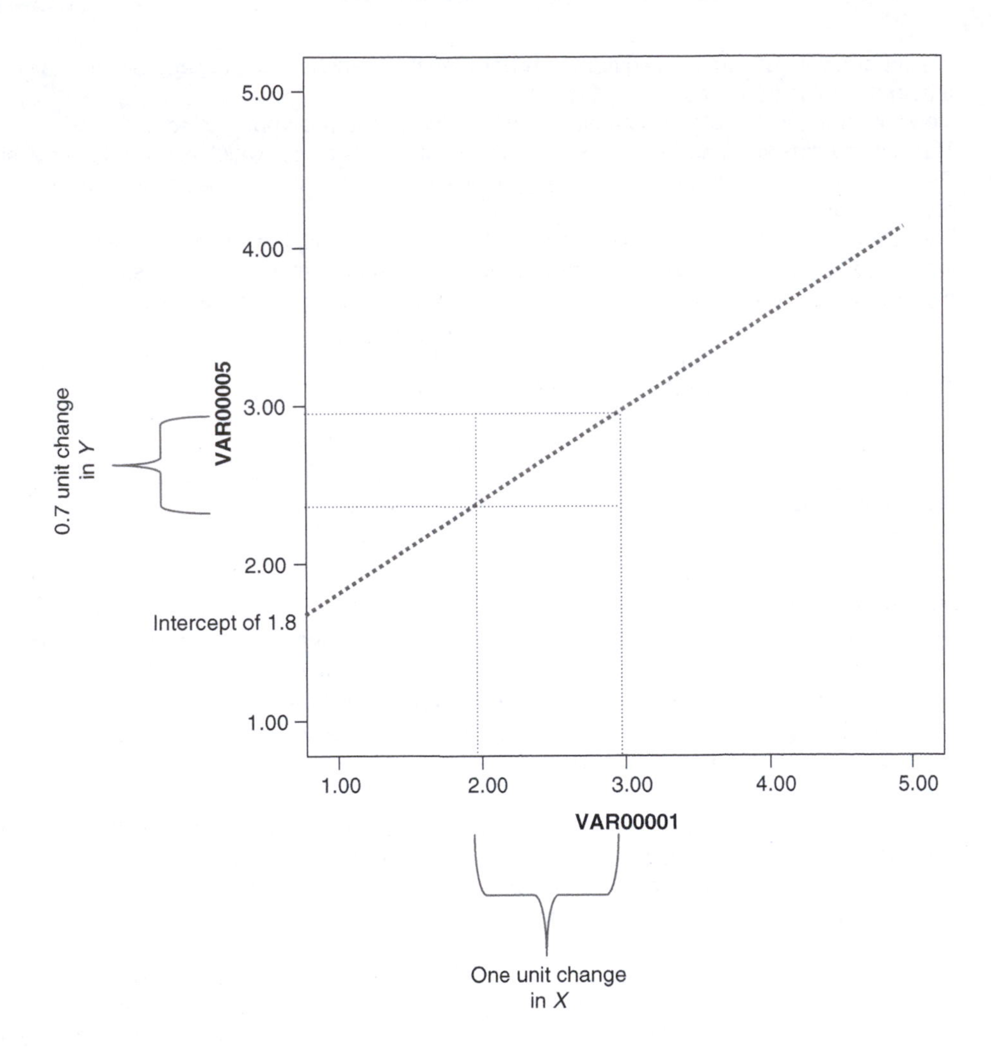

Figure 14.10 A regression line

a cross-sectional/longitudinal perspective. Explore and discuss how all the parts of the research process fit together.

   a. How else could you examine this theory?

3. Look at the line in Figure 14.10, and the information given with it. Use this information to create the regression equation which will allow you to predict *Y* (ignore the error term).

   a. Using this equation, predict the value of *Y* you would get for a value of 25 for *X*.

4. What is the *F*-ratio? What does it tell us in a regression context? How about in an ANOVA context?
5. Look at the ANOVA output in Figure 14.9. Even though it is non-significant, is there anything in those results which warrants further investigation
   a. Which groups seem most different from each other?
   b. How could we provide a statistical test of which groups differed and which groups did not?
6. Give yourself a pat on the back, for you have got through most of the difficult stuff in this book! Go and buy yourself a present!

Chapter 15

Mixing methods and paradigmatic incommensurability

SUPERVISOR'S VIEW: PROFESSOR SUZANNE C. BECKMANN

Imagine a consumer who shops in a supermarket that carries only organic produce. An economist would explain this behaviour by suggesting that this consumer has enough disposable income to pay the higher price. A sociologist would say that the consumer belongs to a social group that prefers organic produce. A psychological point of view would describe this consumer as seeking status and strengthening her identity through her purchase. A biologist would suggest that this consumer is in need of the nutritional substances the organic produce contains. A political perspective would regard the purchase as a sign of the consumer expressing her political beliefs. An anthropologist would account for this behaviour as an expression of the fact that this consumer lives in a culture that perceives a difference between conventional and organic produce. This list of examples could continue *ad infinitum*. The point should be obvious, however: from each given point of view (or paradigm) we choose to focus on different aspects of the phenomenon observed.

Yet, as the example illustrates, it would seem sensible to apply several perspectives in order to explain this consumer's purchase behaviour, because any of the above perspectives makes perfect sense. And indeed we see more and more studies subscribing to methodological pluralism (not to be confused with paradigmatic pluralism!). This, however, necessitates transparency and explanation of assumptions. This constant presentation of theories and methods, though, does not in itself achieve the classic aim of social sciences, namely to strive for certain knowledge about the world and about the way society functions. *Perspectivism* is the solution to this challenge. Different perspectives provide knowledge about precisely that part of a phenomenon that is enlightened by that perspective. Hence, the more perspectives that are involved, the more complete will be our knowledge about a phenomenon. In an abstract logical sense this means that by involving all perspectives of a phenomenon this leads to complete and final knowledge about that phenomenon. As a thought experiment this is nice, but as practical research it is impossible. The more modest aim would then be to acquire more usable knowledge by mixing methods within a given general paradigm. And when doing so one could follow my preferred motto: *Research is different from common sense because it is conducted to achieve specific goals, is grounded in theory, relies on specific methods and is done systematically.*

VIEW FROM THE TRENCHES: JO BROWN

Mixing methods is cool. It's trendy. Funding organisations love it (I'm convinced I got my Ph.D. funding because I took a 'multi-method approach'). However, there are four important things to bear in mind before you reach randomly into your bag of methodological tricks.

First, using three different methods requires three times as much work as using a single method. This may or may not be a problem for you – after all, if you want to do interesting and challenging research, you need to be creative and work hard. Each method needs to be thoroughly researched to ensure that it is relevant to your research question. In particular, you need to be clear about what kind of data each method will generate and how that data will address your research question. This is critical when it comes to writing up your methodology chapter and your viva – you will be required to justify why you have chosen these methods to answer your specific research question. Second, additional resources may be needed, such as training in the use of specific techniques/software. Take care when choosing cutting edge techniques – they may be popular now, but may fall out of favour by the time you are facing examiners. My third point also relates to the writing-up process – you have a word limit on your thesis, yet three methods require a methodology chapter three times as long, never mind the results and discussion chapters. In writing mine, I had to focus on one main method and bring in evidence from the other methods I used to support the outcomes in the discussion chapter! This may make you feel as if you've wasted a lot of time and effort for no real benefit; however, you will have a large amount of data with which to write papers. Finally, there is the important issue of your external examiners – if you are using innovative methods, or just methods from another discipline, it may be difficult to identify potential examiners who will understand, let alone applaud, your choices.

Despite this, remember that this is ***your*** Ph.D. and you should use methods that excite and interest you – just make sure you can justify them.

The main subject of this chapter is one which I can't find in too many research guides and textbooks. I find this very surprising, because since I have started teaching research methods, the questions addressed in this chapter are perhaps the most common ones I get asked by my students. This is especially so as they get further into the course and begin thinking about their own work. Furthermore, the issues I am going to talk about here are also the sources of some of the most common problems and misunderstandings by students and researchers.

This chapter is concerned somewhat with the mixing of methods, but more importantly it is concerned with the mixing (or not) of *paradigms* of research. If you cast your mind back to Chapters 2 and 3 (which seem so far away now), you'll remember I introduced various paradigms for research. There are many ways of framing the paradigms, but I settled on **realism** and **interpretivism** as nice handles with which to grasp the concepts. However, as I have repeatedly emphasised throughout the book, methods are independent of paradigms, it just so happens that the data collected by different methods tends often to be suited to answering the questions which are generally posed by different paradigms. Confusion over this issue seems to me to be at the source of the questions and problems I find myself repeatedly trying to explain.

The key issue in this chapter, therefore, is not mixing methods. Instead, it is the concept of **paradigmatic incommensurability**. This rather impressive phrase will be dealt with in some depth at the beginning of this chapter, but in essence it refers to whether or not one can understand, and more importantly to judge the 'quality' of, the findings of research conducted in one paradigm, from the perspective of another. This issue leads naturally on to the question of whether one can ever be engaged simultaneously in a research project which somehow 'mixes paradigms'. I've spent considerable time with scholars in my own field debating (read: arguing) this, and I do want to convey something of the flavour of this as a 'debate' rather than a simple case of 'right and wrong'. I certainly have my position, and this is my book after all so you'll be getting it right between the eyes,[1] but my real aim is to set out the issues and give you the tools to understand for yourselves how to approach this important question.

[1] And if you have got the impression that writing a book is really one long ego trip, you'd be right. After all, it's certainly not about the money!

At the end of this chapter I really hope you have come to terms with these key ideas:

- That a philosophical paradigm is slightly different from a paradigm as Kuhn talked of it.
- That incommensurability is concerned with how we can interpret research and findings from paradigms different to our own.
- That in a strong sense the inherent differences between paradigms make it impossible to really interpret research from different paradigms coherently, but that instead we can define a weaker form which looks for common ground across paradigms. This makes research from alternative paradigms of some use to us.
- However, it is not possible to actually *conduct* research from different paradigms simultaneously.
- This is even the case if you use multiple methods, which itself is perfectly possible, and can even lead to strong advantages.

Why is it Important to Know This Stuff?

It's important to know the material in this chapter for many reasons, which some of you I suspect will already be thinking about. In fact, I bet that some of you thought about the questions I am going to cover here way back at the end of Chapter 3. As I said earlier, the theories in this chapter are the subject of many questions from beginning researchers, and even more experienced ones too.

The key reason that this material is important is similar to why the material in Chapters 2 and 3 was important. Simply put, without understanding the link between the philosophies of knowledge generation, and your practical attempts to generate knowledge, your project will always run the risk of serious inconsistency and error. Furthermore, you will struggle to create your own original research and thinking, always relying on others. However, it is not enough to understand the philosophies in isolation from each other – although it is a great start. Instead, in order to really get deep understanding of these issues, we need to try to deal with the inherent contradictions involved in how they interrelate. You can never really appreciate where you stand without appreciating why you don't stand somewhere else – and I only did half the job with Chapters 2 and 3.

Furthermore, another really important goal of the material in this chapter is to set out very clearly the demarcation between *methods* and *paradigms* once and for all. As you will by now be aware, I have nagged you about this for what probably seems like forever. At last here is the final capstone on the discussion, which hopefully makes things crystal clear – the happy ending if you like.

So, this chapter returns to the basic subject matter of the earlier sections of the book, the connection between theory and reality, and vice versa (see Figure 15.1, which should look very familiar). In a nutshell, this should show to you that you can never escape the philosophical underpinnings of your research, *even if you ignore them, they are still there, lurking...* Of course, this means that the material is relevant to all researchers, from all different perspectives. Even those of you who say you don't have a perspective at all. Plus, we're nearing the end, if you've come this far you might as well keep going.

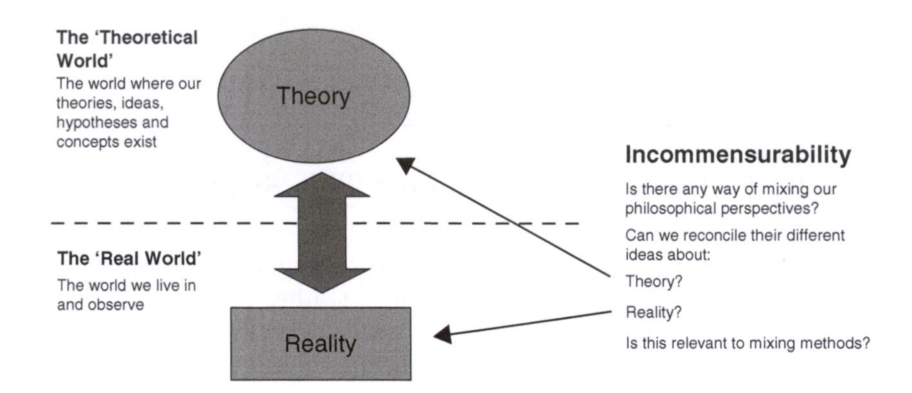

Figure 15.1 Mixing paradigms and methods

Paradigms and incommensurability

I think the first issue to deal with for the purposes of this chapter is that of *incommensurability* itself. Apart from being an irritating word to have to constantly type out (as I am beginning to discover), incommensurability is in essence the principle that it is impossible to compare theories in one paradigm with those within another. However, before we even get to the nitty-gritty, there are two different ways of looking at the issue which should be outlined first. The term 'incommensurability' was coined (or at least popularised) by Thomas Kuhn in his book *The Structure of Scientific Revolutions*, which has already been mentioned as a quality read. But Kuhn's take on the issue is actually rather different from the one I want to deal with. Kuhn was interested in paradigms not in the way which we talked about them (as general philosophies of scientific inquiry), but as overall theoretical frameworks for a given scientific discipline. In this sense a paradigm is a set of practices which define what a given scientific discipline actually 'does'. In other words, the methods used, questions asked, phenomena examined and observed, and the interpretation of results, are all part of the overall paradigm of a discipline. For example, at the beginning of the 20th century, Newtonian mechanics was such a dominant paradigm in physics that Lord Kelvin was moved to say; 'There is nothing new to be discovered in physics now. All that remains is more and more precise measurement'. While of course I would applaud his emphasis on measurement, the eternal embarrassment of Lord Kelvin was sealed by Einstein's work on relativity, which relegated Newtonian mechanics to a special case, rather than the dominant paradigm. Such *paradigm shifts* are how Kuhn characterised the development of a 'mature science', and we can look at the history of science and see many of them (e.g. the shift in biology caused by Darwin's work on evolution). That said, later theorists have argued that such a viewpoint is too limited to describe how science actually develops, and we should also consider that a more 'incremental' progress goes on simultaneously, punctuated by occasional paradigm shifts.

Kuhn considered that paradigm shifts were only done through a process of painful revolution, when exponents of 'old' paradigms rail against incoming ones. Max Planck even suggested that proponents of the old must die before the new can fully take hold![2] According to one reading of Kuhn, theories and research conducted from the perspective of one paradigm are not interpretable from another, as they are based on different research ideas, different languages, different methods, and ultimately different worldviews about the discipline. Further, to Kuhn new paradigms are always better than old, leading to their ultimate supplanting. This view is a natural result of a historical approach to science, which would observe the criticism that incoming paradigms were subjected to, only to win out in the end. This view is also strongly based around a natural science focus, not a social science one. In fact, one could argue that social sciences tend not to have dominant paradigms in the way Kuhn thinks of them.

Of more use to the social scientist in my opinion is the take on paradigms of Paul Feyerabend (our witchdoctoring friend from Chapter 2). Feyerabend's thoughts are somewhat consistent with Kuhn, but Feyerabend goes further to characterise the scientific method itself as a form of paradigm.[3] In this sense then, the idea of incommensurability relates to whether discoveries, results, or research in general, which is conducted from one set of epistemological or ontological principles (e.g. realism or interpretivism) is able to be judged from the standpoint of another. Such a question has implications for how you conduct your research. Feyerabend of course famously argued that 'anything goes', and that in the history of science researchers indeed did do whatever it took to get their theories accepted. Thus, in his view there was no way of judging whether one form of research or knowledge was better than another (hence his visits to witchdoctors as well as medical doctors). But does this mean that as researchers we should follow this example?

---

[2]Well, he meant 'eventually die of old age' really, but it sounds more dramatic the way I wrote it.

[3]Kuhn's natural science focus seems to me to assume that researchers all conduct science using 'the scientific method' – i.e. the methods talked about in Chapter 2.

The problem of objective evaluation across paradigms

Now, the reason I said above that Feyerabend's notion of incommensurability was a bit more useful for our purposes than Kuhn's is bound up with the nature of social sciences as opposed to natural sciences. Within a social science context, we are very rarely in the situation which Kuhn's work is implicitly concerned with, i.e. that of a stable, generally agreed-upon theoretical paradigm of investigation. Instead, social sciences for whatever reason (be it their relative immaturity or the very nature of social phenomena) tend to be constantly operating with multiple *theoretical* paradigms co-existing, sometimes in conflict with each other, sometimes progressing quite happily along distinct paths. Rather than research within a given social science being almost completely based on a single overarching theory, such as, for example, geology being based on plate tectonics, or biology being based on evolution by natural selection, most social sciences have multiple versions of such worldviews. So it is no big deal for a social scientist to regularly be exposed to multiple theories and viewpoints about their subject.

However, it *is* more of a big deal when we consider the very epistemological and ontological bases of the knowledge we look to create within our branch of social science. In this case, most social sciences (or branches within) tend to have a dominant *philosophical* paradigm. For example, Davies and Fitchett (2005) give a very readable introduction to paradigmatic issues within marketing research. The basic question is; If I am a realist(interpretivist), how can I judge the quality of research conducted from an interpretivist(realist) perspective in such a way that I am 'standing outside' my own paradigmatic viewpoint, and judging it purely on its own merits?[4] Feyerabend's answer was that you simply can't, and that even to consider the question was pointless, as it stood outside the domain of logic. Not very helpful to the practical researcher!

But for the social scientist this is a vital question, because at the very least we have to look at work which is conducted from an alternative philosophical paradigm, and also to engage with researchers who appear committed to viewpoints which stand in direct opposition to our own. Furthermore, the beginning (and sometimes the more experienced) researcher is often confused about whether or not it is possible to conduct research simultaneously from multiple philosophical paradigms.

I'll set up the problem with a simple example, which by now you should understand very well. Take the research study outlined in IDE 15.1. It's clearly conducted from a realist philosophical standpoint. Imagine then that you operated within an interpretivist type of paradigm. If you look at Chapter 3 closely you can develop a set of basic principles which could guide your general type of enquiry. They would probably include things like the need to participate within the social context you are studying, recognise the inherent subjectivity of the social constructions involved, or maybe even involve the subjects in 'co-creating' the

---

[4]To give you a picture of the inherent difficulty of this question, consider that the very idea of 'standing outside' is steeped in the rhetoric of realist/positivist worldviews!

research and interpreting the data. Interpreting the research study in IDE 15.1 from such a viewpoint may lead you to come to the conclusion that it can tell you virtually nothing of interest along these lines. Judged from within an interpretivist-type paradigm, such a study would be so far removed from the actual social situation, that the findings would be meaningless. For example, the reliance on abstract quantitative measures of concepts would ignore the idea that individuals each experience such things in unique and subjective ways, making it impossible to capture some kind of 'objective' value for such complex social constructions.

IDE 15.1: A typical realist-type study

Aim: To develop a generalisable explanatory model of the influencing factors of job-related stress and psychological strain in the work place.

Procedures:

1. Conduct thorough review of relevant literature
2. Small-scale qualitative interview study with employees of multiple firms and industries.
3. Develop explanatory model from stages 1 and 2.
4. Create quantitative measures of relevant variables.
5. Collect random sample of 1,000 employees.
6. Analyse data using multiple regression to determine the effects of influencing factors on the dependent strain variable.

On the other hand, a researcher working within a realist-type paradigm would believe that objective value-free research methods and measurement are absolutely necessary to gain a picture of the real social situation going on underneath our subjective perceptions. Instead, such subjective social constructions may be viewed as harmful 'biases' which distract the researcher from the core truth of the situation, which can be generalised (within definable limits). Thus, one should try as much as possible to 'stand outside' the social context and observe it in a detached and abstract manner, in the same way one is able to observe the physical interaction between two snooker/pool balls on a table. Such researchers may consider the findings of interpretively based research as almost meaningless, as they are so inextricably located within a given context that they have little or no meaning outside it. Sure, such results may be of general interest, but they could not be counted as 'knowledge'. At best, we could use them as inputs into further research.

This, in a nutshell, is the problem of paradigmatic incommensurability. The very nature of the epistemological and ontological viewpoints of the realist and interpretive type paradigms unavoidably renders research conducted from outside the worldviews meaningless in a philosophical sense (rather than a 'general interest' sense). Most practical researchers, however, would recoil at such a statement. Some may then argue that they will instead ignore the philosophy of science altogether and just do whatever they feel is appropriate. This is at heart a Feyerabend-style 'anything goes' statement, which leads ultimately to anarchy, and the idea that we are unable to judge any research in terms of its quality. Most practical researchers would also recoil at *this* in horror. In fact, as you have hopefully already understood from this book, the very process of knowledge creation itself is inextricable from epistemological and ontological viewpoints – whether or not you explicitly understand or subscribe to them. Ignoring the issue won't make it go away, it will just leave your research stunted and ill-formed, like a tree without strong roots. Unfortunately, while incommensurability may be unpalatable in a practical sense, in a theoretical sense it is inherent to the philosophical viewpoints themselves.

But all is not lost! Paradigmatic incommensurability can itself be viewed in a 'softer' way, which allows the philosophical perspectives to retain their crucial distinctions, yet still allow us to find meaning and use in research conducted from different viewpoints to our own.

Strong- and weak-form incommensurability

The idea that research conducted from one philosophical paradigm is totally uninterpretable, and thus meaningless, from another is what could be called **strong-form incommensurability**. Apparently, Kuhn was somewhat dismayed with the strong-form implications of his theory, and repeatedly insisted that he did not want to suggest that those from opposing scientific paradigms could never communicate in a rational form. Feyerabend, on the other hand, seemed to revel in the idea that one should not even bother to try to compare one's work with other paradigms.

The idea that alternative paradigms were completely uninterpretable was challenged strongly by the philosopher Donald Davidson in his 1974 essay 'On the very idea of a conceptual scheme'. I'm not sure about you, but that title alone gives me a picture of a withering attack on the idea of incommensurability. Actually, it's a well-argued statement on how there is no defensible argument that conceptual schemes (i.e. paradigms) are so different as to be uninterpretable. Instead, the trick when considering ideas and concepts – and by association research – from alternative paradigms appears to be to look for common ground somewhere. As Davidson says, this method: 'is not designed to eliminate disagreement, nor can it; its purpose is to make meaningful disagreement possible, and this depends entirely on a foundation – *some* foundation – in agreement' (2006, p. 207). The message for us is that there is always some shared or common ground to start from when one is considering research conducted from differing philosophical paradigms, and in fact the differences between the approaches are all the more sharp when we share some underlying principles.

Weak-form, or partial, incommensurability in this sense can be taken to mean that we can indeed examine and evaluate research conducted from alternative philosophical paradigms, without totally dismissing it as meaningless.[5] One simply has to maintain that there is some form of common ground across the approaches, which I like to take at minimum to be the overall aim of research itself. In other words, from whatever philosophical perspective you look at research from, *your objective is to generate some form of knowledge*. The differences arise when we start to define exactly what knowledge is possible, and even what knowledge itself should be. But without agreeing that we are all essentially in the search for some kind of knowledge, research itself becomes a rather unintelligible concept.

The upshot for this is that one can interpret knowledge created from an alternative philosophical perspective in a number of ways. First, it seems clear that a realist(interpretivist) researcher can evaluate and utilise research (e.g. for a literature review) conducted from an interpretivist(realist) perspective. In the first instance, the researcher must judge how usable that research is for their own purposes. This evaluation would tend to be done from within the boundaries of one's own paradigm. For example, is such research usable as 'background', or as critical foundations of a theory? You need to be very clear on what you define as knowledge here, to remain consistent across multiple situations.

However, it is also clear that the paradigms are not completely unintelligible from the outside. So a researcher must somehow also be able to evaluate the 'quality' of the research. To my mind, it is only fair to do this with an understanding of the philosophical perspective which that particular research was conducted from. A realist researcher is not able to say a piece of research is weak simply because it is conducted from an interpretive paradigm. Of course, this is not to ignore the fact that research from *any* of the different paradigms may indeed lack rigour, but one should be very clear on the criteria of quality before making that judgement. Such a framework for the evaluation of research from alternative paradigms allows us to give maximum breadth to our own knowledge generation process. Furthermore, we reduce the chances of destructive and (as I see it) unnecessary disagreement between research and researchers from alternative paradigms. As Davidson said: 'We make maximum sense of the words and thoughts of others when we interpret in a way that optimizes agreement (this includes room … for … differences of opinion) … we improve the clarity and bite of declarations of difference, whether of [paradigm] or opinion, by enlarging the basis of shared (translatable) language or of shared opinion' (2006, p. 207).

Multi-paradigm research?

The previous section essentially rejected the idea that research from a paradigm different from your own is of no use to you. However, I still haven't dealt with the question of whether it is possible to conduct research itself from multiple philosophical paradigms. First, let me

---

[5] It's important to note that Davidson actually dismisses all forms of incommensurability in his essay. However, I personally like to retain the idea of weak-form incommensurability because I think it makes clear the idea that the different philosophical paradigms do actually have some very key distinctions, and thus stresses the idea that we do need to 'make an effort' to interpret work from alternative paradigms to our own.

make one thing abundantly clear; *mixing methods is not mixing paradigms*. Please write this out 10 times right now. Simply because you are conducting qualitative and quantitative research in a single project does not mean you are (for example) mixing interpretive and realist philosophical paradigms. Remember, methods are independent of philosophical paradigms. In fact, when you look at things more closely, it is clear that qualitative researchers sometimes rely on the fundamental ideas of positivist or realist paradigms, and quantitative researchers can sometimes tap into interpretive or constructionist concepts of research. Bryman (2004, pp. 439–446) gives a useful discussion of this, and sums the issues up with the contention that 'the connection between research strategy, on the one hand, and epistemological and ontological commitments, on the other, is not deterministic' (p. 442). So methods are not the major factor in any conception of 'multi-paradigm' research.

In fact, when we talk about paradigms in the context of the philosophy of science (as opposed to different sets of theoretical assumptions), then I don't think it is possible to conduct a research project from multiple philosophical paradigms. 'But *surely* I can mix interpretive and realist approaches to research' I hear you cry! In order to justify my position, let's look at exactly what this might mean in some more depth. Imagine you begin a large-scale research project (maybe a Ph.D.) by conducting some in-depth participant observational studies, which hinge on the assumption that you become highly involved in the social milieu you are studying. You may consider that this type of research might be done from an interpretive perspective, without knowing much else about the project. So, then you continue the research by designing a mail-out questionnaire which you send to 1,000 individual respondents, and go through a quantitative analysis process similar to that described in Chapters 13 and 14, i.e. an archetypal realist approach. This is actually pretty typical of a lot of social science research, which begins with some quite exploratory work, and gets progressively more tightly focused as time moves on.

But does this mean that such a study is 'multi-paradigm'? Certainly, if you take the individual sections as stand-alone projects you could argue that they were conducted from different paradigms. However, these are not two separate projects, they are in fact different stages of the *same project*, with a single overall set of aims and objectives. It is these overarching objectives, along with the implications they have for the epistemology and ontology of the researcher, which define the paradigm of the project. For example, if the aim of the project in my earlier example was to develop and test a generalisable model of the antecedents and consequences of psychological strain in university lecturers, the project would certainly be coming from a realist (or even positivist) set of paradigmatic assumptions. This would be the case *even if I were to use methods or assumptions which may seem based on an interpretive paradigm* at some stages of the research – for example the participant observation study at the beginning.

In essence, research projects will always be based on a single philosophical paradigm, which is defined by and around the overall objectives of the research. One can cut a large-scale research project into as many different slices as one wishes, and indeed these can be conducted using methods which seem appropriate to different philosophical standpoints. If these 'slices' are considered projects in their own right, they may even be considered to have a distinct philosophical viewpoint. But at the instant these research 'slices' are considered to be part of a single project, the *overall philosophical paradigm of that project dominates*. It is simply impossible for one project with a single set of research objectives to mix paradigms. This should make sense when you consider the fundamental incompatibility of the epistemological and ontological assumptions of the different philosophical paradigms. For example, how can a single project consider knowledge to be socially constructed by researcher and subject, at the same time as considering it to be objective, unbiased, and pre-existing? Once you commit to one paradigm, the other one becomes unavailable to you – at least for that particular project. Just like getting married, or so they tell me.

Mixing methods

Unlike the idea of mixing paradigms, which I spent ages on above, it's not really a big deal to mix methods. Simply put, some methods are best at getting different types of information, which is needed to answer different types of questions. So almost all good social researchers will at some point in time use different methods within their careers. Many will utilise different methods in the same project, often in a sequential fashion. For example, a researcher might want to begin a project with qualitative methods to gain a grounding in the area, and follow it up with quantitative and experimental work. Conversely, a quantitative model might benefit from the rich context afforded by subsequent qualitative work. In this section, what I want to do is focus on the overlap between qualitative and quantitative methods, and show how they aren't really as different as you might think. As well as that, I'll take a look at some examples of how you can fruitfully combine the different methodological approaches.

Hammersley (1996) proposed three main approaches to mixed-method research. First is the idea of **triangulation**, which you should have come across before in this book. The idea of triangulation of course, is that if you approach a given idea from multiple angles (i.e. mixed methods), you can gain a more accurate picture of it. Nevertheless, you should make sure that this is consistent with your epistemological and ontological viewpoint. Secondly, Hammersley argues that each method can **facilitate** the other, for example by providing raw material for later investigation using one or the other method. Finally, Hammersley also considers the **complementarity** of each method, where each of the methods is employed in a planned manner to deal with different aspects of a study. For example, by filling in gaps which the other method is incapable of capturing data on.

Qualitative approaches in quantitative research

Qualitative research is commonly applied by researchers who would primarily consider themselves to be quantitative. In fact, this is so much the case that many qualitative scholars have complained that such strategies implicitly restrict qualitative research to 'merely' exploratory scene-setting or context-building. Nevertheless, it can still be a highly beneficial strategy. Qualitative research can be employed in the task of generating rich, unstructured information in order to develop hypotheses, or measurements, to be later quantified. Such strategies are very common, although you'll often find that scholarly articles reduce the discussion of such work to something like 'qualitative interviews were used to generate hypotheses and measurement items', or even totally avoid talking about them. This probably gives a rather inaccurate picture of how commonly qualitative research is used in many studies.

Qualitative research can also be highly useful at the end stages of a quantitative study. For example, qualitative research can be used to explore the relationships you find in your data, particularly the unexpected ones. More specifically, a good piece of quantitative research should generally have a strong theoretical base for its hypotheses, so support for them in turn supports the theory (i.e. hopefully you shouldn't need more information). But what if your data does *not* follow your theoretical expectations? Whereas many researchers (myself included) tend to scrabble around for logical explanations, it is probably a far more rewarding strategy to get back out into the field and investigate these relationships with a qualitative approach. Such a strategy can add significant weight to your study, and also set up many avenues for future work.

Finally, one could also take a qualitative approach to actual quantitative data. In fact, it can be argued that interpreting quantitative data itself is a fundamentally qualitative process. Looking at matrices of numbers in a factor analysis, playing around with structural models, and even presenting/writing about your results, all rely to a greater or lesser extent on some kind of qualitative interpretation. For many of the more advanced methods, there are many decision points where qualitative considerations *could* come into play. A good researcher should be cautious when looking at their data, and fully aware of the influence of their own perspective on its interpretation.

Quantitative approaches in qualitative research

Similar to the use of qualitative work in quantitatively oriented research, quantitative approaches can be useful at the beginning of a qualitative study. In particular, social surveys can be used to identify the appropriate sample to select, either in terms of their attitudes or characteristics. For example, if one needs certain levels of representation of certain population groups or attitudes, it may be useful to get a picture of a larger sample of the population than to make assumptions about the population. Short, quantitative questionnaires can also be used to gather basic information about respondents, e.g. their backgrounds, social class, education, and other demographic measures.

Quantitative approaches can also be used to generate static 'snapshots' of a social situation, which can add depth and perspective to the more dynamic process-oriented results which tend to be generated by the qualitative approaches. Such a combination can allow the qualitative results to attain even more resonance, as their 'fit' with the overall picture of the social context is made clear. Quantification can also help researchers refute the common criticism of the 'anecdotalism' of qualitative research to some extent. For example, giving quantified data on the frequency of examples or analysis units (e.g. quotes) can reassure reviewers and readers that the exemplary quotes reported are not isolated instances of support for the theory, but 'typical' examples.

Finally, it should also be clear that many qualitative techniques seem to implicitly rely on the logic of quantification. For example, it is common in qualitative research reports to see vague uses of terms like 'many', 'often', 'some' and the like – which seem to refer to an attempt to quantify the occurrence of phenomena or utterances. Such words mean little without any explicit definition, and seem to be used in an attempt to give some 'veneer' of respectability to the results. In the same way that quantitative researchers should be conscious of implicit qualitative interpretation of their results, qualitative researchers should be vigilant for their own implicit quantification of results. If such quantification is desired, it should be done only when appropriate, and clearly expressed, such as giving explicit numbers or percentages of the occurrence of data units.

Overall strategic approaches to mixing methods

Before finishing up this chapter – the last on the actual *conduct* of research – I'll talk about some of the basic logics and decisions you might need to think about when mixing methods. I think a useful strategy is provided by Morgan (1998b) with his two-dimensional typology (see Figure 15.2), which identifies four different strategies for mixing methods.

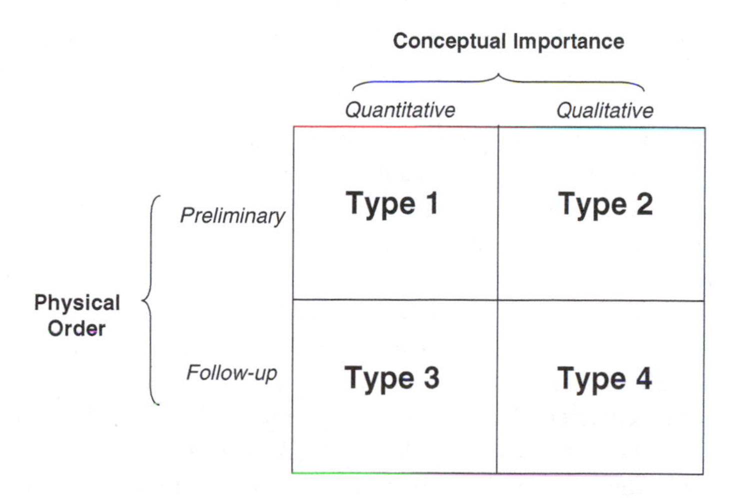

Figure 15.2 Morgan's typology of research approaches
Source: Adapted from Bryman (2004: 455).

The first dimension of the typology is **conceptual priority**, which refers to which method will be used as the primary method of gathering data. Secondly, Morgan refers to the actual **physical sequence** of data gathering, i.e. which comes first? This is quite handy for designing your research, because it allows you to clearly plan what is going to be done. From this typology, I would tend to define aims and objectives for each methodological stage, and how they relate to your overall research question(s). The typology could also be extended, as there is no necessary need to restrict the sequence to just 'preliminary' and 'follow-up'. In fact you might have a further 'follow-up' stage, as we have seen above. The assumption in this model is also that there is a clear dominance or priority of one method over the other, which is not *always* the case. In fact, the idea of 'priority' is also an interesting one, as it can be defined in many ways. What does it mean for one method to have 'priority' over another? In this case, it may also be relevant to think about a 'paradigmatic' dimension to the model, where you make clear your overall philosophical worldview, which then feeds into the research goals, which in turn feed through to the appropriate ways of achieving these goals. This is what I have tried to touch on by using the term 'conceptual priority' to capture this broad idea.

Final notes and reflections

I think the material in this chapter is a nice way of both finishing off discussion about how to do and think about research, as well as tie together a lot of material in this book. By now you should be pretty comfortable with thinking about different epistemologies and ontologies, as well as how the underlying philosophy of knowledge influences exactly what you want to get out of your research project (axiology). You should also now be sharply aware of how the different philosophical paradigms influence the methods you will employ in your research.

However, in the spirit of Donald Davidson's work, you should also now be aware that these paradigmatic differences are *not* irreconcilable. In fact, looking at the shared characteristics of different paradigms, and also exploring how similar methods can be used across the paradigmatic divide, actually helps us to understand the real differences in viewpoint which are inherent to the different paradigms.

That said, it is undeniable that this chapter will have made little sense if you are not comfortable with most of the material I have presented in the earlier parts of this book. If you found yourself struggling, then you really need to go back and re-read the earlier chapters – especially Chapters 2 and 3. Although you may think that this philosophical material is less important than the technical and practical methods I have written about elsewhere, it's really the reverse. The practicalities of research are actually the things that are less important, and understanding the underlying ideas and theories *behind* our practical quest for knowledge is the difference between an 'android' who simply copies the methods of their supervisor or peers, and a fully formed researcher who is able to think for themselves, and make a real contribution to their field. Bearing these things in mind, you need to make sure you are comfortable with the following ideas from this chapter:

- The work of Kuhn and Feyerabend was instrumental in popularising the idea of a 'paradigm'. For our purposes, a paradigm is the set of epistemological and ontological principles which lie behind the search for knowledge.
- Because of the fundamental differences in philosophical assumptions in each paradigm, comparison of work across paradigms is problematic, which gives rise to the term *incommensurability*.
- However, we can define a 'weak-form' incommensurability, which considers the common ground across all paradigms, allowing us to interpret and use research conducted from alternative paradigms.
- Actually conducting research from multiple paradigms simultaneously is not logically possible, *even if you use multiple methods*. One overall paradigm will always dominate when you look carefully.
- On the other hand, mixing methods is perfectly possible, and in fact can lead to some strong advantages in many situations.

Further reading

There's really not a huge amount of work around on this kind of thing, but you can read the works of Kuhn and Feyerabend (see also Chapter 2) which are referred to earlier in the book, and also the book by Bryman (2004) which I have referred to in this chapter and others. Professor Beckmann has also written a book with two colleagues which covers a lot of these issues nicely. Feyerabend's key works are given in the corresponding section of Chapter 2, but the others are:

- *Essentials of Social Science Research Methodology* by Erik S. Rasmussen *et al.*: A nice introduction to the field, and one of the few introductory works which looks seriously at philosophical issues.
- *The Structure of Scientific Revolutions* by Thomas Kuhn: A surprisingly short book for one which has such a vaunted reputation. Do try to make sure you get later versions though, as Kuhn constantly seemed to update, interpret, and re-evaluate his work.
- *Social Research Methods* by Alan Bryman: A very good introduction to some of the multi-method issues appears in the later chapters.

You could also look at the following articles or essays:

- Andrea Davies and James Fitchett (2005) 'Beyond incommensurability? Empirical expansion on diversity in research', *European Journal of Marketing,* 3/4, 272–293.
- Donald Davidson (1974) 'On the very idea of a conceptual scheme', which is available in a 2006 collection titled *The Essential Davidson*. Incidentally, that's where the quotes in this chapter are from.

Finally, a nice book on mixing methods is:

- *Mixing Methods in Psychology* which is edited by Zazie Todd *et al.*

EXERCISES

1. Using the material in Chapters 2, 3, and this one primarily, explain why committing to the principles of an interpretivist philosophical perspective would correspondingly preclude you from conducting research from a realist perspective.
2. Similarly, outline the overlaps between both perspectives – where do they share key features and aims?
3. By now you should have a good feel for your own perspective on research, so think about how you would use research conducted from alternative perspectives in your own work, for example in a literature review. How would you judge whether or not to include such work, and how much weight to give it.
4. How can qualitative methods be used in a realist project?
5. How can quantitative methods be used in an interpretive project?
6. Why is mixing methods not the same as mixing paradigms? You should be able to answer this question very clearly before moving on.
7. Why don't you call someone you haven't spoken to for a while, I bet they miss you!

Chapter 16

Writing and talking about your work

Nick Lee and Ian Lings

SUPERVISOR'S VIEW: PROFESSOR DAN BELLO 

Writing, Talking, and Thinking! A major reason for rejecting academic work at journals and conferences lies in a failure to articulate and communicate the value of the research. Although research may be technically well done, it will not be widely disseminated unless researchers can answer the 'So what?' question and convincingly explain how and why it adds value to the field. Four specific problems can retard the dissemination of an otherwise sophisticated research effort: uninteresting research question; ambiguous positioning; unconvincing contributions; and literature summarisation. While most phenomena are potentially interesting areas of research (there is no short list of hot topics), many studies fail to motivate their research question adequately. There is a failure to establish what is poorly or not understood about a phenomenon and to identify what new or important insights are needed. Create interest by explaining what there is to learn about the phenomenon. Second, studies often suffer from ambiguous positioning by not explaining how the new effort fits into the existing stream of research on the phenomenon. Some extant literature may extend over many decades, so a researcher must articulate how and where a new study fits into the existing body of knowledge. Third, studies frequently fail to explain how the research changes our understanding of the phenomenon. A study must identify how it contributes to the literature; it must specify how it incrementally improves our understanding. Finally, some studies error by merely summarising past literature rather than synthesising and integrating the extant body of knowledge. Existing conceptualisations and empirical findings should be used to support a point of view so that new insights emerge about the phenomenon, presaging the research hypotheses.

Dramatic improvements in these four areas occur during the cycle of revision and resubmission. In fact, an invitation to revise means the research has correctable weaknesses but no 'fatal flaws'. Since revision means 're-seeing' and 're-thinking', re-writing involves the two-step process of new articulation and communication. Prior to the act of re-writing, a researcher may only have the vaguest notion of why the research is interesting and what it contributes to the body of knowledge. First, re-writing involves a creative process of generation and discovery where these key issues are better articulated and understood. During revision, the researcher utilises feedback from reviewers not only to clarify meaning but also to create new meanings that reflect deeper insights into the research and the extant literature. The very act of re-writing leads the researcher to re-think the purpose and outcomes of a study in a way that more effectively articulates its positioning and contributions. Second, in addition to improving articulation, re-writing enhances communication – more effectively conveying and revealing to others what the researcher now better understands. Communication is crucial; writing or speaking that presents material in an unorganised and confusing manner fails to inform and persuade. Importantly, improved communication is preceded by greater clarity in thought – and both are required before an 'acceptance' decision can be made.

VIEW FROM THE TRENCHES: DR MIRELLA KLEIJNEN

'Most of the fundamental ideas of science are essentially simple, and may, as a rule, be expressed in a language comprehensible to everyone.' (Albert Einstein)

Going public with your work is the scariest thing in the world. Up to that moment you can pretend that everyone likes your work and agrees with your thoughts. The reality, though, is an entirely different thing. Horror descended upon me when I first entered the review process, only to find that the reviewers did *not* explode with the same enthusiasm as me when reading my work! Opening yourself up to such criticism can be quite intimidating, not to say discouraging at first. However, the best advice a professor once gave me was 'do not fall in love with your own work'. If reviewers don't understand what you are trying to tell them, you need to rewrite your piece until they do. There is no point in holding on to a piece of paper that doesn't convince anyone of your viewpoint. If you want to be part of the research community, you have to gain an understanding of and appreciation of its rules, and treat those with respect.

Another issue I'm still struggling with is making choices. Page limits are my worst nightmare, as there is always so much to explain yet so little space for it. My strategy here has become one of collecting upon all the favours owned to me by my fellow research friends, just before submitting papers to a journal. I ask them for friendly but candid reviews that signal problems in the positioning of the paper and the clarity of my explanations. While criticism from friends might be even harder to take than criticism from strangers, if even your friends with the best of intentions don't see your point, who will?

You might wonder where you would find such friends. One good way is to go to conferences. Going to conferences serves two major purposes. First of all you can show the research community what you are all about by presenting your work, while simultaneously taking a sneak preview at issues that reviewers might come up with. In some ways this is actually worse than the review process as you cannot retreat into anonymity. However, *neither can your audience*. So here is a great opportunity for civil, constructive discussions on your work, and getting a feel for which outlet might be suitable for your work. Second, and maybe even more importantly, you get to meet lots of new and interesting people. While few people in your social network will understand what on earth you are doing when writing a dissertation, conferences are crowded with people that are all in the same boat. Having connections to fellow researchers will help you to improve your work as well as lift your spirits when the rules of the game do not seem to be working out in your favour. So get out there, and show them what you are made of. You might be pleasantly surprised!

So, you've reached the final chapter – 'at last' many of you will doubtless be thinking. This chapter is about different ways of reporting and defending what you have done. It's at the end of the book not because it is the last thing you need to think about, but because there isn't really any other logical place to put it. In fact, you should really be thinking about what you are going to write about as soon as you start. Of course, that's not to say you should be able to write final drafts of your work before you have finished your research, but you should always be writing. In fact, you might work out later that we actually consider 'writing' to be our main job in the context of research. In many cases though, you will also have to present your work orally, maybe in a presentation, or even an oral examination. Interestingly many people find this side of the research job much more stressful than any other.

The purpose of this chapter is really to give you some useful tools about disseminating your work via the written or spoken word. What we've tried to do here is to add to some of the stuff that is out there in other books, with things we've learnt through our experience, and the experiences of others. We also want to get across our own perspective on the writing and presenting process, and demystify some of the areas which we, and our own colleagues and students, have found difficult in the past. Perhaps the most important section of this chapter is the first one, which deals with what we believe to be the correct 'mindset' to put yourself in when you are disseminating your work to others.

So, for the last time, we'll say, at the end of this chapter we really hope you have come to terms with these key ideas:

- Disseminating your work is of critical importance, and learning to do it well has a big impact on the success of your research.
- Each type of dissemination has a specific purpose, and it is important to understand this.
- You should consider dissemination right the way through your project, not just at the end.
- Keep organised!
- Your write-up should be a carefully structured argument, not just a history of what you have done for the project.
- Different outlets have different styles, and you need to understand these styles to be successful.
- Confidence and preparation are the keys to your success in your viva or a presentation.

Why is it Important to Know This Stuff?

Why is it important to know about writing or talking about your work? If you need to ask that question, then perhaps you need to think about why you are doing research in the first place. As you will hopefully come to understand soon, the process of disseminating your work is really the whole point of doing it! Of course, you could keep the results to yourself, but then you might wonder exactly why you did it in the first place.

However, the dissemination process can be traumatic for many people, and not just new researchers or Ph.D. students either. Some people have little confidence in their own skills at writing or speaking in front of others, and find the whole business of doing so something of a nightmare. One thing which can help reduce this 'fear factor' is the realisation that many other people feel like that too, sometimes even the people who seem to be really confident and brilliant at it. We both remember being surprised at various points, when many of our academic heroes confessed (often at the bar) that they often got very nervous before presentations and the like. It certainly helps to find you are not alone!

But perhaps even more crucially, the writing-up or oral presentation process is one of the most important stages in your success as a researcher. In essence, while it is of course absolutely vital to conduct rigorous research (as much of the rest of this book has covered), learning the most effective way to disseminate that work can move you on to another level. Basically, a well-written thesis or paper, or a great oral presentation or defence, can help you avoid a lot of thorny problems later on. While it is not enough to save a poor piece of research (or maybe we should say it *shouldn't* be enough), a poorly written report or weak oral presentation can most definitely ruin a great piece of research. To find out why, and how you can avoid this problem, read on…

Why disseminate your research? The right mindset to be in

When we are asked about the dissemination of research, we are often reminded of an old saying which is highly relevant: 'If a tree falls in the woods and nobody hears it, did it fall?' Modifying this to the present context; 'If a piece of research gets conducted and nobody hears about it, did it ever get done?' To us, the answer might as well be no. If you go all the way back to Chapter 1, you should remember that part of the duty of the researcher is to disseminate their findings, and this is very important in almost all cases. If you hold a research grant or scholarship, then part of your duty is to disseminate your findings to the funding body, and I imagine you should have already shown them how you will do this before you even got the money. If you are working within a university, part of your duty is to disseminate your findings to relevant outlets, which then helps the university's reputation. You also have a duty to your own field of research, to extend knowledge and *make a contribution*. This contribution is only made when the work is disseminated. Even if you are a commercial researcher (which we aren't really concerned with here), someone needs to know about your findings.

There are many ways of disseminating your work. For example, many of you will be writing a thesis, many of you may want to publish your work in academic or other journal articles, you may have to give an oral defence of your thesis, or do a presentation at a conference. In this chapter we are going to cover both writing and speaking about your work, and the main focus will be on writing a thesis, and then orally defending it. However, we've always thought of these things as simply 'extended remixes' of a journal article or conference presentation, which need the same key features and techniques. So most of this material is relevant whatever stage of your academic career you have reached. That said, the writing and presenting process is a rather personal one, so your own methods and opinions may differ significantly from these. Our intention is that you will take what you need from us, and supplement it with your own experiences and methods. Like a lot of the rest of this book, there is no black and white 'best way' of doing things. In this section, we want to talk about some general issues to do with getting yourself in the right frame of mind to write about or present your work. These are things which will help you throughout your career to see the dissemination process as an enjoyable thing rather than just the chore you have to do at the end.

Perhaps the most important thing to get under control when you start the writing-up and dissemination process for your research is a mental one. If you look back to Chapter 11, and Andrew's 'View from the trenches', you'll see that he talked about the data collection process being totally out of your control, dependent on the whims of your respondents. We felt this too, and it's pretty stressful. However, when it comes to writing about your research, the total opposite is true! This is the only part of your research project that *you are totally in control* of. If you want to work 24 hours a day to finish, the only person to stop you is yourself, you aren't dependent on anyone else, it's just you and your computer (or whatever it is that you use). After all the hassle of actually *doing* research, we both found this process rather liberating. As an aside, it's also good to think of the various dissemination activities as a genuine part of the research itself, not just something you have to tag on to the end. In writing about or otherwise disseminating your work, you are of course 'reporting what you did', but the process can also help you come up with new ideas and directions, and can even have an impact on your conclusions. Of course, it is likely that the more interpretive researcher will be more comfortable with this idea – which is very close to reflexivity – but nevertheless it is worth being aware of it early on in the process. In this way, the dissemination process becomes an integral part of your research activity.

Another major factor in the success of your dissemination efforts – and one which both of us are generally poor at – is *organisation*. We both learnt the hard way that you really need to be well-organised right from the start of your research project in order for the writing up or presentation of that work to go smoothly. Well, we say learnt the hard way, but that implies we have learnt! To be perfectly honest, our organisational skills are still somewhat suboptimal, and we are both lucky to have worked with so many well-organised colleagues! Perhaps the most important thing to keep well-organised is your analysis. Simply put, you need to remember exactly what it is that you did! If you are conducting quantitative analysis good organisation is especially vital, since by the end of a research project you will have done so many bits and pieces of analysis you will never remember exactly what it is that you did. Our motto is to keep records of *every single thing* that you do, to the extent that you could go right back to the start and do it all over again – even down to the mistakes you made. We each kept notebooks when we did our dissertations, but now we use word processor documents. In these documents is every single little piece of information, step-by-step, describing exactly what was done to the data, from collection to final analysis, naming data files, and everything like that. If you could give this record to a colleague, and have them do exactly the same thing as you did, then you are on the right track.

Probably the other major thing you need to keep organised is your literature review, which Ian discussed in Chapter 4. As we shall explain later, it's most likely to be the case that you won't have your final literature review complete until very near the end of the writing process. So it's massively important that you keep a good record of all the literature you used so you can find it again later. There is nothing worse than finding a citation in the text, and then not being able to find exactly what that article is for the bibliography – and almost every one of our colleagues has done this, including us! Different people use different methods, and there are software packages you can use as well, but the method you use is immaterial, just as long as you have a good one!

Finally, make sure you have a way of keeping track of all the brilliant ideas and insights which will occur to you in the course of your life while you are doing your research. Some people have a notebook by their bed, others have a little tape recorder, but whatever it is, make sure you keep it with you. If you are truly engaged in your work, you will tend to think of things at the oddest moments, and trust us *you will forget them if you don't write them down*! The only memory you will have is that the idea was amazing. Mobile phones are actually quite useful here, and we often find ourselves writing little text messages when we come up with something. In fact, Aarti (from Chapter 7's 'View from the trenches') can relate quite a funny story where Nick was driving and came up with a great idea. With no other way of recording it he had to call Aarti[1] to ask her to let him leave a message on her answering machine, and in the process drove straight through an intersection without looking! Fortunately it was a quiet Sunday so no harm was done, but it's a good example of how important it is to record a great idea. Or maybe just that Nick can be an absent-minded fool sometimes.

Our final general point about the 'dissemination mindset' is one that a lot of people have trouble with. Ironically, these people also tend to have done the highest-quality research, but when it comes time to disseminate that work – to 'let it go' so to speak – they struggle. Basically, you have to look at the dissemination process from a somewhat detached mindset, especially when you are writing a thesis or dissertation. This somewhat contradicts our earlier advice to treat dissemination as part of the research itself, but you should be well aware that each of your dissemination efforts are done for a specific purpose as well. For example, the Ph.D. thesis is written and orally defended in order for you to get a Ph.D. degree. Seems obvious, we know, but as we shall show later it is not as easy as it sounds. For example, this means that the Ph.D. is not a demonstration of how many amazing things you did in the last three years, it is a tightly constructed piece of work which tells a clear, coherent story. In many cases, this means *not even talking about* some of the things you did, but we'll get into this in some more depth in the next section. You also have to be fully prepared to send your work out into the world, and in doing so it will become subject to evaluation, and yes, criticism. Accepting this is a key component of your success, and we'll spend time on it during the rest of this chapter. Some of us react to criticism worse than others! We sometimes liken this general idea to sending a child out into the world, eventually you have to let him or her go and once you do that, it's out of your hands. Not easy. Our general advice at this point is to be careful about seeing the research as an extension of yourself or your identity,

---

[1] You may wonder 'why Aarti?' Well, her name comes first in Nick's address book!

and this point is often especially hard for the more interpretive researchers. Try to straddle the line between being fully committed to and excited by your work, and getting your own sense of self and well-being bound up with your research. Although we know it is not that easy. We often find that keeping in mind the overall goal of your research is helpful. Why are you doing this research? If you have a defined goal in mind this helps a lot. For example, what do you hope to achieve with this Ph.D.? An academic career? Or, what do you hope to achieve with this research? An article in the *Journal of Guaranteed Tenure*?[2] Keeping these objective goals in mind helps you focus your efforts on achieving what you want, and seeing the research as a *means to this end.*

Writing about your work

Writing about your research is really the act of 'making it real'. Does research even exist without the written word? This is an interesting question, but it's somewhat beyond the scope of this chapter to discuss it. Either way, have a think about the question while you are reading this section, which deals with some very general and some more specific aspects of writing about your work. The common thread of all the issues we will cover here is that we have seen them cause problems to various researchers in the past, including ourselves, and also that we haven't really seen them dealt with in much depth in other research books.

The first thing to deal with is probably the most common problem that we have seen in written dissertations, and it also has some relevance to those who are writing articles and other types of research write-ups, and it relates to the overall goal of your write up. Remember, the write-up (thesis, article, or similar) is done for a specific reason. You must always remember that reason, and *construct your document completely ruthlessly* to achieve that goal. Essentially, separate your write-up from the act of conducting the research itself. The research has given you the raw material to construct the document. What we are trying to say is **do not think of your write-up as a chronological history of the research project**. This is vital. Your write-up should be a finely constructed argument, designed to achieve a goal. In many cases, you will actually have done many things in the course of your research which you shouldn't include in your write up. For example, when you review the literature, you probably read and wrote many pages of information which you will realise have very little to do with the overall research project as it stands now. Or you might collect data well beyond what you can include in a single project write-up (maybe you included extra measures of additional constructs for future use for example). You must be ruthless about excluding such additional work in your write-up, because including it will not strengthen

[2] This isn't a real journal of course; well, the *name* isn't real anyway!

your work, it will just dilute the quality of your write-up. Research evolves as it proceeds, and what you end up with is very rarely exactly what you set out for. When you write up that research, you need to revisit this earlier work, and make sure everything 'hangs together'. If you read a novel, wouldn't you think it weird if the last few chapters seemed to be telling a story different from the start? It's the same principle for a research write-up. Everything should be focused towards the single goal, not on simply demonstrating 'all the things I did in the last few years'. Alternative View 16.1 gives a slightly different take on this issue.

Alternative View 16.1: The Write-up as Hermeneutic Circle

Perhaps you might remember Chapter 3, when Nick wrote about the 'hermeneutic circle', and how it can be applied to interpretive work? Well, the same basic principle can be applied to writing up a piece of research. Think about a thesis, article, book, or whatever as comprising a lot of different parts (chapters, sections, etc.) The quality of these parts of course determines the quality of the whole document. But the document as a whole is *more* than the simple sum of those parts. The way those parts fit together, support each other, strengthen other parts, and the like, also makes a big contribution to the success of your write-up. You can't take one section out of a larger document and analyse it without any knowledge of the rest of the document. Each individual part influences the whole, and the whole influences the reader's evaluation of the individual parts. It's a difficult thing to get your head around, but if you keep this in mind when you are writing-up your research projects it will help you to consider the whole as well as the individual sections. When you are in the middle of writing-up it's difficult to keep sight of the fact that your document will be treated as a whole, but do try not to forget.

Personally, we think if you internalise and understand the last few pieces of advice, you will already have made major progress towards a great write-up. However, there are a few interesting stylistic issues you might want to think about when writing as well. First of all, make sure you are completely clear on the audience you are writing for. If you are writing an article for a trade magazine, the required style will be completely different from if you are writing an article for the *Journal of Applied Psychology*. In turn, the style for that journal may be different from the style for *Long Range Planning* or *Management Decision*. Again, if you are writing a thesis the style you are using may be different from that for writing a book about research methods! While it is impossible to say exactly how you should write in every situation, there are some useful pointers that can be offered. First and foremost, if you are writing for a particular journal, **make sure you read plenty of articles in that journal**. You can then try to mimic that style. Also, try to make sure that the topic and the methodology you used will 'fit' with the type of things which are usually in that journal. This can be a major impact on your success in publishing.

If you are writing a thesis, the issue of style is a little more complicated. In general though, you can be pretty sure that you should not be writing your work in a 'journalistic' style, or that of a 'blockbuster airport paperback'. You must demonstrate the ability to write clearly, concisely, and usually formally. Of course, make sure you discuss this issue with your supervisor as well, because in some more interpretive frameworks you can justifiably be a little more personal and reflexive. However, if you are in doubt, it is almost always better to err on the side of formality rather than use a casual, personal style. Yes, we know this is boring, but remember the earlier advice – keep your mind focused on the goal of the write-up, not the process.[3] Furthermore, if you are in *any* doubt about your writing, then **get help and advice**. Virtually nobody is a natural writer, and of those that are, even fewer are naturally good at writing about research formally.[4] So practise, ask others for feedback, and don't take it too personally when that feedback comes! And if your first language is not the one you are writing in, please make sure you are able to express your ideas clearly in that language. There is nothing worse than a great piece of work that is hampered by poor writing.

Structuring and actually writing the document

When it comes to the actual task of structuring your write-up, it is hard to give advice that fits everyone. Indeed, entire books have been written on how to write about research. However, we think there are some general issues which are relevant to all scholars who need to write-up their research. A research write-up should usually be structured into a number of parts. First and perhaps foremost is what we call the 'positioning' of the piece. This section (often titled 'introduction') has a key task, and that task is in essence to convince the reader to spend their time reading the rest of the work. If you screw this up, you will fall at the first hurdle. The positioning usually contains four key parts: (a) a compelling introduction into the topic, usually defining some kind of theoretical or practical problem which needs solving; (b) a short discussion of what we do know, and, more importantly, what we don't know about that topic; (c) how *your* research is going to contribute to this topic by building knowledge in the area; (d) how this knowledge will contribute, usually by helping to solve the problem first mentioned in (a). These parts are closely linked, and you want them all to

---

[3]This recalls a comment reportedly made in 2007 by the football manager Jose Mourinho. On the eve of a Cup final against Manchester United, who were at that time renowned for attacking, enjoyable football, he asked his team 'Do you want to enjoy the game, or enjoy *after* the game'. His team, Chelsea, played a defensive, boring, game, winning by a single goal in extra time. Nobody enjoyed that game (it was one of the worst matches of the season), but Chelsea and their fans sure enjoyed it afterwards.

[4]Actually, in our experience, the more gifted a writer you are, the harder you will find it to reign yourself in to write in the formal manner, which is often expected in research articles and theses.

logically follow. For example, in section (b), what you say we don't know should be pretty much what in section (c) you say you are going to discover! These sections should build towards a clear statement of the research objectives, which naturally flows from the previous discussion. Subsequently, you often see a short description of how the rest of the write-up is structured too. The positioning is vital, and you should be very clear on what you want the reader to think by the end of it, then be ruthlessly focused on leading them towards this as you write. Basically, what you want them to think is 'hmm, that *is* a key issue, and we *don't* know some important things about it, but hey, this project is really going to help us understand this important issue better'. If you can't do this, why would anyone read on?

After this, things get a little simpler, because the sections tend to be clearly based on key parts of your actual research. Next should usually come a section where you discuss the existing knowledge on the topic (sometimes called the 'literature review'). This was covered in depth in Chapters 4 and 5 by Ian. When you are writing about the existing literature you need to demonstrate two things very clearly to the reader. First of all you need to make the reader confident that you have covered all of the previous knowledge which is relevant to your topic. Secondly, you will need to convince the reader that this body of knowledge is *not enough* to answer the research question of interest. In other words, by the end you have clearly shown a **gap** in our knowledge. Which, of course, you are going to fill. It's also to your advantage if you can somehow structure the previous knowledge in some new way, which adds insight. You may be able to link previously unrelated strands of theory together, or show how research has focused on one area, to the detriment of our knowledge of others. If you can somehow throw a new light or perspective on extant research, this can really add to the strength of your work. It is around now that hypotheses also begin to rear their head. The only thing we will say here about writing hypotheses is that you must *make sure they have sufficient theoretical back-up*. What we mean here is **not** that you can only formulate hypotheses which have been suggested in previous literature. No, what is meant here is that each hypothesis must be supported by strong logic and theory. In other words, *why* do you propose that hypothesis? In Chapter 5 Ian referred to a great book chapter by Sutton and Staw (2003), which provides some discussion of this point, and we recommend reading it in some depth.

Following the theoretical chapters, we generally find a section on the methodology. This section should really be quite easy, but many have trouble with it, and find it very intimidating. What you are doing here is simply reporting what you did, and to some extent explaining why it was an appropriate method to achieve your research objectives. The only thing you need to provide is a clear description of what you did and why. Sometimes this involves discussing pros and cons of various other methods, but not always! Simply regurgitating 10 pages of text from a research book on 'qualitative versus quantitative methods' and then saying 'that's why I chose quantitative surveys' is *not* a methodology section. Reporting the specific quantitative method you chose, then discussing very clearly why you made that decision and how it is appropriate to the task in hand, is the correct way to write about it. You basically need to do two things here: (a) report your methods in enough detail that they can be replicated; and (b) show that these methods were an appropriate way to answer your questions. Then, the reader can judge for themselves whether you did things appropriately. Perhaps the most important thing to keep in mind when writing about your methods is that you need to show the reader that **your methods did not unduly influence your results**. For example, is your sample likely to have influenced your findings? Keep this in mind when writing about your methods, and also when making your conclusions.

After your methods are detailed, the results are reported and discussed. There are different ways of writing this section, depending on your own background, discipline, and, indeed, method. In quantitative studies, we often first see a short section reporting the raw results and hypothesis tests (e.g. 'Hypothesis 1 was supported with a beta value of ...' etc.) followed by a longer discussion of the results. However, in more qualitative work the results are often reported and discussed at the same time, in keeping with a more reflexive, interpretive standpoint. Either way, you need to show a few things in this section. First you need to make sure the reader actually understands your results clearly. If you used novel or complex analysis methods, don't assume that the reader will naturally understand what you are talking about. Be very clear about what result 'x' actually means in the context of your overall research project. Then, when you are discussing your results, make sure you show clearly how they fit in with our existing knowledge. Do they contradict what we thought we knew? Do they extend our knowledge? How do they relate to other parts of theory which are already in existence? What relevance do they have to future researchers? If you are working in an applied field, such as business research, you should also be able to provide a discussion of how your results can help practitioners (such as business people). In fact this is often a part which many people find difficult, and it is usually the case that first attempts have to be re-written plenty of times. You also have to keep in mind the implications of your methods for the conclusions you can draw. For example, if you only sampled females, can you be justified in drawing conclusions which apply to males as well? Or are your conclusions industry or context-specific? Did you miss out important variables which may have shown your key relationships to be spurious? Keep this in mind, as your readers must be sure that your results are not totally dependent on your methods.

Finally, there tends to be a final 'summing up' section. Often this section includes things like overall conclusions, limitations of your work, and directions for future research. Conclusions should be clear statements of what your work has discovered, and how it relates to what we know already. Clearly state how it has made a contribution to existing knowledge, so the reader is left in no doubt that this is indeed an important piece of work. That said, don't over-egg the pudding by being too confident – saying things like 'these results prove x causes y' is unlikely to be convincing, unless of course you can justify this![5] Researchers

[5]If you don't understand why you shouldn't talk about either 'proof' or 'causality' then perhaps you should go back to Chapters 2 and 3 at least.

often have trouble with discussing the limitations of their work. This is understandable, as you need to walk a fine line between being honest but not completely invalidating your work. Here, you are trying to give the reader a full set of knowledge about how to interpret your results, and whether your methods have unduly influenced those results. No one expects the 'perfect' piece of research as this is pretty much impossible, so reporting genuine limitations on how your findings can be interpreted is completely accepted. Together, all this information should point quite clearly towards some directions for future research. Here you should make useful and interesting suggestions for how your work can influence future research in the area. Indeed, if your work doesn't make an impact on future work, what was the point of it in the first place? Researchers often neglect this section, and just dash it off at the end. But when you think about it, it's arguably one of the most important. After all, your research should fit in with an ever-growing body of knowledge, influencing future work. Your academic reputation is built by others using your work, and making compelling suggestions about how this could be done is a vital first step.

After all of this information on 'what' to write, it is probably going to be useful to provide a short discussion on some key technical aspects of writing about your work. Firstly, make sure you know exactly how you should be formatting your work, according to the relevant regulations. It's most helpful to do this at the start, *especially* if you are writing a long document such as a thesis. There is nothing worse than finding out at the end that you have to change all of your formatting for 300 pages to something completely different. Make sure you get comfortable with your word-processor as well, as it will probably contain features that will make your life *much* easier. Invest in a book of tips and instructions for it, as the manual and help files for most software are rubbish. Make sure before you submit your thesis, or journal article, that it is **perfectly in the required format**. As an editor, there is nothing worse than a manuscript where the author has not even bothered to format it correctly; we often think 'do they even want to publish this?' This brings us to another key point, that of **referencing**. Now, there are hundreds of different formats for referencing, so our key advice is to make sure you follow the required format for your intended outlet absolutely. When in doubt of the required format, we would usually advise using the 'Harvard' style of citing and referencing (see IDE 16.1).

IDE 16.1: The Harvard Referencing Style

While the Harvard referencing style is not the only one you can use, it is a handy one to know, and when in doubt we think this is a great fall-back option. It is also a good tool with which to get used to the idea of referencing. But when you are actually writing for a specific purpose, **make sure you are clear on the style expected of you**

for that particular outlet beforehand – don't assume it will be this, or any other style you are aware of.

Harvard referencing is basically the style you will have seen in this book. It is based on short in-text citations, which refer the reader to a section at the end of the document which collects the full citations or references. In the text, if you wish to cite a source, you would use the authors' second names, and the year of publication. These are normally cited in brackets, for example (Lee and Hooley, 2005), but in some cases only the year is in brackets, for example Lee and Hooley (2005) said … You should include a page number if you are citing a particular section, and always when you make a direct quote. If the same authors have published more than one work in that year which you cite, use letters (e.g. Smith and Jones, 2007a, Smith and Jones, 2007b), but make sure you keep these consistent in the reference section! Also, if you are referring to a reprint of the original work, the original date should be included in square brackets, for example (Blalock [1961] 1972).

When you collect the references together at the end of your work, you need to make sure you do so in the format preferred by your outlet. These should be formally given somewhere, and you need to make sure you follow the guidelines closely. For example, a book reference usually takes the general form of: Smith, Alan, and Jones, Fred (2007a) *One Million Monkeys on One Million Typewriters.* London, Made-Up Book Publishing.

You can see that all the relevant details are given. If the city is small you should also give the country, or state and country for the US. An article reference in general would look similar to: Smith, Alan and Jones, Fred (2007b) 'A monkey-based theory of literary fiction', *Journal of Guaranteed Tenure*, Vol. 42: 1124–1178.

Here, you can see you give the journal name, volume number, and page references. Sometimes you might give the issue number, for example, Vol. 42 (3).

There are many other details to be learned about effective referencing, so make sure you are clear on the relevant guidelines.

However, so many people have trouble with referencing that maybe it will help to think about the actual purpose of referencing. When you provide a reference for an idea, you are showing the reader that you did not think of this yourself; you are reporting what somebody else has said to support your own arguments. When you provide the reference, you are giving the details so that the reader can then go and see for themselves that individual piece of work. So of course, in the reference section at the end of the document, you must provide all the relevant details so the reader can find the article. The in-text *citation* (e.g. 'Lee and Hooley, 2005') is simply there to (a) show exactly where you have built on the work of others, and (b) point the reader to the right place in the reference section at the end. Get these two things right, and you won't have any problems with referencing. Finally, we both remember being confused by the stylistic abbreviations that are often used in academic articles, such as 'cf.', or 'ibid' and the like. So in IDE 16.2 we have provided examples and definitions of these to help you use them correctly.[6]

IDE 16.2: Those Confusing Abbreviations and Their Use

There are lots of bits and pieces that cause confusion for those who are writing about research. In particular are the 'technical details', and chief among these are those strange little abbreviations of Latin that you see in articles. These often have specific meanings in certain fields, such as Law, and the sciences, but here we are discussing how they might be used in more general research writing. Few people know how to use them, and even fewer know what they mean. So here are the most commonly used (and abused), along with their meaning, and how you should use them.

Cf. is short for the Latin *confer*, which means 'consult' or 'compare'. It is used quite commonly in articles to signify when you are asking the reader to go and have a look at another article – but not quite giving a direct reference or example. We always found this one the hardest to use appropriately, especially when it comes to deciding whether to use 'e.g.' or cf.

e.g. is short for the Latin *exempli gratia*, or basically; 'for example'. While you probably knew that, it's important to make sure you use it correctly (especially in relation to i.e. as we show below). As a general rule, only use the abbreviation e.g. inside brackets and the like. In the general flow of your writing, you should use longer forms such as 'for example' or 'by way of example'.

i.e. is short for the Latin *id est*, which means 'in other words'. Use this instead of e.g. when you are clarifying, elaborating, or explaining, rather than giving examples. One useful point is that American style tends to prefer a comma after e.g. or i.e., while British style does not.

etc. is short for the Latin *et cetera* which means 'and other things'. It should be used to represent logical continuation of a list. You should always precede it by a comma.

et al. is short for the Latin *et alii* which means 'and others'. It is used to refer to articles with long lists of authors. There are various rules as to how many authors it takes before you can use *et al.* If in doubt, we usually use *et al.* when there are more than three authors. It is general convention in social science to only use *et al.* in the actual body of the article or thesis, with the full list of authors in the later reference section. However, the natural sciences often allow *et al.* in the reference list also.

[6] That said, we don't guarantee that we have used them correctly in this book ourselves!

ibid. is short for the Latin *ibidem* which means 'the same place'. It is sometimes used to provide a citation to the source which was cited in the immediately preceding citation. This tends to be used only when one is using endnotes or footnotes for citations, rather than the more traditional social scientific in-text citation style.

op cit. is short for the Latin *opera citato*, meaning 'from the cited work'. This is again rarely used in social science writing. It is used to refer the reader back to a previous citation in an endnote or footnote. For example, if in a footnote you cite 'Lee and Hooley, Classical Mythology in Marketing Measure Development, *European Journal of Marketing*, 2005: page x', and later on you want to save yourself the effort of writing all that in the footnote or endnote the next time you want to cite the article, you might say 'Lee and Hooley *op cit.* page y'. Personally, we hate *op cit.* as it is really putting your ease above the ease of the reader. Which as a general rule should never be done.

Talking about your work

Talking about your work is a little bit more difficult to advise you on than writing about it. Specifically, there are so many different 'styles' of oral presentation which work well, that we think it is probably better to find the style you feel comfortable with, rather than try to 'fit in' to a role somebody else tells you to. However, there are some key pointers which will be useful to everybody, in our opinion that is. There are probably two main occasions that your typical academic researcher will have to talk about their work. First and foremost for many of you will be your *viva voce*, or oral defence of your thesis. However, almost all academics will at one time or another have to present their research in front of an audience, perhaps at a conference, or even within their own faculty. Many scholars feel almost as apprehensive about this as they do/did about their viva. We'll primarily focus on the oral defence, but also spend some time on conference presentations, as they do have some significant differences.

The *viva voce* is something which causes a lot of stress to almost every research student, and for many this stress is far in excess of the actual difficulty of the viva. Our key task in this section is to try to reduce that stress a little, by focusing on the one attribute which will have more bearing than any other on your success in all forms of presentation – **confidence**. If you are confident in yourself and your work, things will go a lot smoother, even when unexpected difficulties crop up. The first thing to say in this regard is that if you are stressed and nervous before your viva or presentation, then *you are not alone*. Almost everybody is, even the people who do not seem to be. In fact, if you are not nervous in some way, you should be worried. Usually this means you are either (a) completely uninterested in the result, or (b) over-confident. Both these situations cause problems, and the audience or examiners can see them very clearly. So embrace your nerves, they are the body's way of helping you perform. It is only when you get *too* nervous that you should start thinking about getting some help to reduce your nervousness. And don't be ashamed if you need to do this. Some people remember that Nick was so nervous before his first ever presentation that he needed pills to calm him down!

The first thing you need in order to build your confidence is an appreciation of what the *viva voce* is there to do. It takes many different forms in different countries, but we will try to focus on the general concept of an 'oral defence' of your work'. *Viva voce* is Latin for 'by live voice'. There are three basic things you need to convince your examiners of during this process: (a) that it is your own work; (b) that you are a competent researcher; and (c) that you can justify anything about your work that your examiners might be unsure of. So let's take these one by one. Regarding whether or not it is your own work, rest assured that in general the examiner believes that it is! They are just trying to make sure you really know it inside out, and that it was *you* that was responsible for it all. They'll be asking you stuff about what the work is about, which theoretical framework(s) it is located in, what contribution(s) to knowledge it makes, and a lot of other broad questions like that. You also need to demonstrate in general that you are worthy of the title 'Ph.D.', which they worked hard to get themselves. So they might ask you plenty of questions which allow you to demonstrate your knowledge and capabilities. However, much of the time will probably be spent on the third task. It is natural that your work will have some limitations, things you might have done differently, and things which the examiner either doesn't understand or doesn't agree with. This is the point where you need to 'defend' what you did.

The 'defence' component can be the source of problems if it is not handled well either by the student or the examiner. First, realise that this should not be an 'argument' between you and the examiner, it is a discussion between different viewpoints. Second, realise that by now you are supposed to be the expert in the topic of your thesis, but you are not necessarily the expert in everything! Remember your examiners were generally chosen because they are highly respected in the field, so give them and their opinions the respect they deserve. On the other hand, you need to defend your own point of view. Most importantly, this is hardly ever a case of saying 'viewpoint x is *the most appropriate* view', more that it is *an appropriate* view. There is no shame or problem in disagreement, as long as both views are well-justified.

Hopefully, if you have read this entire book, you should realise that there are rarely black or white, right or wrong situations in research. In this spirit then, do not get defensive in attitude when your examiners query the decisions you made. Do **not** interrupt before they have finished, or jump in with your answer, and do **not** take it personally, even if you feel that way. Simply consider their question, and then state your own viewpoint and why it was an appropriate course of action or thought.

Perhaps the best description either of us has ever heard of the purpose of a viva was from one of Nick's external examiners, Professor Adamantios Diamantopoulos. He told Nick that his view was that the viva was a 'chance for the student to shine', not a chance for the examiner to tear them apart and make themselves look smart. We think this is the way a viva should be approached. You are being given the opportunity to explain in depth what you did and why you did it, to a renowned expert. It is relatively rare for a student to fail their degree solely as the result of a poor viva. However, a poor viva can give you a lot more work to do afterwards to modify your thesis, whereas a good viva can save you a lot of time and trouble afterwards. So make sure you know exactly *why* you did the things that you did, and be prepared to defend and justify them.

In fact, **preparation** is probably the biggest factor in building your confidence up before your viva. Do not submit your written work (no matter how brilliant it is) and then forget about it until the day before your viva appointment. Sure, submit it and then take a few days off as a reward. However, quickly get back into it to prepare for your viva. First things first, make sure you read the whole thing cover to cover. When you write stuff in separate chapters, you will be amazed at how different things look and feel when taken as a whole (remember Alternative View 16.1 above). Then you will want to clearly understand exactly what each chapter and section is aimed at doing. You may wish to write very brief summaries of each chapter as well; this can help you really cut to the core of what you are trying to say. After this, talk with your supervisor, together, think about the areas you are likely to get criticised on, and prepare justifications for why you did the things you did. If you *have* done things which might be a little suboptimal (a common example is that your sample was small or context-specific), prepare answers which explain how these factors do not invalidate your results. Then prepare answers – really good answers – for basic questions like 'what is your thesis about', 'why did you choose this topic', 'what is your contribution to theory' and that kind of thing. When it gets close to the viva date, try to have a 'mock viva' with someone, ideally not your supervisor. This will help you more than you realise.

When you're actually in your viva, try to stay calm and focused as much as possible. Make sure beforehand that you have found out what you are allowed to bring in, normally you are able to bring in notes and your thesis. If so, prepare your notes and thesis, perhaps with markers to key areas so you can flip to it easily. When you are asked questions, make sure you understand the question before you answer. If necessary ask your questioner to repeat the question. Do not be defensive – yes we realise that we said it was a 'defence' earlier, but this does not mean you need to jump down your examiner's throat or attack them aggressively. Take each question as a chance for you to demonstrate that what you did was appropriate, or to demonstrate your wide knowledge of the area. But not as a chance to prove you are 'smarter' than everyone else. If you are able to answer your questions convincingly, you will often persuade your examiner not to ask for major changes to your work, even if they disagree with your approach from their own perspective. However, if they *do* ask for changes, make them as quickly as possible. There is no point arguing about it if they are unwilling to be convinced; after all they are the examiner. So after your viva, just get on with making those changes as soon as you can, whether or not you thought they were justified!

Doing a presentation of your work, for example at a conference, is kind of similar to a viva, but at the same time different. In fact, some oral defences are actually mainly presentation-based. All of the things we said above apply, especially the importance of preparation and confidence. However, when you are presenting, you have to make a special effort to make your work **interesting** to the audience. The worst kind of presentation is one where the presenter just reads out their paper. We've both seen these presentations before, and they are painful. If your audience just wanted the information in the paper, they wouldn't have bothered turning up! Offer something different, not different work of course, but maybe something they can't get in the written paper. In fact, unless you are given a specific brief that your audience are there to see something in particular, assume your audience are there to see someone else, and that you need to 'sell yourself' to them.

Perhaps most importantly when it comes to presentations, **practice makes perfect**. It will probably take you quite a few presentations before you find your own style. Some people are more 'flashy' than others, there's no problem with this, as long as you are comfortable with it. However, always keep your eyes open for tips you can learn from others who you admire. Never be too proud to shamelessly steal a trick or two! Furthermore, we are both fully committed advocates of *practising your presentation* before doing it. This makes you so much more confident and smooth in your delivery, and allows you to focus on making it a great presentation.

Final conclusions, and Goodbye!

In general, the dissemination process is one which should be kind of enjoyable. However, for too many people it is seen as the 'chore' that has to be done after the research is finished. In reality, it is the quality of your written or oral presentations which is what the rest of the world actually sees! Only you are party to the actual research in its rawest form; everybody else just sees your work. So in many ways your dissemination activities are your actual 'products', which you ultimately get judged on. Learning how to write and present your work well certainly won't turn a poor researcher into a good one, but being a poor writer or presenter can lead a good researcher to be seen as less than s/he deserves. It's kind of like being a photographer – the raw material is on the film, but without developing it properly it will never be a good photograph.

Perhaps the best way to learn to enjoy writing or presenting is just to get started doing it. Don't wait until the end of the research to start thinking about what you are going to do with it; get on with it *now*. If you are doing a research degree, think about writing an article for a journal now, or even better, for a conference (then you will get to present it too). You might not like the idea of doing this right now, but in the end you are going to have to, so you might as well get used to it as early as possible.

In fact, the dissemination process is where everything you have learnt about research, and all the material we have written about in this book, comes home to roost. If you don't understand *why* you did things, you are unlikely to ever be able to write convincingly about your work. Even more so, you will not be able to talk about or defend your work in any convincing manner to somebody who does not necessarily agree with you. Remember, one of the messages of this book is that research is not about agreement, it is about *disagreement*. People have different opinions on the same topic. On many of these occasions both views will be perfectly justified – even if you completely disagree with one of them! This is not a case of 'right or wrong', but an opportunity to learn and develop, which – after all – is what being a researcher is all about.

Just to finish off, they key points to this chapter were:

- Both writing and talking about your work are important, and both require separate skills.
- Consider the dissemination process as another component of the research, not just the bit at the end of it.
- Make sure you understand the purpose of your dissemination activities, and ruthlessly structure your work to achieve these goals.
- Understand the key technical skills and stylistic aspects of writing for your outlet, and put these into practise carefully.
- Develop confidence and your own style when presenting or otherwise talking about your work.
- Prepare and practise any presentation you have to give!
- Take the oral presentation process as an opportunity to get feedback, not as a battle between you and an audience. Don't take things too personally.
- Finally, enjoy it if you can!

Further reading

Just like the previous chapter, there isn't a lot of dedicated work on this topic either. Many of the books covered in previous chapters are useful here. However, some other books which you might find helpful are:

- *Researching and Writing A Dissertation For Business Students* by Colin Fisher. A handy book with some original content which many people will find a useful introduction to the area.
- *Researching and Writing Dissertations in Business and Management* by Michael Riley *et al.* Similar to the book by Fisher cited above, this is a good general overview of the process.
- *Tricks of the Trade* by Howard S. Becker. Not specifically a book on writing, but a very interesting perspective on the research process in general.

EXERCISES

1. No more real exercises here, just some advice: *Get writing!*
2. Oh, and don't forget to **have fun!**

Bibliography

Adams, D. (1979) *'The Hitchhiker's Guide to the Galaxy'*, Pan Macmillan, London.

Adorno, T. W. and Horkheimer, M. (1997) *'Dialectic of Enlightement'*, Verso, London.

Althiede, D. L. (1996) *'Qualitative Media Analysis'*, Sage, Thousand Oaks: CA.

Amit, R. and Schoemaker, P. J. H. (1993) 'Strategic assets and organizational rent', *Strategic Management Journal*, 14 (1): 33.

Andrews, M., Sclater, S. D., Squire, C. and Tamboukou, M. (2004) 'Narrative research', in C. Seale, G. Gobo, J. F. Gubrium and D. Silverman (eds), *Qualitative Research Practice*, Sage, London.

Armstrong, J. S. (1995) 'Publication of research on controversial topics: The early acceptance procedure', *International Journal of Forecasting*, 11, Notes: 1–4.

Armstrong, J. S., Brodie, R. J. and Parsons A. G. (2001) 'Hypotheses in marketing science: Literature review and publication audit', *Marketing Letters*, 12 (2), 171–187.

Armstrong, J. S. and Overton, T. S. (1977) 'Estimating nonresponse bias in mail surveys', *Journal of Marketing Research,* XIV (August), 396–402.

Babbie, E. (2006) *'The Practice of Social Research'*, International Thomson Publishing, London.

Bagozzi, R. P. and Edwards, J. R. (1998) 'A general approach for representing constructs in organizational research', *Organizational Research Methods*, 1 (1): 45–87.

Baumgartner, H. and Steenkamp, J-B. E. M. (2001) 'Response styles in marketing research: A cross-national investigation', *Journal of Marketing Research,* 38 (2): 143–156.

Becker, H. S. (1998) *'Tricks of the Trade: How to Think About Your Research While You're Doing It'*, University of Chicago Press, Chicago: IL.

Bell, J. (2007) *'Doing Your Research Project: A Guide for First-Time Researchers in Education, Health and Social Science'*, 4th edn, Open University Press, London.

Bird, A. (1998) *'Philosophy of Science'*, Routledge, London.

Blaikie, N. (2004) 'Interpretivism', in M. S. Lewis-Beck, A. Bryman, T. F. Liao (eds), *The Sage Encyclopedia of Social Science Research Methods*, Sage, London, 508–510.

Blalock, H. M. (1982) *'Conceptualization and Measurement in the Social Sciences'*, Sage, Beverly Hills: CA.

Bollen, K. A. (2002) 'Latent variables in psychology and the social sciences', *Annual Review of Psychology*, 53: 605–634.

Borsboom, D. (2005) *'Measuring the Mind: Conceptual Issues in Contemporary Psychometrics'*, Cambridge University Press, Cambridge.

Brown, D. (2003) *'Angels and Demons'*, Corgi, London.

Brown, S. (1995) *'Postmodern Marketing'*, Thomson, London.

Brown, S. (1997) *'Postmodern Marketing 2'*, Thomson, London.

Bryman, A. (1988) *'Quantity and Quality in Social Research'*, Routledge, London.

Bryman, A. (2004) *'Social Research Methods'*, 2nd edn, Oxford University Press, Oxford.

Burr, V. (1995) *'An Introduction to Social Constructionism'*, Routledge, London.

Buzzell, R. D. (1963) 'Is marketing a science?', *Harvard Business Review*, 41 (1): 32–40.

Calder, B. J., Phillips, L. W. and Tybout, A. M. (1982) 'The concept of external validity', *Journal of Consumer Research*, 9 (3): 240–244.

Carmines, E. G. and Zeller, R. A. (1979) *'Reliability and Validity Assessment'*, Sage, Beverly Hills, CA.

Cattell, R. B. and Kline, P. (1977) *'The Scientific Analysis of Personality and Motivation'*, Academic Press, London.

Churchill, G. A., Jr. (1979) 'A paradigm for developing better measures of marketing constructs', *Journal of Marketing Research*, 64–73.

Churchill, G. A. and Iacobucci, D. (2004) *'Marketing Research: Methodological Foundations'*, 9th edn, South-Western, Mason: OH.

Clayman, S. E. and Gill, V. T. (2004) 'Conversation analysis', in M. Hardy and A. Bryman (eds), *Handbook of Data Analysis*, Sage, London.

Cohen, J., Cohen, P., West, S. G. and Aiken, L. S. *'Applied Multiple Regression/Correlation Analysis for the Behavioral Sciences'*, 3rd edn, Lawrence Erlbaum, Mahwah: NJ.

Combe, I. and Greenley, G. (2004) 'Capabilities for strategic flexibility: a cognitive content framework', *European Journal of Marketing*, 38 (11/12): 1456–1480.

Craig, C. S. and Douglas, S. P. (2005) *'International Marketing Research'*, John Wiley and Sons, London.

Creswell, J. W. (2007) *'Qualitative Inquiry and Research Design: Choosing Among Five Approaches'*, 2nd edn, Sage, London.

Daniels, S. and Martin, J. (1999) 'It's Darwinism – survival of the fittest: How markets and reputations shape the ways in which plaintiffs' lawyers obtain clients', *Law & Policy*, 21 (4): 377–399.

Davidson, D. (1974) 'On the very idea of a conceptual scheme', *Proceedings and Addresses of the American Philosophical Association*, XLVII: 5–20.

Davidson, D. (2006) *'The Essential Davidson'*, Oxford University Press, Oxford.

Davies, A. and Fitchett, J. A. (2005) 'Beyond incommensurability? Empirical expansion on diversity in research', *European Journal of Marketing*, Vol. 39 (3/4): 272–293.

Dennett, D. C. (1996) *'Darwin's Dangerous Idea'*, Penguin Books, London.

Denzin, N. K. and Lincoln, Y. S. (eds) (1998) *'Collecting and Interpreting Qualitative Materials'*, Sage, Thousand Oaks: CA.

DeVellis, R. F. (1991) *'Scale Development: Theory and Applications'*, Sage, London.

Diamantopoulos, A. and Shlegelmilch, B. (1997) *'Taking the Fear Out of Data Analysis'*, Thomson Learning, London.

Diamantopoulos, A. and Winklhofer, H. M. (2001) 'Index construction with formative indicators: An alternative to scale development', *Journal of Marketing Research*, 38 (2): 269–277.

Diamantopoulos, A., Reynolds, N. and Schlegelmilch, B. (1994) 'Pretesting in questionnaire design: the impact of respondent characteristics on error detection', *Journal of the Market Research Society*, 36 (4): 295–315.

Dillman, D. A. (2006) *'Mail and Internet Surveys: The Tailored Design Method'*, John Wiley and Sons, London.

Eisenhardt, K. and Martin, J. (2000) 'Dynamic capabilities: What are they?' *Strategic Management Journal*, 21 (10/11): 1105.

Feyerabend, P. K. (1985) *'Realism, Rationalism, and Scientific Method: Philosophical Papers Volume 1'*, Cambridge University Press, Cambridge.

Feyerabend, P. K. (1993) *'Against Method'*, 3rd edn, Verso, London.

Field, A. (2005) *'Discovering Statistics Using SPSS'*, Sage, London.

Fisher, C. (2004) *'Researching and Writing a Dissertation for Business Students'*, Pearson Education, Harlow: UK.

Flick, U. (2006) *'An Introduction to Qualitative Research'*, 3rd edn, Sage, Thousand Oaks, CA.

Franzosi, R. P. (2004) 'Content analysis', in M. Hardy and A. Bryman (eds), *Handbook of Data Analysis*, Sage, London.

Gaarder, J. (1997) *'Sophie's World'*, Orion Children's Books

Gane, L. and Chan, K. (2005) *'Introducing Nietzche'*, Icon Books, Duxford, Cambridge.

Gerbing, D. W. and Anderson, J. C. (1988) 'An updated paradigm for scale development incorporating unidimensionality and its assessment', *Journal of Marketing Research*, 186–192.

Gerbing, D. W. and Hamilton, J. G. (1996) 'Viability of exploratory factor analysis as a precursor to confirmatory factor analysis', *Structural Equation Modeling* 3 (1): 62–72.

Glaser, B. G. (1992) *'Basics of Grounded Theory Analysis'*, Sociology Press, Mill Valley: CA.

Glaser, B. G. and Strauss, A. L. (1967) *'The Discovery of Grounded Theory: Strategies for Qualitative Research'*, Aldine, Chicago.

Gruber, M. and Harhoff, D. (2001) 'Generierung und Nachhaltige Sicherung Komparativer Wettbewerbsvorteile' *ODEON Center for Entrepreneurship/Institut für Innovationsforschung und Technologiemanagement.*

Guba, E. G. and Lincoln, Y. S. (1994) 'Competing paradigms in qualitative research', in N. K. Denzin and Y. S. Lincoln (eds), *Handbook of Qualitative Research*, Sage, Thousand Oaks, CA.

Gummesson, E. (2000) *'Qualitative Methods in Management Research'*, Sage, Thousand Oaks: CA.

Hackley, C. (2000) 'Silent running: Tacit, discursive and psychological aspects of management in a top UK advertising agency', *British Journal of Management*, 11 (3): 239–254.

Hackley, C. (2003) *'Doing Research Projects in Marketing, Management and Consumer Research'*, Routledge, London.

Hair, J. F., Black, B., Babin. B., Anderson, R. E. and Tatham, R. L. (2005) *'Multivariate Data Analysis'*, 9th edn, Prentice Hall, Harlow, UK.

Hambrick, D. C. (1983) 'Some tests of the effectiveness and functional attributes of miles and snow's strategic types', *Academy of Management Journal*, 26 (1): 5.

Hammersley, M. (ed.) (1992) *'What's Wrong with Ethnography? Methodological Explorations'*, Routledge, London.

Hammersley, M. (1996) 'The relationship between qualitative and quantitative research: Paradigm loyalty versus methodological eclecticism', in J. T. E. Richardson (ed.) *Handbook of Research Methods for Psychology and the Social Sciences*, BPS Books, Leicester, UK.

Hammersley, M. (2004) 'Phenomenology', in M. S. Lewis-Beck, A. Bryman, T. F. Liao (eds), *The Sage Encyclopedia of Social Science Research Methods*, Sage, London: 815.

Hand, D. J. (2004) *'Measurement: Theory and Practice: The World Through Quantification'*, Hodder Arnold, London.

Hart, C. (1998) *'Doing a Literature Review: Releasing the Social Science Research Imagination'*, Sage: London.

Hawking, S. (1998) *'A Brief History of Time'*, 10th Anniv. Edn, Bantam Doubleday Dell.

Helfat, C. and Peteraf, M. (2003) 'The dynamic resource-based view: Capability lifecycles', *Strategic Management Journal*, 24 (10): 997–1010.

Helfat, C., Finkelstein, S., Mitchell, W., Peteraf, M., Singh, H., Teece, D. and Winter, S. (2007) *'Dynamic Capabilities: Understanding Strategic Change in Organisations'*, Blackwell Publishing, Malden.

Hirschman, E. C. (ed.) (1989) *'Interpretive Consumer Research'*, Association for Consumer Research, Provo: UT.

Hodges, W. (2001) *'Logic'*, Penguin Books, London.

Holloway, R. J. (1961) 'Which automobiles will be here tomorrow?' *Journal of Marketing*, 25 (3): 35.

Hubbard, R. and Armstrong, J. S. (1997) 'Publication bias against null results', *Psychological Reports*, 80: 337–338.

Hunt, S. D. (1991) *'Marketing Theory: The Philosophy of Marketing Science'*, Irwin, Homewood: IL.

Hunt, S. D. (2002) *'Foundations of Marketing Theory: Towards a General Theory of Marketing'*, M. E. Sharpe, Armonk: NY.

Hunt, S. D. (1990) 'Truth in marketing theory and research', *Journal of Marketing*, 54 (July): 1–15.

Hunt, S. D. (2003) *'Controversy in Marketing Theory: For Reason, Realism, Truth and Objectivity'*, M. E. Sharpe, Armonk: NY.

Kachigan, S. K. (1982) *'Multivariate Statistical Analysis: A Conceptual Introduction'*, Radius Press, New York: NY.

Kerlinger, F. N. and Lee, H. (1999) *'Foundations of Behavioral Research'*, 4th edn, Thomson, London.

Kidwell, R. E., Jr. (1995) 'Social Darwinism and the Taylor system: A missing link in the evolution of management?' *International Journal of Public Administration*, 18 (5): 767.

Kincaid, H. (1994) 'Defending laws in the social sciences', in M. Martin and L. C. McIntyre (eds), *Readings in the Philosophy of Social Science*, MIT Press, Cambridge, MA: 111–131.

King, M. F. and Bruner, G. C. (2000) 'Social desirability bias: A neglected aspect of validity testing', *Psychology and Marketing*, 17 (2): 79–103.

Kitzinger, C. (2004) 'Feminist approaches', in C. Seale, G. Gobo, J. F. Gubrium and D. Silverman (eds), *Qualitative Research Practice*, Sage, London.

Kline, P. (2000) *'The Handbook of Psychological Testing'*, Routledge, London.

Kuhn, T. S. (1970) *'The Structure of Scientific Revolutions'*, 2nd edn, University of Chicago Press, Chicago: IL.

Lather, P. (1993) 'Fertile obsession: Validity after poststructuralism', *Sociological Quaterly*, 34 (4): 673–693.

Law, K. S., Wong, C. and Mobley, W. H. (1998) 'Towards a taxonomy of multidimensional constructs', *Academy of Management Review*, 23 (4): 741–755.

LeCompte, M. D., Preissle, J. and Tesche, R. (1993) *'Ethnography and Qualitative Design in Educational Research'*, Academic Press, San Diego.

Lee, N. and Hooley, G. (2005) 'The evolution of "classical mythology" within marketing measure development', *European Journal of Marketing*, Vol. 39 (3/4).

Lee, N. J. and Cadogan, J. W. (1998) 'A qualitative analysis of key patterns of the meanings of managerial ruthlessness: Preliminary findings and an agenda for future research', *ANZMAC 1998 Conference*, Otago University, New Zealand.

Losee, J. (2001) *'A Historical Introduction to the Philosophy of Science'*, Oxford University Press, Oxford.

MacCorquodale, K. and Meehl, P. E. (1948) 'On a distinction between hypothetical constructs and intervening variables', *Psychological Review*, 55: 95–107.

Magee, B. (1997) *'Popper'*, Fontana/Collins, Glasgow: UK.

Mann, C. and Stewart, F. (2000) *'Internet Communication and Qualitative Research: A Handbook for Researching Online'*, Sage, London.

Manning, P. K. (2004) 'Semiotics and data analysis', in M. Hardy and A. Bryman (eds), *Handbook of Data Analysis*, Sage, London.

Marshall, C. and Rossman, G. B. (1999) *'Designing Qualitative Research'*, 3rd edn, Sage, Thousand Oaks: CA.

Mason, J. (1996) *'Qualitative Researching'*, Sage, London.

Mautner, T. (ed.) (2000) *'The Penguin Dictionary of Philosophy'*, Penguin, London.

Meehl, P. E. (1991) *'Selected Philosophical and Methodological Papers'*, University of Minnesota Press, Minneapolis: MN.

Miles, M. B. and Huberman, A. M. (1994) *'Qualitative Data Analysis'*, Sage, Thousand Oaks: CA.

Miles, R. and Snow, C. (1986) 'Organizations: New concepts for new forms', *California Management Review*, 28 (3).

Mintzberg, H. (1978) 'Patterns in strategy formation', *Management Science*, 24 (9): 934.

Morgan, D. L. (1998a) *'Planning Focus Groups'*, Sage, Thousand Oaks: CA.

Morgan, D. L. (1998b) 'Practical strategies for combining qualitative and quantitative methods: Applications for health research', *Qualitative Health Research*, 8 (3): 362–376.

Nelson, R. and Winter, S. (1982) *'An Evolutionary Theory of Economic Change'*, Harvard University Press, Cambridge: MA.

Nicholls, A. and Lee, N. (2006) 'Purchase decision-making in fair trade and the ethical gap: "Is there a Fair Trade Twix?"', *Journal of Strategic Marketing* Vol. 14 (4).

Nunnally, J. C. (1967) *'Psychometric Theory'*, McGraw-Hill, New York: NY.

Pankhania, A., Lee, N. and Hooley, G. (2007) 'Within-country ethnic differences and product positioning: A comparison of the perceptions of two British sub-cultures', *Journal of Strategic Marketing*, 15 (2/3): 121–138.

Penrose, E. (1959) *'The Theory of the Growth of the Firm'*, John Wiley & Sons, New York: NY.

Phillips, E. and Pugh, D. (2007) *'How to Get a Ph.D.: A Handbook for Students and Their Supervisors'*, 4th edn, Open University Press, London.

Podsakoff, P. M., MacKenzie, S. B., Lee, J-Y and Podsakoff, N. P. (2003) 'Common method biases in behavioral research: A critical review of the literature and recommended remedies', *Journal of Applied Psychology*, 88 (5): 879–903.

Porter, M. (1985) *'Competitive Advantage: Creating and Sustaining Superior Performance'*, The Free Press, New York: NY.

Potter, J. (1997) 'Discourse analysis as a way of analysing naturally occuring talk', in D. Silverman (ed.), *Qualitative Research: Theory, Method and Practice*, Sage, London.

Potter, J. (2004) 'Discourse analysis', in M. Hardy and A. Bryman (eds), *Handbook of Data Analysis*, Sage, London.

Rasmussen, E. S., Østergaard, P. and Beckmann, S. C. (2006) *'Essentials of Social Science Research Methodology'*, University Press of Southern Denmark.

Riley, M., Wood, R. C., Clark, M. A., Wilkie, E. and Szivas, E. (2000) *'Researching and Writing Dissertations in Business and Management'*, Thomson Learning, London.

Roberts, M. J. and Russo, R. (1999) *'A Student's Guide to Analysis of Variance'*, Routledge, London.

Rossiter, J. R. (2002) 'The C-OAR-SE procedure for scale development in marketing', *International Journal of Research in Marketing*, 19 (4): 305–336.

Rozeboom, W. W. (2005) 'Meehl on metatheory', *Journal of Clinical Psychology*, 61: 1317–1354.

Saunders, J. and Lee, N. (2005) 'Reasons to be cheerful: Foreword to the special issue on the state of marketing research.' *European Journal of Marketing* Vol. 39 (3/4).

Savage, C. W. and Ehrlich, P. (1992) *'Philosophical and Foundational Issues in Measurement'*, Lawrence Erlbaum Associates, Hillsdale: NJ.

Scott, J. (1990) *'A Matter of Record'*, Polity, Cambridge.

Seale, C. (2004) 'Quality in qualitative research', in C. Seale, G. Gobo, J. F. Gubrium and D. Silverman (eds), *Qualitative Research Practice*, Sage, London.

Seale, D., Gobo, G., Gubrium, J. F. and Silverman, D. (eds), (2004) *'Qualitative Research Practice'*, Sage, London.

Shadish, W. R., Cook, T. D. and Campbell, D. T. (2001) *'Experimental and Quasi-Experimental Designs for Generalized Causal Inference'*, Houghton Mifflin, CA.

Silverman, D. (2005) *'Doing Qualitative Research'*, 2nd edn, Sage, Thousand Oaks: CA.

Smart, B. (2000) 'Postmodern social theory', in B. Turner (ed.) *The Blackwell Companion to Social Theory*, Oxford: Blackwell.

Spector, P. E. (1992) *'Summated Rating Scale Construction: An Introduction'*. Sage, London.

Steenkamp, J-B E. M. and Baumgartner, H. (1998) 'Assessing measurement invariance in cross-national consumer research', *Journal of Consumer Research*, 25 (1): 78–90.

Stewart, D. W. and Zinkhan, G. M. (2006) 'Enhancing marketing theory in academic research', *Journal of the Academy of Marketing Science*, 34 (4): 477–480.

Strauss, A. and Corbin, J. M. (1998) *'Basics of Qualitative Research: Techniques and Procedures for Developing Grounded Theory'*, Sage, Thousand Oaks: CA.

Sutton, R. I. and Staw, B. M. (2003) 'What theory is not', in L. L. Thompson (ed.) *The Social Psychology of Organizational Behavior*, Psychology Press, New York: NY.

Tarnas, R. (1996) *'The Passion of the Western Mind: Understanding the Ideas that have Shaped our World View'*, Pimlico: London.

Teece, D., Pisano, G. and Shuen, A. (1997) 'Dynamic capabilities and strategic management', *Strategic Management Journal*, 18 (7): 509.

Todd, Z., Nerlich, B., McKeown, S. and Clarke, D. D. (2004) (eds) *'Mixing Methods in Psychology'*, Psychology Press, Hove: UK.

Tolkein, J. R. R. (2007) *'The Lord of the Rings'*, HarperCollins Publishers, London.

Tranfield, D., Denyer, D. and Smart, P. (2003) 'Towards a methodology for developing evidence-informed management knowledge by means of systematic review', *British Journal of Management,* 14 (3): 207–222.

Tukey, J. W. (1977) *'Exploratory Data Analysis'*, Addison Wesley, London.

Tukey, J. W. (1986) 'Sunset salvo', *American Statistician*, 40 (1): 72–76.

Wallace, M. and Wray, A. (2006) *'Critical Reading and Writing for Postgraduates'*, Sage, London.

Webster, J. and Watson, R. (2002) 'Analyzing the past to prepare for the future: Writing a literature review', *MIS Quarterly*, 26 (2): xiii–xxiii.

Yin, R. K. (2003) *'Case Study Research: Design and Methods'*, Sage, London.

Zinkhan, G. M. and Hirschheim, R. (1992) 'Truth in marketing theory and research: An alternative perspective', *Journal of Marketing*, 56 (April): 80–88.

Index